Europe's Radical Left

Europe's Radical Left

From Marginality
to the Mainstream?

Edited by
Luke March and Daniel Keith

ROWMAN &
LITTLEFIELD
INTERNATIONAL

London • New York

Published by Rowman & Littlefield International, Ltd.
Unit A, Whitacre Mews, 26-34 Stannary Street, London SE11 4AB
www.rowmaninternational.com

Rowman & Littlefield International, Ltd. is an affiliate of Rowman & Littlefield
4501 Forbes Boulevard, Suite 200, Lanham, Maryland 20706, USA
With additional offices in Boulder, New York, Toronto (Canada), and Plymouth (UK)
www.rowman.com

British Library Cataloguing in Publication Data
A catalogue record for this book is available from the British Library

ISBN: HB 978-1-7834-8535-2
        PB 978-1-7834-8536-9

Library of Congress Cataloging-in-Publication Data

Names: March, Luke, editor. | Keith, Daniel.
Title: Europe's radical left : from marginality to the mainstream? / edited by
    Luke March and Daniel Keith.
Description: London ; New York : Rowman & Littlefield International, Ltd.,
    2016. | Includes bibliographical references and index.
Identifiers: LCCN 2016035293 (print) | LCCN 2016043018 (ebook) |
    ISBN 9781783485352 (cloth : alk. paper) | ISBN 9781783485369
    (pbk. : alk. paper) | ISBN 9781783485376 (Electronic)
Subjects: LCSH: Political parties—Europe. | Radicalism—Europe. |
    Right and left (Political science)—Europe. | Communist parties—Europe. |
    Socialist parties—Europe. | Europe—Politics and government—21st century.
Classification: LCC JN50 .E88 2016 (print) | LCC JN50 (ebook) |
    DDC 324.2/17094—dc23
LC record available at https://lccn.loc.gov/2016035293

∞™ The paper used in this publication meets the minimum requirements of American
National Standard for Information Sciences—Permanence of Paper for Printed Library
Materials, ANSI/NISO Z39.48-1992.

Printed in the United States of America

Contents

List of Figures

List of Tables

Acknowledgements

This book had its germination in the conference 'The radical left and crisis in the EU: from marginality to the mainstream?' held at the University of Edinburgh on 17 May 2013, which was kindly funded by the Edinburgh University Europa Institute/Jean Monnet Centre for Excellence. The authors wish to give great thanks to all of those who contributed to that conference, even if, owing to a number of necessary editorial decisions (e.g. the need to spread the geographical coverage more widely), not everyone could be involved in the final volume. Many thanks are also due to our chapter authors, whose contributions have been exceptional. We also wish to thank our friends and family for support and patience during the completion of the project.

List of Abbreviations

This list contains those abbreviations most commonly appearing in the text or tables. All other uncommon abbreviations are always accompanied by the full title when they first appear.

AKEL	Anorthotikó Kómma Ergazómenou Laoú (Progressive Party of Working People, Cyprus)
BE	Bloco de Esquerda (Left Bloc, Portugal)
CDU	Coligação Democrática Unitária (United Democratic Coalition, Portugal)
CP	Communist Party
EL	Enhedslisten – De Rød-Grønne (Red-Green Alliance, Denmark)
ECB	European Central Bank
EP	European Parliament
FdG	Front de Gauche (Left Front, France)
GDR	German Democratic Republic
GJM	Global Justice Movement
GUE/NGL	Confederal Group of the European United Left/Nordic Green Left
IDS	Iniciativa za demokratični socializem (Initiative for Democratic Socialism, Slovenia)
IMF	International Monetary Fund
IU	Izquierda Unida (United Left, Spain)
KKE	Kommounistikó Kómma Elládas (Communist Party of Greece)
KSČM	Komunistická strana Čech a Moravy (Communist Party of Bohemia and Moravia, Czech Republic)

KPRF	Kommunisticheskaya partiya Rossiiskoi Federatsii (Communist Party of the Russian Federation)
KPU	Komunistychna Partiya Ukraïny (Communist Party of Ukraine)
KSS	Komunistická strana Slovenska (Communist Party of Slovakia)
LÉNK	Déi Lénk (The Left, Luxembourg)
LP	Die Linke (The Left Party, Germany)
LSP	Latvijas Sociālistiskā partija (Latvian Socialist Party)
NPA	Nouveau parti anticapitaliste (New Anti-Capitalist Party, France)
PASOK	Panellínio Sosialistikó Kínima (Panhellenic Socialist Movement, Greece)
PCE	Partido Comunista de España (Communist Party of Spain)
PCF	Parti Communiste Français (French Communist Party)
PCI	Partito Comunista Italiano (Italian Communist Party)
PCP	Partido Comunista Português (Portuguese Communist Party)
PCRM	Partidul Comuniştilor din Republica Moldova (Party of Communists of the Republic of Moldova)
PEL	Party of the European Left/European Left Party
PRC (or Rifondazione)	Partito della Rifondazione Comunista (Party of Communist Refoundation, Italy)
PS	Parti Socialiste (Socialist Party, France)
PSOE	Partido Socialista Obrero Español (Spanish Socialist Workers' Party)
RCS	Rifondazione Comunista Sammarinese (Sammarinese Communist Refoundation)
RLP	Radical left party
RRP	Radical right party
SF	Socialistisk Folkeparti (Socialist People's Party, Denmark)
SP	Socialistische Partij (Socialist Party, Netherlands)
SV	Sosialistisk Venstreparti (Socialist Left Party, Norway)
Synaspismós	Synaspismós tīs Aristerás tōn Kinīmátōn kai tīs Oikologías (Coalition of the Left of Movements and Ecology, Greece; until 2003 called Synaspismós tīs Aristerás kai tīs Proódou, Coalition of the Left and Progress)

Syriza	Synaspismós Rizospastikís Aristerás (Coalition of the Radical Left, Greece)
Troika, the	Committee led by the European Commission, European Central Bank and the International Monetary Fund, that organised loans to the governments of Greece, Ireland, Portugal and Cyprus
TU	Trade Union
V	Vänsterpartiet (Left Party, Sweden)
VAS	Vasemmistoliitto (Left Alliance, Finland)
VG	Vinstrihreyfingin–grænt framboð (Left-Green Movement, Iceland)

Chapter 1

Introduction

Daniel Keith and Luke March

> It's no exaggeration to say that Alexis Tsipras, the head of the
> left-wing SYRIZA party in Greece, is the most feared man right
> now in all of Europe.[1]

Beyond the obvious ludicrousness of this statement (most of Europe had
hardly heard of Alexis Tsipras when this was written in mid-2012, let alone
trembled before him), such a view throws up several questions. How could
the young leader of a formerly marginal party in a peripheral European country demand such feverish attention? Why was paranoia the dominant reaction
from a business correspondent? Last, and most pertinently, why was a left-
wing party being seen as a threat to Europe, rather than the more common
'usual suspects', the anti-immigrant Right or terrorism?

One obvious riposte (and one to which we will return) is that mainstream
European economic orthodoxy is now so rigid that even moderate social
democratic challenges to the status quo are regularly seen as at worst dangerous, at best obsolete and 'politically far fetched'.[2] But the longer-term reality
is that parties of the radical Left (i.e. those to the left of social democracy that
aim to transform capitalism), which were usually pronounced obsolete and
moribund immediately after the collapse of the Soviet Union, are now more
relevant actors in Europe than at any time since. At the same time, left-wing
ideas have appeared to move from marginality to the mainstream, particularly in the wake of the post-2008 Great Recession. In the early years of the
crisis, there was renewed interest in Marxian and Keynesian classics.[3] Later,
Thomas Piketty's critique of capitalist inequality, *Capital in the Twenty-
First Century,* became an unlikely bestseller. To take just the UK example,
public figures such as Owen Jones and Russell Brand have brought left-wing
anti-establishment sentiment to the mainstream, while in Jeremy Corbyn, the

1

UK Labour Party now has a leader who would scarcely be out of place in a radical left party. Admittedly, the question of radical left 'relevance' and 'mainstreaming' needs significant qualification, but it is one of the primary purposes of this volume to provide such an analysis.

The success of parties such as Syriza and the Spanish Podemos have latterly garnered the radical Left greater media attention as part of the wave of so-called 'left populism'.[4] Nevertheless, even prior to the rise of these 'new' parties, the study of radical left parties (hereafter RLPs) as important phenomena has been gaining momentum. Whereas a decade or so ago, there were barely any in-depth, up-to-date comparative studies, making RLPs the poor relation of party politics fields, this is now decreasingly the case. There are now important studies with five main aims[5]: first, *overcoming the empirical deficit* by a profusion of single-party and comparative case-study approaches; second, *providing conceptual clarity about the radical Left as party family*.[6] Third has been *analysing RLPs' views on Europe* and transcending the simplistic 'Eurosceptic' label often applied to the radical left in the comparative literature.[7] Fourth has been a focus on *RLPs and government participation*.[8] The final focus has been on *understanding RLPs' divergent electoral performance and social support*.[9] This reflects that although stabilisation and even an improvement in the electoral performance of RLPs became evident even before the crisis, their electoral trajectories are very variable: for every Syriza there is a 'Pythonised' party, whose fate is recrimination and marginalisation.[10]

Yet despite major advances in our understanding, these newer studies are hardly the last word, not least for the simple reason that the field is dynamic and changes with every election. There are still relatively few researchers involved in systematic study of the radical Left, and vital work could be done simply by updating, broadening and deepening the existing empirical base and in analysing and critiquing the categorisations and hypotheses already advanced. Moreover, there are several areas of RLP activity that have been so far less studied, where further research is most urgent. Perhaps the weakest areas of the existing literature are (1) RLP party organisations; (2) RLPs in the extra-parliamentary realm; (3) the radical Left and populism; (4) RLPs and gender politics.[11]

This is where the current volume fits in. Its overall aim is to further the comparative study of the radical Left in general by expanding the number of cases studied and scholars studying them and thereby to refine and test the contributions of the existing literature. The book developed from a conference at the University of Edinburgh in May 2013. It is dedicated to studying the radical Left's response to the international economic crisis, and aims to broaden the networks and knowledge base among those studying the radical Left. We have accordingly tried to incorporate a range of more established and newer scholars, as well as 'usual suspect' case studies (e.g. Germany, France) alongside those far less known (e.g. Iceland, Latvia).

Within this aim, our first main research focus is the reasons for the divergent growth (and possible mainstreaming) of radical left parties since the collapse of the Soviet Union. Consistent with addressing weaknesses in the existing literature, we will pay special attention to the contribution of party organisations and extra-parliamentary links to RLP electoral and policy performance. We will also consider the issue of populism, particularly as it has become increasingly significant even prior to the international economic crisis.

Our second, related but narrower, main research focus is the precise impact of the Great Recession on the radical Left. This volume is the first large-scale comparative academic analysis of the effect of the crisis on RLPs.[12] Since changes in parties' environments have the potential to engender processes of party change, it is important to question the extent to which RLPs have indeed been able to move from the marginality to mainstream of European politics. Mindful both that the effects of the crisis are ongoing, and of Sir Walter Raleigh's warning that 'whosoever in writing a modern history, shall follow truth too near the heels, it may haply strike out his teeth', we will take a longer-term historical perspective and analyse the impact of the crisis in the context of RLPs' previous performance and trajectories.[13]

Such an approach is needed when major gaps exist in our knowledge of RLPs, and not least those that have risen to prominence or governed in the context of the Great Recession. We have three principal research questions that guide the volume and which aim to provide such a historically-informed account of the effect of the Great Recession on RLPs, taking into account the need to focus more on organisation and extra-parliamentary links than hitherto:

1. What characterises RLPs' *intellectual/programmatic* responses to the crisis – that is, how do RLPs conceptualise the causes of the crisis and its consequences? How has this affected their concrete policy proposals? Has it provoked major changes in ideology/world view or discrete policies, or has it simply re-confirmed existing pre-conceptions?
2. What characterises RLPs' *organisational* responses – that is, has the crisis resulted in new methods of organising? Has the crisis affected parties internally, for instance in terms of structure, internal tendencies or organisational integrity?
3. What characterises RLPs' *electoral* responses to the crisis – that is, has the crisis led to changes in the strategies that RLPs follow in election campaigns? Has the crisis materially aided or weakened RLP electoral success and why? How has it affected the social and electoral sources of support for RLPs and affiliated movements?

The particular focus on the crisis is apposite, because until the rise of Syriza and Podemos in 2015, it was widely understood (not least among activists and supporters) that the Left had *not* had a good crisis (at least in terms of party electoral performance). The 2009 European Parliament (EP) Elections, as the first pan-European post-crisis elections, were the first benchmark. The broader Left (social democrats and the radical Left) actually lost ground (their combined EP seat share fell from 32.8 per cent to 30.1 per cent). Despite recovering to 32.2 per cent in 2014, the Left clearly still falls far short of a majority, even when the Greens are considered.

Why should the Left have expected a good crisis? On the face of it, this was the 'perfect storm'. It originated in processes that can be broadly speaking attributed to the Left's major bugbear of 'neoliberalism' (e.g. lack of regulation of the financial sector, the cowardice of states before markets); it resulted in processes that show much more continuity than change (the 'age of austerity', the retrenchment of the state and the socialisation of private debt), and has had pernicious social consequences (e.g. rising unemployment, inequality and social tension). Indicatively, in 2012 Francis Fukuyama asked where was the 'Tea Party on the left' (a populist uprising against the political establishment) given that a crisis rooted in the 'model of American liberalized finance' had led to rising inequality, distrust and dissatisfaction with democracy.[14] Arguably, the 2011 'year of the protester' and the various insurrections spearheaded by Occupy and the Indignants (the Spanish 15M and Greek 'Squares' movement) showed precisely the social basis for such a left-wing populist movement, but at that point, the *party* element of the equation was distinctly missing.

The absence of any 'crisis bounce' for the social democrats is on reflection not surprising. After all, this is a party family long considered to be suffering a crisis of identity, with its future in question.[15] The Great Recession has revealed this only too starkly: the social democratic parties were unable to benefit from the crisis of neoliberalism since many had been co-architects of that neoliberalism and legitimated the 'logic of no alternative' discourse.[16] Most social democratic parties had long given up not only any aspiration to a serious alternative to capitalism, but anything beyond a timid critique of it.

However, the situation for the radical Left looks on the face of it more damning, not least because those who have lost faith in social democracy as an agent of radical change have pinned their hopes on parties and movements to the left of social democracy.[17] The sense of a historical opportunity beckoning is recognised by the radical Left themselves. The philosopher Slavoj Žižek has argued that 'the field is open' for radical change[18]; the Marxist academic Leo Panitch similarly claimed that 'the scale of the Crisis and the popular outrage today provide a historic opening for a renewal of the kind of radical politics that advances a systemic alternative to capitalism'.[19]

The apparent rise in popularity of left-wing ideas might indicate the same tendency.

However, it is precisely the degree to which such ideas have found political expression that it is in doubt. Whereas Syriza and Podemos may represent a 'renewal of radical politics', it is not yet clear whether they are presagers of the future or exceptions to the rule. As this volume will explore throughout, the degree to which either extant or 'new' RLPs themselves offer a convincing 'systemic alternative to capitalism' is very questionable. It is certainly true that the all-too-common idea that the radical Right has most benefitted from the crisis can be doubted, given the divisions within and sporadic representation of this party family.[20] Nevertheless, the fact remains that at the time of writing (March 2016), there has been no switch of socio-economic paradigm. Neoliberalism may be on the defensive, but reports of its death have been greatly exaggerated.[21] There is no evidence of a Gramscian 'historical bloc', that is, a new configuration of ideologies, material capabilities and sociopolitical institutions, which can define a new socialist 'common sense' for individual and collective action. Rather, the overall hegemony of neoliberal ideas remains. As David Bailey will further illustrate in this volume, there is little evidence that the crisis will become a system-shaking 'crisis of capitalism' rather than a cyclical 'capitalist crisis' that enables capitalism to be reformed and reconstituted.

DEFINING THE RADICAL LEFT

Compared with the 'war of words' over the precise definition of the radical right party family, the definitional and conceptual consensus concerning RLPs is now high.[22] There is still a plethora of terms in use (e.g. 'Far Left', 'extreme Left', 'Left'). However, many academic works now employ the term 'radical Left', and even those that do not concur, albeit with nuances, with the essence of the term as outlined by March and Mudde, that this radical Left is *left* by its commitments to equality and internationalism and *radical* in its aspirations to fundamental transformation of capitalism.[23] There is also general agreement over the core members of the radical left party family, notwithstanding several 'fuzzy cases', such as the Danish Socialist People's Party (which became a full member of the European Green Party in 2014 and therefore ceased to be an RLP).[24] Similarly, some consider the Irish Sinn Féin part of the radical Left, but the chapter by Richard Dunphy in this volume argues that it has a number of idiosyncratic positions (including nationalism and inconsistent anti-neoliberalism).

We utilise the term 'radical Left', partly because it is used by many radical left actors (e.g. Syriza [Coalition of the Radical Left]). More significantly, the term (deriving from the Latin *radix* and used in this sense by Marx) indicates a broad aspiration for 'root-and-branch' systemic transformation (of national political systems, of the international system and capitalism *tout court*). Of course, not all of those we term as being on the radical Left actually endorse the term. Nevertheless, the wish to radically *transform* and not just reform contemporary capitalism remains the key distinction between RLPs and social democratic and Green parties, who partially share aspirations to equality, internationalism and anti-neoliberalism.

The nature of this 'radicalism' is obviously questionable. What indeed constitutes 'radical' or 'transformative change'? RLPs are themselves often vague, and rarely spell out in detail either the nature of or the road to their socialism. Parties such as the French Communist Party and Italian Communist Refoundation have long talked not of revolution, but of 'overcoming' or 'surpassing' capitalism. As Amieke Bouma's chapter in this book underlines, commitment to 'Transformation Theory' has been a defining feature of the German Die Linke's response to crisis. Such terms raise as many questions as they do answers. At the very least, all RLPs oppose 'neoliberal' globalised capitalism, broadly associated with the so-called 'Washington Consensus' (trade liberalisation, marketisation, privatisation etc.). However, this blanket opposition still conceals differences between truer anti-capitalists who utterly reject private property and profit incentives or any co-operation with capitalist forces, and those anti-neoliberals who emphasise reforming capitalism in a largely Keynesian fashion. Often such distinctions cause internal divisions within parties and they may not publicly take a clear stance on them.

Such differences do not quite map onto the older divisions between 'reformists' and 'revolutionaries', which have lost a lot of salience. Most of today's major parties are self-evidently 'reformist', and in most European countries true revolutionary forces are largely confined to the marginal extra-parliamentary extreme Left (extreme in the sense of opposing 'bourgeois' democracy as a whole rather than just aspects of liberal democracy). However, they do point to an identity issue at the core of today's radical Left. Whereas the communist parties of yore had a distinct ideological and organisational template originally laid down by the Comintern's '21 Conditions', today's RLPs have many more problems in maintaining distinct stances.

Compared with the international communist movement before 1989, the European radical Left has undoubtedly undergone a process of profound *de-radicalisation*, under the pressures of transforming from agents of a defunct international movement into viable national parties.[25] Indeed, some have long argued that the gradual neoliberalisation of social democracy to adopt Blairite 'Third Way' positions has led to the social-democratisation of the radical Left.[26] There are good reasons to be less categorical: RLPs still maintain extra-parliamentary links and very distinct positions, in rhetoric if not always practice, from post-World War II social democrats. The key differences remain RLPs' commitment to political-economic transformation, their outright opposition to Euro-Atlantic institutions (the IMF, World Bank and NATO) and their 'Euroscepticism'. However, as will be seen throughout this volume, this commonly-used term is very misleading, concealing a kaleidoscope of critiques of the direction of European integration and the European Union.

Nevertheless, the degree to which RLPs can offer any distinct socio-economic vision has come into greater focus in the post-crisis context. Whereas previously, most RLPs were loath to acknowledge that their core economic positions were basically Keynesian, they have had to articulate their economic positions more clearly in the current conjuncture. Podemos leader Pablo Iglesias has voiced this most cogently:

> Today, the option of a socialist strategy, or a Marxist critique of neoliberalism, poses immense problems in the practical, political sense – to articulate an actual opposition that could have even the option of countering the current state of affairs. … Those ambiguities and contradictions are related to something that we openly acknowledge: we are not opposing a strategy for a transition to socialism, but we are being more modest and adopting a neo-Keynesian approach, like the European Left, calling for higher investment, securing social rights and redistribution. That puts us on a difficult terrain open to the standard criticisms of neo-Keynesian claims.[27]

A still bigger example of the contradictions is the first Syriza government of 2015. Syriza promised to break the grip of the Troika (the European Union, IMF and the European Central Bank) and spearhead the European anti-austerity movement. After months of stalemate in negotiations with the Eurogroup, Syriza won a dubiously democratic referendum in July 2015, the Όχι (*Okhi*: 'No') against the terms of a bailout agreement, then proceeded to perform a complete about-turn and adopt an austerity package (the Third Memorandum) still harsher than the one that it had rejected. Many leftists share the view that this was a 'brutal strategic defeat' and 'betrayal' since Syriza has conceded 'the neo-liberal core-argument that There Is No Alternative [TINA]; no strategy for continuing the fightback against financial despotism'.[28] According to some critics, Syriza's problems stem from failing to make a choice between a radical left identity and becoming a 'responsible' centre-left party, which are two seemingly incompatible programmes.[29]

Generally the radical Left's radicalism can often be regarded as 'situational', that is, falling short of full anti-capitalism, but still articulating issues that are radical *in the party's national situation*, for example campaigns promoted by Portugal's Left Bloc (BE), such as the promotion of gay marriage with the right of adoption (passed in March 2016). Such ideological 'fuzziness' is not always a disadvantage, helping RLPs to become more attractive coalition partners and to bridge some of their highly divisive historical differences: it's now usual to find former Stalinists, Maoists and social democrats in the same party. It has allowed the party family to become less ideological and more pragmatic. Today's European radical Left is often seen as a 'mosaic left': a constellation of variegated parties and movements from motley backgrounds.[30] The degree to which these divergent backgrounds still matter is an open question, since the central emphasis has moved from (eternal) fragmentation to limited fusion.

Nevertheless, and particularly since some of these categories will be used by authors within this volume, it is worth briefly elucidating the main radical left subtypes.[31] We can identify four main groups, the *conservative communists*, *reform communists*, *democratic socialists* and *revolutionary extreme leftists*. Their views are further illuminated in Table 1.1.

The conservative communists are so-called because they attempt to conserve the Soviet tradition, define themselves as Marxist-Leninist, maintain a relatively uncritical stance towards the Soviet Union, organise their parties by means of distinctive Leninist democratic centralism and still see the world through the Cold War prism of 'imperialism'. Many of these parties are now marginal, but the communist parties of Greece and Portugal are still significant parties within the European radical Left. Research suggests that, despite there being some differences between these parties, overall they still have fairly similar interpretations of Marxism and Leninism.[32]

The *reform communists* are a more eclectic and pragmatic sub-grouping. They still possess important elements of the communist model (especially traditional organisational linkages in the case of the Cypriot Progressive Party of the Working People, AKEL), but in most other respects their ideological and strategic position is closer to the democratic socialists outlined next, particularly in terms of being (relative to the conservative communists) open to broader alliances, governmental participation, the market economy and elements of the post-1968 'new left' agenda (feminism, environmentalism, grass roots democracy and so on).

Democratic socialist parties comprise the majority of the significant European RLPs, who try to define a position distinct from both communism (which they may regard as highly authoritarian, 'totalitarian' or simply obsolete) and social democracy (seen as insufficiently left or 'neoliberal'). They are a broad church. Some parties (such as the Dutch Socialist Party, as analysed by Dan Keith in this volume) are arguably little distinct from left-wing social democrats with a greater accent on anti-neoliberalism and extra-parliamentary mobilisation. Others (especially the so-called 'Nordic Green Left', encompassing among others the Icelandic Left-Greens, Danish Red-Green

Alliance and Swedish Left Party) have a more cohesive 'red-green' position, more fully combining 'old left' emphases on economic equality and redistribution with 'new left' themes including environmentalism and support for alternative lifestyles and minorities.[33]

The *revolutionary extreme Left* is very marginal. Most countries have several such parties, which rarely directly impact outside their milieu, but usually have adherents within the larger parties. Generally inspired by Leninist, Trotskyist or Maoist views, they share with the conservative communists adherence to elements of the Soviet model, but generally reject conservative communists as bureaucratic and doctrinaire 'Stalinists'. These parties tend towards anti-systemic sectarianism towards the rest of the radical Left (and each other), rejecting broader electoral alliances, parliamentary politics and 'electoralism'. Instead, they focus on grass roots mobilisation and links with (class-based) social movements. Their revolutionary views find expression in the need for socialism to be achieved by a 'rupture' with capitalism, involving mass insurrection, general strikes and/or power achieved by variants of workers' councils. Parties such as the UK Socialist Workers Party, the various Irish Trotskyist parties and the New Anti-Capitalist Party in France illustrate this trend.

It is important not to reify such tendencies, which rarely parlay exactly into divisions among the radical Left; rather they are intended as a heuristic device for illuminating a complex reality. These categories should certainly not be seen as rigid or unchangeable and some parties move between categories over time. Consistent with the aforementioned, more unites than divides today's RLPs. Moreover, divisions often emerge over concrete policy issues rather than abstract ideology (most notably over attitudes to the European Union), or over 'old left' (materialism and class) vs. 'new left' (post-materialism and identity) issues.[34] Nevertheless, these sub-categories are useful because they help to clarify significant divisions. For example, conservative communists tend to regard other tendencies as ideologically suspect 'reformists' and organise their own international organisations, notably the International Meeting of Communist and Workers' Parties. For their part, the revolutionary extreme Left regards the conservative communists as 'Stalinists' and the other categories as 'social democrats' or 'left reformists'.

We have chosen to exclude left-wing populists (*populist socialists* and *social populists*) as a separate sub-category, unlike earlier iterations of this typology.[35] Along with many contemporary scholars, we regard populism as a neutral and not an intrinsically negative phenomenon, a political ideology that 'considers society to be ultimately separated into two homogeneous and antagonistic groups, "the pure people" versus "the corrupt elite," and which argues that politics should be an expression of the of the *volonté générale* (general will) of the people'.[36] Populist socialists add to the democratic socialist

Table 1.1 RLP Sub-types

	Conservative Communists	Reform Communists	Democratic Socialists	Revolutionary Extreme Left
Typical parties	Greek Communist Party, Portuguese Communist Party, Latvian Socialist Party, Communist Party of Bohemia and Moravia (partly)	Communist Refoundation (Italy), Communist Party of Spain, Progressive Party of Working People (Cyprus), Communist Party of Bohemia and Moravia (partly), French Communist Party	Die Linke (Germany), Syriza (Greece), Left Bloc (Portugal), Red-Green Alliance (Denmark), Left-Green Movement (Iceland), Left Unity (UK), Initiative for Democratic Socialism (Slovenia)	Socialist Party (Ireland), People Before Profit (Ireland), New Anti-Capitalist Party (France), Socialist Party, Socialist Workers Party (UK)
Ideological inspiration	Soviet Marxism-Leninism	Marxism and Marxism-Leninism, social democracy and domestic socialist traditions	Post-1968 Marxism, social democracy and domestic socialist traditions	Leninism, Trotskyism, Maoism
Attitude to USSR	Largely positive	Mildly critical or ambiguous	Generally negative	Positive (towards Leninist period); negative (towards Stalinism)
Critique of capitalism	Anti-capitalism, anti-imperialism; class conflict pivotal	Anti-capitalism and anti-neoliberalism; class conflict supplemented by ecological and gender conflicts	Breadth of critiques; anti-capitalism and anti-neoliberalism; ecological and gender conflicts as important as (or more so than) class	Anti-capitalism, anti-imperialism; class conflict pivotal
Alternative offered	Communism achieved via revolution or evolutionary process	Socialism achieved by peaceful transformation	Democratic, socialist and emancipatory society	Capitalist 'rupture' furthered by mass participatory movement/insurrection

Electoral constituency	Focussed on traditional working class, trade unions; sometimes broader populist appeal to all who oppose existing elite	Traditional working class at core; supplemented by appeal to social sectors, pensioners, jobless and low-salaried; populist appeal to all who oppose existing elite	Try to combine traditional worker milieus with white-collar strata or appeal largely to latter; appeal to 'precarious workers'; populist appeal to all who oppose existing elite	Focussed on traditional working class, trade unions; 'entrism' into parliamentary parties; populist appeal to all who oppose existing elite
Attitude to national governmental co-operation	Usually negative	Increasingly pragmatic	Increasingly pragmatic	Entirely negative unless following capitalist rupture
Allies and alliances	Alliances only with ideologically sound, loyal groups	Semi-permanent alliances with non-communist left envisaged	Semi-permanent alliance with other radical left groups envisaged; broader pragmatic alliances increasingly considered	Alliances only with ideologically sound, loyal groups; entrism
International links	International Meetings of Communist and Workers' Parties; INITIATIVE of Communist and Workers' Parties	European Left Party (member/observer)	European Left Party (member/observer); Nordic Green Left Alliance	European Anti-Capitalist Left (defunct); fourth/fifth internationals and equivalents (e.g. Committee for Workers' International, International Socialist Tendency)

Source: Authors' conceptions, developed from C. Hildebrandt, 'Fragmentierung Und Pluralismus Von Linksparteien in Europa'. In B. Daiber, C. Hildebrandt and A. Striethorst (eds.) *Von Revolution Bis Koalition: Linke Parteien in Europa*, (Berlin: Dietz Berlin Verlag, 2010), pp. 9–38; Fabien Escalona and Mathieu Vieira, 'The Radical Left in Europe: Thoughts About the Emergence of a Family', *Fondation Jean-Jaurès / Observatoire de La Vie Politique* (19 November 2013).

ideological core a strong emphasis on moralistic anti-elite discourse, whereas social populists have more developed anti-establishment discourse still, a weaker socialist ideological core and develop further many identitarian appeals (e.g. nationalism) that have not traditionally coexisted with radical left politics.

Whereas focusing on these categories helped identify some important new elements of RLPs' appeal, the original populist socialist parties (e.g. the Dutch Socialist Party and German Die Linke) have become little distinct from other democratic socialist parties. At the same time, the concept is less useful because of the transversal nature of populism.[37] So many RLPs (including the otherwise orthodox Greek communists and Trotskyist parties such as the Irish Socialist party, as described in Richard Dunphy's chapter in this book) now use populist anti-establishment appeals that having populism as a separate category seems otiose.[38] Clearly, parties such as Syriza and Podemos have developed their populist appeals to such a degree that they are often seen as populist parties pure and simple.[39] Nevertheless, this is a similar over-simplification to calling the radical Left 'Eurosceptic', and it is important to remember that they combine both populist and socialist appeals, as demonstrated in this statement by Syriza: 'The "red lines" of the Greek government are also the "red lines" of the Greek people. They express the interests of the workers, self-employed, pensioners, farmers and the youth.'[40]

THE GREAT RECESSION AND PARTY CHANGE

With the main actors now outlined, we can explore the nature of the crisis and how we would expect it to affect RLPs. We will refer to the crisis as the international financial crisis or Great Recession interchangeably throughout the work. The former formulation reflects that whereas the crisis was felt internationally, it was not a true *global* crisis, with many areas of the globe (e.g. Latin America and Australasia) largely avoiding its most pernicious effects.[41] The latter indicates that political consequences and post-crisis perceptions have been equal or in some cases more lasting and pernicious than the economic consequences.

Indeed, the peak period of the economic crisis was from 15 September 2008 (when the bankruptcy of Lehman Brothers fundamentally shook the global financial system) until the last quarter of 2010, by which time most countries had returned to (often anaemic and sporadic) growth. The crisis took on different forms and outcomes in each case. Nevertheless, the general impetus was three interrelated crises[42]: a banking crisis as undercapitalised banks lost liquidity and solvency; a competitiveness crisis driving slowing growth across Europe; and finally, the sovereign debt crisis (the most serious manifestation in southern Europe particularly), where countries could no longer fund public debt independently as a result of rising bond yields and bank bailouts, and therefore had to seek large bailouts from the Troika.

Outside the financial sector, the socio-economic conditions have proved more lasting. Many countries received an initial sudden jolt of declining growth, financial instability and rising unemployment. But the austerity measures promoted across the continent brought with them their own woes, especially a reduction in wages and public spending/social benefits and tax rises as governments aspired to reduce deficits and return to competitiveness. Such effects ensured that a short-term financial crisis became a longer-term social and political one.

In their study of the effects of the crisis on (right and left-wing) populism, Kriesi and Pappas noted the differential nature of the crisis across Europe, and so categorised several European states according to the severity of their economic and political crises.[43] They argue that a deep economic crisis (as evidenced by high unemployment, low growth and high public debt) is likely to lead to a political crisis (evidenced by increased electoral volatility, declining trust in parliament and satisfaction with the way democracy works in one's country). Since they used a slightly different country selection than us, we have categorised all the countries focused on in our case selections to come up with the following categorisation of crisis effects (Table 1.2).

As the authors themselves admit, this is a rough typology using a limited number of criteria that does not account for additional country-specific factors such as scandals or government crises. Nor does it account for national perceptions of crisis, which may be more subjective and judged according to that country's specific experience and/or culture rather than by comparative criteria. Therefore, when assessing the impact of crisis in each country in our conclusion, we will note this comparative categorisation, as well as the more detailed evidence given in our specific country case studies. Before we

Table 1.2   Typology of Crises

Economic Crisis	Political Crisis	
	Weak Impact	*Strong Impact*
Weak impact	Denmark, France, Germany, Netherlands	
Strong impact	UK, Latvia	Czech Republic, Cyprus, Greece, Iceland, Ireland, Portugal, Slovenia, Spain

Source: Developed from Hanspeter Kriesi and Takis S. Pappas, 'Populism during Crisis: An Introduction', in *European Populism in the Shadow of the Great Recession*, ed. Hanspeter Kriesi and Takis S. Pappas (Colchester: ECPR Press, 2015), 17.

outline the structure of our work, however, we will present our expectations of how the crisis should affect the radical Left.

As noted above, we have two main research foci in this volume: (1) to analyse the general reasons for the divergent performance of the radical Left: (2) to analyse the specific ways in which the Great Recession has affected this performance and how RLPs have responded to this change in the environment. The literature gives us three contrasting stories of how the crisis should play out.

The most obvious story, consistent with Žižek's view of an 'open field', is what we call the *radical insurgency thesis*: that the crisis should prove a boon for RLPs. It appears logical that 'under the right political conditions, economic hard times can provide fertile ground for the development of far-Left politics and policies that aim to redirect or constrain market forces'.[44] After all, most parties, and not just the most obvious newsmakers like Syriza, have long critiqued national and EU-level governments for leading elitist neoliberal projects imposing unacceptable sacrifices on unwitting populations. Moreover, RLPs have spent the last two decades recovering from post-Soviet collapse, consolidating, coalescing and becoming ready for government. Given the dire socio-economic post-crisis conditions in many countries, 'radical' left-wing arguments *should* therefore look less like ideological fantasy and more like hard fact and mainstream 'common sense'. Even if neoliberalism remains dominant, the crisis (particularly the European sovereign debt crisis) has revealed fault lines in its core ideas and policies (the Washington Consensus, hyper-globalisation, the huge reduction of state functions, deregulation of financial and other markets, etc.), as well as institutional problems with EU economic and monetary integration.[45] In addition, since the social democratic party family in the European Union has acquiesced in such policies, whereas RLPs have long fought them, this should at least lead to significant recalibration on the left in favour of RLPs.[46]

We have already flagged up some potential problems with this argument, principally that, except in a few cases, an obvious 'boon' for RLPs has been hard to discern. Nevertheless, the recent electoral successes of Syriza and Podemos perhaps indicate that there is truth in the hypothesis that *a deep economic crisis enables increasing support for the radical Left* (Hypothesis 1a). We would particularly expect *a deep economic crisis combined with a political crisis to increase RLP support* (H1b). Parties are unlikely to dramatically increase their support, or new parties to form, without the perception that 'there is something wrong': at the most a 'deep division or cleavage caused by a major social or political transformation'.[47] However, such a cleavage is unlikely to have political consequences unless there are openings in the political space, for example, there are major changes in voter sentiment that existing parties are unwilling and unable to address that give potential for new challengers.[48]

Additionally, when political systems do not address insurgents' concerns, this is traditionally considered a major incentive for social movement mobilisation.[49] Even prior to the crisis, RLPs placed increasing priority on both 'participatory linkages' (ties with members and voters) and 'environmental linkages' (ties with organised civil society groups).[50] Therefore, they might be expected to benefit from any increase in anti-austerity movement mobilisation. Mainstream parties' implication in austerity measures that directly immiserate their populations is potentially a major factor in promoting such voter realignment and social mobilisation.

A linked issue is that we would expect *those RLPs that have most developed their populist appeal to benefit in conditions of combined economic and political crises* (H1c). This is because populism is an archetypal protest discourse that emerges in times of crisis.[51] Populism posits an insurmountable antagonism between elites and the people, which will appear to face an ideal incubator in conditions of economic immiseration, rising inequality combined with popular dissatisfaction with their leaders. Austerity policies, where (particularly via the Troika) economic rigour imposes a painful straightjacket over democratic choices, appear tailor-made to incentivise populist arguments about remote, technocratic elites. Needless to say, such arguments are also grist to the mill of right-wing populists, who can highlight the actions of nefarious foreign elites and/or allegedly greedy debtor nations.[52] Nevertheless, a left-wing populist critique that focuses on the crimes of economic elites (bankers, multinationals, capitalists in general) might be expected to have traction.

The second story is the *'no change' thesis*. There is a strong argument that there has been no particular ideological direction to political responses to the crisis.[53] No party family, right or left, has benefitted more than another. Rather the main result, in accordance with retrospective voting models, is that incumbents have been evaluated on their economic management during the crisis, and voted for accordingly.[54] Thus, part of the reason for the ostensible weakness of the social democrats in the crisis is that many social democratic parties (e.g. in the United Kingdom, Spain, Portugal and Greece) were the incumbents at the beginning of the crisis. However, this is no defeat for the Left as such, because the electoral process has caused the Right to suffer the same fate, and resulted in the Left returning to power in post-crisis elections in several countries (such as Portugal, Slovakia, Denmark and indeed Greece).

It is fair to say that this thesis concentrates on governing parties, and gives scant attention to changes within the wider party system, unless new challengers offer governing options.[55] But, the implication is that, since most RLPs are relatively small parties, they will be largely bypassed by the most significant electoral changes. So we can expect that *RLPs will not benefit from the crisis unless they become viable governing alternatives to incumbent parties* (H2a). RLPs have a very mixed record in coalition government, being usually unable to demonstrate concrete benefits to their supporters.[56] So, we would expect that *the main benefits will only occur in the very rare cases where RLPs become the dominant governing partner* (H2b).

The final story is the *'success shock' thesis*: that the crisis is more challenge than opportunity. Like all parties, RLPs are relatively conservative organisations. They are only likely to dramatically change their party strategies after changes to the dominant intra-party coalition, leadership rotation, or a substantial 'external shock'.[57] Could the Great Recession be such a sufficient external shock? The radical insurgency thesis certainly implies that this is a positive shock, impelling RLPs to greater success if they 'seize the day' and adopt suitable ideological and organisational strategies to benefit from the propitious external environment. But what if RLPs do not conceive the crisis as propitious? There are several reasons for such a supposition. One is the nature of the crisis itself. If we understand the crisis as a 'capitalist crisis' with neoliberalism battered but not broken, then insurgency opportunities for the radical Left are more restricted than they might otherwise appear. Moreover, the European Union is an actor with a powerful market-making bias.[58] It has a powerful homogenising impetus with 'embedded neoliberalism' hard-wiring free trade, market deregulation and state rationalisation into its DNA.[59] The 'strategic defeat' of the Syriza government in 2015 could be seen to confirm the way in which the international institutions can force even mildly Keynesian propositions to kowtow to market orthodoxy.

The specificities of the current crisis notwithstanding, some argue that, for ideological reasons, times of crisis rarely benefit the Left. Perhaps it is normal for the Right to benefit most, because during crisis, voters become risk-averse and focus on 'reassurance rather than radicalism'.[60] Similarly, it is arguable that the Left's traditional focus on programme and progress rather that identitarian issues means that the Right has traditionally spoken better to people's emotions at times of crisis.[61] Other ideological reasons are also compelling: do leftist parties have a fundamental uncertainty about how to deal with capitalist crises? Often brought to power the wake of crises, they are allegedly fundamentally unsure whether they are the 'doctor[s] at the sickbed of capitalism or ... the heir[s] waiting to inherit'.[62] They usually respond by managing capitalism before they can even consider replacing it. The final ideological reason is perhaps the simplest. Given that *prima facie* the crisis vindicates much of the radical left critique, do RLPs need to change anything particular to adapt or exploit the crisis? Is it not proof of the inherent rectitude of their strategy so far? It would perhaps be an understandable historical reflex if RLPs thought that the crisis showed the seeds of capitalism's own destruction beginning to sprout.

All of these arguments indicate a 'success shock': that an opportunity that one is ill-prepared to exploit can become a catastrophe. This can have two variants, first an 'electoral success shock' when previously opposition parties struggle to deal with unprecedented electoral success[63]; second is a 'dashed expectations shock', when a failure to benefit from a supposed golden opportunity turns (as in the Syriza case) relative success into strategic defeat. Defeats are in turn a major fact in instigating party change.[64] The above reasons lead us to our final hypotheses. First, *ideological reasons make RLPs ill-prepared to benefit from the crisis* (H3a). Similarly, we might expect that the more doctrinaire and less pragmatic parties might be most so afflicted. Granted, the relative 'ideological' nature of RLPs is difficult to measure, but, from the above party sub-categories we might assume that, owing to their doctrinaire traditionalism, *the conservative communists and revolutionary extreme Left are least able to benefit from the crisis* (H3b). As noted above, due to their relative pragmatism and eclecticism, we might expect parties with a more populist profile to benefit most.

Overview of the Volume

The book has three main sections. The first presents four chapters analysing RLPs in comparative perspective. The aim of this section is to provide a wider spatial and temporal lens than the case studies, therefore adding context and depth for the overall analysis. We start with a focus on RLP electoral performance before the crisis, which will firm up our expectations of how RLPs will perform post-crisis. We focus on general trends in radical left conceptualisations of the crisis, interactions with social movements before and after the crisis, and how the radical Left responds to the related challenges of immigration and the radical Right.

The second section of the book presents 11 country case studies. While recognising that we could not cover every European country, these cases were chosen to maximise geographical breadth and to include countries that have been affected by the Great Recession to varying degrees. The countries that are analysed allow us to cover a range of RLPs to provide variation in both type of party and party response to crisis. The parties differ in potential independent variables such as presence in government/opposition, size and ideological subgroup within the radical Left. Moreover, they have taken a range of programmatic and organisational responses to the crisis and experienced diverse electoral fortunes since its onset.

The country cases are not limited to EU countries (we include a chapter on Iceland), first because (as in the Icelandic case) some of the largest RLPs are outside the European Union; second because the European radical Left aspires to a politics beyond the European Union; third, because links between

EU and non-EU members are increasing, and therefore the broader aspirations of the radical Left need to be analysed. However, except for occasional references throughout, we do not analyse former Soviet Eastern Europe in depth. Although in many respects parties there are generally comparable, the crisis period there encompasses very different phenomena, for example, the absence of any real possibility to politicise the crisis in authoritarian Russia.[65]

Although the precise form, structure and content of the case studies is necessarily divergent, the case-study authors have concentrated on the following areas:

- What the radical Left represented before the crisis. Who the main parties were, their significance and general stances.
- What the crisis has represented in each country: what the overall economic situation has been; whether and how the crisis has been politicised within each country. Our authors analyse to what degree the crisis has opened up political opportunities for the radical Left (e.g. changes in the positions of main rivals such as the social democrats and Greens, governing prospects).
- Whether there has been any specific programmatic impact of the crisis upon the radical Left. The authors analyse how RLPs have portrayed and explained the crisis and how they have responded. Have they radicalised or moderated, developed new ideological approaches (such as populism), or new specific policy proposals? Have their responses been shaped more by existing party ideology or by engaging with salient issues in the electorate?
- Whether there has been any specific organisational impact of the crisis upon the radical Left. For instance, have there been any membership divisions over strategy? Has party unity come under strain? Have there been any identifiable developments in participatory linkages (ties with members and voters) or environmental linkages (ties with organised civil society groups)? Above all, they analyse whether RLPs are able to use the crisis to forge new links with social movements.
- Finally, they ask whether there has been any specific electoral impact of the crisis in national and European elections. What accounts for national parties' success and failure?

The third and final section of the book consists of one chapter analysing the pan-European policy and organisational response of the radical Left. Understanding the extent to which the radical Left is able to put forward a transnational solution to a transnational problem is a vital element of understanding its response to the crisis. We conclude with a systematic consideration of where the crisis leaves the radical Left, and the study of it.

NOTES

1. Joe Weisenthal, 'I Just Saw the Most Feared Man in All of Europe,' *Business Insider*, 14 June 2012, http://www.businessinsider.com/alexis-tsipras-rally-2012-6.

2. Cf. S. M., 'The Bernie Manifesto: How Much of a Socialist Is Sanders?,' *The Economist*, 1 February 2016, http://www.economist.com/blogs/democracyinamerica/2016/02/bernie-manifesto.

3. For example, Stuart Jeffries, 'Why Marxism Is on the Rise Again', *The Guardian*, 4 July 2012, http://www.theguardian.com/world/2012/jul/04/the-return-of-marxism.

4. For example, Dan Hancox, 'Why Ernesto Laclau Is the Intellectual Figurehead for Syriza and Podemos,' *The Guardian*, 9 February 2015, http://www.theguardian.com/commentisfree/2015/feb/09/ernesto-laclau-intellectual-figurehead-syriza-podemos; Marina Prentoulis and Lasse Thomassen, 'The Winds Are Changing: A New Left Populism for Europe', *openDemocracy*, 27 January 2015, http://www.opendemocracy.net/can-europe-make-it/marina-prentoulis-lasse-thomassen/winds-are-changing-new-left-populism-for-europe.

5. For further details see Luke March, 'Radical Left Parties and Movements: Allies, Associates or Antagonists?,' in *Radical Left Movements in Europe*, ed. Magnus Wennerhag, Christian Fröhlich and Grzegorz Piotrowski (Farnham: Ashgate, 2016); Luke March, 'What We Know and Do Not Know about the Radical Left (and What Do We Want to Know?),' (ECPR General Conference, Bordeaux, 2013).

6. For example, Luke March and Cas Mudde, 'What's Left of the Radical Left? The European Radical Left after 1989: Decline *and* Mutation', *Comparative European Politics* 3 (2005): 23–49; Jonathan Olsen et al., eds., *Left Parties in National Governments* (Basingstoke: Palgrave Macmillan, 2010); Luke March, *Radical Left Parties in Europe* (Abingdon: Routledge, 2011); Fabien Escalona and Mathieu Vieira, 'The Radical Left in Europe: Thoughts About the Emergence of a Family,' Fondation Jean-Jaurès/Observatoire de La Vie Politique (Fondation Jean-Jaurès, 19 November 2013).

7. For example, Giorgos Charalambous, 'All the Shades of Red: Examining the Radical Left's Euroscepticism,' *Contemporary Politics* 17, no. 3 (2011): 299–320; Richard Dunphy, *Contesting Capitalism?: Left Parties and European Integration* (Manchester: Manchester University Press, 2004); Nicolò Conti and Vincenzo Memoli, 'The Multi-Faceted Nature of Party-Based Euroscepticism,' *Acta Politica* 47, no. 2 (2012): 91–112; Michael Holmes and Knut Roder, eds., *The Left and the European Constitution: From Laeken to Lisbon* (Manchester: Manchester University Press, 2012).

8. For example, Olsen et al., *Left Parties in National Governments*; Tim Bale and Richard Dunphy, 'In from the Cold Left Parties and Government Involvement since 1989,' *Comparative European Politics* 9, no. 3 (2011): 269–91.

9. For example, Luke March and Charlotte Rommerskirchen, 'Out of Left Field? Explaining the Variable Electoral Success of European Radical Left Parties', *Party Politics* 21, no. 1 (2015): 40–53; Luis Ramiro, 'Support for Radical Left Parties in Western Europe: Social Background, Ideology and Political Orientations', *European Political Science Review* 8, no. 1 (2016): 1–23; Mark Visser et al., 'Support for

Radical Left Ideologies in Europe', *European Journal of Political Research* 53, no. 3 (2014): 541–58; Raul Gomez et al., 'Varieties of Radicalism: Examining the Diversity of Radical Left Parties and Voters in Western Europe', *West European Politics* 39, no. 2 (2016): 351–79.

10. The phrase refers to the 1979 film *Monty Python's Life of Brian*, in which a fictional Judean People's Front parodied sectarian splits among the radical Left.

11. March, 'Radical Left Parties and Movements'; March, 'What We Know and Do Not Know about the Radical Left'. Nevertheless, an early contribution to developing the literature on RLPs and gender is Bice Maiguashca, Jonathan Dean and Dan Keith, 'Pulling together in a crisis? Anarchism, feminism and the limits of left-wing convergence in austerity Britain,' *Capital & Class* (2016): doi: 0309816815627388.

12. Although for shorter analyses from an activist perspective, see the issue 'The Radical Left in Europe', *Socialism and Democracy*, 69 (2015).

13. Sir Walter Raleigh, Preface to *The History of the World*, 1614, at http://www.bartleby.com/39/17.html (accessed 30 March 2016).

14. Francis Fukuyama, 'Where Is the Uprising from the Left?', *Spiegel Online*, 2 January 2012, http://www.spiegel.de/international/world/0,1518,812208,00.html.

15. Perry Anderson, 'Renewals', *New Left Review* 1 (2000): 1–20.

16. David J. Bailey et al., 'Introduction', in *European Social Democracy during the Global Economic Crisis : Renovation or Resignation?*, ed. David J. Bailey et al. (Manchester: Manchester University Press, 2014), 1–15.

17. Ashley Lavelle, 'Postface: Death by a Thousand Cuts,' in *European Social Democracy during the Global Economic Crisis : Renovation or Resignation?*, ed. David J. Bailey et al. (Manchester: Manchester University Press, 2014), 270–83.

18. As cited in Luke Cooper and Simon Hardy, *Beyond Capitalism? The Future of Radical Politics* (Winchester: Zero Books, 2012), 108.

19. Leo Panitch and Sam Gindin, 'The Current Crisis: A Socialist Perspective,' in *The Great Credit Crash*, ed. Martijn Konings (London: Verso, 2010), 392.

20. Cas Mudde, 'The Far Right in the 2014 European Elections: Of Earthquakes, Cartels and Designer Fascists,' *The Washington Post*, 30 May 2014, https://www.washingtonpost.com/news/monkey-cage/wp/2014/05/30/the-far-right-in-the-2014-european-elections-of-earthquakes-cartels-and-designer-fascists/.

21. Colin Crouch, *The Strange Non-Death of Neoliberalism* (Cambridge: Polity Press, 2011).

22. Cas Mudde, 'The War of Words Defining the Extreme Right Party Family,' *West European Politics* 19, no. 2 (1996): 225–48.

23. March and Mudde, 'What''s Left of the Radical Left?'; Cf. Olsen et al., *Left Parties in National Governments*.

24. Several authors in this book do refer to the SF, since its evolution is relevant to the radical Left. For example, McGowan and Keith (chapter 5) show how its positions on immigration changed as it went through a process of de-radicalisation.

25. For example, Andreas Fagerholm, 'What Is Left for the Radical Left? A Comparative Examination of the Policies of Radical Left Parties in Western Europe before and after 1989', *Journal of Contemporary European Studies* (March 2016): doi:10.1080/14782804.2016.1148592.

26. David Arter, "'Communists We Are No Longer, Social Democrats We Can Never Be": The Evolution of the Leftist Parties in Finland and Sweden', *Journal of Communist Studies and Transition Politics* 18, no. 3 (2002): 1–28.

27. Pablo Iglesias, 'Spain on Edge', *New Left Review* 93 (2015): 27–8.

28. Andreas Karitzis, 'The "SYRIZA Experience": Lessons and Adaptations', *open-Democracy*, 17 March 2016, https://www.opendemocracy.net/can-europe-make-it/andreas-karitzis/syriza-experience-lessons-and-adaptations-0.

29. Cas Mudde, 'After One Year in Government, Syriza and Greece Are More Isolated Than Ever,' *The World Post*, 25 January 2016, http://www.huffingtonpost.com/theworldpost/.

30. Mario Candeias, 'From a Fragmented Left to Mosaic,' *Zeitschrift Luxemburg*, April 2010, http://www.zeitschrift-luxemburg.de/from-a-fragmented-left-to-mosaic/. See also Kate Hudson, *The New European Left: A Socialism for the Twenty-First Century?* (London: Palgrave Macmillan, 2012).

31. For more see March, *Radical Left Parties in Europe*; Luke March, 'Problems and Perspectives of Contemporary European Radical Left Parties: Chasing a Lost World or Still a World to Win?,' *International Critical Thought* 2, no. 3 (2012): 314–39.

32. See Dan Keith and Giorgos Charalambous, 'On the (non) distinctiveness of Marxism-Leninism: The Portuguese and Greek communist parties compared,' *Communist and Post-Communist Studies* (2016), http://dx.doi.org/10.1016/j.postcomstud.2016.04.001.

33. Cf. Escalona and Vieira, 'The Radical Left in Europe.'

34. Gomez et al., 'Varieties of Radicalism'.

35. March, 'Problems and Perspectives of Contemporary European Radical Left Parties'; March, *Radical Left Parties in Europe*.

36. Cas Mudde, 'The Populist Zeitgeist', *Government and Opposition* 39, no. 4 (2004): 543.

37. Gomez et al., 'Varieties of Radicalism'.

38. Matthijs Rooduijn and Tjitske Akkerman, 'Flank Attacks. Populism and Left-Right Radicalism in Western Europe', *Party Politics* (2015), doi:10.1177/1354068815596514.

39. For example, Takis S. Pappas, 'Populist Hegemony in Greece', *openDemocracy*, 25 September 2015, https://www.opendemocracy.net/can-europe-make-it/takis-s-pappas/populist-hegemony-in-greece.

40. 'The "red Lines" of the Greek Government – Are the "red Lines" of the Greek People', *Australia-Greece Solidarity Campaign*, 19 May 2015, https://australiagreecesolidarity.wordpress.com/2015/05/19/the-red-lines-of-the-greek-government-are-the-red-lines-of-the-greek-people/.

41. For example, Andrew Filardo et al., 'The International Financial Crisis: Timeline, Impact and Policy Responses in Asia and the Pacific', BIS Papers (Bank for International Settlements, July 2010), http://www.bis.org/publ/bppdf/bispap52c.pdf.

42. Jay C. Shambaugh, 'The Euro's Three Crises', Brookings Papers on Economic Activity, Spring 2012, http://www.brookings.edu/about/projects/bpea/latest-conference/shambaugh.

43. Hanspeter Kriesi and Takis S. Pappas, 'Populism during Crisis: An Introduction,' in *European Populism in the Shadow of the Great Recession*, ed. Hanspeter Kriesi and Takis S. Pappas, Studies in European Political Science (Colchester: ECPR Press, 2015), 9–18.

44. Mark Vail and Benjamin Bowyer, 'Poverty and Partisanship: Social and Economic Sources of Support for the Far Left in Contemporary Germany,' *Comparative European Politics* 10, no. 4 (2011): 17.

45. Mark Blyth, *Austerity : The History of a Dangerous Idea* (Oxford: Oxford University Press, 2013); Dani Rodrik, *The Globalization Paradox* (Oxford: Oxford University Press, 2012).

46. Ashley Lavelle, 'Postface: Death by a Thousand Cuts', in *European Social Democracy during the Global Economic Crisis : Renovation or Resignation?*, ed. David J. Bailey et al. (Manchester: Manchester University Press, 2014), 270–83.

47. Charles Hauss and David Rayside, 'The Development of New Parties in Western Democracies since 1945,' in *Political Parties: Development and Decay*, ed. Louis Maisel and David Cooper (London: Sage, 1978), 36.

48. March and Rommerskirchen, 'Out of Left Field?'; Hauss and Rayside, 'The Development of New Parties in Western Democracies since 1945,' 45–53.

49. Charles Tilly, *From Mobilization to Revolution* (Reading, MA: Addison-Wesley, 1978).

50. Myrto Tsakatika and Marco Lisi, 'Zippin up My Boots, Goin' Back to My Roots': Radical Left Parties in Southern Europe,' *South European Society and Politics* 18, no. 1 (2013): 1–19.

51. Ernesto Laclau, *On Populist Reason*, Reprint (London: Verso, 2007).

52. Kriesi and Pappas, 'Populism during Crisis: An Introduction', 8.

53. Larry M. Bartels, 'Ideology and Retrospection in Electoral Responses to the Great Recession,' in *Mass Politics in Tough Times*, ed. Larry Bartels and Nancy Bermeo (Oxford: Oxford University Press, 2014), 185–223.

54. Hanspeter Kriesi, 'The Political Consequences of the Economic Crisis in Europe,' in *Mass Politics in Tough Times*, ed. Larry Bartels and Nancy Bermeo (Oxford University Press, 2014), 297–333.

55. Ibid., 300.

56. Richard Dunphy and Tim Bale, 'The Radical Left in Coalition Government: Towards a Comparative Measurement of Success and Failure,' *Party Politics* 17, no. 4 (2011): 488–504; Olsen et al., *Left Parties in National Governments*. See also chapter 2.

57. March, *Radical Left Parties in Europe*; Jonathan Olsen et al., 'From Pariahs to Players? Left Parties in National Governments,' in *Left Parties in National Governments*, ed. Jonathan Olsen, Michael Koß, and Dan Hough (Basingstoke: Palgrave, 2010), 1–15.

58. Chad Damro, 'Market Power Europe,' *Journal of European Public Policy* 19, no. 5 (2012): 682–99.

59. Bastiaan van Apeldoorn, 'The Struggle over European Order: Transnational Class Agency in the Making of "Embedded Neo-Liberalism",' in *Social Forces in the Making of the New Europe : The Restructuring of European Social Relations in the*

Global Political Economy, ed. Andreas Bieler and Adam David Morton (Basingstoke: Palgrave, 2001), 70–89.

60. Andrew Gamble, *The Spectre at the Feast: Capitalist Crisis and the Politics of Recession* (Basingstoke: Palgrave Macmillan, 2009), 112.

61. George Lakoff, Howard Dean and Don Hazen, *Don't Think of an Elephant!: Know Your Values and Frame the Debate – The Essential Guide for Progressives* (White River Junction: Chelsea Green, 2004).

62. Fritz Tarnow, cited in Anthony Wright, 'Social Democracy and Democratic Socialism', in *Contemporary Political Ideologies*, ed. Roger Eatwell and Anthony Wright (London: Pinter, 1993), 87.

63. Olsen et al., 'From Pariahs to Players?', 57.

64. Peter Mair, Wolfgang C. Müller and Fritz Plasser, 'Introduction: Electoral Challenges and Party Responses,' in *Political Parties and Electoral Change: Party Responses to Electoral Markets*, ed. Peter Mair, Wolfgang C. Müller and Fritz Plasser (London: Sage, 2004), 1–19.

65. Luke March, 'The Russian Duma "Opposition": No Drama out of Crisis?,' *East European Politics* 28, no. 3 (2012): 241–55.

PART I

THE INTERNATIONAL ECONOMIC CRISIS AND THE CRISIS OF THE LEFT

Chapter 2

Radical Left 'Success' before and after the Great Recession

Still Waiting for the Great Leap Forward?

Luke March

In recent years, several analysts have argued that the radical Left has stabilised and even been growing in European party systems.[1] However, such prognoses often appeared confounded, with initial dividends from the Great Recession meagre, and many successes counteracted by debacles. However, 2015 marked an apparent step-change. Syriza's stunning victory in the January Greek legislative elections elected the first anti-austerity radical left government within the European Union, at a time when the austerity consensus appeared under renewed assault. This led to a profusion of sympathetic articles proclaiming that Syriza would start a wave of hope and solidarity that would radically transform Europe and finally undermine TINA (Thatcher's adage that 'There Is No Alternative' to neoliberal transformation).[2] Such hopes took a battering with Syriza's submission to the August 2015 Third Memorandum. Nevertheless, impressive results for RLPs in Spain and Portugal in late 2015 reinforced the sense of an upward trajectory. Was this really the case?

The main question of this chapter is whether the Great Recession has indeed marked change rather than continuity in RLPs' performance. It identifies long-term trends to provide a comparative overview examining RLP 'success' both before and after the crisis. Although 'success' here mainly addresses the electoral and policy realms, I recognise that most RLPs judge their own performance reflecting extra-parliamentary linkages.[3] Therefore, such elements as links with social movements will also be mentioned, prior to being fleshed out more fully in the case-study chapters.

The chapter shows how by the mid-2000s, the European radical Left was indeed emerging as a more electorally consolidated party family that was, in certain circumstances, able to challenge mainstream (particularly social democratic) parties. Nevertheless, this was a relative gain: the party family was unable to become more than the sum of its parts. Even prior to 2008, external socio-economic conditions in many European countries were propitious for RLPs. However, internal factors within such parties (particularly the absence of a sufficiently electorally attractive vision and still-persistent ideological and strategic conflicts) and divisions between them often prevented RLPs benefitting. To this degree, the party family had not fully overcome its own communist-era crisis. Initially, the post-2008 environment showed more continuity than change, as few parties exploited deteriorating economic conditions. Nevertheless, as the crisis has developed, opportunities have demonstrably increased. Such opportunities include not only changes to the external environment (the intensification of economic distress and the breakdown of established party systems), but also new strategic possibilities within RLPs themselves. The Syriza and Podemos 'magic equations' demonstrate the effectiveness of combining new forms of populist electoral appeal with programmatic flexibility and enhanced party-movement linkages.[4] Nevertheless, most other parties lack this combination of external opportunities and internal resources, meaning that similar success is unlikely to be repeated *imminently* elsewhere. Similarly, dramatic ruptures in European politics remain, as yet, remote possibilities.

THE PATCHWORK OF ELECTORAL SUCCESS AND FAILURE

A longer-term historical perspective confirms several pertinent facts (Figure 2.1). Even at its post-World War II zenith, when boosted by its role

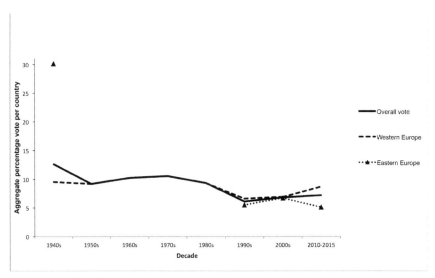

Figure 2.1 The Electoral Performance of the Radical Left in Europe, 1945–2015.
Source: Authors' calculations from www.parties-and-elections.eu and www.parlgov.org.

in the resistance and the relatively benign image of the Soviet Union, the European radical Left was only ever a 'small party family', seldom polling over 15 per cent of the vote.[5]

Table 2.1 (showing the aggregate national percentage vote across all European countries) confirms a sharp decline from the 1940s until the 1950s in overall performance (12.6 to 9.2 per cent), followed by upwards stabilisation in the 1960s and 1970s (10.2 and 10.5 per cent, respectively).[6] A collapse started in the 1980s and especially 1990s (9.3 then 6.1 per cent, respectively), followed by a marginal uptick in the 2000s (6.8 per cent), enhancing in the 2010s (7.2 per cent). Despite this recovery, today's radical Left remains way below its historical high, and is weaker in former Eastern Europe (just 5.1 per cent in the 2010s). Moreover, the radical left vote has become increasingly fragmented domestically. The vote *per party* decreased from 14.9 per cent in the 1940s to 5.2 per cent in the 1980s and merely 3.7 in the 1990s, before recovering to reach 4.5 per cent in 2010–2015. This data reflects that, even at the peak of Western European Communist Party (WECP) strength, few parties (in Cyprus, Finland, France, Iceland, Italy, Portugal and San Marino) ever hit the 15-per cent mark. Many WECPs were nationally insignificant after the 1950s and by the 1970s, 90 per cent of West European communists belonged to the CPs of Italy and France.[7] Various 'new left' parties helped sustain aggregate strength, but were often relatively tiny and/ or ephemeral themselves.

The contemporary situation confirms that RLP support has become geographically broader, but electorally shallower and more nationally variable still than in the communist era. Whereas France, Italy and other historical heartlands no longer make up its core, it is infinitesimal across much of the continent (in 21 of 42 European countries, RLPs poll less than 3 per cent *on aggregate*!) Focusing on the pre-crisis electoral performance of the most relevant European parliamentary (EP) RLPs makes the diversity very apparent (Table 2.1). Despite a marginal recovery (to 9.7 per cent) by 2008, aggregate growth cannot conceal that the fortunes of individual parties much differed. In some countries, party support drastically improved after 1990 (notably the Netherlands); in others it markedly declined (e.g. former WECP heartlands such as France and [especially] Italy); in most the position was stable over time, but volatile from one election to the next. Some general trends are evident. Only six of the 25 most relevant parties polled double digits in the 2000s. Moreover, the pockets of above-average strength were generally in poorer and/or smaller countries (e.g. Greece, Cyprus and Moldova), (only some) post-Soviet countries and outside the European Union. Crucially, RLPs had below-average strength in several core EU countries (e.g. France, Italy and Germany). In some (e.g. the United Kingdom and Austria) there was *no* relevant party whatsoever.

Table 2.1 The Electoral Performance of the Most Relevant RLPs, 1980–August 2008[§]

Country/Party	Average Vote 1980–9	Average Vote 1990–9	Average Vote 2000–2008	Vote Change 1989–2008	Vote Change 1999–2008	Post-1989 High	Post-1989 Low
EU-28							
Cyprus (AKEL)	30.1	31.7	32.9	2.8	1.2	34.7 (2001)	30.6 (1991)
Czech Republic (KSČM)	CP	12.1	15.7	n/a	3.6	18.5 (2002)	10.3 (1996)
Denmark (EL)	8.7 (a)	2.5	2.7	-6.0	0.2	3.4 (2005)	1.7 (1990)
Denmark (SF)	12.6	7.7	8.5	-4.1	0.8	13.0 (2007)	6.0 (2005)
Finland (VAS)	13.5 (b)	10.7	9.4	-4.1	-1.3	11.2 (1995)	8.8 (2007)
France (PCF)	12.4	9.6	4.6	-7.8	-5.0	9.9 (1997)	4.3 (2007)
Germany (LP)	CP	4.0	6.4	n/a	2.4	8.7 (2005)	2.4 (1990)
Greece (KKE)	10.4	5.1	6.5	-3.9	1.4	8.2 (2007)	4.5 (1993)
Greece (Syriza) (c)	6.8	6.1	3.8	-3	-2.3	10.3 (1990)	2.9 (1993)
Greece (DIKKI) (d)	n/a	4.4	2.2	n/a	-2.2	4.4 (1996)	1.8 (2004)
Ireland (Sinn Féin)	1.0	2.1	6.7	5.7	4.6	6.9 (2007)	1.6 (1992)
Italy (PRC) (e)	28.2 (e)	6.7	3.6	-24.6	-3.1	8.6 (1996)	3.1* (2008)
Latvia (LSP)	CP	5.6	(coalition)	n/a	n/a	5.6 (1995)	5.6 (1995)
Luxembourg (LÉNK)	5.3 (f)	3.3	2.6	-2.7	-0.6	3.3 (1999)	1.6 (1994)
Netherlands (SP)	0.4	2.4	9.6	9.4	7.2	16.6 (2006)	1.3 (1994)
Portugal (PCP)	15.6*	8.8*	7.3*	-8.3	-1.4	9.0* (1999)	7.0* (2002)
Portugal (BE)	n/a	2.4	4.6	n/a	2.2	6.4 (2005)	2.4 (1999)
Slovakia (KSS)	CP	2.1	5.1	n/a	3.0	6.3 (2002)	0.8 (1992)
Spain (PCE)	5.9*	9.2*	4.8*	-1.1	-4.4	9.2* (1993/6)	3.8* (2008)
Sweden (V)	5.6	7.6	7.2	1.6	-0.4	12.0 (1998)	4.5 (1991)
Average EU-28	*11.2*	*7.2*	*7.6*	*-3.6*	*0.4*		
Non-EU countries							
Iceland (VG)	15.4 (g)	12.6	11.6	-3.8	-1.0	14.3 (2007)	8.8 (2003)
Moldova (PCRM)	CP	30.1	48.1	n/a	18.1	50.1 (2001)	30.1 (1998)
Norway (SV)	6.8	7.0	10.7	3.9	3.7	12.5 (2001)	6.0 (1997)
Russia (KPRF)	CP	19.7	12.1	n/a	-7.6	24.3 (1999)	11.6 (2007)
San Marino (RCS)	26.6 (h)	3.4	6.1	-20.5	2.7	8.7* (2006)	3.3 (1998)
Ukraine (KPU)	CP	18.7	9.7	n/a	-9	24.7 (1998)	3.7 (2006)
Average non-EU	*16.3*	*15.3*	*16.4*	*0.1*	*1.1*		
Overall average	**12.1**	**9.1**	**9.7**	**-2.4**	**0.6**		

Key: [§] For simplicity and clarity, the relevance threshold is defined as obtaining at least 3 per cent of the vote and gaining parliamentary seats in at least one national election; only parties still extant at end of this period are included; * signifies in coalition. Coalitions not led by RLP are excluded; CP signifies ruling Communist Party; (a) Four constituent parties later forming EL; (b) Finnish People's Democratic League (SKDL; in 1987 SKDL + Democratic Alternative); (c) until 2004 as Synaspismós; (d) Democratic Social Movement. Joined Syriza in 2007; (e) Italian Communist Party (PCI); (f) Communist Party of Luxembourg (KPL) until 1999; (g) People's Alliance (AB) until 1995; (h) Sammarinese Communist Party (PCS).

Source: www.parties-and-elections.eu.

What therefore explains common trends and variations in RLP success before 2008? The ensuing analysis summarises the main reasons, focusing first on *demand-side factors* (long-term socio-economic and electoral variables), then the *external supply side* (party-system and institutional factors) and finally the *internal supply side* (factors internal to RLPs themselves). Recent scholarship argues that the demand side provides a necessary, albeit differential and not sufficient 'breeding ground' for RLPs across Europe and therefore the supply side explains much of the divergence in their trajectories.[8] For instance, the ideological support for the radical Left averages approximately 11 per cent across European electorates.[9] Particularly when protest voting is considered, this means that the potential RLP vote is usually *much* greater than achieved success. Even in the Soviet era, explanations were similar. Whereas countries with traditions of strong (particularly) class cleavages and economic impoverishment provided helpful milieux for WECPs, they did not determine party success, and parties needed 'clever exploitation' of the demand side to perform well.[10] Therefore, as for the radical Right, widespread demand should be 'a given, rather than the main puzzle' and the most pertinent research questions focus on 'why have so few parties been successful given the generally fertile breeding ground?'[11] Although the following sections outline general answers to this question, a significant degree of national variation is to be expected. After all, despite the imposed conformity of Leninism, WECPs were increasingly nationally specific by the 1980s. Therefore, in the absence of Moscow's guiding hand, identical post-Soviet trajectories would be more surprising still.

The Modernisation Crisis

The general context for the rise of anti-establishment parties since the 1980s (whether of right, left or green orientation) has been a 'modernisation crisis'.[12] This term encapsulates many things: the transition from industrial economies to post-industrialism; a declining role for class identities and the traditional proletariat; the end of the post-war 'social democratic consensus', whereby mainstream parties pursued Keynesian economics and protected the national welfare state and the flourishing of neoliberal globalisation since the 1970s. Most pertinent for the Left has been the structural disaggregation of social democrats' links to traditional electorates and affiliated organisations like trade unions. This has left social democrats' traditional Keynesian solutions at the mercy of financial markets, central banks and ratings agencies, leading to the neoliberalisation of social democracy itself.[13] Together, these factors have produced strata of the population who perceive themselves as 'modernisation losers', materially and psychologically threatened by the contemporary capitalist state's apparent inability to control borders, the economy and welfare. New forms of protest have emerged to reflect this trend.

The Populist Zeitgeist

One prevalent new form of protest is populism. Many European political actors have become increasingly prone to using elements of populism that is presenting themselves as 'ordinary' representatives of the 'common people', and depicting their opponents as the mainstream, elitist, 'Establishment'.[14] An accelerator of this process has been EU integration, which, as an elite-led project that impinges on national sovereignty with a pronounced market-making bias, has become the favoured target for new populists as the phantom of unaccountable and anti-popular policies imposed by a faceless bureaucratic elite.[15]

RLPs have certainly benefited directly from such sentiments. Their vote potential increases where an electorate's anti-globalisation and anti-EU sentiments are high.[16] Most contemporary RLPs can be regarded as 'Eurosceptic', although, as Michael Holmes and Simon Lightfoot argue in this volume, this term conceals varied and contradictory stances towards the European Union. Nevertheless, a core part of RLPs' appeal has long been critiquing the European Union for acting as globalisation's vanguard in favouring free-market integration over state-led regulation. Their common cause with the global justice movement (GJM) is based on defending 'globalisation losers' against new forms of economic insecurity ('precarity').[17]

Historical Legacy

The past matters, most obviously because RLPs are rarely newcomers: they either have a long historical pedigree (e.g. the Greek Communist Party [KKE], founded in 1924) or are recompositions of older organisations (e.g. Syriza, often seen as a 'new' party, has distant origins in the KKE-Interior of 1968–1987). The past is most evident in post-communist countries, where most RLPs (including Die Linke) are 'successor parties' – that is, they have partially inherited the former ruling parties' organisational and ideological legacy.[18] Yet in Western Europe too, an (albeit slowly diminishing) appeal to revolutionary traditions dating back to the early 1920s underpins sub-cultural support for parties such as the Cypriot Progressive Party of Working People (AKEL). Overall, the most successful RLPs today generally exist where their predecessors were successful. Weak legacies also mean weak RLPs today. With very few exceptions (e.g. Germany and the Netherlands), where there was no successful RLP in the 1980s (e.g. Britain, Austria and Belgium), there is none now.

However, although heritage usually underpins contemporary success, it is certainly not sufficient, and is sometimes an obstacle. In most post-communist countries outside the former Soviet Union, there has been no consistently successful RLP since 1989. This reflects how many ruling communist regimes lacked domestic legitimacy, particularly where communism was seen as an imported imposition. Generally, outside the Soviet Union communism simply lacked sufficient domestic legitimacy to sustain a post-communist RLP. In most cases (e.g. in Hungary and Poland), the former communists became social democrats and RLPs were marginalised. Throughout the 1990s until declining fortunes thereafter, such ex-communist social democratic parties monopolised links with trade unions and significant numbers of activists who might otherwise have formed independent RLPs.[19]

The Czech Communist Party of Bohemia and Moravia (KSČM), which remains one of Europe's stronger RLPs, represents an exception to this general trend. As Vladimír Handl and Andreas Goffin argue in this volume, at root is a strong interwar domestic socialist culture that continued during communist rule and underpins a strong traditionalism. Ammon Cheskin and Luke March's chapter also shows how the 'success' of the Latvian Socialist Party (LSP) results from coalition with other Russophone parties, with an appeal more focused on ethnic sentiments than left-wing policies. The LSP never exceeded 6 per cent of the vote when running independently. Overall, the communist past is a very mixed blessing, particularly for unabashed communist parties. With the exception of AKEL, no European CP (either in East and West) has avoided secular decline. Even when they have apparently stable ratings (e.g. 6–8 per cent in Greece and Portugal), this is far below their historical zenith.

Economic Distress

One of the factors most helping RLPs is a poor economic environment (especially high unemployment and low growth). This is unsurprising, given RLPs' emphasis on economic and job-security issues, particularly affecting lower-status constituencies.[20] Nevertheless, there has been no *direct* relationship between economic distress and RLP success (principally because the mainstream opposition and other protest parties may also benefit). Certainly, there were cases where the economy did directly matter prior to the Great Recession. For example, the Portuguese Left Bloc grew as Portugal's economy faltered in the mid-late 2000s (although it suffered a reverse in 2011 in the midst of Portugal's crisis). However, there are more counter-examples: RLP support *grew* alongside rising GDP and declining unemployment in several countries until 2007 (Denmark, Greece and the Netherlands), and fell despite rising unemployment in others (e.g. Spain in 2008 and the Czech Republic in 2005). Despite an average unemployment rate of 13.47 per cent between 1990 and 2016, there is no successful RLP in Poland. Clearly then, economic factors play an important background role, but are far from all-determining.

Political Institutions

Turning to the external supply side, it is evident that, as a small party family, RLPs are very susceptible to the influence of political institutions and other party competitors. For example, when electoral systems are not very proportional, or there are high parliamentary thresholds, these generally weaken small parties' prospects, and RLPs are no exception.[21] Generally, higher electoral thresholds in East-Central Europe have contributed to RLP marginalisation there. For example, the Hungarian Workers' Party (*Munkáspárt*) polled 3–4 per cent in the 1990s (enough for parliamentary representation in countries like the Netherlands), but it never crossed Hungary's 5-per cent parliamentary threshold. In addition, many Eastern European RLPs have suffered from restrictive legislation. In 1991–1993, new anti-communist authorities often banned communist parties and expropriated their resources. Although in much of the former Soviet Union the bans were eventually rescinded, in several states (e.g. the Baltic states), communists remain illegal or face continuing legal difficulties. This is one reason why the LSP has been unable to replicate the success of the Russian communists.

The Social Democratic Vacuum

One of the biggest factors affecting RLP performance is whether there is an open electoral field. In particular, the 'vacuum thesis' argues that social democrats' rightwards drift since the late 1990s has created a vacuum, meaning that former social democratic core constituencies are now available for capture by new actors.[22] Similarly, social democrats' uncritical adaptation to the European Union's market-integration policies has allowed RLPs to adopt 'Euroscepticism' as an identity marker vis-à-vis the Centre-Left.[23] Certainly, RLPs have often presented themselves as the real Left, appealing to former social democrats who feel deserted by their erstwhile parties. Such a strategy is potentially lucrative, because whenever RLPs attract protest votes, a significant proportion (often upwards of 25 per cent of their vote gained) comes from disaffected social democrats.

A potent symbol of the neoliberalisation of social democracy has been 'grand coalitions' between the Centre-Left and the Centre-Right. In several countries (e.g. Germany and especially Austria), these have a long tradition. Nevertheless, when the mainstream parties regularly collaborate in this way, such 'establishment party convergence' can boost 'outsider' parties (particularly populists) who claim that the 'Establishment' are all the same.[24] Certainly, such a populist critique of the social democrats as an integral component of the neoliberal establishment gave the Dutch Socialist Party and Die Linke much traction in the 2000s. In the post-crisis environment, this trend has intensified. Syriza's dramatic breakthrough in 2012–2015 is intimately related to 'Pasokification' – the collapse of the social democratic party (PASOK) following its implementation (in left-right coalitions) of austerity.[25] Consequently, Syriza successfully persuaded many former PASOK supporters that it was the only credible left party remaining.

However, over-fishing social democrats' electorates can backfire, weaken the RLP vote and increase social democratic support. RLP support proves particularly vulnerable if the main social democratic party can demonstrate it is a better 'useful vote' to defeat the Right. As Dan Keith argues in this volume, this dynamic helps explain why the SP vote first ballooned then returned to Labour in the September 2012 Netherlands elections. Moreover, opportunities to exploit social democrats do not always transpire. Not all social democrats have 'neoliberalised' – for example, the Socialist Party in Wallonia never fully embraced Blairism. As Fabien Escalona and Mathieu Vieira show (this volume), the French Socialist Party's avoidance of full austerity has weakened the RLPs' traction.

Moreover, competition from other non-establishment parties, including the Greens and the radical Right, constrains RLPs' ability to exploit the social democratic vacuum. Although most European green parties are no longer radical, in some countries (e.g. Finland and Western Germany), their espousal of non-mainstream concerns means that they can rival RLP support among the white-collar electorate.[26] In southern and (particularly) Eastern Europe, the Greens remain less viable as competitors because of the relative weakness of post-materialist politics.

That radical right parties (RRPs) compete with RLPs is no paradox. Historically, this phenomenon was most noted in the decline of the French Communist Party (PCF) in the 1980s, when working-class PCF voters defected to the French Front National en masse.[27] Contemporary competition between RLPs and RRPs is rarely so direct – each has very ideologically distinct core supporters that do not intersect.[28] However, competition for protest voters disaffected by the 'modernisation crisis' is more salient. As Escalona and Vieira note (this volume), it is the radical Right's 'agenda-setting' among the 'popular classes' with issues such as anti-immigration and defence of sovereignty that may limit RLPs' potential to exploit anti-EU, anti-globalisation and anti-establishment sentiments. In addition, many contemporary RRPs (such as the British National Party) and nationalist-populist parties (such as the Finns Party) combine identity issues with a Left-sounding 'welfare chauvinist' economic platform that defends indigenous workers' rights against 'outsiders'.[29]

Overall, even prior to the Great Recession, there were sufficiently advantageous external conditions for RLPs to succeed in many European countries. However, far from all European countries developed strong RLPs. Therefore, such external factors should be regarded as contextual, not causative, and we must focus more on factors internal to the RLPs themselves. The chief of these are now summarised.

Party Origins

Parties that took the initiative in reforming communism prior to communism's collapse (especially in Scandinavia, where transitions from orthodox Marxism-Leninism began in the early 1960s) were best placed to survive it. Overall, the evolution of many RLPs since their re(founding) in the late 1980s/early 1990s corroborates arguments that the ability of a party to use its Soviet-era legacy positively depends much on how elite struggles in the transition from communism were resolved in the early 1990s.[30] This lastingly affected whether a party was able to adopt a clear post-communist policy direction. For example, the Dutch SP's consistent ideological moderation was predicated on its rapid centralisation and de-Leninisation after 1991.[31] Where internal conflicts were not decisively resolved (e.g. the Italian *Rifondazione Comunista* never developed a party programme), RLPs potentially remain hampered by internal strategic disputes deriving from the Soviet era.

The Intra-Party Balance

Party organisation is also an important factor in shaping RLP success. Traditionally, over-dependence on Leninist democratic centralism was a critical weakness of CPs, and those that interpreted it most flexibly were also the most adaptable. In the post-Soviet era, this pattern has recurred: some parties have combined democratic centralism with ideological and strategic flexibility (e.g. the Cypriot AKEL), while many (e.g. the KKE, LSP, Portuguese Communist Party [PCP]) have demonstrated the strategic ossification common to parties upholding democratic centralism. In general, however, many RLPs have replaced democratic centralism with *Basisdemokratie* (grassroots democracy), which enhances linkages with the GJM.[32] This has improved pluralism and democracy, but the flip side can be more open internal tension (for instance, Die Linke has numerous internal platforms, making consensus over programmatic issues a 'tortuous process').[33]

Many RLPs experience conflict between policy purist *Fundis* and more pragmatic *Realos*. Nevertheless (as with the Greens of the 1980s), the Realos are increasingly dominant: many more successful parties (e.g. the Dutch SP and Portuguese Left Bloc) are led by pragmatists who focus less on abstract Marxist theory and more on practical campaigns that try to implement concrete policies and to build support broader than the party. Even (ex-) Trotskyist parties such as People Before Profit (Ireland) have grounded their increased popularity in becoming campaigning organisations (e.g. by being central to the anti-water charges movement in Ireland in 2014–2015). Similarly, most parties, even the more pragmatic, have become more 'populist' in terms of addressing the *vox populi* more than the proletariat.[34] Leadership Realism can often conflict with parties' orientation towards *Basisdemokratie*. Certainly, inveterate strategic/doctrinal disputes (e.g. over parliamentarism vs. movementism) have not entirely dissipated, and many CPs in particular retain conservative and sectarian practices. Even ostensibly ex-communist parties (such as the Finnish Left Alliance) have often been troubled by disputes predating 1991.[35]

Party Leadership

This related factor has great influence. For example, where conservatives retained control in the early 1990s (e.g. in the LSP or the KSČM), these parties continue 'introverted' doctrinaire strategies, focused on keeping party activists happy rather than broadening their electorate or making policy compromises. This has preserved stability but not dynamism. Where pragmatic leaders have been able to centralise, professionalise and de-ideologise their parties (as in the Dutch SP), they have often been largely able to respond flexibly to their environments with minimal risks of party splits.

In the most effective parties, the role of leadership has also changed. Rather than the dour 'democratically centralised' bureaucrats such as former PCF leader Georges Marchais (replicated today in the PCP's Jerónimo de Sousa or LSP's Alfrēds Rubiks, who have minimal appeal beyond the party base), many modern RLP leaders are non-dogmatic, media-savvy performers who are considered effective, if not 'charismatic' even by political opponents. For instance, interlocutors have recognised Alexis Tsipras' solidity, statesmanship and charm: 'He comes across neither as a fervent ideologue nor as an aggressive *enfant terrible*.'[36] Of course, poor leadership is often evident. The PCF's long electoral slide since the 1970s results from continually reforming 'too little, too late'. Generally, leadership change is one of the most significant factors impacting on party success: many parties have suffered electorally after leadership changes (e.g. the Dutch SP after Jan Marijnissen in 2008); in other cases a new leader has soon brought electoral gain (e.g. Syriza after Tsipras's entry into parliament in 2009).

Party Goal

Introverted strategies that prioritised policy purity over electoral success were once traditional to most RLPs, who, after all, were highly ideological actors.

Certainly, this remains partially true: several communist parties (e.g. the KSČM, KKE and PCP), have appeared relatively content with niche positions concentrating on programmatic purism. For others (e.g. the Italian Rifondazione or French PCF) the prospects of broader coalition or government have caused serious internal ructions. However, as outlined below, most RLPs now find the notion of governing in so-called left-left coalitions (between the Centre-Left and radical Left) at national-level uncontentious, at least under favourable conditions. Even where governing possibilities remain remote, many RLPs have sought new constituencies and allies. Several now exist in semi-permanent coalitions (such as the Portuguese Democratic Unity Coalition [CDU], Spanish United Left [IU] and [less stably] the French Left Front).

Overall, some advantageous party strategies can be observed. Many of the more electorally dynamic parties have relied decreasingly on abstract ideological slogans and doctrine; they try to encapsulate all radical left trends under an umbrella of opposition to neoliberalism (or austerity) that makes little *electoral* reference to Marxism or socialism (this is most noticeable in the Portuguese Left Bloc and the Dutch SP). Symptomatic was the 2009 refounding of the French Communist Revolutionary League as the New Anti-Capitalist Party, whose spokesperson (Olivier Besancenot) claimed no longer to be a Trotskyist. Parties that have espoused specific campaigns or practical actions have often received electoral dividends (e.g. both the French and Dutch Left got boosts from their 2005 opposition to the European Union's Constitutional Treaty). It is now unproblematic for most parties to adopt non-Marxist ideological accents, such as environmentalism, feminism and regionalism. One of the most noticeable new accents is the left-wing populism that focuses more on identity than on theory. For all that Syriza and Podemos are presented as the harbingers of a new left-populist spectre haunting the continent, the fact is that many other successful RLPs have attempted elements of similar strategies over the last decade, albeit less successfully.[37] Even Syriza's dogmatic opponent, the conservative communist KKE, has dallied with populism and nationalism.[38]

THE CRISIS AND RLPS: PLUS ÇA CHANGE?

Given the above, there was every reason to expect that RLPs might be chief beneficiaries of the post-2008 crisis, providing they could exploit the favourable milieu. Falling output, rising unemployment and Euroscepticism, as well as ideological support for RLPs even where such parties were absent, appear a potent growth formula. However, this section will show that RLPs' electoral gains were meagre prior to the rise of Syriza. It is still unclear whether the tide has substantially or lastingly turned.

The EP elections make a comparative benchmark. In June 2009, the European United Left-Nordic Green Left parliamentary group (GUE/NGL) actually dropped from 42 MEPs to 35, with its seat share declining from 5.2 to 4.8 per cent. However, the GUE/NGL won big in May 2014, increasing its seat share to 6.9 per cent (52 seats) to become the biggest radical left EP group since 1986. This total was, however, disproportionately boosted by stellar results in Greece and Spain (providing 13 of the new MEPs), while as Holmes and Lightfoot show in this volume, the radical left transnational Party of the European Left barely gained.

In national elections since the crisis began, the picture is similarly mixed. Table 2.2, focusing on the parliamentary RLPs, shows that these *have* certainly benefited electorally from the crisis. On average, RLP results have increased by nearly 60 per cent of their previous vote since September 2008. Simultaneously, it is unsurprising that this increase has barely registered in political consciousness – many parties are still so small that even significant vote improvement (2.7 percentage points on average) hardly increases their political weight. Moreover, Syriza and Podemos are rather exceptional and skew the results upwards: nowhere else apart from Moldova and Cyprus are RLPs polling over 20 per cent. There are some countries (e.g. Belgium and Slovenia), where RLPs have made parliamentary breakthroughs. Elsewhere, increases are much more incremental.

Indeed, the trajectory for the majority of parties in major European states (e.g. France, Germany and Italy) is one of relative stability, whereas in some (e.g. the Netherlands, the United Kingdom and Finland), RLPs appear to be doing *worse* during the crisis. Certainly, the major growth appears to be in some countries hardest hit by the crisis (e.g. Greece, Spain, Portugal and Ireland). Nevertheless, it is reasonable to ask whether RLPs should not have done better, sooner and more often. The previous discussion indicated that there is rarely a direct relationship between economic woes and RLP success. Several factors (some related to those already indicated) have played a particular role in the crisis, and help explain how RLPs have been as yet unable fully to capture the moment.

Lack of Policy Impact

RLPs often struggle to demonstrate clear policy achievements, because they lack national governing experience and are often perceived, even if no longer as pariahs, then as lacking competence. This is partially a product of the Soviet era, when Leninist parties often put policy purity before effectiveness and used parliaments as 'tribunes' simply to disown bourgeois politics. Before 1988, RLP participation in government was very exceptional: only the Finnish Communist Party (12 years total), Icelandic People's Alliance/

Table 2.2　European RLPs' National Electoral Performance (September 2008–February 2016)

Country/Party	Post-Crisis Performance	Post-Crisis Vote Change	Percentage Vote Retained Post-Crisis
EU Countries			
Belgium (Workers' Party of Belgium)	2.8 (average 2010–2014)	+2.0	350
Cyprus (Progressive Party of Working People)	32.7 (2011)	+1.6	105.1
Czech Republic (Communist Party of Bohemia and Moravia)	13.1 (average 2010–13)	+0.3	102.3
Denmark (Red-Green Alliance)	7.3 (average 2011–15)	+5.1	331.8
Finland (Left Alliance)	7.6 (average 2011–15)	−1.2	86.4
France (Left Front)	6.9 (2012)	+2.6	160.5
Germany (Left Party)	10.3 (average 2009–13)	+1.6	117.8
Greece (Communist Party of Greece)	6.3 (average 2009–15)	−1.9	76.9
Greece (Syriza)	24.0 (average 2009–15)	+19.0	480.4
Ireland (Anti-Austerity Alliance – People Before Profit)*	3.1 (average 2011–16)	+2.0	281.8
Ireland (Sinn Féin)	11.9 (average 2011–16)	+5.0	172.4
Italy (Left Ecology Freedom)	3.2 (2013)	+0.1	103.2
Luxembourg (The Left)	4.1 (average 2009–13)	+2.2	215.8
Netherlands (Socialist Party)	9.8 (average 2010–12)	−6.8	59.0
Portugal (Portuguese Communist Party)	8.0* (average 2009–15)	+0.4	105.7
Portugal (Left Bloc)	8.4 (average 2009–15)	+2.0	131.3
Slovenia (United Left)*	6.0* (2014)	+6.0	n/a
Spain (PCE/United Left)*	5.3* (average 2011–15)	+1.5	139.5
Spain (Podemos)	20.7 (2015)	+20.7	n/a
Sweden (Left Party)	5.7 (average 2010–14)	−0.2	95.8
UK (Respect)	0.1 (average 2010–15)	−0.3	16.7
Average EU Countries	9.4	+2.9	164.9
Non-EU Countries			
Iceland (Left-Green Movement)	16.3 (average 2009–13)	+2.0	114.0
Moldova (Party of Communists of Republic of Moldova)	37.8 (average 2009–14)	−8.2	82.2
Moldova (Party of Socialists of Republic of Moldova)	20.5 (2014)	+15.5	410
Norway (Socialist Left Party)	5.2 (average 2009–13)	−3.6	59.1
Russia (Communist Party of the Russian Federation)	19.2 (2011)	+7.6	165.5
San Marino (United Left)*	8.9* (average 2008–12)	+0.2	101.7
Switzerland (Labour Party of Switzerland)	0.6 (average 2011–15)	−0.1	78.6
Ukraine (Communist Party of Ukraine)	8.6 (average 2012–15)	+3.2	159.3
Average Non-EU Countries	14.6	+2.1	146.3
Average (excluding Syriza and Podemos)	10.0	+1.4	147.0
Overall average	**10.8**	**+2.7**	**159.4**

Key: *Coalition. Calculations from www.parties-and-elections.eu. Parliamentary parties only. Correct at 1 April 2016.

United Socialist Party (10 years total) and FCP (three years total), joined governmental coalitions during this period.[39] The situation has ameliorated as RLPs (although seldom the extreme Left) have become increasingly open to 'left-left' coalitions with social democrats (and Greens). At the very least, they will consider parliamentary support for social democrat minority governments.[40]

In general, as Table 2.3 shows, RLP participation in government has not been a particularly happy experience. In most cases, RLPs have lost support after governmental participation (the average loss is 1.3 percentage points; after government they retain only 84 per cent of their previous vote). Generally, this results from the dilemma of small coalition partners everywhere – sharing policy responsibility with larger parties without significant ministers, power or visibility to demonstrate an independent profile.

RLPs join such coalitions in order to mitigate governmental neoliberalism, advance their own agenda and provide a 'left-wing conscience' for social democrats. Yet to date, even such minimalistic aims have been hard to corroborate. At best, RLPs can demonstrate limited *reforms* in office (e.g. incremental increases in benefits, halting privatisation and pioneering socially liberal legislation), but this is hardly a 'radical' reconfiguration of capitalism. Certainly, RLPs have been involved in key campaigns both internationally (e.g. opposing the EU Constitutional/Lisbon treaties) and nationally (e.g. Portuguese legalisation of abortion and gay marriage) that have had wider resonance, and indeed, one of their key aspirations (the Tobin financial transactions tax) is now widely supported in continental Europe (but unimplemented). However, many such campaigns also had considerable support in other parties (including social democrats), and RLP contributions have hardly been pivotal.

There are only three European countries where RLPs have been the dominant government partner since 1990: Cyprus (2003–2013), Moldova (2001–2009) and Greece (2015–). Despite significant differences, these are all small, peripheral states. In the former two cases, RLP governmental policies were little different from those of a social democratic government, greater emphasis on economic dirigisme and scepticism towards Euro-Atlantic institutions notwithstanding (e.g. in 2011, the AKEL government adopted [without significant protest] the EU fiscal treaty imposing penalties if countries' budget deficits exceeded 3 per cent). Not only did these parties not fundamentally challenge neoliberalism domestically or abroad, but their governments failed to survive post-crisis elections. Such travails explain why RLPs have put such hopes on the Syriza government. It remains a work in progress but its acceptance of austerity measures after the Third Memorandum indicates it may not fundamentally buck the odds.

Table 2.3   RLP Government Participation 1990–2015

Country	Party	Date	Type of Participation (a)	Party Vote Change At Election Following Participation	Percentage of Vote Retained
Cyprus	AKEL	1988–1991	Coalition	+3.2	111.7
	AKEL	1991–1993	Coalition	+2.4	107.8
		2003–2006	Coalition	–3.6	89.6
		2006–2011	Coalition	+1.6	105.1
		2011–2013	Coalition	Not yet known	n/a
Denmark	SF (b)	1994–1998	Support	+0.2	102.7
		1998–2001	Support	–1.1	85.3
		2011–2014	Coalition	–0.5	45.7
	EL	1994–1998	Support	–0.4	87.1
		1998–2001	Support	–0.3	88.9
		2014–2015	Support	+1.1	116.4
Finland	VAS	1995–1999	Coalition	–0.3	97.3
		1999–2003	Coalition	–1.0	90.8
		2011–2014	Coalition	–1.0	87.7
France	PCF	1989–1993	Support	–1.9	81.4
		1997–2002	Coalition	–5.1	48.5
Greece	SYN/KKE	1989–1990	Coalition	–0.7	93.6
	Syriza	2015 (Jan–Sept)	Coalition	–0.8	97.8
	Syriza	Sept 2015–	Coalition	Not yet known	n/a
Iceland	VG	2009–2013	Coalition	–10.8	49.3
Ireland	Democratic Left	1994–7	Coalition	–0.3	89.3
Italy	PRC	1996–8	Support	–1.9 (total PRC and	77.9
	PdCI	1998–2001	Support	PdCI)	
Italy	PRC/PdCI	2006–8	Coalition	–7.1 (total PRC, PdCI and Greens)	38.3
Moldova	PCRM	2001–5	Government	–4.1	91.8
		2005–Feb 2009	Government	+3.5	107.6
		2009 (April–July)	Government	–4.8	90.3
		2015 (Feb–July)	Support	Not yet known	n/a
Norway	SV	1993–7	Support	–1.9	75.9
		2005–9	Coalition	–2.6	70.5
		2009–2013	Coalition	–2.1	66.1
Portugal	Left Bloc	2015–	Support	Not yet known	n/a
Portugal	PCP	2015–	Support	Not yet known	n/a
Russia	KPRF	1998–9	Support	+2.0	109
Spain	IU	2004–2008	Support	–1.2	76
Sweden	V	1998–2002	Support	–3.6	70
Sweden		2002–2006	Support	–2.5	70
Ukraine	KPU	2006–7	Coalition	+1.7	145.9
		2010–12	Support	+7.8	244.4
		2012–14	Support	–9.3	29.5
Average				*–1.26*	*84.43*

Key: (a) 'Coalition' is where a party is formally included in government portfolio allocation, 'support' is where a party is not formally included in government, but lends legislative support to (at least some of) its main initiatives to guarantee its position in the legislature; (b) SF is counted as an RLP until 2014.

Source: T. Bale and R. Dunphy, "In from the cold? Left parties and government involvement since 1989", *Comparative European Politics*, 9(3), 2011 pp. 269–291; author's calculations from www.parties-and-elections.eu. Data correct at 1 March 2016.

RLPs increasingly consider governmental participation even where they have not governed to date (e.g. in Sweden and the Netherlands). As detailed elsewhere in this volume, the post-crisis scenario has brought RLPs ever more into coalition contention (e.g. in Portugal and Spain). Parties increasingly develop a sober calculation of risks and rewards, and try to enter formal coalitions where possible, regarding the risks as no worse than electoral losses when in opposition.[41] This perception is not entirely borne out by the facts: when they join left-left coalitions, the principal beneficiaries are often the larger social democrats (as in Norway in 2005). Increasingly, RLPs have to weigh up unpredictable gains when in opposition against similarly unpredictable losses when in government. Such is the lot of a small party family.

Lack of Extra-Parliamentary Mobilisation

Until the 1980s, communist parties had links to whole 'counter-societies' of affiliated trade unions and social movements that multiplied their social weight.[42] In most cases, these are history: the Cypriot AKEL is the only European RLP to retain affiliated organisations in every 'nook and cranny' of society.[43] Although RLPs of all stripes have reinvigorated their pursuit of extra-parliamentary linkages, these have rarely been able to approach their historic influence.

For instance, RLPs were becoming attractive to trade unionists disaffected with social democratic parties even prior to the crisis. After all, trade unionists defecting from the German Social Democratic Party were instrumental in the founding of Die Linke in 2005; sections of the Communication Workers' and Rail, Maritime and Transport Unions left UK Labour to support the Scottish Socialist and Respect parties in 2004–2007. Often (as in Scandinavia) the trade unions have been the major advocates of left-left coalitions. Austerity has brought trade unions and RLPs closer, as evidenced by the European Trade Union Confederation's address to the European Left Party's 2013 Madrid congress. Nevertheless, more intensive rapprochement between RLPs and trade unions is unlikely as long as social democrats remain governing parties that represent the best lobbying points for NGO interests.

Usually, RLPs have long-standing links with diverse social movements, including peace, environmental and solidarity groups deriving from the 1970s. RLP ties with the GJM acccelerated during the European Social Forums in the 2000s, with RLP activists, networks and logistical support becoming critical to these bi-annual festivals of workshops, seminars and rallies for NGOs, civil society and trade unions. However, RLP links with the GJM remain problematic, and is questionable whether there is really a left-wing 'movement' as such. This is the core of Alex Callinicos' (exaggerated) claim that RLPs are still in deep crisis, as 'left reformist' parties with weak social bases incapable of exploiting class discontent.[44] Indeed, while left-wing activists comprise much of the movement, many of them (particularly in Northern Europe) orientate themselves to moderate NGOs and social democratic parties; whereas the GJM has also had a strong autonomist and anarchistic tradition, which regard all parties' politics with suspicion.

Nevertheless, after initially indicating continuity, the Great Recession has expanded opportunities for renewed RLP-movement ties. On the one hand, the crisis arguably accelerated the demise of the European Social Forums (last held in 2010). The earliest anti-austerity manifestations (e.g. Occupy and the Indignants) initially appeared to replicate the anti-party sentiment of the GJM – as one *Indignado* claimed: 'In Syntagma square the people didn't want to hear about political parties, even left ones.'[45] On the other hand, as illustrated further in this volume, RLPs, trade unions and social movements have played integral roles in anti-austerity actions (e.g. the general strikes in Portugal in 2012–2013). Moreover, other trends within the GJM have shown a renewed acceptance of internal organisation and engagement with state power.[46] The recent success of parties such as Syriza, Podemos and the Slovenian United Left Coalition is intimately connected with strong links to anti-austerity movements and to this degree appears to represent 'the rejection of the rejection of the parliamentary process'.[47]

Overall, most RLPs' extra-parliamentary possibilities barely match those the biggest CPs used to have. Moreover, the lack of obvious, direct policy repercussions ensuing from often transient movements (Occupy, most recently), remind us that these are often capable at most of influencing the political climate rather than fundamentally changing any state's policy direction. Nevertheless, the crisis has (gradually) increased RLPs' extra-parliamentary mobilisation potential.

Ideological/Strategic Divisions

Although RLPs have made major efforts to surmount them, divisions often linger from Marxism-Leninism's obsession with correct doctrine and exegesis: most obviously many countries still have several 'dwarf' extra-parliamentary RLPs that 'salami-slice' an already-small electorate. Some of the divisions mirror profound ideological-cultural cleavages. For example, old left-new left divisions are still very salient.[48] Certainly, there are many parties, principally the conservative communists, who remain more socially authoritarian, not supporting libertarian issues such as LBGT rights, drugs decriminalisation and opposition to nuclear power.

Moreover, parties are often internally fissiparous. Indeed, internal divisions have been behind some of the radical Left's most spectacular failures, for example, the auto-combustion of the Italian Left, which cost both communist parties their national and EP representation in 2008–2009. Other examples of party divisions hindering crisis responses abound: most recently, tensions between Podemos and the United Left, and divisions between Europeanist and pro-'rupture' tendencies within Syriza. Indeed, the starkest divisions are over the European Union. As the chapter by Holmes and Lightfoot shows, the inability to find common understandings over how to interpret the European Union prevents RLPs from developing a shared strategic vision of Europe. Therefore, RLPs cannot move from a defensive position towards actively shaping European politics.

The Eastern Deficit

Another legacy-influenced weakness is in former communist countries, where relevant RLPs are generally absent outside former Soviet countries, which are not likely to become EU members anytime soon. This weakness matters, because the more that former Eastern Europe joins the European Union, the potentially weaker the radical Left becomes. The 2004–2013 enlargements incorporated countries where RLP's 2014 votes totalled just 1.5 per cent.[49] Moreover, because of the vastly different significance of 1968 in both West and East, Eastern parties have often been less engaged with new left traditions, adding to the existing ideological heterogeneity of the party family. The situation does show signs of changing. For instance, Die Linke's Rosa Luxemburg Stiftung has 'built a major infrastructure for the left in Eastern Europe'.[50] Younger radical left groups are playing increasingly important roles in protests in Eastern Europe (e.g. Bosnia, Croatia and above all Slovenia). The 2014 parliamentary breakthrough of the Slovenian United Left shows that new actors can emerge. Nevertheless, this success has yet to be replicated more widely, and it remains critical to building the Left in the East.

Lack of the Vision Thing

Undoubtedly most debilitating for contemporary RLPs is the failure to develop a distinct popular vision for contemporary Europe. Hopes of activists notwithstanding, TINA was emphatically reinforced by Syriza's capitulation to the Third Memorandum. Despite the evident crisis of neoliberalism, most European political, economic and media elites regard fundamental challenges to the consensus as impossible and RLPs as dangerous and irresponsible populists/extremists. There is exceedingly narrow scope for publicly articulated alternatives. For instance, many media stories described the Dutch Socialists in 2012 as a 'far left' party, whereas (as Dan Keith shows in this volume), the SP's moderated policies are little different from a Eurosceptic social democratic party!

Moreover, the nature of the Great Recession itself has challenged the Left's economic credibility. Although its origins are rooted in private sector irresponsibility, the result is unprecedented state indebtedness. RLPs' main alternative economic solutions are essentially Keynesian. Their chief weakness has always been doubt over their viability in the contemporary world of globalised financial flows (and, as the Syriza example revealed, creditors and ratings agencies). Recognising this, many RLPs have insisted on reforming the international financial architecture, principally the IMF and European Central Bank. However, the dominant narrative of a bloated state sector makes it much harder for the Left to advocate higher state spending and interventionism. In the initial crisis years, when neo-Keynesian solutions were more in vogue, it did not help that centre-left governments were in office in some of the most crisis-hit nations (Greece, Portugal and Spain), and anti-incumbent sentiment therefore brought the Right back to power.

It is not that (as often proclaimed), RLPs lack practical solutions. They have plenty, including models of participatory budgeting and local democracy developed in Latin America, Iceland and elsewhere. However, local solutions do not compensate for their lack of governing experience in major European countries. Overall, the radical Left lacks a distinct metanarrative now that this is no longer (for most parties) communism. Additionally, RLPs often fail to communicate their core messages in ways that resonate as much as anti-immigration or environmentalism, and so cede intellectual and electoral ground to the Right and the Greens. Often, rightly or wrongly, electorates still perceive RLPs as too nostalgic and 'old left'. As illustrated elsewhere in this volume, many RLPs argue that the crisis has vindicated their economic programmes. But rather than necessarily bringing electoral benefit, this often results in a Cassandra complex: as former European Left Party chair Lothar Bisky argued: 'Nobody votes for you just because you've known things from the start.'[51] The diminution of RLPs' message is reinforced by *red-washing* (the appropriation of their slogans and ideas by other parties), something inconceivable in the Soviet era. Greens and social democrats have increased their (rhetorical) criticism of neoliberalism, while newer formations like the Italian Five Star movement, with their anti-elite rhetoric, 'neither left nor right' image, and emphasis on new social media, can often better appeal to younger voters for whom parties in general and left parties in particular appear antiquated. It is only the more populist formations, such as Podemos and Syriza, that have fully engaged with more general anti-establishment sentiment beyond RLPs' traditional ideological comfort zones.

CONCLUSION

In the post-Soviet era, the European radical Left's impact has been mixed at best. There is demonstrably an increase in electoral performance. RLPs are more organisationally and ideologically consolidated (and confident) than they have been for several decades. Many have become stable actors in their party systems, and increasingly in government, and as such need to be reckoned with by political elites and social democratic parties alike. They have been able to affect the political climate, and some of their long-articulated policies have entered the political mainstream.

The weaknesses of RLPs are equally apparent and difficult to surmount. Historical legacy still looms large, evident in the absence of relevant parties in many European countries, above all in the East. Several parties still face internal ideological and strategic divisions, particularly over the balance between national and EU-level policies. Though far less doctrinaire than hitherto, they still remain among the most ideological of party families, making the absence of a cohesive vision still more problematic. Overall, RLPs remain on the defensive, the central strategic problem being first to successfully mount a rear-guard defence of the Keynesian welfare state before even considering a more proactive transformation of capitalism, for which there still remains no credible blueprint.

The Great Recession has undoubtedly offered great growth potential: after all, core ideological support, buttressed by socio-economic stress, Euroscepticism and anti-establishment sentiment demonstrably aided RLPs even *before* the crisis, although far from all benefited. Even if Europe returns to stable growth, lasting socio-economic side effects will likely provide excellent mobilisation potential for the radical Left (although they face a crowded field with a resurgent radical Right, Greens and newer actors).

However, the principal caveat is that most RLPs remain small actors that are barely the masters of their own environments. Developments in 2015 appeared to indicate this situation was changing, with Syriza and Podemos showing that RLPs could become both major domestic actors and examples to the rest of Europe. Yet, these two parties remain largely exceptional: products of particularly intense socio-economic crisis, the discrediting of the political establishment and (in Syriza's case) 'Pasokification', all of which has helped parties with a populist image and strong ties to social movements. Rarely are all these components in place for RLPs elsewhere, at least yet. Accordingly, only precipitate declines in economic and party-system stability will give other RLPs similarly dramatic opportunities for growth. Most likely, where RLPs are established they may well get bigger, but where they are small they are likely to remain small(ish), and where they are microscopic, they are unlikely to make major breakthroughs. Therefore, the most likely medium-term scenario is no 'great leap forward', but a succession of baby steps. But perhaps European elites should beware: babies eventually learn to run!

NOTES

1. For example, Luke March, 'Problems and Perspectives of Contemporary European Radical Left Parties: Chasing a Lost World or Still a World to Win?,' *International Critical Thought* 2, no. 3 (2012): 314–39. See also Fabien Escalona and Mathieu Vieira, 'The Radical Left in Europe: Thoughts about the Emergence of a Family,' Fondation Jean-Jaurès/Observatoire de La Vie Politique (Fondation Jean-Jaurès, 19 November 2013).

2. For example, Peter Bratsis, 'The End of TINA,' *Jacobin*, 13 January 2015, https://www.jacobinmag.com/2015/01/syriza-greece-election-tina/.

3. Myrto Tsakatika and Marco Lisi, '"Zippin" up My Boots, Goin' Back to My Roots': Radical Left Parties in Southern Europe,' *South European Society and Politics* 18, no. 1 (2013): 1–19.

4. The term (albeit used for Syriza only) is from Stathis Kouvelakis, 'Syriza's Magic Equation,' *Jacobin*, 9 February 2015, https://www.jacobinmag.com/2015/02/tsipras-parliament-speech-austerity/.

5. Peter Mair, 'The Electoral Universe of Small Parties,' in *Small Parties in Western Europe*, ed. Ferdinand Müller-Rommel and Geoffrey Pridham (London: Sage, 1991), 41–70.

6. Data in this figure includes all European countries and all RLPs included in the databases, parliamentary and non-parliamentary.

7. Neil McInnes, *The Communist Parties of Western Europe* (London; New York: Published for the Royal Institute of International Affairs by Oxford University Press, 1975), 2.

8. For example, Luke March, *Radical Left Parties in Europe* (Abingdon: Routledge, 2011).

9. Mark Visser et al., 'Support for Radical Left Ideologies in Europe,' *European Journal of Political Research* 53, no. 3 (2014): 541–58.

10. R. Neal Tannahill, *Communist Parties of Western Europe: A Comparative Study* (Greenwood Press, 1978), 105.

11. Cas Mudde, 'The Populist Radical Right: A Pathological Normalcy,' *West European Politics* 33, no. 6 (2010): 12.

12. Hans-Georg Betz, *Radical Right-Wing Populism in Western Europe* (New York: St. Martin's Press, 1994).

13. For example, Ashley Lavelle, *The Death of Social Democracy: Political Consequences in the 21st Century* (Farnham: Ashgate, 2008). See also chapter 3 in this book, authored by David Bailey.

14. Cas Mudde, 'The Populist Zeitgeist', *Government and Opposition* 39, no. 4 (2004): 542–63.

15. Margaret Canovan, 'Trust the People! Populism and the Two Faces of Democracy,' *Political Studies* 47, no. 1 (1 March 1999): 2–16.

16. Luke March and Charlotte Rommerskirchen, 'Out of Left Field? Explaining the Variable Electoral Success of European Radical Left Parties,' *Party Politics* 21, no. 1 (2015): 40–53.

17. Luke March and Cas Mudde, 'What's Left of the Radical Left? The European Radical Left after 1989: Decline *and* Mutation,' *Comparative European Politics* 3 (2005): 23–49.

18. Andras Bozóki and John T. Ishiyama, eds., *The Communist Successor Parties of Central and Eastern Europe* (Armond: M.E. Sharpe, 2002).

19. Ibid.

20. March and Rommerskirchen, 'Out of Left Field?'.

21. Ibid.

22. For example, David F. Patton, 'Germany's Left Party. PDS and the "Vacuum Thesis": From Regional Milieu Party to Left Alternative?,' *Journal of Communist Studies and Transition Politics* 22, no. 2 (2006): 206–27; Lavelle, *The Death of Social Democracy*.

23. Gerassimos Moschonas, 'The EU and the Identity of Social Democracy,' *Renewal* 17 (2009): 17.

24. Richard S. Katz and Peter Mair, eds., *How Parties Organize: Change and Adaptation in Party Organizations in Western Democracies* (London: Sage, 1994).

25. James Doran, 'Democratic Wealth and Building up the Institutions of the Left,' *openDemocracy*, 15 October 2013, http://www.opendemocracy.net/ourkingdom/james-doran/democratic-wealth-and-building-up-institutions-of-left.

26. Richard Dunphy, *Contesting Capitalism?: Left Parties and European Integration* (Manchester: Manchester University Press, 2004).

27. Nonna Mayer, *Ces Français Qui Votent FN* (Paris: Flammarion, 1999).

28. Luis Ramiro, 'Support for Radical Left Parties in Western Europe: Social Background, Ideology and Political Orientations,' *European Political Science Review* First View (December 2014): 1–23. See also chapter 5 in this book, authored by McGowan and Keith.

29. Cf. Cas Mudde, *Populist Radical Right Parties in Europe* (Cambridge: Cambridge University Press, 2007), 130–1.

30. Anna M. Grzymała-Busse, *Redeeming the Communist Past: The Regeneration of Communist Parties in East Central Europe* (Cambridge: Cambridge University Press, 2002); Bozóki and Ishiyama, *The Communist Successor Parties of Central and Eastern Europe*; Herbert Kitschelt et al., *Post-Communist Party Systems: Competition, Representation, and Inter-Party Cooperation* (Cambridge: Cambridge University Press, 1999).

31. Dan Keith, 'Party Organisation and Party Adaptation: Western European Communists and Successor Parties' (DPhil Thesis, University of Sussex, 2011).

32. Myrto Tsakatika and Marco Lisi, 'Zippin' up My Boots, Goin' Back to My Roots': Radical Left Parties in Southern Europe', *South European Society and Politics* 18, no. 1 (2013): 1–19.

33. Dan Hough, 'From Pariah to Prospective Partner? The German Left Party's Winding Path towards Government,' in *Left Parties in National Governments*, ed. Jonathan Olsen, M. Koß and Dan Hough (Basingstoke: Palgrave, 2010), 145.

34. Luke March, 'From Vanguard of the Proletariat to Vox Populi: Left-Populism as a "Shadow" of Contemporary Socialism,' *SAIS Review* 27, no. 1 (2007): 63–77.

35. Richard Dunphy, 'In Search of an Identity: Finland's Left Alliance and the Experience of Coalition Government,' *Contemporary Politics* 13, no. 1 (March 2007): 37–55.

36. 'Merkel's Unintended Creation: Could Tsipras' Win Upset Balance of Power in Europe?', *Spiegel Online*, 30 January 2015, http://www.spiegel.de/international/europe/greek-election-makes-euro-zone-exit-real-possibility-a-1015907.html.

37. Marina Prentoulis and Lasse Thomassen, 'The Winds Are Changing: A New Left Populism for Europe,' *OpenDemocracy*, 27 January 2015, http://www.opendemocracy.net/can-europe-make-it/marina-prentoulis-lasse-thomassen/winds-are-changing-new-left-populism-for-europe.

38. Emmanouil Tsatsanis, 'Hellenism under Siege: The National-Populist Logic of Antiglobalization Rhetoric in Greece,' *Journal of Political Ideologies* 16, no. 1 (2011): 11–31.

39. Thanks to Andre Freire for this information. We could also count the Sammarinese Communist Party, which governed in coalition from 1945 to 1957 and 1978 to 1992.

40. For in-depth analyses see Tim Bale and Richard Dunphy, 'In from the Cold? Left Parties and Government Involvement since 1989,' *Comparative European Politics* 9, no. 3 (2011): 269–91; Jonathan Olsen et al., eds., *Left Parties in National Governments* (Basingstoke: Palgrave Macmillan, 2010).

41. Bale and Dunphy, 'In from the Cold?'.

42. Annie Kriegel, *The French Communists: Profile of a People* (Chicago: University of Chicago Press, 1972).

43. Tsakatika and Lisi, 'Zippin' up My Boots', 13.

44. Alex Callinicos, 'Thunder on the Left', *International Socialism*, 26 June 2014, http://isj.org.uk/thunder-on-the-left/.

45. A. Nunns, 'More than a Demonstration, Less than a Revolt', *Red Pepper* 183 (2012): 17–19.

46. R. Reitan, 'Coordinated Power in Contemporary Leftist Activism,' in *Power and Transnational Activism*, ed. T. Olsen (Abingdon: Routledge, 2011), 51–72.

47. David Bailey, 'The European Left after Recession and Representation: Social Democracy or Bust?', *E-International Relations*, 14 June 2015, http://www.e-ir.info/2015/06/14/the-european-left-after-recession-and-representation-social-democracy-or-bust/.

48. Raul Gomez, Laura Morales and Luis Ramiro, 'Varieties of Radicalism: Examining the Diversity of Radical Left Parties and Voters in Western Europe,' *West European Politics* 39, no. 2 (2016): 351–79.

49. Paolo Chiocchetti, 'The Radical Left at the 2014 EP Election,' *Transform!*, 27 June 2014, http://www.transform-network.net/en/blog/blog-2014/news/detail/Blog/-c5f323c33b.html.

50. Vladimir Unkovski-Korica, 'Where Next, after Syriza? A View from the Left in South-Eastern Europe,' *Counterfire*, 8 February 2016, http://www.counterfire.org/articles/analysis/18164-where-next-after-syriza-a-view-from-the-left-in-south-eastern-europe.

51. Lothar Bisky, 'European Parliament Elections: Ambivalent Results for the Left,' *Transform! European Network for Alternative Thinking and Political Dialogue*, 2009, http://transform-network.net/journal/issue-052009/news/detail/Journal/european-parliament-elections-ambivalent-results-for-the-left.html.

Chapter 3

Capitalist Crisis or Crisis of Capitalism?

How the Radical Left Conceptualises the Crisis[1]

David J. Bailey

The way in which radical left actors have perceived and conceptualised the international economic crisis and its consequences has the potential to shape the way in which they have sought to engage with it. Therefore, this chapter asks questions such as: what causal processes are considered by the radical Left to have brought the crisis about? What social structures are considered to have generated those processes? In particular, it asks whether RLPs conceptualised the crisis as a capitalist crisis or a crisis of capitalism. Whereas a 'capitalist crisis' enables capitalism to be reconstituted and restructured in a more profitable form, in a 'crisis of capitalism' the very existence of capitalism itself is threatened.[2] This distinction highlights the importance of understanding how crises are conceptualised and how they are produced in the present.[3]

How radical left actors conceptualise the crisis may also affect the type of crisis that it becomes, especially in contexts where they have significant influence over public policy, public opinion or mass social movements. For instance, if radical left actors perceive a capitalist crisis as taking place, then we might expect them to seek to intervene in or resist any process of 'restructuring' capitalism. If a crisis of capitalism is perceived to be occurring, however, then this is likely to inform a more militant response as left actors anticipate and seek to accelerate the transcendence of capitalism. This echoes debates within the socialist movement of the early twentieth century, between those pursuing reform of a near-permanent capitalism and those seeking social revolution.[4] It also draws our attention to questions of ontology and epistemology, in that it requires us to consider the degree to which RLPs see social structures as fixed or immutable, the role of ideas regarding those structures, and the actions that are required to transform or disturb those structures.[5]

It is now clear that the post-2008 crisis period has been a capitalist crisis rather than a crisis of capitalism. The initially destabilising effects of the collapse of Lehman Brothers resulted in efforts by the state to shore up the financial sector and to restructure the capitalist economy. In doing so, advanced industrial democracies entered an 'age of austerity' characterised by an acceleration of welfare state retrenchment and a decline in real wages.[6] Capitalism was stabilised, despite ongoing instances of insubordination and obstinacy.[7] It is through this course of events that this chapter maps the different conceptualisations of crisis adopted by radical left actors.

In exploring such conceptualisations, this chapter highlights how developments during the pre-crisis period helped to shape perspectives and strategies that were drawn upon to inform radical left actors' interpretations of, and responses to, the crisis.[8] While recognising that the responses of the radical Left to the crisis have manifested themselves in a range of ways (conceptual, ideological developments, electoral strategy and organisational change), the present chapter focuses more directly on conceptions of crisis, with a secondary focus on how these have informed electoral and organisational developments. The chapter analyses four types of radical left actor: radical left parties (both renewed and conservative communist); autonomous social movements; and new anti-austerity RLPs.

Prior to the international economic crisis, RLPs and the autonomous anti-globalisation movement grew increasingly disconnected from each other. RLPs tended to regard the anti-globalisation movement as uncoordinated and as being unable to develop into a coherent and consistent political movement, and sought only in certain cases to connect with and provide leadership to it.[9] Meanwhile, (renewed) RLPs increasingly moved to occupy positions on the political spectrum that were once adopted by social democratic parties. The anti-globalisation movement undertook a more thoroughgoing rejection of formal institutions of political authority. Instead, it pursued an attempt to 'change the world without taking power'.

The chapter argues that these different positions subsequently fed into and informed the response of radical left actors to the international economic crisis. In particular, this meant that both radical left parties and autonomous anti-austerity social movements generally perceived the crisis as a product of the worst excesses of neoliberalism. In response, renewed RLPs continued to attempt to build electoral support for an alternative Keynesian programme. In contrast to RLPs, anti-austerity social movements sought to prefigure alternatives to neoliberalism through practices of direct action and the fuller rejection of the state and the formal political process. The critique within autonomous movements of the unrepresentative state was, however, more ambiguous than perhaps recognised at the time. While some within the anti-austerity movement rejected the process of representation per se, others viewed representation as flawed by virtue of the co-opted nature of the existing political class (established RLPs included). This, the chapter argues, opened up possibilities for the emergence of new anti-austerity RLPs, who could claim to be untarnished by prior engagement with the political establishment. Finally, the chapter argues that the more recent experience of the Syriza government nevertheless highlights the structural problems faced by *both* older and newer radical left parties in seeking to build an anti-austerity electoral programme. The chapter concludes by highlighting the need for an anti-capitalist *and* anti-representational political movement if neoliberalism is genuinely to be challenged in the future. It is argued that the anti-austerity movement should make a more serious commitment to autonomist principles if it is to navigate the difficult course between co-optation and marginality.

THE LEFT PRIOR TO THE CRISIS

Two key events have been central to the development of the European radical Left during the period prior to the onset of the international economic crisis. First, the collapse of the Soviet Union represented the end of the heavily centralised, bureaucratic and state-oriented form of communism that came to be associated with Stalinism. This called into question what (if anything) the Left should do now that 'actually existing Socialism' had ceased to exist and we appeared to have reached the 'End of History'.[10] The second key event was the move by social democratic parties towards the so-called *Third Way* position.[11] The demise of the Bretton Woods System and the crisis of the Keynesian consensus in the 1970s, combined with the experience of slowing growth and 'stagflation', and a number of electoral defeats, was met throughout the 1980s by most social democratic parties moving towards a new, neoliberal, policy consensus.[12]

The combined effect of these two developments was to foreclose what had for much of the twentieth century been viewed as the two major alternatives facing political actors on the Left. Clearly this raised important questions for the Left. If both moderate and radical left strategies had failed, then what (if anything) was left for the Left?[13]

This is the context for understanding the development of the radical Left. Prior to the crisis, three main radical left groupings emerged. First, the alter-globalisation movement emerged onto the stage with the 1999 Battle of Seattle, in opposition to the apparent global hegemony of neoliberalism; it is commonly associated with groups such as the Zapatista Solidarity Network and Ya Basta![14] Second, 'renewed RLPs' (such as the Italian Party of Communist Refoundation [*Rifondazione Comunista*], Die Linke, and the Dutch Socialist Party), underwent a process of transformation and revision after the

1970s or 1980s, in many cases rejecting their communist past and moving into the ideological space being vacated by social democratic parties.[15] Third, a smaller group of RLPs remained more consistent with their long-standing historical positions, retaining a more 'conservative communist' identity (including the Portuguese Communist Party [PCP] and Greek Communist Party [KKE]). In addition, we might include the conservative and traditional factions within the Czech Communist Party of Bohemia and Moravia (KSČM). The influence of a modernising faction over party policy in the latter means that it might be more accurate to describe it as spanning both the conservative communist and renewed RLP categories.[16] These groupings and their subsequent development are set out in Table 3.1.

The alter-globalisation movement and the renewed RLPs were highly critical of the core features of neoliberalism, including its rapid financialisation, unfettered global economic integration, growing inequality, the heightening of social insecurity and precarity.[17] As Steger and Wilson show, alter-globalisation actors were united around their condemnation of market-driven globalisation, and on the need for alternative forms of globalisation.[18] Similarly, Luke March concludes that 'opposition to "neo-liberal" third way social democracy, defence of the traditional policies abandoned by it, and appeal to its disaffected supporters' have each come to 'play increasingly vital roles as identity markers' for RLPs.[19]

Conservative communist parties, in contrast, tended to focus more on capitalism in general, rather than its specific neoliberal manifestation, alongside a more thorough rejection of the process of European integration. Moreover, the alter-globalisation movement and renewed RLPs adopted different political strategies for challenging neoliberalism.[20] Additionally, they diverged over their understanding of why and how the neoliberal consensus had been formed, and the role of the state within that process. It is possible to characterise this key distinction as that of whether the problem of the neoliberal state originated from either its *unresponsiveness* or its *inherent unrepresentativeness*.

From the perspective of renewed RLPs a number of developments had taken place. The state had become unresponsive, the labour movement in most advanced industrial democracies had become demobilised, and the Centre-Left had been overwhelmed by the dominance of neoliberal thinking (among the political elite and large sections of the electorate) and lost confidence in its core programme. In this process, a significant section of the population of contemporary advanced industrial democracies were seen to have become detached from a political elite that is unresponsive to their views and welfare requirements. Furthermore, many RLPs viewed themselves as the only organised force contesting neoliberalism, with social movements considered too weak and disorganised to offer any significant response. From

Table 3.1   Radical Left Actors: Conceptualising Struggle and the Crisis, Pre- and Post-2008

Pre-Crisis

Radical Left Actor	Examples	Core Socio-Economic Critique	On Political Authority (state)	On Political Authority (EU)	Bridge-building with Other Radical Left Actors?
Renewed radical left parties	(PG/FdG), *Die Linke*/PDS, IU, *Rifondazione*, SP* (KSČM – modernisers)	Neoliberalism	Unresponsive	Expansionist Euroscepticism	Attempted – but largely unsuccessful
Conservative communist RLPs	PCP, KKE (KSČM – conservatives/ traditionalists)	Capitalism	Bourgeois state	Hard Euroscepticism	Mostly uninterested
Anti-globalisation movement (pre-crisis)/Autonomous anti-austerity movements (post-2008)	Global Justice Movement, Zapatista Solidarity Network, Ya Basta!	Neoliberalism	Unrepresentative	Unrepresentative	Sceptical of cynical political opportunism
New anti-austerity radical left	*Indignados*, Occupy, UK Uncut, Syriza, Podemos	–	–	–	–

Post-2008

Radical Left Actor	Examples	Cause of Crisis	On Political Authority (state)	On Political Authority (EU)	Bridge-building With Other Radical Left Actors?
Renewed radical left parties	(PG/FdG), *Die Linke*/PDS, IU, *Rifondazione*, SP* (KSČM – modernisers)	Neoliberalism	Unresponsive	Expansionist Euroscepticism	Attempted – but largely unsuccessful
Conservative communist RLPs	PCP, KKE (KSČM – conservatives/ traditionalists)	Capitalism	Bourgeois state	Hard Euroscepticism	Mostly uninterested
Anti-globalisation movement (pre-crisis)/ Autonomous anti-austerity movements (post-2008)	Global Justice Movement, Zapatista Solidarity Network, Ya Basta!	Neoliberalism	Un-representative *and* unresponsive	Unrepresentative *and* unresponsive	Sceptical of cynical political opportunism
New anti-austerity radical left	*Indignados*, Occupy, UK Uncut, Syriza, Podemos	Neoliberalism	Unresponsive and a need to renew	Unresponsive and a need to renew	Yes, successful as parties 'of the movements'

Note: *The SP is an outlier within this group in that it is more Eurosceptic than a number of the other renewed radical left parties.
Source: Author's conceptualisation.

this perspective, therefore, there remained a need to continue to advocate state policies to ameliorate poverty, manage and regulate capitalism in such a way that would avoid its harshest excesses, and to seek to implement redistributive measures.

In this sense, RLPs essentially went through the same turn towards Keynesianism and redistributive/reformist politics that many social democratic parties underwent during the interwar period. RLPs denounced the turn away from 'traditional' social democracy by social democratic parties, and viewed this move as mistaken given the ongoing existence of an electoral constituency prepared to support such 'traditional' policies. Renewed RLPs attempted to make the unresponsive neoliberal state respond anew to its marginalised citizens via re-appropriating these 'traditional' policies (higher tax-and-spend, reversals of privatisation and welfare cuts etc.), now increasingly jettisoned by a social democratic party family that had lost faith in its historic commitment to redistribution.

For instance, Rifondazione adopted a position of 'pale communism little distinguishable from left-wing social democracy'.[21] Similarly, the Dutch Socialist Party adopted a pragmatic programme that evoked 'a past "homeland" where workers had security and respect under the Keynesian welfare consensus, whose foundations [were] considered to have "started to rot" under neo-liberalism".[22] This position, sometimes referred to as 'social democracy plus', represented an office-seeking move initiated during the 1990s, when many RLPs dropped direct reference to socialism and the abolition of capitalism in favour of more moderate opposition to neoliberalism and defence of the welfare state.[23] For example, in France, the Front de Gauche focused its 2005 campaign against the European Constitutional Treaty, on a strategy 'that breaks with the [neo]liberal system'.[24]

The development of Die Linke in Germany during the 2000s also illustrates these trends well. The party moved rightwards throughout the decade and in the process filled the space vacated by the SPD.[25] Indeed, Die Linke's party programme, although adopted after the onset of the crisis, nevertheless sets out very clearly the conceptualisation of contemporary struggles common to renewed RLPs both before and during the crisis. Die Linke viewed democracy as having been significantly undermined by financialisation and neoliberalism: 'The possibility of exerting democratic influence ... recedes as the power of the corporations and of finance capital grows and privatisation and liberalisation of the economy reduce the scope for political and public action.'[26] At the same time, however, it acknowledged the need for improved responsiveness: 'Representative bodies need the corresponding rights and resources so that they can act on an equal footing with governments and administrations. ... The positions of trade unions, social, environmental, consumers, tenants and disabled associations, selfhelp organisations and democratic movements must be heard at an early stage.'[27]

In contrast to the renewed RLPs, the third, smaller group of conservative-communist RLPs defended a more traditional communist identity during this period. The key features that distinguish the conservative communist RLPs from the renewed RLPs are: a stronger focus on capitalism as the target of socio-economic critique, with neoliberalism viewed as a symptom of a wider problem inherent to capitalism; and stronger opposition (and in most cases outright rejection of) the European Union as both the main institution through which neoliberal capitalism is imposed within Europe and a key mechanism through which the depoliticisation of the political process is secured. In terms of concrete policy programmes, however, the PCP has tended to adopt policies relatively similar to the other renewed RLPs, albeit typically at a national level, with an outright rejection of the European Union, and with a stronger focus on nationalisation of industry and fiscal redistribution.[28] The KKE, in contrast, has advocated a position of 'revolutionary sovereigntism', which includes a radical rejection of European integration and the advocacy of militant action such as general strikes and demonstrations.[29]

In contrast to renewed RLPs, the alter-globalisation movement has been more sceptical towards the state. Indeed, rather than a critique focusing on *unresponsiveness*, much of the alter-globalisation movement viewed the state as being *unrepresentative*. As a result, many of the activities undertaken by the movement were informed by a conviction that direct action was both the most efficacious and most desirable means by which to achieve global social change.[30] Underpinning this view, for many activists, was a widespread commitment to the notion of 'prefiguration'. That is, the need for social mobilisation to incorporate and seek to embody the principles that it aims to realise.[31]

In rejecting the notion that means and ends could be separated, the alter-globalisation movement came to be linked to John Holloway's rallying cry: *change the world without taking power!*[32] Direct action was considered important as both a means to challenge neoliberalism, but also as a means by which desirable social change could be put into effect. In words from an earlier syndicalist age, prefigurative action created the 'structure of the new society within the shell of the old'.[33] As Tormey puts it, 'The rejection of politicians clearly goes beyond a sense of exasperation with the mannerisms and gestures of the political class and embraces the very idea at the heart of representation, that some should be elevated to a position of power whilst everyone else is placed in the position of passive spectators, *the represented*.'[34]

Put simply, the process of representative democracy was considered an attempt to construct a fundamental divide between those who are 'represented' and those who act as 'representatives'. A difference in the interests of those who represent and those who were represented thereby precluded the possibility of a common identity between the two; attempts to present such a common identity necessitated limiting the demands of the represented. Contemporary representative democracy was not criticised primarily because it was failing to fulfil its promise of representation. Rather, it was challenged on the basis that representation itself was unachievable and its pursuit undesirable. This sentiment was expressed in the Zapatistas' influential *Fourth declaration of the Lacandón jungle*, issued on 1 January 1996:

> We invite national civil society without party affiliations, social and citizen movements, all Mexicans, to build a new political force. ... A new political force whose members do not hold or aspire to hold public office or government posts at any level. A political force that does not seek to take power. ... A political force that can find solutions to collective problems without the intervention of political parties or the government.'[35]

THE LEFT DURING THE CRISIS

The response of the radical Left to the economic crisis in 2008 should be understood as a continuation and consolidation of the key trends discussed above. This is also depicted in Table 3.1.

Established RLPs: A Crisis of Neoliberalism and Calls for a Keynesian U-Turn

Following the onset of economic crisis, renewed RLPs consolidated their occupation of the vacant social democratic ideological space. In conceptualising the crisis as one of neoliberalism and an unresponsive neoliberal state, renewed RLPs promoted Keynesianism as an alternative programme that could avoid the need for austerity and secure a return to growth. The international economic crisis therefore witnessed RLPs consolidating their espousal of a Keynesian alternative, including through associations such as the transnational Party of the European Left (PEL), its think-tank network Transform! and more indirectly through the EuroMemo Group, a network of European economists committed to promoting full employment, social justice with an eradication of poverty and social exclusion.[36] However, as detailed in the previous chapter, this has largely failed to result in a significant impact in policymaking (there is little sign of the sought-after Keynesian U-turn) or electoral performance.

Die Linke again presents an illustrative case, as it conceptualised the cause of the crisis clearly in terms of neoliberal mechanisms: 'Through deregulation, liberalisation and privatisation, neo-liberal policy planted the roots of the present crisis, which may grow into a catastrophe if no political counteraction is taken.'[37] Moreover, the solution proposed by Die Linke was a 'traditional' social democratic one, including state management of the economy to ensure full employment, higher incomes, the strengthening of public finances and Keynesian-style demand management ('[d]omestic demand must be strengthened through redistribution in favour of low and medium incomes and the expansion of public services'). It also included state-led investment, public sector job creation schemes improved employment protection, and an increase in progressive tax revenues such as wealth and inheritance taxes.[38] These were not, however, successful initiatives: Die Linke lost over 3 per cent of the vote between the Bundestag elections of 2009 and 2013, with the Merkel coalition government promoting austerity all the while.

A similar position was adopted by other renewed RLPs, often with a strong focus on the neoliberal policies being produced by the process of European integration. For instance, the Dutch SP explicitly chose *not* to focus on capitalism as the cause of the problem.[39] Instead, the SP's analysis of the crisis focused on neoliberalism and greed, and even went so far as to accept the need for austerity measures. It called for a modest stimulus package as the best form of response to the crisis, alongside more stringent financial regulation.[40] The Spanish United Left (IU), with the Spanish Communist Party as its primary member, focused explicitly on a rejection of the 'neoliberal orientation of the existing EU treaties', and argued instead for more redistributive and regulatory policies, many of which should be implemented through reforms made to the European Union. For instance, the IU called for EU policies to be developed in the area of 'labour law, wage setting, and taxation policy' and for 'a social Europe to set a counter-point to the dominant neoliberal concept'. This, the IU claimed, should also be developed alongside a democratisation of the process of European integration, especially the creation of a democratically controlled ECB.[41] These shared goals of countering neoliberalism and proposing a greater democratisation of the institutions of representative democracy were also visible within the PEL. Thus, the PEL's core programmatic goals have included strengthening the European Parliament, socio-economic policies that would create/improve the minimum income available to workers and citizens, and replacing the current Stability and Growth Pact with a 'new pact for growth, full employment, social security and environmental protection'.[42]

In contrast, the conservative communist RLPs' response to the international economic crisis differs principally in their much more explicit focus both on capitalism as the cause of the crisis, and relatedly, the EU's role as a fundamental contributor both to the crisis and to austerity policies arising in response. Whereas most of the renewed RLPs focused on reforms to the European Union as a potentially positive response (with the Dutch SP being an obvious exception), the conservative communist RLPs were much more hostile towards the European Union and the measures imposed by the Troika, arguing for full withdrawal from the European Union as the best means by which to challenge the austerity agenda. The PCP focused on the role of EMU in creating the crisis, advocating its dissolution.[43] For the KKE, opposition to capitalism was stated perhaps more clearly still, viewing the post-2008 crisis as one 'of capital over-accumulation', occurring 'under the impact of the law of uneven capitalist development', and condemning 'the framework of the Eurozone and the EU and the international imperialist pyramid in general'.[44]

The Anti-Austerity Movement: A Dual Crisis of Neoliberalism and Representative Democracy

Since 2008 we have also witnessed the mobilisation of a widespread grassroots anti-austerity social movement across Europe (and beyond). In many ways this continued the trajectory of the preceding alter-globalisation movement, being informed by its commitment to principles of prefiguration, horizontality and a critique of the unrepresentativeness of the state.[45] In contrast to RLPs, who largely failed to achieve their goal of connecting with popular sentiment, this developed into a vibrant and innovative social movement, albeit one taking different forms in different countries. The most visible of these forms was the widespread occupation of public squares.[46] This includes the *Indignados* protests of Puerta del Sol (15-M) and Syntagma Square; but also extends to the Occupy movement, Blockupy, UK Uncut and a wave of anti-tuition fee protests (which often included occupations of university buildings).[47]

Another key development, especially in Southern Europe where the anti-austerity movement was (by necessity) most advanced, has been the development of grassroots movements seeking to develop autonomous associations providing alternative means of social reproduction, most obviously in the form of housing provision and housing rights organisations such as the Platform for People Affected by Mortgages (*Plataforma de Afectados por la Hipoteca*, or PAH).[48] A radicalisation of the labour movement has also been evident, with an upturn in the militancy of (sometimes more independent) trade unions, especially those representing the more precarious and flexible workers associated with the post-Fordist period.[49]

Southern Europe's New Anti-Austerity Left Parties: Challenging Neoliberalism and Re-embracing Representative Democracy

Following an apparent peak in 2011, we have witnessed an 'electoral turn' by Europe's anti-austerity social movements from around 2013 onwards, resulting in the emergence of newer anti-austerity left-populist parties, albeit so far limited to Southern Europe (Spain and Greece). Such parties include Syriza, Podemos and the myriad new experiments with party and electoral democracy in the form of different citizens' initiatives and municipalist platforms in Spain (perhaps most notably with the election of *Barcelona en Comú* leader, Ada Colau, as mayor of Barcelona in May 2015).[50] The newer left anti-austerity parties, which in Spain and Greece have secured enough votes to gain access to office, represent a genuine and dramatic change to the party system of each country, both of which had been relatively stable following their consolidation as democracies in the 1970s and 1980s.

Such parties have sought to adopt a 'mass connective party' strategy – that is, an attempt to connect with social bases outside the formal party organisation. In doing so, each has tried to adapt to the groundswell of social mobilisation created by the anti-austerity movements in their respective countries.[51] This is a particularly significant development, because it represents a substantial break with the previous consensus around prefigurative politics among extra-parliamentary left actors that appeared to hold before 2008 and for much of the post-2008 period. Indeed, prior to 2013, the anti-austerity movement appeared to be *consolidating* its distance from representative and parliamentary politics alike, replacing representation with prefiguration and 'Real Democracy Now!'[52] The new left anti-austerity parties epitomised by Syriza and Podemos clearly don't 'fit' with this trajectory. In fact, they seem to represent 'the rejection of the rejection' of the parliamentary process, at a time when prefiguration appeared to have become something of a shibboleth for the extra-parliamentary Left and a principle that had underpinned the development and vibrancy of the anti-austerity movement.[53]

In order to explain this development two observations are key. First, in conceptualising the crisis and seeking to highlight the processes that have caused it, there has been a tendency within the anti-austerity movement to focus on neoliberalism and some of its key symptoms, including financialisation, sharpening inequality, shrinking welfare state and rising precarity. It is significant in that for much of the anti-austerity movement neoliberal capitalism, rather than capitalism per se, has been the key social process of concern. For instance, the Occupy London Economics Statement included a number of goals to reform and regulate neoliberalism and reverse austerity measures. These include greater accountability of the financial industry, measures to tackle the impact of debt on individuals and to tackle economic inequality, a clamping down on tax avoidance and greater economic regulation.[54]

Similarly, the key demands agreed by the 15-M protesters who occupied Puerta del Sol in Madrid in 2011 included: employment protection legislation, improved unemployment benefits, improvements to public health care, education and transport and increased tax revenues (especially from capital and finance).[55] A central part of the analysis of much of the anti-austerity movement was the need to reverse some of the key elements of neoliberalism. These might include, for instance, measures to alleviate poverty, to regulate or minimise financialisation, to abandon attempts to impose austerity measures or to improve working conditions and labour market regulation to create greater social security. Neoliberalism was thus conceptualised as the cause of the crisis and therefore the principal phenomenon needing to be reversed in any attempt to respond to it.

Second, and partly in contrast to the depiction above, the anti-austerity movement's conceptualisation of the crisis of representation was more ambiguous in terms of its critique of the neoliberal state's unrepresentativeness than was commonly appreciated by observers prior to 2015. Thus, rather than adopting an outright rejection of representative politics, the position was nuanced and even contradictory: on the one hand, representation was considered problematic per se; on the other hand, it was the operation of representative democracy *in the contemporary context* that was the focus of critique.

Both of these positions can be found in the language, discourse and slogans of the anti-austerity movement. For instance, in the demands adopted by the 15-M occupiers, we see a strong criticism of representative democracy and the need for it to be replaced by a more direct, participatory, form of democracy. This included a call for 'mandatory and binding referendums on the wide-ranging issues that change the lives of citizens'.[56] At the same time, however, the movement sought to introduce reforms that would ensure that the channels of representation within representative democracy would be made to operate more effectively. Thus, there was a demand for 'amendment of the Electoral Act to ensure a truly representative system that does not discriminate and that is proportional to any political or social will, where the blank vote and the no-vote also have representation in the legislature', and for the 'establishment of effective mechanisms to ensure internal democracy in political parties'.[57]

Cristina Flesher Fominaya alludes to this ambiguity when she notes that 15-M 'combine[d] prefigurative practices of radical democracy within social movements spaces with a highly organized attack on the illegitimacy of representative democratic institutions using the courts (both national and international) and the law to hold politicians and officials accountable for their actions within the legal frameworks of the state itself'.[58] Yet, this turn to the use of the state against the state occurred *despite* an ongoing and fierce commitment to horizontalism, prefiguration and anti-representation. Thus, 'group after group stressed the centrality of horizontality and non-representation as fundamental and defining organizing principles'.[59]

A similar ambiguity was witnessed in the square occupations in Greece. For instance, when the first popular assemblies were created in May 2011, their call 'Direct Democracy Now!' echoed the 15-M's 'Real Democracy Now' slogans and similarly symbolised a rejection of parliamentary democracy. However, those protests were centred on Syntagma Square, chosen because it was immediately in front of the national parliament and enabled parliament to be targeted. As Marilena Simiti put it, 'The majority of demonstrators took an extremely negative view of representative democracy as a practical political project. However, they continued to take a positive view of representative democracy as a model of constitutional government.'[60] This ambiguity is particularly noteworthy because it appears at first sight impossible to reconcile the two views: that representation is problematic per se, and that it is worthwhile seeking to renovate existing channels of representation. After all, for those with a more fundamental critique of representation, it is the act of seeking to create channels of representation itself that *causes* the very same problems observed within representative democracy.

However, these two key strands of the anti-austerity movement help us understand the turn to newer left anti-austerity parties. The movement's focus on critiquing key elements of neoliberal capitalism, including financialisation, sharpening inequality, shrinking welfare state and rising precarity, comes with an implied search for alternative ('Keynesian', or 'traditional social democratic') public policies. These might include financial regulation, heightened welfare provision, labour market regulation, and/or fiscal redistribution.

Similarly, the critique of representation found in the anti-austerity movement, at least that part of it criticising the *channels* of representation (rather than a critique based on the *impossibility* of representation), opens up the possibility for more representative channels of representation to be sought. It is this combination of the search for an alternative traditional social democratic programme pursued through alternative channels of representation that informs the turn to the newer left anti-austerity parties of Syriza, Podemos and the other experiments with new parties and citizens' initiatives in Spain.

This therefore prompts us to ask why it was possible for RLPs such as Syriza and Podemos to successfully build bridges with the autonomous social movements that developed during the economic crisis, while parties such as Rifondazione and the Portuguese Left Bloc had been trying (without sustained success) to do likewise for many years.[61] Part of the answer lies in the relatively untarnished nature of parties such as Syriza, Podemos and the Spanish municipalist initiatives, in terms of their entanglement with the political establishment. These newer parties were able to claim (with much more plausibility than the longer-standing RLPs, both renewed and conservative communist) to be parties 'of the movements'. This bolstered their ability to promise a Keynesian reversal of neoliberalism and an improvement in the representativeness of the state, thereby enabling a more successful connection with the autonomous anti-austerity movements than the more established RLPs were able to do.

Indeed, each of these twin goals – the reversal of neoliberalism and the improvement of channels of representation – can be seen in the programmes of the three most evident instances of newer anti-austerity RLPs. In the case of Syriza, for instance, its pre-election Thessaloniki Programme included proposals for a moratorium on debt so that public policies could be more focused on growth, an EU-led investment programme and fiscal demand management to stimulate the economy. Thus, Syriza was committed to 'measures to restart the economy. Priority is given to alleviating tax suppression on the real economy, relieving citizens of financial burdens, injecting liquidity and *enhancing demand*.'[62] In addition, democratic renewal was to be achieved through 'the institutional and democratic reconstruction of the state', including an empowerment of 'the institutions of representative democracy' and initiatives to ensure greater representation for citizens.[63]

Similarly, the Podemos party leader, Pablo Iglesias, talked of how the international economic crisis made it 'feasible to aim at sovereign processes that would limit the power of finance, spur the transformation of production, ensure a wider redistribution of wealth'.[64] Democratic renewal, moreover, would see a transition from a situation in which (following the election of the centre-right PP in the 2011 general election) 'politicians and parties that were utterly discredited, perceived as the main problem by the citizens, were apparently inescapable, still dominating the realm of formal democracy', to one in which, in the words of Podemos' 2015 manifesto, 'we can see that this wall is not unbreachable. ... It is possible to put a stop to these processes that are dismantling our democracies.'[65]

Finally, in the case of the Spanish municipalist movements, we again see a focus on the search for a traditional social democratic U-turn. In the words of Ada Colau, the new mayor of Barcelona, who rose to prominence as a PAH activist, 'This is about taking back politics to kick out the corrupt, stop evictions, end hunger, guarantee basic services and, above all, put our resources at the service of the majority of the population.'[66] We also see a clear attempt to renovate the channels of representative democracy. This was to be done through a radically open process of candidate selection, the collective drafting of a 'code of political ethics', and the open and collective writing of a manifesto. As Colau put it, 'We drew up our election manifesto in an open, participatory way. Over 5000 people took part in its development, resulting in a programme that focuses on guaranteeing basic rights, making the city more liveable, and democratizing public institutions.'[67] Therefore, as Flesher Fominaya points out, this represents 'a key role not only in redefining the crisis but also in redefining Spanish democracy and reshaping Spain's political landscape'.[68]

CONCLUSION

As we have seen, relative to more established RLPs, the newer anti-austerity RLPs have been better able to position themselves as genuine electoral representatives of the anti-austerity movement. A significant factor in this was that the movement was broadly anti-neoliberal (rather than anti-capitalist) in its critique of the crisis and, at least in part, critical of the *operation* of contemporary representative democracy (rather than solely sceptical of its very *possibility*, as was often argued). It was also significant that some parties had a relatively untarnished status as regards to the political establishment. Because these RLPs articulated a critique that combines anti-neoliberal economic prescriptions with measures to address representation deficits, they have been able to align themselves with sentiments from within the movements and to successfully present themselves as being 'of the movement'.

This position does, however, raise the question of what an anti-capitalist, anti-representational conceptualisation of the crisis might look like. For those who adopt an anti-capitalist (rather than anti-neoliberal) conceptualisation, it is crisis tendencies inherent to capitalism that explain the occurrence of the global economic crisis, and not the defining features of the *neoliberal phase* of capitalism (which are better considered a symptom rather than cause). According to this view, capitalism is both dependent upon profit as its primary objective, and simultaneously driven by internal pressures that result in a reduction in the rate of profit.[69] This contradiction creates crisis tendencies that result in the ever-present need to seek intensified commodification of all aspects of human life, in an attempt to offset the crisis tendencies created by the declining profit rate.[70] This search for intensified commodification, moreover, occurs in a context in which capital is systematically privileged such that it will be able to ensure that the necessary commodifying reforms are likely to be instantiated.[71] It is only when there exists a militant opposition movement that is able to operate *autonomously* of established within-system institutions that we can expect an effective opposition to the pressure for commodification to occur.[72]

Likewise, for those who adopt a more fundamental critique of representation, we should expect that any attempt to construct a radical anti-austerity movement will be hampered in proportion to the degree to which it submits to the requirements of representative democracy.[73] The leadership, or representative elite, of political parties have a tendency to seek to limit, restrict and modify the demands of their constituents – for each of the reasons identified above in our discussion of the critique of representation – and this tendency thereby hampers attempts to mobilise anti-austerity movements.

To what extent do such critiques help us to understand the development of anti-austerity radical left-populist parties? In the case of Syriza, at the time of writing (January 2016) it is undeniable that its leader Alexis Tsipras has spent the last six months ensuring that the bailout deal imposed upon him by the European Union is, in turn, accepted by his own party, the Greek parliament and the Greek people – and in doing so he has sought to limit the demands of his own constituents. This would seem to chime almost exactly with the critique of capitalism and representation spelt out above.

In the case of *Barcelona en Comú* (a more experimental attempt to circumvent the constraints highlighted by the anti-capitalist, anti-representational position), the question is whether the safeguards introduced by the movement/party to ensure against co-optation are sufficient. While this is ultimately an empirical question yet to be answered, the experiment echoes earlier attempts by the German Green Party to form an 'anti-party-party' in an (ultimately unsuccessful) attempt to safeguard against co-optation and the 'iron law of oligarchy' by building constitutional safeguards within party rules.[74]

Thus perhaps the real goal remains the search for an effective *mode of organisation* that is both anti-capitalist and anti-representational, and therefore has the greatest likelihood of disrupting, rather than succumbing to, the pressures systematically generated by capitalist crises, and thereby bringing about a crisis of capitalism. Groups such as Syriza's Left Platform (and the splinter party, Popular Unity, which eventually grew from the Platform) have been attempting to give the electoral route one last chance (again).[75] In contrast, it is perhaps the novel forms of activity geared towards more autonomous and alternative forms of social reproduction that present the greatest prospect for hope in the present. These include the well-documented activities of groups such as the PAH in Spain, and the scores of grassroots solidarity groups in Greece that emerged during the crisis as a means to provide alternative access to a range of human necessities, including food, education and health care.[76] A more general extension of such activities would require that popular social movements, such as the anti-austerity movement, take more seriously still their comment to autonomist principles, avoiding the fateful lure of direct input into public policy. In other words, the problem remains an eternal one: how to navigate between co-optation and marginality? In this sense, the challenge remains largely unchanged, and still unresolved, from when it was worded by the First International in its General Rules of 1864: how to ensure that 'the emancipation of the working classes must be conquered by the working classes themselves'.[77]

NOTES

1. I presented an earlier version of this chapter at the PSA annual conference, 1 May 2015, and received helpful comments from Laura Jenkins, Adam Morton and Nick Taylor.

2. For similar distinctions, see Barry K. Gills, 'The Return of Crisis in the Era of Globalization: One Crisis, or Many?,' *Globalizations* 7, no. 1–2 (2010): 3–8; see also Bob Jessop's distinction between a crisis *in* and crisis *of* capitalism, in Jessop, 'The

Symptomatology of Crises, Reading Crises and Learning from Them: Some Critical Realist Reflections,' *Journal of Critical Realism* 14, no. 3 (2015): 238–71.

3. Jessop, 'The Symptomatology of Crises'; Amin Samman, 'Making Financial History: The Crisis of 2008 and the Return of the Past', *Millennium* 42, no. 2 (2014): 309–30.

4. Rosa Luxemburg, *Reform or Revolution* (London: Militant Publications, 1900 [1986]). Available here: https://www.marxists.org/archive/luxemburg/1900/reform-revolution/.

5. This chapter adopts a broadly critical realist position in that it views social structures as relatively stable but continuously open to contestation and therefore change. For more detail, see: David J. Bailey and Stephen R. Bates, 'Struggle (or Its Absence) during the Crisis: What Power Is Left?' *Journal of Political Power* 5, no. 2 (2012): 195–216.

6. Nancy Bermeo and Jonas Pontusson, 'Coping with Crisis: An Introduction', in *Coping with Crisis: Government Reactions to the Great Recession*, ed. Nancy Bermeo and Jonas Pontusson (New York: Russel Sage Foundation, 2012), 1–31.

7. Nikolai Huke et al., 'Disrupting the European Crisis: A Critical Political Economy of Contestation, Subversion and Escape,' *New Political Economy* 20, no. 5: 2015: 725–51.

8. For similar arguments about continuity between the pre- and post-crisis period, see Cristina Flesher Fominaya, 'Debunking Spontaneity: Spain's 15-M/Indignados as Autonomous Movement,' *Social Movement Studies* 14, no. 2 (2015): 142–63; and Jerome Roos and Leonidas Oikonomakis, 'We Are Everywhere! The Autonomous Roots of the Real Democracy Movement' (paper delivered at ECPR general conference, Sciences Po Bordeaux, 4–7 September 2013). Available: https://www.academia.edu/4342422/The_Autonomous_Roots_of_the_Real_Democracy_Movement.

9. Cristina Flesher Fominaya, 'Autonomous Movement and the Institutional Left: Two Approaches in Tension in Madrid's Anti-globalization Network,' *South European Society & Politics* 12, no. 3 (2007): 335–58.

10. Chamsy El-Ojeili, *Beyond Post-Socialism: Dialogues with the Far-Left* (Basingstoke: Palgrave Macmillan, 2015), 21.

11. Andrea Volkens, 'Policy changes of European Social Democrats, 1945-98', in *Social Democratic Party Policies in Contemporary Europe*, ed. Giuliano Bonoli and Martin Powell, (London: Routledge, 2004), 21–42.

12. David J. Bailey, *The Political Economy of European Social Democracy: A Critical Realist Approach* (London: Routledge, 2009); Ashley Lavelle, *The Death of Social Democracy: Political Consequences in the 21st Century* (Aldershot: Ashgate, 2008).

13. *Parliamentary Affairs* (56:1), Special Issue: 'What's Left? The Left in Europe Today', 2003.

14. Lesley J. Wood, *Direct Action, Deliberation, and Diffusion: Collective Action after the WTO Protests in Seattle* (Cambridge: Cambridge University Press, 2012).

15. A number of studies differentiate between different types of 'renewed radical left parties'. For example, Luke March, *Radical Left Parties in Europe* (Abingdon: Routledge, 2011); Dan Keith, 'Opposing Europe, Opposing Austerity: Radical Left

Parties and the Eurosceptic debate', in *The Routledge Handbook of Euroscepticism*, ed. Nick Startin and Simon Usherwood (Abingdon, Routledge, 2016, forthcoming).

However, here they are treated here as a single grouping, because of their lack of explicitly anti-capitalist position and their broadly social democratic programme against neoliberalism.

16. Vladimír Handl and Andreas Goffin, 'Czech Communists and the crisis: Between radical alternative and pragmatic Europeanization', this volume.

17. Manfred B. Steger and Erin K. Wilson, 'Anti-Globalization or Alter-Globalization? Mapping the Political Ideology of the Global Justice Movement,' *International Studies Quarterly* 56, no. 3 (2012): 439–54; March, *Radical Left Parties*.

18. Steger and Wilson, 'Anti-Globalization or Alter-Globalization?'.

19. March, *Radical Left Parties,* 205.

20. Flesher Fominaya, 'Autonomous Movement and the Institutional Left'.

21. March, *Radical Left Parties,* 70.

22. Ibid., 130.

23. Dan Keith, 'Failing to capitalise on the crisis: the Dutch Socialist Party', this volume.

24. Fabien Escalona and Mathieu Vieira, 'The French Radical Left and the Crisis: 'Business as usual' rather than "*le Grand Soir*"', this volume.

25. Hilde Coffé and Rebecca Plassa, 'Party Policy Position of *Die Linke*: A Continuation of the PDS?' *German Politics* 16, no. 6 (2010): 721–35.

26. *Die Linke*, 'Programme of the *Die Linke* Party', Resolution of the Party Congress, Erfurt, 21–23 October 2011, approved through a vote by the party membership on December 2011. Available: en.die-linke.de/fileadmin/download/english_pages/programme_of_the_die_linke_party_2011/programme_of_the_die_linke_party_2011.pdf.

27. 'Programme of the Die Linke Party'.

28. André Freire and Marco Lisi, 'The Portuguese Radical Left and the Great Recession: Between New Challenges and Old Responses', this volume.

29. Thilo Janssen, *The Parties of the Left in Europe: A Comparison of their Positions on European Policy Leading into the 2014 European Elections* (Berlin: Rosa-Luxemburg-Stiftung, 2013), 38–9.

30. David Graeber, 'The New Anarchists,' *New Left Review* 13 (2002): 61–73.

31. Ben Franks, 'The direct action ethic: From 59 upwards,' *Anarchist Studies* 11, no. 1 (2003): 16–41.

32. John Holloway, *Change the World without Taking Power: The Meaning of Revolution Today: New Edition* (London: Pluto, 2005).

33. IWW, 'Preamble to the IWW Constitution', 1905. Available: http://www.iww.org/culture/official/preamble.shtml.

34. Simon Tormey, *The End of Representative Politics* (Cambridge: Polity, 2015), 62–3.

35. Quoted in Gloria M. Ramirez, *The Fire and the Word: A History of the Zapatista Movement* (San Francisco: City Light Books, 2008), 133–4.

36. As pointed out by Michael Holmes and Simon Lightfoot in this volume, the PEL is the 'Euro-party' incorporating most EU RLPs. For Transform!, see http://www.transform-network.net/home.html. The EuroMemo Group publishes an annual

Memorandum that provides a critical analysis of recent developments in the European Union and has informal links to Transform! See: http://www.euromemo.eu/index. html.

37. 'Programme of the Die Linke Party'.

38. Ibid.

39. Keith, 'Failing to capitalise on the crisis'.

40. Ibid.

41. Janssen, *The Parties of the Left in Europe*, 20.

42. Ibid., 13.

43. Freire and Lisi, 'The Portuguese Radical Left'.

44. KKE, *Programme of the KKE* (2013). Available here: http://inter.kke.gr/en/ articles/Programme-of-the-KKE/.

45. Roos and Oikonomakis, 'We Are Everywhere!'.

46. Benjamin Tejerina, Ignacia Perugorría, Tova Benski and Lauren Langman, 'From Indignation to Occupation: A New Wave of Global Mobilization', *Current Sociology* 61, no. 4 (2013): 377–92.

47. N.b. Die Linke was closely involved in the organisation of the Blockupy movement. For a discussion of these developments in the British context, see David Bailey, 'Palliating Terminal Social Democratic Decline at the EU-level?', in *European Social Democracy During the Global Economic Crisis: Renovation or Resignation?*, ed. David J. Bailey, Jean-Michel De Waele, Fabien Escalona and Mathieu Vieira (Manchester: Manchester University Press, 2014), 233–51.

48. Huke, Clua-Losada and Bailey, 'Disrupting the European Crisis'; Flesher Fominaya, Cristina. 'Redefining the Crisis/Redefining Democracy: Mobilising for the Right to Housing in Spain's PAH Movement,' *South European Society and Politics* 20, no. 4 (2015): 465–85.

49. For example, Wolfgang Streeck, 'The strikes sweeping Germany are here to stay', *The Guardian* 22 May 2015. Available: http://www.theguardian.com/ commentisfree/2015/may/22/strikes-sweeping-germany-here-to-stay.

50. Although of course Syriza is not, strictly speaking, a new party.

51. Michalis Spourdalakis, 'The Miraculous Rise of the "Phenomenon SYRIZA"', *International Critical Thought* 4, no. 3 (2014): 354–66; Mimmo Porcaro, 'Occupy Lenin', in *Socialist Register: The Question of Strategy*, ed. Leo Panitch, Greg Albo and Vivek Chibber (London: Merlin Press, 2013), 84–97; Jan Rehmann, *'Connective Party or Return to a "War of Maneuver"?'* (Berlin: Rosa Luxemburg Stiftung, 2013).

52. Tormey, *The End of Representative Politics*; Roos and Oikonomakis, 'We Are Everywhere!'.

53. Roos and Oikonomakis, 'We Are Everywhere!'.

54. Occupy London, 'Economics Statement', 6 December 2011. Available: http:// occupylondon.org.uk/about/statements/statement-on-economy/.

55. 15-M, 'List of specific demands from the 15-M movement', 27 May 2011. Available: http://roarmag.org/2011/05/list-demands-spanish-protesters-15-m-madrid/.

56. Ibid.

57. Ibid.

58. Flesher Fominaya, 'Debunking Spontaneity', 154.

59. Ibid., 157.

60. Marilena Simiti, 'Rage and Protest: The case of the Greek Indignant movement', GreeSE Paper No. 82 Hellenic Observatory Papers on Greece and Southeast Europe, February 2014. Available: http://www.lse.ac.uk/europeanInstitute/research/hellenicObservatory/CMS%20pdf/Publications/GreeSE/GreeSE-No82.pdf.

61. Luke March, 'Radical Left Parties and Social Movements: Allies, Associates or Antagonists?', in Christian Frohlich, Magnus Wennerhag and Grzegorz Piotrowski (eds.), *Radical Left Parties and Social Movements in Europe* (Farnham: Ashgate, forthcoming, 2016).

62. Syriza, *The Thessaloniki Programme*, 2014, emphasis added. Available: http://www.syriza.gr/article/SYRIZA---THE-THESSALONIKI-PROGRAMME.html.

63. Ibid.

64. Pablo Iglesias, 'Understanding Podemos,' *New Left Review* 93 (2015): 10, emphasis added.

65. Podemos, 'Turning outrage into political change,' English translation of the 2014 Podemos manifesto: *Mover ficha*. Available: https://hiredknaves.wordpress.com/2014/01/20/podemos-translated-manifesto/.

66. Ada Colau, 'Making the Democratic Revolution Happen,' *Diario Público*, 5 December 2014. Available: http://adacolau.cat/en/post/making-democratic-revolution-happen.

67. Ada Colau, 'First we take Barcelona ...', *Open Democracy* 20 May 2015. Available: https://www.opendemocracy.net/can-europe-make-it/ada-colau/first-we-take-barcelona.

68. Flesher Fominaya, 'Redefining the Crisis/Redefining Democracy'.

69. Andrew Kliman, *The Failure of Capitalist Production: Underlying Causes of the Great Recession* (London: Pluto Press, 2012).

70. David Harvey, *A Brief History of Neoliberalism* (Oxford: Oxford University Press, 2005).

71. Bob Jessop, *State Theory: Putting Capitalist States in their Place* (Cambridge: Polity, 1990).

72. David J. Bailey, 'Resistance Is Futile? The Impact of Disruptive Protest in the "Silver Age of Permanent Austerity,"' *Socio-Economic Review* 13, no. 1 (2015): 5–32.

73. David J. Bailey, 'The Transition to "New" Social Democracy: The Role of Capitalism, Representation, and (hampered) Contestation,' *British Journal of Politics and International Relations* 11, no. 4 (2009): 593–612.

74. Margit Mayer and John Ely (eds.), *The German Greens: Paradox Between Movement and Party* (Philadelphia: Temple University Press, 1998).

75. It should be noted that this alternative electoral strategy has so far been without success, with Popular Unity failing to win a single seat in the second 2015 general election.

76. For a comprehensive list, see http://omikronproject.gr/grassroots.

77. International Workingmen's Association, 'General Rules', October 1864. Available at: http://www.marxists.org/archive/marx/iwma/documents/1864/rules.htm.

Chapter 4

Uplifting the Masses?

Radical Left Parties and Social Movements during the Crisis

Óscar García Agustín and Martin Bak Jørgensen

The financial crisis has impacted upon European countries to different extents and with diverse consequences. While in Southern Europe the drastic economic and social adjustment has been followed by a crisis of representation in the political system, in the Nordic countries economic reforms are being carried out gradually without massive protests.[1] In Eastern Europe as in Southern Europe there have been massive uprisings reinventing popular democracy and confronting political power. In Western Europe, the form and scope of protests has differed. Although austerity policies may not have been as harsh as elsewhere in Europe, some countries (e.g. Belgium) have witnessed popular mobilisations in the form of demonstrations and rallies.

In this chapter we analyse how RLPs have connected with popular mobilisations and responses to the economic and political crisis in four countries: Denmark, Slovenia, Spain and the United Kingdom. The crisis has affected Spain the worst but Slovenia has also suffered from a retraction of the welfare state. The United Kingdom has been less directly affected by the Troika but has experienced internal austerity policies, continued privatisation and cuts to public services.[2] In Denmark neoliberal reforms have slowly led to a transformation of the welfare state that has had severe effects for people who depend on social benefits (unemployed, early retirement pensioners, immigrants, etc.).[3] The four countries selected illustrate relations between RLPs and social movements in countries from Northern, Eastern, Central and Southern Europe. They are interesting to compare due to their different welfare state traditions, which are affected differently by the economic crisis and austerity measures: Spain has a conservative-corporate model, Slovenia a particular post-socialist mix of social democratic and conservative-corporate models, Denmark a social democratic/universalist model, and United Kingdom a liberal welfare state. Furthermore, the comparison offers the possibility of discussing whether the strong social mobilisations in Southern (and to some degree in Eastern) Europe have been proxies for similar developments in Central and Northern Europe.

Here, we focus on three new parties that emerged after the economic crisis: the Initiative for Democratic Socialism (*Iniciativa za demokratični sociali-zem*, IDS) in Slovenia, Podemos in Spain and Left Unity (LU) in the United Kingdom. We also focus on the Red-Green Alliance in Denmark (*Enhedslis-ten – De Rød-Grønne*, EL), founded in 1989. The selection of these parties results from the choice of country cases (discussed above) but also allows us to investigate different constellations of relations between RLPs and social movements. In particular, the four parties/countries allow us to analyse differ-ent scenarios such as strong movement mobilisation and political realignment (IDS and Podemos); no strong mobilisation but partial political realignment (EL); and some mobilisation but no political realignment (LU). Although some of these parties are not discussed in detail elsewhere in this volume, they fit Luke March's definition of RLPs as parties that are anti-capitalist, which demand equality and stronger economic redistribution.[4] The parties also share the goals of grassroots mobilisation and of retaining strong link-ages with social movements. Moreover, we understand these parties as hav-ing elements of left populism, since their juxtaposition between the elite and the people presents an important dimension of their political demands.[5]

To compare RLP relations with movements in the four countries, we have selected three key dimensions of analysis. First, we analyse the nature of social mobilisations during the crisis to determine how the existence (or lack) of large-scale protests and movements influence the institutionalisation of new social agendas; second, we discuss the strategies used to link the social with the political focusing on what we can term intersectional or transversal features; and finally, we discuss the possibility of political realignment(s) taking place on the left and the way in which the positions of RLPs can shape the political system. By analysing these three dimensions we address the potential for new political organisations to emerge that possess the capability to promote an 'uplifting of the masses'. Furthermore, the analysis contrib-utes to our understanding of why RLPs vary in terms of electoral success. We show that it is above all the size and persistence of the mass mobilisa-tions; the organisational forms; the ability to expand collective claims; and power positioning that are decisive factors in shaping the composition and success of RLPs.

Overall, we argue that the recession and austerity measures have had several effects that have promoted a transition from the social to the politi-cal.[6] In particular, economic crisis has been augmented with political crisis, because the party systems have been perceived as being unable to respond to the interests of the citizenry. At the national and European levels, the crisis therefore enhanced what Donatella della Porta (citing John W. Kingdon) has called the 'window of political opportunity' for new parties.[7] The strong links between the social and political actors indicate points to the need for further research on organisational change in RLPs and their linkage strategies.[8]

SOCIAL MOBILISATIONS

Since 2011 we have seen a cycle of protests that included social mobilisations including Occupy Wall Street and the 15M in Spain. According to della Porta, such mobilisations usually entail two phenomena: the institutionalisation of mobilisations, especially when these are declining; and the emergence of party-movements, that is, parties born from social mobilisations whose aim is to translate some of the new modes of 'doing politics' into the electoral arena.[9] However, key features of the 2011 cycle of protests also include manifestations against neoliberalism and corruption in the political system, and a distrust of politicians. The critique of a lack of representation was central to the protests and the occupations of public squares. Among the four countries that we analyse, Spain and Slovenia have experienced large-scale mobilisations and these help to explain the emergence of new parties as 'party-movements'.

These parties possess a stronger articulation of political indignation and a clear stance towards renewing the political system through a 'democratic turn' based on a serious commitment to exploring new ways of organising and participating. They share political programmes with other RLPs, but they incorporate a self-identification of the party as a 'democratic' organisation that emanates from the recent cycle of protests. The lack of a wider social mobilisation is clear in the case of the United Kingdom where the anti-austerity movement faces difficulties in articulating different protests and rallies. LU has experienced difficulties in channelling this discontent, especially since the renewed leadership of the Labour Party has assumed part of the critique against austerity measures. In Denmark, on the other hand, the lack of mobilisations has made it difficult to foster an alternative anti-neoliberal agenda. We will now discuss the social mobilisation in each country in turn.

Austerity measures in Spain were mostly carried out by the conservative party (Spanish People's Party, PP), but were already initiated by the social democratic Socialist Workers' Party (PSOE). This explains why the reaction against austerity was not just aimed against one party but against the two-party system where policy differences had become almost imperceptible and corruption became a major issue. The 15M movement in 2011 was an uprising against austerity that involved the occupation of public squares and experimentation with forms of direct and participatory democracy through assemblies and deliberation. Interestingly, the rejection of the limitations of representative democracy and austerity measures were manifested, according to Cristina Flesher Fominaya, by a 'democratic turn', which reclaimed new organisational processes from below and articulated alternatives to representative democracy through placing 'emphasis on democratic reform and renewal and a reclaiming of the constitution, with its guarantees of basic social rights (housing, education)'.[10] There was no immediate political outlet for the combination of distrust in the political class and political institutions, despite the enormous sympathy and mobilisation awakened by the 15M. Indeed, the conservative government won the local and regional elections a few days after the first protests and later, in November 2011, won an absolute majority in the general elections. However, from the perspective of Podemos' leaders, 15M offered an opportunity to develop a new political culture and a broader articulation of the movement could be carried out by institutional means.

Although Podemos is not the same as 15M, as one of the party's leaders, Iñigo Errejón, points out, Podemos would not exist without the small transformations in the 'common sense' provoked by 15M, which contributed to opening of a window of opportunity.[11] However, in terms of party organisation, Podemos has sought to overcome the tension between movement and party-form with innovative methods of organising. These include the so-called 'circles' (*círculos*), which reproduce the assembly and deliberative dynamic of 15M, and a centralised leadership, characteristic of traditional parties. These two sides are reflected in the internal debates in which the populist strategy assumed by the party has been contested by the assembly one. Indeed, when party founder Juan Carlos Monedero left the party in 2015, he cited the party's loss of movement origins as one of his reasons.[12] Podemos appears to promote a 'democratic turn' and a new way of doing politics by oscillating between horizontal and centralised ways of organising, but with the latter becoming dominant so far. Nevertheless, it is clear that the strong mobilisations initiated by 15M and its positioning against the two-party system enhanced the possibility of articulating a completely new political alternative.

In Slovenia, IDS was founded in 2014 after a long period of mobilisation since the end of 2012. The 'Maribor uprising' in Slovenia was the largest protest movement in 20 years and started as a protest against the right-wing mayor of Maribor's plans to set up a traffic control network of speed radars based on public-private partnership.[13] The protests spread throughout the country and grew to attack the right-wing government's austerity measures for harming the public sector. The demonstrations rejected austerity as well as the political system, which blurred the ideological difference between left and right. An element of left populism was evident in IDS as well. The slogan

'They are all the same' showed a lack of interest in making compromises with the political class since the uprisings 'radically challenged the very meaning of democracy'.[14]

IDS' founders had been members of the Workers and Punks' University (WPU).[15] They interpreted the protest moment in terms of class and reclaimed the need for radical change and a socialist project to fight against capitalism and corruption. In this sense, the university struggles offered an opportunity to develop a political organisation that was able to unite the forces and experiences of heterogeneous actors. Without the movement, IDS 'as such would have never been born or ... would be born only much later on'.[16] IDS was rooted in the protest movement, but was aware of the fact that these experiences should be augmented with struggle in official institutions.[17] The protests led IDS to understand the situation as a political opportunity to create a new party, whose intention was to renew socialism in order to capture the dynamics fostered by the 'Maribor uprising'.

The case of Denmark is quite different because the economic crisis had a lower impact than in the other countries and although unemployment increased, the public sector has remained relatively strong.[18] However, austerity measures were applied and aroused protests over cuts to unemployment benefits, the reform of the education system as well as privatisations (e.g. of public energy providers). The protests were particularly intense in the educational area where a lock-out led to the intervention of the government without accepting the demands of the teachers. Yet overall, mobilisations against austerity were relatively weak and from 2011 to 2015 the centre-left government (Social Democracy [S] and the Socialist People's Party [SF]) was responsible for the application of such measures. This meant that protests were not against a right-wing government as in many other countries and the EL found difficulties in combining support for the government in Parliament with its role in social protest.

As a result, although several groups were extremely critical of the government, including EL, which, for example, took a leading role in opposing the reform of unemployment benefits, the limited opportunities to mobilise or radically criticise austerity measures did not open a political 'window' for other alternatives. Nor was the radicalisation of EL possible, since it was not in a position to force a direct confrontation with the government. Critical, albeit minority, voices within the party reproached its leaders for not being capable of assuming a major opposition position.[19] Although traditionally EL is a party of activists with strong connections to grassroots movements, its support role to the former government has, according to those critics, led the party to shift from activism to parliamentarism.[20] It remains to be seen whether major mobilisations will appear that might strengthen RLPs in Denmark.

In contrast, the application of austerity measures in the United Kingdom was carried out by the Conservative-Liberal Democrat government elected in 2010, which aimed to lower the deficit through the largest public spending cuts since World War II. In 2010, UK Uncut emerged as a grassroots mass movement whose main priority was to fight austerity politics and to use direct action in protests against corporations. It appealed to the 'ordinary people' and appropriated Vodafone's 'Power to you' slogan in order to empower citizens and take action against austerity. As in the case of Spain and the rise of 15M we here see clear elements of left populism emphasising the distinctions between the ordinary people vs. the corrupt elite as well as a critique of the lack of democracy.

Later, in 2013, the People's Assembly Against Austerity was launched, supported by unions and anti-austerity parties, among others the Green Party and Left Unity, and some Labour MPs including now-Labour Party leader Jeremy Corbyn.[21] The assembly's goal is to shape a broad opposition against the government cuts which were barely represented in Parliament. Its capacity for social opposition became evident 44 days after the Conservative Party won the 2015 general election when large protests took place in the United Kingdom against government plans for more austerity policies. The protesters presented the marches as a step towards building a stronger movement that could have a real influence on government policies. Corbyn emphasised that mass movements were also the root of the Labour movement.[22]

However, RLPs in the United Kingdom struggled to develop strong links with such radical mobilisations. Left Unity certainly had such an intent.[23] It was officially established in London on 30 November 2013 following an appeal by filmmaker and socialist/activist Ken Loach after his film *Spirit of '45*, which lauds the radical achievements of the post-war welfare state that have been undermined in recent decades. Academic and writer Kate Hudson and anti-war activist Gilbert Achcar also signed the appeal, which was supported by more than 10,000 people and quickly developed into LU. Unlike the multiple existing micro-parties on Britain's radical Left, LU explicitly aspired to replicate the examples set by other electorally successful RLPs (e.g. Syriza and Die Linke) or those which had shown potential to mobilise broadly (Podemos). Basically, the hope was to become a strong alternative RLP in the new European tradition.

Nonetheless, LU's results have been meagre to date. As a party of activists, LU was involved in mobilisation against austerity but has failed to gain a position as an electoral alternative to the Labour Party. Unlike existing RLPs, in the United Kingdom, it adopted an anti-sectarian approach to cooperation with grassroots movements. It sought to become part of them, and to assuage their suspicions it avoided a top-down perspective. But the characteristics of LU, such as activism, community work and unity initiatives, have not led to a bigger political project so far. The question of 'being a party that people would want to *join*, rather than work with' is relevant.[24] Instead, the People's Assemblies gave room for Corbyn to promote an anti-austerity discourse and contributed towards the reinvigoration of the left wing of the Labour Party. After the 2015 elections, and Corbyn's surprise victory as Labour leader, the anti-austerity mobilisations provided a potential pool of support for Labour and Corbyn's intention to make Labour more of a social movement. However, this provided a strategic dilemma for LU whose sympathies for the Corbyn movement have driven many of its activists to re-connect to the Labour Party. Consequently, the space for RLPs to expand electorally to the left of Labour appears to have been closed for the time being.

PARTY-BUILDING THROUGH INTERSECTIONAL AND TRANSVERSAL POLITICS

The second dimension concerns the intersectional and transversal relations between social movements and parties. We argue that RLPs emerging during the crisis have expanded the conflict-lines by foregrounding *intersectional perspectives*, that is, opened to issues of gender, sexuality, race, ethnicity, religion and other inequalities, and *transversal politics*, that is, the redefinition of conflict in terms of 'above' (the elite) and 'below' (the people) to include social actors who do not identify with traditional parties. This implies not only a discursive dimension but also an organisational dimension regarding the incorporation of diversity.

Podemos represents the strongest example of transversal politics in practice and how this has influenced party formation. The heterogeneity of the 15M movement led to a diffusion and fragmentation of the social groups comprising the movement. This development caused concerns and calls for action from two founders of Podemos, Ariel Jerez and Carolina Bescansa.[25] These activists wanted to avoid the further dispersal of the movement as there were no existing parties that could reflect and encompass the growing pressure for social and political change. They argued that it was necessary to support the 'transversal efforts undertaken by the social protesters and groups' to unify the struggle in a political space and to confront political power. Like 15M, the base of Podemos is constituted by a transversal class united through precaritisation as a result of the economic crisis. It consists of young and old, of the unemployed, of the highly educated, of activists, minorities, students, as well as leftists. Podemos has deliberately striven to develop the party through participation – connecting with the decision-making processes initiated by 15M.

The approach taken by Podemos has been based on developing an organisation that reflects and enhances its diverse social composition. Its 'circles' therefore act as autonomous groups which allow it to encompass diverse and intersecting issues. However, the populist strategy assumed by Podemos, which identifies social conflict between elite and people (creating a signifier capable of capturing the transversal composition of its constituencies) makes it difficult to adopt an intersectional approach since categories like gender or ethnicity become relegated. Such problems have led to attempts to promote a more clearly feminist approach in aims of dealing with different identities in a more inclusionary way.

In Slovenia, transversal politics was also a decisive factor in the formation of IDS. From the start, the party drew on the heterogeneity of protesters in the mobilisations of 2012–2013. The protesters included leftists, unionists, activists from the Occupy movement, former members of the Global Justice Movement, anti-racist groups, immigrants and broad segments of the population. Yet, despite this, IDS draws explicitly on socialism. Party international spokesperson Anej Korsika emphasised this in 2014: 'Our orientation is socialist, even communist and is fed from the history of workers' struggles; we acknowledge this loudly and clearly.'[26] This seems to indicate a more traditional leftist party ideology. The challenge has, therefore, been to redefine and expand the left-right distinction.

IDS has sought to do this through expanding the category of 'the people' that are understood to be struggling against neoliberalism and the Troika.[27] This means supporting and integrating the emancipatory struggles of workers, immigrants, women and peasants. Class differences are linked to inequalities and subordination, which creates a position defining a collective subject.[28] Korsika describes an example of this dynamic through the linkage to the LGBT community. Indeed, the IDS parliamentary group succeeded in pushing through a bill that ensures equal rights for hetero and homosexual couples. The prioritisation of this minority issue shows how IDS seeks to expand the limits of the political debate.

The Danish EL was established in 1989 as a coalition of small RLPs; its party programme from 1996 underlines that it is not a party in the traditional sense but the voice of social mobilisations and organisations which do not have access to established political channels.[29] Its conception of political identities is understood in relation to the socialist project. Its agenda combines socialist ideology with issues of racism, sexual discrimination, gender equality, etc. Recently, the party has struggled with internal disputes between reformists and revolutionaries and it has assumed more pragmatic positions and even approached the 'left populist turn' fostered by Syriza and Podemos.

This became particularly evident in debates on formulating the party's programme at its convention on 16–18 May 2014. In the months before the convention several discussions took place on the online leftist forum *Modkraft* discussing future leftist strategies, and trying to combine experiences from Southern Europe with more orthodox socialist approaches.[30] EL has emphasised that socialism and feminism are inseparable struggles and promotes the rights of gays, lesbians and transgender people. However, despite its opposition to racism and support for multiculturalism, EL has struggled to include minorities within the party structure and in the selection of candidates for general elections. These difficulties were reflected in the case of Asmaa Abdol-Hamid, an electoral candidate in 2007, whose Muslim identity was criticised by feminists and socialists within the party.

In the United Kingdom, LU has been an attempt to not only create linkages with social movements but also to develop a party from below through letting them shape policymaking processes. The party organisation has established caucuses for youth, disabled, LGBTQ, 'black' and ethnic minority-members and for women. Where LU differs from its predecessors is in the way in which it puts issues of race, gender and non-citizens to the fore in struggling against capitalism.[31] For example, during the 2015 election the party presented an immigrant-tolerant alternative to the UK Independence Party (UKIP) as both the Labour Party and the Conservative Party promoted restrictive positions on immigration.

The way that LU seeks to translate social indignation into a political alternative representing an inclusive 'we' illustrates its transversal approach. For example, it argues that 'the ruling class tries to divide us – saying they are saving services and resources for the "indigenous" people by excluding the "foreigners." We need to say "we are all in this together"'; or that 'any anti-austerity movement with any chance of success must therefore be persuaded to foreground the issue of anti-racism, to argue that working class people, of whatever background, are indeed all in it together'.[32]

LU did not develop from a social movement, however. Neither does it unite the landscape of protests and social mobilisations. The party has developed through intersectional and transversal politics with campaigns like 'No More Austerity', collaborating with groups like Black Activists Rising Against the Cuts (BARAC), or being involved in the My Belly is Mine campaigns, which aim at keeping abortion legal in Spain. Alliances are established nationally with UK Feminist Action, The Women's Assembly (and other groups) and transnationally with *La Asamblea de Mujeres* in Spain. The repercussions of the crisis have kept the anti-austerity protests strong. However, the leading role now assumed by Jeremy Corbyn makes LU's development dependent on its position towards the Labour Party.

POLITICAL COMPETITION AND LEFT REALIGNMENT

The economic crisis has led to changes in the positions assumed by parties on the left in varying ways. For instance, in both Spain and Denmark, the main social democratic party remains dominant (albeit under increasing pressure, particularly in the former). EL has an increasing monopoly over the radical left space since the formerly radical left Socialist People's Party (SF) has moved to more social liberal positions during the period. Conversely, Podemos has grown larger than Spain's other main RLP, United Left (IU). In Slovenia, IDS is similarly new, but represents the appearance of an electorally success-ful, self-defined, RLP in Slovenia for the first time since the fall of the Soviet Union. In the United Kingdom, there is also a new RLP, Left Unity, but it has been in no way able to shake the hegemony of the Labour Party over the Left.

We now consider the extent to which the above-mentioned discourses and ways of organising (and strengthening linkages with social movements) have shaped the positions of Social Democrats (SD) and other RLPs and whether a recomposition of the Left has taken place. Podemos has had a dramatic impact on the left political space in Spain and gained five MEPs at the 2014 European Parliamentary elections. In its rapid development, Podemos obtained greater success still in the 20 December 2015 general elections with 69 mandates and 20.66 per cent of the vote, very close to the 22.01 per cent for the Spanish Socialist Worker's Party (PSOE), while IU gained only two mandates with 3.67 per cent of the vote. On the one hand, Podemos' emergence contributed to the realignment of the Left, and on the other to resituating the parties on a new axis differentiating between traditional and new parties. Indeed, the recently established centre-right party Ciudadanos also represents a new politics. This meant that Podemos encountered elec-toral competition from Ciudadanos and lost part of its transversal discourse since some centrist voters were able to move their preferences towards Ciudadanos.

Podemos' populist turn made it possible for the party to compete with the PSOE for the hegemony of the Left in a way that had never happened with IU. The leading role played by social movements in recent years as the only opposition against the PP was inherited by Podemos and the PSOE experi-enced difficulties in recovering its image as the major electoral alternative to the PP. While appearing to eschew ideology, Podemos' leader, Pablo Igle-sias, has claimed that his party occupies the space of social democracy, since the space of welfare and social rights has been left empty. This movement towards the Centre-Left has been so far combined with Podemos' consolida-tion as the biggest RLP. As further detailed by Luis Ramiro in this volume, IU reacted late to the 2011 mobilisations and it was not until 2015 (when Alberto Garzón, linked to the 15M, was elected new leader of the party) that the intention of regenerating the party became visible. Nonetheless, IU has continued to face problems in relation to Podemos: it is perceived as a marginal party which cannot win elections nor gain significant influence; the relations with social movements are of cooperation but also mistrust; and it is considered as an 'old' party, sharing some of the problems of other political parties. The attempt to expand its electoral scope in 2015 through the coalition IU-Popular Unity was likewise a late reaction with insufficient (but not insignificant) support.

Having questioned the hegemony of social democracy and grown significantly Podemos faced several challenges. How could it maintain a left politics and avoid assuming the centre-left position of its main adversary the PSOE? How to set up a left agenda for the majority without being perceived as a minority party? How to involve IU in this process? How should it foster democratic renovation from the Left and avoid a non-ideological position in this sense (which Ciudadanos can also assume)? It remains to be seen whether Podemos is able to answer these challenges and to present a viable alternative to the right-wing parties.

Slovenia had parliamentary elections on 13 July 2014. Elections took place in a situation characterised by electoral volatility and new parties emerged as voters rejected established parties. The most popular party was founded only six weeks before the elections under the name of its leader, the Party of Miro Cerar (SMC). It ultimately obtained 34.6 per cent of the votes (36 out of 90 seats). This centrist, social liberal party benefited from Cerar's position as an outsider and the SMC changed its name into the Modern Centre Party after winning the elections and forming a coalition government with the Democratic Pensioners' Party of Slovenia (DESUS) and the SD. The success of new parties was based on the need to regenerate the political system, the extensive corruption among traditional parties, and debates surrounding an international bailout for the banks and fulfilling European Union programmes through privatisations and control of public expenses.

Within this limited political space for leftist parties, one of the major surprises was the fifth position achieved by United Left (ZL) with six seats and almost the same number of votes as the SD. ZL is an alliance between Democratic Labour Party (DSD), Party for Sustainable Development of Slovenia (TRS), and IDS. The radical Left thus gained its best result since the disintegration of Yugoslavia and for the first time had the possibility to promote its agenda in Parliament. The fact that ZL is not participating in the governmental coalition, whose popularity has been in free fall, benefits the party to lead the struggle against privatisations or for social rights (like LGBT rights) in a versatile way. According to the December 2014 polls, the two most popular parties would be the main opposition party the Democratic Party (SDS), with just 13.7 per cent and the ruling party, SMC, with merely 12.4 per cent. In this situation, ZL has an opportunity to modify the Left by overcoming the SD and to develop support for radical left politics. It may have potential to create a new political panorama both in Slovenia and in the Balkan region in general.

In the Danish context, EL found itself in a completely different situation. From 2011 to 2015, Denmark was governed by a centre-left coalition composed of the SD, the Social Liberal Party and Socialist People's Party (SF, who withdrew in 2014). EL supported this government in order to gain influence and ensure an alternative against a right-wing government, which had been in power for 10 years by 2011. Having been a marginal parliamentary party, EL obtained its best results in 2011 with 12 seats (doubling its result in 2005). The ascendancy of EL continued in 2015 with 14 seats and it became the second most popular party of the 'red' bloc after the SD. EL appeared to have managed the difficult balance of supporting the government (through a more pragmatic approach than before) and offering an alternative agenda based on the defence of welfare and social rights.

While the SD became the largest party in the 2015 general elections and gained four seats more than in 2011, the other members of the government coalition, the Social Liberal Party and the SF, lost seats and obtained eight and seven, respectively. SF left the government owing to an internal crisis. Over recent years it has moved from the radical Left to the Centre-Left. Moreover, while it was in office it struggled to promote a left agenda. This thereby provided EL with an opportunity to become the major party on the radical left.

This situation led to calls to 'modernise' EL as it formulated a new programme of principles in 2014. Some called for EL to abandon class politics and the left-right spectrum for a populist approach that reflected the conflict between 'ordinary' Danes and the elite. Despite arguments that this would help to expand EL's position within the left, a survey from *Ugebrevet A4* showed problems for this strategy as more Danes say they would never vote for EL than for any other party.[33] The Danish general electoral results in 2015 also saw the appearance of a new centre-left party, The Alternative, which obtained nine seats despite being established only a few months prior to the election. The Alternative seeks to enhance relations between politicians and citizens and to practise new ways of participation and involvement in politics. In this sense, The Alternative has commonalities with new parties like Podemos that espouse the importance of changing political culture. EL is thus now challenged by a party who shares the importance of being a party of activists and capable of connecting with people who are disenchanted with the political system.

In the United Kingdom, the general election of 7 May 2015 gave an increased majority to the Conservative Party and showed again how the majoritarian electoral system favours the biggest parties and does not distribute seats with any concern for proportionality. The Labour Party, whose proposals were characterised by LU as 'austerity lite', was in contrast framed as being too left wing by British right-wing media such as *The Daily Mail*, particularly its leader 'Red' Ed Miliband.[34] Arguably, the Green Party became the biggest anti-austerity party on the left. However, despite assuming anti-austerity discourse, the party cannot be considered as an RLP, since it lacks any class analysis for understanding the mechanism of redistribution and the sense of connection with the poorest.[35] With 3.8 per cent of votes and just one seat, the Greens have few possibilities to lead anti-austerity politics (albeit still much more than LU).

LU's ability to promote a realignment of the Left remains limited since it faces other anti-austerity parties (not just the Greens but now the Scottish National Party) as well as bigger anti-establishment parties (chiefly UKIP). More significantly, Corbyn's left turn makes the possibility of creating any alternative to the left of Labour, a 'British Syriza', still more complicated. The pitifully low percentage of votes in 2015, with just 10 national candidates (three gaining just 455 votes between them, and seven joint candidates with the Trade Unionist and Socialist Coalition [TUSC]), reflected the lack of electoral impact from the party's work in the streets. Nonetheless LU has not abandoned the project of constituting a radical left alternative to Labour with efforts relying on work with local communities. Yet it remains unclear how LU as a party of activists can develop into a significant electoral party. At a party conference in November 2015 entitled 'New Challenges, New Opportunities', LU developed an uneasy compromise: a large majority of delegates voted for LU to continue as an independent party of the radical Left, yet giving strong support to Jeremy Corbyn's Labour leadership and encouraging members to join his movement Momentum.[36]

CONCLUSIONS

This chapter has shown that some movements turned anti-austerity protests into a struggle for democracy. The cycle of protests emerging during the economic crisis constituted a window of opportunity, particularly in countries where large-scale mobilisations led to a 'democratic turn' that identified the political system as being part of the problem. This had consequences for the Left, where new parties emerged in search of new ways of doing politics. Other existing left parties have likewise had to consider their role and how to reflect the demands of democratising the political system. We have shown how the nature of mass mobilisation in society; RLP organisational forms and composition, RLP political strategies, RLP inclusion in government and wider political realignments on the left shaped the development of the four parties studied here (see Table 4.1).

We have shown how large-scale mobilisations in Spain and Slovenia enabled the unexpected emergence of new parties. IDS and Podemos were capable of institutionalising strong movements such as the Maribor uprising

Table 4.1 Patterns of Mobilisation and Left Party Realignment

Party (country)	Foundation	Mass Mobilisations	Organisational Forms	Organisational Composition	Political Strategy	Power Positioning	Left Political Competition/ Realignment
Left Unity (UK)	2013	Protests against austerity (Trade Unions, UK Uncut, students, The People's Assembly against Austerity)	Fostering horizontality	Transversal and intersectional (inclusive us – class, gender, ethnicity)	Socialist	Without parliamentary or local representation	Hegemonic Labour, the tiny TUSC (Trade Unionist and Socialist Coalition)
Initiative for Democratic Socialism	2014	Maribor (2012–13): against political elite and corruption	Fostering horizontality	Transversal (domination and class differences)	Socialist	Opposition party	Weak social democratic party
Podemos	2014	15M: for more democracy and against political corruption	Combination of horizontality and vertical leadership	Transversal (precaritisation and class, ordinary people)	Left-populist	Office-oriented	Weakening social democratic party and United Left
Red-Green Alliance	1989	Few social conflicts (teachers, reform of unemployment benefits)	Increasing leadership and maintaining grass-root activism	Class and nation	Socialist-reformist	Supportive of center-left government / opposition	Stable social democratic party, weakening Socialist People's Party, new The Alternative

Source: Authors' conceptualisations.

and the 15M and open up the political space from the Left to other ideological approaches (democratic socialism in Slovenia and left populism in Spain) as well as other political actors and subjectivities excluded from the representative system. These parties have also spearheaded experiments with other forms of organisation based on more horizontality and participation, despite the difficulties presented by parliamentary politics and electoral competition.

While these new political parties in Spain and Slovenia compete with social democratic parties and aspire to take a leading role on the left, in Denmark and the UK RLPs are still not capable of challenging the hegemonic role of the social democrats. In Denmark, the lack of such mobilisations in a period led by a ruling centre-left coalition contributed to the consolidation of EL as the main RLP. The EL is still trying to find the best balance between parliamentarism and support for centre-left governments, versus its earlier commitment to grassroots activism. Despite the relative lack of anti-austerity protests, the general crisis of trust in the political system has (to some extent) produced a new competitor for EL in the form of the centre-left party The Alternative.

In the United Kingdom, the efforts of LU to become a 'British Syriza' through community work and social activism have not produced any electoral dividends, despite promising mass mobilisations beforehand. Instead, the potential for developing links with social movements have been captured by Labour, with its left turn under Jeremy Corbyn and his intention of making the party more social movement-oriented. Thus (albeit with much difficulty), there is the possibility of an existing mainstream party institutionalising anti-austerity protests. Any capacity LU had to lead the political articulation of the anti-austerity movement has been diminished.

In sum, the financial and economic crisis has presented different political opportunities for RLPs to develop links to social mobilisations. Despite these contextual differences we find a common intention among the RLPs in the countries studied here to do politics differently and an increased orientation towards social movements and their organisational forms. It is currently difficult to tell whether the new parties or the substantial changes within existing ones outlined here will result in the achievement of a radical left agenda or at least the radicalisation of the Left overall, and there are certainly reasons for doubt. Nevertheless, a redefinition of the political space of the Left is taking place and along with it the *possibility* of further advancing left-wing agendas.

NOTES

1. Myrto Tsakatika, and Marco Lisi, 'Zippin'up My Boots, Goin'Back to My Roots': Radical Left Parties in Southern Europe', *South European Society and Politics* 18, no. 1 (2013): 19.

2. Peter Taylor-Gooby, 'Root and Branch Restructuring to Achieve Major Cuts: The Social Policy Programme of the 2010 UK Coalition Government', *Social Policy & Administration* 46, no. 1 (2012): 61–82.

3. Bent Greve, 'Denmark: Still a Nordic Welfare State after the Changes of Recent Years?,' *Challenges to European Welfare Systems* (Springer International Publishing, 2016), 159–176.

4. Luke March, *Radical Left Parties in Europe* (Abingdon: Routledge, 2011).

5. Ibid.

6. Martin Bak Jørgensen and Óscar García Agustín, 'The Postmodern Prince: The Political Articulation of Social Dissent,' in *Politics of Dissent*, ed. Martin Bak Jørgensen and Óscar García Agustín (Frankfurt am Main: Peter Lang, 2015), 31–52.

7. Donatella della Porta, 'Del 15M a Podemos: resistencia en tiempos de recesion,' *Encrucijadas, Revista Crítica de Ciencias Sociales* 9 (2015): 1–11.

8. For similar claims, see Óscar García Agustín, 'Podemos som postkrise-parti: Mellem populisme og radikalisme', *Arbejderhistorie* 1 (2015): 34–57; Dan Keith, 'Radical Left Parties and left Movements in Northern Europe,' in Magnus Wennerhag et al. Grzegorz Piotrowski; Christian Fröhlich *Radical Left Movements*, Farnham: Ashgate (2016); Luke March and Cas Mudde, 'What's Left of the Radical Left? The European Radical Left after 1989: Decline *and* Mutation,' *Comparative European Politics* 3, no. 1 (2005): 23–49; March, *Radical Left Parties in Europe*; Jørgensen and Agustín, 'The Postmodern Prince'; Ezequiel Adamovsky, 'Autonomous Politics and its Problems: Thinking the Passage from Social to Political', *Choike* (2006), accessed 30 November 2015, http://www.choike.org/documentos/adamovsky_autonomous.pdf.

9. della Porta, 'Del 15M a Podemos'; Herbert Kitschelt, 'Social Movements, Political Parties, and Democratic Theory,' *The Annals of the American Academy of Political and Social Science* 528 (1993): 13–29.

10. Cristina Flesher Fominaya, 'Debunking Spontaneity: Spain's 15M/Indignados as Autonomous Movement,' *Social Movement Studies: Journal of Social, Cultural and Political Protest* 14, no. 2 (2015): 154.

11. Iñigo Errejón and Chantal Mouffe, *Construir pueblo. Hegemonía y radicalización de la democracia* (Barcelona: Icaria, 2015).

12. For example, Francesco Manetta, 'Podemos co-founder criticizes mainstream drift in his own party,' *El País*, 30 April 2015, http://elpais.com/elpais/2015/04/30/inenglish/1430403454_148415.html?rel=mas.

13. Anej Korsika and Luka Mesec, 'Slovenia: From Spontaneous Protests to Renewal of the Social Left,' *Kurswechsel* 1 (2014): 80–8.

14. Gal Kirn, 'Slovenia's Social Uprising in the European Crisis: Maribor as Periphery from 1988 to 2012,' *Stasis* 2, no. 1 (2014): 106–29.

15. The Workers and Punks' University in Ljubljana is an educational project that since 1998 has organised a series of lectures based on social theories critical towards neoliberalism.

16. Korsika and Mesec, 'Slovenia,' 85.

17. Gal Kirn, 'The emergence of the new left party in Slovenia: Initiative for Democratic Socialism,' *Chronosmag* March 2014, http://chronosmag.eu/index.

php/g-kirn-the-emergence-of-the-new-left-party-in-slovenia-initiative-for-demo-cratic-socialism.html.

18. Mikkel Mailand, 'Austerity Measures and Municipalities: The Case of Denmark,' *Transfer: European Review of Labour and Research* 20, no. 3 (2014): 417–30.

19. Marianne Rosenkvist et al., 'Enhedslistens forspildte muligheder – Hvad kan vi lære af Folketingsvalget 2015?' *Modkraft*, 14 July 2015, accessed 30 November 2015, http://modkraft.dk/blog/marianne-rosenkvist/enhedslistens-forspildte-muligheder-hvad-kan-vi-l-re-af-folketingsvalget.

20. Keith, Dan. 'Radical Left Parties and Left Movements in Northern Europe and Scandinavia,' in *Radical Left Parties and Social Movements in Europe*, ed. Christian Fröhlich, Magnus Wennerhag and Grzegorz Piotrowski (Farnham: Ashgate, forthcoming, 2016).

21. Bice Maiguashca et al., 'Pulling Together in a Crisis? Anarchism, Feminism and the Limits of Left-wing Convergence in Austerity Britain', *Capital & Class* (2016). doi: 0309816815627388.

22. Damien Gayle, 'Anti-austerity protests: tens of thousands rally across UK,' *The Guardian*, June 20 2015, accessed 30 November 2015, http://www.theguardian.com/world/2015/jun/20/tens-thousands-rally-uk-protest-against-austerity.

23. See Maiguashca, et al., 'Pulling Together in a Crisis?'.

24. Joordinarybloggs, 'After the Election: What Next for Left Unity,' *Facing Reality*, May 24 2015, accessed 30 November, 2015, https://bloggingjbloggs1917.wordpress.com/2015/05/24/after-the-election-what-next-for-left-unity/.

25. Agustín, 'Podemos'; Ariel Jerez and Carolina Bescansa, 'Coyuntura fluida y nuevo sujeto constituyente,' *El Diario*, 2 February 2013, accessed 30 November 2015, http://www.eldiario.es/zonacritica/Coyuntura-fluida-nuevo-sujeto-constituy-ente_6_99100110.html.

26. Anej Korsika, 'The formation of a European Movement is Key,' *LeftEast* March 14, 2014, accessed 30 November, 2015, http://www.criticatac.ro/lefteast/interview-anej-korsika-ids-1/.

27. Initiative for Democratic Socialism, *Manifesto of the Initiative for Democratic Socialism* (2013), accessed 30 November 2015, http://www.demokraticni-socializem.si/programski-dokumenti/manifesto-of-the-initiative-for-democratic-socialism/.

28. Jørgensen and Agustín, 'The Post-Modern Prince'.

29. Enhedslisten, *Partiprogram* 1996, accessed 30 November 2015, http://www.arbejdermuseet.dk/index.php?option=com_docman&task=cat_view&gid=21&Itemid=238.

30. See http://modkraft.dk/artikel/diskussionsoversigt for an overview, accessed 30 November 2015.

31. Jørgensen and Agustín, 'The Post-Modern Prince'; Richard Seymour, 'Left Unity: A Report from the Founding Conference,' *New Left Project* December 1, 2013, accessed 30 November 2015, http://www.newleftproject.org/index.php/site/article_comments/left_unity_a_report_from_the_founding_conference.

32. Left Unity, 'Policy passed at Left Unity National Conference Manchester,' – 29 March 2014, http://leftunity.org/policy-passed-at-left-unity-conference-29-march-2014/.

33. Michael Braemer, 'Vælgerne: EL er de mindst stuerne,' *Ugebrevet A4*, October, 2014, accessed November 30, 2015, http://www.ugebreveta4.dk/vaelgerne-el-er-de-mindst-stuerene_19867.aspx.

34. Ivor Gaber, 'The "Othering" of "Red Ed," or How the Daily Mail "Framed" the British Labour Leader,' *The Political Quarterly* 85, no. 4 (2014): 471–9.

35. Suzanne Moore, 'Forget the Greens – if the UK wants a truly leftwing party, it might have to grow its own,' *The Guardian*, 28 January 2015, accessed 30 November 2015, http://www.theguardian.com/commentisfree/2015/jan/28/forget-greens-grow-your-own-leftwing-party-election.

36. Left Unity, 'Final motions and amendments,' 21–22 November 2015, accessed 30 November 2015, http://leftunity.org/motions-passed-at-left-unity-conference/.

Chapter 5

The Radical Left and Immigration

Resilient or Acquiescent in the Face of the Radical Right?

Francis McGowan and Daniel Keith

Expectations that the Great Recession would result in greater support for RLPs have been fulfilled only partly (see chapters 2 and 18 of this volume). The general picture is one of moderate and uneven growth. While electoral gains for radical right populist parties have also been varied, they appear to have gained more in both national elections and in elections to the European Parliament (not least in the early stages of the Great Recession).[1] What can explain these apparently counter-intuitive developments? Luke March has highlighted that RLPs 'lack a vision' in contrast to the relative success of radical right parties (hereafter RRPs) in crafting a narrative that resonates with many voters' sense of grievance and insecurity.[2] Moreover, while Cas Mudde found reasons to caution against linking the crisis to a growth in the salience of anti-immigration sentiment, recent data highlights a need for further scrutiny.[3]

There has been considerable debate regarding whether or not mainstream parties have adopted less tolerant policy stances on migration control and integration in response to the growth of the radical Right, indicating a 'contagion effect'. In this chapter, we ask whether the radical Right's exploitation of migration-related issues has also obliged RLPs to change their policies. It could be argued that RLPs are caught between two key responses: on the one hand, defending a universalist position of (international) solidarity with often marginalised and oppressed communities; on the other, being wary of immigration as a manifestation of globalisation at home, undercutting wages and job security. Odmalm and Bale identify a similar dilemma facing the Left as a whole, but it is arguably more acute for RLPs given their adherence to critiquing globalisation and to making common cause with the oppressed.[4] This might also coincide with a strategic dilemma of building support from migrant communities versus the fear of losing votes of the working class (often seen as a traditional source of RLP support).

Below, we explore how RLPs have responded to these dilemmas where parties of the radical Right have grown significantly since the crisis (see Table 5.1). Taking the examples of Denmark (Socialist People's Party [SF] and Red-Green Alliance [EL]), Sweden (Left Party), the Netherlands (Socialist Party [SP]) and Greece (Syriza), we contrast parties that have maintained a broadly 'solidaristic' stance on immigration with those who have adopted (or sustained) more restrictive and integrationist policies. We analyse these parties because they come from the largest of the RLP sub-categories that March identifies – the democratic socialists.[5] This provides a basis for future comparative research with other RLP subgroups.

Our analysis draws on interviews with party elites and is supplemented by aggregate data from the Comparative Manifestos Project (CMP) and the Chapel Hill Expert Survey. The interviewees included members of the parties' leading bodies and immigration spokespeople. These interviewees were selected because they were well positioned to provide information regarding debates on immigration within their parties and actions (e.g. protests) that the parties engaged in as they responded to the radical Right.[6]

We begin by reviewing divisions in the existing literature regarding the way that we should expect RLPs and RRPs to interact. On one side, writers such as Arzheimer view RLPs and RRPs as occupying totally different parts of the spectrum and as not being in competition. Yet there is another prevalent view, which has become stronger with Syriza's more populist turn, that left and right radicalism are part of the same protest phenomenon or are more similar than they might otherwise appear.[7]

The following section compares the stances of RLPs on the three particularly salient migration-related issues of immigration, asylum and integration. We find only limited evidence of contagion, although it would be wrong to say that RLPs are entirely immune. A degree of variation does, however, exist in RLP immigration policies and in their responses to the radical Right, with the main explanation being party origins and office-seeking strategies. What stands out, however, is that even the RLPs that are most restrictive (i.e. seek to restrict levels of net immigration) are still relatively inclusive and promote rights for migrants in their programmes.

The chapter then analyses the organisational and electoral strategies pursued by RLPs. We examine the extent to which RLPs compete with the radical Right for support and to which they have confronted the radical Right in campaigns and protests. We argue that the leaders of the RLPs studied here do not perceive electoral competition as coming from the radical Right. Instead, most seek to present their parties as a repository for disaffected supporters of social democratic parties when these parties adopt more restrictive immigration policies. While the RLPs had generally been active in protesting

Table 5.1 RLP and RRP Electoral Results in Parliamentary Elections as Share of the Vote (and Recent Opinion Poll Data)

	The Netherlands		Sweden		Greece		Denmark		
	RLP	RRP	RLP	RRP	RLP	RRP	RLP	RLP	RRP
Year	Socialist Party	Party for Freedom	Left Party	Swedish Democrats	Syriza	Golden Dawn	Red-Green Alliance	Socialist People's Party	Danish People's Party
2015	19 (Sept 2015 poll)	22 (Sept 2015 poll)			36.3 and 35.5	6.3 and 7	7.8	4.2	21.5
2014			5.7						
2013									
2012	9.7	10.1		12.9	16.8 and 26.9	7.0 and 6.9			
2011							6.7	9.2	12.3
2010	9.9	15.5	5.6	5.7					
2009					4.6	0.3			
2008									
2007					5		2.2	13	13.9
2006	16.6	5.9	5.9	2.9					

Sources: Parties and Elections in Europe, 'The Netherlands', available at http://www.parties-and-elections.eu/. 2015. (election results); Ipsos, Politieke Barometer, IPSOS. 'Political Barometer' available at: http://www.ipsos-nederland.nl/content.asp?targetid=1155 (opinion polls), 2015. Poll average taken from: http://peilingwijzer.tomlouwerse.nl/. 1 September 2015.

against the radical Right, we show that RLPs have made only limited achieve-ments in forging links with migrant community groups.

THE RADICAL RIGHT AND CONTAGION

As Joost van Spanje notes, the conventional wisdom has been that the elec-toral success and increased prominence of the radical Right in political debate has had a significant impact on other political parties and promoted a tough-ening of policies on immigration.[8] How far might we expect RLPs to have been susceptible to such 'contagion effects'? This depends on the extent to which such a contagion effect exists and how far it extends across the politi-cal spectrum. Indeed, recent attempts to gauge the impact of RRPs on other party families have come to rather divergent conclusions.

First, Tjitske Akkerman's analysis of Western European party positions on immigration since the early 1990s finds that while some centre-right par-ties adopted restrictive positions on immigration and migrant rights, this has not spread to social democratic parties.[9] Aside from some more restrictive positions on labour migration, the mainstream Left has generally followed 'a fairly consistent cosmopolitan course'.[10]

Similarly, Sonia Alonso and Sara Claro da Fonseca highlight the ideologi-cal and strategic dilemmas facing mainstream left parties.[11] To them, such parties' memberships consist of two groups: a well-educated group with lib-eral values and 'an inclination towards … social egalitarianism and solidarity that is defined in universalist … terms'; the other, the traditional working class who feel threatened by elements of globalisation such as immigration. Their research, based on analysis of the party stances using CMP data, sug-gests that mainstream left parties have shifted towards 'tougher' migration policies. Last, Tim Bale et al. use a qualitative analysis of responses by social democrats to the radical Right in Denmark, Norway, the Netherlands and Austria to highlight considerable variation.[12]

RLPs are generally overlooked in these studies. Nevertheless, van Spanje calls into question the idea that the impact of contagion is greater for par-ties of the Centre-Right than the Left or that that parties of what he calls the 'niche' Left are the least affected by contagion. His analysis indicates that some of these parties have shifted their position (he cites the French and Greek communists and Danish and Italian Greens as examples).[13]

In contrast, Alonso and da Fonseca suggest that left-libertarian radical parties may be beneficiaries of the dilemmas which immigration presents the Centre-Left. Any move towards a tougher immigration stance risks alienat-ing the Centre-Left's more universalist-inclined supporters who may prefer more radical parties maintaining such policies. Similarly, Kai Arzheimer argues that RLPs are least likely to be affected since they have a very different demographic of support and 'occupy diametrically opposed positions in West European policy space'.[14] Overall, then, recent research is divided and unclear on the extent to which the radical Right has redefined RLP positions on migration. The positions of RLPs on immigration, should however, be of interest to political scientists when Bale et al. find that the positions of RLPs are significant in shaping the positions of the Centre-Left. More concretely, when RLPs politicise immigration it becomes harder for social democratic parties to avoid the issue.[15]

Furthermore, the dilemmas facing RLPs over immigration issues are not entirely new. During the 1970s the French Communist Party, adopted a 'welfare chauvinist' position towards migrant communities in its traditional power bases of working-class communities. This policy became most visible when a communist mayor of a Parisian suburb oversaw the destruction of accommodation for migrant workers.[16] This has even been interpreted as effectively facilitating rather than pre-empting the emergence of the radical Right.

PROGRAMMATIC RESPONSES

This section analyses RLP positions on immigration, asylum and integration. It demonstrates that our case studies generally promote policies inconsistent with the idea that they have undergone significant contagion from the radical Right. While it points to a general overlap in the parties' policies on immigration issues, it highlights several important differences.

Immigration

Starting with the parties that favour less restrictive immigration policies, the Left Party has maintained a relatively open immigration policy compared with other Swedish parties (excluding the Greens). It opposes restrictive EU-level policies and visa regulations and calls for an easing of 'Fortress Europe' policies.[17] It has generally viewed labour migration as a good thing and while it is concerned that migrants are used as a source of cheap labour to undercut wages and conditions for Swedish workers, it campaigns for all workers to be included in trade union collective bargaining arrangements rather than for migration restrictions.[18] In addition, the Left Party calls for social policies to combat inequalities that migrants face.

Syriza also has relatively flexible programmatic positions on immigration. It has sought an easing of rules on Greek citizenship and to grant citizenship to large numbers of 'illegal' migrants. It argues that Greece is suffering a humanitarian crisis because of large migration flows but rather than tighter restrictions, it wants migrants to be freer to travel into the European Union to their favoured destinations.[19] Syriza also opposes laws that deny citizenship (and social and political rights) to the children of migrants born in Greece. It wants better regulation of labour contracts for migrant workers. It seeks to address their exploitation, in terms of lower wages and poor working conditions, to provide help for migrants receiving physical abuse from their employers.[20] The party also seeks to give migrants access to welfare services and education.

In contrast, the SP has taken a more ambiguous stance on immigration policy. It has held a rather restrictive position on levels of immigration for nearly 30 years. Its arguments are largely on economic grounds, claiming that open labour markets are a feature of neoliberalism that exploits the migrant and the national worker.[21] The SP does not think that the Netherlands is full, but that immigration should take place at a more manageable rate that does not destabilise the Dutch labour market.[22] Overall the party's stance combines some restrictions on immigration, including restoration of work permits to East European workers, with policies to combat discrimination against migrants. It wants to see Dutch labour standards applied to migrant working conditions and fines for companies that violate these rules.[23] It opposes policies of repatriation suggested by the radical Right or plans to restrict migrants' voting rights and access to social security.

In Denmark, the SF did not agree with Denmark's controversial '24 year' rule (a law restricting the right for family reunification to those over the age of 24 years old in order to prevent forced marriages). However, before the SF entered office in coalition with the social democrats in 2011 it accepted the need to compromise on the issue, since the social democrats are more restrictive on immigration.[24] SF seeks to remove application fees for residency; however, it argues that migrants seeking family reunification should demonstrate that they are engaged in work or education and talks more of attracting skilled workers.[25] In comparison, the EL has been more open to increased immigration. It has sought to make it easier for migrants to obtain citizenship and to facilitate family reunification by abolishing the '24 year rule'.[26]

A clear distinction has been apparent between the approaches of the Left Party, EL and Syriza compared with the more restrictive immigration policies of SF and SP. Nevertheless, we also find areas of overlap between the parties. While none of them favoured an open borders policy, even the more restrictive policies of the SP and SF are designed to slow the pace and to focus on integration first, but do not oppose increased immigration rates in the future. Where the parties have called for restrictions on immigration, this has largely been based on opposition to neoliberalism and the distortion of labour markets. All the parties have opposed employers seeking to lower wages through cheap migrant labour and all claim to seek to prevent the exploitation of migrants by ensuring that they receive equal pay and employment rights. There is little sign of welfare chauvinism, with most parties seeking equal or additional benefits for migrants. However, while Syriza and the Left Party most clearly emphasise cosmopolitanism/internationalism, the other parties tend to emphasise national solutions to immigration problems.

Asylum

The Left Party criticises Swedish government asylum policies, calling for a more generous approach, including full respect for international conventions, and arguing that too many asylum-seekers have been forced to return to their country of origin despite risks of persecution.[27] It calls for more funding to be provided for local authorities dealing with asylum cases and to ensure that welfare payments to asylum-seekers are raised to allow a decent standard of living.[28] In Greece, Syriza was also generally sympathetic to the rights of asylum-seekers, arguing that their predicament was a humanitarian crisis that must be addressed. However, it saw the problem as one for the European Union as a whole and not just for Greece. In particular it criticised the Dublin II Convention that makes the first EU country that asylum-seekers enter responsible for providing asylum. Instead, Syriza called for reforms to spread the burden imposed upon Greece, a speeding up of asylum procedures and the granting of travel papers to migrants. Since coming to power, however, the party has been obliged to adopt policies which are at odds with its opposition rhetoric. While initially the new government appeared to be acting on its commitments, aiming to close the detention camps set up to cope with the large number of asylum seekers, the intensification of the asylum crisis and pressures from the EU to engage in a broader asylum agreement with Turkey have led to a very restrictive policy. As part of the EU-Turkey agreement, Greece has been deporting some asylum seekers and detaining others in conditions as bad as those in place under previous governments.[29]

The SP is closer to the other RLPs on asylum issues than on other immigration-related policy areas. It has called for changes to make it harder to send asylum-seekers back to dangerous states including Iraq and Somalia and giving child asylum-seekers the right to stay after five years. It opposed detention centres, and wanted to provide aid to Greece on the EU border to improve the conditions facing asylum-seekers.[30]

Similarly, the SF has called for more humane conditions for asylum-seekers and for reforms to ensure that asylum-seekers can work outside asylum centres after staying in Denmark for a period of six months.[31] It seeks better protection for child refugees and to tackle human trafficking. However, while the SF wanted to maintain Denmark's annual quota of 500 refugees, the EL called for this to be expanded.[32] The EL campaigned to make it harder to send asylum-seekers back to Iraq where they could face persecution.[33] It called for improvements in the conditions for asylum-seekers and to make it easier to apply for asylum.[34]

In sum, all the parties examined have had more in common over asylum policy than in the other two policy areas (at least until Syriza entered government). They have generally wanted more open asylum policies (or at least to defend existing commitments) and sought to prevent the return of asylum-seekers to states where they were at risk from persecution. They have demanded better conditions for asylum-seekers (including access to welfare benefits and the right to live outside detention centres) as well as fairer and speedier procedures. Internationally, they have sought conflict prevention in asylum-seekers' states of origin, and some seek to abolish or reform the Dublin II Accord. To most RLPs, it is necessary to reform this process to relieve the burden on southern European states.

Integration

The Left Party has maintained a policy of multiculturalism and has called for interaction between communities. It supported language courses for migrants but opposed citizenship or cultural tests. Instead it has wanted greater emphasis on encouraging the recruitment of migrants into employment and opportunities for communities to study in their native language.[35] Syriza has also adopted a broadly multicultural approach, respecting the different values of communities (e.g. criticising the publication of cartoons portraying the Prophet Mohammed). It seeks to remove the requirement of speaking Greek as a criteria for residency, promotes intercultural schools and education schemes for migrants to notify them of their social rights.[36]

In comparison, the SP has stressed the importance of integration in protecting migrant workers from segregation.[37] It argues that the over-representation of migrant communities in crime statistics, and their experiences of educational underachievement and poor housing would have been prevented had the party's integration policies been applied.[38] The SP has stressed the need for education and citizenship tests but has sought to prevent these from becoming a financial burden on migrant communities.[39] While critics of the SP's stance have argued that it effectively places the blame upon the migrant communities and that its original policies on integration were racist, SP politicians have argued that their policy is not rooted in religion or ideas of cultural superiority and that it sought to ensure that migrants are treated fairly.[40]

The Danish RLPs have been split on the issue of integration. The SF sought to send a message that migrants must integrate and respect the ways of Danish society – including democracy, freedom of speech and equality – and to counter the radicalisation of migrants. It demanded housing and education policies to dismantle ghettos and to relocate migrants by ensuring all schools have 30 per cent socially vulnerable migrants to ensure wealthy municipalities take greater responsibility. While the SF opposed a citizenship test it supported language tests and giving migrant families vouchers to help them experience cultural activities.[41]

These policies were fiercely criticised by the EL, which adopted a multicultural approach. Unlike the SF, it argued that counselling rather than Denmark's '24 year rule' should tackle forced marriage.[42] The EL opposed language tests and argued that children from migrant backgrounds should learn their parents' native languages.[43] It also criticised the SF for stigmatising immigrants by talking of breaking up 'ghettos' and associating them with crime.[44] Instead, it called for community mentors to provide role models for young migrants and urban regeneration to combat the poverty faced by migrants.[45]

All five parties have wanted to reduce the cost of obtaining citizenship and most took a liberal position towards the rights of migrant communities to freedom of speech. Generally they have supported rights to wearing religious dress including the Burqa and shared a willingness to tackle Islamophobia. The parties have also largely agreed on helping migrants to succeed through integrating into the labour market, through better language training, work placements with industry and expanding access to education.

However we can identify three differences between RLPs on integration. First, some parties called for greater levels of cultural integration such as citizenship or language tests while others favour a multicultural society. Second, the parties have differed in terms of their willingness to link migrant communities to crime and social problems. Third, some parties promoted integration through using housing and education policies to avoid segregation and to break up so-called 'ghettos'. Others sought to help migrants where they reside through urban regeneration policies and argued that it is immoral to encourage migrants to move location.

Summarising the results of our analysis we have found a high degree of overlap on a number of immigration policies in the five RLPs. In general terms it appears that they have maintained a principled position on immigration, indicating that RLPs have experienced limited contagion from the radical Right. Data from the CMP (see Table 5.2) and Chapel Hill Expert Survey (see Table 5.3) also show that all five RLPs maintained positions that oppose highly restrictive migration policies and tough positions on integrating migrants. Moreover, this data indicates that since 2008 V and the SP may have become less restrictive on immigration (see Table 5.3).

However, we have also found some important differences between the policies of RLPs. Some (V, EL, Syriza) were more engaged in taking and promoting multiculturalism and have less restrictive immigration policies than others (SP, SF). This is again reinforced by the Chapel Hill data and to some extent by manifesto data on multiculturalism (summarised in Tables 5.2 and 5.3).

Table 5.2 Comparative Manifesto Project Data: Multiculturalism Positive or Negative Expressed as a Percentage of the Manifesto

	RGA Positive	RGA Negative	SF Positive	SF Negative	SP Positive	SP Negative	Syriza* Positive	Syriza* Negative	V Positive	V Negative
2014										
2013										
2012					0.913	0.0	1.667	0.0		
2011	6.7	0.0	0.6	0.0						
2010					0.4	0.4			0.4	0.0
2009							0.0	0.0		
2008										
2007							0.0	0.0		
2006					1.2	0.7			1.0	0.0
2005	0.0	0.0	0.0	0.2						
2004							2.5	0.0		
2003										
2002					0.1	0.0			0.0	0.0
2001	0.0	0.0	0.0	0.0						
2000							0.487	0.0		

*Formerly Synaspismós

Source: Pola Lehmann, Theres Matthieß, Theres Merz, Nicolas, Regel, Sven, Annika Werner. Manifesto Corpus. Version: 2000–2014 (Berlin: WZB Berlin Social Science Center, 2015).

Table 5.3 Chapel Hill Expert Survey Data on Immigration and Multiculturalism

	SP	SF	Red-Green Alliance	Syriza	Left Party
Immigration Policy	2006: 5.3	2006: 1.8	2006: 1	2006: 0.71	2006: 1.88
	2010: 6	2010: 3.7	2010: 1.3	2010: 0.6	2010: 1.4
	2014: 4.11	2014: 2.8	2014: 1.6	2014: 2.22	2014: 0.55
Multiculturalism vs Integration	2006: 6	2006: 2.8	2006: 1.4	2006: 2.14	2006: 2.25
	2010: 6.2	2010: 3.1	2010: 1.5	2010: 0.64	2010: 1.3
	2014: 3.77	2014: 2.8	2014: 1.5	2014: 1.88	2014: 0.66

Key: Position on immigration policy: 0 strongly opposes tough policy, 10 strongly supports tough policy. Importance/salience of immigration policy: 0 not important at all, 10 very important.
Source: Ryan Bakker, Erica Edwards, Liesbet Hooghe, Seth Jolly, Jelle Koedam, Filip Kostelka, Gary Marks, Jonathan Polk, Jan Rovny, Gijs Schumacher, Marco Steenbergen, Milada Vachudova, and Marko Zilovic. *1999–2014 Chapel Hill Expert Survey Trend File. Version 1.1* (Chapel Hill, NC: University of North Carolina, Chapel Hill, 2015). Available at: chesdata.eu.

EXPLAINING RLP RESPONSES TO THE RADICAL RIGHT

This section will show that RLP responses to the radical Right (and their immigration policies more generally) have been shaped by both contextual factors and internal party developments. The wider environment and the nature of the radical Right clearly matter. For example, the humanitarian crisis in Greece and the actions taken by Golden Dawn made the nature of immigration debates more immediate. Golden Dawn is qualitatively different from the parties in the other countries studied here as it is on the extreme Right, rather than simply being a radical right populist party.[46] Consequently, Syriza encountered additional pressure to engage in seeking protection for migrants, through housing shelters and educating the police due to the physical attacks on migrants. Institutional factors also come into play with Syriza having called for the removal of immunity for MPs in response to violence by politicians from Golden Dawn.[47]

However, the more restrictive immigration policies and tougher integration policies of the SP and SF are not simply a direct result of contagion from the Right but have been shaped by internal factors. The SP has had the most restrictive and integrationist policies. These were motivated by ideological conviction and its own attempts to prevent divisions between migrants and workers in the 1980s that pre-date the rise of the radical Right in the Netherlands. In Denmark, SF politicians claimed it was not a fear of losing votes that led it in this direction but the adoption of an office-seeking strategy and its attempt to forge cooperation with the social democrats (who did fear the loss of votes to the Right).[48] This is supported by reports that its attempts to develop relations with the social democrats involved major compromises.[49] In this respect a form of indirect contagion can be identified. Chapel Hill data also indicates that Syriza adopted a more restrictive position on immigration in 2014, which may reflect its office-seeking strategies.

RLPs have had some impact in terms of enacting immigration policy reforms while participating in coalition governments during the crisis. Syriza was criticised for coalescing with the anti-immigration right-wing populist Independent Greeks (ANEL) in January 2015. However, as the junior partner, ANEL appeared to have had limited impact on immigration policy and a human rights activist, Tassia Christodoulopoulou, became minister for immigration. Syriza passed reforms to make it easier for migrants to gain Greek nationality (without support from ANEL but from the social democratic PASOK). While these reforms may have been narrower than those Syriza had promised, this represented a significant change.

In contrast to the position encountered by Syriza, it has been more common for RLPs to be junior partners in governing coalitions. In Denmark, the SF worked to relax internal EU border controls introduced by the previous government.[50] Having been constrained by its coalition agreement in 2011, it only sought minor reforms including the relaxation of family reunification for migrants. Since it was only a support party to the government and not a coalition member, the SF's rival EL appeared to have more success in negotiating concessions in 2012, including a deal to reduce the time that refugee children spent in asylum centres. This raises questions as to whether RLPs may have more influence over immigration policy by remaining outside the coalition, ironically perhaps mirroring the practice of radical right parties.

Elizabeth Gautier of the PCF argues that 'Left Parties don't yet have a successful strategy to contest the extreme right'.[51] Indeed, none of elites from the RLPs studied here thought that their parties' organisational or programmatic responses to the radical Right had been particularly successful given the ongoing growth of the latter. Studies of Swedish municipalities show that a stronger stance against the Sweden Democrats from the Left Party correlates with stronger gains for the Right and simply brings more attention to the radical Right.[52]

ORGANISATIONAL RESPONSES: CONFRONTING THE RADICAL RIGHT?

Interviews with officials responsible for immigration policy from our case studies suggest that they do perceive the Great Recession to have contributed to the growth of the radical Right. The RLPs studied here, have however differed in the extent and nature of their readiness to confront RRPs directly during the economic crisis. The Swedish Left Party has a strong anti-fascist tradition, and has been to the fore in opposing the right-wing populist Sweden

Democrats.[53] Left Party politicians initially refused to share the stage with Sweden Democrats while forcefully arguing against their policies. Prior to the 2010 election, the Left Party was active in organising counterdemonstrations and rapid response tactics to oppose Sweden Democrat meetings.[54] Since the Sweden Democrats gained parliamentary representation in 2010, the adversarial strategy of the Left Party continued; however it focused on parliamentary debates and social media to counter the radical Right's claims.

Syriza too has been active in organising protests against the radical Right and has regularly organised conferences to promote migrant rights. It has run a 'Solidarity for all' campaign to encourage Greeks to show solidarity with migrants throughout the economic crisis. The party sought to educate the police to break Golden Dawn's influence and visited schools to educate children about migrant issues and racism, in order to limit Golden Dawn's appeal and to promote a cultural change. At the European level, it has worked with groups including European Antifascist Manifesto and organised protests and seminars against the threat from the Right.[55] Activists in the party have wanted to go further, however, in holding counterdemonstrations and organising 'defence committees' to protect migrants.

By contrast the Dutch SP has been critical of Geert Wilders, the leader of the radical right Party for Freedom, but has also been reluctant to organise protests and to engage in such direct confrontation with the radical Right. Instead, the party's vote- and office-seeking strategies have seen its leaders seek to campaign on issues that they believed would deliver more votes, rather than to spend time organising to fight the radical Right. In Denmark, the SF has opposed the Danish People's Party. Its youth organisation was active in organising counterdemonstrations against them. Since the economic crisis, however, immigration became less of an issue for the SF and the more radical EL became more engaged in campaigns on immigration. The EL was highly active in protesting against the Danish People's Party (e.g. at demonstrations in May 2013 in Copenhagen). This has become one of the EL's top priorities.[56]

The RLPs have all tolerated the right of RRPs to contest elections but they have all opposed the radical Right in parliament, in publications and in the media. The policy documents of V and Syriza now identify the radical Right as their main 'enemy' due to the nature of their policy proposals.[57] It is clear that some RLPs have also taken an adversarial approach towards confronting RRPs through organising counterdemonstrations.

LINKS WITH MIGRANT COMMUNITIES

Most of the RLPs studied here have developed some links with migrant communities. The Swedish Left Party has long maintained links with migrant community organisations.[58] The Dutch SP has also been active in campaigning to promote increased rights for refugees in The Hague where politicians are active in helping to organise refugee shelters. Of our case studies, however, only Syriza has really made it a priority to develop such links during the crisis. This was when the problems faced by migrants had become a major humanitarian problem. Where Syriza has governed at the local level it has engaged in providing free food and shelter for homeless migrants, and protecting them from attacks by the Far Right. Syriza also engaged in direct action to provide meals for migrants. In Denmark, the EL worked with asylum-seekers, who have gone underground having left government centres and protested in Copenhagen alongside Iraqi refugees facing deportation in 2011.[59]

To at least a limited extent, however, our case studies suggest that RLPs have encountered internal divisions over immigration and their responses to the radical Right. Both the SP and the EL experienced internal debates about the selection of migrant candidates for parliamentary elections. For example, when a female Muslim candidate, Asmaa Abdol-Hamid, gained a place on the EL's list for the parliamentary elections in 2007, a debate unfolded as to whether this broke the party's secular image. Similarly, feminists within V have regularly criticised the treatment of women in migrant communities and changes to SF's immigration policies resulted in internal criticisms. In 2010, the SP's then-leader Agnes Kant faced internal dissent when she labelled scapegoating of migrants by Geert Wilders' PVV as the number one threat to Dutch society.

Migrants remain poorly represented as parliamentarians in several of our case studies (EL 0 per cent; SF 0 per cent; Syriza 6.5 per cent; SP 6.6 per cent; conversely the Left Party has 24 per cent).[60] No party had implemented quotas to ensure the representation of migrants in their parliamentary groups or national leaderships (however the data for the Left Party warrants further investigation). The Left Party's congress has, however, made a vague commitment to increasing the proportion of its elected representatives from immigrant backgrounds.[61] Whether or not this has contributed to its higher levels of representation of migrant candidates warrants further investigation.

Most of the parties studied (including the Left Party, SP and SF) have failed to launch new links with migrant communities since the onset of the crisis and only Syriza has explicitly invited migrants to join. It appears that RLPs may be lagging behind trade unions in terms of launching initiatives to recruit members from migrant communities.[62] While researchers have found that data on the proportion of RLP party members from migrant backgrounds is not available, this is generally regarded as lower than their relative share of the general population.[63] Moreover, SP politicians argue that their party sees migrant groups as relatively disparate, rather than a united group, and prefers to deal with them on class terms.[64]

While RLPs including Syriza organise conferences on migration and the radical Right alongside other organisations including the Rosa Luxemburg Foundation, they appear to have struggled to conceptualise the position of migrants in society. These conferences have revealed tensions as RLP politicians have portrayed migrants as the 'most working class' or revolutionary group in society, while representatives from migrant organisations have argued that this takes a reductionist approach to their experiences.[65]

ELECTORAL RESPONSES: COMPETING WITH THE RADICAL RIGHT?

Research on the radical Right shows that a major source of its increased support has come from the male urban working class, historically seen as more likely to vote left than right. This group tends to have lower educational qualifications and fears that competition from immigrants threatens its welfare, jobs and culture.[66] Several RRPs have also promoted interventionist welfare policies that may appeal to these groups. The extent to which RLPs find themselves in competition with RRPs seems likely to be shaped by the extent to which they depend on working-class support. RLPs often claim to be parties 'for the working class' and therefore appear susceptible to contagion.

However, party elites and spokespeople on immigration issues interviewed for all case studies claimed that that there were several reasons why their parties only encountered limited electoral competition from the radical Right. First, they believed their parties to be insulated by significant levels of middle-class, public-sector or highly educated supporters who were unlikely to defect to the Right. Second, their working-class supporters may have values that are directly opposed to the radical Right, making an oppositional strategy towards the radical Right popular. In Denmark, for example, the EL gained support from the SF following a shift by the latter to more restrictive approaches to immigration.[67]

Third, geographical differences can mean that the parties compete in different regions. In Sweden, for example Left Party politicians highlighted their party's support from unionised voters in the North while the SD has tended to get support from non-unionised voters in the South. Last and most significantly, they believed that their parties mostly competed with social democratic and other left/green parties for voters, providing little reason for contagion to occur.

RLP elites might be expected to downplay processes of contagion to present their parties as having stuck to their ideals. However, their arguments are consistent with our analysis of party programmes and gain some support from the available literature on RLP voters. For instance, Luke March and

Charlotte Rommerskirchen find that the presence of a successful radical right party can reduce RLP electoral results by 3 per cent; however, they show that RLP's are *mostly* in competition with social democratic parties.[68]

The idea of a large transfer of votes between RLPs and RRPs is rejected by Ramiro's analysis of European Social Study data that finds only marginal overlap between their voters in most countries.[69] Ramiro argues that the vast majority of those who end up voting for a RLP are not the same individuals who consider voting for a RRP. Despite some degree of overlap in their voters' social groups, it appears that RLP voters have different values. The literature on the SP adds support to this finding. Both the SP and Geert Wilders' Party For Freedom (PVV) attract lower educated and income groups, working and lower-middle class; however, there is little evidence of voters switching between the parties.[70] This is reinforced by research from the Netherlands that finds little overlap between the votes of the SP and PVV in parliament (and particularly on migration).[71] In Sweden, Left Party voters also tend to be 'immigrant friendly', freeing the party to take an adversarial approach.[72] More broadly, Eurobarometer surveys indicate that 'left-wing' voters are the least likely to say that immigrants do not contribute to the economy.[73] This indicates that the core voters of RLPs and RRPs are fundamentally different. However, we do not discount room for overlap between the peripheral protest voters that the parties try to attract.

The literature on our case studies supports the idea that their electorates might present barriers to contagion. The RLP electorate is essentially split between working class and highly educated groups.[74] More specifically, European Social Survey data suggests that all of our cases derive less than half of their support from those identifying as working class (Left Party 34 per cent; SP 29 per cent; Syriza (plus KKE) 28 per cent and EL and SF combined 18 per cent).[75] For example, the Left Party draws more heavily on support from the middle classes, students and public-sector workers than the working classes.[76] Studies also show that in 2012 the typical Syriza voter had a degree or was still in university and that the party gained little support from industrial workers.[77]

Several RLPs including the EL, SP and Syriza increased their vote simultaneously with RRPs, which some party leaders interpreted as a sign they were not at risk of losing their voters.[78] However, success may also give new reasons for competition. After 2012 Syriza's new-found success involved expansion beyond the middle-class intelligentsia, to include a wider spectrum of poor and working-class voters, it came into more direct competition with Golden Dawn. Similarly, the EL's politicians have targeted winning voters from the Danish People's Party and sections of the working class after their party expanded in 2010.[79] Even so, however, we find limited evidence of contagion.

Support from Migrant Voters

While migration may or may not be an issue that could lose RLPs working-class supporters, it may also be one that could generate new sources of support including support from migrant communities (as might related issues such as the easing of citizenship rules). The evidence available on the voting intentions of migrant communities is, however, patchy. Individual country studies and some collective research projects (analysed below) have tried to tease out voting intentions, but their findings are quite variable and inconsistent between cases. However, most of these studies find that the Left tends to benefit from migrant votes.

One of the few comparative studies of migrant voting behaviour draws upon the perspectives of national experts making use of available national data to parse the allegiances of migrant communities.[80] The analysis of the Netherlands indicates lower levels for support for RLPs among migrant communities than for the country as a whole: instead migrant communities overwhelmingly supported the Labour Party (*Partij van de Arbeid* – PvdA). While this may have been due to the SP's ambivalent stance on immigration, more recent studies suggest higher levels of migrant community support for the SP – of up to 22 per cent of migrant community support.[81] In Sweden, non-European migrants were nearly three times as likely to support the Left Party as other voters and high levels of support from migrants for RLPs were also apparent in Denmark.[82] Syriza's policies have also been reciprocated by support from those migrants who are able to vote.[83]

In explaining these trends, some analyses point to the relative youth of many migrant communities, while others highlight rationalist explanations in that RLP welfare policies may be appealing due to migrants' lower socio-economic status.[84] There may be significant 'group effects' in shaping migrant voting behaviour but the factor which seems less significant is ideology – indeed most analyses highlight the paradox that migrants may hold values that are more conservative than the parties for whom they vote.[85] Since most studies of migrant voting are based on research carried out before the crisis, research is needed to investigate how migrants' voting may have been affected by austerity measures or increases in anti-migrant rhetoric. Research is also needed to explore the way in which legal restrictions on migrant voting may impact on RLPs.

CONCLUSION

Several of the RLPs studied here appear to be developing a distinctive narrative on immigration issues, which emphasises internationalism and open migration and which often sets them apart from social democratic rivals.

However, they have generally struggled to express this in a way that has been convincing to voters or has been able to prevent the growth of the radical Right. It remains to be seen whether RLPs can successfully emulate Syriza's attempts to promote solidarity between migrants and workers.

Our analysis of RLPs in countries where the radical Right has grown during the crisis finds little evidence of contagion in terms of a tightening of immigration policy. This is reflected in the positions on immigration we have identified in RLP programmes as well as data from interviews regarding the attempts RLPs have made to protest against the growth of the radical Right. It is also supported by data from the CMP and Chapel Hill datasets. Questions remain, however, as to the extent to which the growth of the radical Right has contributed to the increased tendency of RLPs to promote left-populist appeals (a theme highlighted by several chapters in this volume).[86]

The long-term implications of this remain unclear. On the one hand, engaging in left populism might encourage RLPs to emulate Syriza's inclusive approach to migrants and to appeal to a range of social groups on a local level. On the other, it could foreseeably lead to the promotion of restrictive and integrationist positions similar to those developed by the SP in the 1980s. It also remains to be seen whether the anti-establishment appeals made by left-populist RLPs make them any better positioned to win votes from the radical Right.

The findings of this chapter are significant in several respects. First, they point to the norm that RLPs adopted more policy-oriented than office-seeking positions on immigration issues. This may pose significant barriers to their inclusion in office as junior coalition partners alongside social democratic parties. Indeed, the case where contagion was most evident, was that of the SF in Denmark where the social democrats had undergone a process of contagion. The SF's office-seeking strategy required it to make significant compromises on immigration policy before it could gain acceptance as a coalition partner. There are some signs that in office, Syriza has also taken a more restrictive approach to immigration. While the SP has also adopted office-seeking strategies, there is little sign that this has coincided with more restrictive immigration policies. This may be because, for an RLP, the SP already had relatively restrictive immigration policies and therefore faced less pressure to make such compromises.

Second, it is significant that the RLPs studied here have maintained a policy-seeking approach on a number of immigration-related issues. The finding that RLPs have generally been committed to internationalism and more open migration systems may not surprise those familiar with these parties. However, that such positions have been largely maintained despite the growth of the radical Right, is significant in that it suggests that contagion across the party system from the radical Right is not as significant as some writers suggest. Moreover, it presents a way in which RLPs and RRPs are not as similar as is often claimed. Our findings suggest that the 'theory of two extremes' struggles to account for the immigration policies of RLPs as these significantly differ from those of RRPs.

Third, our findings suggest that any electoral overlap between the parties may come from peripheral protest voters rather than their core supporters. Overall, however, taking principled positions on immigration issues does not appear to have gained RLPs much electoral traction, in all likelihood due to the popularity of anti-immigration positions. Questions also remain regarding the extent to which migrants can constitute a source of support for RLPs. We also find that RLPs' programmatic commitments to defending migrant rights have not been accompanied by new or sustained attempts to build links with migrant organisations or to field migrant candidates in parliamentary elections.

NOTES

1. Sofia Vasilopoulou, 'Far-Right Euroscepticism in the 2014 European Parliament Elections'. Paolo Chioccetti, 'The Radical Left at the 2014 European Parliament Election,' in *The Left in Europe After the EU Elections: New Challenges*, ed. Cornelia Hildebrandt (Berlin: Rosa Luxemburg-Stiftung, 2014), 7. in *Is Europe afraid of Europe?* ed. Kostas Ifantis (Athens: Wilfried Martens Centre, 2014).

2. Luke March, 'Problems and Perspectives of Contemporary European RLPs: Chasing a lost world or Still a World to Win?,' *International Critical Thought* 2, no. 3 (2011): 336.

3. Cas Mudde, *The Relationship between Immigration and Nativism in Europe and North America* (Washington, Migration Policy Institute: 2012), 30. Mudde found that the proportion of EU citizens viewing immigration as one of the two main challenges facing their country actually fell in the early years of the crisis. However, this increased from 8 per cent in 2011 to 18 per cent in 2014. Moreover it increased from 9 per cent in 2008 to 15 per cent in 2015 and may thereafter have contributed to RRP success. Given the growing debate surrounding the immigration crisis, this tendency seems likely to increase further. See Eurobarometer 2015, accessed 20 September 2015, http://ec.europa.eu/public_opinion/cf/showtable.cfm?keyID=2212&nationID=16,&startdate=2003.11&enddate=2014.11.

4. Pontus Odmalm and Tim Bale, 'Immigration into the Mainstream: Conflicting Ideological Streams, Strategic Reasoning and Party Competition,' *Acta Politica* (2014) Accessed 20 September. doi: 10.1057/ap.2014.28.

5. Luke March, *Radical Left Parties in Europe* (Routledge: London, 2012, 17). Notwithstanding that the SP was, until recently widely seen to be a left-populist party and that the Socialist People's Party has can be understood as having ceased to be an RLP by 2014 when it became a Green Party.

6. References to the interviews are curtailed in the text to preserve readability.

7. This is the so-called 'mirror thesis' or the 'theory of the two extremes'. See Daphne Halikiopoulou, Nanou Kyriaki and Sofia Vasilopoulou. 'The Paradox of

Nationalism: The Common Denominator of Radical Right and Radical Left Euroscepticism,' *European Journal of Political Research* 51, no. 4 (2012): 504–39. Alistair Clark, Karin Bottom and Colin Copus, 'More similar than they'd like to admit? Ideology, Policy and Populism in the Trajectories of the British National Party and Respect,' *British Politics* 3, no. 4 (2008): 511–34. Also in online blogs Othon Anastasakis, 'The Far Right in Greece and the Theory of the Two Extremes,' Open Democracy, 31 May 2013, available at https://www.opendemocracy.net/othon-anastasakis/far-right-in-greece-and-theory-of-two-extremes-0.

8. Joost van Spanje, 'Contagious Parties: Anti-Immigration Parties and Their Impact on Other Parties' Immigration Stances in Contemporary Western Europe,' *Party Politics* 16, no. 5 (2010): 570.

9. Tjitske Akkerman, 'Immigration Policy and Electoral Competition in Western Europe. A Fine-Grained Analysis of Party Positions over the Past Two Decades,' *Party Politics* 21 (2015): 60.

10. Ibid., 9.

11. Sonia Alonso and Sara Claro da Fonseca, 'Immigration, Left and Right', *Party Politics* 18, no. 5 (2012): 865–84.

12. Tim Bale et al., 'If You Can't Beat Them, Join Them? Explaining Social Democratic Responses to the Challenge from the Populist Radical Right in Western Europe,' *Political Studies* 5 (2010): 424.

13. Joost van Spanje, 'Contagious Parties', 576.

14. Kai Arzheimer, 'Working Class Parties 2.0? Competition between Centre Left and Extreme Right Parties,' in *Class Politics and the Radical Right*, ed. Jens Rydgren (London: Routledge: 2013), 77.

15. Tim Bale et al., 'If You Can't Beat Them, Join Them?', 423.

16. See David Bell and Byron Criddle, 'The Decline of the French Communist Party', *British Journal of Political Science* 19, no. 4 (1989): 515–36.

17. Left Party, 'Party Programme,' Published 5–8 January 2012, accessed 20 September 2015, http://www.vansterpartiet.se/material/partiprogram.

18. Left Party, *Partiprogram på lättläst svenska*: Stockholm, 2015. Available at http://www.vansterpartiet.se/assets/Partiprogrammet-lattlast-svenska.pdf, 25.

19. Syriza ΟΙ ΠΡΟΣΦΥΓΙΚΕΣ ΚΑΙ ΜΕΤΑΝΑΣΤΕΥΤΙΚΕΣ ΡΟΕΣ ΕΙΝΑΙ ΕΝΑ ΟΙΚΟΥΜΕΝΙΚΟ ΖΗΤΗΜΑ. Available at, http://www.syriza.gr/theseis/pros_diavoulefsi_metanasteytiko.pdf (Syriza: Athens, 2014), 2.

20. Ibid., 3.

21. SP, Nieuw Vertrouwen: Verkingsprogramma 2013–17 (SP: Amersfoort 2012) Available at, https://www.sp.nl/verkiezingen/2012/programma/gedeelde-toekomst, 13.

22. Kox interview.

23. SP, European Election Manifesto, 'No to this EU' (SP: 2014 Amersfoort), 9.

24. Inger Johansen, 'The Left and Radical Left in Denmark', in *From Revolution to Coalition, Radical Left Parties in Europe*, ed. Birgit Daiber, Cornelia Hildebrandt and Anna Striethorst (Berlin: Rosa Luxemburg Stiftung, 2012), 15.

25. SF, 'Plads Til Alle Der Vil', accessed 20 September 2015, http://sf.dk/det-vil-vi/et-mangfoldigt-danmark/udlaendinge-og-integration. SF Copenhagen.

26. RGA, 'Udlændingepolitik og statsborgerskab' Published online 29 October 2013, accessed 20 September 2015, http://enhedslisten.dk/artikel/udlpercentC3percentA6ndingepolitik-og-statsborgerskab-71981.

27. Left Party, 'Handledning Flyktingmottagande' (Stockholm: Left Party, 2015), accessed 20 September 2015, http://www.vansterpartiet.se/assets/Handledning-flyktingmottagande1.pdf.

28. See Vasterpartiet, 'Förbättrat flyktingmottagande'. Stockholm, 2008. Available at, http://www.vansterpartiet.se/assets/frbttrat_flyktingmottagande.pdf.

29. Syriza, 'ΟΙ ΠΡΟΣΦΥΓΙΚΕΣ', 4.

30. SP, 'No to this EU', 15.

31. SF, *Socialdemokraternes og SF's Forslag Til en Integrationsreform for Danmark*, SF, Copenhagen 2011, 6.

32. EL, 'Udlændingepolitik og statsborgerskab'.

33. Johansen, 'The Left and Radical Left in Denmark', 20.

34. EL, Sprgsmål og svar om flygtninge i Europa, accessed 20 September 2015, http://enhedslisten.dk/spoergsmaal-og-svar-om-flygtninge-i-europa.

35. Left Party, *Parliamentary motion 2013/14:A301*. Published online 3 October 2013, accessed 20 September 2015, http://www.riksdagen.se/sv/Dokument-Lagar/Forslag/Motioner/Inkludering-och-antidiskrimine_H102A301/?text=true.

36. Syriza 'ΟΙ ΠΡΟΣΦΥΓΙΚΕΣ', 8.

37. SP, 'Nieuw Vertrouwen: Verkingsprogramma 2013-17', 13.

38. Kox interview

39. SP, Nieuw Vertrouwen: Verkingsprogramma 2013-17, 13.

40. Kox interview.

41. SF, 'Integrationsreform for Danmark', 3.

42. Ibid., 6.

43. EL, 'Udlændingepolitik og statsborgerskab'.

44. Rohleder interview.

45. EL, 'Udlændingepolitik og statsborgerskab'.

46. See Sofia Vasilopoulou and Daphne Halikiopoulou, eds. *The Golden Dawn's 'Nationalist Solution': Explaining the Rise of the Far Right in Greece* (Basingstoke: Palgrave Macmillan, 2015).

47. See Syriza, *The Election Programme of Syriza for the Election 6 May 2012*. Syriza: Athens 2012.

48. Enevoldsen interview.

49. Copenhagen Post, 'Justice Ministry grants seven year old second chance at residency,' 9 January 2012, accessed 20 September 2015, http://cphpost.dk/news14/immigration-denmark/justice-ministry-grants-seven-year-old-second-chance-at-residency.html. See also Johansen 'The Left and Radical Left in Denmark,' 16.

50. Thomas Larson, 'Heading towards a change of government in Denmark', EU Observer. 14. September 2011, accessed 20 September 2015, https://euobserver.com/political/113620.

51. Speaking at the Rosa Luxemburg-Stiftung Conference in Berlin 8 July 2015.

52. Carl Dahlström, and Anders Sundell, 'A losing gamble. How mainstream parties facilitate anti-immigrant party success,' *Electoral Studies* (2012) 31: 353–363.

53. Carl Dahlström and Peter Esaisson. 'The Immigration Issue and Anti-Immigrant Party Success in Sweden 1970-2006: A Deviant Case Analysis', *Party Politics* 19 (2011): 343.

54. Barbara Steiner, 'The Swedish Left party', in *From Revolution to Coalition, RLPs in Europe*, ed. Birgit Daiber, Cornelia Hildebrandt and Anna Striethorst (Berlin: Rosa Luxemburg Stiftung, 2012), 67.

55. Thilo Janssen, *The Parties of the Left in Europe* (Berlin: Rosa Luxemburg Stiftung, 2014): 20.

56. Pernille Skipper, 'Tale: KRGAbenhavn er for alle,' 26 May 2013, accessed 20 September 2015, https://enhedslisten.dk/artikel/tale-kbenhavn-er-alle-71430.

57. Syriza (Founding Statement) 'Τι είναι και τι θέλει ο Συνασπισμός Ριζοσπαστικής Αριστεράς'. Published online July 2013, accessed 20 September 2015, http://www.syriza.gr/page/idrytikh-diakhryksh.html#.VfQCQbxViko.

58. Henning Süssner, 'Sweden', in *The Left in Government in Latin America and Europe*, ed. Birgit Daiber (Rosa Luxemburg-Stiftung: Brussels, 2010), 49.

59. Per Clausen, 'Ehl. opfordrer til at stRGAtte flygtninge under jorden,' Published 14 September 2009, accessed 20 September 2015, https://enhedslisten.dk/artikel/ehl-opfordrer-til-sttte-flygtninge-under-jorden-11483.

60. The proportion of the population that is foreign born in these countries is as follows: Denmark 8.5 per cent, Netherlands 11.6 per cent, Sweden 16 per cent, Greece, 10 per cent. See OECD, 'Migration and Foreign Born Population,' 2015, accessed 1 March 2016, https://data.oecd.org/migration/foreign-born-population.htm. Also, Trading Economics, 'International Migration Data,' accessed 1 March 2016, http://www.tradingeconomics.com/greece/international-migrant-stock-percent-of-population-wb-data.html.

61. Left Party, 'Strategy for the future of the Left Adopted by the Left Party's 39th Congress,' 5–8 January 2012 (Left party: Stockholm, 2012).

62. Gregory Mauzé, 'The Left and Migrants: How to think about Struggles in Common by Migrants, Non-migrants and Minorities?' 21 June 2013, accessed 1 March 2016, http://www.transform-network.net/cs/blog/blog-2013/news/detail/Blog/the-left-and-migrants-how-to-think-about-struggles-in-common-by-migrants-non-migrants-and-minoriti.html.

63. Anna Striethorst, *Members and Electorates of Left Parties in Europe* (Berlin: Rosa Luxemburg Stiftung: 2011).

64. Interview with SP immigration spokesperson Sharon Gestuizen.

65. For example debates between officials from RLPs and migrants at the Rosa Luxemburg-Stiftung Conference, 'The Left and Immigration' 29–30 May 2013, Brussels.

66. Tim Bale, 'Cinderella and Her Ugly Sisters: the Mainstream and Extreme Right in Europe's Bipolarising Party Systems,' *West European Politics* 26, no. 3 (2003): 71.

67. Johansen, 'The Left and Radical Left in Denmark', 22.

68. Luke March and Charlotte Rommerskirchen, 'Explaining Electoral Success and Failure,' in *Radical Left Parties in Europe*, ed. Luke March (Abingdon: Routledge: 2011), 192.

69. Luis Ramiro, 'Support for RLPs in Western Europe: Social Background, Ideology and Political Orientations,' *European Political Science Review* 5 (2014): 2.

70. Stijn van Kessel and Andre Krouwel, 'Fishing in the Same Pond? Comparing the Electorates of the Socialist Party and the Freedom Party in the Netherlands.' Paper for the Dutch-Flemish annual political science conference Politicologenetmaal, 31 May to 1 June 2012.

71. Simon Otjes and Tom Louwerse, 'Populists in Parliament: Comparing Left-Wing and Right-Wing Populism in the Netherlands,' *Political Studies* 63 (2015): 75.

72. Dahlström and Esaiasson, 'The immigration issue'.

73. Tim Bale, 'Turning Round the Telescope: Centre-right Parties and Immigration and Integration Policy in Europe', *Journal of European Public Policy* 15, no. 3 (2008): 315–30.

74. Ramiro, 'Support for RLPs', 14.

75. We thank Louis Ramiro and Laura Morales for providing this recoded data from the European Election Study data. Currently there is no separate data available for the Danish and Greek RLPs.

76. Steiner, 'The Swedish Left Party', 70.

77. Julian Marioulas, 'The Greek Left', in *From Revolution to Coalition, Radical Left parties in Europe*, ed. Birgit Daiber, Cornelia Hildebrandt and Anna Striethorst (Berlin: Rosa Luxemburg Stiftung 2012), 295.

78. Interview Tiny Kox, SP Senate Group Leader.

79. Inger Johansen, 'The Danish People's Party – A success story' Situation on the Left,' in *Europe after the EU Elections*, ed. Cornelia Hildebrant (Rosa Luxemburg Foundation: Berlin, 2014), 100.

80. Karen Bird, Thomas Saalfeld and Andreas Wust, eds. *The Political Representation of Immigrants and Minorities: Voters, Parties and Parliaments in Liberal Democracies* (London: Routledge, 2010).

81. Clemens Wirries, 'A party for the "Simple People" The Socialist Party of the Netherlands', in *From Revolution to Coalition, RLPs in Europe*, ed. Birgit Daiber, Cornelia Hildebrandt and Anna Striethorst (Berlin: Rosa Luxemburg Stiftung, 2012), 144.

82. Bird, Saalfeld and Wust, *The Political Representation of Immigrants and Minorities*.

83. Paul Mason, 'Trying to understand Syriza' 14 May 2012, accessed 20 September 2015, http://www.bbc.co.uk/news/world-europe-18056677.

84. Wirries, 'A Party for the "Simple People,"' 158.

85. Johannes Bergh and Tor Bjrgarklund, 'The Revival of Group Voting: Explaining the Voting Preferences of Immigrants in Norway,' *Political Studies* 59 (2011): 308–27.

86. Syriza has taken a 'populist turn': see Giorgos Katsembekis, 'The Rise of the Greek Radical Left to Power: Notes on Syriza's Discourse and Strategy', *Linea Sur* 9 (2015): 159. However, we also see that some RLPs such as the SP have engaged less in populist appeals since the beginning of the international economic crisis: see Stijn van Kessel, 'Dutch Populism During the Crisis', in *European Populism in the Shadow of the Great Recession*, ed. Hanspeter Kriesi and Takis S. Pappas (Colchester: ECPR, 2015), 109.

PART II

NATIONAL RESPONSES TO CRISIS

Chapter 6

The French Radical Left and the Crisis

'Business as Usual' rather than 'le Grand Soir'

Fabien Escalona and Mathieu Vieira

Since 2008 radical left parties in France have attempted several internal regroupings with uneven electoral results. Yet, it would be a mistake to deduce from this chronology that the crisis *caused* these regroupings: its roots actually predate the outburst of contradictions in the world economy. More-over, the way in which the crisis has been experienced in France helps explain why the fortunes of France's radical Left are so different from those of the Eurozone's peripheral countries. Nevertheless, the major developments on the left, including the rise of the *Front de Gauche* (Left Front, FdG) and the marginalisation of the extreme Left after 2009, have other causes. Similarly, variations in the radical Left's post-2008 electoral performance cannot be attributed solely to the crisis. The crisis did, however, contribute to ideological and strategic reflection and the most significant impact of the crisis on the French RLPs has been felt in *programmatic* terms. In particular, more promi-nence has been given by the FdG to resisting European integration, even if the scope and possible consequences of this resistance remain controversial between the members of this coalition. Important actors within the FdG, and especially the former socialist dissenters around Jean-Luc Mélenchon, sought to adapt their discourse to the austerity measures in the Eurozone. Ironically, the Communist Party (*Parti communiste français*, PCF) had previously fol-lowed a course of moderation on this issue given its highly anti-EU stances of the past. It accepted the need for making compromises within the FdG insofar as they were not too audacious and because they were seen as a price worth paying to escape its long-term marginalisation and weakening role within the French Left.

   This chapter begins by analysing the development of the FdG to show how this new coalition has restructured the radical Left in France at the expense of the extreme Left, which now occupies a negligible role.[1] The FdG formed as the result of long-standing developments (principally efforts to resist European integration) and of the strategies of key protagonists (among them the defection of Mélenchon from the Socialist Party). The second section explains the disappointing electoral results of the FdG after the 2012 presidential election and asks why the radical Left has performed less well in France than in Greece or Spain. It demonstrates that this should be explained not only through considering the effect the crisis has on society but also the nature of political competition and the internal features of the FdG. In the third part, we show that the Eurozone crisis has altered the programmatic and strategic conceptions of some radical left actors in France in terms of their resistance to European institutions. In this sense, the crisis contributed more to the *ideological* change of the radical Left than the creation of the FdG in itself, which was almost an organisational novelty. Finally, we conclude that the rise of a new RLP in France is constrained by institutional, organisational and cultural factors.

THE REGROUPING OF FRANCE'S RADICAL LEFT: FROM 1995 TO THE PRESENT

In this first section, we show that the most dramatic changes in the radical Left during the international economic crisis – the changes in the inter-party competition between RLPs – are explained by dynamics *predating* the crisis. Beforehand, the radical Left in France was split between several components of more-or-less similar electoral weight. Although the PCF had significantly more elected officials than the extreme left parties (Worker's Struggle [*Lutte Ouvrière*, LO], and the New Anti-Capitalist Party [NPA], formerly the Revolutionary Communist League, LCR) its electoral results were low in the 2002 and 2007 presidential elections (see Table 6.1). However, in the three years from 2009 to 2012 another configuration emerged as the PCF became the backbone of an alliance called the *Front de Gauche*, which gained hegemony within the radical Left at the expense of the small now-marginalised Trotskyist parties. We trace the construction of this coalition to show how while it took place during the crisis, its emergence has its roots in the long-term evolution of the PCF, the defections of socialist and Trotskyist dissenters and their earlier participation in common struggles against European integration.

The PCF, had been the largest party of the Left in France between 1945 and 1978, but thereafter suffered significant electoral decline due to its anchorage in a declining working-class milieu, its loyalty to the decaying Soviet Union and its ideological sectarianism. From 1994 to 2002, it went through a 'mutation' process under the leadership of Robert Hue who replaced Georges Marchais. During this period, its organisational model was de-Stalinised, its

Table 6.1   National Electoral Results of the French Left, 1995–2014

Elections	Extreme Left			PCF/FdG			Total Left		
	Votes	%	Seats	Votes	%	Seats	Votes	%	Seats
P 1995	1,599,969	5.30		2,598,720	8.64		12,104,383	40.56	
L 1997	633,235	2.56		2,450,875	9.89	36	11,707,909	47.26	312
E 1999	914,811	5.18	5	1,196,491	6.78	6	7,701,262	43.63	42
P 2002	2,946,175	10.44		954,880	3.37		11,868,506	42.89	
L 2002	706,922	2.74		1,267,789	4.91	21	10,305,624	39.91	179
E 2004	571,568	3.33		1,009,976	5.88	3	7,935,267	46.23	40
P 2007	2,110,248	5.75		707,268	1.93		13,377,302	36.44	
L 2007	888,250	3.41		1,115,663	4.29	20	10,351,838	39.77	231
E 2009	1,050,016	6.10		1,115,021	6.48	5	7,806,356	45.34	33
P 2012	594,804	1.71		3,900,147	11.10		15,000,631	43.75	
L 2012	253,386	0.98		1,793,192	6.91	15	12,642,689	48.71	346
E 2014	302,436	1.60		1,252,730	6.61	4	6,451,699	34.04	23

Source: Ministry of Interior.

account of the Soviet experience was revised and stances more favourable to cultural liberalism and European integration were introduced. Above all, the PCF integrated into the alliance system (called *gauche plurielle* [plural left]) that was headed by the Socialist Party (PS). It proved to be a failure (see below). Neither isolation nor subordination to the PS countered the decline of the PCF. Consequently, its leaders (Marie-Georges Buffet from 2002 to 2010 and Pierre Laurent since 2010) returned to an oppositional profile but tried to strengthen links to other RLPs and movements.[2] As shown below, this was only realised when Jean-Luc Mélenchon came onto the stage.

Meanwhile, the extreme-left parties had become a new electoral competitor. Whereas their influence in the past had been mostly cultural, the pro-socialist turn of the PCF helped them to reach unusual numbers of votes at different types of elections.[3] However, even before the FdG was formed, their development was hampered by their ideological sectarianism and rigid organisational structures. LO, which had always been a closed and small group, suffered from the withdrawal of its famous candidate, Arlette Laguiller. The NPA (the LCR's successor founded in 2009) quickly suffered a massive loss of activists and voters. Three principal factors explain this collapse: first, its party culture and organisational structure did not adapt well to an influx of new activists with little or no political education; second, it was quickly criticised for being sectarian, especially in comparison to the FdG's attempt to present itself as a continuation of an ongoing effort to achieve a 'union of the (true) left'[4]; and third, the popular Olivier Besancenot relinquished his role as principal NPA spokesperson in order to avoid playing the game of 'politics as entertainment'. Therefore, the fate of these extreme-left parties is best explained by their own strategic and ideological inertia rather than the Great Recession.

The following subsections outline the developments that led to the foundation of the FdG. It is shown that three events laid a 'unified dynamic' on the Left in the 2005 referendum against the European Constitutional Treaty (TCE). After that it took four more years before a genuine party coalition emerged. A major factor in shaping this process was the creation of the *Parti de Gauche* (Left Party, PG) by Jean-Luc Mélenchon in 2008.

1995–2005: The Early Stages of Unification

The first of the three events just mentioned was the formation of a social movement in 1995, which campaigned against the Juppé government's pension reforms. The November-December 1995 strikes marked the transition to a new cycle of protest by social movements, as seen in the successful emergence of the anti-globalisation movement in France. At the time, this new wave of opposition had no political outlet, but subsequently, it contributed to the emergence of a new radicalism. The second unifying event occurred on 21 April 2002 when the lack of a left candidate in the second round of the presidential election (PS candidate Jospin being outflanked by *Front National* candidate Jean-Marie Le Pen) gave incentives for future candidates to cooperate in the future. The poor result of the communist candidate Robert Hue also added weight to calls for a more coherent anti-capitalist position, that could oppose the alleged 'slide towards social liberalism' of the Jospin government.[5] Hue, who had previously governed with the PS, only received 3.37 per cent of votes (five points less than in the previous election), while extreme-left candidates doubled their 1995 result by polling 10.44 per cent. Finally, the 'Appeal for a Left Alternative' (known as the Ramulaud Appeal), launched in July 2003, attempted for the first time to found an organisation of different components of the radical Left.[6] Through the appeal, the latter resolved to 'work for the convergence of all who refuse to resign themselves to capitalism'. This create the foundations of the campaign for the 'No' to the TCE and also facilitated dialogue between RLPs and social movements.

The 'No'-To-The-TCE Campaign in 2005

The 'No'-to-the-TCE campaign presented a decisive break for PS dissidents and contributed to bringing together key protagonists and organisations that formed the '*Front de Gauche* galaxy'.[7] The 'Appeal of the 200 Against the European Constitutional Treaty' initiated by the Fondation Copernic on 19 October 2004 was the founding moment of the unified campaign.[8] The signatories included the spectrum of forces behind the Ramulaud Appeal as well as most of the future leaders of the PG/FdG. The appeal sought to mobilise opposition to the constitutional treaty to present 'a left "no" that breaks with the liberal system and which can translate into votes what the social and alter-globalisation mobilisations of recent years have expressed with the support of the majority of the population, workers and youth'. On the ground, the National Collective and the Unified Local Collectives became platforms for interaction between the future parts of the FdG.[9] Hundreds of meetings gave room for building connections that had previously been difficult to create between the parties, trade unions and radical left intellectuals. These relations had been underdeveloped, having been strained by the dogmatic turn of the PCF in the Marchais era, which prompted disillusioned intellectuals to withdraw from public debates. In part this was also due to the tradition of independence of the trade unions in France.

The 'No' campaign prompted a restructuring of the left wing of the PS, as Mélenchon created the *Trait d'Union* current within the party. This was an extension of the political association *Pour la République Sociale* (PRS), an association that was a platform for discussion between supporters of the 'No' campaign. It gave them opportunities to have a degree of autonomy from the PS, and played a similar role to that of the club *République Moderne* before Jean-Pierre Chevènement's split in 1993.[10] Amandine Crespy is right to portray the 2005 campaign as 'a moment of crystallization of latent resistance to European integration within the French left'.[11] What is more, this campaign should be seen as a moment of polarisation, when divisions emerged within the PS that were significant in the emergence of the FdG.

From Faction to Mélenchonist Dissidence

The Mélenchon dissidence of 2008 was another major ingredient in the formation of the FdG. Rather than simply being a split, it needs to be understood as a process that significantly weakened the loyalty of PS supporters to the party. The roots of this process are to be found in the marginalisation suffered by the Mélenchon faction within post-2002 intra-PS politics.[12] The split became feasible because the Mélenchon current constituted a genuine faction in Zariski's understanding of the term, that is, being a clearly identifiable group within the party, characterised by a common identity and strong collective organisation.[13] It had become a 'parallel faction' that forged links to the wider Left outside the party, in contrast to an 'organisational faction', that would have adhered to the majority line.[14] The structure and the homogeneity of this highly ideological current (in an increasingly moderate PS) explain the 2008 split. The majority of the leaders of the *Trait d'Union* current and the PRS association gained positions in the National Secretariat or the National Bureau of the PG, while approximately 1,000 activists who left the PS to join this new formation became active in the new party. Although

Mélenchon seized an important 'window of opportunity' and was encouraged by the example of the German Die Linke, the creation of such a new formation appeared very risky given France's bipolar party system in which the left bloc had been dominated by the PS for three decades.

The split thus appeared to be the fruit of a number of strategic tensions within the party.[15] From 2002 onwards the 'socialist left' current within the PS grew exponentially, which resulted in Mélenchon having a weakened position within the PS Left between 2005 and 2008. While Mélenchon seemed prepared to break with the PS after the 2005 referendum campaign, the split – which only occurred at the Reims Congress in November 2008 – was not yet feasible for two reasons. First, after the socialist defeat in the 2002 presidential election and the return of factional rivalries, the PS left-wing currents had good overall numbers at the Dijon Congress in 2003 (35.7 per cent) and the Mans Congress in 2005 (44.6 per cent), held following the referendum.[16] Given these good results for the Left, justifying a split on the basis of the triumph of the social liberal line was unfeasible. Second, the 2006 internal primary reactivated what Cole calls 'presidentialised faction-alism'; since then the battle of potential presidential candidates has taken precedence over structured currents. Therefore, it was not beneficial for the leaders of PS currents to express dissidence on the eve of a major election.[17] Yet, once the 2007 presidential campaign was over, conditions grew ripe for a split. The Mélenchon faction remained marginalised within the left wing of the PS, which was itself weakened at the Reims Congress in 2008. Mélenchon also developed positive contacts with the PCF and the Chevène-ment dissidents.

The Creation of the Parti de Gauche
and the 2009 European Elections

After the 'cultural shock' of 2005, the 'anti-liberal committees' that emerged from the anti-TCE campaign failed to agree on a common candidate for the 2007 presidential election. At that time, Mélenchon's membership of the PS removed him from contention; however, this obstacle was overcome when he left the PS on 7 November 2008 and subsequently founded the PG on 1 February 2009. The timing of the break with the PS and the creation of a new party exploited the opportunity to contest the June 2009 European elections. Mélenchon also used the left wing's disappointing results at the PS' Reims congress (14–16 November 2008) to justify his long awaited exit.[18] Since its founding, the PG has presented itself as a 'melting-pot' composed of different left traditions and as a force capable of forging a broader FdG. Thereafter, the latter has been defined as a left opposition to 'social liberal-ism', although in reality it encompasses the groups that supported the 'No' in

2005. The PCF also sent Mélenchon a positive signal by stating that for the first time it favoured 'left fronts made up of personalities and organisations'.[19]

The European issue helped to establish the FdG. The radical left organisations that stayed outside FdG's banner appeared to be sects hostile to uniting against 'Euro-liberalism' just as in 2005.[20] The European campaign's objective was to be the largest force of the 'No spectrum'. This objective was achieved: with almost 6.5 per cent of votes, as the FdG lists marginally improved on the PCF's 2004 results (5.88 per cent) and redeemed its disastrous 2007 electoral result (1.93 per cent). By contrast, the NPA lists fell beneath the 5-per cent electoral threshold, which helped to give credibility to the idea that the FdG was achieving a regrouping of the Left.

It is probable that the PCF would not have risked running within the FdG (and autonomously from the PS) in the 2010 regional elections if the 2009 vote had not shown the viability of this coalition. Indeed, the PCF could have secured its existing seats by pursuing alliances with the socialists. However, having seen how damaging subordination to the PS had proved in the past, the FdG had the advantage of enlarging the appeal of the PCF while remaining under its control. The FdG could also be portrayed as a variant of the 'radical left pole' that had been promoted by some communist 'renovators' in the late 1990s. The respectable European result reinforced this direction, after it had been strongly disputed at the PCF's 2008 Congress. The party leadership's motion was opposed by other motions insisting on the preservation of communist identity, and received just 60 per cent of members' votes. Moreover, the election for the party's National Council was also highly contested, as the 'official' list attracted 68 per cent of votes, compared with 91 per cent in 2006. By contrast, at the 2010 and 2013 Congresses, the more orthodox motions receded and the leadership lists regained a dominant position. The 2009 European elections thus enabled the consolidation of the FdG and it went on to establish a leading role within the space to the left of the PS.

The Difficult Construction of a Coalition of Parties: 2009–2015

Following the electoral agreement by the PCF and the PG for the 2009 European elections, the FdG has remained an electoral 'coalition' rather than an integrated political organisation, such as Germany's Die Linke or Greece's Syriza. Indeed, the FdG does not have statutes, written rules or direct individual membership. The PCF's reluctance to abandon its name (or more generally its role in activism and financial resources) explains why the electoral coalition has not been transformed into a new party structure, which was the option advocated by the PG.

Some flexible structures have been established to ensure regular contacts between the groups involved in the FdG and to coordinate its initiatives and electoral campaigns. More concretely, at the national level, the FdG has two bodies: the National Council, which functions as a sort of legislature for the FdG, and the National Coordination, which is the executive and decision-making body that brings together its main leaders during electoral campaigns. The FdG also has local bodies, the Citizens' Assemblies, which are spaces for both discussion and action. The Front of Struggles coordinates collective mobilisation, oversees Thematic Fronts and programmatic development. Since 2011, the various components of the FdG have been meeting at summer universities, the *Estivales* in Grenoble.

From 2009 to 2012, the FdG was successfully enlarged to include seven additional organisations.[21] In November 2013, four components of FdG (FASE, C&A, GA and *Alternatifs*), some *Gauche unitaire* activists and the *Tous Ensemble* activists, along with *Trait d'Union*, launched the movement *Ensemble* ('Together, movement for a left, environmentalist, and solidary alternative'). Ensemble was personified by Clémentine Autain and aimed to become the third force in the FdG, alongside the PCF and the PG. After the 2014 municipal elections, Gauche unitaire announced an end to its participation in the national bodies of the FdG and withdrew those candidates whom it judged had been placed in low positions on the European electoral lists.

Despite the ongoing erosion of the PCF's membership, having lost nearly 150,000 members from 1997 to 2013, it remains the biggest force within the FdG (see Table 6.2). The biggest losses occurred during the communists'

Table 6.2   RLP Membership in France, 1997–2015

Year	Left Front			NPA
	PCF	PG	Ensemble	
1997	203,590			
2001	164,181			
2003	131,239			
2004	97,000			
2006	92,954			
2008	78,779			
2009		6,000		10,000
2010		8,000		8,000
2011	69,227			
2012		12,000		6,000
2013	64,184	12,000	2,500	
2014		9,000		2,500
2015		4,000		2,100

Note: for the PCF, membership figures are those reflected in internal votes. For the other parties only estimates are available.

Sources: Dominique Andolfatto and Fabienne Greffet, 'La "semi-cartellisation" du parti communiste français', in *Les systèmes de partis dans les démocraties occidentales. Le modèle du parti-cartel en question,* ed. Yohann Aucante and Alexandre Dézé (Paris: Presses de Sciences Po, 2008), 321–46; the present authors.

participation in the *gauche plurielle* governments. However, the decline continued well after this as the party lost local authorities and was slow to adapt to structural demographic changes in France. Although the PG was able to double its modest forces from the presidential election campaign in 2012, it has also faced a loss of members and within three years had lost two-thirds of its members. The losses can be attributed to both general factors (the overall lack of advances for the radical Left) and internal ones (the widely criticised authoritarianism of the party executive). After three waves of dissidence since its creation in 2009, the NPA also lost activists and could count little more than 2,000 members in 2015. LO claims to have 8,000 members but this figure is unverifiable. Overall, it is clear that the crisis has not boosted the membership of the French RLPs and their failure to attract supporters is also reflected in their electoral (mis)fortunes that are analysed below.

THE RADICAL LEFT'S ELECTORAL TRENDS – THE CRISIS DOES NOT EXPLAIN EVERYTHING

The 2012 presidential election was a success for the FdG's candidate Jean-Luc Mélenchon who received just under 4 million votes (11.10 per cent). It was the first time since 1981 that a radical left candidate attracted so many votes. The radical Left expanded its geographic base as Mélenchon's vote expanded beyond the PCF's historic strongholds (the old industrial areas, the *banlieue rouge* of the Île-de-France, the egalitarian rural zones), to increase support in metropolitan areas and encroach on the areas favourable to the socialists and the Left Union.[22] This development reflects the appeals made by the FdG to groups with academic degrees and skilled wage earners. Moreover, the extreme Left saw its worst score in presidential elections with less than 600,000 votes (1.71 per cent). However, polls also suggested that the radical Left could have performed better; as a whole its results totalled 12.81 per cent – clearly above its results from 2007 but slightly below its 2002 and 1995 performance.

The FdG's greatest failure lies in not building on the results from the presidential election. Following a less personalised and less national campaign, the coalition scored a national average of 6.91 per cent in the June 2012 legislative elections, which was translated into 15 seats in the National Assembly against 20 in the preceding PCF group (see Table 6.1). While the extreme Left was collapsing, the radical Left as a whole grew by little more than one per cent from the results in 2007. The situation became worse at the 2014 European election. This time, the overall radical left vote declined by 4.4 per cent compared with 2009 and the FdG had a near-identical result. At the local elections (municipal in 2014 and departmental in 2015), the extreme Left was further marginalised, while the FdG's electoral performance stagnated as it lost elected officials and local governments, although it did score some breakthroughs in left-leaning metropolitan areas. These results make the 2012 presidential elections look like a blip.

It is hard to establish a connection between the economic crisis and this sequence of electoral results. The 2012 presidential campaign was indeed a success in comparison with 2007, but the FdG in essence mobilised an *already existing* electoral potential. Moreover, if the crisis was the sole explanation for Mélenchon's score in 2012 (three years after the 2009 recession), it should have also led to better results in the mid-term elections. After all, during the first years of François Hollande's presidential mandate (which began in 2012), GDP stagnated and unemployment and poverty continued to advance (see Table 6.3). If the PS had indeed lost great numbers of voters due to its government's economic failures, then this was translated into widespread abstention among left voters, rather than large-scale transfer of votes to the radical Left. For that matter, these losses were not sufficient to threaten the status of the PS as the leading force on the left.

Therefore, the radical Left in France has been unable to overturn the electoral order in contrast to its counterparts in Greece and Spain. How can this be explained? First of all, the austerity practised by successive governments has been moderate and has not led to the nominal income and price decreases seen in southern Europe. It mostly consisted of tax increases, limits on public expenditure and deregulation of the labour market. During the 2010–2015 period, purchasing power per household receded to pre-2004 levels.[23] However, there were no cuts to the wages of public servants, nor attacks on permanent contracts, meaning that the interests of the labour force have been *relatively* preserved. Youth unemployment peaked in autumn 2012 (at almost 26 per cent), but this is well below figures recorded in southern Europe. Thus, the FdG lacked opportunities to present itself as the natural outlet for

Table 6.3   French Socio-economic Data, 2007–2014

Year	GDP Growth	Unemployment Rate*	Deficit Ratio	Debt Ratio
2007	2.4	7.7	−2.5	64.4
2008	0.2	7.1	−3.2	68.1
2009	−2.9	8.7	−7.2	79
2010	2	8.9	−7.1	81.7
2011	2.1	8.8	−5.3	85.2
2012	0.2	8.8	−4.8	89.6
2013	0.7	9.8	−4.1	92.3
2014	0.2	10.1	−4	95

Note: *International Labor organization's definition.
Sources: INSEE; OFCE.

the movements (as did Podemos and Syriza), due to the lack of large social movements opposed to austerity. Moreover, the French trade union organisations remained weak, rather unrepresentative and divided. The impact of the crisis was therefore relatively limited, and this allowed the French socialists to maintain their status as the main alternative to the Right.

Secondly, Syriza and Podemos' common features include popular leaders and relatively united organisations that maintain complete independence to social democracy. However, the FdG's internal organisation has proved less effective. Each group has different resources and weaknesses, and none can lay claim to fully representing the FdG on the political stage. Moreover, the strategies defended by each of its main groups have not been entirely compatible. Particularly problematic has been the way in which the groups (PG and Ensemble) that have the ideas most capable of helping the FdG to expand through attracting younger and well-educated middle-class voters as well as those in precarious employment are also weaker in organisational terms. Indeed, the FdG would probably be relegated to political marginality without the activist apparatus and local anchoring of the PCF. However, the latter's relative organisational and programmatic conservatism makes it harder to build a more integrated political movement. Thus, not only has the crisis not significantly expanded demand for the radical Left in France but the 'supply side' has remained confusing and unattractive for ordinary citizens.

The structures of political competition in France present a third reason for the FdG's stagnation.[24] France's party system is particularly hard for any new competitor that seeks to compete with the PS and the Union for a Popular Majority (UMP, now The Republicans [LR]) and significantly disadvantages smaller parties. From the primacy of the presidential election to the two-rounds, first-past-the-post, balloting at the legislative elections, various obstacles confront other parties. So in France, compared with the more proportional systems in Spain and Greece, decisive ballots involving national power are stacked against small parties and those who are unallied to larger parties. This also helps to explain why the radical right FN, although far ahead of the radical Left, remains unable to establish itself as a party of government at the national level.

It would be wrong to see the existence of the FN as a major obstacle for French RLPs. FN voters still exhibit partisan similarities and attitudes (on authority and universalism) that strongly anchor them within the Right. The radical Right would become an obstacle if the goal of the radical Left was to become one of the country's leading political forces. However, for the moment, the FdG is not even positioned to attract enough disillusioned socialist voters to contest the PS' domination of the Left. At intermediate and by-elections held since 2012, such voters mostly abstained while a small minority may have been attracted by the FN in some constituencies.[25]

The radical Left must first expand its support within the left electorate to gain credibility. This said, the biggest threat presented by the FN to RLPs is its attraction for significant sections of the popular classes. At present, France's radical Left is incapable of competing with the FN's agenda-setting and ability to focus media attention on its preferred issues of immigration, protectionism and the defence of sovereignty. By contrast, in Spain or Greece, the radical Right is either contained within a mainstream right-wing party, or is more marginal. The FN is able to present itself as the only party that has not held responsibility in government, while laying claim to offering protection against foreign, cultural and free-market threats. Whereas the FdG defends a loosely defined post-capitalist project without jettisoning its internationalism, the FN offers an arguably still more fantastical autarchic capitalism rid of the perceived threats of immigration and of uneven economic competition.

THE CRISIS AS A CATALYST OF IDEOLOGICAL AND STRATEGIC DEVELOPMENTS

Overall, the French RLPs' approach to the crisis has been unsurprising. It has been consistent with their previous programmatic stances, as they have interpreted it as the exhaustion of neoliberal capitalism. The parties believe that the fault is in the 'system' rather than in an alleged excess of public expenditures or rules and have therefore given outright opposition to austerity. The French RLPs assert that any enduring response to the crisis requires more fundamental changes to the capitalist economy. Such an approach differs from that promoted by the Centre-Left, including the socialists (even those who remained faithful to Keynesian economics). That said, Mélenchon and his supporters have developed a number of ideological and strategic innovations in the FdG. Once again, the crisis is not the ultimate source of these changes, but it did provoke debates and to some extent challenge pre-existing conceptions. The PG felt the need to adapt to the economic crisis through moving closer to the experiences at the heart of Europe's radical Left. Despite the small size of this organisation, this approach enabled it to have a significant influence on the discourse of France's radical Left.

On the ideological level, the PG has promoted two key themes. One of them is based on eco-socialism, the thesis that environmental problems cannot be resolved within the capitalist order. This line of thought has roots in France that predate the *Manifeste pour l'écosocialisme*, adopted by the PG in March 2013.[26] Previously, however, only the NPA had supported this orientation in France. The PG has been effective in promoting eco-socialism and brought it to the forefront of debates within the French radical Left. It also managed to get a motion on the subject adopted by the Party of the European Left in December 2013.

Ideas derived from eco-socialism enabled the PG to present an analysis of the crisis that distinguished the radical Left from social democracy and opened the possibility of an alliance with the Greens. The crisis is seen in civilisational rather than narrowly economic terms. It therefore demands a politics that is not only anti-capitalist but also anti-productivist, and that concerns all of humanity and not just a proletariat whose class-consciousness has faded away. Mélenchon and his colleagues have thus used the crisis to legitimise the ideological syncretism that might be used in further building a nationally specific alternative Left.[27] Yet, for the moment, eco-socialism is not part of the FdG's established doctrine, even if 'ecological planning' and the 'Green Rule' ('do not extract from nature more than it can reconstitute') were included in the 2012 programme (*L'Humain d'Abord* – 'People Come First').

The impact of the PG's theorists has been clearer on the issue of 'disobedience' against the European Union. In this instance, the crisis has acted as a powerful stimulus to rethink conceptions of European integration. The European Union's policies towards the indebted nations of southern Europe, followed by drastic austerity measures imposed by the European Union and the IMF, prompted those advocating an alternative economic policy to clarify their strategies of resistance. In particular, what was to be done to subordinate the goals of deficit and inflation reduction to human well-being, and what if conversely European markets and institutions put pressure on a government of the radical Left? Since its 'refounding' under Robert Hue in the 1990s, the PCF has largely contented itself with the vague promise of 'another Europe'.[28] In contrast, in 2012, the FdG's programme pledged to 'disobey' existing treaties. The detailed argument underlying this position had been made available in the previous year in (then economy secretary of the PG) Jacques Généreux's book.[29] Disobedience towards the treaties was not presented as a goal in itself, but only as a tool for achieving anti-neoliberal, or even anti-capitalist, objectives. The PG thus claimed to reconcile respect for popular sovereignty with internationalism. It advocated a position midway between minority groups of the radical Left, which have long advocated an exit from the European Union, and abstract appeals for a reorientation of the European Union 'from above'.

The PG developed more precise criticisms of the single currency, which represents a genuine change from the pre-2008 period. According to the party's economists, a change in monetary policy was possible if France took responsibility for a conflict within the European Union, the Euro being described as an instrument of anti-social discipline. The series of alternative scenarios for a common currency, including a more desirable 'Euro-South' zone, or a return to national currencies were envisaged as successive fall-back solutions. It is clear that PG leaders rejected the 'sanctifying' of the Euro and that a large section of the party was ready to assume at the end of a debate 'if other countries reject it, there will be an exit from the Euro'.[30] In contrast, the PCF has taken more careful positions and its economists have constantly taken pro-Euro stances. It claims that the only viable solution would be to turn the ECB into a genuine lender of last resort, which would enact rules to ensure funding for social and environmental projects.[31] The risk of being isolated within the FdG (and Europe's radical Left) partly explains why the PG has not gone further in contesting the common currency. Conversely, the sovereign debt crisis in Greece and Spain, followed by the ECB's pressure on Cyprus, pushed PG leaders to go beyond promoting customary appeals for 'another Euro'.

With 'disobedience' being part of the FdG's heritage, discussions are ongoing as to whether the Front can make sharper 'ruptures' with the European Union. For example, the Third Memorandum accepted by the Syriza government in summer 2015 triggered an informal debate between the leaders of the coalition. PG and Ensemble clearly promoted a 'plan B' if a putative French radical left government failed to transform the Eurozone from inside, whereas the PCF did not contemplate such a prospect.[32]

The crisis has also had an indirect effect on the strategic options advocated within the FdG. Syriza's victory in Greece and the emergence of Podemos have led the coalition's forces to compare their own political practice to the 'successful' courses adopted in Greece and Spain.[33] Solidarity with the Tsipras government unites all the components of the FdG. The French communists saw the new Greek government as a point of reference for a general reorientation of the European Union. For their part, the PG and Ensemble noted that Syriza had become the leader of Europe's Left, all the while preserving its independence vis-à-vis the crisis-ridden social democrats. They also viewed the Greek situation as a practical case of resistance to European 'ordoliberalism'.

In contrast, the PCF kept a distance from Podemos and maintained its historic ties to Podemos' competitor *Izquierda Unida* (United Left). The fact that Podemos has adopted populist stances inspired by the theorist Ernesto Laclau and refuses to situate itself along the right/left spectrum constitutes a cultural challenge for the European radical Left. Mélenchon and his colleagues have displayed more sympathy and sense of connection with this new arrival on the Spanish political stage. In particular, they share Podemos' interest in Latin American experiences and, like Podemos' leaders, consider the old political references to be obsolete and insufficient to bring the people together.[34]

Mélenchon has sought to create an alternative political space focused on the issue of sovereignty and capable of expanding beyond the 'natural' base of the radical Left through the recent launch of the Movement for the Sixth Republic (M6R), which operates outside of the FdG. The PCF criticised this campaign, fearing a loss of FdG control and a dilution of traditional left values. Ensemble has been more enthusiastic, approving of its constituent process, while rejecting a slide towards plebiscitarianism and seeking greater autonomy for local governments (issues on which Mélenchon is perceived as being more traditional). Ensemble has also helped initiate the *Chantiers d'Espoir* (Projects Hope), which seeks to develop alternative policy proposals through a participatory process in which civil society and the social-transformative Left interact. At the time of writing, there is little sign that M6R has gained momentum, and it appears that the FdG's organisation is suffering from a degree of inertia. The roots of this are internal and external: internally, they result from a lack of direct membership (which has never been seriously discussed) and the asymmetry of resources among the three main groups within the FdG. Externally, the sluggishness of civil society movements while austerity remains 'bearable' and the lack of popular engagement with the groups' appeals has made it hard for the FdG to develop further.

CONCLUSION

In the first section we argued that the constitution of the FdG and the crisis of the NPA were not a direct result of the international economic crisis. We then showed that the crisis was only one factor among others that need to be considered when explaining the electoral, ideological and strategic development of the radical Left in France. The incompleteness of the radical Left's regrouping under a common banner and the FdG's stagnation can only be explained with consideration of the configuration of protagonists that crystallised between 2009 and 2012 and the 'closed' character of the French party system. The crisis has not led to the collapse of either of the two main forces of this bipolar system (the PS and UMP), and oppositional forces have only been able to 'blur the margins' of the PS. France's radical Left therefore has to overcome *three obstacles*: (1) the absence of opportunities for a left revolt of the precarious middle classes; (2) a political system that is impervious to outsiders; (3) its organisational and cultural diversity, which impedes a common and effective response to the challenges that face the radical Left.

The 2014 municipal elections and the 2015 departmental elections demonstrated the local limitations of the FdG and revealed its strategic dilemmas and internal divisions. These two elections revived the strategic disagreement between the PCF, attached since the 1970s to a strategy of left unity that includes the PS, and the other components of the FdG, which advocate autonomy vis-à-vis the PS. Despite having exhausted the left unity strategy, the PCF continues to privilege it as part of its objective of preserving what has traditionally constituted its strength – 'municipal communism'. Reacting to the Communist Party's standstill and convinced by the 'winning formula' of Grenoble, where the ecologists and the PG presented common lists and won the city in opposition to the socialists, the PG opted for an alliance with the green party *Europe Écologie-Les Verts* (EELV) in 395 cantons in the first round of the 2015 departmental elections. For the time being, however, a national agreement is not in sight between any of the FdG's components and the ecologists. Nor does it appear that any of these components could benefit significantly from the break-up of the FdG coalition. Nevertheless, its strategic outlook has never been so blurred. In 2012, a minority of the PCF refused to be represented by a former socialist, but it was accepted that the FdG would have a common candidate. Looking ahead to the 2017 presidential elections, each member of the FdG claims its wants to develop a popular movement but as yet no coordinated effort is visible.

NOTES

1. We consider that extreme-left parties are part of the radical left party family, but constitute a component of their own. See Fabien Escalona and Mathieu Vieira, 'The Radical Left in Europe. Thoughts about the Emergence of a Family', *Fondation Jean-Jaurès* 2 (2013): 1–17.

2. Dominique Andolfatto, *PCF: de la mutation à la liquidation* (Paris: Editions du Rocher, 2006); Bernard Pudal, *Un monde défait: les communistes français de 1956 à nos jours* (Bellecombe-en-Bauges: Editions du Croquant, 2009).

3. Christine Pina, 'L'extrême-gauche, la vraie gauche?', in *Les partis politiques français*, ed. Pierre Bréchon (Paris: La documentation française, 2011): 181–203.

4. The Left Union (*Union de la Gauche*), associated with the Popular Front in 1936 or the 1972 Common Programme of the socialists and the communists, also designates the 'culture' of left cooperation that motivates large sections of the electorate for whom differences within the Left are less important than a common dynamic. Mélenchon and his comrades tried to rejuvenate this ideal by painting the PS as more centrist than leftist and the extreme Left as content with purist impotence.

5. French left-wing intellectuals coined the term 'social liberalism' to criticise the pro-market orientations of supposedly socialist rulers who try to submit social-democratic aspirations to an uncontested free-competition framework (i.e. similar to New Labour 'third wayers').

6. 'Appel pour une alternative à gauche', accessed 11 February 2016, http://www.democratie-socialisme.org/spip.php?article115.

7. Fabien Escalona and Mathieu Vieira, 'Le sens et le rôle de la résistance à l'UE pour le Parti de gauche', *Politique européenne* 43, no. 1 (2014): 68–92.

8. 'Appel des 200 contre le Traité constitutionnel européen,' Fondation Copernic, accessed 11 February 2016, http://www.fondation-copernic.org/index.php/2004/10/14/appel-des-200-contre-le-traite-constitutionnel-europeen-octobre-2004/.

9. These loosely structured collectives gathered left parties, trade unions and independent citizens who wanted to discuss and publicly contest the TCE.

10. See Benoît Verrier, 'Chronique d'une rupture. De Socialisme et République au Mouvement des Citoyens', *Politix* 12, no. 45 (1999): 87–113.

11. Amandine Crespy, 'La cristallisation des résistances de gauche à l'intégration européenne: les logiques de mobilisation dans la campagne référendaire française de 2005', *Revue internationale de politique comparée* 15, no. 4 (2008): 590.

12. Fabien Escalona and Mathieu Vieira, 'France', in *The Palgrave Handbook of Social Democracy in the European Union,* ed. Jean-Michel De Waele et al. (Basingstoke and New York: Palgrave Macmillan, 2013), 127–62.

13. Raphael Zariski, 'Party Factions and Comparative Politics: Some Preliminary Observations,' *Midwest Journal of Political Science* 4, no. 1 (1960): 372–90.

14. Alistair M. Cole, 'Factionalism, the French Socialist Party and the Fifth Republic: An Explanation of Intra-party Divisions,' *European Journal of Political Research* 17 (1989): 77–94.

15. Françoise Boucek, 'Rethinking Factionalism: Typologies, Intra-party Dynamics and Three Faces of Factionalism,' *Party Politics* 15, no. 4 (2009): 455–85.

16. The first is the cumulative result of the motions *Nouveau Parti Socialiste* (NPS – led by Arnaud Montebourg, Vincent Peillon, and Benoît Hamon), *Nouveau Monde* (co-founded by Jean-Luc Mélenchon and Henri Emmanuelli), and of *Forces Militantes* (led by Marc Dolez); the second, the cumulative result of the motion led by Laurent Fabius (supported by Mélenchon) and the NPS (which Henri Emmanuelli joined).

17. Cole, 'Factionalism.'

18. Motion C 'A World in Advance', led by Benoît Hamon, which gathered together all the components of the left wing, only reached fourth place with 18.5 per cent of votes, behind Ségolène Royal's Motion E (29 per cent), Bertrand Delanoë's Motion A (25.2 per cent), and Martine Aubry's Motion D (24.3 per cent).

19. Lilian Allemagna and Stéphane Alliès, *Mélenchon le plébéien* (Paris: Editions Robert Laffont, 2012).

20. The left supporters of the 'No' used Euro-liberalism' to designate the neoliberal architecture of the European Union and the Eurozone. Euro-liberalism is perceived to be supported by social liberalism and the neoliberal Right.

21. These being *Gauche unitaire* (United Left, GU), emerging from the 'Unir' current of the ex-LCR; *République et Socialisme* (R&S), dissidents from the Mouvement Républicain et Citoyen (MCR); the *Fédération pour une alternative sociale et* écologique (FASE), grouping the 'unified communists' coming from the PCF's 'Réformateur' current, along with a galaxy of small radical left organisations; *Convergences et alternative* (C&A), dissidents from the NPA, who also came originally from the ex-LCR's 'Unir' current; the *Parti communiste des ouvriers de France* (PCOF); the *Gauche anticapitaliste* (GA), dissidents from the NPA, coming from the 'United for Ecosocialism' current; the *Alternatifs*, a movement bringing together several tendencies from the environmentalist, anti-globalisation and self-government Left.

22. See Bruno Cautrès, 'Le vote Mélenchon. Le poids de l'héritage communiste et les limites d'une dynamique,' in *Le vote normal*, ed. P. Perrineau (Paris: Presses de Sciences Po, 2013): 111–32.

23. 'Austerity and purchasing power in France', *Le blog de l'OFCE*, 5 January 2015, accessed 19 August 2015, http://www.ofce.sciences-po.fr/blog/austerity-purchasing-power-france/.

24. Peter Mair, *Party System Change: Approaches and Interpretations* (Oxford: Oxford University Press, 1997).

25. Martial Foucault and Florent Gougou, 'Regard rétrospectif sur les élections municipales de mars 2014. Un vote sanction dans la logique des élections intermédiaires,' *Revue Politique et Parlementaire* 1075 (2015): 109–27.

26. The origins of the motion go back to the 1970s.

27. The challenge of climate change would also make it possible to reconcile republicanism (there is a general human interest that only popular and sovereign choices can defend), communism ('common goods' need to be managed collectively, without mediation by the market), and environmentalism (the priority is to save humanity from climate change and prepare for a world without growth).

28. Nicolas Azam, 'Européanisation et dynamique de changement partisan – Le Parti communiste français et l'Union européenne (1989-1999),' *Politique européenne* 43, no. 1 (2014): 46–67.

29. Jacques Généreux, *Nous on peut!* (Paris: Seuil, 2011).

30. Jacques Généreux, 'La priorité, c'est de sauver l'Europe, pas l'euro', *Rue 89*, 16 November 2013, accessed 10 June 2015, http://rue89.nouvelobs.com/2013/11/16/jacques-genereux-priorite-cest-sauver-leurope-leuro-247475.

31. For example, Frédéric Boccara, 'Une autre BCE et un autre euro, contre l'austérité,' *L'Humanité*, 12 May 2014.

32. Clémentine Autain, 'Prendre la mesure du tournant historique,' *Regards*, 17 July 2015, accessed 23 July 2015, http://www.regards.fr/je-vois-rouge-par-clementine/article/prendre-la-mesure-du-tournant; Alexis Corbière, 'Au PG, notre "plan B" envisage la sortie de l'euro,' *Marianne*, 27 July 2015, accessed 27 July 2015, http://www.marianne.net/alexis-corbiere-au-pg-notre-plan-b-envisage-sortie-euro-100235722.html; Pierre Laurent, 'Une sortie de la zone euro n'empêche pas la pression des marchés,' *Marianne*, 25 July 2015, accessed 27 July 2015, http://www.marianne.net/pierre-laurent-sortie-zone-euro-n-empeche-pas-pression-marches-100235637.html.

33. Notwithstanding that Mélenchon expressed harsh criticisms of Tsipras following the Third Memorandum bailout agreement in August 2015.

34. Alexis Carles, 'Mélenchon, de la Gauche au Peuple 2/2', *Ballast*, 11 March 2015, accessed 12 June 2015, http://www.revue-ballast.fr/melenchon-de-la-gauche-au-peuple-22/.

Chapter 7

Ideological Confirmation and Party Consolidation

Germany's Die Linke and the Financial and Refugee Crises

Amieke Bouma

Germany's main RLP, Die Linke ('The Left') emerged in 2007 from a fusion of the east German PDS-Linkspartei (a successor to the GDR's ruling party, SED) and a new west German protest platform, Electoral Alliance for Labour and Social Justice (*Wahlalternative Arbeit und soziale Gerechtigkeit* [WASG]). The merger of two organisationally and ideologically distinct parties was followed by a process of institutional and ideological consolidation. The international financial crisis provided Die Linke with additional arguments against neoliberalism, and became a common reference point in its debates surrounding its ideological development and linkage strategies. Yet after Die Linke's success in the 2009 elections, support for the party declined again, despite the seemingly beneficial conditions of the crisis.

This chapter argues that Die Linke was confronted with several major obstacles. First, its internationalist positions with regard to Greece were difficult to sell to the German electorate. Germany's economic performance during the crisis differed markedly from the situation in other EU countries, and has not been conducive to the traditional left agenda of international solidarity. Second, the emergent refugee crisis took the wind out of Die Linke's sails. The party developed a number of strategies to cope with these challenges, including attempts to launch new links with civil society and to strengthen relations within the European radical Left. It also developed a new ideological platform, the *Transformationstheorie* ('Transformation Theory'). Nevertheless, the communist legacy in east Germany continues to haunt the party, and there are ongoing tensions between those who advocate active involvement in government coalitions and those who see Die Linke as a protest party.

FROM PDS AND WASG TO DIE LINKE

The Party of Democratic Socialism (*Partei des demokratischen Sozialismus*, PDS) was the successor party to the German Socialist Unity Party (*Sozialistische Einheitspartei Deutschlands*, SED), which once ruled the GDR. Throughout the 1990s and the early 2000s, the PDS maintained a stable support base of around 20 per cent of the vote in east German provinces. In west Germany, however, continuing association with the former SED hindered the party's image and resulted in national election results below the 5-per cent threshold. The few members the PDS did attract in the west usually came from 'left dogmatists': micro-parties such as the German Communist Party (DKP) and the Marxist-Leninist Party of Germany (MLPD).[1] Nonetheless, in the 1990s, the PDS gained some representation in the Bundestag due to a transition law securing seats for parties supported by a considerable amount of east German voters. It built on this to win 5.1 per cent of the vote in 1998. However, in 2002 the PDS fell below the 5-per cent electoral threshold and its national representation fell to two MPs elected through east German single-mandate districts.

However, a political opportunity opened in west Germany as the result of widespread discontent with the then-ruling Social Democrat/green coalition, and in particular their proposed reforms to welfare and labour relations ('Agenda 2010'), including a reduction of unemployment benefits ('Hartz IV'). In 2004–2005, opposition to Agenda 2010 prompted groups of west German trade unionists, disappointed SPD members, anti-globalisation activists and PDS representatives to form the 'Electoral Alliance for Labour and Social Justice' WASG. WASG expanded quickly in the western provinces of Germany but remained small in the east, largely due to the strong position of the PDS, which also protested against Agenda 2010.

The PDS and WASG began to informally cooperate to avoid marginalisation.[2] Anticipating a merger, the PDS changed its name to Linkspartei.PDS and included WASG representatives on its election lists. The prospect of a new left party was rewarded in the September 2005 national election, when the Linkspartei.PDS obtained 8.7 per cent of the votes. After the full merger in 2007 the new party (now called Die Linke) tried to avoid the impression that WASG had simply been swallowed by the larger Linkspartei.PDS. Thus the new Bundestag faction was initially led by the two driving forces behind the rapprochement: charismatic PDS veteran Gregor Gysi and former leading Social Democratic Party (SPD) politician Oskar Lafontaine.

Die Linke also adopted the principle of dual East-West leadership: it is currently chaired by Katja Kipping, a Dresden-born PDS leader, and Bernd Riexinger, a west German WASG trade unionist. When Gysi resigned as faction leader in October 2015, he was replaced by his two vice-chairs: the reform-minded advocate of 'red-red-green' (SPD-Die Linke-green) coalitions Dietmar Bartsch and Sarah Wagenknecht, the long-term speaker of the party's Communist Platform. Such a construction reflects significant fault lines between different constituencies of the traditional and new Left, and between east and west.[3]

Die Linke continued to grow at the 2009 election when Germany was most clearly experiencing the economic effects of the crisis. These were the first (and so far only) elections in which the party passed the 5-per cent threshold in every German province, securing 11.1 per cent nationally. Yet it was unable to sustain this success in the 2013 Bundestag election, and returned to its 2005 support levels, both in terms of proportional party list support (now 8.6 per cent) and in single-mandate constituencies (four; all Berlin). The losses were most dramatic in the western province of Saarland, where the WASG had originated. As a result, Die Linke's centre of gravity continues to lie in the old PDS constituencies (see Table 7.1). These developments raise questions as to whether the party's success in the 2009 election was essentially an anomaly as it benefited from protest votes from those unhappy with the SPD's role in government.

Fluctuations in membership figures show a similar pattern. After Die Linke formed in 2007, it boasted 71,711 members, increasing to 78,046 in 2009. This growth was, however, short-lived. In east Germany we see the continuation of long-term processes of membership decline, and Die Linke had just 60,551 members overall in 2014.[4] While both the PDS and WASG may well have vanished if the merger had not taken place, the establishment of Die Linke has failed either to maintain the organisational strength of the (former PDS) in east Germany or attract a significant membership base in west Germany. Clearly, the financial-economic crisis failed to reverse the trend.

DIE LINKE IN REGIONAL GOVERNMENTS

Die Linke's success in 2009 may be attributed to the party's 'successful mobilization of feelings of social unrest and latent dissatisfaction' in the context of the Hartz IV reforms and the economic crisis, and perhaps its 'simplistic policy solutions'.[5] Yet Die Linke thereafter failed to substantially shape public policy or debates on the economic crisis. The party's 'ideological and programmatic heterogeneity' made it hard for it to present a coherent political strategy in response to the crisis.[6] In addition, its SED past remained a continuing fault-line between old and new constituencies within the party, and meant that other parties avoided cooperation with it at national level.[7] The past has been a serious dilemma for Die Linke. Although the PDS had already declared a break with the past, GDR-era cadres remain Die Linke's most stable support base, a fact others have viewed with suspicion.[8]

Table 7.1 Election Results PDS/*Die Linke*, 1990–Present

	2 Dec. 1990 (PDS)	16 Oct. 1994 (PDS)	27 Sept. 1998 (PDS)	22 Sept. 2002 (PDS)	18 Sept. 2005 (Die Linke)	27 Sept. 2009 (Die Linke)	22 Sept. 2013 (Die Linke)
Germany (total)	2.3	4.1	4.9	4.3	8.0	11.1	8.2
Baden-Wuerttemberg	0.3	0.3	0.6	0.9	3.1	6.4	4.2
Bayern	0.2	0.2	0.3	0.6	2.9	5.8	3.4
Berlin	**9.7**	**16.8**	**16.7**	**14.5**	**17.4**	**20.7**	**18.7**
Brandenburg	**11.0**	**20.3**	**21.1**	**20.6**	**27.0**	**29.7**	**23.9**
Bremen	1.1	2.0	2.1	1.9	7.1	12.7	8.7
Hamburg	1.1	1.1	0.7	1.6	4.7	9.7	7.5
Hessen	0.4	0.6	1.2	1.3	4.2	7.1	5.3
Mecklenburg-Vorpommern	**14.1**	**24.4**	**24.8**	**16.4**	**23.3**	**29.5**	**23.6**
Niedersachsen	–	0.4	1.0	1.0	3.5	7.5	4.3
Nordrhein-Westfalen	–	0.4	0.7	1.1	4.2	7.1	5.1
Rheinland-Pfalz	–	0.0	0.3	0.9	4.7	8.1	4.8
Saarland	–	*0.4*	*0.5*	*1.1*	*17.3*	*18.4*	*8.7*
Sachsen	**9.2**	**17.2**	**19.7**	**17.7**	**22.3**	**24.2**	**21.5**
Sachsen-Anhalt	**10.0**	**17.6**	**20.1**	**15.8**	**25.5**	**32.0**	**25.4**
Schleswig-Holstein	–	–	1.0	1.2	2.8	7.1	4.1
Thüringen	**8.8**	**16.4**	**21.0**	**19.0**	**25.4**	**29.1**	**24.3**

Note: Data displayed is proportional party list votes in national elections. Berlin and East German provinces in bold.
Source: Combined figures adapted from Informationen des Bundeswahlleiters, *Ergebnisse früherer Bundestagswahlen. Stand: 3. August 2015* (Wiesbaden: Der Bundeswahlleiter, 2015), http://www.bundeswahlleiter.de/de/bundestagswahlen/downloads/bundestagswahlergebnisse/btw_ab49_gesamt.pdf (accessed 18 February 2016).

Die Linke was more successful on the regional level (excluding some regions such as Saxony), where it pursued an office-seeking strategy and displayed a willingness to compromise. The PDS had already become an accepted coalition partner for the SPD in two eastern provinces (Mecklenburg-Vorpommern, 1998–2006, and Berlin 2002–2011). In 2009 in the eastern province of Thuringia, Die Linke had been ready to form a red-red-green coalition with an SPD prime minister, despite itself being the larger party. However, ultimately the SPD opted for a junior partner position in a grand coalition with the Christian Democratic Union (CDU).[9] In addition to the usual concerns about Die Linke's image, the SPD was unwilling to join a coalition with a stronger left-wing competitor.[10] This changed in 2014 when the SPD and Greens agreed to join a Linke-led coalition government in Thuringia on condition that Die Linke publicly acknowledge that the GDR was a 'state of injustice' (*Unrechtsstaat*) which was even acknowledged in the Coalition Agreement.[11] This development aroused strong sentiments, yet it made Bodo Ramelow the first Linke prime minister of a German province.

GERMAN DEBATES ON CRISES: THE INTERNATIONAL ECONOMIC CRISIS AND THE 'REFUGEE CRISIS'

That on the national level Die Linke's electoral success peaked in 2009 (as it fell back to an 8–10 percent share of the vote) indicates that the crisis played out somewhat differently in Germany than in other EU countries. The number of refugees applying for asylum and the relatively mild economic effects of the crisis within Germany soon made the influx of refugees the most salient political issue in German political discourse, popular perception and the media.

Germany's economy has indeed been performing well throughout the crisis period. German GDP figures indicate a crisis impact primarily for 2009, and already in 2010 Germany had growth rates doubling the Eurozone average. In 2012 and 2013, when the majority of the European Union experienced negative growth, Germany's GDP continued to grow, if minimally (see Table 7.2). Similarly, German employment rates have seen a positive trend throughout the crisis. In 2014, according to Eurostat, unemployment was 5.0 per cent, less than half the EU average, and less than half the 12.6 per cent peak German unemployment figure in March 2005. In 2014, German youth unemployment was 7.7 per cent, compared with a 23.8 per cent average in the Eurozone. Furthermore, the percentage of the population at risk of poverty and social exclusion remained rather stable, around 20 per cent. In spring 2015, 86 per cent of Germans judged the situation of the national economy as good, a sharp rise of 8 per cent compared with autumn 2014.[12]

Table 7.2   German GDP Growth

	2004	2005	2006	2007	2008	2009	2010	2011	2012	2013	2014
EU 28	2.5	2.0	3.4	3.1	0.5	−4.4	2.1	1.7	−0.5	0.0	1.3
Eurozone	2.2	1.7	3.3	3.1	0.5	−4.5	2.0	1.6	−0.8	−0.4	0.9
Germany	1.2	0.7	3.7	3.3	1.1	**−5.6**	4.1	3.6	0.4	0.1	1.6

Source: Eurostat, http://ec.europa.eu/eurostat.

Election results showed that citizens largely credited Chancellor Merkel's administration, led by the centre-right CDU, with the relative absence of crisis in Germany after 2009. Moreover, between 2008 and 2014, trust in the national government grew (+6, compared with −14 throughout the European Union).[13] Eurobarometer polls also show that Germans regard immigration as the most important issue facing the European Union (mentioned by 55 per cent of Eurobarometer respondents), followed by the state of public finances in the member states (34 per cent) and unemployment (19 per cent).[14] These figures suggest that many Germans experienced the economic crisis as a foreign rather than a domestic issue; and that worries about the economy were overshadowed by debates on immigration.

The International Economic Crisis

There was therefore little fertile soil where Die Linke's arguments regarding the economic and Euro-crises might grow. The party saw the current crisis as a reflection of structural problems inherent in capitalism, and argued that the crisis of capitalism should not lead to emergency measures to keep the system intact. Rather, what was needed was a radical restructuring of the global and European economy. This included the cancellation of debts of crisis-hit countries, and a 'radical redistribution of wealth' in Europe.[15] While debates in Germany focused on solidarity at home, in the form of saving 'German taxpayers' money', Die Linke called for international solidarity.

In response to mainstream debates, Die Linke provided a different reading of how the European crisis was linked to the situation at home. According to Kipping and Riexinger, the nation was wrong to experience the crisis as an external threat. Instead, 'this in itself is the outcome of the neoliberal politics that pushed the crisis to southern Europe. The German government is self-congratulatory on the improvements in Germany, although what has increased most is the gap between rich and poor.'[16] The catastrophic results of austerity measures in southern Europe were compared with the decline of social welfare provisions in Germany, especially through the Hartz IV reforms; both phenomena were seen to be products of the capitalist system. In response, Die Linke proposed classic redistribution policies at the

European and national level, including a 'millionaires' tax' to increase the purchasing power of the poor.[17]

The financial crisis was thus understood within existing ideological frameworks. Two decades after the fall of the GDR, many in Die Linke saw the crisis as a historical vindication of socialism. Party documents gleefully announced that 1989 did not mark an 'end of history' after all.[18] Syriza's January 2015 success was celebrated as an important victory that heralded a resurrection of the European radical Left. In particular, older Die Linke members experienced the Όχι in the Greek bailout referendum on 5 July 2015 as a catharsis.

Yet, being identified with the SED/GDR remains a present problem for Die Linke. Therefore, it has been careful not to reject capitalism as such; rather, it attacked 'neoliberal capitalism' or 'finance market capitalism' for bringing about 'crisis capitalism'. Such rhetorical choices suggested that other, better forms of capitalism might be available (or existed in the past). Die Linke thus made a distinction between the system (capitalism) and the ideology (neoliberalism), and called for a struggle against the latter in order to positively change the former. This was already the position of the PDS in the 1990s.[19] Ultimately, however, the problems of capitalism were seen to be inherent in the system, so that only a systemic change could solve the crisis.[20]

For Die Linke, the German government was responsible for the problems in southern Europe. By allowing below-subsistence wages and a 'flexible labour market', Agenda 2010 directly contributed to budget deficits in other countries. The Troika, under Angela Merkel's influence, 'left a picture of social devastation in the crisis-hit countries of Europe'.[21] Die Linke co-chair Riexinger referred to Germany as 'the motherland of austerity'.[22] Because Die Linke believed that the debts of European countries were ultimately caused by the system (or even by Germany) rather than by their respective governments, these countries were 'victims' of the crisis, and should be supported.

Consequently, Die Linke demanded more lenient budget norms within the Eurozone and direct loans from the ECB to member states. The party also called for a 'democratic process' for deciding which debts were to be repaid (and more importantly) which would not be repaid.[23] As the idea of debt cancellation is unpopular in Germany, Die Linke's call for a 'Europe-wide radical redistribution of wealth' was unlikely to garner much domestic support.[24] Nevertheless, the party advocated annulling all current EU agreements in order to substantially change the institutional make-up of Europe, and demanded Europe-wide social standards.[25] It also called for investment programmes to help indebted regions; these would lead to a social-ecological restructuring of the economy, strengthen parliaments against lobbying from businesses and industry, and deprive the financial sector of its power.[26]

However, so far most German political parties and the media blame the crisis in Greece and other countries on their governments' unwillingness to reform, which is not conducive for the promotion of international solidarity. This even seems to be the case for Die Linke's own support base: Linke supporters have been more divided on Syriza than the party hierarchy, and apparently even in mid-July 2015 (right after the Greek referendum) about half of the party's electorate actually supported Angela Merkel's negotiation line with Greece.[27] The Die Linke leadership has thus consciously swum against the tide of public opinion.

Overall, the Eurozone crisis damaged Germany's reputation within the European Union, but did not bring Die Linke concrete dividends. The crisis turned Merkel into the face of EU austerity measures, and the identification of the Troika with Germany was enhanced by the location of the European Central Bank in Frankfurt. Yet the strict line of the Merkel administration in terms of demanding budgetary discipline and reforms from Greece was supported by most German citizens, and until the July 2015 Greek referendum this position could count on broad, if not necessarily enthusiastic, parliamentary support. While many people resented paying for the irresponsible behaviour of foreign governments, they grudgingly accepted Germany's 'historical responsibility' for the European project.[28] At the same time, Euroscepticism has become more widespread in Germany – as noticeable in the rise of the right-populist Alternative for Germany *Alternative für Deutschland* (AfD). Nevertheless, it has been difficult for Die Linke to benefit, not least because Greek anti-austerity protesters compared Merkel to Hitler; and the Syriza-led government reinforced this perception when it demanded, in the midst of bailout negotiations, that Germany pay Greece 278.7bn Euros as World War II reparations.

The German votes on financial aid also presented a political problem for Die Linke (and the Greens): both saw substantial flaws in government policy towards Greece, but, at least until the July 2015 referendum, preferred to vote in favour of financial aid rather than against. In February 2015, Die Linke supported the second financial aid package to Greece (and of the 32 MPs voting against, 29 came from Merkel's own CDU/CSU).[29] In the debate about the aid package, the Greens agreed to the principle of conditionality, yet demanded that an expected third aid programme be designed in such way that 'at the end, Greece is more stable and prosperous', whereas Die Linke threatened to withhold support for future aid packages if these would 'lead to further social destruction'.[30] In July 2015, after the Greek referendum, the Greens were divided on negotiations over a third aid package but in August they voted overwhelmingly in favour of the Third Memorandum.[31] In contrast, none of Die Linke's parliamentarians voted in favour of the negotiations over a new financial aid package nor of the eventual package negotiated as initial euphoria over the Greek Όχι was soon followed by disillusionment when the Syriza-led government was forced to accept EU terms on further financial aid.[32]

The Refugee Crisis

Debates emerged surrounding the issue of whether Germany's economic performance and relatively lenient asylum laws were leading to an influx of refugees via the Balkans and the Mediterranean. Merkel's initial claim that Germany could resolve the refugee problem (*Wir schaffen das!*: 'We can do it!') were attacked as an open invitation to seek asylum in Germany. In response, Germany has been advocating a European solution to the refugee crisis (by national quotas), but such plans have failed to find support among European leaders.

The refugee crisis strengthened right-wing populism. The AfD was originally founded in 2013 as a party against the rescuing of the Euro, but turned to more open anti-immigrant discourse.[33] AfD is now close to Pegida ('Patriotic Europeans against the Islamisation of the Occident'), a group originating in eastern Germany that has since December 2014 organised weekly 'Monday marches' in Dresden and other cities. While Pegida marches began as a statement 'against Islamisation', they soon became a reservoir for anti-establishment resentment, and have attracted members of Germany's extreme Right.

Tensions over the influx of immigrants also led to violent incidents, such as arson attacks on buildings earmarked for use as refugee asylums. Initially, Merkel's policy gained grudging support. Many Germans thought their government did too little to stop extreme right groups, but at the same time believed the chancellor was reacting too slowly to the refugee crisis. Still, by September 2015, 63 per cent of Germans continued to support Merkel's policies.[34]

For Die Linke, the refugee influx into Europe demonstrated 'the inequality of our economic system', characterised by 'a double exploitation' of natural resources and human labour in the countries of origin.[35] Anti-immigrant violence in Germany was likewise the result of the deeper systemic crisis of capitalism, which created a 'society of fear' that threatened the middle classes with social descent.[36] Accordingly, violence against minorities was seen to be an outcome of the growing gap between rich and poor. Consequently, Die Linke understood AfD and Pegida as 'national-conservative' proponents of a 'radicalised neoliberalism'.[37] Moreover, if the economy was not democratised, then 'crisis capitalism' would bring 'more competition, more brutality' and 'the defence of an ever-smaller group's welfare against .the others.'[38] In response, Die Linke demanded more social provision and refugee rights.[39]

Die Linke's opposition to anti-immigrant extremism was shared by most German parties, including Merkel's centre-right CDU, and in late 2015

Germans organised many local activities to welcome refugees, independent from parties. Die Linke found itself caught in a dilemma: it condemned CDU/CSU calls to discourage and confine the stream of refugees but approved government proposals on the allocation of extra funds to improve the situation of refugees.[40] When Merkel was criticised for her policy towards asylum-seekers from CDU/CSU politicians, she was defended by Die Linke Bundestag faction leader Dietmar Bartsch.[41]

Yet this defence came when general attitudes towards the refugee crisis were hardening. Between late September 2015 and January 2016, the number of people positive about Merkel's policy declined from 63 to 39 per cent (although since this appears to be recovering). Her personal popularity dropped and Finance Minister Wolfgang Schäuble (CDU) became Germany's most popular parliamentary politician, another indication that dissatisfaction was based around immigration not economic policies.[42] The political rhetoric concerning refugees radicalised still more after the New Year's Eve events in Cologne, where hundreds of women were assaulted and robbed. The local police initially denied that the assailants were of 'North-African descent', reportedly in order not to arouse xenophobia. This apparent cover-up backfired spectacularly, and despite the police's later factual clarification that the assailants were long-standing residents of Moroccan or Tunisian origin, a narrative of refugee-instigated violence took hold. The governing CDU/CSU-SPD coalition announced that it would look into denying criminal offenders the right to asylum, and into speeding up the deportation of immigrants who have no right to asylum.[43]

It could be argued that the change in the other parties' positions marks an opportunity for Die Linke, since it is now the only parliamentary party continuing to fully advocate asylum-seekers' rights. Party chiefs Kipping and Riexinger reiterated that the 'right to asylum is a human right', which cannot be restricted, and pointed out the need for a more equal and integrative society with 'more social justice' for Germans and refugees alike.[44] However, Die Linke now advocates a position that few Germans fully identify with and, polls from January 2016 suggest that Die Linke's popularity remains about 10 per cent.[45]

IDEOLOGICAL RESPONSES

Die Linke did not benefit from the crisis in electoral terms, the crisis did, however, become an important point of reference in party documents and debates.[46] The development of a new ideological platform was a potential minefield for Die Linke, uniting as it does two constituencies with different histories and traditions. On the national level Die Linke is a protest party that campaigns against welfare cuts, but in the eastern provinces it is also a broad People's Party (*Volkspartei*).[47] Moreover, in east Germany Die Linke is an established party with long experience in local politics, whereas in west Germany it remains 'a party under construction'.[48] Although Die Linke presents its 'pluralism' as a strength, it struggles with ideological discrepancies among its supporters.[49]

Traditional communist-leaning party members have understood the crisis as the result of over-accumulation and increased competition between capitalist countries. For them, the conflict between capital and labour was central, and the remedy was active resistance to the capitalist system. Accordingly, Die Linke should focus on the working class, and must prioritise the collective over the individual. The party should participate in governing coalitions only when this can bring goods and services back into state responsibility and meet its aim of creating full employment and equal remuneration.[50]

In contrast, Die Linke's 'democratic socialist' ('new left') currents understand capitalist society as developing through 'struggle between the dominant logic of capital', on the one side, and a 'social and democratic logic that creates potential for emancipation', on the other.[51] They saw the crisis as the confluence of 'finance-market capitalism' and a civilisational crisis. The crisis could lead to 'authoritarian capitalism', in the worst case, but might also lead to a 'social-ecological transformation'. The crisis was characterised by several mutually constitutive lines of conflict (capital-labour, north-south, racism, sexism, etc.) that could only be overcome via a wholesale transformation of society, one brought about by a 'coalition of middle and lower classes' and leading to a society that celebrates plurality and individual freedom.[52] This freedom was endangered by measures such as the Hartz IV reforms, which pushed people to work to remain eligible for welfare.

Such divergent views reflect differences between the 'traditional Left' and the 'new Left', between socio-economic (egalitarian) and sociocultural (libertarian) values, and specific west-east discrepancies among the German Left.[53] Die Linke's lack of ideological consolidation is reflected in party documents and those of its research foundation, the Rosa Luxemburg Foundation (*Rosa-Luxemburg-Stiftung*, *RLS*), which still repeatedly refer to the concept of 'democratic socialism', which had been consciously removed from the party name during the merger process as many WASG members found the term 'outdated'.[54] Clearly, the discourse of the former PDS remains prevalent almost a decade after the merger.

Ideological consolidation had certainly been emphasised before the merger, when the PDS and WASG had established joint working groups to delineate the 'new left project'. The common platform during the merger included a number of 'ideological cornerstones', which were either concrete actions that both parties could easily agree upon, or they were sufficiently vague to allow for multiple interpretations.[55] It took until 2011 for a Die Linke programme to be formulated and adopted via a membership vote.[56] Again, this programme called for 'deep-rooted change' of the current system but was unclear on what precisely this change consisted of, and how it was to come about. Thus the party chose to be inclusive of as many members as possible. This strategy was itself a continuation of the PDS transformation from the SED in December 1989, when an inclusive strategy was adopted to stem dramatic membership loss and ensure the erstwhile state party's survival. Moreover, ideological pluralism was also meant to facilitate cooperation with extra-parliamentary movements.

Therefore, from the start in 2007, Die Linke strove to mobilise people behind a broad left agenda, supplying 'isolated short-term actions with wide-ranging visions for the future', in order to convince people that there were real alternatives to neoliberalism.[57] Die Linke takes its claim to pluralism seriously, and various ideological subdivisions are permitted within the party (including, among others, the Communist Platform, the Emancipatory Left and the Forum for Democratic Socialism). The Rosa Luxemburg Foundation and its *Institut für Gesellschaftsanalyse* (IfG), established in December 2008, developed this mobilisation strategy into the so-called 'Transformation Theory' (*Transformationstheorie*), Die Linke's main intellectual response to the crisis. With 17 regular and seven freelance employees, the Institute investigates strategies for the Left to promote 'a democratic-socialist transformation of capitalist societies'.[58]

The IfG presented its first analysis of 'the left in society in the current crisis' in 2009.[59] Rolf Reißig (political scientist and member of the RLS scientific advisory board) also published a monograph on 'current societal changes', in which he described the global and European financial and economic crisis as the trigger of a 'Second Great Transformation'.[60] A year later, then-chair of the IfG Dieter Klein published a 32-page essay entitled 'A second great transformation and the left'.[61] This paper marked the beginning of the *Transformationstheorie* as an important ideological parameter in Die Linke. Since then 'transformation' has remained a major key word in RLS publications, conferences, discussions and meetings.[62]

Following the influential socialist economist Karl Polanyi, the Transformation Theory sees the first great transformation in the transition from feudalism and other pre-capitalist socio-economic formations to a commodity-based capitalist society. The international financial and economic crisis demonstrated the failure of this particular capitalist system, and prepared the ground for a second transformation from capitalism to 'democratic socialism', 'a just and sustainable society based on solidarity'.[63] This 'emancipatory, social, ecological and feminist' transformation will lead to 'a society of individual freedom, in which all citizens participate and enjoy a self-determined life in social security and solidarity'. This future society must be ecologically sustainable, something at present 'impossible due to the profit-dominated mechanisms of the market'.[64] Moreover, it is argued that ecological change requires that economic growth be consciously limited, with the losers of this process being compensated by redistributionist policies.[65]

According to this perspective, the transformational process will start 'in the midst of bourgeois society, and will lead beyond it'.[66] Yet Die Linke is clearly not advocating system change through revolution. Instead, transformation will be a 'third way' between revolution and reform.[67] This approach is oriented towards a broad left electorate, and leaves room for partnerships with social democrats and the Greens, on the basis of common 'short-term' practical goals that can be reached through coalition politics. Such coalitions are also sanctioned through the notion of the 'strategic triangle': political change can be achieved by a three-pronged strategy of presenting alternative political visions through protesting against policies, through parliamentary politics and through creating socialist alternatives outside parliament.[68]

As Klein argued, there would be a double transformation, one 'within the system' and one 'system-crossing'. For the time being, left actors should work towards an 'inner-capitalist transformation' towards a socially regulated bourgeois capitalist society with green elements. This was seen as an entry point for a second Great Transformation. While the strategy to work for concrete goals within capitalism was primarily aimed at finding broader support for the left project, the concept of a 'double' transformation maintained the goal of ultimately establishing a socialist society.[69]

In this way, the Transformation Theory justifies not only the attempts to create extra-parliamentary bonds but also Die Linke's office-seeking strategy, and also preserves longer-term strategic goals that explicate the party's radical left ideology. In spite of its vagueness, the eventual 'transformation' signals a clear departure from the more communist-minded egalitarian, traditional left outlook still shared by some of the older party cadres, whom the PDS struggled to keep on board through all its ideological adjustments after the early 1990s.[70] It is more geared towards a new left that cherishes diversity and individual freedom, as well as sustainable development and environmental protection. Consequently, several old members and sympathisers have accused Die Linke of having effectively given up its socialist agenda in order to become a 'normal' political party and some even liken the current party to the Weimar-era SPD.[71]

LINKAGE STRATEGIES

These theoretical debates, and Die Linke's claims to be a new, pluralistic left party, have clear implications for its linkage strategies. Die Linke wants to provide a discussion platform open to a broad 'societal left' (*gesellschaftliche*

Linke). The party explicitly invites members and sympathisers to discuss new ideas, to send in proposals and to join organised debates and events.[72] The financial crisis was a new source of inspiration. In the words of party leaders Kipping and Riexinger, the crisis raised spirits 'of an awakening, against the desolation of the ruling neoliberal politics', and created an opening for the Left as social protests and movements against the crisis inspire people to pursue the struggle for 'real [socialist] democracy'.[73]

A recent such campaign to stimulate debate was the 'Left Week of the Future' (*Linke Woche der Zukunft*) in Berlin on 23–26 April 2015, featuring 85 public meetings and events with Linke and other left politicians, as well as activists and scholars.[74] Debates focused on issues such as 'the future of social work', 'equality as opportunity', and 'the appropriation of democracy'. Similarly, Die Linke's most recent campaign against precarious forms of employment was described by party-chairs Kipping and Riexinger as 'a self-organised learning process', and as a space for exchange and for developing organisational skills, that is, for connecting and recruiting.[75] The party has sought to enhance both participatory linkage (discussion within the party) and environmental linkage (cooperation with left actors and social movements).[76] The crisis, however, only intensified existing strategies as such efforts at environmental linkage pre-date the establishment of Die Linke and the crisis.[77] Since 2006, the parliamentary faction of Linkspartei/Die Linke had hosted a 'contact point for social movements' (*Kontaktstelle soziale Bewegungen*), in order to become more accessible to 'social movements, NGOs and trade unions, groups and initiatives of the extra-parliamentary left'.[78]

During the crisis, Die Linke participated in anti-austerity protests, especially in the Blockupy protests against the European Central Bank in Frankfurt starting in 2011. Through Blockupy, the party also cooperated with Occupy and Attac, trade unions, unemployed, youth and student organisations, as well as anti-fascist, environmental and peace movements.[79] These networks are important to Die Linke's ambition to unite various left forces in practical cooperation. As one IfG official (and also an official from the Kontakstelle soziale Bewegungen) Corinna Genschel argued, 'The answer to the crisis will not be a unitary force but a *mosaic* of diverse movements.'[80] Yet it took serious internal party discussion for Die Linke to prioritise links with social movements in contentious actions such as Blockupy.[81] Previously, cooperation had long been hampered by mutual mistrust deriving from very different organisational cultures and perceptions that Die Linke had a centralised structure. Die Linke therefore celebrated the new-found understanding with social movements as a success.[82] Nevertheless, anti-austerity protests in Germany have been relatively small-scale, and the general weakness of the protest movement is probably one of the reasons why cooperation developed within the Blockupy campaign.

EUROPE

Die Linke's approach to the crisis needs to be seen within the context of its internationalist and generally Europeanist positions, as well as intra-party divisions over such strategies. The party has been one of the main instigators of international cooperation between RLPs. Already in 1998, the PDS was one of the founders of what ultimately became the Party of the European Left (PEL), the first exploratory meeting of which took place in Berlin.[83] Despite its downward trend in national elections, Die Linke maintained a stable presence in European Parliament (EP) elections through the crisis, receiving 7.5 per cent of the vote in 2009, and roughly the same in 2014. This helped the party become an influential member of the radical left EP group, the European United Left/Nordic Green Left (GUE/NGL). With seven MEPs after the 2014 elections, it hosts the largest national delegation within the GUE/NGL group of 52 MEPs. Since 2009, GUE/NGL has been led by Die Linke chairs: first by Lothar Bisky, and since 2012 by Gabi Zimmer.

At European level, Die Linke has called for a broad left platform uniting different types of left party and non-party organisations, in line both with its national-level practice and with the GUE/NGL's confederal structure.[84] In RLS analyses, the party identifies a need for a more substantial common platform to carry out reforms to the European Union.[85] Die Linke does, however, recognise that agreement is unlikely in the short term because of substantial differences between RLPs.[86] Meanwhile, the RLS Brussels office published Klein's article on 'The Second Great Transformation and the Left' in English, apparently in an attempt to promote the Transformation Theory as a unifying factor for the international radical Left's response to the crisis.[87] The RLS has also directly supported activist organisations beyond Germany: it maintains 18 regional offices around the world, including in eastern and south-eastern Europe, and it invites international groups to conferences and training. Through the RLS, Die Linke also gives financial support to the Transform!Europe network, the European political foundation of the European Left Party.

Like other parties of the European Left, Die Linke strongly opposes the Transatlantic Trade and Investment Partnership (TTIP) agreement with the United States, which it sees as an 'economic NATO'.[88] Die Linke has also been critical of any western, and specifically German, involvement in international conflicts, thereby continuing the SED's ideology of 'antifascism', but also the PDS' opposition to the 1999 NATO bombings in Yugoslavia and to the US-led invasions in Afghanistan and Iraq. Die Linke has also taken a pro-Kremlin position in the Ukrainian conflict, a position that seems to derive from the party's 'historical affinity' with Russia and, again, the shared narrative of 'antifascism'. This position is not uncontroversial, and has led to debates within the party as well as within the European Left. Again, this can be seen as the outcome of deep-rooted cleavages within Die Linke.

Die Linke has also developed a position of activist solidarity towards Greece. In 2012 the RLS established a liaison office in Athens.[89] Die Linke MEPs have also directly supported the Syriza government throughout the Greek crisis, depicting the austerity measures in Greece as a German device for robbery.[90] The broad support that Syriza enjoyed in Greece in early 2015 was portrayed as an inspiring example for other RLPs, including Die Linke itself. The Syriza-led government's forced acceptance of new austerity measures in return for loans after the Third Memorandum was seen as a sign of stalled democracy in Europe.[91] The failure of the Greek referendum (5 July 2015) to change relations between the European Union and Greece was largely blamed on the failure of European RLPs to support their Greek comrades by organising protests against EU austerity measures, thus strengthening Die Linke's narrative about the need for a strong and united European radical left project.[92] At the same time, Die Linke criticised the European Union for depriving any democratically elected radical left government of room for manoeuvre.[93]

However, beyond such common themes, the situation in Greece has re-ignited debates within Die Linke over the party's attitude towards the European Union. Broadly speaking, three different strands can be identified: The first group wishes to continue Die Linke's existing 'reform programme' for Europe by first focusing on the 'radical democratisation' of all EU institutions, and on building strong left coalitions to make this happen.[94] Yet a more disappointed group argues that meaningful balance of power within the European Union's will forever be blocked and advocates 'Lexit' (left-wing exit from the European Union). This standpoint has the support of prominent Linke-politicians, including those connected to the party's 'Marx21' network.[95] Finally, a third group has recently evolved around the new initiative for a 'Plan B in Europe' spearheaded by Yanis Varoufakis, but also by Die Linke co-founder Oskar Lafontaine and the leader of the French Parti de Gauche, Jean-Luc Mélenchon. This approach combines calls for radical reform of the European institutions ('Plan A') with appeals to mobilise forces against the reactionary elements who 'crushed the Athens spring' ('Plan B').[96] It remains to be seen whether or not the Plan B initiative can unite these policy preferences into a common platform or develop links with the closely connected 'Democracy in Europe Movement 2025' (Diem25) initiated by Yanis Varoufakis, and whether either project can surpass Die Linke's previous agenda-setting position among European RLPs.

CONCLUSION

Die Linke emerged in its present form only in 2007, and the process of party consolidation largely coincided with the economic crisis. The crisis initially helped to bring different party constituencies closer together, by providing a common reference point against neoliberalism. In this context, Die Linke has tried to respond to the crisis through seeking to expound on it theoretically (the *Transformationstheorie*) and by launching new links with civil society. The crisis, however, has supplemented existing ideas and organisational strategies rather than fundamentally changing Die Linke's direction.

Die Linke has also been unable to expand or to reconcile internal divisions in recent years. After a peak in 2009, both its membership and electoral support have declined, except in European elections. At the European level, the party has continued to be a prime mover in promoting international solidarity and RLP cooperation, but with limited success. Indicatively, initial euphoria over developments in Greece was soon crushed by disappointment over Syriza's inability to reset the terms of negotiation with the European Union. Die Linke felt a sense of responsibility for this failure through not having been active enough in support of Greece.

Overall, Die Linke's regular vote share (8–10 per cent) could be seen as relatively good, given that there has not been a widespread rejection of the mainstream parties in Germany. Moreover, its failure to expand further can also be partly attributed to the strength of the German economy and the government's ability to claim that it avoided the worst of the crisis. Furthermore, Die Linke has struggled to promote its solutions to the refugee crisis, which has become a more salient issue. However, and perhaps above all, while Die Linke has established itself as an important player nationally, it continues to be constrained by its past and the need to appeal to various internal constituencies. This means that a unified response to the crisis, both domestically and internationally, has been hard to discern.

NOTES

1. Michael Chrapa, 'Interne Konfliktpotentiale und Modernisierungschancen der PDS. Situation, Anforderungen, Optionen,' *UTOPIE Kreativ* 113 (2000): 278.

2. Charles Lees et al., 'Towards an Analytical Framework for Party Mergers: Operationalising the Cases of the German Left Party and the Dutch Green Left,' *West European Politics* 33, no. 6 (2010): 1306.

3. Dan Hough and Michael Koß, 'Populism Personified or Reinvigorated Reformers?' The German Left Party in 2009 and Beyond,' *German Politics and Society* 91, no. 27 (2009): 80–1.

4. Die Linke, 'Mitgliederzahlen 2014', http://www.die-linke.de/partei/fakten/mitgliederzahlen/.

5. Hough and Koß, "Populism Personified,' 83.

6. Ibid., 89.

7. Amieke Bouma, 'Left without Its Party: Interest Organizations of Former GDR Elites and the Transformation of the PDS/Linke,' in *Radical Left Movements*, ed. Magnus Wennerhag, Christian Fröhlich and Grzegorz Piotrowski (Farnham: Ashgate, forthcoming).

8. On the necessity for successor parties to break with the past early, see Anna Grzymala-Busse, *Redeeming the Communist Past. The Regeneration of Communist Parties in East Central Europe* (Cambridge: Cambridge University Press, 2002), 69–82.

9. Dan Hough, 'From pariah to prospective partner? The German Left Party's winding path towards government', in *Left Parties in National Governments*, ed. Jonathan Olsen, Michael Koß and Dan Hough (London: Palgrave, 2010), 148.

10. Tania Verge and Dan Hough, 'A Sheep in Wolf's Clothing or a Gift from Heaven? Left-left Coalitions in Comparative Perspective,' *Regional and Federal Studies* 19 (2009): 4–6.

11. 'Koalitionsvertrag zwischen den Parteien DIE LINKE, SPD, BÜNDNIS 90/DIE GRÜNEN für die 6. Wahlperiode des Thüringer Landtags: Thüringen gemeinsam voranbringen – demokratisch, sozial, ökologisch'. 2014, 2, http://www.otz.de/documents/12936/0/Koalitionsvertrag+Rot-Rot-Gr%C3%BCn/cd8995b4-da16-4816-8284-03dcb3cfbe2e.

12. First results Eurobarometer 83 (Spring 2015), http://ec.europa.eu/public_opinion/archives/eb/eb83/eb83_first_en.pdf.

13. Eurobarometers 70 (2008), 72 (2009), 82 (2014), http://ec.europa.eu/public_opinion/.

14. First results Eurobarometer 83 (Spring 2015).

15. Katja Kipping and Bernd Riexinger, 'Die Kommende Demokratie: Sozialismus 2.0. Zu den Aufgaben und Möglichkeiten einer Partei der Zukunft im Europa von Morgen,' 24 April 2015, 26, http://www.katja-kipping.de/de/article/887.die-kommende-demokratie-sozialismus-2-0.html.

16. Ibid., 12.

17. Die Linke, *100% Sozial. Wahlprogramm zur Bundestagswahl 2013*, 26, http://www.die-linke.de/die-linke/wahlen/archiv/archiv-fruehere-wahlprogramme/wahlprogramm-2013/wahlprogramm-2013/.

18. Kipping and Riexinger, 'Die Kommende Demokratie,' 7.

19. Helge Meves, 'Das Selbstverständnis der PDS, der Neoliberalismus und die Mitte-Unten-Optionen,' *UTOPIE kreativ* 152 (2003): 528–32.

20. Kipping and Riexinger, 'Die kommende Demokratie', 26; Anna Striethorst, 'Aktuelle Themen und Debatten der europäischen Linksparteien', in *Von Revolution bis Koalition. Linke Parteien in Europa*, ed. Birgit Daiber, Cornelia Hildebrandt and Anna Striethorst (Berlin: Karl Dietz Verlag, 2010), 52.

21. Bernd Riexinger, 'Eine Vision: Einstieg in ein anderes Europa', *Europalinks. Beilage der Tageszeitung Neues Deutschland in Zusammenarbeit mit der Zeitschrift Luxemburg* (2014): 23.

22. Ibid., 23–24.

23. Mario Candeias, Lukas Obendorfer and Anne Stecker, 'Neugründung Europas? Strategische Orientierungen,' *Europalinks* (2014): 4.

24. Kipping and Riexinger, 'Die kommende Demokratie', 26.

25. Ibid.; Riexinger, 'Eine Vision', 24.

26. Kipping and Riexinger, 'Die kommende Demokratie', 24.

27. 'Schuldenstreit mit Griechenland: Grünen-Wähler begrüßen Merkels Krisenkurs,' *Spiegel Online* (14 July 2015).

28. According to the ARD DeutschlandTrend Survey of 13 July 2015, 62 per cent of Germans thought Greece should stay a member of the European Union, 52 per cent supported the third aid package to Greece, although only 18 per cent expected the Greek government to fulfil its conditions.

29. Bundestag website, http://www.bundestag.de/bundestag/plenum/abstimmung/grafik?id=327.

30. Bundestag website, https://www.bundestag.de/dokumente/textarchiv/2015/kw09_de_griechenland/360760.

31. Bundestag website, http://www.bundestag.de/bundestag/plenum/abstimmung/grafik/?id=352; Tagesschau.de, 'Bundestagsabstimmung zu Griechenland' (19 August 2015), https://www.tagesschau.de/inland/griechenland-abweichler-101.html.

32. Ibid.

33. Michael Jankowski, Sebastian Schneider and Markus Tepe, 'Ideological Alternative? Analyzing Alternative für Deutschland candidates' ideal points via black box scaling', *Party Politics* (12 January 2016), 2.

34. Infratest Dimap, 'ARDDeutschlandTREND September 2015. Eine Studie im Auftrag der Tagesthemen,' https://www.tagesschau.de/inland/deutschlandtrend-399.pdf.

35. Prager Frühling Magazine, 'This is a movement. Massendissidenz in Merkelland? Überlegungen zur Flüchtlingspolitikkrise', *Rosalux* 3 (2015): 6.

36. Kipping and Riexinger, 'Die Kommende Demokratie', 13.

37. Felix Korsch and Volkmar Wölk, *National-Konservativ und Marktradikal. Eine politische Einordnung der 'Alternative für Deutschland'* (*Analysen* series, Berlin: Rosa-Luxemburg-Stiftung, 2014).

38. Kipping and Riexinger, 'Die Kommende Demokratie', 14.

39. Rosa-Luxemburg-Stiftung, 'Flüchtlinge willkommen – Refugees welcome? Mythen und Fakten zur Migrations- und Flüchtlingspolitik', *Luxemburg Argumente* 8, no. 2 (2015): 45–50.

40. Axel Troost, 'Die Flüchtlingsfrage als europäische und gesamtdeutsche Aufgabe,' http://www.die-linke.de/nc/die-linke/nachrichten/detail/artikel/die-fluechtlingsfrage-als-europaeische-und-gesamt-deutsche-aufgabe/ (4 September 2015). Troost is *Die Linke* vice-chairman and financial spokesman of its parliamentary group.

41. ARD, *Panorama*, 17 December 2015; 00:27:00-20, http://www.ardmediathek.de/tv/Panorama/Panorama-die-ganze-Sendung/Das-Erste/Video?documentId=32347834&bcastId=310918.

42. ZDF Politbarometer, 'Merkel stürzt ab' (15 January 2016).

43. 'Übergriffe in Silvesternacht: Union plant nach Kölner Gewaltexzessen schärfere Gesetze,' *Spiegel Online* (8 January 2016).

44. Katja Kipping and Bernd Riexinger, 'Asylrecht ist Menschenrecht', 13 January 2016. http://www.die-linke.de/nc/mediathek/videos-pressekonferenzen/archiv/2016/januar/.

45. Opinion polls from several agencies can be found at http://www.wahlumfrage.de/t/die-linke/.

46. Giorgos Charalambous, 'Taking party ideology development seriously,' *Rivista Italiana di Scienza Politica* XLIV, no. 2 (2014): 208.

47. Birgit Daiber, 'Über den Gebrauchswert der Linksparteien', in Daiber et al. (eds.) *Von Revolution bis Koalition*, 45.

48. Anna Striethorst, 'Mitglieder und Elektorate von Linksparteien in Europa,' in Ibid., 93.

49. Hough and Koß, 'Populism Personified,' 80–1.

50. Cornelia Hildebrandt, 'DIE LINKE in Deutschland,' in Daiber et al. (eds.) *Von Revolution bis Koalition*, 170–2.

51. Ibid.

52. Michael Brie and Cornelia Hildebrandt, 'Solidarische Mitte-Unten Bündnisse und Anforderungen an Linke Politik,' *Luxemburg. Gesellschaftsanalyse und Linke Praxis* 2 (2015), http://www.zeitschrift-luxemburg.de/solidarische-mitte-unten-buendnisse/.

53. Cf. Bouma, 'Left without Its Party'.

54. Lees et al. 'Towards an Analytical Framework for Party Mergers', 1309.

55. Die Linke, 'Programmatische Eckpunkte – Programmatisches Gründungsdokument der Partei DIE LINKE. Beschluss der Parteitage von WASG und Linkspartei. PDS am 24. und 25. März 2007 in Dortmund,' http://www.die-linke.de/fileadmin/download/dokumente/alt/programmatische_eckpunkte.pdf.

56. Die Linke, 'Programmentwurf', accessed 28 August 2015, http://www.die-linke.de/programm/programmdebatte/leitantrag-an-den-erfurter-parteitag/programmentwurf/.

57. Kipping and Riexinger, 'Die Kommende Demokratie', 16.

58. www.rosalux.de.

59. Institut für Gesellschaftsanalyse, 'Die gesellschaftliche Linke in den gegenwärtigen Krisen,' *Kontrovers* 2 (2009).

60. Rolf Reißig, *Gesellschafts-Transformation im 21. Jahrhundert. Ein neues Konzept sozialen Wandels* (Wiesbaden: VS Verlag für Sozialwissenschaften, 2009).

61. Dieter Klein, 'Eine zweite Grosse Transformation und die Linke,' *Kontrovers* 01 (2010).

62. Searching the electronic RLS webpage (www.rosalux.de) for the word 'transformation' results in 419 hits since 2010, overwhelmingly in the context of the present and future transformation of society (*gesellschaftliche Transformation*).

63. Klein, 'Eine zweite Grosse Transformation, 3–4.

64. Ibid., 6–7.

65. Ibid., 8.

66. Ibid., 6.

67. Dieter Klein, *Das Morgen tanzt im Heute. Transformation im Kapitalismus und über ihn hinaus* (Hamburg: VSA Verlag, 2013), 110–27.

68. Hildebrandt, 'DIE LINKE in Deutschland', 166. The concept of the 'strategic triangle' was adopted by the PDS party congress of 2004.

69. Klein, *Das Morgen tanzt im Heute*, 14–15.

70. See also André Brie, Michael Brie, Michael Chrapa, 'Für eine moderne sozialistische Partei in Deutschland. Grundprobleme der Erneuerung der PDS,' *RLS-Standpunkte* 7 (2002): 4–5.

71. Sebastian Carlens, 'Wohin geht Die Linke?,' *Junge Welt* (18 June 2015); Herbert Meißner, 'Geht es um die Transformation des Kapitalismus oder der Partei Die Linke? Über Täuschungsmanöver der gehobenen Art,' *RotFuchs* 17, no. 209 (2015): 15.

72. Kipping and Riexinger, 'Die Kommende Demokratie', 4–5.

73. Ibid., 8; 16.

74. http://www.linke-woche-der-zukunft.de/linke-woche-der-zukunft/, accessed 31 August 2015).

75. Kipping and Riexinger, 'Die Kommende Demokratie', 29–30.

76. Cf. Myrto Tsakatika and Marco Lisi, '"Zippin'up My Boots, Goin' Back to My Roots": Radical Left Parties in Southern Europe', *South European Society and Politics* 18, no. 1 (2013): 1–19.

77. Christoph Spehr, 'Wem gehört die Partei? Moderne Linkspartei, Offene Organisation, Offener Sozialismus,' in *Parteien und Bewegungen. Die Linke im Aufbruch*, ed. Michael Brie and Cornelia Hildebrandt (Berlin: Karl Dietz Verlag, 2006), 48–9.

78. Hannah Hoffmann, 'Man muss immer wieder von vorn anfangen können,' *Clara* 22 (14 December 2011).

79. http://2012.blockupy-frankfurt.org/sites/european-resistance.org/files/files/doku/faqs_1.pdf (accessed 31 August 2015).'

80. Hoffmann, 'Man muss immer wieder,'.

81. http://2012.blockupy-frankfurt.org/de/aufrufe/transnational_call_de.html (accessed 31 August 2015); Die Linke, 'Für ein Ende der neoliberalen Traurigkeit – Europa anders machen. Resolution des Bielefelder Parteitages,' Resolution adopted at the Die Linke party congress, 6–7 June 2015, *Disput* (June 2015): 55–6.

82. Katja Kipping, 'Eine starke LINKE ist die Garantie dafür, dass sozialen Worten soziale Taten folgen,' speech at the 2013 Die Linke party congress, 15 June 2013, http://www.die-linke.de/index.php?id=12344.

83. http://www.european-left.org/about-el (accessed 18 February 2016).

84. Die Linke, 'GUE/NGL – die Fraktion der LINKEN im Europäischen Parlament', http://www.dielinke-europa.eu/article/8985..html.

85. Bernd Riexinger, Pierre Laurent, Maite Mola and Theodoros Paraskevopoulos, 'Hoffnung für einen demokratischen Aufbruch in Europa,' 17 February 2015, http://www.die-linke.de/nc/die-linke/nachrichten/detail/artikel/hoffnung-fuer-einen-demokratischen-aufbruch-in-europa/.

86. Cf. Daiber et al., *Von Revolution bis Koalition*.

87. Dieter Klein, *The Second Great Transformation and the Left* (Brussels: RLS, 2010).

88. EuroMemo Gruppe, 'EuroMemorandum 2015, Die Zukunft der Europäischen Union. Stagnation und Polarisierung oder eine grundlegende Neuausrichtung?' Supplement to the *Zeitschrift Sozialismus* 3 (2015).

89. http://rosalux.gr/de/foundation/verbindungsburo-griechenland, accessed 1 December 2015.

90. Gabi Zimmer, 'Three proposals for a real rescue package for Greece and its people. Statement by GUE/NGL President Gabi Zimmer on the Greek bailout deal,' 15 August 2015, http://www.guengl.eu/news/article/three-proposals-for-a-real-rescue-package-for-greece-and-its-people.

91. Brie and Hildebrandt, 'Solidarische Mitte-Unten Bündnisse,' 107.

92. Lutz Brangsch, 'Haben wir etwas gelernt? Was Syrizas scheitern für Linke in der Europäischen Union bedeutet,' *Rosalux* 3 (2015): 19–20.

93. Alex Demirovic, 'Regieren reicht nicht. Der Fall Griechenland zeigt: Europa muss radikal demokratisiert werden,' *Rosalux* 3 (2015): 13.

94. See also Mario Candeias, 'Nichts mehr wie zuvor. Den Widerstand für ein anders Europa von Unten zusammenbringen,' *Rosalux* 3 (2015): 16.

95. Nicole Gohlke and Janine Wissler, 'Escaping the Euro Dream', *Jacobin Magazin*, 31 July 2015, https://www.jacobinmag.com/2015/07/germany-greece-austerity-grexit/.

96. 'A Plan B in Europe'; https://www.euro-planb.eu/?page_id=96&lang=en (accessed 17 February 2016).

Chapter 8

Failing to Capitalise on the Crisis

The Dutch Socialist Party

Daniel Keith

The Dutch Socialist Party (SP) has developed out of a tiny Maoist party in the 1970s to play a significant role in Dutch politics. Its socialist, populist and Eurosceptic appeals helped the party to expand during the 1990s. Subsequently, it replaced populism with an office-seeking strategy by 2008 in an incremental process of change.[1] This history has led scholars to point to the SP's highly adaptive, 'chameleonic' characteristics.[2] Given this, it is surprising that the economic crisis has not prompted the SP to revert to greater radicalism or the populist 'anti-establishment' appeals so successful in Greece and Spain. Certainly, the SP has criticised austerity measures and bank bailouts to be at the forefront of debates about the crisis in the Netherlands, yet the party has neither re-radicalised nor gained obvious sustained electoral benefit to date.

This chapter seeks to explain these rather puzzling developments. It begins by discussing the SP's historical development and highlights the significant role played by the party's leaders in shaping its strategies. It then identifies how the politicisation of the economic crisis has presented several opportunities for the SP to expand. Second, the party's programmatic responses to the economic crisis are analysed to show how that despite critics' attempts to portray the SP as a threat to the system, it has promoted a relatively moderate response to the crisis, certainly when compared with other RLPs. It is argued that this process can be explained as a result of the SP's leaders responding to the crisis firmly within the context of their existing strategies.[3] Its leaders have been cautious to avoid a return to former positions and to have sought to maintain their office-seeking strategy.

Third, while the SP is shown to have undergone only limited organisational changes during the period, it has experienced a dramatic electoral ride. In particular, at the 2012 parliamentary election the SP threatened the position of the mainstream parties and came to the attention of the press across Europe.[4] Yet since then it has largely failed to capitalise on such dramatic growth in parliamentary election opinion polls, notwithstanding success at the 2015 provincial elections. One of this chapter's key questions is why the SP has been unable to significantly expand its support during the economic crisis?

Indeed, this chapter shows that the SP's responses to the Great Recession and the disappointment following its 2012 election defeat have been characterised by continuity rather than change. The SP still maintains moderate policies as it searches for a way to gain inclusion in a governing coalition. It has shown itself to be more willing to compromise with centre-right parties in coalition formation at the local level. Such a consistently pragmatic approach to entering office is somewhat unusual for an RLP. Nevertheless, a slight recalibration vis-à-vis the party's relationship with the social democratic Labour Party (*Partij van de Arbeid*, PvdA) can be identified after their rivals entered government in 2012. The SP has been more critical of the PvdA for implementing austerity measures and breaking campaign commitments. It is significant, however, that this change resulted largely from changes in the SP's external environment rather than from a significant change within the party itself.

THE RISE OF THE SP

The SP formed in 1972 from a Maoist splinter group of the Communist Party of the Netherlands. It soon broke with Mao but remained Marxist-Leninist into the late 1980s. This sect of around 500 members was transformed by a handful of powerful local councillors under the leadership of the charismatic Jan Marijnissen to become the third largest party in the Netherlands in 2006 with over 50,000 members and 25 MPs. There have been three main stages in the 'Long March of the SP'.[5] First, following the collapse of communism, the SP's leaders pursued a vote-seeking strategy by abandoning Marxism-Leninism and the nationalisation of the means of production for a vague brand of socialism in 1991.[6] The SP sought to set itself apart from the political establishment and a populist 'Vote Against!' slogan and the image of a tomato (as thrown by its activists) now symbolised its oppositional role.[7] It offered something different through providing direct help for workers; its activists campaigned actively to talk to the 'ordinary people'; and elected officials paid a large proportion of their wages to the party, so that they lived on a normal wage.[8]

After the SP gained its first national parliamentary seats in 1994, a second stage in its development began. The PvdA broke tradition by pursuing allegedly neoliberal policies under Ruud Lubbers' (1989–1994) and Wim Kok's 'Purple Governments' (1994–2002).[9] This provided the SP with an opportune

Table 8.1   Dutch Parliamentary Election Results

	1998	2002	2003	2006	2010	2012
Labour (PvdA)	29.0	15.1	27.3	21.2	19.6	24.9
Liberals (VVD)	24.7	15.4	17.9	14.6	20.5	26.6
Chr. Democrats (CDA)	18.4	27.9	28.6	26.5	13.6	8.5
Democrats 66 (D66)	9.0	5.1	4.1	2.0	7.0	8.0
GroenLinks	7.3	7.0	5.1	4.6	6.7	2.3
SP	3.5	5.9	6.3	16.6	9.9	9.7
Christian Union (CU)	3.2	2.5	2.1	4.0	3.2	3.1
Freedom Party (PVV)				5.9	15.5	10.1

Source: DNPP. 'Socialistische Partij', available at: http://dnpp.ub.rug.nl/dnpp/pp/sp, 2015.

moment to moderate as its leaders re-positioned the party as a credible alternative for disaffected PvdA supporters.[10] They moved away from commitments to socialism, the planned economy and abolishing capitalism towards vaguer concepts of human dignity, equality and solidarity. During the late 1990s the SP increasingly focused on criticising neoliberalism, welfare cuts and privatisations.[11] This led to the party combining more moderate appeals with activism, radical left credentials and opposition to European integration to provide 'social democracy plus'.[12] The SP's new moderate approach saw it drop opposition to NATO and the Dutch royal family. Moreover, the SP's central role in campaigning for the 'No' vote in the referendum on the European Constitution in 2005 helped it win over supporters from the PvdA and GreenLeft (*GroenLinks*). This strategy saw the SP expand its electoral support (see Table 8.1).

Third, having expanded and gained experience of administration at local and provincial levels, the SP's leaders adopted an office-seeking strategy, changing the party's slogan to 'Vote For, Vote SP'. In 2006, the SP's' more moderate programme demanded 'A better Netherlands for the same money'.[13] In line with this approach, in the years running up to the crisis, the SP made Eurosceptic appeals that criticised the neoliberal basis of European integration and called for a slimmed down, social Europe. This would be based on limits to the EU budget and reductions in Dutch contributions to the EU. The SP also rejected restrictions on national level budgets under the Stability and Growth Pact (SGP). It called for powers to be returned to national parliaments while expanding the power of the European Parliament vis-à-vis the unelected and bureaucratic European Commission.[14]

THE ECONOMIC CRISIS IN THE NETHERLANDS

The 2008 crisis had major political consequences in the Netherlands and the SP encountered significant opportunities to pursuing its policy of trying to win over disgruntled social democratic voters. In 2007, the GDP of the

Netherlands grew by 3.7 per cent, but this fell to 1.7 per cent in 2008 before contracting by 3.8 per cent in 2009.[15] While an economic recovery appeared to take place, GDP again contracted by 1.1 per cent in 2012 and 0.5 per cent in 2013; subsequently, GDP has grown at approximately 1 per cent a year. Unemployment also increased from 3.6 per cent in 2008 to 5.8 per cent in 2012 and 7.4 per cent in 2014.[16]

As the crisis unfolded, Wouter Bos, the PvdA leader and the minister of finance in the Balkenende cabinet (consisting of the Christian Democratic Appeal [*Christen-Democratisch Appèl* – CDA], PvdA and Christian Union parties) rescued Dutch banks ING and ABN AMRO through implementing state purchase of their shares.[17] Amid a growing budget deficit, the government then proposed cuts of 35 billion euros that also involved increasing the age for receiving a state pension from 65 to 67 years in 2009.[18]

Following the 2010 election, the Liberal People's Party for Freedom and Democracy (*Volkspartij voor Vrijheid en Democratie* – VVD) and CDA formed a minority government that sought to implement this rise in the retirement age. However the government could not rely on its support party the right-wing populist Party for Freedom (*Partij voor de Vrijheid* – PVV) and concluded a deal with the PvdA, which won concessions for retirees on low incomes.[19] The PvdA and GreenLeft also supported the government over loans for Greece in 2011, which the SP and PVV opposed on the basis that investors rather than Greek and Dutch taxpayers should foot the bill. The PvdA continued to play an important role in supporting the government in passing legislation to tighten the budgetary rules of the SGP in December 2011.

Divisions over austerity measures meant that new elections were called after the PVV also refused to support large cuts to welfare spending in March 2012. However, with cuts needed to meet the Netherlands' SGP commitments of a 3 per cent of GDP maximum budget deficit and the European Commission requiring a new budget that May, the government negotiated for support from other parties including GroenLinks, D66 and Christian Union under a five-party agreement.

The economic crisis became highly politicised during the 2012 Dutch parliamentary election as the campaign focused on austerity measures and for the first time in a national election campaign European integration became a major issue. In particular, important debates revolved around austerity measures and the future of the welfare state as well as debt bailouts for Southern European counties.[20] While all parties proposed spending cuts, the VVD sought the largest cuts (€22 billion) and the PVV the smallest (€11 billion).[21] A major debate surrounded cuts to healthcare as the VVD sought to increase personal payments for healthcare, while the PvdA and GroenLinks called for such payments to be income-dependent. In contrast, the SP called for a more limited payment and the PVV opposed payments altogether.

The result of the election was the unexpected formation of a PvdA-VVD minority coalition government. Subsequently, the SP encountered new opportunities to criticise the PvdA as it negotiated with the liberal D66 and Christian Union parties to pass a budget with an additional €6 billion cuts.[22] The parties also reached an agreement to increase the retirement age and to pass a further €3 billion of spending cuts and to reduce tax breaks on savings for retirement. The PvdA had performed well in the 2012 election, in part because it did not support cuts made under the earlier five-party coalition.[23] In office, however, the PvdA has fallen significantly in opinion polls as it supported austerity measures including those to the care for the elderly. It faces a credibility problem having dropped its fierce opposition to the VVD's cuts and calls for a post Third Way 'back to the roots' reorientation of social democracy.[24]

Since the early 1990s, GreenLeft (the successor to the former Communist Party) abandoned its socialist principles for left-libertarian politics, making the SP the clearest 'left' alternative to the PvdA.[25] GreenLeft's support for austerity measures has helped position the SP at the forefront of campaigning against welfare cuts. Moreover, GreenLeft's 'europhilia places it on the wrong side of the fence'.[26] Instead, the SP's opposition to austerity measures appears to have more in common with that of the right-wing populist PVV, and the SP has claimed that the PVV has sought to 'steal' its welfare policies. The SP remained the only major party without government experience (or a support role) meaning that it cannot be blamed for the crisis or austerity measures. In principle, it should have been well-placed to offer an alternative in a context of high unemployment and a slow economic recovery.[27]

THE SP'S RESPONSE TO THE CRISIS

The SP's leaders maintained an office-seeking strategy, and tried to propose prudent and detailed responses to the crisis. The party's 2008 thirty-point programme on the economic crisis was written by Ewout Irrgang, a moderate member of its parliamentary group.[28] The programme adopted a traditional social democratic approach to position the SP just to the left of the PvdA. In the words of SP Member of the European Parliament Eric Meijer 'It was as if we were saying that we wanted the capitalism of twenty years ago, rather than to radically change the economic system.'[29]

The SP has clearly avoided engaging with the crisis in overtly ideological terms; it did not, for example, argue there was 'a crisis of capitalism' or 'show that capitalism is a system that the party is trying to combat'.[30] In 2008, the SP reluctantly accepted the need for the government to bail out Dutch banks because they were too big to fail, making it necessary 'to avert a bigger social cost'.[31] As one SP politician put it, '[First] ... we had to save the system and now we can try to change it.'[32]

Instead of radical social transformation, the SP has made rather vague criticisms of neoliberal economics, unregulated markets and a culture of greed for causing the crisis.[33] Its politicians claim that their long-standing critique of neoliberalism (understood as a socio-economic system that prioritises profit above human dignity, solidarity, the environment and democracy[34]) had predicted the economic crisis, giving them little reason for a significant change of policy.[35]

The SP has generally argued that austerity measures would damage the economic recovery because they were badly targeted and too severe. To symbolise the party's commitment to moderation, however, its 2010 election programme called for building 'a better Netherlands with less money' and it accepted that some cuts were necessary.[36] This strategy was continued in the party's 2012 programme, which called for a 'frugal' approach.[37]

Alongside cuts, the SP has proposed a rather modest €10 billion injection into the economy.[38] This stimulus package was based on social policies to create jobs through increased spending on renovating schools and nursing homes and investing in renewable energy.[39] The SP, however, generally opposed cuts to the public sector in response to budget problems that it argued were caused by the financial sector.[40] It claimed that its package would provide a deficit of 3.1 per cent of GDP in 2013 before eventually complying with European rules. Increased spending would also be offset against measures including taxes on banks, legalised soft drugs and property tax increases.[41]

The SP had called for more regulation of financial services for years and developed these policies through the international economic crisis. In the early stages of the crisis, its politicians believed that some SP policies were being incorporated into government policy.[42] Subsequently, however, the SP called for more far-reaching regulations to the financial sector, laws to ban bonuses that encourage risky speculation and the prosecution of bankers for inappropriate actions.[43] Proposed regulations have also included laws banning lobbying by the financial sector with EU institutions, separating banks' consumer and investment activities, and laws restricting the speed of financial transactions to reduce speculation.[44]

The SP has expressed solidarity with debt-stricken Southern European countries but opposed sovereign debt bailouts. Its politicians feared 'that tax money sent to Greece will not come back'.[45] Bailouts were rejected as a 'poisoned pill' that add to countries' debt burdens and line the pockets of German and French creditors rather than the people they intend to help. Instead, the SP argued for large-scale debt cancellation so that shareholders of foreign banks rather than taxpayers and poor states paid the costs. The party refrained from calling for the Netherlands to leave the Euro but called for 'two Euros' to let Southern European states fluctuate their exchange rates.[46]

The SP's Eurosceptic ideas provided a basis for its response to the international economic crisis. The SP's elites have criticised the introduction of additional funds that the Netherlands needed to pay to Brussels.[47] In response to such developments, the SP has reiterated earlier calls for reforms to democratise the European Union through increased use of referendums and the return of national sovereignty over social and economic policy.[48] There have also been signs of nationalism in the SP's response to the crisis. While the SP encourages a move to a German shareholder model whereby shareholders are kept at a distance to ensure long-term planning, the party's politicians have identified the German government and banks as being obstacles to solving the economic crisis.[49] The SP has also maintained its decision not to join the Party of the European Left and has not seen the development of formal transnational networks as a route to solving the crisis.[50]

Organisational Responses

The SP has undergone only a limited degree of change to its linkage strategies during the economic crisis. For instance, the party has long engaged in extra-parliamentary activism and during the crisis it participated in anti-austerity protests at which its activists handed out tomato soup. In September 2015, the SP joined protests by the People's Petition movement against healthcare cuts by PvdA health minister Martin van Rijn.[51] The SP also developed some links with the Occupy movement as its activists helped to organise Occupy Amsterdam in October 2011. The party began working with anarchist activists on the local level in The Hague to promote rights for refugees. Furthermore, the SP maintained existing links to anti-capitalist movements like ATTAC, and campaigned at G20 protest marches in London 2009 and European Social Forums (Malmo in 2008 and Brussels in May 2011).

Generally, however, the SP's leaders have seen social movements as being weak in the Netherlands in recent years.[52] Therefore, the party has placed relatively little emphasis on forging more sustained links with new movements such as new anti-capitalist, anarchist movements and Occupy in response to the crisis. As one leader argued, 'We are the anti-capitalist movement in the Netherlands.'[53] Moreover, as MP Sharon Gesthuitzen argues 'we don't go out of our way to make links with anarchists'; these groups are seen as too small to be influential beyond local level campaigns.[54]

The most significant change in SP organisational strategy during the crisis, however, has been in its leaders' attempts to strengthen links with trade unions to provide them with an alternative to the PvdA. In 2010, SP leaders met with the main Dutch trade union federation Federatie Nederlandse Vakbeweging (FNV) to discuss the crisis.[55] Thereafter, the SP organised protests with the unions against cuts to healthcare services in 2010 and protested with the FNV against austerity measures in November 2013 and April 2014. While the SP historically had weak links to unions and it still lacks much of an organised presence therein, an increasing number of union members are voting SP.[56] Such changes, however, proved unable to prevent an overall decline in membership during the international economic crisis. The SP's membership peaked at 50,000 in 2009; by 2015 this had fallen to 42,600 (see Table 8.2).[57]

There have been few calls for a radicalisation of policy during the crisis at SP congresses.[58] This is partly because the SP's centralised organisational practices give little room for discussion of party strategy or how to respond to the crisis at grassroots level.[59] The leadership has also appeared relatively united in seeking continued policy moderation. The more radical Trotskyist group Socialist Alternative joined the SP in 1998 but was expelled in 2009 for seeking to become a 'party within a party'. There have only been occasional calls for a change of strategy, including SP senator Anja Meulenbelt's resignation in 2014 as she called for a more radical and extra-parliamentary approach.[60] Generally, criticisms of party strategy have only come when small groups of radical activists have broken ranks.[61] Overall, there has been little sign of any significant shift in party strategy. Indicatively, while Sharon Gesthuizen and Ron Meyer, the candidates to succeed Jan Marijnissen as party chairperson in 2015, were from a younger generation of party elites, both pledged to continue the strategy of combining office-seeking with extra-parliamentary activism.[62] While Gesthuizen's campaign promised reforms to the SP's centralised internal structures, Meyer was chosen to succeed Marijnissen as party chairman.[63] Meyer's background as an FNV official may offer opportunities to strengthen the SP's presence in the unions but his victory does little to indicate that there will be significant changes in the SP's strategies in the near future.

THE ELECTORAL IMPACT OF THE CRISIS ON THE SP

The SP struggled to make the most of the opportunities it encountered during the crisis and was unable to sustain the success it achieved in the 2006 election (see Table 8.2). A major reason for this was that the party failed to find a successor to its charismatic leader Jan Marijnissen.[64] He had been the SP's leader in parliament from 1994 to 2010. However, after Marijnissen stepped down as the SP's parliamentary leader he continued to lead from the sidelines as party chairman until 2015 (a role he had occupied since 1988). Following disappointing results in the March 2010 municipal elections, Agnes Kant, his successor as SP parliamentary leader, resigned. Subsequently the SP lost ten of its twenty-five seats in the 2010 parliamentary elections under the leadership of Emile Roemer. It appears that most of these seats went to the SP's left-wing rivals PvdA and GroenLinks.[65]

Table 8.2   SP Party Membership

2006	2007	2008	2009	2010	2011	2012	2013	2014	2015
44,853	50,740	50,238	50,444	46,507	46,308	44,186	45,815	44,240	42,679

Source: DNPP. 'Socialistische Partij', available at: http://dnpp.ub.rug.nl/dnpp/pp/sp, 2015.

By the beginning of 2012, however, the SP had bounced back and was ahead of PvdA in opinion polls. Austerity and the economic crisis were the key issues running through the 2012 parliamentary election campaign.[66] The SP's strategy was shaped by its experiences in 2006 when it had sacrificed some radical policies, only to be excluded from a governing coalition by mainstream parties.[67] The SP's leaders perceived the need to go further in countering claims by rivals to that it was too radical to govern, which they feared might make voting SP appear a wasted vote.[68] The process outlined below reinforces the idea that the SP's long-term strategic goals have made it one of the most office-seeking and least radical RLPs.

During the 2012 election campaign the SP's leaders continued to moderate their policies with an election programme that made detailed and modest spending commitments of an extra €3 billion in 2013. The SP proposed few nationalisations other than bringing the rail system back under public control.[69] The aim was to highlight that it was 'keen to govern, willing to compromise'.[70] Therefore it presented a 'social route', rather than a socialist one based on increased spending on social housing, accessible healthcare and funding to fight child poverty. This approach was based largely on progressive social democratic politics including taxes on banks, increased tax on incomes over €150,000 a year from 52 to 65 per cent, and a separate property tax.[71] In particular, the SP tried to keep spending plans within the 3 per cent deficit rule, in order to gain a moderate score in the Central Planning Bureau's analysis of the cost of party programmes and thereby to show that it could govern within tight constraints.[72]

During the campaign, some SP politicians even called for the party to change its name to show it had broken from its radical past and had become social democratic.[73] The SP made a major concession in accepting that retirement at 65 was no longer a sacred principle and might have to rise to 67 from 2020.[74] This was a considerable step back from earlier commitments for '65 remaining 65'.[75] The change took place after party leaders saw that support for the policy had fallen in opinion polls, which illustrates their commitment to electoral success.[76]

The SP also took steps to develop closer relations with other parties, forming a new electoral alliance or *lijstverbinding* with GroenLinks and PvdA. It was hoped that this would help the parties to win an extra seat in parliament through a technicality in the way that vote shares are converted into seats under the Dutch electoral system. This could have allowed them to combine any shared 'surplus votes' that had not been translated into seats. SP politi-cians also tried to remove potential obstacles to their inclusion in a governing coalition through hinting that they might accept market forces in healthcare and reforms to working rights in an attempt to forge links with the centre-right VVD. The SP also announced that it would be prepared to coalition with any party other than the right-wing populist PVV as governing was, in Party Chair-man Jan Marijnissen's words, 'a logical step in the development of the party'.[77]

It appeared that this strategy was going to be successful, and in mid-2012 the VVD and the SP were competing for first place in opinion polls.[78] Later, that summer, however, the SP and PVV were in the lead. Polls showed that up to 39 per cent of PvdA voters had switched to the SP and it looked as if the election might mark a major realignment in Dutch politics.[79] The SP held talks with the PvdA, which accepted the idea of governing alongside the SP, remarkable given that a radical left party has not governed in the Netherlands since the Political Party of Radicals (*Politieke Partij Radikalen*) participated in the Den Uyl cabinet (1973–1977). The big questions seemed to be whether or not the SP would enter government as the largest party and whether Emile Roemer would become prime minister with the SP set to win 35–37 seats in parliament.[80] SP politicians expected the party to govern and argued that SP ministers would comply with its rules requiring SP elected officials to donate significant proportions of their salaries to the party.[81]

A centre–left coalition was, however, unrealistic when most of the SP's increased popularity came from the PvdA and GroenLinks, leaving the three parties short of a majority in parliament.[82] The SP's support in polls col-lapsed during August as the PvdA recovered.[83] At the election the SP only maintained its existing 15 seats. Subsequently, the VVD and PvdA formed a minimum-winning coalition and the SP's leaders were left to argue that the PvdA had betrayed its voters by returning the VVD to power.

EXPLAINING THE SP'S FAILURE TO EXPAND

By 2012, it appeared that the economic crisis had provided the SP with an excellent opportunity to gain electoral success through appeals based on Euroscepticism and its critique of neoliberalism. For the first time it domi-nated much of a parliamentary election campaign. So why as Luke March noted, did it end up like a 'squashed tomato' in 2012?[84] Moreover, why has it struggled to expand its support since?

First, to some extent, the PvdA showed in 2012 that it was capable of shift-ing to the left or 'red-washing' its campaign to take away the SP's distinctive-ness. Indeed, new PvdA leader Diederik Samsom had a left-wing profile and campaigned on policies of protecting working rights and healthcare.[85] As one of the leaders of the SP's campaign argued: 'Labour copy and pasted our programme and leader.'[86] What is more, when the PvdA strongly criticised the SP, its campaign team failed to respond as they stuck to their strategy of trying to show they could cooperate with their rival to form a coalition.[87] Thereafter, PvdA politicians realised that the SP had no 'Plan B'.[88]

The televised leadership debates presented a major turning point in the 2012 campaign as PvdA leader Samsom was generally acknowledged to have outperformed Roemer.[89] Roemer was also criticised for being inconsistent when he announced that he would refuse to pay fines should the Netherlands break the 3 per cent budget deficit rule and then promoted the party's policy that it would follow the 3 per cent rule after two years.[90] These problems serve to highlight the difficulty that the SP has found in finding an effective replacement for its long-serving leader Jan Marijnissen.

The PvdA was also quick to criticise Roemer for being too inexperienced to be prime minister in a time of economic crisis.[91] As the PvdA Chairman put it, 'This is no time for experimentation, making Roemer a risk, and he would be unable to keep promises, for example of retirement at 65.'[92] Pollsters found that the PvdA's greater experience in office was central in contributing to the flow of votes away from the SP.[93] As Cas Mudde argues, undecided voters went for the mainstream parties at the last minute in a search of economic stability.[94]

Having gained a lead in the polls, the SP also appeared unprepared when other parties targeted their criticisms on it.[95] Similarly, it encountered considerable opposition in the media as newspapers highlighted its Maoist past and argued that it would ruin the economy and burden future generations with debts of up to 25,000 euros per capita.[96] The largest newspaper in the Netherlands, the right-leaning *De Telegraaf* ran alarmist headlines such as 'SP costs jobs' while business magazine *Quote* proclaimed, 'If Roemer becomes Prime Minister, we'll all move to Switzerland.'[97]

REASSESSING THE SP'S STRATEGY

The SP has now twice stood a chance of entering government only to lose out. It might appear surprising that the SP's inability to consolidate its support in opinion polls has, however, only been met with limited criticism of its leadership from party members. The SP maintained its centralised organisational structures following the 2012 election and there has been little room provided for discussing its failure to significantly expand in 2012. It was significant however, that members of the SP's elite and its Party Council did criticise the hesitancy shown by its election campaign team and the party's attempt to hide differences with the PvdA to the extent that the SP lost its distinctiveness.[98] The SP's leaders also argued that it was a mistake to campaign so strongly on the idea of their leader becoming the prime minister.

The SP's leaders also, however, rejected the idea of returning to more radical, niche positions. As one politician put it, 'If only 5 per cent of the public support policies then we will not support them.'[99] The party's elite did conclude, however, that it should pursue a new strategy of trying to weaken voter confidence in the PvdA. This saw them attempt to present the SP as a way to prevent the PvdA going to the right in coalition formation negotiations. We can also see this more assertive strategy being followed in the 2015 provincial election campaign, when Roemer argued that the PvdA had 'sold its soul' in working with the VVD to cut care for the elderly, introduce student loans and close housing shelters.[100] The SP's leaders continue to try to reach out to Labour supporters that are disaffected with austerity measures. The aim is to show that while the SP party is not that radical, unlike the PvdA it is sufficiently radical to offer an alternative to large-scale austerity measures.

In 2012, the PvdA was able to recover because it could claim to have no responsibility for controversial cuts under the 'five party agreement' in the budget in 2012.[101] It was also able to run a more left-wing campaign. Now, however, the PvdA appears more vulnerable to the SP's criticisms of its austerity measures and its argument that the PvdA 'talks left but goes right' in coalition formations.[102] The early stages of this strategy proved successful for the SP in terms of winning votes as it become the largest left-wing party in the Netherlands in the 2014 European elections (when it increased its share of the vote by 2.5 per cent) and the 2015 provincial elections as the PvdA's support collapsed.

By September 2015, the SP was gaining between 21 and 23 per cent in opinion polls compared with 9–11 per cent for the PvdA. However, by early 2016, the SP's attempt to expand appears to have lost ground, despite the ongoing weakness of the PvdA. While there has been little sign of parties to the left of SP, GroenLinks has managed to strengthen its standing in the polls.[103]

There were brief signs of more populist appeals by SP politicians in 2010. This occurred as they criticised the role of 'economic elites' for causing the crisis. However, this diminished and populism remains 'more of an auxiliary rhetorical device than an ideological core attribute' of the SP.[104] As Gerrit Voerman has argued, following Marijnissen's resignation as party leader, the SP's leaders have been less well equipped to make such appeals.[105] The SP's elites argue that rather than resort to anti-establishment appeals, the party needs to maintain its current policies to place itself at the forefront of election campaigns and to gain credibility through entering government.[106]

The SP's preference is for a left-left coalition with the PvdA and GroenLinks. While this remains unlikely for numerical reasons, the SP's relations with other parties continue to change. In 2012 the SP expressed willingness to open to coalition negotiations with any party other than the PVV and a coalition alongside the CDA might become feasible. While a national level coalition with the VVD may appear unlikely given the parties' disagreement over austerity measures, this did not prevent the parties forming an unexpected coalition government in Amsterdam in 2015.

CONCLUSION

The SP has been at the forefront of Dutch debates surrounding the post-2008 international economic crisis. Its criticisms of austerity and the direction of European integration have featured strongly in election campaigns. This chapter has shown that the SP maintained its primary goals, and continued to moderate through the economic crisis in line with its leaders' long-term office-seeking strategy. Its leaders were not tempted towards policy radicalisation during the crisis. The party primarily seeks 'to get enough votes to gain inclusion in a government coalition'.[107] The crisis has only had a limited organisational impact on the SP; however, it is developing a stronger influence in trade unions. Nevertheless, the party only had a moderate degree of success in developing links with new protest groups.

The major impact of the economic crisis on the SP can be found in terms of its election results and opinion poll ratings. The SP has enjoyed periods of expansion in inter-election opinion polls but again demonstrated that it struggles to consolidate such growth.[108] In the early stages of the economic crisis, the SP struggled to retain its distinctiveness from the PvdA while it avoided radical positions that might alienate social democratic voters. This led commentators to argue that by 2012, the SP had reached a crossroads and it needed to decide whether to move further to the centre or return to its roots as an anti-neoliberal protest party.[109] However, with the PvdA participating in a coalition that has introduced austerity measures from 2012, the SP's leaders have been able to present themselves as 'the real social democrats' and promoted a more critical approach towards their social democratic rivals. In this context, the SP's leaders showed that they retain the ability to adapt their party's positions to a changing environment. It remains to be seen, however, whether the SP will be able to exploit the opportunity it has to become the largest party of the left in elections to the House of Representatives (*Tweede Kamer*) scheduled for 2017.

NOTES

1. Luke March, *Radical Left Parties in Europe* (Abingdon: Routledge, 2012), 17.

2. Gerrit Voerman, 'Een politieke kameleon', *Vlaams marxistisch tijdschrift* 38 (2004): 48.

3. Daniel Keith, 'Ready to Get Their Hands Dirty: The Dutch Socialist Party and GroenLinks,' in *Left Parties in National Governments*, ed. Jonathan Olsen, Michael Koβ and Dan Hough (Basingstoke: Palgrave, 2010), 155–72.

4. Roel Janssen, 'How anti-euro sentiment is fuelling the rise of the Dutch socialists,' *The Guardian*, 15 May 2012, accessed 10 September 2014, http://www.theguardian.com/commentisfree/2012/may/15/anti-euro-sentiment-rise-dutch-socialist-party.

5. Alex de Jong, 'The Long March of the Dutch SP, Institute for Research and Education,' Working Paper 35 (2015).

6. SP, *Handvest 2000* (Rotterdam: SP, 1991).

7. P. van der Steen, 'De doorbraak van de "gewone mensen"-partij: De SP en de Tweede-Kamerverkiezingen', in *Kroniek 1994*, ed Joop Hippe, Paul Lucardie and Gerrit Voerman (Groningen: DNPP, 1994).

8. Keith, 'Ready to Get Their Hands Dirty', 157.

9. So-called because of the combination of the colour of the social democrats (red) and liberals (blue).

10. Gerrit Voerman, 'The Disappearance of Communism in the Netherlands', in *Communist and Post-Communist Parties in Europe*, ed. Uwe Backes and Patrick Moreau (Gottingen: Vandenoek and Ruprecht, 2008), 35.

11. Gerrit Voerman and Paul Lucardie, *Sociaal-democraie nu definitief verdeeld: Met volwassen SP is het adonnement van de PvdA opde linkse stem verlopen* (Groningen: DNPP, 2007).

12. Voerman and Lucardie, '*Sociaal-democraie nu definitief verdeeld,*' 1202.

13. SP, *A Better Netherlands for the Same Money. Election Programme 2006-2010* (Amersfoort: SP, 2006).

14. SP, *A Better Europe Starts* (Amersfoort: SP, 2006).

15. The World Bank, 'GDP growth', accessed 1 April 2016, http://data.worldbank.org/indicator/NY.GDP.MKTP.KD.ZG/countries/NL?display=graph.

16. Statista, 'Netherlands unemployment rate,' accessed 1 April 2016, http://www.statista.com/statistics/263703/unemployment-rate-in-the-netherlands/.

17. Paul Lucardie, 'The Netherlands,' *European Journal of Political Research (EJPR) Political Data Yearbook* 48, no. 7 (2009): 1131.

18. Paul Lucardie and Gerrit Voerman, 'The Netherlands,' *EJPR Political Data Yearbook* 49, no. 7 (2010): 1095.

19. Paul Lucardie and Gerrit Voerman, 'The Netherlands,' *EJPR Political Data Yearbook* 51, no. 1 (2012): 215.

20. Stijn van Kessel and Saskia Hollander, 'Europe and the Dutch Parliamentary Election September 2012', in *European Parties, Elections and Referendums Briefing Paper* 71 (Sussex: Sussex European Institute, 2012).

21. Simon Otjes and Gerrit Voerman, 'The Netherlands,', *EJPR Political Data Yearbook* 52, no. 1 (2013): 1624.

22. Simon Otjes and Gerrit Voerman, 'The Netherlands,', *EJPR Political Data Yearbook* 53, no. 1 (2014): 234.

23. Otjes and Voerman, 'The Netherlands', 2013, 165.

24. Rene Cuperis, 'Electoral bloodbath for Dutch Labour,' *Policy Network* 26 March 2014, accessed 10 August, 2015, http://www.policy-network.net/pno_detail.aspx?ID=4604&title=Electoral-bloodbath-for-Dutch-Labour-.

25. Keith, 'Ready to Get Their Hands Dirty', 163.

26. Daniel Finn, 'Order Reigns in the Hague,' *New Left Review*, 77, 2012.

27. Eurostat 'Unemployment Statistics', Eurostat accessed 1 September, 2015, http://ec.europa.eu/eurostat/statistics-explained/index.php/Unemployment_statistics. World Bank GDP Growth Rate, World Bank, accessed 1 September 2015, http://data. worldbank.org/indicator/NY.GDP.MKTP.KD.ZG/countries/NL?display=graph.

28. SP, *Lessons from the Credit Crisis* (Amersfoort: SP, 2008).

29. Interview with Eric Meijer, SP party functionary, former MEP, 15 April 2013.

30. Interview with Frank Futselaar, SP Local Councillor, 10 April 2013.

31. Interview with Tiny Kox, Senator, member of the SP's 2012 election campaign, 25 April 2013.

32. Futselaar Interview.

33. SP, *Nieuw Vertrouwen*.

34. Teun Pauwels, *Populism in Western Europe: Comparing Belgium, Germany and the Netherlands* (Abingdon: Routledge, 2014), 131.

35. Interview with Arjan Vliegenthart, Senator, Political scientist and member of the SP's 2012 election campaign team, 3 May 2013.

36. SP, *Better Netherlands for Less Money: Election Programme 2011-2015* (Amersfoort, SP, 2010), 5.

37. See SP, Nieuw Vertrouwen: Verkiezingsprogramma 2013–2017 (Amersfoort: SP, 2012).

38. SP, *Crisis Plan SP: A new course for Netherlands* (Amersfoort: SP, 2009).

39. SP, *Lessons from the Credit Crisis*, 5.

40. SP, *Nieuw Vertrouwen*.

41. SP, *Crisis Plan SP: A New Course for Netherlands*.

42. Kox interview.

43. SP, 'Bonusverbod Voor alle Banken en Verzekeraars', 31 January 2012, accessed 1 September 2015, http://www.sp.nl/nieuwsberichten/11251/120131-pvda_en_sp_bonusverbod_voor_alle_banken_en_verzekeraars.html.

44. SP, 'Crisis Plan SP; Dennis De Jong Europese Bankenwetgeving Gatenkas', 16 April 2013, accessed 1 September 2015, https://www.sp.nl/nieuws/2013/04/jong-europese-bankenwetgeving-gatenkaas.

45. SP, 'Bonusverbod Voor alle Banken en Verzekeraars', 2012.

46. Dennis de Jong, *The Euro has a plan B, SP,* accessed 20 September 2014, http://www.sp.nl/nieuwsberichten/8151/101123-de_jong_de_euro_heeft_plan_b_nodig.html.

47. Metro news Roemer: Kabinet wist van naheffing, accessed 1 September 2015, http://www.metronieuws.nl/nieuws/2014/10/roemer-sp-kabinet-wist-van-naheffing 26 October 2014. SP *Nieuw Vertrouwen*.

48. SP, A better Netherland for the same money: Election Programme 2006–2010; SP, 'De Jong wil referendum over Europese Economische Regering', 14 November 2011, accessed 1 September 2015, https://www.sp.nl/nieuws/2011/11/jong-wil-referendum-over-europese-economische-regering.

49. SP, *Lessons from the Credit Crisis*, 5.

50. For more see March, *Radical Left Parties in Europe*, 164.

51. SP, 'Kom naar de red de zorg demonstratie,' 21 August 2015, accessed 1 September 2015, https://www.sp.nl/nieuws/2015/08/kom-naar-red-zorg-demonstratie.

52. Interview with Hans van Heijingen, SP Party Secretary, 10 March 2015; Kox interview.

53. Kox interview.

54. Interview with Sharon Gesthuizen, SP Member of Parliament, 25 April 2013.

55. Dennis De Jong,' De Euro Heeft Een Plan B Nodig', SP, 23 November 2010, accessed 1 September 2015, https://www.sp.nl/nieuws/2010/11/jong-euro-heeft-plan-b-nodig.

56. De Jong, 'The Long March': 22.

57. Documentatiecentrum Nederlandse Politieke Partijen, 'SP ledentallen 1992-2015,' 25 February 2015, accessed 1 September 2015, http://dnpp.ub.rug.nl/dnpp/pp/sp/leden.

58. Meijer interview.

59. Keith 'Ready to Get Their Hands Dirty', 169.

60. Alex De Jong, 'From Sect to Mass Party', *Jacobin*, 10 July 2014, accessed 1 September 2015, https://www.jacobinmag.com/2014/10/from-sect-to-mass-party/. See also: Anja Meulenbelt, 'Afscheid van de SP- de lange versie', 5 August 2014, accessed 1 September 2015, http://www.anjameulenbelt.nl/weblog/2014/08/05/afscheid-van-de-sp-de-lange-versie/.

61. See Finn, 'Order Reigns in the Hague'.

62. SP, 'Kandidaat-Vooritters: Maak Kennis Met Sharon Gestuizen en Ron Meyer,' 14 August 2015, Accessed 1 September 2015, https://www.sp.nl/nieuws/2015/08/kandidaat-voorzitters-maak-kennis-met-sharon-gesthuizen-en-ron-meyer.

63. NU, 'Gesthuizen wil 'linkse en activistische,' SP in de regering', NU 30 August 2015, accessed 5 September 2015, http://www.nu.nl/politiek/4115846/gesthuizen-wil-linkse-en-activistische-sp-in-regering.html.

64. Clemens Wirries, 'A Party for the "Ordinary People": The Socialist Party of the Netherlands,' in *From Revolution to Coalition – Radical Left Parties in Europe,* ed. Birgit Daiber, Cornelia Hildebrant and Anna Striethorst (Berlin: Rosa Luxemburg Stiftung, 2012): 157.

65. Paul Lucardie and Gerrit Voerman, 'The Netherlands,' *EJPR Political Data Yearbook* 50, no. 7 (2011): 1071.

66. van Kessel and Hollander, 'Europe and the Dutch Parliamentary Election', 1.

67. Keith, 'Ready to Get Their Hands Dirty,' 162.

68. Will Wroth, 'Rise and Rise of the Dutch Socialist Party: New Perspectives for Socialism or naïve, hip, left parliamentarism?' *International Journal of Socialist Renewal*, 1 September 2012.

69. Wroth, 'Rise and rise of the Dutch Socialist Party'.

70. SP, *Nieuw Vertrouwen*.

71. Alex De Jong, 'Netherlands Elections: A Hangover Instead of an Earthquake', *International Journal of Socialist Renewal*, 12 September 2009.

72. Futselaar interview.

73. NRC, 'Harry van Bommel: SP-top overweegt nieuwe partijnaam'. 2 June 2012, accessed 1 September 2015, http://www.nrc.nl/nieuws/2012/06/02/harry-van-bommel-sp-top-overweegt-nieuwe-partijnaam/.

74. SP, *Nieuw Vertrouwen*.

75. De Jong, 'A Hangover Instead of an Earthquake'.

76. Meijer interview.

77. NRC, 'SP wil in cabinet en is bereid tot compromissen'. 1 June 2012, accessed 1 September 2015, http://www.nrc.nl/nieuws/2012/06/01/sp-wil-in-kabinet-en-is-bereid-tot-compromissen/.

78. Otjes and Voerman, 'The Netherlands', 2013.

79. NRC, *Peiling De Hond: verlies SP vooral door terugkerende PvdA-stemmers*. 2 September 2012, accessed 1 September 2015, http://www.nrc.nl/verkiezingen/2012/09/02/peiling-de-hond-verlies-sp-vooral-door-terugkerende-pvda-stemmers/.

80. NRC, *Buitenlandse media waarschuwen voor anti-Europa-partij van Roemer.* 30 August 2012, accessed 1 September 2015, http://www.nrc.nl/stevendejong/2012/08/30/buitenlandse-media-waarschuwen-voor-anti-europa-partij-van-roemer/.

81. NRC, *Marijnissen voorziet 45 zetels voor SP*. 28 August 2012, Accessed 1 September 2015, http://www.nrc.nl/verkiezingen/2012/08/28/marijnissen-voorziet-45-zetels-voor-sp/.

82. Wroth, 'The Rise and Rise'.

83. NRC, *Buitenlandse media waarschuwen voor anti-Europa-partij van Roemer.* 2012.

84. Luke March 'Squashed Tomatoes – will the SP miss the target?,' Extremis Project September 10, 2012, accessed 1 September 2015, http://extremisproject.org/2012/09/squashed-tomatoes-will-the-socialist-party-miss-the-target/.

85. Finn, 'Order Reigns in the Hague,' 79.

86. Kox Interview.

87. De Jong, 'A Hangover Instead of an Earthquake'.

88. NU, 'SP had no plan B in campaign', NU, 13 September 2012, accessed 1 September 2015, http://www.nu.nl/.

89. Otjes and Voerman, 'The Netherlands', 2013.

90. De Jong, 'The Rise and Rise'.

91. NRC, *Buitenlandse media waarschuwen voor anti-Europa-partij van Roemer.* 30 August, 2012, accessed 1 September 2015, http://www.nrc.nl/stevendejong/2012/08/30/buitenlandse-media-waarschuwen-voor-anti-europa-partij-van-roemer/.

92. NRC, *PvdA-voorzitter: Nederland kan zich geen kabinet met SP permitteren*. 3 August, 2012, accessed 1 September 2015. http://www.nrc.nl/nieuws/2012/08/03/pvda-voorzitter-nederland-kan-zich-geen-kabinet-met-sp-permitteren/.

93. NRC, *Insiderspanel: kan de PvdA zich nog profileren ten opzichte van de SP?* 22 August, 2012, accessed 1 September 2015, http://www.nrc.nl/verkiezingen/2012/08/22/insiderspanel-kan-de-pvda-zich-nog-profileren-ten-opzichte-van-de-sp/.

94. Cas Mudde, 'The Dutch Elections and the Eurosceptic Paradox', *Open Democracy* 2012, accessed 1 September 2015, http://www.opendemocracy.net/cas-mudde/dutch-elections-and-eurosceptic-paradox.

95. NRC, *Roemer onder vuur om 'rabiate standpunten' over begrotingstekort*, 16 August 2012, accessed 1 September 2015, http://www.nrc.nl/verkiezingen/2012/08/16/roemer-onder-vuur-om-eu-dreigement/.

96. Wroth, 'Rise and Rise'.

97. NRC, *Wientjes noemt SP-programma rampzalig,* 25 August 2012, accessed 1 September 2015, http://www.nrc.nl/verkiezingen/2012/08/25/wientjes-noemt-sp-programma-rampzalig/.

98. Meijer interview.

99. Meijer interview.

100. Metro, 'Roemer (SP): PvdA onbetrouwbaar en ongeloofwaardig,' *Metro,* 31 January 2015, accessed 1 September 2015, http://www.metronieuws.nl/binnenland/2015/01/roemer-sp-pvda-onbetrouwbaar-en-ongeloofwaardig.

101. Otjes and Voerman, 'The Netherlands,' 2013.

102. 'Roemer: Samsom is ongeloofwaardig,' *Telegraaf,* 17 March 2015, accessed 1 September, 2015: http://www.telegraaf.nl/verkiezingen/ps2015/23813194/___Samsom_is_ongeloofwaardig___.html.

103. Peil 2016, The Netherlands Poll 10 April 2016. Paeil.nl, accessed 11 April 2016, http://www.electograph.com/2016/04/the-netherlands-april-2016-peilnl-poll_10.html.

104. Stijn van Kessel, 'Dutch populism during the crisis', *European Populism in the Shadow of the Great Recession* (ECPR, 2015) 122.

105. Giorgos Katsambekis, 'Left Wing Populism and the Dutch SP: An interview with Professor Gerrit Voerman', *Populismus Interventions* 2 (2015), accessed 1 September 2015, http://www.populismus.gr/wp-content/uploads/2015/05/interventions2-voerman.pdf.

106. Vliegenthart interview.

107. Kox interview.

108. Mudde, 'The Dutch Elections and the Eurosceptic Paradox'.

109. De Jong, 'A Hangover Instead of an Earthquake'.

Chapter 9

The Icelandic Left-Green Movement from Victory to Defeat

Silja Bára Ómarsdóttir and Andrés Ingi Jónsson

In this chapter, we explore the impact of the financial crisis on the Left-Green Movement in Iceland. A small and marginal party in Icelandic politics from its establishment in 1999, the Left-Green Movement (VG) was catapulted into government after the breakdown of the ruling coalition in January 2009. Working in a minority coalition with the Social Democratic Alliance from February that year, the two parties won an impressive victory in the late April elections, establishing a two-party coalition on the left for the first time in Icelandic history. Nevertheless, the VG's electoral results after four years in power were very disappointing.

We begin by providing a historical overview of the radical Left in Iceland, which traces its roots to the socialist movement in the early twentieth century. We then assess the way that the crisis unfolded in Iceland, how it affected the party system and the impact of the Icesave disputes and subsequent referenda. A section follows that analyses the experience of the Left-Greens in office and the way in which policies pursued by the left-wing coalition tested their commitment to remaining in the coalition. Before concluding, we analyse the longer-term impact of the financial crisis on the VG.

The VG had contested neoliberal policies in Iceland in the years before the crash; however, we argue that on entering office it found itself forced by systemic constraints (the confines of coalition, tight fiscal restraints during the post-crisis budget years and international pressures) to collaborate with the international financial system, in particular the International Monetary Fund (IMF). The party soon faced difficulties adhering to its commitment to social justice. Its achievements in office amounted to a piecemeal reconstruction of the pre-existing order, rather than any restructuring of the economy based on alternative ideas, such as the operation of state-owned banks.

In this chapter, we also show that the rapid growth in the Left-Greens' parliamentary group (from seven to 14 members) resulted in growing pains in the party's internal organisation. Subsequently, internal struggles within the Left-Green Movement resulted in a number of elected representatives leaving the party during its time in government. These representatives, as well as a share of the left-wing electorate, felt that the government had prioritised power over the protection of the 'average Icelander'. As a result, despite most economic indicators showing marked improvement at the end of the left-wing government's term, both of the coalition parties suffered significant electoral losses in the 2013 election. Yet the crisis has so far resulted in more continuity than change for the Left-Green Movement, which continues to operate with most of its former personnel at the helm, and has not made significant ideological or organisational revisions even after leaving government.

ICELAND'S RADICAL LEFT

Following intense public protests for a number of months in the winter of 2008–2009, early elections were called in Iceland. This led to a landslide victory of left-wing parties and the first purely left-wing coalition government in Iceland's history (Table 9.1). This coalition was composed of the Social Democratic Alliance and the Left-Green Movement, representing the country's Centre-Left and radical Left, respectively.

The Left-Green Movement was founded in 1999 by major players from the People's Alliance (Alþýðubandalagið), which started as an electoral alliance around the Socialist Party, itself a scion of the Communist Party (which had split from the social democrats in 1930). As Ólafur Þ. Harðarson states, a 'major characteristic of Icelandic politics in the twentieth century had been that the Social Democratic Party was one of the weakest social democratic parties in Europe (usually obtaining around 14 per cent of the vote) while the [People's Alliance] was able to take advantage of Iceland's proportional electoral system [and} was one of the strongest left socialist parties (gaining around 17 per cent of the votes)'.[1] Between 1983 and 1999 the Women's List also had a significant level of representation in Parliament, however, as Table 9.1 shows, the parties of the Left fell far short of a majority until 2009.

Despite the electoral weakness of the left-wing parties, the People's Alliance became a junior coalition partner six times from 1944 to 1999. Most often it was in a three-party coalition on the left with the Social Democratic Party and the centrist Progressive Party at the helm. These coalitions tended to be short-lived, and in one case a splinter group from the right wing was brought in to maintain power. The exception to this was in 1980, when the

Table 9.1   Left Parties' Vote Percentage

Year	Social Democrats	Radical Left	Women's List	Total Left
1963	14.2	16		30.2
1967	15.7	17.6		33.3
1971	10.5	26		36.5
1974	9.1	22.9		32
1978	22	22.9		44.9
1979	17.4	19.7		37.1
1983	19	17.3	5.5	41.8
1987	15.2	13.3	10.1	38.6
1991	15.5	14.4	8.3	38.2
1995	18.6	14.3	4.9	37.8
1999	26.8	9.1		35.9
2003	31	8.8		39.8
2007	26.8	14.3		41.1
2009	29.8	21.7		51.5
2013	21.1	10.9		32

Key: Social democrats: Social Democratic Party (Alþýðuflokkur), Alliance of Social Democrats (Bandalag jafnaðarmanna), Social Democratic Alliance (Samfylkingin), Bright Future (Björt framtíð), People's Movement (Þjóðvaki). Radical Left: Union of Liberals and Leftists (Samtök frjálslyndra og vinstri manna), People's Alliance (Alþýðubandalag), Left-Green Movement (Vinstrihreyfingin – grænt framboð). Women's List (Kvennalistinn).
Source: Authors' calculations.

Alliance joined a coalition on the Right, with a splinter group from the centre-right Independence Party leading the Alliance and Progressive Party.[2]

A reformulation of the left-wing parties in Iceland occurred at the turn of the twentieth century. This was an attempt to respond to the parties' consistent failure to build successful coalitions on the left through unifying the Left within a single party. Consequently, numerous parties, such as the People's Alliance, Social Democratic Party (*Alþýðuflokkurinn*), The Women's List (*Kvennalistinn*) and the People's Movement (*Þjóðvaki*) ran together in the May 1999 elections and finally came together to formally establish the Social Democratic Alliance (*Samfylkingin* [S]) in May 2000. Nevertheless, divisions had already become apparent, as individuals from most of the founder parties who did not approve of the founding of S established the Left-Green Movement in February 1999. While the two left-wing parties have come to share a commitment to social issues such as the welfare system and gender equality, they diverge when it comes to EU accession, international trade, and significantly, membership of NATO.

In particular, the Left-Greens oppose EU membership, as they believe the cost of accession would outweigh the benefits.[3] In their view, too much legislative power would be moved from Iceland to Brussels, resulting in a democratic deficit. The European Union has also been seen to represent the interests of global capitalism. The Left-Green Movement has based its policies on five cornerstones: Conservation of the environment; equality and social justice; a fair and prosperous economy; an independent foreign policy, and feminism.[4] At the international level, the Left-Green Movement is affiliated with the Nordic Green Left Alliance, a regional grouping established in 2004. However, it has not participated in the European Left Party, nor (not being within the European Union), the European Parliamentary group the European United Left-Nordic Green Left (GUE/NGL).

The two left-wing parties in Iceland have held similar roles in Icelandic politics throughout their many previous incarnations. The Left-Green Movement and its predecessors have been the more radical of the two and more likely to adhere to more ideological positions. Its parliamentary group, for example, has strongly opposed the sale of Iceland's energy companies to foreign competitors.[5] The Social Democratic Alliance has historically been the larger of the two parties. It is closer to the centre and more willing to collaborate with right-wing parties and it participated in a coalition with liberal-conservative Independence Party in the Haarde II cabinet from 2007 to 2009, up until the economic collapse.

During these years, the Left-Green Movement remained on the margins of Icelandic politics, with minimal impact on public policy and weak links to other opposition parties. As demonstrated by the Left-Green MPs' statements in Parliament and public, the party opposed the expansion and overheating of the economy,[6] and sought to alert the government[7] and the public alike to the dangers entailed in the operations of the financial system.[8] These warnings were largely ignored and media commentators and bankers frequently derided the party for raising them. Examples of this can be found as far back as 2003, when the editor of the *Fréttablaðið* daily noted that perhaps the Left-Greens needed more causes to oppose, as they were losing their campaigns against selling of profitable public banks and building hydropower plants.[9]

THE CRISIS IN ICELAND

When Iceland's financial system, which was dominated by three large banks, collapsed within 10 days in 2008, Iceland became a symbol of the international financial crisis. The banks had been privatised by the end of 2003. At this time their financial assets amounted to just over one year of Iceland's GDP; however, by the time of the collapse they amounted to nine times the GDP of Iceland.[10] The growth was high in risk, and the Special Investigation Committee, set up by Parliament to investigate the causes of the financial crash, stated: 'It is clear that the FME, the main banking supervisor, did not grow at the same rate as the parties subject to its control and, for that reason, was not able to fulfil its tasks properly.'[11]

The gradual privatisation of the banks was initiated by the government (composed of the right-wing Independence Party and the centrist Progressive Party) in 1995 and then implemented by successive right-wing governments. The electoral term from 1999 to 2003 saw some of the largest privatisations of banks and also of the national telephone company and several industrial companies. Nine enterprises were privatised in total.[12] The privatisations were carried out by committees that aimed to ensure the profitability and diverse ownership of the new companies. Nonetheless, the Special Investigation Commission report on the causes of the financial crash concluded that the conditions placed on the prospective owners of banks were weakened.[13] As a result owners lacked experience in financial services and had strong connections to the ruling political parties – Landsbankinn being bought by individuals close to the Independence Party and Búnaðarbankinn by people connected to the Progressive Party.[14] The banks, however, grew quickly after they were privatised.

Rather than decreasing public spending to cool down an overheating economy, economic processes were further exacerbated by continued state intervention, for example the construction of the Kárahnjúkar Hydropower Plant in the east of Iceland by the national power company Landsvirkjun. In the years leading up to the crash, unemployment fell as low as 0.8 per cent and foreign labourers were brought in to meet the demands of the market.[15] Most politicians seemed convinced that the boom would continue and warnings from foreign market analysts were largely ignored. In one case, a government minister suggested that an analyst needed re-education or had ulterior motives.[16]

The Left-Green Movement's MPs had previously made two major criticisms of the government's strategy for economic growth. First, they opposed massive state investments in heavy industry, and in particular the building of the Kárahnjúkar plant (the country's largest) which started in 2003, and of the associated Fjardaál aluminium smelter a year later.[17] Aside from the environmental argument, the Left-Greens argued that the electricity would be severely undervalued, with prices pegged to the world market price of aluminium, resulting in the state bearing excessive risk.[18] In 2005, the Left-Green parliamentary group put forward a motion to ensure economic stability through a moratorium on new large-scale, energy-intensive industrial projects.[19]

Second, the parliamentary group challenged the dominant position of financial services in the economy and called for a risk assessment.[20] In particular, the Left-Greens argued that the banks paid relatively low taxes and were under-regulated. In response to such criticisms the banks threatened to move their headquarters abroad. On one such occasion, in the autumn of 2006, Left-Green MP Ögmundur Jónasson argued that they could leave if they so desired to but as more favourable conditions were hard to find they were unlikely to do so.[21] However, positive news coverage of the banks outnumbered negative coverage by a factor of almost seven to one.[22] Jónasson was, perhaps unsurprisingly portrayed in the media as being out-of-touch and seeking to return to a form of pre-industrial society.[23]

The first signs of the collapse appeared in March 2008, when the Icelandic Króna took a steep dive in international markets. Government ministers (from the Independence Party and the Social Democratic Alliance) responded by touring neighbouring countries in an effort to reassure them that the Icelandic economy was not at risk. In March 2008, Ingibjörg Sólrún Gísladóttir, Minister of Foreign Affairs (and Social Democratic Alliance chairwoman), rejected warnings from Danish banks on the state of the Iceland's economy as being misguided.[24] In April of the same year, she told Danish newspapers that the banks could count on the full support of the Icelandic government.[25] At the same time, Geir Haarde, Prime Minister and Chairman of the Independence Party, claimed that nothing could be further from the truth than Iceland needing IMF assistance.[26]

The government was proven wrong within six months as Iceland's currency collapsed in value.[27] The government responded by seeking to secure credit from neighbouring states to prop up the currency.[28] The central banks of Denmark, Norway and Sweden entered currency swap agreements with the central bank of Iceland, on the precondition that the Icelandic government reduce the size of the Icelandic banks' balance sheets. An agreement was signed in May 2008, along with a declaration by ministers that these measures would be taken. However, 'the declaration was not made public, nor was it presented at a government meeting. The aforementioned promises by the government in the summer of 2008 were not kept.'[29] By late September 2008, these states stopped providing assistance and Iceland was left to fend for itself. The banks fell, one by one, within the space of ten days and the currency dropped in value by half. The government then turned to the IMF for assistance.

Consequently, within a couple of weeks protesters started organising; academic conferences were held, town hall meetings took place, and weekly gatherings outside the Parliament followed. Two of the major activist groups formalised during this time were *Opinn borgarafundur* and *Raddir fólksins*. Opinn borgarafundur ('Open town hall meeting') was a group of citizens who organised eight town hall meetings at which a range of experts spoke. Raddir fólksins ('Voices of the people') was an activist group which held a series of demonstrations each Saturday from 15 November 2008 until 14 March 2009 outside Parliament. Numerous groups worked within these venues. In response to the crisis, feminists, environmentalists, anarchists, as well as those who had previously been largely apolitical, converged on demands for political reform and calls for a 'new republic'.[30] Noticeable demands included the removal of the Central Bank's governing council and the board of the Financial Supervisory Authority (FSA), and a call for new elections.[31]

The government continued regardless until things started to change in January 2009. With the *Alþingi* (Parliament) scheduled to reconvene after a relatively long holiday break of nearly a whole month, it drew criticism for prioritising the legalisation of alcohol in supermarkets rather than fixing the economy. Subsequently, the protests grew and thousands protested at Parliament. In an attempt to disrupt the meetings of Parliament, the protesters took up suggestions on social media to bring pots and pans to bang on to the square in front of the house of Parliament, and the protests became known as *Búsáhaldabyltingin* ('The pots and pans revolution'). The protests caused a degree of disruption as MPs complained they felt unsafe and sessions were cancelled due to the level of noise.[32] The following day, the Reykjavik chapter of the Social Democratic Alliance called on the party leadership to leave the governing coalition and for elections to be scheduled for the spring.[33]

After the government fell, the left-wing parties formed a minority coalition, protected from a vote of no confidence by the Progressive Party. The two-party left-wing coalition was enabled because VG was untainted by previous participation in government. Moreover, S had also only served in government for two years and had been relatively uninvolved in the attempts to liberalise the economy. The minority government 'promised an election as soon as possible, welfare measures and support for indebted homes, greater emphasis on ethics and accountability in government, continuation of the IMF programme instigated by the previous government and, not least, the revision of the Constitution'.[34] This latter was a demand of the protesters, who argued that the existing Constitution had failed to prevent executive over-reach and cronyism in the economy.[35]

The Progressive Party's support for the interim left-wing government was conditional on guarantees that elections would take place no later than April, and steps taken towards writing a new Constitution.[36] The new government faced several challenges, including pressure to stabilise the economy, to respond to demands from the 'pots and pans revolution' to replace the boards of the Central Bank and the FSA, as well as to continue to collaborate with the IMF. Elections were held in April, and the two governing parties secured a combined 51.5 per cent of the electorate, which translated into 34 members of the 63-member Alþingi.[37]

FINANCE BEFORE WELFARE

The 2009 coalition agreement between the Social Democratic Alliance and the Left-Green Movement provides a clear indication of the parties' understanding of the crisis. It highlighted that the parties believed that the interim government demonstrated that they were suitable partners in a coalition and that they could cooperate to rebuild Iceland's economy and political system through promoting welfare provision and equality.[38] At the same time, however, the agreement suggested an adherence to the foundations of the capitalist system and stability. In particular, it emphasised the need for a credible economic plan and working towards a balanced budget, indicating that the coalition partners saw the situation as a crisis of capitalism, but not the end of it. The agreement also showed that the left-wing parties explained the economic result as a lack of transparency and corruption in the financial system.

Building on this theme, the coalition agreement expressly identified 'moral hazard' (when one party takes excessive risks knowing that someone else will bear the burden of those risks), as a significant problem in the financial sector before the crash. The new coalition argued that regulations were needed to counter such problems. However, despite this being the most left-wing government in Iceland's history, it is noteworthy that the first steps identified by the agreement focused on the economy and the financial system; the commitment 'to defending the welfare system to the furthest extent possible' was only the fourth item.[39]

CONSTRAINTS FACING THE LEFT-GREENS IN OFFICE

In the election campaign, Left-Green vice-chair, Katrín Jakobsdóttir argued that she would refuse to make easy promises. She stated that a mixed approach to the crisis would be needed, that included reducing the state budget on one hand and raising taxes on the other.[40] In office, however, VG struggled to manage internal divisions surrounding the nature of their coalition with the social democrats and the growth of their parliamentary group, from 7 to 14 members at the 2009 elections. A major consequence of the crash was that Iceland's government needed to collaborate with the IMF, a development that was ideologically problematic and divisive for the Left-Greens, and one that threatened to compromise the party's 'radical' identity. Some central committee members stated that the party should remain outside of government; however, the view prevailed that a left-wing government was needed to guide the country out of the crash and ultimately only five members voted against the Left-Greens joining the coalition.[41]

The IMF programme was linked to Iceland's willingness to comply with demands to settle the Icesave dispute. As Eiríkur Bergmann notes, the 'IMF would not consider [Iceland's] loan application until the dispute with the UK and Dutch governments over the Icesave deposit accounts was settled'.[42]

The dispute centred on whether the Icelandic government had to guarantee the deposits in the Icesave scheme (high-yield savings accounts offered outside Iceland by Landsbanki, which collapsed during the crisis), as it had done for domestic deposits in Iceland, or if they should fall under British and Dutch deposit guarantee schemes.

Considering the size of the Icesave deposits and the scale of the financial collapse, (which seemed insurmountable given the size of the Icelandic economy), the government went so far as to maintain a force majeure defence for not covering the Icesave accounts. Instead, it argued that the Depositors' and Investors' Guarantee Fund should shoulder the burden of the Icelandic part of the banks' collapse and cover domestic deposits. In autumn 2008 the government had agreed to negotiate with the foreign creditors, and the left-wing coalition continued this approach. However, a group, calling itself InDefence, formed and argued that negotiation with foreign creditors involved the unfair exploitation of Iceland's small size by larger, more powerful countries.

The leaders of InDefence helped to politicise the Icesave dispute in January 2009 when one member, Sigmundur Davíð Gunnlaugsson, became the chairman of the Progressive Party. The left-wing government (having taken over the negotiations in April 2009) soon became portrayed as an agent of foreign interests by the right-wing opposition in Parliament. While the government maintained that its main post-crisis objective was to maintain the integrity of the welfare state, critics regularly pointed at the Icesave agreements as evidence that the interests of global finance were higher on the government's agenda. Such criticisms were echoed by several VG representatives who voiced concern over the way that austerity measures were being used to offset the cost of settling the dispute.[43]

InDefence and the Progressive Party subsequently ran an active campaign in opposition to Iceland accepting responsibility for the Icesave accounts (the scale of this responsibility equalled roughly half of Iceland's 2008 GDP).[44] An emergency law had been passed right after the crash, guaranteeing the deposits in domestic banks. The law caused the UK and Dutch authorities, as well as one of the owners of Landsbanki, to believe that the guarantee covered the branches of Icelandic banks abroad, when this was not the intent of the Icelandic authorities.

After lengthy negotiations, a deal was brought back to Parliament in which Icelandic authorities provided a guarantee for the repayment of the Icesave deposit insurance if it turned out that the Landsbanki assets would not cover them. The deal was strongly resisted in Parliament and having been passed by a slim margin in December 2009, and with two members of the Left-Greens voting against the deal, the President of Iceland then vetoed it. This forced the bill into a referendum (6 March 2010), where an overwhelming majority of voters also rejected it. The government redoubled its efforts to negotiate a more agreeable deal, and by the end of 2010 a new version was presented to Parliament. It was met with more leniency by the parliamentary opposition, but was nonetheless rejected by the president before being put to another referendum. Initially, polls showed over 60 per cent support for the deal.[45] However, two months of intense campaigning by InDefence turned the situation around and it was ultimately rejected on 9 April 2011 by a 60/40 margin.

The Icesave disputes were not the only problem facing the Left-Greens in Parliament during this time. A major conflict surrounded Iceland's application to join the European Union. The Social Democratic Alliance saw membership of the European Union as a solution to the crisis. While the Left-Greens were opposed to membership, they accepted the application in the coalition agreement, which had recognised the differing opinions of the parties. This caused huge rifts within the Left-Greens, and from some of its MPs who were also active within *Heimssýn*, Iceland's 'No to EU' movement. Consequently, many disillusioned members left the party, claiming that the decision contradicted its core principles.

Secondly, the process of revising the Constitution became problematic. The Progressive Party had supported the minority coalition in early 2009 on the basis that an independent nationally elected body be put in charge of the process.[46] Subsequently, this body was tasked with exploring such options as converting to a more presidentialist political system, increasing the use of referenda, and with scrutinising the transfer of sovereignty to international organisations.[47] However, the Progressive Party's new chairman dropped support for revising the Constitution, which had by now become one of the left-wing government's main priorities. When the Constitutional Council presented its proposals in early 2011 these were resisted by both the Progressive Party and the Independence Party. The complications in the process also created rifts within the Left-Greens. After the Supreme Court ruled the election of 25 members to the Constitutional Council null and void, the government nonetheless decided to nominate these 25 individuals to the Council (February 2011). Some members of the Left-Green parliamentary group were unwilling to support this as they felt it would risk the rule of law.[48]

The Left-Greens faced numerous parliamentary rebellions as the government dealt with these issues. One minister, Ögmundur Jónasson, resigned in protest against the government's position on Icesave.[49] Other Left-Green members of Parliament refused to work with the government, claiming that the party leadership was breaking with its ideological foundations and undermining Iceland's interests. The same arguments were made when it finally came to the party's support for the EU application. While some Left-Green parliamentarians left the party, others remained but refused to toe the party line, thus weakening its cohesion in Parliament.

THE WIDER IMPACT OF THE CRASH
ON THE ICELANDIC LEFT

The financial crisis of 2008 had a pronounced impact on the Left-Greens and the social democrats. The parties explained the crisis with reference to corruption and a lack of transparency and sought to correct it through political reforms such as revising the Constitution and protecting the welfare state. Such an approach contributed to the electoral success that catapulted them into government in the spring of 2009. The inclusion of apolitical ministers (civil servant Ragna Árnadóttir became Minister of Justice and professor of business Gylfi Magnússon became Minister of Business Affairs and later Minister of Economic Affairs) in the minority coalition also demonstrated a willingness to look beyond traditional politics and to reach out beyond their traditional supporters.

The broader Icelandic political system also underwent remarkable changes following 2008. Intense demonstrations in front of the Parliament focused on a number of issues around the central theme of a politically reformed 'New Iceland'. New parties emerged and in 2009, seven parties participated in the elections. However, the 5-per cent threshold for parliamentary representation meant that the Civic Movement was the only new party to enter parliament. These elections were also held too soon after the crash for emerging parties to fully organise. However, by 2013, fifteen parties contested the election.[50] Yet only six parties secured seats, with the Pirate Party and a new centre-left party, Bright Future entering the Parliament for the first time, while the Civic Movement lost all the mandates it had gained in 2009.[51]

Entering government placed pressure on the radical and Eurosceptic Left-Greens to moderate their policy positions. To begin with, their senior partner in the coalition was closer to the centre and less willing to contest IMF conditions or to freeze the assets of capitalists associated with the crash.[52] The coalition declaration demonstrated that the goal of the coalition was to rebuild and not to restructure the state and the market economy. The government was also formally bound to collaborate with the IMF, which placed significant limits on the type of restructuring that would be possible. This was in sharp contrast to the agenda of the Left-Greens, who at their party congress in 2009 agreed that the Icelandic authorities should press for changes in the international financial system, for example by reducing the power of international corporations and democratising international financial organisations.[53]

Despite being the junior member of the coalition, the Left-Greens still managed to implement some left-wing policies. The party advocated the use of the tax system to reduce social inequalities through a more progressive income tax and imposing a wealth tax on individuals with considerable net worth. Companies in export industries which had gained windfall profits due to the collapse of the Króna were taxed to provide new revenue, and companies whose operations were based on exploiting common natural resources were made to pay a special resource tax.[54] These measures were successful in increasing the state's revenue, and reducing the need for austerity measures. Temporary adjustments were also made to compensate homeowners for an increase in mortgage interest rates. Overall, while the Left-Greens had previously prioritised policy-seeking goals based on radical left ideology, during their time in government it is safe to say that they presented economic stability as the primary issue to be addressed. The ideological foundation of the party's agenda was not entirely ignored, but it was clearly overshadowed by the need to rebuild the economy.

Having been in opposition in the years before the crisis, the Left-Greens benefited from having maintained a vocal and visible opposition to the financial industry in the 2009 elections. Yet it is clear that the VG was insufficiently prepared to enter government in 2009. The parliamentary group doubled in size, adding coordination problems as its MPs struggled to shoulder the responsibilities of governing. As a small opposition party, one of the group's strengths had been that its parliamentarians could operate without much consultation or interference from the leadership, but this became a weakness when the party entered government. Subsequently, a greater degree of coordination was needed to ensure support for the government. The small size of the party meant that it had a small number of party employees and activists, when most of them were pulled into working to support the government and parliamentary group, the party struggled to maintain its engagement in grassroots activism and campaigns.

With the party being the only one of the four large parties untainted by the pre-crash years, it gained new members. Some of the party's new members of Parliament, however, felt that they had been elected on personal terms and that they did not need to follow the party line. The divisions were not just within the parliamentary group, and became particularly pronounced at national assemblies and meetings of the party's governing council where the EU application was discussed. A vocal group within the party saw support for the application as a betrayal, and a group abandoned the Left-Greens and formed a splinter party, *Regnboginn* (The Rainbow). This new party stood in the 2013 elections but received negligible support (1.1 per cent), although it did draw some votes away from the Left-Greens. While smaller groups also left the party over a range of disputed policy issues to form their own parties, they gained little support in national elections. Nevertheless, these developments highlighted the problems stemming from the lack of internal cohesion in the Left-Greens.

Ultimately, the reforms pursued by the left-wing coalition government did little to enhance the popularity of the governing parties, despite evidence that the policy agenda had popular support. Both suffered dismal results in the 2013 elections. The VG has struggled to respond to competition from new parties campaigning on an environmental agenda, and from other parties who have also promoted feminism and gender equality. Numerous fractions and splits indicate that the Left-Greens face continued threats to their role as the main RLP in Iceland.

On leaving office, the Left-Greens faced several challenges. First, the parliamentary group shrank to seven members of Parliament. It thus seems likely that the party will require a three-party coalition in order to return to government. Such a situation would force the Left-Greens to negotiate a range of issues that would require the party to compromise on its radical programmatic appeals. While this may place added pressures on activists, the party's previous fissures mean that it is more unified, with potential dissidents having already chosen 'exit' strategies to form political parties that are largely ineffectual at the national level (at least so far). Conversely, those who remained active within the party throughout the 2009–2013 term were more willing to accept concessions and are likely to be more pragmatic if the party faces the possibility of forming a coalition following the next elections. Second, the party's MPs, including its chairwoman Katrín Jakobsdóttir, remain overshadowed by the previous chairman, Steingrímur J. Sigfússon, who is currently Iceland's longest serving MP and was previously in government from 1988 to 1991. Third, in organisational terms the Left-Greens have been unable to significantly reverse the decline in membership that began in office (Table 9.2).

In electoral terms, the Left-Greens have returned to a position similar to that which they faced before the crisis. Despite the current chairwoman's personal popularity, the party is not gaining support in opinion polls. Instead, the Pirate Party has expanded its appeal through its ability to claim to be outside the establishment. Having taken the helm during the economic crisis, the Left-Greens, at least for now, appear to be a part of the 'system'. It is possible that support for the radical Left in Iceland has returned to its 'natural' level of around 10 per cent. However, it is also possible that the Left-Greens'

Table 9.2   Left-Green Movement Membership 2010–2014

Year	Membership
2010	5796
2011	5132
2012	4975
2013	5048
2014	5189

Source: VG party office; personal correspondence, November 2015.
Membership numbers are only available from 2010 onwards. The membership count refers to party rosters at the end of the calendar year.

engagement in rebuilding, rather than reforming, the system when in government has done long-term damage to its electoral appeal.

After returning to opposition, the VG sought to reformulate its manifesto through organising a series of working groups on policy issues in the run-up to the party's national convention in 2015. While this process did not completely re-write the party's platform, it presented a significant update. The party's chairwoman Katrín Jakobsdóttir sought to emphasise its increased focus on the equal distribution of wealth, commitment to the welfare and education systems, and presented an ambitious plan regarding environmental and climate issues.[55] Furthermore, at the 2015 convention, a number of resolutions were passed that reaffirmed the VG's position as a radical left-wing and green party. The VG's resolutions ruled out oil production off Iceland's shores and called on the state to use its ownership of Iceland's largest bank to transform it into an ethical bank.[56] The meeting was more sedate than in previous years, but referring to such resolutions and policy changes, Jakobsdóttir described the party as having taken a sharp turn to the left.[57]

CONCLUSION

This chapter has shown how major social upheavals following the financial crisis of 2008 catapulted the Left-Greens into power for the first time. There, the party found it difficult to promote its radical goals. Participation in office also revealed weaknesses in the organisational infrastructure of the Left-Greens. A lack of cohesion among the parliamentary group proved to be particularly problematic and drew attention away from the policy issues that the party wanted to promote. The left-wing government sought to soften the effect of the crisis on the general population by reducing unemployment, reining in inflation and subsidising mortgage payments, and at the same time protecting the welfare system from the austerity measures recommended by the IMF.[58]

While in office, the Left-Greens were criticised for being subservient to international financial powers, rather than defending the interests of 'average Icelanders'. This caused disillusion among the electorate, and contributed to the sense that the party was unable or unwilling to promote its radical political agenda. However, the party remained substantially ideologically and organisationally intact following its involvement in government. Although a number of elected representatives left the party during the post-crisis period, most of the parliamentary group remains the same as before the crisis. While the party got a new leader in 2013 with the election of a new chairwoman, her personal popularity has not yet benefited the party. She had also been part of the leadership as vice-chairwoman for the previous ten years and the former chairman remains a visible member of the parliamentary group. The party's appearance therefore remains much the same. However the significant difference now is that, having formerly had the image of opposing the international financial system, the Left-Greens now struggle to overcome perceptions that not only were they captured by the system, but that they were active in reconstructing it.

NOTES

1. Ólafur Þ. Harðarson, 'Republic of Iceland,' *World Encyclopedia of Political Systems and Parties,* ed. N. Schlager and J. Weisblatt (New York, Facts on File, 2006), 576.

2. Stjórnarráð Íslands, 'Ríkisstjórnatal frá stofnun lýðveldis', accessed 30 June 2015, http://www.stjornarrad.is/Rikisstjornartal/.

3. Vinstrihreyfingin – grænt framboð, 'Friðsöm alþjóðahyggja', accessed 5 November 2015, http://vg.is/stefnan/fridsom-althjodahyggja/.

4. Auður Lilja Erlingsdóttir, 'The Left in Iceland', in *From Revolution to Coalition – Radical Left Parties in Europe.* ed. Birgit Daiber, Cornelia Hildebrandt and Anna Striethorst (Berlin: Rosa-Luxemburg-Foundation, 2012), 44–5.

5. *Eyjan.is,* 'VG með kröfu um riftun Magma-samningsins – Samfylkingin áminnt', 24 July 2010, accessed 5 November 2015, http://eyjan.pressan.is/frettir/2010/07/24/vg-med-krofu-um-riftun-magma-samningsins-samfylkingin-ihugi-sina-stodu/.

6. Ögmundur Jónasson, 'Staða efnahagsmála', 21 March 2006, accessed 5 November 2015, http://www.althingi.is/altext/raeda/132/rad20060321T140101.html.

7. Steingrímur J. Sigfússon, 'Umræður utan dagskrár (skuldastaða þjóðarbúsins),' 10 March 2003, accessed 5 November 2015, http://www.althingi.is/altext/130/03/r10160721.sgml.

8. Steingrímur J. Sigfússon et al., 'Tillaga til þingsályktunar um aðgerðir til að tryggja efnahagslegan stöðugleika,' accessed 13 September 2015, http://www.althingi.is/altext/131/s/1014.html.

9. Gunnar Smári Egilsson, 'Vantar fleiri mál til að vera á móti,' *Fréttablaðið* 20 January 2003, 14.

10. Special Investigation Commission, 'Orsakir falls íslensku bankanna – ábyrgð, mistök og vanræksla,' *Skýrsla Rannsóknarnefndar Alþingis* 7 (2010): 1.

11. Special Investigation Commission, 'Orsakir falls íslensku bankanna', 3.

12. Framkvæmdanefnd um einkavæðingu, '*Einkavæðing 1999-2003*,' Reykjavík: 2003.

13. Special Investigation Commission, 'Einkavæðing og eignarhald bankanna,' *Skýrsla Rannsóknarnefndar Alþingis* 1 (2010): 301.

14. Ingi Freyr Vilhjálmsson, 'Halldór og Guðni skrifuðu undir,' *dv.is,* 9 October 2013, accessed 30 June 2015, http://www.dv.is/frettir/2013/10/10/halldor-og-gudni-skrifudu-undir-4ZOMBY/.

15. Special Investigation Commission, 'Orsakir falls íslensku bankanna', 3.

188 *Silja Bára Ómarsdóttir and Andrés Ingi Jónsson*

16. Björn Þór Sigbjörnsson, 'Óskhyggja og fögur orð duga skammt,' *Fréttablaðið*, 26 July 2008.
17. Landsvirkjun, 'Fljótsdalur Power Station', accessed 5 November 2015, http://www.landsvirkjun.com/Company/PowerStations/FljotsdalurPowerStation/.
18. Vinstrihreyfingin – grænt framboð, 'Ályktun um stóriðju og virkjanir,' ályktanir landsfundar VG. (2001), accessed 5 November 2015, http://eldri.vg.is/wp-content/uploads/2013/02/%C3%81lyktanir-landsfundar-2001.pdf, 12–13.
19. Steingrímur J. Sigfússon et al., 'Tillaga til þingsályktunar um aðgerðir til að tryggja efnahagslegan stöðugleika.' accessed 13 September 2015, http://www.althingi.is/altext/131/s/1014.html.
20. Steingrímur J. Sigfússon, 'Fjármálafyrirtæki', 14 October 2003, accessed 5 November 2015, http://www.althingi.is/altext/130/10/r14143923.sgml.
21. Ögmundur Jónasson, 'Gróði og samfélag,' Ögmundur.is, 1 November 2006, accessed 30 June 2015, http://ogmundur.is/samfelagsmal/nr/2896/.
22. Special Investigation Commission, 'Appendix II,' *Skýrsla Rannsóknarnefndar Alþingis* 8 (2010): 263–4.
23. Viðskiptablaðið, 'Lausn að handan,' 30 July 2008, accessed 5 November 2015, http://www.vb.is/skodun/lausn-a-handan/15242/.
24. Special Investigation Commission, 'Stefna stjórnvalda um stærð og starfsemi íslenskra fjármálafyrirtækja,' *Skýrsla Rannsóknarnefndar Alþingis* 1 (2010): 216.
25. Elías Jón Guðjónsson, 'Mikilvæg skilaboð utanríkisráðherra,' *24 stundir,* 15 April 2008, accessed 30 June 2015, http://www.mbl.is/greinasafn/grein/1207015/.
26. *Mbl.is*, 'Kerfið fjarri því hrunið,' 22 November 2008, accessed 30 June 2008, http://www.mbl.is/greinasafn/grein/1256305/.
27. Vísir, 'Markaðurinn í mínus og krónan fellur áfram,' *Vísir,* 18 March 2008, accessed 30 June 2015, http://www.visir.is/markadurinn-i-minus-og-kronan-fellur-afram/article/200880318021.
28. Ingimundur Friðriksson, 'Aðdragandi bankahrunsins í október 2008,' *Seðlabanki* Íslands 2009.
29. Special Investigation Commission, 'Einkavæðing og eignarhald bankanna,' *Skýrsla Rannsóknarnefndar Alþingis* 1 (2010): 13.
30. Jón Gunnar Bernburg, Berglind Hólm Ragnarsdóttir and Sigrún Ólafsdóttir, 'Hverjir tóku þátt í búsáhaldabyltingunni?,' in *Þjóðarspegillinn 2010,* ed. Helga Ólafs and Hulda Proppé, (Reykjavík: Félagsvísindastofnun Háskóla Íslands, 2010).
31. Guðni Th. Jóhannsson, 'Búsaháldabylting? Hvaða búsáhaldabylting?' *gudnith. is,* 2010, accessed 30 June 2015, http://gudnith.is/efni/b%C3%BAs%C3%A1hald abylting_hva%C3%B0a_b%C3%BAs%C3%A1haldabylting_2010.
32. Lára Hanna Einarsdóttir, 'Ári síðar - þingið og byltingi,' *eyjan.is,* 23 January 2010, accessed 30 June 2015, http://blog.pressan.is/larahanna/2010/01/23/ari-sidar-thingid-og-byltingin/.
33. *Mbl.is*. 'Ingibjörg vill kosningar í vor'. 21 December 2009, accessed 30 June 2015, http://www.mbl.is/frettir/innlent/2009/01/22/ingibjorg_vill_kosningar_i_vor/.
34. Ólafur Þ. Harðarson and Gunnar Helgi Kristinsson, 'Iceland.' *European Journal of Political Research* 49 (2010): 1012.

35. Thorvaldur Gylfason, 'Democracy on Ice: A Post-Mortem of the Icelandic Constitution,' *Open Democracy*, 19 June 2013, accessed 30 June 2015, http://www.opendemocracy.net/can-europe-make-it/thorvaldur-gylfason/democracy-on-ice-post-mortem-of-icelandic-constitution.

36. Birkir Jón Jónsson, 'Stefna ríkisstjórnarinnar: skýrsla forsætisráðherra,' 4 February 2009, accessed 30 June 2015, http://www.althingi.is/altext/raeda/136/rad20090204T203725.html.

37. Landskjör, 'Úrslit kosninga til Alþingis 25 Apríl 2009,' *Landskjor.is,* accessed 30 June 2015, http://www.landskjor.is/media/frettir/Urslit2009_mai2009.pdf.

38. Stjórnarráð Íslands, 'Samstarfsyfirlýsing ríkisstjórnar Samfylkingarinnar og Vinstrihreyfingarinnar – græns framboðs,'. accessed 30 June 2015, http://www.stjornarrad.is/media/Skjol/rikisstjorn_8mai09.pdf, 2009.

39. Samstarfsyfirlýsing ríkisstjórnar Samfylkingarinnar og Vinstrihreyfingarinnar – græns framboðs.'

40. Alþingi. 'Störf þingsins.' 132. Fundur, accessed 30 June 2015, http://www.althingi.is/skodalid.php?lthing=136&lidur=lid20090415T103240.

41. Vinstrihreyfingin – grænt framboð: 'Ríkisstjórnarsamstarf með Samfylkingu', accessed November 5, 2015, http://vg.is/um-vg/flokksradsfundir/mai-2009/.

42. Eiríkur Bergmann, 'The Icesave Dispute: Case Study into Crisis of Diplomacy During the Credit Crunch,' *ECPR General Council* (2014): 3.

43. Guðfríður Lilja Grétarsdóttir, 'Ríkisábyrgð á lántöku Tryggingarsjóðs innstæðueigenda og fjárfesta,' 21 August 2009, accessed 12 February 2016, http://www.althingi.is/altext/raeda/137/rad20090821T203143.html.

44. FSCS, '£4.5bn Paid out to Nearly 230,000 UK customers – FSCS Reveals Icesave's Impact Five Years After its Collapse,' *FSCS,* 8 October 2013, accessed 30 June 2015, http://www.fscs.org.uk/uploaded_files/07_icesave_five_year_anniversary_08_10_13_final_pdf.pdf.

45. Vísir, 'Rúm 60% segja já við Icesave,' *Vísir,* 25 February 2011, accessed 30 June 2015, http://www.visir.is/rum-60-prosent-segja-ja-vid-icesave/article/2011702259957.

46. Halla Gunnarsdóttir, 'Stjórnlagaþing gæti tekið til starfa í haust', *Morgunblaðið,* 30 January 2009: 14.

47. Framsóknarflokkurinn, 'Ályktun um stjórnlagaþing frá flokksþingi', 19 January 2009, accessed 5 November 2015, http://wayback.vefsafn.is/wayback/20090403105814/http:/www.framsokn.is/Flokkurinn/Fyrir_fjolmidla/Frettir/?b=1,3719,news_view.html.

48. *Mbl.is*, 'Ögmundur ítrekar andstöðu við stjórnlagaráð', 26 February 2011, accessed 30 June 2015, http://www.mbl.is/frettir/innlent/2011/02/26/itrekar_andstodu_vid_stjornlagarad/.

49. Viðskiptablaðið, 'Ögmundur segir af sér ráðherradómi', *Viðskiptablaðið,* 30 September 2009, accessed 30 June 2015, http://www.vb.is/frettir/4369/.

50. Statistics Iceland, 'General elections to the Althingi 27 April 2013,' *Statistical Series, Elections,* 2015.

51. Ólafur Þ. Harðarson and Gunnar Helgi Kristinsson, 'Iceland,' *European Journal of Political Research* 52 (2014): 157.

52. *Mbl.is*, 'Greinir á um kosningar', 28 January 2009, accessed 30 June 2015, http://www.mbl.is/frettir/innlent/2009/01/28/greinir_a_um_kosningar/.

53. Vinstrihreyfingin – grænt framboð, 'Samþykkt á landsfundi 2009,' accessed 5 November 2015, http://vg.is/wp-content/uploads/2015/02/Landsfundaralykanir_2009.pdf, 10.

54. Philip Daniel et al., 'Iceland: Advancing Tax Reform and the Taxation of Natural Resources,' *IMF*, Country Report No 11/138 (2011).

55. Vinstrihreyfingin – grænt framboð, 'Stefnan.' accessed 5 November 2015, http://vg.is/stefnan/.

56. Vinstrihreyfingin 'Landsfundarályktanir 2015'.

57. Stefán Rafn Sigurbjörnsson, 'Tóku skarpa vinstri beygju á Selfossi', *Visir.is* 26 October 2015, accessed 5 November 2015, http://www.visir.is/toku-skarpa-vinstri-beygju-a-selfossi/article/2015151029193.

58. Björn Valur Gíslason, 'Besta ríkisstjórn lýðveldissögunnar,' 30 September 2013, accessed 12 February 2016, http://www.bvg.is/blogg/2013/09/30/besta-rikisstjorn-lydveldissogunnar.

Chapter 10

Struggling for Coherence

Irish Radical Left and Nationalist Responses to the Austerity Crisis

Richard Dunphy[1]

After the so-called 'Celtic Tiger' years of unprecedented economic growth during the 1990s and 2000s, the Republic of Ireland became the first Euro-zone country to officially enter recession in September 2008. The international financial crisis exposed three fatal weaknesses at the heart of the Irish 'economic miracle': over-reliance on foreign investment, a corrupt and unregulated banking and financial sector, and an overheated property market. As recession bit, unemployment in Ireland reached, by February 2009, its highest levels since 1967, and continued to rise thereafter, reaching 14.8 per cent by 2012. Large-scale emigration recommenced. Tens of thousands of families faced crippling negative equity as housing prices collapsed. The country became scarred by half-built 'ghost towns' – large suburban sink estates leaving families trapped in unfinished housing developments, sometimes without basic infrastructure such as connection to the sewage system.

This would appear to be fertile ground for the Irish radical Left. However, the main electoral fallout from the crisis would see a shift in the balance of power between the two big conservative centre-right parties – from Fianna Fáil (FF) to Fine Gael (FG). This chapter argues that, despite the emergence of a large and diverse anti-austerity protest movement, internal divisions on the radical Left, combined with the conservative nature of Irish political culture, would contribute to this outcome and ensure a rise in support for populist nationalism (Sinn Féin, SF) and for Independent politicians rather than any major radical left upswing. It is arguably these latter Independents that show the greatest potential for future radical left gains.

POLITICAL FALLOUT

When recession first hit, Ireland was governed by Fianna Fáil, a populist-nationalist Catholic centre-right party with strong links to the construction industry and the banking sector, in coalition with the small Green Party. FF's response to the crisis was to secure the Irish banks' position by guaranteeing their liabilities, via a National Asset Management Agency (NAMA), established in 2009 to take over major loans from the banks. By 2010, the cost of bank bailouts, NAMA and other government borrowing was pushing the national debt upwards. That September, following renewed bank failure, the FF Taoiseach (prime minister) Brian Cowen entered negotiations with the European Union, the European Central Bank (ECB) and the International Monetary Fund (IMF). In December 2010, Cowen signed the so-called Economic Adjustment Programme for Ireland with the Troika, which involved a three-year bailout of around 85 billion euros in exchange for a far-reaching austerity programme that slashed public expenditure. The most controversial aspects included cuts to spending on health, education, social welfare and pensions; a household tax (essentially an annual levy on every individual or family who owned their own home); and the introduction of bin and water charges. Above all, it would be the water charges that would galvanise opposition.

Since 2008, Ireland has seen repeated, and sometimes mass, street protests testifying to the unpopularity of the austerity programme. Students, pensioners, teachers, farmers, civil servants, police officers and taxi drivers are among the many groups that have staged marches and rallies, drawing many into political protest for the first time. For instance, 2010 saw trade unions holding one of Ireland's biggest protests ever with 100,000 participating, and some 40,000 took part in the biggest student march ever seen. In 2011, Occupy camps were established in Dublin, Cork, Galway and Waterford. In 2014–2015 huge protest rallies were held in many towns and cities against water charges. Radical left parties were prominently involved in the water charge protests, in particular.

Yet, despite this evidence of a political reawakening of at least part of Irish civil society, popular discontent has not resulted in a really significant political breakthrough for parties of the radical Left, although some important gains have been registered, especially in the period 2011–2014. The Irish Left has always been weak – electorally, ideologically and organisationally. There are many reasons for the weakness. Ireland has never experienced a full industrial revolution and the urban proletariat has remained numerically small and politically weak. Until the 1980s, Ireland was a largely agricultural country, dominated by a powerful conservative and Catholic farming lobby. Trade unions have tended to accept the leadership of a moderate and centrist

Labour Party – or even FF, which has dominated Irish politics since 1932, with its position often described as hegemonic. Furthermore, Irish political culture has been dominated until recently by Catholicism and nationalism, both of which have proven hostile to class politics. Radical energies have often been channelled into militant nationalism.

Moreover, Irish political culture has exhibited marked personalism – a tendency to judge politicians on their personal merits or popularity. This personalism (in turn facilitated both by the small size of the country and by the STV electoral system) also militates against the emergence of RLPs in two ways: even when voters are disillusioned with traditional parties, some such voters continue to vote for popular individuals within those parties; secondly, protest voters often vote for popular or charismatic Independent candidates rather than ideologically motivated parties. Indeed, Ireland's political system tends to reward individuals over ideology.[2]

The immediate and most dramatic casualty of the popular backlash against austerity was FF, which crashed to a spectacular defeat (and third party status) in the 2011 general election. Its Green Party coalition allies were wiped out altogether (see Table 10.1). Most disillusioned Irish voters, however, turned not to the radical Left but to the other two traditional parties, the centre-right FG and the centrist Labour Party. (To a lesser extent, the populist-nationalist party SF benefited, significantly increasing its parliamentary presence in 2011 and rising in opinion polls thereafter.) These two then formed a coalition government with the largest parliamentary majority in the history of the State – and proceeded to implement the austerity policies agreed to by FF in office. Local and European elections in 2014 showed a marked decline in support for the government parties, above all Labour, which has borne the brunt of popular anger over austerity since 2011 (see Tables 10.2 and 10.3).

Table 10.1 Summary of 2011 Irish General Election Results (with 2009 results for comparison)

Party	Percentage of Votes	Seats in Dáil	2009 Election Percentage	2009 Seats
FG	36.1	76	27.3	51
Labour	19.4	37	10.1	20
FF	17.4	20	41.6	77
SF	9.9	14	6.9	4
Marxist parties	2.7*	5	1.3	0
Greens	1.8	0	4.7	6
Independents	12.7	14	8.1	8
Total	100	166	100	166

Key: *Socialist Party (1.2% – 2 seats), People Before Profit Alliance (1% – 2 seats), Unemployed Workers' Action Group (0.4% – 1 seat), Workers' Party (0.1% – 0 seats)
Source: Author's calculations.

Table 10.2 Summary of 2014 European Parliament Elections in the Republic of Ireland (with 2009 results for comparison)

Party	Percentage of Votes	2009 Election Percentage	Seats in EP	2009 Seats
FG	22.3	29.1	4	4
FF	22.3	24.1	2	3
Labour	5.3	13.9	0	3
SF	19.5	11.2	3	0
Green party	4.9	1.9	0	0
Marxist parties	3.3*	2.7	0	1
Others and Independents	22.4	17.1	2	1
Total	100	100	11	12

Key: *Socialist Party (1.8%), People Before Profit Alliance (1.5%).
Source: Author's calculations.

Table 10.3 Summary of 2014 Local Government Elections in the Republic of Ireland

Party	Seats Won	Change from Previous	Percentage of First Preference Votes	Change from Previous
FF	267	+49	25.3	+0.3
FG	235	−105	24.0	−10.7
SF	158	+105	15.2	+7.4
Labour	51	−81	7.2	−7.0
Greens	12	+9	1.6	+0.5
Marxist parties*	31	+19	3.4	+1.2
Other minor parties	2	No change	0.7	+0.5
Independents	193	+71	22.6	+7.6
Total	949		100	

Key: *Socialist Party (1.2% and 14 seats), People Before Profit Alliance (1.7% and 14 seats), Unemployed Workers' Action Group (0.1% and 1 seat), Workers' Party (0.2% and 1 seat), United Left (0.2% and 1 seat). The WP subsequently gained another seat with the defection of an Independent councillor, bringing the Marxist tally to 32.
Source: Author's calculations.

Ireland officially exited the Economic Adjustment Programme in late 2013 and returned to modest economic growth in 2014. Labour hoped that this might allow it to recover ground before the 2016 general election (held on 26 February). SF hoped to overtake both Labour and FF. A total of 14 Independent parliamentary deputies were elected in the Irish general election of 2011, of whom a small number were left Independents who had chosen to agitate against austerity outside of formal party structures. By 2015, with splits and defections from most political parties, including both the small Trotskyist parties (the Socialist Party [SP] lost Clare Daly and the People Before Profit Alliance [PBPA] lost Joan Collins), the number of Independents had risen to over 20. The 2016 election saw a similar strong showing for Independents (see Table 10.4). It is therefore, timely to consider what contribution left Independents might make to a reconfiguration of the Irish radical Left.

Table 10.4   Summary of 2016 Irish General Election Results

Party	Percentage of Votes	Seats in Dáil
FG	25.5	50
Labour	6.6	7
FF	24.4	44
SF	13.9	23
AAA/PBPA*	3.9	5
Greens	2.7	2
Renua**	2.2	0
Social Democrats**	3.0	3
Independents	17.8	23
Total	100	158***

Key: *The two RLPs – the Anti-Austerity Alliance (incorporating the Socialist Party) and the People Before Profit Alliance – presented a single list at the 2016 election, despite publishing separate manifestos. Many left independents did not participate in this list.
**Renua and the Social Democrats are two new parties, of the centre-right and centre-left respectively.
*** In 2016, the number of seats in the Dáil was reduced from 166 to 158.
Source: http://www.irishtimes.com/election-2016/results-hub (accessed 1 March 2016).

THE IRISH RADICAL LEFT AND THE (NOT SO) LEFT NATIONALISM OF SINN FÉIN

Until the 1980s, there was never much of a class-based or Marxist Left in the Republic of Ireland and most Irish left-wing groups and parties struggled to come to terms with the legacy of militant, radical nationalism (republicanism). At various times in its history, the republican movement (a collective name for the IRA and Sinn Féin combined) has sought to expand its support by redefining itself as 'social republican' or 'left republican'. Such terms tend to indicate attempts to harness greater worker and small farmer support for the nationalist cause by emphasising wealth redistribution and social justice – not that the movement has abandoned nationalism in favour of 'socialism'.

'Social republicanism' has always provoked a mixed and contradictory response from the socialist (non-nationalist) Left.[3] For example, are republicans who seek to mobilise people on the grounds of national rather than class identity, and who oppose links between Northern Ireland and Great Britain rather than support class solidarity, part of the Irish Left? Some Irish socialists accept left republicans as a force for progressive change. Others argue that they seek only to manipulate social issues and workers' grievances to gain support for a nationalist and reactionary agenda. Given the rise in support for SF in recent years, this is a central issue. If one accepts SF's claims to be a left party, and of republicanism (or radical nationalism) to be a left ideology, then by definition the Irish Left is nationalist since SF outnumbers everyone else put together. However, if one defines the radical Left in terms of class-based ideology, or even anti-capitalism, and as being distrustful of

radical nationalism, then the rise of SF is not an advance for radical left politics but an obstacle. Sinn Féin is, quite explicitly, not anti-capitalist.

The SF issue has provoked contradictory responses from the two small
RLPs – the Anti-Austerity Alliance (AAA), led by the SP, and the PBPA, led
by the Socialist Workers' Party (SWP). Despite forming a united list for the
2016 general election, the parties were divided on what advice to give their
supporters on transferring second and third preference votes to SF. The AAA/
SP does not regard SF as part of the Irish Left and sees it as determined to get
into government office at all costs; it rejected SF's plea for a votes transfer
agreement. The PBPA regards SF as part of the broader progressive movement and endorsed its votes transfer proposal.[4]

The Marxist Parties

Until the recent agitation against Troika-imposed austerity, the most successful class-based Marxist party in the Republic of Ireland was the Workers' Party (WP) during the 1980s.[5] Although it emerged from the republican
movement, the WP abandoned republicanism and developed into a Marxist-
Leninist party along pro-Soviet lines. In effect, it became Ireland's communist party. It built up a solid block of local and disciplined activists and
reached 7.5 per cent of the national vote in 1989, winning seven seats in the
Irish parliament and one seat in the European Parliament (EP). However, the
WP split and declined following the collapse of the Soviet Union. A pro-
Gorbachev, or pro-Eurocommunist, majority formed a new party, Democratic
Left, which failed to achieve much success and merged with the Labour Party
in 1999. A hard-line Marxist-Leninist minority continues as the WP to this
day. The WP, during the 1980s, had radically reassessed its policy on the
European Union, moving away from opposition to Ireland's EU membership
towards accepting it as potentially progressive and campaigning for change
to the European Union from within.[6] Yet more recently, the hard-line rump
WP has reacted to the austerity crisis by moving back towards a position of
outright rejection of EU membership, reassuring hard-line communist allies,
such as the Greek Communist Party (KKE) that 'the EU is a centralised,
militarised, imperialist inter-state alliance which acts in the interests of big
capital and the monopolies'.[7] However, the WP has ceased to be of any electoral significance.

Nevertheless, agitation against austerity since 2008 has seen the re-emer-
gence of a Marxist, class-based Left of some electoral significance, above all
in Dublin, which is exactly where the WP has its greatest successes in the
1980s. This time, it is parties of a Trotskyist (not a pro-Soviet) orientation
that have tapped into this substantial urban reservoir of support for a non-
nationalist, class-based radical Left. There are currently two small Trotskyist

parties that have played prominent roles in anti-austerity agitation in Ireland, and have begun to reap modest but significant electoral rewards as a result.

The SP took its present name in 1996, prior to which it was known as Militant Labour (and before that, the Militant Tendency). Like its British sister-organisation, the Irish Militant Tendency was expelled from the Labour Party for 'entryism' in 1989. Reborn as the SP, it tasted some success in 1997 with the election to the Dáil of its popular leading activist, Joe Higgins. He held his seat for ten years, losing it in 2007. In the 2009 EP elections, the SP scored a real triumph in Dublin when Higgins polled more than 12 per cent of first preference votes, winning a seat in the Dublin European constituency (at the expense of SF). He sat with the GUE/NGL group in the EP. Higgins stood down as an MEP in 2011 and was replaced by the young party activist Paul Murphy. Higgins regained a seat in the Dáil, while Clare Daly won a second seat for the SP. However, Paul Murphy lost his EP seat in 2014; he was much less well known than Higgins and faced competition from a rival Trotskyist party (see below). There was, nevertheless, a significant compensation for the SP. In a by-election in Dublin West, its candidate, Ruth Coppinger, who had a very high local profile, polled over 20 per cent of first preference votes and won the seat, defeating strong challenges from both FF and SF. Arguably her victory proves yet again that, for Irish voters, the prioritisation of strong local appeal over ideology can lead to electoral success, even for a small, revolutionary Trotskyist party.

Further success came in October 2014 when Paul Murphy won a by-election in Dublin South West, where SF was expected to achieve success. Admittedly, Murphy stood under the banner of the AAA, a tactic used by the SP since 2013 to suggest that it stands at the head of a mass movement against austerity, but which most commentators, including ex-SP members, regard as nothing more than a flag of convenience for the SP. Without doubt it was the small Marxist party's involvement in agitation against the water charges, and its defiant calls for non-payment, that chimed with the working-class electorate of Dublin and led to its defeat of SF on transfer votes.

SF, preparing itself for coalition government and moving towards the centre, refused to back a non-payment campaign, with its spokesperson branding calls for non-payment as 'irresponsible'. Only in the wake of its by-election defeat did SF commit itself to abolishing water charges, while still refusing to back a non-payment campaign. As the *Irish Times* put it, 'It is probably the first election in recent years where Sinn Féin has had to deal with the fact that other credible contenders are capable of outflanking it on the left, in a manner as ruthless as it has targeted Fine Gael, Labour and Fianna Fáil.'[8] Indeed, the campaign against water charges has proven to be the lynch-pin of anti-austerity agitation in Ireland with the Irish Water Authority reporting in July 2015 that two-thirds of the population were failing to pay the charges.

SF's ambiguous position on the issue is symbolic of its reluctance to translate anti-austerity rhetoric into social protest that is so radical as to jeopardise its chances of a future coalition government deal with one or more of the mainstream parties.

The other small Trotskyist party is the SWP, which rebranded itself in 2005 as the PBPA. It, too, has been very active in the anti-austerity protest movement and in 2011 the PBPA secured the election of two members of parliament (TDs), Richard Boyd Barrett and Joan Collins. Bitter sectarian hatred between the two camps, both long claimants to the Trotskyist legacy, led the PBPA to field the popular Dublin councillor, Brid Smith, as its own candidate against the SP's Murphy in the Dublin constituency in the 2014 EP elections. This decision, together with the failure of voters for the two small Trotskyist parties to transfer to each other's candidate in sufficient numbers, cost the SP the seat (which went to SF), causing further political bitterness. The decision to split the Marxist vote appears surprising given the lack of any discernible difference in either policies or ideology between the two groups, but is explained by long-standing sectarian rivalry.

In the 2014 local and European elections, both Marxist parties ran vigorous, class-based campaigns, emphasising the fight against water and housing taxes, poverty and unemployment, women's and gay rights, environmental issues, class inequality and social injustice. The parties called for rent controls and a public or social house building programme; new taxes on the rich; and emphasised their fight for abortion rights in Ireland.[9] This message proved to have substantial appeal in Dublin, where the two Marxist parties polled around 13 per cent, despite failing to win a seat (see Table 10.2). Although the class-based Left only polled around 3.4 per cent nationally, in the local elections held on the same day as the European elections it achieved a solid core of local councillors (31 in all), including some 17 councillors in Greater Dublin, which promises potential expansion in the future (see Table 10.3).

For the most part, the ideological thinking behind both parties' campaigns seems to resemble classical Marxism-Leninism – old-fashioned class-against-class politics, rather than populism. An exception might be the rhetoric used in the water charges campaign that sought to oppose the rage of a victimised 'people' against the complacency of a corrupt political elite.[10] Yet such streaks of populism tend to be exceptional. For the most part, both Marxist parties are keen to emphasise what SP secretary Laura Fitzgerald calls 'our analysis of capitalism's rule [and of] the rigid class divide that is at the root of austerity and economic crisis and inequality' as opposed to SF's nationalist 'all class view' of society.[11]

Certainly, neither of the two Marxist parties consciously adopts populist rhetoric in the manner of Spain's Podemos party. For example, in a recent interview, Podemos leader Pablo Iglesias admitted that the adoption of a classically populist stand of attacking "'the Caste," privileged elites who have hijacked the power from the people' was a useful way of diverting accusations that the party is a classic radical left party, hidebound by the limitations of that tradition.[12] By contrast, both of Ireland's small Marxist parties seem willing to pay the price of stunted growth and influence if this means preserving their ideological purity as class-against-class Marxist-Leninist parties.

Despite their advances, both Trotskyist parties-cum-alliances suffer from a number of serious in-built problems that will almost certainly affect their potential for further growth and evolution. First, both see themselves as classical vanguard parties, despite their small size, and they tend to exhibit many of the dogmatic, sectarian and elitist features of such Leninist parties. For example, they stand accused by former members and by non-party activists in the social movements of seeking to rigidly control the social protests that they have been involved in – and of trying to destroy or discredit that which they cannot control.[13]

There is little or no evidence of any new ideological thinking as a result of the recent prolonged recession. For instance, in July 2015, one of the PBPA's leading theoreticians, Kieran Allen, penned a damning indictment of the Greek Syriza party's 'surrender' to 'a dysfunctional, imperial project known as the EU'.[14] Syriza, he wrote, had 'embraced a reformist strategy' and 'operates within the framework of capitalism … at the core of its strategy was a belief that the machinery of the state could be used to ameliorate the lives of workers'. It was now paying the price for its legacy of Eurocommunism: 'After the Greek crisis, the Irish left needs to drop any idea about the progressive nature of a social EU. It should note that Syriza was wrong to believe that it could combine an anti-austerity programme with support for the EU.' According to Allen, the Irish Left 'should make it clear that it favours the break-up of the EU in its current form and will seek its replacement by a federation of peoples based on democracy and control of capital'. Such views were echoed by the SP, which denounced Alexis Tsipras and the Syriza leadership as 'reformists' who have 'led the Greek working class to a significant defeat' through 'capitulation' to the European Union.[15] What is interesting about this analysis is that it could have been penned, word for word, by the Greek Communist Party – or indeed by the PBPA or AAA several years earlier.

Second, neither party has encouraged an influx of new members despite the obvious evidence that the impact of austerity has politicised and radicalised many Irish people for the first time. Both seem more concerned with maintaining ideological purity than with organisational expansion. Despite the undoubted opportunities that the past seven or eight years have presented for mass recruitment, the SP TD Ruth Coppinger claims a national membership of just 500–600.[16] This figure is hotly disputed by her former party colleague,

Clare Daly TD, who estimates the total membership at only 200–300.[17] Former PBPA (now Independent) TD Joan Collins estimates that group's membership at around '100 in Dublin with maybe the same throughout the rest of the country'.[18]

Third, both parties seem incapable or unwilling to tolerate internal dissent and have struggled to work together effectively – they have been prone to splits and splinters, forcing dissenters to choose 'exit' over 'voice'. In 2011, both parties, together with the small Unemployed Workers' Action Group (led by another Trotskyist) formed a United Left Alliance (ULA). This front had five parliamentary seats after the 2011 general election. If it had held together, subsequent by-election victories could have pushed its membership to seven by 2014. The ULA, however, fell apart in 2013 after the withdrawal of the SP. Both the SP and the PBPA then suffered splits, apparently driven by personal animosity rather than any major ideological or policy difference, with Clare Daly TD leaving the SP and Joan Collins TD leaving the PBPA. These two parliamentary deputies then formed a short-lived United Left party, which was never more than a flag of convenience, and by 2015 were in effect Independent TDs.

Learning the lessons of division and vote splitting to some extent, the two Trotskyist parties agreed a joint list of candidates for the 2016 general election but remained unable to publish a joint manifesto or to agree upon a vote transfer strategy vis-à-vis SF. The development of a formal unitary structures that might enable them to raise their profile must still contend with a legacy of great mutual antipathy and bitterness and a profound distrust of working with others. Moreover, in the case of the SP in particular, any strategy involving alliance or cooperation with Labour or SF, for example, has been explicitly ruled out. The SP is also uncompromising in its denunciation of the leadership of Ireland's main trade unions as 'class traitors'. This outlook presents considerable obstacles to the forging of durable alliances.

The Marxist Left has made some impressive, if limited, electoral advances in recent years. A solid tier of local councillors means that a larger pool of candidates from which future TDs might be drawn was available at the 2016 general election. In Dublin, and elsewhere in urban Ireland such as Cork, a class-based, Marxist alternative to the nationalist populism of Sinn Féin now exists, calling SF to account as it moves towards the centre in its desire for government office. Those are significant achievements. However, the lack of ideological or organisational innovation, the dogmatic inflexibility and internecine bitterness, and the small size of these parties mean that they are unlikely to generate the sort of new politics that many in Ireland are crying out for. It may be to the ranks of Independents (see below) that those in search of a new radical Left that is not driven by nationalism have to look.

Sinn Féin

Without doubt, the most high-profile anti-austerity campaign in recent elections has been that run by SF, which makes no claim to be a Marxist party. Nor does it usually describe itself as 'radical left' (unless addressing a European audience), still less 'anti-capitalist'. It does, however, describe itself as 'left republican'. It has combined calls for defence of national sovereignty and the 'Irish national interest' against any increase in EU powers, with anti-austerity rhetoric. This combination proved attractive in the 2014 local and European elections, and again in 2016. Indeed, given the nature of Irish political culture, it is perhaps an easier combination for many anti-austerity voters to identify with than the class-based political ideology of the smaller Marxist parties. The strongly nationalist theme was evident even in the title of the party's 2014 European manifesto, 'Putting Ireland First'. SF, moreover, is a well-known brand name, with deep roots in Irish history. The fact that that brand name is no longer associated with the deeply unpopular campaign of IRA terrorist violence in Northern Ireland has allowed many voters to feel more comfortable with it than with the small Marxist parties.

That said, SF remains vulnerable on its left flank, above all in Dublin – as the 2014 Dublin South West by-election shows. Its populist rhetoric against the 'corrupt political elites' loses credibility, both as a result of its own participation in coalition government in Northern Ireland, which has implemented austerity cuts, and as its ambitions to enter coalition government in the Republic become ever more obvious. Moreover, even though increasing numbers of Republic of Ireland voters seem willing to ignore the fact that SF has never withdrawn its legitimation of the IRA's past terrorist campaign, or accepted that 'armed struggle' was ever morally wrong, many others remain reluctant to trust the party. Its poor record at attracting second, third and fourth preference transfers from other parties has cost it parliamentary seats and perhaps shows that for sections of the electorate it remains a 'slightly constitutional' or 'semi-democratic' party.

SF has certainly run highly professional campaigns in recent years, proving that it now has a reliable thousands-strong core of party cadres in the Republic that can get its message across. Given its reputation for strong local activism and a strategy of deliberately embedding its activists in local community projects, the decision to hold the 2014 European elections on the same day as local government elections probably played in its favour and increased its ability to get its voters to turn out. In its campaign the party emphasised:[19]

- Decent wages, an end to zero hours contracts, legislation to protect the right to strike, and the need for social progress clauses in EU Treaties;

- Opposition to proposed cuts in the Common Agricultural Policy (CAP), arguing instead for a 'well-funded CAP' to protect the interests of Irish farmers;
- Strong support for small and medium-sized private businesses;
- Support for an EU-wide Convention to identify competencies to be returned to member states;
- Support for a reduction in European Commission powers;
- Support for more MEPs from smaller member states, and for smaller member states to retain their right to one Commissioner each;
- A pledge that the party would campaign for EU funding to promote Irish reunification by supporting cross-border integration;
- Support for attempts to utilise the European Union to put pressure on the British and Irish governments for a poll in Northern Ireland on Irish reunification;
- A demand for members of the Northern Ireland executive to participate in the Council of Ministers;
- A demand for upgraded recognition of the Irish language to create '180 jobs in the EU institutions for Irish language speakers for jobs such as interpreters, translators, lawyer-linguists'.

In short, SF fought a strongly nationalist and republican campaign, opposed to further European integration, in favour of rolling back EU powers in favour of greater national sovereignty, but with specific policies aimed at urban workers, farmers and the petite bourgeoisie. Many of these proposals were rather vague, however, and arguably not that radical. The manifesto is interesting for what it does not mention – there are no calls for an extension of public ownership, for example, and no mention of capitalism, or even neoliberalism. Throughout its campaign, SF explicitly rejected calls (such as those made by the Irish radical Left) for Ireland to leave the European Union, arguing that the European Union is potentially a force for progressive change. SF rejects the label 'Eurosceptic', insisting that it sees itself as Euro-critical, but not opposed to the European Union. It is also worth noting that the SF manifesto never once mentioned such words as 'socialism', 'socialist', 'left', or 'left-wing' and was the only European manifesto of a major Irish political party to make no mention at all of its EP grouping – in SF's case, of course, this is GUE-NGL.

However, the outcome of the 2014 European elections left SF in a position to present itself as the voice of the Irish Left in Europe and the main electoral success story as its share of the vote rose to 19.5 per cent, compared with 11.2 per cent in 2009. It won three seats as opposed to none in 2009. Without doubt, SF has benefited most from the anti-austerity backlash (after the Independents, of course). Its radical nationalism has enabled it to draw support from FF while its leftist rhetoric and anti-austerity message has proven attractive to former Labour voters. Despite polling significantly less in the local elections (15.4 per cent), it still scored a huge success, trebling its number of local councillors from 53 to 158. This provided a very strong launch-pad for further parliamentary success. Indeed, SF significantly increased its number of seats at the 2016 general election (Table 10.4), albeit falling short of its own ambition of becoming part of a new coalition government.

For some years, the SF leadership has aspired to enter coalition government in the Republic, as it has done in Northern Ireland since 2007. Of course, government participation in Northern Ireland has been alongside its once-derided Unionist enemies. The price for such a coalition has been criticism that it is losing credibility as it engages in the rhetoric of opposition to neoliberalism while, in government, it implements privatisations, hospital closures and public-private finance initiatives in the public sector. This 'collusion in austerity' has generated enormous strains within SF and forced its leadership to symbolically stall the Northern Ireland government in protest against new austerity cuts imposed by the newly elected conservative government at Westminster in 2015.

In short, despite the rhetoric, SF in government in the north has for some years acted like any other centre-right or centre-left party in Europe that has chosen to work with neoliberalism rather than going against the tide. One of the figures on the left of SF, Eoin Ó Broin, admitted that such redistributive and welfarist policies as it advocated in Northern Ireland remain within the 'same economic consensus on generating growth as the other parties'.[20] Yet, SF seems to think that government participation in both parts of Ireland can be presented to its supporters as tangible evidence of progress towards a united Ireland. From this perspective, getting into government on both sides of the border becomes a republican imperative, and overrides such concerns as its choice of coalition partners or the actual content of the policies implemented in government – as long as they are all-Ireland policies.

SF president Gerry Adams indicated to a special party conference on 21–22 June 2014 that he hoped SF would be ready to enter government soon: 'For our part Sinn Féin needs to be ready for government in this State on our terms, agree our policy priorities and political platform. Our commitments need to be deliverable. We are ambitious for change and believe we can deliver on jobs, housing and health.'[21] Interviewed on Irish radio shortly afterwards, he indicated that the one core principle that SF would not compromise on as part of coalition deals was 'a strategic plan for Irish unity'.[22] Any coalition of which SF was a part would have to be committed to pressurising the UK government into holding a new referendum on Irish unity. However, radical economic and social policies, such as a new wealth tax on anyone earning over 100,000 euros, would evidently not be a stumbling block to coalition compromises. Adams indicated that SF had not yet settled on such a tax and that it would be the subject of internal discussions.

Many on the left of SF, though reluctant to voice any criticism of the leadership, are concerned that a move towards the centre on economic policies might be the price for a coalition with FF. Eoin Ó Broin, for example, would prefer a coalition with Labour, the Greens and smaller socialist parties. Yet even this vision is not particularly radical as both Labour and the Greens have never been more than moderate centre-left parties and have track records of implementing austerity policies. The problem for this approach is that neither Labour nor the Greens trust SF, nor are they willing to contemplate any alliance. In any case, the parliamentary seat numbers have been insufficient to date. This SF strategy may lead to downplaying radical policies and left-wing rhetoric in the next few years and an emphasis on economic policies that are at best Keynesian.

There are certainly precedents for such changes. Frampton talks of how Gerry Adams moved the party towards the centre in the late 1990s, reassuring the business community that SF was 'business-friendly', urging multinationals to play a role in stimulating growth, and telling the Dublin Chamber of Commerce in 2004 that SF had no plans to raise taxes.[23] Former SF/IRA activist Tommy McKearney adds that Adams told the same meeting that 'Sinn Féin was not as socialist as its opponents claimed' and that he went on to defend its support for public-private partnerships in government while party policy was officially opposed to them – citing this as an example of 'pragmatic politics'.[24]

Ó Broin admits that pursuit of a coalition with FF led to the abandonment of 'left' policies in 2007 when SF made an economic U-turn on fiscal policy; it supported low taxes, offered no meaningful job creation or public finances policy and abandoned wealth/tax redistributive policies a week before polling day. He argues that such a stance alienated left-wing voters and contributed to a poor electoral result in 2007.[25] He claims that a post-election internal review left many dissatisfied because ideological and strategic issues were left unaddressed. Similarly, the party's relaunch 'in September 2007, under the heading Engaging Modern Ireland, contained a mixture of common sense and political spin, but again avoided engagement with the more substantive issues that lay behind the electoral disappointment.'[26]

Naturally, the collapse of the Irish economy since 2008 has afforded greater opportunity for anti-establishment and anti-austerity rhetoric, above all since the financial constraints imposed on Irish governments can be seen as a violation of national sovereignty. This has enabled SF to present itself as the opponent of austerity cuts and the Irish equivalent of Spain's Podemos, at least rhetorically: for example, SF MEP Martina Anderson sent a leaflet to constituents proclaiming, 'In Spain it is called Podemos, In Greece, Syriza.

And in Ireland, Sinn Féin.'[27] But the implication of the above is that the SF leadership may feel forced to restrain any really radical 'left turn' that could jeopardise its hopes for government participation.

Given that SF has always been first and foremost a nationalist and republican, rather than socialist or left, party, its sacrificing of social radicalism for advancing nationalist objectives is unsurprising. Nevertheless, it may provoke unease and possibly dissent within SF ranks. Some of the more left-wing members of the party would find a move towards the centre and the compromises undoubtedly imposed by a coalition-seeking strategy very difficult to stomach. The 2016 general election proved the most inconclusive in the history of the Republic with the prospects of new elections within a year or two giving hope to the SF leadership of further advancement towards government inclusion. But SF's participation in coalition in current conditions could lead to a loss of votes and members, above all in Dublin. This would of course create renewed opportunities for a non-nationalist radical Left.

ANOTHER POSSIBILITY: LEFT INDEPENDENTS IN IRISH POLITICS

We have seen that the Single Transferable Vote (STV) electoral system in Ireland combines with aspects of Irish political culture such as the emphasis on personality and strong local ties and the weakness of ideology to encourage the election of Independent politicians. Many such Independents are in reality former party members who have deliberately excluded themselves or provoked expulsion from their parties because they know that standing up against the central party leadership, in defence of local interests, will make them local heroes and guarantee re-election. Ireland has always had more independent members of parliament than most European democracies. On occasion, it has had more Independents elected than *all* other European democracies combined. In the 2011 general election, 14 Independent TDs (out of a total of 166) were elected. By 2014, with additional party defections, this had risen to 20.

Several Independents have been radical left-wingers who have seen no advantage to joining a party. In the 2016 general election, 23 Independents were elected, of whom at least six represented the anti-austerity, anti-capitalist Left. During 2011–2016, the parliamentary Independents included several prominent radical leftists: Clare Daly (ex-SP), Joan Collins (ex-PBPA), John Halligan (ex-WP), Séamus Healy (Workers and Unemployed Action Group, but effectively an Independent), and Thomas Pringle (who resigned from SF accusing it of a lack of internal democracy and of being insufficiently left wing). In addition to the authentic radical leftists, there were several

left-leaning Independents, for example: Finian McGrath (whose maverick
views include outspoken support for the Cuban government and who might
be described as an Irish *Fidelista*); Mick Wallace (campaigner against austerity and police corruption, and for women's equality – but whose credentials
as a radical leftist are somewhat undermined by his status as a successful
business entrepreneur accused of underpaying the revenue commissioners);
and Maureen O'Sullivan (a community activist who has campaigned against
the Transatlantic Trade Investment Partnership [TTIP], and against organised
crime). All were re-elected in 2016.

Many of the themes with which the left Independents are most strongly
identified – opposition to police, political and financial corruption; standing
as lone voices for the common people against an 'out of touch' party political
mainstream – are clearly given to populism. Certainly, Independents of all
shades have long been a source of locally based populism in Ireland. Resign-
ing the party whip in protest against an unpopular constituency-level policy
(e.g. a hospital or school closure) is a good bet for getting re-elected via the
STV system as a defender of the 'common people back home' against the
uncaring Dublin political elite.

Left Independents are certainly no less inclined to using populistic rhetoric
than those on the right or centre. The populist charge has been explicitly lev-
elled against the Independents by SP secretary Laura Fitzgerald, who argues
that this populism reflects the Independents' lack of a class-based political
programme and is an obstacle to the building of a major left force: 'The
obvious limit of being an Independent is how can one person, or a loose connection of individuals without any cohesive programme make fundamental
changes?'[28] Indeed, such an atomisation of politics and rejection of parties
makes it more difficult to forge a radical left alternative nationally. The proliferation of Independents increases fragmentation and diverts energies better
spent building a mass movement into a wide array of individualised electoral
campaigns.

Yet, it is also possible to see the proliferation of Independents as a contradictory phenomenon. It is from the ranks of left Independents that new
thinking, new ways of 'doing' politics and ultimately new parties may yet
emerge. For example, Clare Daly TD believes that the vanguard party is no
longer relevant and that if the radical Left in Ireland has a future then it must
be as the expression of a mass social movement, built from the grassroots
upwards.[29] Both Joan Collins TD and Thomas Pringle TD agree that a new
political structure is needed but argue that it has to emerge from within the
broad social movement, and build on that movement's new ways of doing
politics.[30] All of these TDs cite the example of Spain's Podemos – a new left
movement built from the base upwards – over Greece's Syriza – in their view,
a new party built from top down through alliances between existing parties,

factions and elites. They see the role of the left Independent as being to work within the social movements and with initiatives such as the Right2Water movement. This is an initiative backed by several Irish trade unions that, in 2015, held a conference to assess the future of the Left and published a list of principles for a progressive government.[31]

It is interesting to note that many of the Independents along with the PBPA signed up to these principles, but the AAA/SP refused to do so, seeing the initiative as too reformist. These left Independent politicians believed that any attempt to artificially create a new party from the top down in time for the 2016 election would be doomed to failure. Whether such a new party eventually comes to pass or not is, of course, quite another matter. But, it is interesting that it is among the Independent TDs that new thinking about the reconfiguration of the radical Left in the wake of austerity and recession is to be most readily found.

CONCLUSION

This chapter has argued that despite the fact that the Republic of Ireland has been one of the countries that has endured the full brunt of Troika-imposed austerity policies in recent years, producing widespread popular disillusionment with the political establishment, the radical Left has failed, to date, to take full advantage of the opportunities for ideological, organisational and electoral advancement. A large and diverse anti-austerity protest movement has yet to find its electoral expression. The small Trotskyist parties have made some progress, but these parties are hidebound by sterile dogma and sectarian political instincts and are unlikely to advance much further. Conversely, Sinn Féin has made very significant electoral strides, and this is likely to continue.

The advance of SF is not, however, a straightforward advance for the radical Left for three reasons. First, SF is primarily a radical nationalist party that raises social issues as a means to a nationalist end. Second, SF's credibility as an anti-austerity force is stretched by its record in government in Northern Ireland, where it has gone along with hospital and school closures, public-private partnerships, privatisations and various other 'neoliberal' policies. And third, SF's governmental ambitions are already leading it to moderate its policy stances in the Republic, exposing its left flank to electoral competition. In the words of one former SF representative, 'SF is not a left alternative because it is focussed on power as an end in itself, and will go into coalition with any party that will accept it.'[32] It is, perhaps, to the ranks of left Independents – the real issues of fragmentation and populism notwithstanding – that one needs to look for the sort of new thinking that might facilitate the emergence of a new radical left political formation.

NOTES

1. I acknowledge the kind assistance of Joan Collins TD, Ruth Coppinger TD, Clare Daly TD, Laura Fitzgerald, Thomas Pringle TD, Cllr. Eoin Ó Broin, and four other interviewees who requested anonymity.

2. Basil Chubb, *The Government and Politics of Ireland* (Oxford: Oxford University Press, 1970); John Coakley and Michael Gallagher, *Politics in the Republic of Ireland* (London: Routledge, 2010), 146.

3. See Henry Patterson, *The Politics of Illusion: A Political History of the IRA* (London: Serif, 1997).

4. Fiach Kelly, 'The Anti-Austerity Alliance and the People Before Profit Alliance', *The Irish Times*, 3 February 2016, accessed 3 February 2016, http://www.irishtimes.com/election-2016/the-anti-austerity-alliance-and-people-before-profit-1.2520628.

5. Richard Dunphy and Stephen Hopkins, 'The Organizational and Political Evolution of the Workers' Party of Ireland,' *The Journal of Communist Studies* 8, no. 3 (1992): 91–118.

6. Richard Dunphy, 'The Workers' Party and Europe: Trajectory of an Idea,' *Irish Political Studies* 7 (1992): 21–39.

7. Workers' Party, 'Contribution by the Workers' Party of Ireland to the 17th International Meeting of Communist and Workers' Parties', Workers' Party (2015), accessed 2 November 2015, http://workersparty.ie/wpi-contribution-to-international-meeting/.

8. Fiach Kelly, 'Sinn Féin has taken a hit on its exposed Left flank', *The Irish Times* (13 October 2014).

9. *We Can't Afford to Live: Shift the burden to the Super-Rich* (Dublin: Socialist Party European Election Manifesto, 2014); *Vote Brid Smith. Send a Working Class Fighter to the European Parliament* (Dublin: People Before Profit Alliance European Election Manifesto, 2014).

10. For accounts of populism that incorporate such themes, see Cas Mudde, 'The Populist Zeitgeist', *Government and Opposition* 39, no. 4 (2004): 542–63; Roman Gerodimos, 'The Ideology of Far Left Populism in Greece: Blame, Victimhood and Revenge in the Discourse of Greek Anarchists', *Political Studies* 63, no. 3 (2015): 608–25.

11. Interview with Laura Fitzgerald, Socialist Party Secretary, July 2015.

12. Pablo Iglesias, 'Spain on Edge,' *New Left Review* 93 (2015): 28.

13. Interviews with Clare Daly TD (ex-SP) and Joan Collins TD (ex-PBFA) and with two ex-SP members and two non-party social movement activists who requested anonymity, all July 2015.

14. Kieran Allen, 'The Defeat of Syriza and its Implications for the Irish Left', accessed 23 August 2015, www.peoplebeforeprofit.ie/2015/07/the-defate-of-syriza-and-its-implications-for-the-irish-left.

15. Paul Murphy, 'Why Syriza Capitulated and the Alternative Road of "Rupture,"' *The Socialist* 93 (July–August 2015).

16. Interview with Ruth Coppinger TD, SP, July 2015.

17. Interview with Clare Daly TD, July 2015.

18. Interview with Joan Collins TD, July 2015.

19. Sinn Féin, *Putting Ireland First* (Dublin: Sinn Féin European Election Manifesto, 2014).

20. Eoin Ó Broin, *Sinn Féin and the Politics of Left Republicanism* (London: Pluto Press, 2009), 301.

21. Harry McGee, 'Sinn Féin prepares for government where compromises await,' *The Irish Times* (23 June 2014).

22. John A. Murphy, 'Why we should be wary of Sinn Féin in government,' *The Irish Times* (8 July 2014).

23. Martyn Frampton, *The Long March: The Political Strategy of Sinn Féin, 1981-2007* (Basingstoke: Palgrave Macmillan, 2009), 141–3.

24. Tommy McKearney, *The Provisional IRA: From Insurrection to Parliament* (Dublin: Pluto Press Ireland, 2011), 191.

25. Ó Broin, *Sinn Féin and the Politics of Left Republicanism*, 242.

26. Ibid., 283.

27. *Introducing Martina Anderson, MEP* (Derry: Sinn Féin, 2015).

28. Laura Fitzgerald, 'Organised left force or disparate Independents?' *The Socialist* 93 (July–August 2015).

29. Interview with Clare Daly TD, July 2015.

30. Interview with Joan Collins TD, July 2015; Interview with Thomas Pringle TD, July 2015.

31. Right2Water, *Policy Principles for a Progressive Irish Government* (Dublin: Right2Water 2015).

32. Interview with Thomas Pringle TD, July 2015.

Chapter 11

Czech Communists and the Crisis

Between Radical Alternative and
Pragmatic Europeanisation

Vladimír Handl and Andreas Goffin

The Communist Party of Bohemia and Moravia (KSČM) is the only communist party in East-Central Europe that flourished after the end of the Eastern Bloc without changing its name or giving up its anti-capitalist, anti-liberal and anti-Western appeals. The party still clings to its Marxist-Leninist identity and culture, even though Lenin is hardly mentioned in the party's documents and its programme resembles those of 1970s Western social democratic and labour parties. In terms of membership, the KSČM is the largest political party in the Czech Republic, in terms of parliamentary representation it is third, while in terms of representation in regional assemblies it is second. At the same time, the party has never played an inspiring or integrating role on the Left and has remained largely detached from leftist discourse and action.

In this chapter, we question whether the party was willing or able to use the crisis as an incentive for programmatic innovation or as a basis from which to expand its support. In the first section, we analyse the general characteristics of the party to show how it has been a rallying point for the elderly conservative Left, poorly educated and socially disadvantaged. We then proceed to analyse the party's responses to the crisis. We argue that the KSČM has continued to be a protest party. The party's ability to exploit the political opportunities brought about by the crisis were limited by internal divisions, its limited intellectual capacity and its predominantly conservative identity. While the party interpreted the crisis as proof of its correct ideological and political orientation, it did little to elaborate on its programme, or to establish a leading position on the Czech left.

THE KSČM: A STABILISED *INTROVERT*

The KSCM is the 'successor party' to the notoriously conservative Communist Party of Czechoslovakia (KSČ), which remained largely unreformed until it was swept from power in Czechoslovakia's Velvet Revolution. However, under the weak leadership of Jiří Svoboda (1990–1993) (who was inspired by Alexander Kwaśniewski's successful transformation of the Polish ruling party into the Social Democratic Party of the Republic of Poland [SdRP]), there was an attempt to lead the KSČM on a social democratic path of transformation.[1] Yet Svoboda failed to develop an adequate strategy for such a change. As party structures and procedures were largely democratised and decentralised, the predominantly ideologically and culturally conservative grassroots and the district organisations dominated the process of programmatic transformation.[2]

As a result, the party promoted conservative positions under the leadership of Miroslav Grebeníček (chairman 1993–2005), who was succeeded by the pragmatic centrist Vojtěch Filip (chairman since 2005). Instead of opening the party to new ideas, a new identity and new supporters, the party's leaders have fallen back on traditional ideological and political positions. By doing so, they secured the support of the still-significant membership and electoral base. The party thus adopted a 'survivalist strategy', which Ishiyama and Bozóki labelled a 'strategy of leftist retreat'.[3] The specific path the party has taken since 1992 is explained by several factors:

- *Historical tradition and identity* – the Czechoslovak communist party had adopted Leninism, having been fully Bolshevised back in 1929. It was one of the strongest communist parties in Europe before World War II and won the last democratic elections in May 1946. Strong and victorious, the party had little need to rather search for compromises with the non-communist majority in society. The party was defined by its discipline, ideological purity and flawless organisation before 1989.
- *Weak leadership* – before 1989, party leaders, officials and representatives engaged little with the opposition or voters outside its traditional constituency. Subsequently they did not acquire 'portable skills' needed for negotiation through experience of forging compromises or of political campaigning.[4] Given their limited engagement with society prior to 1989, and the firm ideological discipline within their ranks, party elites were unable to articulate a vision for radical transformation.
- *Anti-communist vs. communist symbiosis* – as anti-communist policies became an important part of the election strategy of liberal and conservative parties, the struggle against anti-communism and radical anti-capitalist rhetoric became a 'mirror project', helping to mobilise the KSČM and its

supporters. As a result of the polarised and ritualistic debate, the KSČM focused on fighting its corner rather than on developing a left alternative. Debate about such an alternative has taken place elsewhere, mostly in internet journals and various NGOs.

The 'class nature' of the KSČM has been shaped, as Daniel Kunštát shows, by low-income membership (pensioners and low-wage employees), and its members have the lowest educational level among all Czech political parties. The electorate of the KSČM generally depends on state welfare policies; for this group, the party represents a better, more secure and understandable past.[5] What is more, half of the pensioners who vote KSČM have been workers, a third having been low-level clerks and technicians and only 10 per cent of them came from the former regime's 'social elite' (senior officials, teachers, researchers, managers, members of the security apparatus).[6] The party has, therefore, possessed limited intellectual capacity.

In terms of its cultural identity, the KSČM has been mainly traditionalist, conservative, anti-liberal and anti-Western. The party did adjust its programmes and accepted liberal democracy, the multiparty system, pluralism of forms of ownership and private property, and protection of human rights.[7] Still, the KSČM has remained internally differentiated as far as attitudes to the party's past, its ideology and attitude to the outer world are concerned.[8] Official intraparty fractions have not been allowed since 1993. Unofficially, however, at least four distinct groups have been discernible. First, a minority group of party intellectuals can be described as modernisers/neo-communists. This group have tried to turn the party into a modern left party and open it towards other leftist formations. The position of this fraction was weakened in 2008, with only one representative remaining in the party leadership (Jiří Dolejš, party deputy chairman, with a strong academic background in economic analysis) and one MEP (the late Miloslav Ransdorf, an academic specialist in philosophy, history and economics).

Ondřej Císař has developed a useful categorisation of the Left that helps us to understand the differences between the modernisers and the other fractions. He differentiates between a *revolutionary Left* (those who seek a radical alternative to capitalism) and a *post-revolutionary Left* (those who seek social reform of capitalism). He further adds two different responses to the challenges of globalisation: anti-globalisation positions (particularistic and sovereigntist) and alter-globalisation positions (seeking a regulated and democratised globalisation).[9] Using Císař's categorisation, the modernisers tend towards an alter-globalist response to the international environment while the other three streams mostly take anti-globalisation responses, seeking nation-state control over global processes.

The conservative fraction (the Marxist-Leninists and neo-Stalinists) believe that the modernisers have betrayed the communist cause. The conservatives represent a widely supported group in the party. This group dominate the Prague city party organisation (headed by Marta Semelová, an MP and Klement Gottwald admirer). Moreover, they demand revision of the KSČM's programmatic documents from 1990 to 1992, a return to Marxism-Leninism, and they reject the programme of the Socialist International and its idea of 'democratic socialism'.[10] The conservatives' anti-globalisation position includes both revolutionary and post-revolutionary tendencies (either focusing on anti-systemic alternatives to capitalist globalisation or stressing rather a return to nation-state protectionism).

A similar attitude is also found among the majority of the party's members, who make up the traditionalist group. They identify with Marxism-Leninism as a 'faith', support 'communist' remaining in the party's name, as well as the use of the traditional historical narrative, symbols and pre-1989 'communist speak'. Unlike conservatives, traditionalists do not represent a distinct tendency but make up the majority of the (mostly elderly) mass membership. The group are not organised or active in developing programmatic positions. Being policy-takers rather than policy producers, the traditionalists are extremely loyal to the party and support its mostly pragmatic leadership, so long as it continues (at least formally) to maintain the party's communist identity. The support of the traditionalist membership base allows the conservatives to exercise a kind of 'cultural hegemony' over much of the party.

Pragmatists represent the last stream. This group, represented by current party chairman Vojtěch Filip, have been growing in importance. The pragmatists control most of the MPs and regional and local level representatives and are primarily policy (and profit) oriented, being ideologically close to the conservatives. The pragmatists tend to speak two 'languages': the language of communist orthodoxy in internal debates and a more moderate language for the general public. Rhetorically, they tend to promote revolutionary anti-globalist stances, whereas in policymaking they tend towards a post-revolutionary anti-globalisation praxis. For example, when addressing the party's Central Committee, Filip fully endorsed 'revolutionary processes in Venezuela, Nicaragua, Bolivia and Ecuador … which prove that through mobilisation of the masses big capital and imperialism can be overpowered'.[11] Yet, cognisant of the generally negative attitude of the Czech population to immigrants (the party's membership base included), Filip sided with the national-conservative Hungarian prime minister Victor Orbán in the context of the refugee crisis in 2015.[12]

Given the growing public frustration over the transformation process and the direction of mainstream party politics, the party experienced electoral success mainly when the other leftist party (the Czech Social Democratic

Party, ČSSD) has formed governments (1998–2005 and since 2014). The KSČM has been successful in attracting frustrated 'protest voters', and those seeking to punish the ČSSD for its unsatisfactory performance. Electoral support for the KSČM has varied between 10 and 15 per cent, reached an impressive 18.5 per cent in 2002 and 12.4 per cent in 2006 (the last parliamentary elections before the crisis).

In response, the Social Democrats intensified co-operation with the KSČM in Parliament in 2005, and subsequently accepted the principle of coalitions at the regional level. National-level governing coalitions have, however, been ruled out over incompatible foreign-policy orientations – the KSČM firmly rejects Czech NATO membership and seeks to leave it; opposes any military missions abroad, and endorses Russian actions in Ukraine and its annexation of Crimea. The KSČM is as a whole a soft Eurosceptic party rejecting the Lisbon Treaty, but is internally divided over European integration. The modernisers tend to accept the Lisbon Treaty, and to believe that the European Union offers opportunities for leftist policies. The other three streams promote hard Eurosceptic and sovereignist positions, perceiving the European Union as an instrument of neoliberal capitalism. For example, Hassan Charfo, an influential member of the conservative fraction and former Head of the Central Committee's Department of International Relations, rejected the Lisbon Treaty as the road to a 'great capitalist power'.[13] The party as a whole thus accepts the European Union's social policies and supports active use of EU structural funds; however, it rejects most other policies and the pooling of sovereignty at the European level.

Electoral success brought with it a number of problems for the KSČM. First, surging self-confidence made it easy to block attempts to modernise the party and the 'Bolshevisation' of the party was viewed as being nearly complete in 2006.[14] Even limited 'Europeanisation' of the party, as it has become involved in EU-related politics, institutions and networks, has contributed to internal divisions. The KSČM's MEPs work actively within the GUE/NGL and the party has gradually become involved the European Left Party (PEL), where it has observer status. The pragmatic chairman Vojtěch Filip raised the question of full membership of the PEL in 2007 but failed as he faced opposition from both the conservatives and traditionalists. In particular, PEL membership was unacceptable for the conservatives who saw it as a 'Eurocommunist' entity. The party's sovereignist preferences and high level of Euroscepticism mean that its policies on foreign-policy issues can resemble those of the conservative-liberal Civic Democratic Party (ODS). Indeed, the KSČM twice helped to elect its candidate (and the architect of contemporary capitalism in the Czech Republic) Václav Klaus as Czech president.

All in all, the performance of the party before the outbreak of the crisis in 2008 supports March and Rommerskirchen's arguments that certain 'demand-side' factors are vital in explaining RLPs' electoral success.[15] Social-economic conditions, Euroscepticism, conservative national values and the past success of the communist party played crucial roles in stabilising the place of the KSČM on the political scene.

THE KSČM'S RESPONSE TO THE CRISIS

The KSČM's response to the crisis has been shaped by several factors including the particular nature of the crisis in the Czech Republic, the party's own characteristics and the changing nature of party competition in the Czech Republic. First, the most important factor that limited the ability to respond to the crisis was the fact that the Euro crisis influenced the Czech economy only indirectly and it avoided a lasting economic crisis in 2008–2013. The economy did contract by 4.8 per cent of GDP in 2009, but returned to growth in 2010 and 2011 (2.3 and 2 per cent respectively) and contracted again in 2012 and 2013 (0.8 and 0.7 per cent respectively).[16] While the first contraction was directly linked to the financial crisis and falling Czech exports, the second was a result of both decreasing economic activity in the Eurozone and 'weak domestic demand – partly due to fiscal consolidation of 2% in 2011 and 2012'.[17] Indeed, the austerity policy of the centre-right government of Mirek Topolánek was criticised by trade unions and the left opposition, including the KSČM. While the economy returned to growth, in 2014 growth rates remained weaker than in other Visegrad states. The centre-left government that came to power in 2014 eased the situation to some extent, by increasing public spending in the aim of promoting growth.

One of the reasons why the financial crisis did not hit the Czech Republic too hard was the fact that Czech banks had been bailed out and the banking sector restructured in the second half of the 1990s. This meant that there was no actual Czech banking crisis, although the financial crisis of 2008–2010 was felt in what resembled a cyclical swing in the Czech Republic that led to the freezing of pensions and loans for three years and increasing unemployment.[18] While such developments contributed to an increased feeling of dissatisfaction, even during the crisis, the Czech Republic remained one of the best-performing European countries in terms of tackling poverty. According to a weighted social justice index, the Czech Republic occupied fifth place following Sweden, Finland, Denmark and Netherlands in 2008–2014.[19] While the unemployment rate increased from 4.4 to 7 per cent during the same period, the Czech Republic took the second lowest rank (following Slovenia) in terms of its Gini coefficient.[20] Subsequently, the political debates surrounding the financial crisis largely treated it as an external phenomenon unrelated to Czech economic or political life. As a non-Euro country, the Czech Republic was also somewhat distanced from the economic crisis in Greece.

Second, by the time the crisis started, the KSČM was becoming less able to maintain an active internal party life and to develop policy. The leadership has focused increasingly on elections and even during the crisis it has failed to reverse the party's organisational decline.[21] The membership base had shrunk to 40,000 by 2015 and the party was dominated by the ageing lower strata of the former executive class (low-level officials and intelligence officers).[22] The average age of members reached 73–74 in 2015, and pensioners made up two-thirds of the party. The KSČM has just 1,000 members under 30 years of age. One-third of its members joined the party after 1990; however, most of them were military officers who renewed their party membership after they became pensioners.[23] This age profile increases the party's propensity to conservativism, anti-liberalism and anti-Westernism and has diminished the party's intellectual capacity. During the 1990s, the party still benefited from its top-down interaction with small circles of intellectual elites and grassroots activists. However, by 2010–2015, most of the party's intellectuals had become too old to produce relevant theoretical analysis and grassroots activists were left behind.[24] Miloslav Ransdorf concluded in 2015 that the party was unable to differentiate between theory, strategy and tactics and even argued that the party was not able to conduct any cognitive activities at all.[25]

Third, the nature of the Czech party system has been changing since 2010. The KSČM become an integral part of the party system, which has been viewed as a situation of 'fragile stability'.[26] However, this 'fragile stability' has started to crumble as voters have turned away from its two main pillars the liberal-conservative ODS and the social democratic ČSSD. Common explanations for this change include increasing disappointment with the established parties, corruption and their detachment from their electorate. The KSČM, an 'old party' itself, was, however, unable to significantly capitalise on these changes. The main beneficiaries have been new actors such as the centrist-liberal 'Movement Yes-2011' (ANO-2011, formerly The Action of Disappointed Citizens [*Akce Nespokojených Občanů 2011*]), created by the tycoon Andrej Babiš, which is currently leading in opinion polls.

DIFFERENT ATTITUDES TOWARDS THE CRISIS

In this section, we evaluate the KSČM's response to the crisis in its programmes as well as the statements made by representatives from the main factions within it and show how they reacted to the crisis differently. The most recent programmatic documents of the KSČM are the 'Election Manifesto for the National Elections 2010',[27] 'Main Tasks & Aims of the Party's Work after

KSCM's VIII Congress'[28] and the preliminary expert study 'Socialism for the 21st Century'.[29] The first of these represents a political response drafted rather hastily by a small circle of party representatives and experts in summer 2009 (as levels of party activity decline between June and September as many of the party's aged members move to their countryside homes). The programme was used for the 2010 elections with little substantial adjustment.[30]

The second document, which sets out the party's main aims, was adopted at the party's VIII Congress in 2012 and was prepared by the Central Committee. The third, in contrast, sums up the laborious (and ongoing) search for a theoretical model of socialism and was drafted by the Center for Strategic and Theoretical Studies of the KSČM under the leadership of its head, Jiří Dolejš. It is presented as an 'expert analysis' and rejects the polarisation that exists between 'nostalgics and Stalinists' on the one side and 'revisionists and renegades' on the other.[31]

A Limited Intellectual and Programmatic Response

It is clear that the documents mentioned above are largely informed by long-standing ideological approaches within the party rather than being the basis for a genuinely new approach that directly engages with the financial/Eurozone crisis. For a brief moment, there was considerable hope among party members and the leadership alike that the Icelandic crisis could bring about a socialist alternative.[32] As yet, however, the party has not published a substantial analysis of the financial and Eurozone crises nor conducted a detailed debate on the issue. Some direct references can be found, for instance, at the beginning of 'Main Tasks & Aims', where the KSČM referred to a 'deep crisis', which was 'a social and economic, thus a political one'. It argued that the public interest was ignored and that 'decisions [were] being made by a smaller and smaller group of owners of transnational companies'.[33] Privatisations and the nationalisation of losses were seen to have led to sovereign deficits and austerity policies are criticised for undermining consumption and deepening the crises.

Beyond this brief narrative, however, the crisis had little impact on the KSČM's programme, which failed to even suggest any measures in response to the crisis. What stands of out is that the crisis is interpreted as proof of the party's traditional standpoints. It therefore fails to make any attempt to develop a more substantive analysis of the causes, dynamics and implications of the process. Instead, more general goals are prioritised including the defence of free medical care and the reintroduction of a progressive tax rate.

A few representatives of the party's intellectual elite have looked beyond this narrow narrative. MEP Miloslav Ransdorf's analysis combined data on the cyclical development of the economy and technological innovation, and drew on Kondratiev and other prominent academics.[34] Ransdorf argued that the party's role should be one of connecting different social groups, strata and classes that have overlapping interests rather than to lay claim to possessing the correct interpretation of history. Secondly, he argued that party's aim should be to capitalise on the end of the post-modern era in the sphere of culture (which the crisis is seen to have brought about) by seeking to construct a Gramscian cultural hegemony in the coming 'neo-modern era'.[35]

Fellow moderniser and deputy chairman Jiří Dolejš argued that the crisis could not be explained nor solved by either monetarist or Keynesian concepts as he rejected both libertarian and state-centred crisis solutions.[36] That said, he argued that countries might need to increase state intervention in strategic areas (e.g. energy, communication, public transport, water supply, sewage systems) and take over struggling firms, while employee ownership of companies was also presented as a solution to the crisis.[37] A deepening of European integration was also seen as part of the solution, not of the problem.[38]

Conversely, the Marxist-Leninist and more conservative stream in the KSČM interpreted the crisis as the final breakdown of the system. Hassan Charfo named the crisis 'The Natural Child of Capitalism' and argued that the problems could not be solved 'within the framework of capitalism' but only 'within the framework of socialism'. The crisis, he argued, was caused by neoliberal policies and the hegemony of the United States.[39] A common conservative communist view is that the breakdown of the current system inevitably pushes capitalists into war, the purpose of which is annihilation of the surplus labour force and of capitalist competitors. In this sense the party's role is to speed up the breakdown of the system and to seize political power.[40]

The pragmatists share a large degree of ideological common ground with the conservatives, shown when they address communist audiences. During the 13th International Meeting of Communist and Workers' Parties (IMCWP) in Athens (2011), KSČM chairman Vojtěch Filip elaborated on 'the advancing death throes of the world capitalist system' and saw Marx's economic teaching as 'celebrating a clear victory in the current world-wide crisis'. He argued that the crisis had been deepened 'by enforcing neoliberal economic models' and voiced apprehension that the United States and other countries involved would 'perversely consider solving the crisis by wars of aggression'.[41] In a more practical vein, Filip also proposed the elimination of 'elements of neoliberalism' in EU treaties, expressed solidarity with Greece, demanded 'abolition of the public debt' and argued that the European Central Bank should 'adopt a regime of low interest loans' for countries most affected by the crisis.[42] Any more intensive engagement with the roots of the crisis or debts was missing.

Tellingly, during the 15th IMCWP in Lisbon (2013) Filip made no mention of the crisis, and instead focused on international conflicts, the refugee problem and the problem of 'anti-communism' in the media. Moreover, the final declaration of the International Conference held in Prague (23–24 May 2015) was devoted to offering support to Russia in its conflict with the West, as the party again failed to engage with the Euro crisis.[43] The party focused on working 'to resist imperialism' and building an 'anti-fascist front', while elaborating its model of socialism.[44]

The KSČM position on the Euro and the Greek debt crisis centred on a critique of the capitalist economic system. While there were expressions of solidarity with the countries of southern Europe, this was not translated into support for Czech financial assistance to southern European countries as the country is not a member of the Eurozone. The predominant economic thinking of the party includes both Keynesian instruments of demand economics and the culture of sound money and fiscal discipline. It is significant that before 1989 the Czechoslovak communist party had strongly emphasised the importance of a balanced budget and maintaining low foreign debt. Therefore, the Greek crisis was viewed as a result of bad fiscal policy by governing elites.

The conservatives blamed the left-wing governments of Greece, Portugal and Spain for imposing austerity on their populations 'for the sake of great capital and banks'.[45] Subsequently, they supported the only 'revolutionary' Left – the Communist Party of Greece (KKE). For example, in the KSČM's statement on the 2012 Greek elections, its Executive Bureau commented on the KKE's result but hardly mentioned the stronger performance of Syriza.[46] Unlike the KKE, however, the KSČM has consistently demanded that Greece remain a Eurozone member.[47] Certainly, for the modernisers, a return to the drachma or economic protectionism represented the wrong type of response.[48]

Rather than articulating a clear response to the crisis, the programmatic document 'Socialism for the 21st Century' does more to offer insight into the way that the KSČM struggles to formulate a socially just and democratic alternative to capitalism. The document briefly elaborates on the inability of capitalism to provide sustainable development. It acknowledges that attempts have been made under capitalism to improve the system of regulation on the global and European levels. However, it argues that capitalism currently faces not only a specific but also a structural or systemic crisis, that it has lost its 'historical legitimacy' and that its ability to adapt to the new conditions is unclear.[49]

During the drafting of this document, the number of references to Marxism decreased as internal ideational divisions within the party came to the fore. In the version adopted during the VII Party Congress (2008), the document still referred to Marx, Engels and even Lenin as an 'essential methodological basis for the scientific concept of socialism'.[50] The 2012 version (adopted during the VIII Congress), however, only mentioned how much the world has changed since 'the founders of Marxism' analysed capitalism.[51] Similarly, while the 2008 version elaborated on the concept of the 'leading' and 'vanguard' roles of the party, the 2012 version argued that the 'vanguard role' did not have to be assigned to only one party and might be implemented by a coalition, block or alliance of pluralist progressive forces.[52] The model of socialism was to be founded on economic democracy, self-government and collective ownership of the tools of mass production.[53]

Formulating the document was difficult, as the radical conservative Prague 1 district organisation had rejected the earlier version of the document, prepared for the VII Congress, as being yet another attempt to abandon the 'communist nature of the party'.[54] Penčo Savov, an active speaker of the conservative stream, blamed the Central Committee for being captured by revisionists of Marxism-Leninism who sought to implement social democratic policies.[55] The 2012 version of 'Socialism 21' also provoked fierce opposition from the conservatives who accused the authors of revisionism.[56] Developing a new vision of a socialist society is no easy task and future progress to this end is complicated by the way in which modernisers and conservatives have differing interpretations of the document. For the former, the document represents an open-ended search for alternatives; for the latter it provides a blueprint for revolutionary changes that a communist-led government should implement once in power.[57]

Foreign-policy issues also reveal the deep lying divisions within the party. Ultimately, the conservatives and the pragmatists seek a geopolitical alternative to the pro-Western orientation of the Czech Republic. In his address to the VIII party congress, Vojtěch Filip did not mention the European Union once, but sought to orientate the party's foreign policy towards the BRICS states as he welcomed the prospective victory of China (allegedly a more socially just system) over the United States in economic competition.[58] In contrast, the modernisers focus on improving the regulatory capacity of the European Union. Thus, Jiří Dolejš agreed with the necessity of strengthening the Stability and Growth Pact as well as other stabilisation mechanisms of the European Union alongside an increase in wages that would strengthen the purchasing power of the population and increase domestic demand.[59]

STRATEGIC, POLITICAL AND ORGANISATIONAL RESPONSES: FIGHTING AUSTERITY THROUGH BROAD COALITIONS

In 2010–2011, the right-wing governing coalition initiated austerity policies that cut the salaries of state employees by roughly 10 per cent each year. The government also cut social benefits by between 5 and 30 per cent and

VAT was increased by 1 per cent in 2010.[60] In response, the KSČM and the ČSSD organised anti-austerity protests that included several mass rallies. This section shows, however, that the KSČM failed to modernise its election and communication strategies and as a result failed to capitalise on the crisis. Moreover, its linkages with the non-communist Left remained marginal.

The KSČM election manifesto of 2010 (the only national elections directly influenced by the financial crisis) began by stating that the 'economic and political crisis as a product of capitalism hit the Czech Republic and our society hard'.[61] What followed was, however, a criticism of particular policies of the liberal-conservative government rather than specific elaboration of the nature of the crisis. Economic solutions to the problems caused by the government focused on the demand side (state investment policies), as well as measures such as support for small and middle-sized businesses, cutting red tape, better regulation of the financial market and banks, increased funding for science and technology and tax reforms (abolition of the flat tax and the introduction of five tax brackets).[62] At the same time, the party argued that eligibility for welfare benefits should be based on merit and that there was a general preference for responsible fiscal policy.[63] This presented an indirect but clear rejection of solidarity with those seen to not work – primarily the Roma population (and later on immigrants as well). The KSČM's European election manifesto did, however, go further in setting out measures to respond to the crisis including regulation of the banking sector on the European level.[64] It demanded an end to social dumping, to downgrading of social security and to tax havens. Overall, however, the party paid less attention to European elections.

The KSČM's electoral campaigns were consistent in using posters and leaflets that promoted slogans such as 'With the people for the people!' and (for European elections) 'We want a Europe for the people!'. Such slogans on campaigning posters changed little in response to the economic crisis. A simple glance election at results in 2010 (Table 11.1) show that the party failed to capitalise on Europe's deepest economic crisis since the great depression in 1930s. All the major parties lost electoral support and the losses also hit the KSČM. The winners of the elections were the newly established liberal TOP09, which exploited the crisis through scaring voters over the Greek debt crisis, and the 'Věci veřejné' (Public Affairs) anti-corruption party. The KSČM performed more strongly during the elections in 2013 as it won more

Table 11.1   National Legislative Election Results of the KSČM since 1996

Year	1996	1998	2002	2006	2010	2013
Result in %	10.33	11.03	18.51	12.81	11.27	14.91

Source: Výsledky voleb a referend. Poslanecká sněmovna Parlamentu ČR (respective years), http://www. volby.cz.

protest votes against the mainstream parliamentary parties (as noted above, however, the greatest gains were achieved by the new party ANO).

The absence of a crisis effect was even more obvious in the 2014 European elections: here, the election results of the party have been continuously decreasing, mainly due to its ambivalent attitude towards the European Union and competition from other Eurosceptic parties (Table 11.2). The actual winner of the election was ANO.

On the regional level, the KSČM was more successful. In 2012, it achieved 20.43 per cent of votes in regional assemblies and became the second most successful party in the Czech Republic. The KSČM was subsequently invited by the ČSSD to build joint governments in nine regions and in one of them its candidate secured the post of the regional governor. The economic crisis played little role in helping the party to expand. More significant explanations are found in the KSČM's ability to exploit local political issues, the view that it is largely isolated and therefore 'has its hands clean' and the way that it placed non-party candidates on electoral lists.

Attempts to analyse the 2010 electoral losses by Vojtěch Filip concluded that the election programme was both well written and offered the right answers to the situation. Filip argued that the problem was that the party was unable to communicate the programme to society, mainly to the young generation. According to him, the way forward was more actively to seek broader societal coalitions. The Central Committee should be more actively using its new competence and directly influencing the lists of candidates on the regional level.[65]

For the modernisers, the problems facing the party are more complex: the above-mentioned demographic change is seen to be compounded by the party's outdated and unattractive party programme.[66] For example, they highlighted that policies that promote employee stock ownership have little resonance with Czech citizens who appear to seek either full independence and engage in start-ups, or to prefer a position as employees. The modernisers agree that the party lacks effective communication strategies – it poured considerable funds into its own radio and TV programmes for several years but neither offered sufficient quality or managed to significantly expand their audience. The KSČM initiated and sponsored the platform 'Společenství práce a solidarity' (SPAS, 'Alliance for labour and solidarity') to co-ordinate

Table 11.2   KSČM Performance during the Elections to the European Parliament

Year	2004	2009	2014
Percentage	20.26	14.18	10.98
Seats	6	4	3

Source: Výsledky voleb a referend. *Evropský parlament* (respective years), http//:www.volby.cz.

social organisations in the search for alternatives to the system. However, although this recieved much praise, it failed to attract new left activists.[67]

The party's attempts to develop links to civil society through discussion platforms and gatherings, have a syncretic rather than synergic effect.[68] For instance, the KSČM supported a small trade union organisation, the Trade Union of Bohemia, Moravia and Silesia (*Odborové sdružení Čech, Moravy a Slezska*, OSČMS), chaired by Stanislav Grospič, communist MP (which has its headquarters in the KSČM's headquarters). The party also has a close but strained relationship with the Communist Youth Union (*Komunistický svaz mládeže*, KSM), a radical organisation of some 750 members. Beyond this, the KSČM also has informal but mostly sporadic contacts with small leftist groups (anarchist, radical socialist, left-leaning intellectual clubs) such as Socialist Solidarity (*Spocialistická solidarita*, SOCSOL, an organisation of c.30 intellectuals), Socialist Circle (*Socialistický kruh*, SOK, a leftist discussion platform of c.50 intellectuals), the Czech Antifa and such like. However, the scope of common activities between these groups and the KSČM remains limited and they view the KSČM as either being too conservative or too pragmatic and too focused on the politics of the nation-state. Moreover, within the KSČM, only the modernisers appear to actually seek an intensive exchange of ideas with social movements.

CONCLUSION

The KSČM remains significant as a protest party; it combines radical anti-systemness with conservative appeals. In terms of Ondřej Císař's model, despite its internal divisions, the KSČM is predominantly a particularistic revolutionary anti-globalist party, that is, one oriented towards the nation-state. The financial crisis and the Eurozone crisis have not changed the situation dramatically. Neither of them has been regarded as a 'Czech crisis'. The Czech Republic was not seriously hit by the crisis and as a non-Eurozone state was only marginally involved in the Greek crisis. As a soft Eurosceptic party, the KSČM remained ambivalent and divided in its attitude to the European Union. Consequently, the KSČM has not elaborated on the crisis intellectually. For the conservatives, the crisis simply confirmed the teachings of Marxism-Leninism and they viewed the European Union as a part of the problem. The few modernisers within the party focused more on the causes of the crisis, and viewed European integration as both part of the problem as well as the solution.

In general, though, the programmatic debate within the KSČM has taken place mostly over the future model of socialism rather than about the economic crisis. In a political sense, the party suffered vote losses during the only crisis-driven elections in 2010 (it lost 1.54 per cent). Its electoral success in 2013 (plus 3.37 per cent) was a result of widespread rejection of the established mainstream parties, not of an anti-crisis mobilisation. The crisis played a minor role even in foreign-policy issues, with more significant topics being the Ukraine crisis, a US Army convoy passing through the Czech Republic in March 2015 and Europe's refugee policies. In general, the KSČM has lacked expertise on international issues and has not been able to generate an active and effective foreign-policy programme in response to such issues.

The exhaustion of the KSČM's intellectual elite and the lack of a flow of ideas within the party is particularly noticeable.[69] The anarchist intellectual and activist Ondřej Slačálek has argued that the KSČM has become a burden for the Czech Left because it has failed to integrate interesting left issues into the public sphere.[70] Indeed, for many on the left, the KSČM represents a conservative party that has become so much a part of the establishment that it cannot be seriously viewed as an anti-system party. Overall, its demographic problems, the 'cultural hegemony' of the conservatives and the stalemate between the conservatives and the modernisers/neo-communists indicate there are only limited chances for further programmatic and political reform of the party.

NOTES

1. Adam Drda and Petr Dudek, *Kdo ve stínu čeká na moc. Čeští komunisté po listopadu 1989* (Praha: Paseka, 2006).

2. Anna Grzymała-Busse, *Redeeming the Communist Past. The Regeneration of Communist Parties in East Central Europe* (Cambridge: Cambridge University Press, 2002), 86.

3. John Ishiyama and Andras Bozóki, 'Adaptation and Change: Characterizing the Survival Strategies of the Communist Successor Parties,' *Journal of Communist Studies and Transition Politics* 17 (2001): 34 and 41.

4. Grzymała-Busse, *Redeeming the Communist Past*, 60.

5. Daniel Kunštát, 'Strana, která neumírá: K příčinám stability volební podpory KSČM,' *Naše společnost* 12, no. 2 (2014): 18.

6. Daniel Kunštát, *Za rudou oponou. Komunisté a jejich voliči po roce 1989* (Praha: Sociologické nakladatelství, 2013), 288–90.

7. Goran Marković, 'Challenges of the Czech Radical Left,' *Journal of Contemporary Central and Eastern Europe* 21, no. 1(2013): 73–4.

8. Stanislav Holubec, 'Die radikale Linke in Tschechien,' in *Die Linke in Europa. Analyse der linken Parteien und Parteiallianzen*, ed. Birgit Daiber and Cornelia Hildebrandt (Berlin: Dietzverlag, 2009): 116–25. Similarly Vladimír Handl, 'Choosing between China and Europe? Virtual inspiration and Policy Transfer in the Programmatic Development of the Czech Communist Party,' *Journal of Communist Studies and Transition Politics* 21, no. 1 (2005): 123–41.

9. Ondřej Císař, 'The Left in the Beginning of the 21st Century,' in *Trajectories of the Left*, ed. Lubomír Kopeček (Brno: CDK, 2005), 11–28.

10. Zdeněk Košťál, 'Dvě poznámky,' in *25 let budování kapitalismu v České republice. Sborník vystoupení na XXXVI Pražské teoreticko-politické konferenci*, Praha 8. 11. 2014 (Praha: KSČM Praha Východ), 74–8.

11. 'Vystoupení předsedy ÚV KSČM Vojtěcha Filipa na 14. zasedání ÚV KSČM 28. 3. 2015,' KSČM, accessed 5 May 2015, https://www.kscm.cz/stanoviska-tiskove-konference-projevy/projevy/96712/vystoupeni-predsedy-uv-kscm-vojtecha-filipa-na-14-zasedani-uv-kscm-28-3-2015.

12. Vojtěch Filip, 'Zrada,' *Haló noviny*, 26 September 2015.

13. KSČM, 'The Lisbon Treaty,' 2008, https://www.kscm.cz/rewrite_url. asp?rew_thema=political-opinions&rew_item=39980&rew_other=.

14. Václav Balín, 'Že by se bolševizace dovršovala?,' 1 January 2006, accessed 20 September 2008, http://www.balin.cz/phorum.php?idDiskuze=656&phorumId=256.

15. Luke March and Charlotte Rommerskirchen, 'Out of Left Field? Explaining the Variable Electoral Success of European Radical Left Parties,' *Party Politics* 21, no. 1 (2015): 47–8. Similar finding by Kunštát, 'Strana, která neumírá,' 20–1.

16. Real GDP Growth Rate – Eurostat 2 February 2015, Czech Statistical Office, accessed 3 November 2015, https://www.czso.cz/csu/czso/makroekonomika421.

17. Czech Republic. OECD Economic surveys. March 2014. Overview (OECD 2014), 4.

18. Interview with a high ranking party representative, Prague, 9 July 2015. See also Daniel Schraad-Tischlera and Christian Kroll, 'Social Justice in the EU – Cross-country Comparative', in *Social Inclusion Monitor Europe (SIM)* (Güttersloh: Bertelsmann Stiftung, 2014), 45.

19. Ibid., 9, 22–3.

20. Ibid., 45 and 58.

21. Martin Polášek, Vilém Novotný, Michel Perottino, *Mezi masovou a kartelovou stranou. Možnosti teorie při výkladu vývoje ČSSD a KSČM v letech 2000-2010* (Praha: Slon, 2012), 164.

22. The figure was referred to by a high party representative during our interview, Prague 9 July 2015. Josef Heller, 'Bída analýzy aneb Co překroutili analytici ČSSD,' *Alternativy* 14 (2003): 28.

23. In Czechoslovakia and the Czech Republic armed forces are strictly non-political and officers may not be members of any political party.

24. Interview with a high ranking party representative, Prague, 9 July 2015.

25. Miloslav Ransdorf, 'Sedíš-li na mrtvém koni, sesedni!,' in *25 let budování kapitalismu v České Republice*, 124.

26. Kevin Deegan-Krause and Tim Haughton, 'A Fragile Stability. The Institutional Roots of Low Party System Volatility in the Czech Republic, 1990-2009,' *Czech Journal of Political Science* 7, no. 3 (2010): 227–41.

27. 'Otevřený volební program KSČM pro volby do PS PCR 2010,' KSČM, accessed 2 July 2015, http://www.kscm.cz/viewDocument.asp?document=5481.

28. 'Main Tasks & Aims of the Party's Work after KSCM's VIII Congress,' KSČM 2012, accessed 10 July 2015, https://www.kscm.cz/our-politics/documents/65189/main-tasks-aims-of-the-partys-work-after-kscms-viii-congress.

29. 'Socialismus pro 21. Století,' KSČM 2012, accessed 10 July 2015, https://www.kscm.cz/volby-a-akce/viii-sjezd-kscm-v-liberci/dokumenty/64118/socialismus-v-21-stoleti).

30. Interview, 9 July 2015.

31. Jiří Dolejš. 'Základní směry v diskusi o socialismu v 21. Století,' accessed 23 August 2015, https://www.kscm.cz/nazory-a-polemika/61135/zakladni-smery-v-diskusi-o-socialismu-v-21-stoleti?previev=archiv.

32. Interview, 9 July 2015.

33. 'Main Tasks & Aims of the Party's Work after KSCM's VIII Congress,' KSČM 2012, accessed 10 July 2015, https://www.kscm.cz/our-politics/documents/65189/main-tasks-aims-of-the-partys-work-after-kscms-viii-congress.

34. Nikolai Kondratiev, economist, the author of the long economic cycle theory. Ransdorf died suddenly in January 2016.

35. Miloslav Ransdorf, 'Sedíš-li na mrtvém koni,' 125–6.

36. Jiří Dolejš, 'Ekonomická krize a krize ekonomů,' *Blog Aktuálně.cz*, 6 April 2010, http://blog.aktualne.cz/blogy/jiri-dolejs.php?itemid=9435.

37. Jiří Dolejš, 'Je tu krize – zbavme se stereotypů,' *Blog Aktuálně.cz*, 9 February 2009, http://blog.aktualne.cz/blogy/jiri-dolejs.php?itemid=5844#more.

38. Jiří Dolejš, 'Sýček Klaus o fiskální unii,' *Blog Aktuálně.cz*, 14 December 2010, http://blog.aktualne.cz/blogy/jiri-dolejs.php?itemid=11588.

39. 'The Natural Child of Capitalism,' KSČM, accessed 10 July 2015, https://www.kscm.cz/rewrite_url.asp?rew_thema=political-opinions&rew_item=40724&rew_other=.

40. Věra Klonza, 'Kolapsy a regenerace společensko-ekonomických systémů. Naše současná situace a možnosti jejího aktivního ovlivnění,' in *25 let budování kapitalismu*, 90.

41. 'Address delivered by Comrade Vojtech Filip, chairman of the Central Committee of the Communist Party of Bohemia and Moravia (CPBM) at the 13th World Meeting of Communist and Workers' Parties in Athens,' KSČM, accessed 8 July 2015, https://www.kscm.cz/international/60503/address-delivered-by-comrade-vojtech-filip-chairman-of-the-central-committee-of-the-communist-party-of-bohemia-and-moravia-cpbm-at-the-13th-world-meeting-of-communist-and-workers-parties-in-athens.

42. Ibid.

43. KSČM, 'The Declaration Communist Party of Bohemia & Moravia's International Conference, Prague, May 23-24, 2015,' KSČM, accessed 8 July 2015, https://www.kscm.cz/our-politics/international-conferences/international-conference-22-24-05-2015/98740/the-declaration-communist-party-of-bohemia-moravias-international-conference-prague-may-23-24-2015.

44. 'Speech by cme. Vojtěch Filip, Chairman of Communist Party of Bohemia & Moravia's Central Committee, on 15th International Meeting of Communist and Workers' Parties, Lisbon 2013,' KSČM, accessed 10 July 2015, https://www.kscm.cz/international/82172/speech-by-cme-vojtech-filip-chairman-of-communist-party-of-bohemia-moravias-central-committee-to-be-delivered-on-15th-international-meeting-of-communist-and-workers-parties-lisbon-2013.

45. See a response by Stanislav Grospič, deputy chairman of the party. Grospič, Stanislav 'Soupeření dolaru s eurem a co je za tím'. *KSČM*, 4 March

2010, accessed 10 July 2015, https://www.kscm.cz/nazory-a-polemika/46809/ grospic-soupereni-dolaru-s-eurem-a-co-je-za-tim?previev=archiv.

46. 'Statements, Elections in the European Union – hope for change,' KSČM, accessed 9 July 2015, https://www.kscm.cz/our-politics/statements/64022/elections-in-the-european-union-hope-for-change.

47. 'Řešení řecké krize přijetím jednostranných opatření povede k diskreditaci levicové politiky,' KSČM 17 July 2015, accessed 5 August 2015, https://www.kscm.cz/politika-kscm/stanoviska-kscm/99605/reseni-recke-krize-prijetim-jednostran-nych-opatreni-povede-k-diskreditaci-levicove-politiky.

48. Jiří Dolejš, 'Co s řeckými dluhy?', in *Blog Aktuálně.cz*, 20 June 2011, accessed 10 July 2015, http://blog.aktualne.cz/blogy/jiri-dolejs.php?itemid=13516.

49. KSČM. 'Socialismus pro 21. Století'. 2012, 183.

50. 'Socialismus pro 21. Století,' 2008.

51. 'Socialismus pro 21. Století,' version adopted by the VIII. Congress, 2012, 181.

52. 'Socialismus pro 21. Století,' version VII. Congress, 2008 and 'Socialismus pro 21. Století,' version adopted by the VIII. Congress, 2012, 194.

53. 'Socialismus pro 21. Století,' 2012, 185.

54. K pracovnímu návrhu materiálu 'Socialismus pro 21. století' (Ze stanoviska OV KSČM Praha 1). 2007. *Dialog* (18) 234, 1. The main topic of the same issue was defence of the achievements of the Russian 1917 socialist revolution.

55. Penčo Savov, 'Teoreticko-analytické pracoviště KSČM a komunisté. Materiál k VII. Sjezdu KSČM je pro marxisty-leninovce nepřijatelný'. Ibid., 2.

56. Dalibor Hozák, 'Usnesení VIII. sjezdu KSČM a realita', in Dialog 289, October 2012, accessed 5 August 2015, http://www.komsomol.cz/clanky/2594_dia-log_sjezd.html.

57. Interview, 9 July 2015.

58. Haló Noviny, 'Úvodní vystoupení předsedy ÚV KSČM Vojtěcha Filipa na VIII. Sjezdu' 21 May 2012, accessed 5 August 2015, http://www.halonoviny.cz/articles/view/324759.

59. Internet discussion between Jiří Dolejš and radical left sociologist Ilona Švihlíková, 29 November 2011, accessed 10 June 2012, http://www.denikreferen-dum.cz/clanek/9782-pakt-euro-plus-je-minusem-pro-obcany.

60. Jan Stuchlík, 'Přehledně: Co Vám vezme Janotův úsporný balíček,' Peníze.cz, 23 September 2009, accessed 15 January 2016, http://www.penize.cz/socialni-davky/59476prehlednecovamvezmejanotuvuspornybalicek. Franče, Václav, Důsledky úsporných opatření v České republice. Nadace Friedricha Eberta, Praha 2012.

61. 'Otevřený volební program KSČM pro volby do PS PCR 2010,' KSČM 2010, accessed 2 July 2015, www.kscm.cz/viewDocument.asp?document=5481.

62. Ibid.

63. See the member of the parliament for the KSČM and speaker for social policy Opálka, Miroslav, 'Podklad k vystoupení na semináři SPaS 26. dubna 2012. Téma – sociální politika,' 2012, accessed 5 August 2015, https://www.kscm.cz/viewDocu-ment.asp?document=5769.

64. 'Volby do EP 2009,' KSČM, accessed 10 January 2015, www.kscm.cz/volby-a-akce/volby-do-ep-2009.

65. Vojtěch Filip, 'Nabízíme spolupráci všem, kteří vyznávají levicové myšlenky,' accessed 10 July 2015, http://www.kscm.cz/article.asp?thema=3892&item=48984.

66. Ibid.

67. KSČM, Zpráva ÚV KSČM o činnosti strany v období od VII. do VIII. sjezdu KSČM. 2012, S. 3.

68. Interview, 9 July 2015.

69. Vlasta Hábová, 'Idea Levicového fóra,' *Britské listy*, 13 May 2013, accessed 20 July 2015, http://blisty.cz/art/68452.html.

70. Ondřej Slačálek, 'Opatrně s tou pravdou', *A2Alarm*, 2015, accessed 10 July 2015, http://a2larm.cz/2014/02/opatrne-s-tou-pravdou/.

Chapter 12

Latvia's 'Russian Left'

Trapped between Ethnic, Socialist and Social Democratic Identities

Ammon Cheskin and Luke March

Following the 2008 economic crisis, Latvia suffered the worst loss of output *in the world*, with GDP collapsing 25 per cent.[1] Latvia has been heralded as a 'poster child' for austerity as the Right has continued to dominate government policy.[2] Yet Latvia's radical Left has shown no notable ideological or strategic response. Existing RLPs did not secure significant political gains from the crisis, nor have new challengers benefited. This chapter explores this puzzle. Although the economic crisis was economically destructive, we argue that the political responses have been consistently ethnicised in Latvia. Additionally, the Latvian Left has been equally challenged intellectually and strategically by the ethnically-framed Ukrainian crisis of 2014.

Special attention is given to the Latvian Socialist Party (*Latvijas Sociālistiskā partija*, LSP), Latvia's most prominent (albeit small) RLP. We argue that one of the principal reasons for the LSP's inability to exploit the crisis is its strategic inertness and stubborn adherence to the ideological tenets of Marxism-Leninism. Second is its preference for sheltering within a wider electoral alliance of 'Russian' centre-left parties.

The 'Russianness' of the LSP and the Latvian Centre-Left has its primary explanation in Latvia's Soviet past, entailing the admixture of socialism with Russification promoted by the 'colonial' Soviet Union. In truth, these legacies remain live because they have been utilised by political entrepreneurs who have conflated appeals based on socialism and ethnicity. Consequently, centre-left and radical left parties have been largely unable (and indeed, often unwilling) to shake off popular associations with communism, the Soviet past and their 'Russianness'.

Precisely because Latvia's political spectrum can be characterised in terms of ethnic, rather than ideological cleavages, the responses of the country's radical Left have been heavily constrained by ethnic considerations that are peculiar to Latvia's post-Soviet political environment (although with some similarities in Estonia).[3] The conflation of ethnic and ideological 'leftness' explains the ultimate failure of RLPs to gain wider appeal in Latvia. Crucially, it has almost entirely prevented the country's extant radical Left from moving beyond its communist roots and articulating an anti-austerity message that could transcend ethnic cleavages.

This chapter illustrates these peculiarities by also focusing on the wider Latvian Left. Because the LSP's political fortunes are deeply contingent on the resonance of its Soviet aesthetics and its appeal to the Russian-speaking electorate, it is impossible to ignore the wider ('Russian') context within which it operates. Accordingly, we show how the positions of the Social Democratic Party 'Harmony' (*Sociāldemokrātiskā Partija 'Saskaņa'*), the LSP's most regular coalition partner and since 2011 the largest party in the Latvian Parliament, impacted upon its response to the economic crisis. The third main 'Russian left' party we examine is For Human Rights in United Latvia (*Par cilvēka tiesībām vienotā Latvijā*, PCTVL), which has latterly developed from a declaratively left-wing, socially oriented party into the ethnicised, radical-right Latvian Russian Union (*Latvijas Krievu savienība*, LKS). In 2002, PCTVL was Latvia's second-largest parliamentary party. However, it failed to gain any seats in the 2010, 2011 and 2014 parliamentary elections.[4]

LATVIA AND THE ECONOMIC CRISIS

The international economic crisis had a major impact on Latvia. Real, year-on-year GDP percentage growth had been in double digits for the three years preceding the crisis.[5] From late 2007, however, Latvia experienced two years of economic recession; a 70 per cent collapse in housing prices and rise in unemployment to 20.7 per cent.[6] One of the most striking aspects of the Latvian case is that, despite such economic hardships, the right-wing governing coalition (at times a numerical minority within the Latvian Parliament [*Saeima*]), was able to push through extensive austerity measures with only one brief period of public protests.

The austerity measures focused on so-called 'internal devaluation'[7]: public-sector wages were cut 35 per cent, 14,000 public-sector workers lost their jobs, 29 of a total 49 hospitals were closed and pensions were cut by 10 per cent.[8] At the same time, the national currency (the Lat) was pegged to the Euro, preventing purposeful currency depreciation and eventually helping Latvia join the Eurozone in 2014.

Public anger at the government's handling of the crisis peaked on 13 January 2009, when approximately 10,000 people took to Riga's streets, demanding the dissolution of Parliament. The protests culminated in violence as shops and vehicles were attacked and protesters tried (unsuccessfully) to force their way into Parliament. The protests had been called for by opposition parties and trade unions, but were largely out of their control and fuelled speculation that Latvian society was moving away from its traditional post-Soviet passivity towards a more radicalised 'Greek' protest model.[9]

Although this appeared a fertile context for exploitation by radical left groups, the protests soon diminished, especially after Prime Minister Ivars Godmanis resigned and Valdis Dombrovskis (of the centre-right New Era party) was appointed to head a re-jigged coalition in March 2009. Thereafter, notwithstanding small-scale, sporadic protests, the Latvian public faced the ensuing austerity drive stoically. After an economic recovery began in early 2010, Prime Minister Dombrovskis, who had overseen many of the harsh reforms, co-authored a book proclaiming the exemplary nature of the reform outcomes: 'Social unrest was minimal, and extremism nearly absent. ... Traditional populism lost out and ethnic tensions were reduced.'[10]

Certainly, the radical Left did not benefit electorally from the economic crisis. Whereas the centre-left 'Harmony Centre' coalition (in which the LSP participates) did dramatically increase its votes in the 2010 and 2011 Saeima elections, Latvian voters explicitly backed right-wing incumbent governments. Unexpectedly, Dombrovskis' Unity coalition received the greatest number of seats (33 of 100) in 2010, and despite repeated coalition turnover thereafter (common to Latvian politics), Unity returned to office in 2011 and 2014. Conversely, the LSP's vote and seat share remained stagnant throughout the crisis, even losing one of four seats in 2010 (see Table 12.1). We now explore the different, but ultimately unsuccessful strategies of the main parties of the Russian Left.

LATVIA'S 'RUSSIAN LEFT'

Latvia's demographic situation has significantly shaped the development of its RLPs. In 1989, ethnic Latvians made up just 52 per cent of the country's population, while Russians, Belarusians and Ukrainians (mostly Russian-speaking) comprised 42 per cent.[11] The bulk of these Russophones were Soviet-era migrants, provoking calls for the 'de-Russification' and 'decolonisation' of Latvia following independence in 1991.[12] Accordingly, the majority of Russophones were initially denied Latvian citizenship and only in 1998 were the majority of non-citizens allowed to apply for naturalisation. To this day, a significant proportion (37 per cent) of Russian speakers do not hold Latvian citizenship and are not eligible to vote.[13] This means that Russian-speaking citizens represent roughly 20 per cent of today's population.

Table 12.1 Parliamentary and European Representation of the 'Russian Left'

Party		1993 (5th Saeima)	1995 (6th Saeima)	1998 (7th Saeima)	2002 (8th Saeima)	2006 (9th Saeima)	2010 (10th Saeima)	2011 (11th Saeima)	2014 (12th Saeima)	2007 (EP)	2009 (EP)
Latvian Socialist Party (LSP)	%	L	5.6	TSP	PCTVL	SC	SC	SC	SDPS	1.7	SC
	Seats	(4)	5	(4)	(5)	(4)	(3)	(3)	(3)	0	1
Harmony (SDPS, TSP, SL)	%	12.0	5.6	14.2	PCTVL	14.4 (SC)	26.0 (SC)	28.4 (SC)	23.0	4.8	19.9
	Seats	13	6	16	(12)	17	29	31	24	0	1
Latvian Russian Union (LKS, PCTVL, L)	%	5.8	LSP	TSP	19.1	6.0	1.4	0.8	1.6	10.8	9.8
	Seats	7	0	(5)	25	6	0	0	0	1	1
Total	%	17.8	11.2	14.2	19.1	20.4	27.4	29.2	24.6	17.3	29.7
	Seats	20	11	16	25	23	29	31	24	1	3

Note: Latvia's Saeima comprises 100 seats. Abbreviations: EP: European Parliament; SC: Harmony Centre; PCTVL: For Human Rights in United Latvia (1993: Equal Rights Movement, L; 2014 Latvian Russian Union, LKS); SDPS: Social Democratic Party 'Harmony' (1993: Harmony for Latvia, SL; 1995–2006: People's Harmony Party, TSP).
Source: www.parties-and-elections.eu, authors' calculations.

Jānis Ikstens notes that, as a consequence of Latvia's demographic peculiarities, the party system has largely been determined by two cleavages – ethnic and socio-economic.[14] Latvia's political spectrum traverses left to right, but often conflates socio-economic positions with ethnic ones.[15] In many respects, this is due to 'a tendency for "Latvian" parties to adopt right-of-centre positions on economic issues, with the "Slavic" parties leaning towards leftist solutions in economic policy'. Consequently, while relatively weak urban-rural and liberal-conservative cleavages are observable, 'the ethnic cleavage has remained the major division shaping the Latvian party system'.[16]

There appears to be a high level of support for leftist social ideals in Latvia. Several surveys have pointed to leftist social preferences not only among Russian speakers, but also many ethnic Latvians.[17] In this respect, Latvia seems little different from other post-communist countries where a paternalistic, egalitarian 'socialist value culture' underpinned strong left-wing parties.[18] However, the post-Soviet Latvian electorate has never elected a left-leaning government. The major explanation for this discrepancy appears to be that the political expression of even the social democratic 'Left' is tied discursively to concepts associated with the Soviet past and, by extension, to Russianness. An overview of the parties of the 'Russian left' helps to illustrate this point.

As well as being a minority, the Russian-speaking electorate is ideologically divided, with three principal tendencies: nostalgic 'Soviet internationalists', 'Great Russia' imperialists and supporters of multi-ethnicity.[19] Such ideological divisions underpin today's Latvian Socialist Party, Latvian Russian Union and Harmony respectively, and explain why their coalitions have often been fractious.

The LSP has been Latvia's most prominent RLP since its formation in 1994. It can be understood as a 'communist successor party': although it does not claim direct continuity with the (former ruling) Latvian Communist Party out of political expediency because the KPL was banned in 1991. Latvian legislation still prohibits communist symbols and prevents those who were KPL members after 13 January 1991 running for national office.

Indeed, the LSP's continuity with the communist past is apparent in both ideology and personnel. It is a Marxist party, which steadfastly clings to Soviet shibboleths such as democratic centralism, class struggle, imperialism and proletarian internationalism. It remains rooted to theories of dialectical and historical materialism.[20] In comparative terms, the party is a nostalgic 'conservative communist' party, evidenced by membership of the International Meetings of Communist and Workers' Parties initiated by the Greek Communist Party. Indicatively, the LSP's leader from 1999 until retirement in 2015 was Alfrēds Rubiks, the last head of the KPL, who was imprisoned from 1995 to 1997 for conspiring to overthrow the new Latvian government while supporting the August 1991 Soviet coup against Mikhail Gorbachev.

Some successor parties have benefited at elections from pointing to their 'usable past', that is, a history of governing competence or independent decision-making in the Soviet era.[21] But the LSP has little usable past to offer: notwithstanding its internationalism, its arch-conservatism is buttressed by a strong link with *Russianness*. Whereas successor parties in Russia, Ukraine and Moldova have been able to utilise (some) positive associations with the Soviet developmental model, in the Baltic states many simply associate this model with Russian colonialism.[22] After all, only about one-third of the KPL membership was ethnically Latvian, making it the least 'national' Soviet communist party, and one perceived as a 'foreign' entity.[23]

Little wonder then, that from 1995 onwards the LSP has occupied a niche position, with three to five deputies (of 100) in the Latvian Saeima (Table 12.1). Additionally, the party obtained one seat in the 2009 European Parliament elections (taken up by Rubiks, because of his ban on standing in domestic elections). Given the Saeima's 5-per cent threshold, these modest results forced the party to canvass within a number of wider left and centre-left alliances (see Table 12.1) since the 1998 Saeima elections.

As a result, it is impossible to understand the development of the Latvian radical Left without also understanding the challenges and opportunities afforded to the broader Left in Latvia. The LSP contested the 1998 elections under the People's Harmony Party list and soon afterwards both parties joined the coalition For Human Rights in United Latvia (PCTVL).

In 2003, both the LSP and the People's Harmony Party left the PCTVL coalition following acrimonious disputes about its strategic direction. The People's Harmony Party then created Harmony Centre (*Saskaņas Centrs* SC) which in 2006 displaced PCTVL as the most electorally successful 'Russian' alliance in Latvian politics, and took most of its 2002 vote. SC united a number of centre-left parties with the more radical LSP. In 2010 the centre-left parties within the alliance merged to form The Social Democratic Party 'Harmony' (SDPS). SC therefore represented a notable shift towards the Centre-Left. In its 2005 programme, the LSP justified its participation within SC by noting that it was forced to cooperate 'under the conditions of bourgeois dictatorship', while all the time maintaining that transition from capitalism to socialism was inevitable.[24]

In 2014, Harmony Centre was officially dissolved and the LSP and Harmony contested the 2014 European Parliament elections separately. After a poor showing in these elections (LSP lost their single seat while Harmony only obtained one European mandate), Harmony allocated LSP three seats from its party list in the 2014 Saeima elections, despite having hinted that it might sever ties completely. Continued cooperation is therefore a marriage of convenience, with both parties sensing that their electoral success is maximised through collaboration. Nevertheless, collaboration remains problematic:

the LSP's obvious continuity with its Soviet predecessor sullies Harmony's increasing aspirations to be coalitionable and reinforces the unofficial *cordon sanitaire* against the 'Russian parties' in Latvian national politics.

At the same time, 'Latvian' left-leaning parties (i.e. parties whose electorates are comprised of significant ethnic Latvians) have long been unable to garner substantial electoral support. Significantly, 1998 was the last time any such 'Latvian' party gained Saeima representation. The Social Democratic Workers' Party (LSDSP) (a merger of the former ex-Menshevik party influential in Latvia's interwar republic and the pro-independence split from the KPL) obtained 14 seats in 1998 but failed to return a single deputy in 2002. The LSDSP has tried to distance itself from the communist past. It sets out a centre-left but anti-austerity programme and supports Latvia's EU membership (unlike the LSP) and NATO membership (unlike the LSP and PCTVL).[25] But not even the predominance of ethnic Latvian members and Latvian-language literature has insulated it from association with Russianness. The very use of 'social' in the party name negatively ties the organisation to the Soviet past.[26]

Indicatively, the principal catalyst for the party splitting disastrously in 2002 was its cooperation with PCTVL in the Riga municipality in 2001–2005. Breaking the taboo on cooperation with 'Russian' organisations has caused lasting damage.[27] Indeed, as Stephen Bloom notes, after the demise of the LSDSP, 'ethnic Latvian voters with leftist political views must either cross the ethnic cleavage and vote for a Russian minority party, or waste their votes by voting for a smaller ethnic Latvian leftist party'.[28]

The discursive association of PCTVL and the LSP with Russianness can therefore be attributed to a number of factors, not least the Soviet experience of communism. Even relatively moderate left-wing parties, however, such as Harmony (which unlike PCTVL and the LSP originated in the independence movement) have been unable to shake the notion that they are exclusively Russian, precisely because they espouse leftist values and aims. At the same time, the majority of parties that wish to be seen as 'normal', 'Latvian' parties have often adopted right-wing policies in order to distance themselves from any association with Russianness and Russia.

Ethnic polarisation has therefore persisted in the context of Latvia's 'ethnic democracy' or 'militant democracy',[29] exemplified by the restrictive citizenship policy which aims at excluding 'Moscow's protégés'.[30] Initially, only citizens of the pre-Soviet Latvian Republic and their direct ancestors were eligible for Latvian citizenship and this excluded the majority of Russian speakers in Latvia who were Soviet-era immigrants.

A major concern for left-wing parties in Latvia has, understandably, centred on the issue of citizenship. The PCTVL and Harmony factions have campaigned extensively for greater minority rights for Latvia's Slavic population, with particular focus on education, citizenship and language policies.[31] Although the pursuit of equal rights is a central aim of left-wing parties the world over, in the Latvian context, this inevitably led to the impression that the Left was fighting for the rights of the Russian population in opposition to the newly-acquired sovereignty of the Latvian Republic.

For Ivars Ijabs, the Left's problem results from the centrality of nation-building to Latvia's democratic institutions and thereby a tension between liberal and ethnic approaches within this militant democracy. He notes that 'the initial exclusion of the Soviet-era immigrants from the Latvian *demos* was seen as a precondition for democracy, and a particular type of nation-building, centred on the ethnic Latvian nation, as a necessary limitation of democracy for the sake of democracy itself'.[32] Consequently, traditionally left-wing concerns are often perceived as inherently threatening to Latvia's nation-building project *and* constitutional order.

Additionally, the 'Russian left' has struggled to avoid entanglement in Latvia's fraught 'memory politics' concerning the Soviet legacy. In 2010 Harmony Centre become the second-largest party in Parliament. Subsequently, it expanded to become the largest party at the 2011 snap general election, and it became possible for the SC to be included a new government coalition for the first time.[33] However, its inclusion in government was blocked, partly because its leftist economic programme advocated increasing public expenditure in contrast to the general consensus among 'Latvian' parties for prolonging internal devaluation. Yet the central argument for excluding SC rested on the party's perceived pro-Sovietism. For example, in the daily newspaper *Diena* V. Liepiņš (Zatlers' Reform Party MP) did not rule out future cooperation with SC, but noted it was then impossible because 'he was not convinced of SC's ability to be loyal to the Latvian state: "the fact of the matter is that they do not acknowledge the occupation. They think that it was a fateful event which occurred and they do not have a problem with that"' (*Diena* 25.09.11, emphasis added).

POLITICAL CONSEQUENCES OF THE ECONOMIC CRISIS

This section shows how ethnic divisions in Latvian politics have shaped the response of political parties to the 2008 economic crisis. Indeed, the economic and social upheavals of the crisis did not fundamentally challenge the clear political boundaries between 'Russian/Slavic' and 'Latvian' political entrepreneurs. Instead, the economic crisis *reinforced* these ethnic boundaries. As such, pan-national intellectual and strategic engagement with economic issues is greatly constrained, which has made it difficult for the Left to translate the crisis into political gains.

In particular, the Left's intellectual responses to the crisis have been constrained by the need to retain core support among Russian speakers. Consequently, the LSP and other sections of the 'Russian' Left have been reluctant to break with Soviet-era aesthetics. The radical Left has largely maintained its focus on the human and political rights of Latvia's non-citizens, the status of the Russian language in Latvia, and (in the case of the LSP) the importance of the memory of Soviet victory in World War II. This has impeded the articulation of a coherent economic argument about the crisis that could be consumed by a broader, non-ethnicised audience. At the same time, whereas Harmony has often tried to transcend such issues and to articulate a coherent, de-ethnicised alternative economic programme, it has been constantly forced to re-emphasise its ethnic credentials or face losing support among its primary electorate.

Abrupt changes in macroeconomic conditions have been found to induce changes in the saliency of ethnicity.[34] It was therefore unsurprising that Latvian politics experienced a renewed spike in ethnicisation following the crisis, most evident in a series of controversial language and constitutional referendums. Although the crisis peaked in 2008–2009, it was not until 2010 that the real ethnicisation started. In the run-up to the October 2010 general election, the nationalist party For Fatherland and Freedom/Latvian National Movement (later forming the National Alliance coalition [NA] with the other main nationalist party All for Latvia!) announced plans to instigate a nationwide referendum to outlaw Russian as a language of instruction in Latvia's publicly-funded schools.[35] Importantly, this issue ensured the continued entrenchment of ethnicity as the most salient political cleavage in Latvian politics.

Harmony Centre had been gradually trying to reduce its image as an exclusively Slavic/Russian party by including more ethnically Latvian names on its party lists and ensuring that its public representatives all spoke fluent Latvian.[36] Its main strategic response to the crisis had been to focus on concrete economic issues over ethnic ones, criticising the austerity reforms of the incumbent government and highlighting the need for greater social guarantees.[37] For example, SC leader Nils Ušakovs noted how the economic crisis brought Latvians and Russians together as 'all are suffering equally from economic problems'.[38]

This strategy looked propitious after Ušakovs became the first ethnic Russian Riga mayor in 2009 and SC was poised to become the largest Saeima party. Harmony Centre's opponents feared that the economic consequences of the crisis might help it make gains among the ethnic Latvian electorate. In response, the National Alliance fell back on a familiar repertoire that forced SC to re-emphasise the interests of its (mainly Russian-speaking) electorate, thereby falling into the trap of increased ethnicisation. When Harmony Centre argued against the referendum initiative, nationalist parties inevitably found it easy to cast SC as pro-Russian and as 'a hateful force towards Latvians'.[39]

Ultimately, although the National Alliance did not succeed in gathering the required number of signatures for a nationwide referendum (10 per cent of the registered electorate), its actions reinforced ethnic boundaries.[40] Perhaps predictably, the failed attempt to initiate a referendum led to a counter-reaction by Russian minority organisations and representatives. The previously fringe extreme leftist United Latvia and Native Language, for example, were able to galvanise support for a counter-referendum that would make constitutional changes to give Russian the status of the second state language of Latvia.[41]

SC initially rejected calls for a referendum. After all, these were supported most prominently by individuals with ultra-radical ethnic agendas (combined with left-wing ideologies). It also had good reason to do so given its intention to appeal to the wider Latvian electorate and move beyond Latvia's ethnicised cleavages. However, in November 2011, the party reversed its stance and gave full support to the referendum.[42]

Consequently, with SC's backing, United Latvia and Native Language were successful in securing 187,378 signatures (from a required 154,379) in favour of staging a referendum. In the end, however, 75 per cent opposed the introduction of Russian as a second language from a referendum turnout of 71 per cent of eligible voters. For David Lublin, this whole episode 'serves as an example of how pressure from more extreme parties can help polarize more moderate ethnic parties and leaders, among both the majority and the minority'.[43]

The referendum clearly illustrated the dilemma that Harmony Centre faced. As prominent SC politicians eventually backed the language initiative, they reinforced arguments portraying their party as pro-Russian and anti-Latvian, and this diverted attention away from their economic programme of increased social spending. At the same time, as the referendum initiative gathered momentum, it simply became politically untenable for SC to ignore the demands of their predominantly Russian-speaking electorate. There was an almost exact match between the ethnicity of voters and their decision to support or oppose the referendum proposals.[44]

Interestingly, the LSP's strategic response to the referendum was generally one of neutrality, despite being part of the SC coalition. Party leader Rubiks stated that he would not participate in it and supported Latvia's 'status quo'.[45] Unlike the extreme Left which championed the referendum, the LSP doggedly upholds the communist ideal of internationalism and makes a point of publishing materials in both Russian and Latvian.

In fact, this apparently virtuous stance is a symptom of the LSP's deeper reluctance to make any meaningful strategic or intellectual changes to its party programme. The party's official publication *Latvian Socialist* simply sidestepped the referendum issue completely.[46] However, Soviet internationalism did not preclude some deeply Russocentric, ethnicised strategies. For instance, the LSP remains fixated on the topic of the Red Army's victory over Nazi Germany in World War II, one of the major issues demarcating ethnic boundaries in contemporary Latvia.[47] The importance of the 'Great Patriotic War' (as it is termed in Russia) in maintaining the political legitimacy both of the Soviet Union and Vladimir Putin's post-Soviet Russia is widely acknowledged. For the LSP, reverence for the Soviet/Russian interpretations of the conflict also underpins its historic role and legitimacy. For example, the December 2009 edition of *Latvian Socialist* reported that the LSP's most important annual achievement was organising the annual gathering for veterans of the Great Patriotic War at the Kurgan Druzhby cemetery in Belarus.

The LSP's Non-Response to the Crisis

The LSP has produced just two-party resolutions specifically mentioning the economic crisis, both at the LSP's 2009 Party Congress. The December 2009 *Latvian Socialist* reproduced the four Congress resolutions. It was notable that two ('No to anti-communism', 'In support of an objective history of the Second World War') focused exclusively on historical memory. The other two emphasised 'support for small and medium-sized employers' and that 'the government needs to take responsibility for the crisis and the catastrophic fall in Latvians' standard of living'. The latter included strong criticism of the right-wing government's austerity policies. It is apparent, however, that this resolution lacked any concrete policy proposals. The LSP has made few detailed economic policies in response to the crisis. It has been rare for such issues to play a central role in its political strategy.

Indeed, the party has long argued that Latvia has undergone a far-reaching socio-economic crisis caused by 'anti-people' market reforms and corrupt elites in the context of imperialist globalisation.[48] The major means whereby the LSP conceptualised the latest crisis was to juxtapose Latvia's disastrous economic situation (high unemployment, shrinking manufacturing sector, critical outflow of labour to other EU countries) with the Soviet model (full employment, thriving manufacturing sector, inflow of skilled labour from the rest of the Soviet Union).

Overall, the party's messages remain ritualistic, and framed in a familiar Soviet lexicon and aesthetics. Images in LSP publications, for example, depict Soviet statues, Red Army war veterans and pictures from World War II. The party, like the Czech KSČM, has preferred to be the 'introverted' guardian of the Soviet sub-culture than to fundamentally adapt to emerging challenges. It is true that the party has long called for mobilisation of left-wing parties, trade unions and social movements against the 'bourgeois' government.

Yet the LSP is utterly unable to realise such a mobilisation. After all, Latvia suffers from the general post-Soviet syndrome of feeble social movements. In particular, trade unions are weak and have few ties to political parties, let alone the Left.[49] The LSP has admitted that its contacts with trade unions are woeful.[50] Moreover, it is an organisation less than 1,000-strong, which struggles to expand or impose internal discipline.[51] Indicatively, the reasons the youth organisation United Latvia gave for leaving the LSP in 2010 were political passivity and being a 'Rubiks fanclub'.[52] The cumulative image is of a nostalgic entity, unwilling and unable to break with the traditions of the 'Russian Left'.

THE CONSEQUENCES OF THE 'ETHNIC' UKRAINIAN CRISIS

It is important to note that the recent development of RLPs in Latvia has also been shaped by external, geopolitical developments. Russia's annexation of the Crimean peninsula in 2014, for example, had direct implications for Latvian RLPs. President Putin justified Russia's actions in Crimea by citing the need to protect Russian speakers, and many were quick to highlight existing and potential parallels with the demographic and ethnic situation in Latvia.

Owing to Latvia's highly ethnicised political system, the 'ethnic crisis' had just as significant an effect on the Left as the economic one and forced the 'Russian Left' to decide how to react to the heightened geopolitical tensions. We refer to the Ukrainian crisis as 'ethnic', not because this was its sole essence, but because it was largely perceived in ethnic terms within Latvia's political debates. As in the economic crisis, it is noticeable how the LSP has largely pursued a 'status quo' position, rarely mentioning this crisis, with the exception of lambasting the interference of US, EU and NATO imperialists in Ukraine's affairs and for supporting 'nationalist' and 'fascistic' forces.[53]

Consequently, this section focuses on the two other most significant 'Russian left' parties in Latvia, Harmony and the Latvian Russian Union (LKS), whose responses to the Ukrainian crisis have been more dynamic than the LSP's. The LKS evolved from the rump For Human Rights in United Latvia (PCTVL), the largest left-wing coalition in 1998–2002. PCTVL changed its name to the LKS in early 2014, which, we argue, indicates noticeable ethnicisation and a departure from some of the core leftist values it had previously espoused. As detailed above, Harmony replaced PCTVL as the most electorally successful left party in Latvia, and remains the partner of choice for the LSP. Examining the political discourse of these two parties helps understand the ethnic pressures that continue to define Latvia's political party system. As such, this section analyses data from the respective websites and party programmes of Harmony and the LKS from February to May 2014.[54]

Harmony's public statements during the period in question continued its attempts to transcend ethnic divisions, a trend evident since the start of the economic crisis. The majority of its statements in news articles focused on concrete policies unrelated to questions of identity or ethnicity. For example, the party called for the reversal of austerity policies that had reduced spending on education and medicine, a policy which, Harmony argued, would stimulate the economy and increase Latvia's investment potential (Harmony, 19.02.14).

Party documents reduced the salience of ethnic issues relative to those of economic prosperity. Consistent with its name, the party advocated interethnic harmony, arguing that 'our home is Latvia, and inhabitants of this land need to be united ... ignoring questions of history, language and such like. Only under these conditions will Latvia become a "prosperous home"' (Harmony, 10.05.14). Harmony's view of prosperity involved Latvia's advantageous investment potential as a bridge between Europe and Russia, thereby conceptualising the European Union and Russia as solutions to, rather than the causes of, the economic crisis (Harmony, 18.03.14). Overall, Harmony's approach envisaged Latvians and Russians as equal participants in a social democratic Latvia engaged in a globalised economy and attracting investment from the European Union and Russia alike.

However, events in Ukraine forced the party to set out its official position on the international crisis (Harmony 05.03.14). Harmony tried to avoid taking sides and gave support for the 'unconditional territorial integrity of Ukraine', the 'immediate, constructive dialogue between the EU, Russia, and Ukraine', and the rights of Ukraine's national and linguistic minorities. It also, however, repudiated efforts of Latvian politicians to escalate the situation in Latvia through criticising representatives of national minorities. Harmony thus, avoided explicit references to Russophones in Ukraine and argued that Russia's actions there did not entail a threat to Latvia.

Harmony's approach however, has reflected the aforementioned tension between liberal and ethnic approaches in Latvia's 'militant democracy'.[55] Despite its 'neutral' stance, Harmony has continued to appeal to the aesthetics of memory among its predominantly Russian-speaking electorate. Victory Day (9 May) is a symbolic date for many Russian speakers in Latvia as it marks Victory of the Soviet Army over Nazi Germany in World War II.[56] Therefore, similarly to the LSP, Harmony employs the 'Great Patriotic War' as a legitimising discourse. For example, Harmony is actively involved in organising annual Victory Day celebrations in Riga.

At the same time, Harmony has attempted to de-ethnicise these celebrations. In 2014, Harmony argued that 'Ušakovs asks for people to protect and love Latvia regardless of nationality' (Harmony 10.05.14). The party also refers to the sacred memory of the people who fought against Nazism, but the discourse is framed in terms of loyalty to Latvia: 'The children of the soldiers and veterans need to be worthy of their memory. They need to respect their state, Latvia, and trust in it.'

Ultimately, the Ukraine crisis seriously compromised Harmony's political neutrality. Russia's annexation of Crimea and the armed conflict in south-east Ukraine were significant themes in the May 2014 European and October 2014 Saeima elections. Harmony suffered a significant setback in May, losing 6 per cent of its vote and one of two EP seats, largely because of its unconvincing stance: 'Hardline Russophones voted for [the LKS] and the populist Alternative party while moderates switched their vote to the governing Unity (*Vienotība*) party.'[57] Harmony's contortions became starkly visible. The day after the EP elections, its website (referring to the LKS), warned that 'Radical Russian forces will enter the next *Saeima*' (Harmony 26.05.14). However, only two days later, the website adopted a more radical, opposing view:

> Ethnic Latvians are scared because they've started to think what they would do if they were in the position of ethnic Russians in [Latvia]. After twenty-five years of persecution and insult they would also have turned to 'radical leaders' or 'little green men' for help.[58] When there is a defender of the oppressed (he's called VVP [Vladimir Vladimirovich Putin]), they are scared that Russian Latvians will turn to him. (Harmony 28.05.14)

Indeed, the 'Putin question' highlights Harmony's problem in balancing economic and ethnic issues. Harmony has long had a cooperation agreement with United Russia (Putin's ruling party), and prior to the May election Ušakovs had announced in a TV interview in Moscow that Putin was the 'best possible' leader for Russia in the current climate. Harmony thereafter articulated a Janus-faced position of 'largely denouncing Russian actions to Latvian audiences while speaking in a more subtle and supportive tone to Russophone ones'.[59]

The pressures to adopt a more ethnicised tone and increased competition for the Russophone vote from radicalised 'Russian' parties were most evident in the emergence of the Latvian Russian Union in early 2014. The LKS' predecessor, For Human Rights in United Latvia had always held Russophone rights central to its agenda, but also articulated a left-leaning economic programme calling for higher social spending and greater state involvement in the economy.[60] For example, its (pre-crisis) 2006 programme prioritised economic goals above ethnic ones, with the issues of status of the Russian language and non-citizenship appearing merely as the ninth and tenth headings.[61] Instead, the programme promised to raise social guarantees 'to the European level', increase pensions and wages to the real living minimum, to spend no less than 8 per cent of GDP on the health service, and to stimulate growth in Latvia's export industries.

Following the economic crisis, PCTVL responded by emphasising its credentials as the party that supported the cultural and linguistic rights of Russian speakers. Its 2010 party programme pledged to turn Latvia into a 'Baltic Luxemburg' by facilitating multilingualism and using the Russian community as a unique economic resource to attract investments from the European Union and Russia.[62] Additionally, PCTVL started to refer to itself specifically as 'the party of the Russian community in Latvia' instead of a party that supported equal rights (as its name suggested).[63] The economic component of the PCTVL programme did not disappear, but became less visible, especially because Harmony Centre's overlapping social and economic messages were being articulated with more success through slicker marketing, and more dynamic (younger) personalities.

In contrast, the Latvian Russian Union demonstrated a much narrower scope of interests and focused exclusively on ethnicised issues such as the protection of Russian schools (LKS 03.03.14), celebration of Victory Day (LKS 16.03.14), calls for protests and pickets in support of Russia's actions in Crimea (LKS 10.03.14), diatribes against corrupt western values (LKS 12.03.14) and highlighting 'Russophobia' and 'anti-Russian' sentiments in the Baltic states (LKS 06.05.14). Policies that went beyond ethnic issues were largely ignored. Unsurprisingly, LKS's stance became almost entirely congruent with contemporary Russian state discourses, with emphasis on the historical-cultural, spiritual and civilisational uniqueness of the Russian nation and its separateness from 'postmodern' Europe and 'fascistic' Latvia.[64] Russia's allegedly benevolent support for Russophone rights in Latvia was endorsed wholesale. On the question of Russia's annexation of Crimea, LKS (20.05.14) adopted an entirely pro-Russian position and argued that 'the Russian army, as is natural, came to the defence of peaceful citizens and its co-citizens'.

Analysis of Harmony and the LKS's discourses on the Ukraine crisis is therefore very telling. Harmony highlights the duality of Latvia's ethnicised and liberal-republican approaches to democracy, caught between focusing on socio-economic arguments and periodically feeling forced to revert to discourses of ethnic discrimination. In contrast, LKS demonstrates how it has transitioned from a socio-economically leftist party to a radicalised ethnic one, as anti-elite ethnic populism increasingly subsumed its economic programme during the economic and Ukrainian crises. In most contexts LKS would now be categorised as a radical right-wing party. However, amidst the peculiarities of Latvian politics, it remains popularly perceived as a party of the radical Left.

The electoral consequences of these processes have, as yet, been minimal. Harmony partially recovered from its May 2014 debacle, and despite losing votes in October 2014, maintained its position as Latvia's biggest Saeima party with 24 seats (previously 31) (Table 12.1). Although LKS leader Tatjana Ždanoka was re-elected as an MEP in May and the party doubled its previous Saeima vote in October, its result of 1.6 per cent remained far below the required 5-per cent Saeima threshold. This gives grounds to suggest that heavily ethnicised Russian discourses lack resonance with the majority of Latvia's Russian speakers, at least among the politically-enfranchised members.

Of course, we may also expect that LKS discourses resonate more with non-voting, non-citizens who generally articulate more allegiance to Russia than Latvia.[65] Nevertheless, these developments point to the continued salience of ethnicity within Latvian politics and demonstrate how the 'Russian Left' has been unable to articulate coherent, de-ethnicised economic policies.

CONCLUSION

This chapter examined why RLPs in Latvia have been unable to mobilise popular support following the 2008 crisis. The crisis, brought acute economic decline and rising unemployment to Latvia and governments enacted austerity-based remedies. These could have boosted support for the radical Left as in Greece, Spain and Portugal. In Latvia, while the centre-left Harmony, with which the radical left Socialist Party has a long-term alliance, benefited electorally in 2010–2011, it failed to capitalise on this success. The LSP's vote has stagnated.

We have argued that the major reason for the failure of the Left and the radical Left has been Latvia's post-Soviet ethnicised party system which results in the Left being viewed as a Russophone 'fifth column' as it struggles to separate leftist socio-economic preferences from ethnic concerns. Consequently, the Left remains divided and partially disenfranchised. In large part this is a legacy of Soviet occupation, which means that concepts such as socialism and a strong welfare state are closely tied to the Soviet experience. Moreover, the Ukrainian 'ethnic crisis' showed that the Soviet-era relationship between the defence of minority rights and Russification is not historically obsolescent and accelerated further ethnicisation of the Left.

Might the Left have solved this problem through adopting more effective supply-side strategies? Certainly, the division of forces into three often-competing parliamentary parties has often divided the Left's potential, albeit this division reflects ongoing ideological divisions (social democratic, socialist and Russophile) among Latvia's Russophones. Moreover, the consequence of Latvia's ethnicisation leaves the Left in a classic electoral bind: moving to the centre risks defection to more hard-line Russophile groups, while nourishing the Russophone electorate risks entrenching a 'Russian' image that is antagonistic to many ethnic Latvians.

The strategies of the major left parties demonstrate how they have limited room for manoeuvre. Harmony's attempts to articulate a coherent, de-ethnicised social democratic position and alternatives to austerity have allowed it to become the dominant left player, eclipsing the more minority-focused PCTVL and attracting some ethnic Latvians. Yet this chapter has shown how nationalist parties diverted attention away from economic issues, forcing Harmony to re-emphasise its 'Russian' positions.

As the most prominent RLP in Latvia, the LSP continues to articulate an all-too-familiar agenda: the lexicon and aesthetics of Soviet Marxism-Leninism in all but name. Whereas its pragmatic alliances have allowed it a parliamentary niche, its subordinate position within these alliances has failed to nurture a sustainable, independent profile. Moreover, it has resisted substantive changes to its intellectual or strategic priorities, leaving it with a conservative communism that both fails to capture new audiences and immediately serves to ethnicise the party (and by extension Harmony), since for many in Latvia, Sovietisation equals Russification.

Finally, the Latvian Russian Union was originally a leftist minority-rights party, and remains a radical left party in Latvian parlance, but now represents a radical-right ethnic Russian party whose strategy has increasingly been to ignore economic issues almost entirely. In these contexts, it is little wonder that the radical Left has been so ineffective and that Latvia's neoliberal consensus has continued to dominate the political scene, despite the effects of a deep and socially devastating economic crisis.

NOTES

1. Mark Weisbrot and Rebecca Ray, 'Latvia's Internal Devaluation: A Success Story?' (Centre for Economic and Policy Research, 2011), 3, http://www.cepr.net/documents/publications/latvia-2011-12.pdf.

2. Josephine Moulds, 'Estonia and Latvia: Europe's Champions of Austerity?,' *The Guardian*, 8 June 2012, sec. World news, http://www.theguardian.com/world/2012/jun/08/estonia-latvia-eurozone-champions-austerity.

3. Ryo Nakai, 'The Influence of Party Competition on Minority Politics: A Comparison of Latvia and Estonia,' *Journal on Ethnopolitics and Minority Issues in Europe* 13, no. 1 (2014): 57–85.

4. In 2014 it canvassed as LKS.

5. Yoji Koyama, 'Economic Crisis in the Baltic States: Focusing on Latvia', *Economic Annals* 55, no. 186 (2010): 99.

6. Anders Åslund and Valdis Dombrovskis, *How Latvia Came Through the Financial Crisis* (Washington, DC: Peterson Institute of International Economics, 2011), 85.

7. Weisbrot and Ray, 'Latvia's Internal Devaluation: A Success Story?'.

8. Anders Åslund, *The Last Shall Be the First: The East European Financial Crisis* (Washington, DC: Peterson Institute for International Economics, 2010), 37.

9. Ellen Barry, 'Latvia Is Shaken by Riots Over Its Weak Economy,' *The New York Times*, 14 January 2009, http://www.nytimes.com/2009/01/15/world/europe/15latvia.html?_r=0.

10. Åslund and Dombrovskis, *How Latvia Came Through the Financial Crisis*, 2.

11. Mark Jubulis, *Nationalism and Democratic Transition : The Politics of Citizenship and Language in Post-Soviet Latvia* (Oxford: University Press of America, 2001), 47.

12. Ammon Cheskin, *Russian Speakers in Post-Soviet Latvia: Discursive Identity Strategies* (Edinburgh: Edinburgh University Press, 2016), 54.

13. Office of Citizen and Migration Affairs, 'Latvijas Iedzivotaju Sadalijums Pec Nacionala Sastava Un Valstiskas Piederibas (The Division of Latvia's Inhabitants by Nationality and Citizenship)', 1 January 2015, http://www.pmlp.gov.lv/lv/assets/documents/statistika/01.01.2015/ISVN_Latvija_pec_TTB_VPD.pdf.

14. Janis Ikstens, 'Does Europe Matter? The EU and Latvia's Political Parties,' in *The European Union and Party Politics in Central and Eastern Europe*, ed. Paul Lewis and Zdenka Mansfeldova (Basingstoke: Palgrave, 2006), 87.

15. For example, Artis Pabriks and Aiga Štokenberga, 'Political Parties and the Party System in Latvia,' in *Post-Communist EU Member States: Parties and Party Systems*, ed. Susanne Jungerstam-Mulders (Aldershot: Ashgate, 2006), 66.

16. Daunis Auers, 'An Electoral Tactic? Citizens' Initiatives in Post-Soviet Latvia', in *Citizens' Initiatives in Europe: Procedures and Consequences of Agenda-Setting by Citizens*, ed. Maija. Setälä and Theo Schiller (Basingstoke: Palgrave, 2012), 62.

17. For example, Richard Rose, 'New Baltic Barometer III: A Survey Study,' *Studies in Public Policy* 284 (1997), http://www.balticvoices.org/documents/spp-284.pdf. Latter at http://www.balticvoices.org/documents/spp-401.pdf; Richard Rose, 'New Baltic Barometer VI: A Post-Enlargement Survey,' *Studies in Public Policy* 401 (2005); Victor Makarov, 'Latvian Political Culture: Democratic or Authoritarian Bias? An Interpretation Attempt Based on a Survey Study,' (Baltic Forum, 2002), http://www.balticforum.org/files_uploads/files/vm_survey2002-1.pdf.

18. Paul T. Christensen, 'Socialism after Communism?: The Socioeconomic and Cultural Foundations of Left Politics in Post-Soviet Russia,' *Communist and Post-Communist Studies* 31, no. 4 (1998): 345–57.

19. Boris Tsilevich, cited in Brita Skuland, 'The Impact of Historical Conflicts and Cleavages on the Formation of New Political Oppositions in Latvia' (University of Oslo, 2005), 63.

20. The party's documents are expounded in detail in A. Rubiks and F. Stroganov (eds.), *SPL: Istoriya v Dokumentakh* (Riga: Latvijas Sociālistiskā partija, 2006).

21. For example, Anna Grzymała-Busse, *Redeeming the Communist Past: The Regeneration of Communist Parties in East Central Europe* (Cambridge: Cambridge University Press, 2002).

22. Vello Pettai and Marcus Kreuzer, 'Party Politics in the Baltic States: Social Bases and Institutional Context,' *East European Politics & Societies* 13, no. 1 (1998): 160.

23. Artis Pabriks and Aldis Purs, *Latvia: The Challenges of Change* (Abingdon: Routledge, 2002), 37.

24. As cited in Aivars Ozoliņš, 'Nebalsotāji Atbalstīs Rubiku (Non-Voters Support Rubiks)', *Diena*, 6 October 2006, http://www.diena.lv/arhivs/nebalsotaji-atbalstis-rubiku-12925970.

25. LSDSP, 'Latvijas Sociāldemokrātiskās Strādnieku Partijas (LSDSP) īsā Programma [The Concise Programme of the Social Democratic Party of Latvia (LSDSP)]', http://www.lsdsp.lv/faili/upload/programma.pdf.

26. Pabriks and Štokenberga, 'Political Parties and the Party System in Latvia', 55.

27. Janis Ikstens, 'Latvia', in *The Palgrave Handbook of Social Democracy in the European Union*, ed. Jean-Michel de Waele, Fabien Escalona and Mathieu Vieira (Basingstoke: Palgrave Macmillan, 2013), 470–87.

28. Stephen Bloom, 'The 2010 Latvian Parliamentary Elections', *Electoral Studies* 30, no. 2 (2011): 381.

29. For example, Graham Smith, 'The Ethnic Democracy Thesis and the Citizenship Question in Estonia and Latvia', *Nationalities Papers* 24, no. 2 (1996): 199–216; Ivars Ijabs, 'After the Referendum: Militant Democracy and Nation-Building in Latvia', *East European Politics & Societies* 30, no. 2 (May 2016): 288–314.

30. P. Kolsto and B. Tsilevich, 'Patterns of Nation Building and Political Integration in a Bifurcated Postcommunist State: Ethnic Aspects of Parliamentary Elections in Latvia', *East European Politics & Societies* 11, no. 2 (1997): 368–71.

31. Ikstens, 'Does Europe Matter?', 89.

32. Ijabs, 'After the Referendum', 4.

33. President Valdis Zatlers dissolved Parliament following MPs' refusal to sanction the home search of prominent businessman and MP Ainārs Šlesers (Latvia's First Party/Latvian Way), following corruption charges.

34. Francesco Caselli and W. J. Coleman, 'On the Theory of Ethnic Conflict', *Journal of the European Economic Association* 11 (2013): 166.

35. Auers, 'An Electoral Tactic? Citizens' Initiatives in Post-Soviet Latvia', 62–4.

36. Following election to the 10th *Saeima*, Harmony Centre deputy Valērijs Kravcovs became the centre of attention for his inability to speak Latvian. MPs from the National Alliance demanded that he be stripped of his parliamentary mandate and an investigation was launched into how he was able to obtain Latvian citizenship (which requires basic knowledge of Latvian). See http://www.tvnet.lv/zinas/latvija/427019-kravcovs_nolemis_kartot_valsts_valodas_prasmes_parbaudijumu (accessed 26 January 2016).

37. Cheskin, *Russian Speakers in Post-Soviet Latvia*.

38. As cited in Vija Sile and Ilze Dzalbe, 'The Financial Crisis and the Discourses of Latvia's Political Parties,' *European Integration Studies* 5 (2012): 105.

39. Personal interview with Saeima deputy Jānis Dombrava (National Alliance), 14 March 2011. See also Ijabs, 'After the Referendum'.

40. 120,433 signatures were gathered out of a necessary 153,232. Inese Šūpule, 'The Construction of National and Ethnic Identity in Online Discussions on Referenda Initiatives in Latvia,' *Baltic Journal of European Studies* 2, no. 1 (2011): 124.

41. United Latvia (*Vienota Latvija*) is a former LSP youth organisation. The more militant NGO Native Language (*Za rodnoi yazyk*, ZaRYA) emerged in 2012 as a union of the populist RLP Osipov Party and '13 January'. The latter was a successor to the banned Russian extreme-left-nationalist National Bolshevik Party (NBP), and was headed by its controversial Latvian leader Vladimirs Lindermans, who has had a confrontational relationship both with the Russian authorities and the Latvian state. More recently, Lindermans has become a vocal supporter of Vladimir Putin.

42. David Lublin, 'The 2012 Latvia Language Referendum,' *Electoral Studies* 32, no. 2 (2013): 386.

43. Ibid.

44. Ibid., 387.

45. 'Rubiks Nepiedalīsies Referendumā Par Krievu Valodu,', *TVNET.lv*, 21 December 2011, http://www.tvnet.lv/zinas/viedokli/404375-rubiks_nepiedalisies _referenduma_par_krievu_valodu.

46. *Latvian Socialist* issues from 2006 to 2015 are available at http://latsocpartija. lv/ru/activities/paper/.

47. Ammon Cheskin, 'History, Conflicting Collective Memories, and National Identities: How Latvia's Russian-Speakers Are Learning to Remember,' *Nationalities Papers* 40, no. 4 (2012): 561–84.

48. Rubiks and Stroganov, *SPL: Istoriya v Dokumentakh*.

49. For example, Magdalena Bernaciak, Rebecca Gumbrell-McCormick and Richard Hyman, *Trade Unions in Europe Innovative Responses to Hard Times* (Berlin: Friedrich Ebert Stiftung, April 2014).

50. LSP, 'Otchetnyi Doklad Pravleniya i Politicheskogo soveta SPL XI s"ezdu Sotsialisticheskoi Partii Latvii Na XIX S"ezde', *Sotsialist Latvii*, 2(51) 2008, 8–9, http://latsocpartija.lv/ru/activities/paper/.

51. LSP, 'Otchetnyi Doklad Pravleniya Sotsialisticheskoi Partii Latvii Na XIX S"ezde', *LSP*, 12 January 2016, http://latsocpartija.lv/ru/news/234/.

52. '"Edinaya Latvia": Rubiks Nas Obmanul', *United Latvia Webpage*, 10 June 2010, http://www.vienotalatvija.lv/index.php?option=com_content&view=article& id=113%3A-l-r-&catid=3%3Anewsflash&Itemid=11&lang=ru.

53. For example, LSP, 'Otchetnyi Doklad Pravleniya Sotsialisticheskoi Partii Latvii Na XIX S"ezde'.

54. Harmony website http://www.saskanascentrs.lv/and LKS website: http://zap-chel.lv/.

55 For example, Ivars Ijabs, 'After the Referendum: Militant Democracy and Nation-Building in Latvia,' *East European Politics & Societies* (2015): 22.

56. Ammon Cheskin, 'History, Conflicting Collective Memories, and National Identities: How Latvia's Russian-Speakers Are Learning to Remember', *Nationalities Papers* 40, no. 4 (2012): 561–84.

57. Daunis Auers, 'The October 4th 2014 Parliamentary Election in Latvia,' *EPERN*, 28 October 2014, https://epern.wordpress.com/2014/10/28/the-october-4th-2014-parliamentary-election-in-latvia/.

58. This was the ironic name given to the armed soldiers who appeared without insignia in the Crimean peninsula before the region was incorporated into the Russian Federation. The Kremlin had maintained that these were local militias, but Putin later admitted to the presence of Russian troops operating in Crimea.

59. Auers, 'The October 4th 2014 Parliamentary Election in Latvia'.

60. Artis Pabriks and Aiga Štokenberga, 'Political Parties and the Party System in Latvia,' in *Post-Communist EU Member States: Parties and Party Systems*, ed. Susanne Jungerstam-Mulders (Aldershot: Ashgate, 2006), 57.

61. 'PROGRAMMA Ob"edineniya Politicheskikh Organizatsii "Za Prava Cheloveka v Edinoi Latvii" Na Vyborakh 9-Go Seima', *LKS Web Page*, 2006, http://zapchel.lv/index.php?lang=ru&mode=party&submode=program&page_id=3989.

62. 'Programma ZaPChEL Na Vyborakh 10-Go Seima', *LKS Web Page*, 2010, http://zapchel.lv/index.php?lang=ru&mode=party&submode=program&page_id=10629.

63. 'Programma ZaPChEL Na Vyborakh Rizhskoi Dumy 2009 G', *LKS Web Page*, 2009, http://zapchel.lv/index.php?lang=ru&mode=party&submode=program&page_id=10628.

64. Cheskin, *Russian Speakers in Post-Soviet Latvia*.

65. Market and public opinion research centre, 'Piederības Sajūta Latvijai: Mazākumtautību Latvijas Iedzīvotāju Aptauja [Feeling of Belonging to Latvia: A Survey of Latvia's Inhabitants],' June 2014, http://www.mk.gov.lv/sites/default/files/editor/atskaite_piederiba_08_2014.pdf.

Chapter 13

The Portuguese Radical Left and the Great Recession

Old Challenges and New Responses

André Freire and Marco Lisi

The implementation of austerity packages in Portugal had devastating socio-economic consequences (e.g. rising unemployment, economic decline and rising public debt ratio to GDP). The crisis became highly politicised as governments were forced to violate their electoral commitments and to promote policies they disliked. This chapter shows how the crisis fostered major change in the Portuguese party system, not least by facilitating cooperation among left-wing parties and providing innovative governmental possibilities. Portugal certainly did not witness the degree of change that engendered new social movements capable of generating successful new parties, as in Spain, Greece or Italy.[1] However, the minority government headed by the Socialist Party (*Partido Socialista*, PS) that took office in November 2015 was supported by the two main Portuguese RLPs, the Portuguese Communist Party PCP (*Partido Comunista Português*, PCP) and Left Bloc (*Bloco de Esquerda*, BE). It thereby ended the marginalisation of Portugal's radical Left that had endured since the beginning of the democratic regime in 1975.

In this chapter we address several questions. What are the major impacts in ideological, strategic, organisational and electoral terms of the crisis upon the radical Left in Portugal? Have RLPs benefited from the crisis, particularly at the electoral level? Finally, what are the reasons behind the historical agreement achieved after the 2015 general elections? We begin by outlining the historical development of the Portuguese radical Left. The second section deals with the effects of the crisis and in particular its impact on the ideological and programmatic adaptation of RLPs in Portugal. Third, we analyse the RLPs' strategies in terms of coalition politics, and show how these ended in an agreement to make the socialist minority government viable after the 2015 legislative elections. We assess the possibility of increasing strategic convergence between the parties. In the fourth section, we consider organisational changes by Portugal's RLPs following the economic crisis, while the fifth section scrutinises their electoral performance over the last decade. The chapter ends by analysing the main challenges that face Portugal's RLPs in the foreseeable future.

We argue that the PCP and BE did not significantly alter their programmes as they responded to the crisis. However, the distance between the Portuguese centre-left and centre-right parties has increased. Consequently, the crisis gave powerful incentives for left-wing parties to compromise and presented new opportunities to overcome forty years in which the radical Left was denied access to executive power and policymaking. We argue that such changes were also possible because of the strategies of adaptation pursued by party elites. The ideas and decisions of party leaders were crucial to enabling cooperation among the left-wing parties. Finally, the BE has shown a greater flexibility and adaptability than the communists, which facilitated governmental agreements.

THE HISTORICAL DEVELOPMENT OF THE PORTUGUESE RADICAL LEFT

During the democratic period, the radical Left in Portugal has faced three main problems. The first is the high level of fragmentation within the Left, which contrasts with the stability and simplicity of the parties on the right of the Portuguese political spectrum. The second is the historical lack of cooperation between left-wing parties, especially in terms of government formation, while the third is related to the major divisions that have existed between the PS and the radical Left.

Following democratisation in Portugal, the PCP became marginalised from the main parties of government (the centre-left PS, centre-right Social Democratic Party [PSD] and right-wing conservative People's Party [CDS-PP]). The PCP played the role of being Portugal's main 'anti-system' party. In contrast, the PS adopted moderate positions, especially with regard to socio-economic issues.[2] Key differences between the communists and socialists revolved around their attitudes towards democracy, the European Union, as well as the legacy of the Carnation Revolution, namely with respect to the nationalisation of big private companies, estates and banks. Despite the erosion of the PCP's electoral support (see below), the communists have generally been able to resist competition from the extra-parliamentary Left and to remain the main institutional alternative to the Left of the PS. Since 1987 the PCP has operated within the Democratic Unitarian Coalition (*Coligação Democrática Unitária*, CDU) with the Green Party (*Partido Ecologista Os Verdes*, PEV), which is, however, widely considered to be a 'satellite' of the communists. Several extreme-left groups have formed, but have almost always been excluded from parliamentary representation (one exception was the former Maoist Popular and Democratic Union [UDP], whose best results were winning one seat in some legislatures prior to 1987).

Notwithstanding failed attempts to revise and moderate the communists' ideological orientations before and after the collapse of the Soviet Union, the PCP remains one of the most orthodox communist parties in Western Europe, fitting the 'extreme left' or 'conservative communist' categories.[3] However, the institutional predominance of the PCP within the radical Left was challenged in 1999 when the BE gained representation in Parliament for the first time. The BE was result of the merging of two RLPs (the former Trotskyist Socialist and Revolutionary Party [PSR] and the former Maoist Popular and Democratic Union [UDP]) and one political movement (*Política XXI*). Despite having strong anti-capitalist positions, the BE differed from the PCP with regard to two main issues: on the one hand, it aimed to reform democracy by enhancing participatory channels while accepting the main institutions of liberal democracy; on the other, it took a very critical view of the Soviet Union and defended new forms of transnationalism such as the anti-globalisation movement. Since 2007, the BE leadership has sought to de-radicalise some economic policy proposals by re-launching the party as an 'eco-socialist' party.[4]

In terms of electoral performance, Portuguese RLPs have always been relevant actors, and have generally performed well compared with most other RLPs in Europe. The initial years of Portuguese democracy were relatively successful for the PCP and it polled above 10 per cent of the vote in the 1970s and 1980s. However, this pattern was to be radically transformed from the mid-1980s, as the PCP faced an accelerating pattern of electoral decline. In 1983, the PCP polled 18.1 per cent of the vote; eight years later, it polled less than half this proportion, obtaining only 8.8 per cent. Over the period 1975–1985, the PCP averaged 16.7 per cent of the national vote; between 1987 and 2011 this average was 8.6 per cent. The PCP witnessed its electoral nadir in 2002, when it polled under 7 per cent. The party was able to achieve more positive results during the first decade of the twenty-first century. However, these results have only seen marginal rises in its share of the vote and suggest that the PCP has reached a plateau rather than being able to reverse its previous decline. Additionally, the period has seen the rise of the BE, which has made steady inroads into the potential PCP electorate since 1999.

The 2005 elections marked the beginning of a new period of socialist majorities (2005–2011), during which both RLPs opposed most of the reforms implemented by the PS, especially with regard to welfare policies (health, social security, education). Yet the distance between the PCP and the BE remained significant, especially over the issue of European integration.

The communists continued to articulate a highly ideological form of Euroscepticism, with very clear nationalist tones and a very negative evaluation of the effects of European integration.[5] By contrast, the BE aimed to reform Europe by strengthening supranational policies and proposing left-wing internationalist cooperation to change the process of European integration.[6] This position was mainly due to the influence of the 'right wing' of the BE led by Miguel Portas, one of the BE's founders and its first MEP (elected in the 2004 European elections).

Following the 2009 elections, the PS formed a minority government after the failure to compromise with other parties. With the worsening of the economic and financial situation, the socialist government was forced by European institutions to implement austerity measures through the adoption of several Stability and Growth Programmes (*Programa de Estabilidade e Crescimento,* PEC). Three PECs were adopted during 2009–2010, all approved with the support of the PSD, whereas both radical left parties rejected them. The response of European partners and institutions led to an increasing convergence among the radical Left, harshening their criticism towards the process of European integration.

THE NATURE OF THE GREAT RECESSION IN PORTUGAL

On 23 March 2011 the PS prime minister José Sócrates resigned following the parliamentary defeat of austerity measures under the fourth Stability and Growth Programme (PEC IV), initiating a process that eventually resulted in the PSD and CDS-PP governing after winning the June 2011 parliamentary elections. Subsequently, upward pressure on Portuguese debt interest rates forced the government to request external assistance. This led the main governing parties to negotiate the Memorandum of Understanding (MoU), which was signed at the beginning of May 2011. The agreement had a strongly neoliberal flavour with a wide-ranging programme of privatisations, ostensibly to pay the debt and to promote competition in monopolistic sectors; extensive deregulation of the labour market, allegedly to promote economic competitiveness by increasing labour flexibility and reducing labour costs; a reduction of the size of the state through pay freezes and a moderate and phased decrease in the number of public-sector employees.

The programme also called for the rationalisation of the state (by reducing the number of local authorities and balancing the deficits in public companies; reform of the pension system; renegotiation of public-private partnerships) and for a reduction in red tape for companies (through streamlining the justice system). Finally, it called for the recapitalisation of the banks, to comply with the new capital ratios demanded by the European Union, but also in order ensure that credit was again available again for businesses. The parties of the radical Left not only opposed the agreement but actually refused to meet the Troika.

There are four main elements that characterise the way that the crisis was politicised in Portugal during the Troika's financial bailout, 2011–2014.[7] First, there were complaints that the right-wing PSD/CDS-PP government's policies exceeded the political mandate it received in June 2011, as well as the Troika's original proposals that had framed the electorate's choices, and that the government was testing the limits of the Constitution. Second, there was dissatisfaction with the enormous imbalance in the sacrifices being required of citizens (wage earners and retired) and capital respectively. Third, as André Freire shows using individual-level data collected between 2012 and 2014, the debt, unemployment and poverty that emerged contributed to erosion of support for the democratic political system.[8] Of course, such a decline may have already been underway before the crisis; however the Troika years and implementation of austerity appear to have had specific effects.[9]

Fourth, the opposition struggled to present viable alternatives to austerity, partly because the PS provided only weak opposition to the right-wing government (at least until the end of 2012) and also because until recently the left-wing parties (PS, BE and PCP-PEV) failed to cooperate in generating a governmental alternative.[10] This means that there was an imbalance between the preferences of left-wing voters (which overwhelmingly supported left-left cooperation in government) and the behaviour of the left-wing parties.

THE IDEOLOGICAL RESPONSES OF THE PORTUGUESE RADICAL LEFT TO THE GREAT RECESSION

The most important change in the programmatic stances of RLPs during the crisis has been the strengthening of opposition towards European integration, while criticisms even emerged within the PS, which traditionally championed support for the European Union.[11] In addition, the left-wing parties adopted a more radical discourse when they were in opposition against the right-wing government, thus strengthening the polarisation of the party system. It is also worth noting that between 2008 and 2015 the crisis did not raise any significant ideological conflicts within Portugal's RLPs, nor any deep debate about their ideology or identity.

Signs of a radicalisation of the PCP's positions can be found in its electoral manifestos for the 2011 national election and 2014 European elections, as well as the new programme and statutes approved at its XIX Congress (2012) and its 2015 electoral manifesto.[12] In particular, the PCP tightened its anti-system stance by criticising the previous 35–40 years of democracy associated with the rule of moderate parties (PS, PSD and CDS-PP) and the predominance of right-wing policies.[13] While these parties were considered responsible for the economic and political crisis, the PCP aimed to defend the values enshrined in the Constitution and to represent the 'spirit' of the Carnation Revolution.

Second, there are signs that the PCP is increasingly becoming nostalgic for the 'real socialism' that existed under the Soviet Union, even if serious problems in the way that it functioned are acknowledged.[14] The PCP's Euroscepticism also has an increasingly strong nationalist tone. For example, the 2015 electoral manifesto was titled *Por uma Política Patriótica e de Esquerda* ('For a Patriotic and Left-Wing Policy'), which was also the main slogan used during the campaign. The communists are now asking for 'the dissolution of the European Economic and Monetary Union', which means the end of the Euro.[15] In addition, the PCP has advocated the need to prepare Portugal's exit from the Eurozone, which ultimately should be decided via referendum.[16] The communists also defend the renegotiation of public debt (in terms of volume, interest rates and maturities). It is also worth underlining that the party supports a diversification of financing the country's public (and private) expenses, both at the domestic and the international levels.[17]

We also find continuities in the PCP's inability to openly criticise socialist dictatorships such as China, North Korea and Angola. It seeks extensive re-nationalisation of strategic sectors of the economy (banks, utilities, etc.).[18] Additionally, the fight for equality and a fairer distribution of income between capital and labour, with a strongly progressive fiscal policy, still lie at the core of the PCP's proposals.[19]

Conversely, the BE shows no nostalgia for the Soviet Union, has been highly critical vis-à-vis North Korea and Angola and does not seek either to leave the Euro or extensive re-nationalisation of strategic sectors of the economy. In many respects, however, the BE's policies during the Great Recession have been similar to those of the PCP.[20] First, like the PCP, the party rejects the Troika bailout, and argues for a renegotiation of Portuguese public debt (in terms of volume, interest rates and maturities) following an audit process.[21] Moreover, as in the case of the PCP, it seeks an alliance of peripheral and debt-laden EU countries to fight the European Union's neoliberal approach to the crisis. Like the PCP, the BE also argues for more fairness in the distribution of income between capital and labour, anchored in a strong role of the state in economy and society, and in strengthening public investment.[22]

The main ideological difference between the BE and the PCP, besides the issues already mentioned, is in terms of the BE's approach towards Europe.[23] Thus, although the party articulates a radical critique of European integration, the BE supports an alternative left-wing and progressive vision for Europe that is not anchored in nationalism (unlike the PCP). Besides an alliance of peripheral EU countries to fight austerity, the party proposes an alternative European Union focused on growth and employment, an increase in the EU budget, common management of European debt (through the creation of Eurobonds and a European rating agency). The BE's vision for European integration is based on the exclusion of public investment from calculations of the public deficit, a tax on capital transactions and regulation of off-shore tax havens.[24] In other words the BE takes a more constructive approach towards defending the reform of European institutions in the aim of fostering economic growth and equality.[25]

The parties offer different explanations for the economic crisis in Europe. However, both criticise the market to some respect. According to the PCP, the European Union is experiencing a deep social and economic crisis, which stemmed from the crisis of capitalism, leading to a growing impoverishment of European countries to the benefit of big business (banks, multinational industries, financial markets).[26] On the other hand, the BE claims that the main failure of the European Union is the lack of convergence among European countries, while national egoisms and competition have led to a general decrease in salaries and people's living conditions.[27]

The economic crisis and developments in Greece in 2015 contributed to a limited degree of convergence between the parties' criticisms of European integration, as evidenced by the October 2015 general elections. Both parties now maintained that the European Union had been detrimental to Portuguese development and the country's interests. Both the PCP and the BE now rejected the further loss of national sovereignty and highlighted the need to recover important instruments of economic, financial and social policies. Both parties also presented supranational decision-making processes in a negative way, not only because they foster the dominance of foreign capital and the transfer of national resources outside the country, but also because supranational actors have eroded the social and economic rights protected by the Portuguese Constitution. In particular, the European Union's crisis management policy has strengthened the Euroscepticism of the BE, fostering internal divergences, especially compared with the communists' cohesion.[28] Nevertheless, the harsher criticism of the PCP with regard to the European Union is still visible. It seeks an exit from the Eurozone, while the BE emphasises solutions such as debt restructuring without seriously considering the 'exit' option.

THE DIFFICULT ROAD TO COOPERATION BETWEEN PORTUGAL'S RLPS

The high level of competition between the two RLPs in Portugal reinforced their fierce opposition towards cooperation with the PS. However, this section shows how the economic crisis decreased the distance between RLPs and the PS, thus facilitating the agreement ultimately made between the parties after the 2015 general election.

Before 2015, Portugal was one of the few West European countries where RLPs had not been included in left-left governments either as members of a coalition and/or as parliamentary support parties for centre-left governments since the fall of the Berlin Wall.[29] Several factors contributed to the PCP's lack of institutional integration. First there was a legacy from the transition to democracy when the communists had tried to take over power through extra-electoral means: the so-called 'hot summer' of 1975. Second, the PCP's use of democratic centralism to control internal dissent led other parties to mistrust it. Third, the PS took a centrist direction and adopted a pivotal role in the party system, which gave it several routes to government without working with the PCP (through single party, coalition or minority governments).

Research suggests that there are differences between subgroups of the RLP family in terms of their willingness to participate in government.[30] In Portugal, however, both the PCP and the BE had long been unable to establish forms of collaboration with the PS. Besides the ideological and policy differences between the three parties on the Left, the inability of party elites to compromise and strategic considerations are important factors that help to account for the lack of cooperation.

How has the economic crisis influenced the patterns of cooperation between left-wing political parties in Portugal? Here we analyse the ideological placement of parties on the left-right continuum before and after the crisis. Surveys of MPs conducted in 2008 and 2012 suggest that there has been a clear move of right-wing parties (PSD and CDS-PP) further to the right, while left-wing parties (PS, BE and PCP) moved further to the left.[31] Thus, the system is now more polarised than ever, but only at the elite level.

These changes have not, however, been replicated at the voter level, resulting in a widening gap between parliamentary elites and the voters. On the left, this mismatch is larger for RLPs than for the PS, meaning that the latter is more in tune with its electorate than the BE or the PCP.[32] Furthermore, a recent study found that although PS MPs are now closer to radical left MPs in terms of left-right self-placement and policy preferences, PS voting behaviour in Parliament (2011–2014) was closer to the right than that of RLPs.[33] Conversely, RLPs have behaved similarly to each other in Parliament.[34] The BE and PCP's voting records showed similar rates of rejection of government bills (56 and 60 per cent, respectively) during the last legislature (2011–2015). This pattern was clearly distinct from the PS which adopted more moderate positions (27 per cent rejection, 52 per cent approval and 21 per cent abstention).

One reason for this strange phenomenon is that the PS has historically been one of the most centrist social democratic parties in Europe[35]; another being the pattern of coalition politics which until late 2015 involved cooperation between the PS and right-wing parties. In any case, the absence of left-left government options in Portugal until the end of 2015 created a gap between the voters (clearly in favour of agreements) and the elites of left parties (who were more sceptical), similar to the one we found in ideological orientations. The results presented in Table 13.1 show that a majority of PCP and BE voters and a large plurality of PS voters are in favour of left-left governments. Moreover, these results are similar to those found in 2009 and 2012.[36]

The 2015 general election confirmed that differences exist between the PS and the radical Left with regard to significant policies such as debt renegotiation, nationalisations and reform of the European Union. These differences did not, however, prevent left-wing parties making a historic agreement after the failure to form a minority right-wing government. The parties of the left made a pact that agreed upon undoing some of the most important measures implemented during the Troika's MoU, especially in terms of fiscal and welfare policies, meaning a return to the pre-Memorandum status quo. The agreement involved concessions from the elites of all of the left parties. The PS, for example, dropped its proposal for conciliatory dismissal (a measure also supported by the Right), yet the pact did not mention debt restructuring. From the RLPs' viewpoint, however, the pact was a strategic instrument to implement anti-austerity measures. Negotiation was easier for the more factionalised and pluralistic BE than for the centralised PCP, which was less enthusiastic about the idea of making compromises with the other left-wing parties, especially due to historical animosities between the PCP and PS at leadership level. Thus, the decision to support a socialist minority

Table 13.1   Party Sympathisers' Attitudes towards a Left-wing Government, 2014

'Imagine that tomorrow legislative elections would be held and that the PS would win without an absolute majority. Which one of the following options would you consider to be better for the country (choose only one option)? It would be better for the country that the PS would ...'

	CDU/PCP	BE	PS	PSD	CDS-PP
Rule in minority	11.1	12.8	21.1	19.3	11.9
Coalesce with the radical left	69.1	66.7	41.8	7.5	7.2
Coalesce with the right	2.5	5.2	21.6	54.1	57.2
Coalesce with all the parties	17.3	15.4	15.4	19.3	23.8
N	81	39	227	161	42

Note: Figures in first four rows are percentage of each group total.
Source: Survey of a representative sample of the adult Portuguese population living in the mainland, N = 1205, fielded between June and October 2014. Ana Belchior et al. 'Survey Portuguese population – Dataset 2014', project *Public Preferences and Policy Decision-Making. A Longitudinal and Comparative Analysis.* PTDC/IVC-CPO/3921/2012, ISCTE – University Institute of Lisbon: CIES-IUL.

government was a reciprocal move, and without the BE's willingness the PCP would not have accepted the idea of cooperating with the other left-wing parties.

PARTY ORGANISATION: BETWEEN
TRADITION AND INNOVATION

The two main Portuguese RLPs have operated under very different organisational models. While social movements and the organisations of other left-libertarian parties clearly influenced the BE's organisation, the PCP has preserved the traditional communist organisation based on democratic centralism.[37] The former has strongly emphasised informal ties with civil society organisations, whereas the latter adopted top-down hierarchical principles and gave limited autonomy to party members. Whereas the internal organisation of the PCP has been characterised by a strong degree of continuity since the emergence of the economic crisis, the organisation of the BE has experienced more significant changes.

The PCP is the only contemporary party in Portugal founded before the fall of the dictatorship and it was one of the main actors during the revolution. The role it played in those years left it with an extensive and hierarchical organisation. The party leadership and party officials control the election of the main national party bodies (the Central Committee, the Secretariat and the Political Commission) and the process of candidate selection, whereas the formation of factions is prohibited and congress decisions are binding, especially with regard to the party programme. In addition, the PCP has followed the traditional communist vanguard model of seeking hegemonic ties to civil society. In particular, it has maintained strong links with its ancillary organisations, mainly trade unions: the Portuguese Workers General Confederation (CGTP), the Agriculture National Confederation (CNA), the National Confederation of Pensioners and Elders (MURPI) and several cooperative associations.

Conversely, the BE's organisation closely resembles the left-libertarian model outlined by Herbert Kitschelt.[38] The party's founding constitution defined it as a 'political movement of citizens' based on a civic culture of participation with the goal of finding alternative ways to capitalism.[39] Social movements were a great inspiration when defining the main features of this new organisation.[40] This influence is visible not only with regard to ensuring an overlap between activism and the party leadership, but also in terms of developing horizontal links between members and participatory and decentralised mechanisms of decision-making. In contrast to the PCP's rigid vertical model, the BE adopted a loose form of party membership and a 'network organisation' based on loose internal structures. Finally, the party rejected the idea of having a dominant leadership and decided to adopt a 'polyarchic' executive. Thus, party statutes do not formally recognise the role of a party leader, although Francisco Louçã played this role on a de facto basis for over ten years (until 2012).

Despite attempts to initiate processes of centralisation within the BE by strengthening the power of party leaders and developing vertical organisational structures, the cohesion of party elites remains one of the main differences between the two RLPs.[41] The fall of communism generated several internal conflicts within the PCP.[42] However, attempts to reform the party from within failed and reformers left or were expelled between 2002 and 2004. Moreover, the PCP's electoral results stabilised and contributed to limiting intra-party dissent. These processes mean that the PCP can now be considered as the most united party in Portugal.

In contrast, factionalism has been an important feature of the BE's internal organisation. The parties that founded the BE gained control over its internal distribution of power, thereby marginalising the influence of independents within the party.[43] This was reflected in the way that whereas Louçã occupied the leadership position, the leadership of the parliamentary group was attributed to one of the other founding groups (most often the UDP). Moreover, representation on the main party bodies privileges the four main factions (the three founding parties and the FER [Revolutionary Left Front], which joined the party in 2000) to the detriment of more recent party members who joined the party directly and without any previous affiliation.

After losses at the 2011 election, the BE faced two main problems. The first was to deal with leadership succession and to reconsider the role of the party leadership. Following Louçã's voluntary resignation in 2012, the main party bodies selected two speakers, one man and one woman, both members of party's Secretariat (the main executive organ). This solution was decided upon by the party's inner circle and was highly criticised by party members. The second challenge came from internal dissent and the difficulties in maintaining unity within the party elite. Conflicts had generally been related to strategic concerns (especially the possibility of coalition with other left-wing parties) and this led to several splits. The first was carried out in 2011 when the FER current and its leader Gil Garcia decided to form a new political party (Alternative Socialist Movement, MAS).

The second split occurred when a right-leaning group brought together several independent and academic figures around the 'Manifesto Forum' (*Fórum Manifesto*). In the wake of the electoral defeat in the 2011 legislative elections, this group disagreed with the party's refusal to cooperate with other left parties. The poor performance registered at the 2014 European elections then triggered a split with the Fórum Manifesto leaving to form a new political movement ('Time to Move Forward', *Tempo de Avançar*) headed by Ana Drago, a former BE MP in aim of cooperating with 'Free' (*Livre*), a new party aiming to represent the 'centre of the Left' and to promote cooperation between left-wing parties.[44] Two main issues were crucial for this split. The splitters criticised the BE's organisation for having a top-down approach to decision-making and called for more influence for party members by adopting open primaries for candidate selection. The splitters also criticised the BE's anti-government stance and were open to developing some forms of cooperation with the socialists with the aim of ending austerity measures.

BE's initial inability to take advantage of the economic crisis and to provide a viable alternative to the socialists exacerbated its internal crisis. The BE's IX Convention of November 2014 was its most divided party meeting to date. The leadership tried to remedy this by proposing reforms to expand the use of internal referenda on strategic issues (i.e. electoral alliances and government participation). Moreover, the result of the election of the main national party body (*Mesa Nacional*), which ended in a 50:50 split between the two main factions, obliged the rethinking of the model of party leadership. A clearer and more consensual role for the party leadership was established. As a consequence, a permanent commission was elected as the party's main executive body (composed of six members, with one speaker as de facto leader [Catarina Martins]).[45]

The two Portuguese RLPs also differ remarkably in their links to civil society. Considering labour organisations, the CGTP has remained basically a 'transmission belt' for the communists, while the BE has been unable to consolidate its position in trade unions.[46] The main trade unions (CGTP and UGT) have opposed austerity politics and have been an important instrument of mobilisation throughout the crisis. However, the level of protest peaked in 2011–2012, and subsequently a period of de-mobilisation has occurred.

We find significant differences between the relations between the two RLPs and anti-austerity protests. The BE played an active role in fostering the emergence and mobilisation of new social movements, especially after the first Mayday protests held in 2007. By contrast, the PCP was less enthusiastic and prioritised formal and institutionalised channels of protest. Alongside partisan mobilisation, new social movements emerged after the 2008 crisis, reaching their peak with the 'struggling generation' (*geração à rasca*) mobilisation held in 2011 when more than 300,000 people rallied against the political and economic crisis.[47] This was a new form of mobilisation due to its spontaneous and non-partisan character, which challenged the traditional role played by mainstream parties and trade unions.[48] Yet these movements failed to consolidate due to the lack of a credible leadership, organisational resources and the inability to build strong alliances with other social and political actors.

THE ELECTORAL PERFORMANCE: RESILIENCE OR SUCCESS?

RLPs in Portugal have followed very different electoral trajectories (Table 13.2). The PCP's electoral support has displayed remarkable stability over the last two decades, while the BE has been more volatile. The crisis has however strengthened the overall performance of Portugal's RLPs in legislative contests, thereby reversing their marginalisation before the crisis. However, RLPs have performed better in second-order elections (2014 European elections vs 2015 general elections) indicating that Portuguese voters still rely more on conventional actors when the highest prize is at stake.

In the aftermath of the Great Recession both RLPs benefited from the crisis, inasmuch as the socialist government was initially held responsible for the bad state of the economy. Therefore, both RLPs were able to attract disgruntled voters, as well as a share of the PS' support. Important differences can, however, be identified in the electoral impact of the crisis on each RLP. Despite the aforementioned volatility, the BE has been overall the more successful of the two parties, due to a combination of having an effective leadership, adopting new issues and its engagement in forms of participatory mobilisation. In contrast, the electoral gains of 2009 were bittersweet for the PCP: while it saw its vote and seat numbers both rise, it was overtaken by the right-wing CDS-PP and also the BE, which left the communists as the fifth strongest party in Parliament. While the PCP was no longer leaking votes, it was unable to significantly expand its appeal to Portugal's increasingly volatile left-wing voters.

Table 13.2   Portuguese RLP Election Results 1987–2015

	Legislative		European		Total Radical Left	
	PCP	BE	PCP	BE	Legislative	European
1987	12.1 (31)		11.5 (3)		12.1	11.5
1989			14.4 (4)			14.4
1991	8.8 (17)				8.8	
1994			11.2 (3)			11.2
1995	8.6 (15)				8.6	
1999	9.0 (17)	2.4 (2)	10.3 (2)	1.8	11.4	12.1
2002	6.9 (12)	2.7 (3)			9.6	
2004			9.1 (2)	4.9 (1)		14.0
2005	7.5 (14)	6.3 (8)			13.8	
2009	7.9 (15)	9.8 (16)	10.6 (2)	10.7 (3)	17.7	21.3
2011	7.9 (16)	5.2 (8)			13.1	
2014			13.7 (3)	4.9 (1)		18.6
2015	8.3 (17)	10.2 (19)			18.5	

Note: We only consider parties of the radical left with parliamentary representation.
Sources: Data elaborated by the authors from *Comissão Nacional de Eleições* (National Electoral Commission).

At the 2015 legislative elections both RLPs increased their proportion of MPs. The BE was the clear winner, achieving its best result ever, both in terms of votes (10.2 per cent) and seats (19). The party grew in nearly all districts, with an impressive performance in the littoral and urban areas. The PCP-CDU also improved its score (8.3 per cent and 17 MPs). Both RLPs ran effective campaigns in terms of both mobilising their supporters and their leaders' performances. The RLPs offered a clear alternative to the other parties. Post-electoral surveys showed, however, that while the PCP-CDU's vote was essentially stable (with losses to abstention offset by attracting former non-voters), the BE was able to expand through attracting new voters, as well as dissatisfied PS and right-wing voters.[49] These results countered the electoral decline of the BE, and helped to consolidate the position of its party leader, Catarina Martins, who was one of its major assets in the electoral campaign.

The more positive results for the BE compared with the PCP can also be explained through its different position on the Euro and the way it promoted new issues that were particularly important for young voters (e.g. the problem of emigration, voting at 16). In addition, the BE moderated its position in 2015 by downplaying the issue of debt restructuring, in all likelihood as a direct consequence of Syriza's failure to make progress on this at European level. Finally, the way in which the BE hinted at cooperating with other left-wing parties during the campaign may have contributed to boosting its electoral performance.

Several reasons help explain the stability of the PCP's vote compared with the more volatile results for the BE. The first is that the PCP's different organisational model gives it a stronger capacity to mobilise its grassroots support. Conversely, the BE has struggled to develop a stable party base that it can mobilise at elections. The more volatile societal base of the BE emerges not only if we look at the ratio of members to voters (an indicator of the 'encapsulation' of civil society by the party) but also in terms of its linkages to social movements and the difficulties it has had in penetrating the labour movement.

The second factor is the stronger party identification of communist voters relative to those of the BE, who are typically more educated, younger and more sceptical of political parties and party elites, as well as being more issue-oriented. Thirdly, the PCP's stable party leadership and its capacity to control internal dissent have been an important electoral asset. In contrast, the BE's problems in terms of party cohesion left it unable to present an image of having a unified leadership to the electorate. Only after the compromise achieved following the BE's 2014 party convention, did the BE manage to address internal tensions and unify behind Catarina Martins' leadership during the 2015 elections. Thus the BE's electoral performance appears heavily dependent on the visibility of its leadership and the electorate's evaluation of its leaders.[50]

Finally, the communists have shown a stable and strong anti-European orientation, whereas the BE has adopted a more flexible discourse that left it more room to adapt its appeals as the Eurozone crisis unfolded. This pragmatic orientation has been an important asset to appeal to moderate voters, especially those who support European integration but are against the implementation of austerity measures.

CONCLUSION

RLPs have played an important role in Portuguese politics during the Great Recession, not only at the institutional level but also in terms of mobilisation. After several years of neoliberal measures and four years of a right-wing government, their anti-austerity discourse gained strength among the electorate. The crisis and in particular the implementation of the MoU in 2011 had important effects on the RLPs. First, they have become more critical of the European Union, and in the PCP's case have increasingly promoted nationalist and patriotic appeals. Second, the implementation of the MoU has led to a degree of convergence between left-wing parties. RLPs in Portugal provide slightly different explanations for the 2008 crisis, propose different policies and have historically struggled to work with the PS. These factors help explain why RLPs struggled to benefit in the immediate aftermath of the crisis; however, following the policies pursued by the right-wing government, it was easier to achieve a compromise based on the reversal of key austerity reforms and to expand their share of the vote. Another possible reason behind this 'late' success is that voters in 2015 had less negative expectations about the national economy than in 2011 and had become more willing to experiment with an alternation of government.

Portugal did not witness new social movements capable of generating successful new parties during the Great Recession. However, the crisis did alter one of the major particularities of politics in Portugal, that is, the previous marginalisation of RLPs from policymaking (despite their electoral and social relevance). The 2015 general elections significantly altered this, and the new minority PS government drew parliamentary support from both the BE and PCP, thereby marking a major change in terms of the parties' ability to cooperate.

Five major factors can explain the development of this new governmental solution. First, the right-wing parties moved to the right during the Troika years, thereby making agreements with the Centre-Left less likely.[51] Second, the austerity measures enacted by the right-wing parties (PSD and CDS-PP) went beyond those required by the Troika (e.g. higher cuts to salaries, pensions, public-sector employment and the welfare state).

Third, there were incentives for the socialist leader António Costa to stay in power as it was clear that he had to become PM under a left-left government or to resign. In addition, a left-left governmental solution would allow the PS to achieve its office-seeking goals. Fourth, there were important institutional incentives that favoured this innovation – namely the fact that the Portuguese president cannot dissolve Parliament in the six months before new presidential elections (January 2016) nor within six months of a new Parliament (i.e. before April 2016). Fifth, this left-left governmental solution was a way for left-wing parties to stay in tune with voters' preferences.

If the current government based on left-left cooperation lasts a whole term in office, it may see the beginning of a new era in Portuguese politics. Consequently, we may see more inclusiveness and a higher congruence between left-wing voters and elites' preferences that may offer a way to restore support for the democratic political system. It remains to be seen whether the new government can survive and implement its reformist leftist programme in such adverse conditions.

NOTES

1. Manuel Nunes Ramires Serrano, 'Why is there no Syriza in Portugal?', accessed 30 December 2015, https://www.opendemocracy.net/democraciaabierta/manuel-nunes-ramires-serrano/why-is-there-no-syriza-in-portugal; Daphne Halikiopoulou, 'Far-Left Euroscepticism in the 2014 European Parliament Elections: A Cross-Europe Comparison,' in *Is Europe Afraid of Europe? An Assessment of the Result of the 2014 European Elections*, ed. Kostas Infatis (Athens: The Wilfried Martens Centre for European Studies, 2014), 244.

2. Anna Bosco, 'Four Actors in Search of a Role: The Southern European Communist Parties,' in *Parties, Politics, and Democracy in the New Southern Europe*, ed. Nikiforos Diamandouros and Richard Gunther (Baltimore: The Johns Hopkins University Press, 2001), 329.

3. Luke March, *Contemporary Far Left Parties in Europe From Marxism to the Mainstream?* (Berlin and Bonn: Friedrich Ebert Stiftung, 2008).

4. Marco Lisi, 'New Politics in Portugal: The Rise and Success of the Left Bloc,' *Pôle Sud* 30 (2009): 127.

5. Marina Costa Lobo, 'A União Europeia e Os Partidos Políticos Portugueses: Da Consolidação à Qualidade Democrática,' in *Portugal Em Mudança (1986-2006)*, ed. Marina Costa Lobo and Pedro Lains (Estoril: Princípia, 2007), 77.

6. Luke March and André Freire, *A Esquerda Radical em Portugal e na Europa: Marxismo, Mainstream ou Marginalidade?* (Porto: Quid Novi, 2012).

7. André Freire, 'The Condition of Portuguese Democracy During the Troika's Intervention, 2011-2015', within the special issue 'Political Parties, Institutions and Civil Society: The Economic Crisis and the Evolution of Southern Europe Political Systems,' *Portuguese Journal of Social Science* 15 (2016 forthcoming).

8. Ibid.

9. Ibid.

10. André Freire, Marco Lisi and Inês Lima, 'Crise económica, política de austeridade e o potencial de coligação da "esquerda radical" portuguesa,' in *Crise Económica, Políticas de Austeridade e Representação Política*, ed. André Freire, Marco Lisi and José Manuel Leite Viegas (Lisbon: Assembleia da República, 2015), 385.

11. Marina Costa Lobo, 'A União Europeia e Os Partidos Políticos Portugueses', 96; Marina Costa Lobo and Pedro C. Magalhães, 'Room for Manoeuvre: Euroscepticism in the Portuguese Parties and Electorate,' *South European Society and Politics* 16 (2011): 81.

12. PCP, *Compromisso por Uma Política Patriótica e de Esquerda – Legislativas de 2011* (Lisbon: PCP, 2011); PCP, *Declaração Programática do PCP para as Eleições para o Parlamento Europeu 2014* (Lisbon: PCP, 2014); PCP, *Política Patriótica e de Esquerda. Soluções para um Portugal com Futuro* (2015), 7–20.

13. PCP, *Compromisso por Uma Política Patriótica e de Esquerda*, 4; PCP, *Declaração Programática do PCP*, 4–5; PCP, *Política Patriótica e de Esquerda*, 7–20.

14. PCP, *Programa e Estatutos aprovados no XIX Congresso. Uma Democracia Avançada, os Valores de Abril no Futuro de Portugal* (Lisbon: PCP, 2012), 77–8.

15. PCP, *Políticas Patrióticas e de Esquerda. Soluções para um Portugal com Futuro* (Lisbon: PCP, 2014) 15; PCP, *Política Patriótica e de Esquerda. Soluções para um Portugal com Futuro* (2015), 76.

16. Interview with PCP leader, Jerónimo de Sousa, *Observador* 23 May 2015.

17. PCP, *Compromisso por Uma Política Patriótica e de Esquerda* (2011), 5–7; PCP, *Política Patriótica e de Esquerda*, 11, 20–1.

18. PCP *Compromisso*, 7–8; PCP, *Política Patriótica*, 5–7.

19. PCP, *Compromisso*, 8–10; PCP, *Política Patriótica*, 5–21.

20. BE, *Compromisso Eleitoral – Bloco de Esquerda 2011: Mudar de Futuro, Pelo Emprego e Pela Justiça Fiscal* (Lisbon: BE, 2011); BE, *Declaração da Comissão Política do Bloco de Esquerda* (Lisbon: BE, 2013); BE, *Resolução Aprovada na VIII do Bloco de Esquerda 2011: A Esquerda Contra a Dívida* (Lisbon: BE, 2013); BE, *Recuperar o que é Nosso. Manifesto Eleitoral Legislativas 2015* (Lisbon: BE, 2015).

21. BE, *Compromisso Eleitoral*, 2 and 8–10; BE, *Recuperar o que é Nosso*, 4–5.

22. BE, *Compromisso Eleitoral*, 3–7; BE, *Recuperar o que é Nosso*, 12–27.

23. Thilo Janssen, *The Parties of the Left in Europe. A Comparison of their Position on European Policy Leading into the 2014 European Elections* (Berlin: Rosa-Luxemburg-Stiftung, 2013).

24. BE, *Compromisso Eleitoral*, 11–12.

25. BE, *Recuperar o que é Nosso*.

26. PCP, *Política Patriótica e de Esquerda. Soluções para um Portugal com Futuro*.

27. BE, *Recuperar o que é Nosso*.

28. Liesbet Hooghe et al., 'Reliability and validity of the 2002 and 2006 Chapel Hill expert surveys on party positioning,' *European Journal of Political Research* 49 (2010): 687.

29. Luke March, *Contemporary Far Left Parties in Europe*; Tim Bale and Richard Dunphy, 'In From the Cold? Left Parties and Government Involvement Since 1989.' *Comparative European Politics* 9 (2011): 269–91; March and Freire, *A Esquerda Radical em Portugal e na Europa*.

30. Luke March, *Radical Left Parties in Contemporary Europe* (Abingdon: Routledge, 2011); March and Freire, *A Esquerda Radical em Portugal e na Europa*.

31. André Freire, Emmanouil Tsatsanis and Inês Lima, 'Portugal in Times of Crisis: Value Change and Policy Representation,' in *Values, Economic Crisis and Democracy*, ed. Malina Voicu, Ingvill C. Mochmann and Hermann Dülmer (Abingdon: Routledge, 2016 forthcoming); Freire, Lisi and Lima, 'Crise económica, política de austeridade e o potencial de coligação da 'esquerda radical' portuguesa', 385.

32. Freire, Tsatsanis and Lima, 'Portugal in Times of Crisis: Value Change and Policy Representation; Freire, Lisi and Lima, 'Crise económica, política de austeridade e o potencial de coligação da 'esquerda radical' portuguesa', 385; March and Freire, *A Esquerda Radical em Portugal e na Europa*.

33. Freire, Lisi and Lima, 'Crise económica', 385.

34. For more information on the methodology adopted, see Elisabetta De Giorgi, Catherine Moury and João Pedro Ruivo, 'Governing Portugal in Hard Times: Incumbents, Opposition and International Lenders,' *Journal of Legislative Studies* 21 (2015): 54.

35. March and Freire, *A Esquerda Radical em Portugal e na Europa*, Part II.

36. Ibid.; Freire, Lisi and Lima, 2015, 'Crise económica', 385.

37. Marco Lisi, 'Rediscovering Civil Society? Renewal and Continuity in the Portuguese Radical Left,' *South European Society and Politics* 18 (2013): 21.

38. Herbert Kitschelt, 'Left-Libertarian Parties: Explaining Innovation in Competitive Party Systems,' *World Politics* 40 (1988): 194.

39. BE, *Começar de novo* (Lisbon: BE, 1999).

40. Lisi, 'New Politics in Portugal,' 127–44, 'Rediscovering Civil Society?', 21.

41. Lisi, 'New Politics in Portugal', 27.

42. Anna Bosco, *Comunisti. Trasformazioni di partito in Italia, Spagna e Portogallo*. (Bologna: Il Mulino 2000); Bosco, 'Four Actors in Search of a Role,' 329.

43. See 'O Bloco e os caminhos da Esquerda' written after the electoral defeat in 2011.

44. Livre was formed in 2014 by ex-BE MEP Rui Tavares, running for the first time at the 2014 European Elections and obtaining 2.2 per cent of the vote. Like the BE, it can be considered a left-libertarian party. It is a member of the Green party family at the EU level.

45. See *Público*, 30 November 2014, http://www.publico.pt/politica/noticia/joao-semedo-despedese-da-lideranca-do-bloco-continua-catarina-martins-1677984?page=-1.

46. Lisi, 'Rediscovering Civil Society?', 21.

47. Britta Baumgarten, 'Geração À Rasca and Beyond: Mobilisations in Portugal after 12 March 2011,' *Current Sociology* 61 (2013): 457–73.

48. José Soeiro, 'Da Geração À Rasca Ao Que Se Lixe a Troika. Portugal No Novo Ciclo Internacional De Protesto', *Sociologia* XXVIII (2014): 55.

49. See Pedro Magalhães' 'As transferências de voto de 2011 para 2015', accessed 15 January 2016, http://www.pedro-magalhaes.org/margens-de-erro/.

50. Lisi, 'New Politics in Portugal', 27.

51. Freire, 'The Condition of Portuguese Democracy During the Troika's Intervention'.

Chapter 14

The Left and the Crisis in Cyprus

'In the Midst of Change They Were Not Changing'[1]

Gregoris Ioannou and Giorgos Charalambous

The Left in Cyprus is dominated by the Progressive Party of Working People (AKEL). AKEL is a hybrid and in some respects unique RLP, because it has operated in exceptional circumstances as a result of the historical division of Cyprus, and its national(ist) consensus. This chapter shows how AKEL has been unable to use the crisis to increase its political influence. AKEL was long expecting a capitalist crisis to arrive, and was leading the government coalition (for the first time in its history) when the economic crisis hit Cyprus. However, it appeared unprepared and unable to mobilise its organisational, cultural and theoretical resources to enhance its position. Rather, the crisis caused AKEL to lose credibility and popular trust and it faced increased difficulties as socio-economic conditions deteriorated.

AKEL's response to the crisis is particularly interesting because of its governmental role, the severity of the crisis in Cyprus and because of the way that the crisis unfolded in the context of the 'national question' that dominates Greek Cypriot politics. This chapter discusses the response of the Cypriot Left to the economic crisis in three sections. First, it analyses AKEL's programmatic responses to the crisis and its actions in office.[2] Second, the chapter questions the extent to which AKEL's positions changed when it was in opposition. Last, it shows how the crisis impacted on AKEL's support base, internal party organisation and relations with the wider extra-parliamentary Left in Cyprus. It demonstrates, however, that anti-austerity movements were generally weak in Cyprus in comparison to much of southern Europe.[3] Left radicalism during the crisis has been largely limited to AKEL in political terms.

We argue in favour of a 'no change' thesis: that AKEL hesitated and was incapable of significantly adapting in either programmatic or organisational terms in response to the crisis. Its ideology, strategy vis-à-vis the extra-parliamentary Left and its favourable attitude towards institutional consensus rather than social confrontation have remained unchanged. It failed to exploit opportunities to engineer a 'left turn' in wider society. AKEL, as always, has acted to distinguish itself from other groups and failed to work in tandem with them. Consequently, there are signs of a decrease in protest mobilisation alongside sustained efforts by AKEL to defend the record of the Christofias government. The crisis appears to have only had a limited impact on the party system in Cyprus, which is only very gradually showing signs of change.[4]

THE DOMINANCE OF AKEL OVER THE LEFT IN CYPRUS

AKEL emerged in the early 1940s as a front organisation of the Communist Party of Cyprus, as an attempt by the latter to broaden its appeal beyond the working class to sections of the 'progressive bourgeoisie' at a time when the colonial regime was liberalising. AKEL was very successful in the 1943 municipal elections and soon became the strongest organised political force on the island, as shown by even bigger success in the 1946 municipal elections. AKEL's strength was based on its ability to establish itself as the political expression of social movements, and to benefit from the move towards participation of the masses into politics.[5] By the end of the decade, with the emergence of the Cold War and the re-organisation of the Right in a virulent anti-communist climate, AKEL lost ground as the leader of the anti-colonial movement. At the same time, however, it managed to initiate a process of organisational consolidation and built a significant party apparatus. In the transition to the independence period (the late 1950s and the early 1960s), AKEL found itself under pressure as the united Right's monopoly over the state was legitimised through the vehicle of EOKA (National Organisation of Cypriot Fighters, the nationalist and anti-communist armed anti-colonial movement).[6] However, AKEL retained a mass base, a social influence and developed links with the Soviet Union. Moreover, its support for Archbishop Makarios' Non-Aligned Movement strategy helped it avoid the threat from the extreme Right.[7]

AKEL was able to step out of its marginalisation by the 1970s as the Centre-Right became divided into pro-Makarios and anti-Makarios factions. AKEL presented itself as the core of a broader coalition of 'patriotic-progressive forces' and maintained its dominance of the Left as small groups and individuals that split from it failed to form rival organisations that could compete with its social influence. During the Cold War, AKEL's orthodox ideology, loyalty to the Soviet Union and cooperation with other communist parties at the international level remained relatively unchallenged.[8] This continued into the post-1990 period. Even following a subsequent course of ideological renewal, the party's core ideology has remained largely untouched by alternative forms of left-wing thinking.

There were only two moments in which AKEL faced serious challenges from left-wing rivals, but both times it managed to maintain leadership over the Left. The first case was in the late 1970s, when extraordinary conditions provoked by the 1974 war saw a group within the youth section of the Movement for Social Democracy (EDEK) articulate an alternative left-wing and quasi-revolutionary discourse. However, this group was unable to capture EDEK and its members were gradually expelled while EDEK drifted to the right (its vote has rarely topped 10 per cent). The second case was in the late 1980s and early 1990s when a battle for succession in AKEL's leadership resulted in a split that saw some AKEL leaders break away to form a new party called ADISOK (the Democratic Socialist Reform Movement). Yet this newcomer was unable to attract a significant section of AKEL's rank-and-file and remained small. It subsequently drifted to the right, merged with liberals and dissolved. Both these moments strengthened AKEL's cohesion and its leadership pointed to them as reasons to avoid internal divisions.

AKEL has traditionally had a risk-averse but centralised organisational culture. This, combined with the salience of the ethnic cleavage on the island, enabled its leaders to develop pragmatic, catch-all, albeit clearly leftist, appeals.[9] This explains AKEL's enduring electoral success. Its level of electoral support has remained strong and stable throughout its history.[10] Since 1991 its share of the vote has ranged between 30 per cent and 34 per cent, reaching its peak in 2001 after almost ten years of a right-wing government (see Table 14.1). AKEL has also managed in alliance with the centrist Democratic Party (DIKO) and EDEK to elect its preferred presidential candidate to office on two occasions (out of five in the post-1991 period). These were DIKO's leader Tassos Papadopoulos in 2003 and then AKEL's own leader, Dimitris Christofias in 2008 after it secured the support of DIKO and EDEK in the second round of voting.

AKEL's membership has also exhibited an exceptional level of stability, despite a decrease in its overall membership density (M/V) due to the gradual increase in the number of registered voters.[11] Its links to society have also been maintained as it colonised parts of the state and promoted diverse and strong (generally top-down) relationships with organised social groups.[12]

Table 14.1   AKEL's Electoral Results

	Parliamentary Elections Per cent / Seats	Presidential Elections	European Elections Per cent / Seats
1991	30.63 per cent / 18 seats	–	–
1993	–	Vasiliou (not elected)	–
1996	33.00 per cent / 19 seats	–	–
1998	–	Iakovou (not elected)	–
2001	34.71 per cent / 20 seats	–	–
2003	–	Papadopoulos (elected)	–
2004	–	–	27.89 per cent / 2 seats
2006	31.13 per cent / 18 seats	–	–
2008	–	Christofias (elected)	–
2009	–	–	34.90 per cent / 2 seats
2011	32.67 per cent / 19 seats	–	–
2013	–	Malas (not elected)	–
2014	–	–	27.0 per cent / 2 seats

Source: Authors' calculations, www.parties-and-elections.eu.

THE CRISIS IN CYPRUS AND PARTY COMPETITION

The crisis in Cyprus has seen an increase in unemployment from 5 per cent in 2008 to 16 per cent in 2015. The crisis as such really began to be felt in 2011 with growing pressures on public finances and when the signs of deep structural problems in the over-extended banking sector became visible.[13] The Christofias government reacted to the crisis in 2009 by trying to boost demand by offering packages of economic aid to the three key sectors of the Cyprus economy: the hotel industry, construction and the banks. The latter received state guarantees for additional liquidity.[14] Following the publication of encouraging economic data in 2010, the government gave reassurances that the economy was under control and that the growing crisis in Greece and the Eurozone would by-pass Cyprus.

The Cyprus problem continued to monopolise the headlines in 2010 but thereafter the economy and rising unemployment moved up the political agenda and there was also a noticeable increase in anti-immigrant rhetoric from far right and populist politicians from the mainstream parties. In 2010, EDEK deserted the government coalition and the 'informal DIKO', the faction of that party led by its current president Nicolas Papadopoulos, made increasingly vociferous attacks on the economic record of the Christofias government. By 2011, with the negotiations regarding the Cyprus problem reaching a stalemate, economic conditions deteriorating rapidly and Cypriot banks headed for collapse, the crisis became highly politicised. The opposition parties increasingly called for the Christofias government to introduce austerity measures.[15] The AKEL-headed government was severely weakened following criticism of its handling of an explosion near the village of Mari in summer 2011, which initiated a gradual retreat that finally culminated in signing the Memorandum of Agreement with the Troika a year later.[16]

In 2011, the handling of the economy became the number one issue in the public debate. Stagnation became apparent and international credit-rating agencies, as well as the European Commission, issued various negative evaluations of Cyprus' public finances.[17] By 2011 the country could no longer borrow from the markets, as credit-rating agencies highlighted the exposure of Cypriot banks to the Greek economy and the country's economy lost credibility.[18] The opposition parties pointed to these developments as evidence of bad management and attacked the government for bankrupting Cyprus through its refusal to cut public-sector salaries. The dominant framing of the issue was the timing, extent and form of austerity measures to be adopted. Union-bashing became the central theme of the financial pages of the newspapers.

By the end of 2011, AKEL caved in. It changed from opposing austerity to supporting mild and 'socially just' austerity as it accepted that public-sector workers were privileged and would have to contribute to solving the crisis.[19] It was noteworthy that the initial austerity measures were adopted in a way that bypassed the unions and the celebrated processes of 'social dialogue among the social partners' because the conditions were seen to be 'extraordinary'. This was a glimpse of the much bigger wage cuts, increased taxes and spending cuts imposed by the Troika a year later, which were voted in without any discussion by parliament.[20]

The AKEL-led government accepted a loan from Russia at the end of 2011 in order to refinance sovereign debt as it remained temporarily blocked from the markets and reluctant to engage with the Troika. However, the severity of the banking crisis became too big to handle. Cypriot banks neared collapse due to risky investments, poor management and their connection with Greece. Moreover, the introduction of stricter re-capitalisation rules by the European Central Bank placed additional pressures on them in June 2012.[21] The banks lost up to 75 per cent of the value of their bonds, an amount equal to around 4.5 billion and close to 25 per cent of the country's GDP. Laiki Bank (Popular Bank) turned to the state for a bailout in June 2012, but when the Bank of Cyprus followed suit, the Christofias government did not have funds to comply. At this point, the government applied to the Troika for a 'rescue'.

So in June 2012, the Cypriot government applied to the European Financial Stability Fund (EFSF), and the Troika visited Cyprus in July in order to begin negotiations. The Troika dealt with the crisis in Cyprus in a similar way to the crisis in Greece. Nevertheless, the causes of the crisis in Cyprus were closer to those in Spain than in Greece in that it was effectively a banking crisis that spilled over to the economy and the state, rather than an example of political and economic crises becoming inextricable. AKEL tried to use this line of defence against accusations of fiscal mismanagement. The opposition parties, however, continued to blame AKEL for the state of public finances and now held it responsible for the banking crisis as well.

In March 2013 the Eurogroup reached an unprecedented decision regarding the Cypriot economic crisis, as well as the Eurozone more broadly. Initial proposals sought to ensure that all bank accounts contributed to solving the crisis, but this was rejected by the Cypriot parliament. The plan eventually adopted imposed a haircut on deposits above 100,000 euros and only those at the Bank of Cyprus and the Popular Bank. At the same time the Popular Bank was dissolved and merged with the Bank of Cyprus. The president, who had pledged to reject any kind of haircut just a few months earlier, said that this was now the only option as Cyprus's partners in the European Union had threatened to let both banks collapse if a haircut were not implemented. Soon after, a Memorandum of Understanding was signed between the Cypriot government and the Troika. The Memorandum extended the austerity measures already adopted in December 2012 with big cuts on the wages of civil servants and employees of semi-governmental organisations providing electricity and communications. The Memorandum also set these organisations, which had traditionally been considered as important parts of the Cypriot social contract, on a path towards privatisation. Furthermore, the Troika imposed an increase in the corporate tax rates, spreading concern that Cyprus's status as an international financial centre would suffer severely.

For the Left, the crisis represented an external development that had spread to the Cypriot economy. The problems of global financial capitalism rather than the Cypriot government had caused the crisis. The only domestic factors responsible were therefore the banks and mismanagement by the Central Bank governor.[22] Similar arguments were made by AKEL and the Christofias government as they responded to criticisms from other parties between 2011 and 2013 and in particular during the presidential elections of 2013 and the European elections of 2014. Conversely, AKEL's main competitors – the conservative Democratic Rally (DISY) and to an extent the centrist party, DIKO – blamed the crisis on the government's 'incompetence', the public sector and Christofias himself. AKEL was criticised for having 'brought' the Troika to Cyprus. The centre and right opposition were neither willing nor able to oppose austerity nor mobilise against it, nor could they initially convince many that austerity was AKEL's fault. However, their messages that the Left was responsible for the economic downturn due to its 'incompetence' and that it was too 'ideologically stuck' for government hit harder. AKEL's position disappointed its own supporters, since it looked too timid, and too prepared to seek compromise for the imperatives of the 'national interest' and the capitalists' 'national economy'.

Additionally, the government's anti-banks rhetoric was criticised by opponents who pointed out that the three Ministers of Economy appointed by Christofias all came from the banking sector. The opposition also ridiculed the occasional use of anti-Troika or anti-austerity rhetoric by AKEL by pointing out that its legislation for austerity in 2011 and 2012 had been voted in unanimously. AKEL faced a significant drop in electoral strength from 2010 to 2013. Christofias did not run for a second term owing to deadlock in reunification talks, and AKEL lost the presidency (and thereby, according to Cyprus' presidential constitution, the executive branch) in February 2013. Particularly important was the poor performance at the 2014 European elections when the party lost approximately 37,000 votes (a drop of 8 per cent compared with 2009). Empirical analysis of voting intentions indicates that voters blamed the previous Christofias government for the economic crisis more than the DISY government, which succeeded it in 2013 and was experiencing a 'honeymoon period' in 2014.[23]

AKEL DURING THE CRISIS

Naturally enough, during the crisis, AKEL focused its energies on supporting the Christofias government. There was limited change in terms of political rhetoric or organisational practices during the period 2008–2013. However, the arrangements that had sufficed in the past proved inadequate in the context of governing during the economic crisis. The most visible change was AKEL's attempt to scale down its affiliated organisations' engagement in protest and criticism. An attempt was made to restrict the scope of grievances and divert the target of criticism away from the government to the international and EU forces and to their 'local allies', the opposition parties in parliament, the Central Bank and other local institutions of power.

Organisational Responses

The need to protect the Christofias government, when it found itself isolated, facing a hostile media and fierce opposition in parliament, meant that AKEL's affiliated organisations issued frequent statements of support to the government. These organisations were forced to remain silent at other times and found themselves in the difficult position of justifying negative developments.[24] For example, AKEL's youth wing the United Democratic Youth Organisation (EDON) and the Progressive Movement of Students opposed the raising of the retirement age and supported the government's attempts to delay this in the course of 2012, only to become quiet when it was voted in as part of the Memorandum measures at the end of that year. The Pancyprian Labour Union (PEO) opposed public-sector cuts but went silent when this issue provoked a conflict between the government and the civil servants' union PASYDY. The Farmers' Union (EKA) was the only ancillary organisation that (slightly) diverged from full-on support of the Christofias government, even participating in protests against government measures along with other farmers' organisations outside the Presidential Palace. By this time, however, the government had changed and EKA shifted its focus to the right's agricultural policies.

More importantly, AKEL's affiliated organisations assumed the role of managing discontent – staging symbolic protest and ensuring that reactions were controlled. Although this proved increasingly difficult as austerity measures became more severe in the course of 2012, AKEL's affiliated organisations pointed to the generous public spending of the initial years of the Christofias government and to the fact that austerity was being imposed from the outside by the Troika and from the inside by the opposition parties that controlled parliament. The pro-austerity positions of all the other political parties made it easier for AKEL's affiliated organisations to retain support from citizens opposed to austerity and those affected the most by the austerity measures. With the exception of the social democratic EDEK, they remained careful in their criticism of the banks, did not challenge the discourse of 'a country in urgent need of reforms' and avoided any substantive Eurosceptic rhetoric.

While there were signs of a general dissatisfaction with representative democratic institutions, including political parties, following the economic crisis, the experience of the Christofias government placed additional strains on AKEL's organisation. AKEL's rank-and-file members were largely excluded from any serious consultation regarding government policy, negotiations with the Troika or austerity measures, and policies that reinforced the logic of TINA ('There is no Alternative'). AKEL's members and its affiliated organisations became increasingly inactive and it is no coincidence that party congresses have emphasised the need for new members and to reach out to disillusioned former members. Internal divisions, however, remained hidden from public view and limited to hearsay in the media about Central Committee discussions (e.g. those at the party's 22nd Congress in the summer of 2015). There were no formal challenges to the leadership nor public criticisms of its austerity policies.

AKEL's internal decision-making processes, which emphasise co-optation from the centre, and its ancillary structures have remained generally unchanged.[25] The party's 2015 Congress identified the need for more volunteers to gain positions in the Central Committee, for more young members to reach leading positions and for a more substantial role for members in debates and decision-making. These statements were not, however, accompanied by concrete proposals that could put them into practice.[26] Changes have remained limited to the introduction of age limits on the holders of party posts and term limits for party members in state elected positions. Activists were most opposed to the use of a special committee at congresses to rank candidates for public office. This was not entirely scrapped, but now two lists will be presented to Congress delegates – one which lists candidates alphabetically and one which indicates whether candidates have been suggested by a new Evaluation Committee (which will replace the existing Ranking Committee).

AKEL's electoral and organisational difficulties prompted its leaders to attempt to enhance the party's standing in wider society. However, AKEL's leaders approached the extra-parliamentary Left in a way that was neither novel nor comprehensive. Instead, it was selective as they focused on developing links with key individuals and using them as personalities in campaigns while their arguments filled the space left by a lack of party intellectual production. Independent intellectuals could say things that were popular with party members and supporters that AKEL's leaders could not or would not say. Therefore, criticisms of austerity and arguments for alternative ways of organising for social change have come only from activists who could not be directly identified with the party leadership.

Such developments have had little effect on AKEL's links with social movements and have done little to dilute the centralism within AKEL's internal party organisation. Indeed, changes to the management of communication with the party's newspaper *Charavgi* indicated processes of centralisation. Members of the Political Bureau are now directly responsible for both the newspaper and the party-affiliated radio station. AKEL has not mobilised emergent social movements in the way that Syriza in Greece or Bloco in Portugal have done. Rather, AKEL's environmental linkage (i.e. its relations to society at large, as well as to particular organised groups) was not enhanced through an open interaction with movements, but was based on a top-down approach similar to that of the communist parties of Greece and Portugal.[27] The social movement structures that were created as part of anti-austerity protests originated mostly from within AKEL and largely functioned under its control or only as online communities. Solidarity initiatives that were organisationally autonomous from the party did not develop.

Ideological and Programmatic Responses

Party congresses in 2014 and 2015 did not concede that the Christofias government was a negative experience nor blame the 'party in government' for the problems facing Cyprus. Instead, congresses implied that AKEL would not shy away from pursuing executive office given the possibility of new alliances. When AKEL lost 37,000 votes in the 2014 European elections, the majority of these voters abstained rather than voting for other parties, indicating that although they were disappointed, a lasting realignment of support was not taking place. Recent polls show that AKEL is regaining its support and a significant proportion of AKEL's disillusioned supporters rejoined the ranks of the Left after the Right entered government.

Defeat in the 2013 presidential elections and opposition to the Troika rescue operation prompted AKEL to re-orient its appeals. It reverted to staunchly anti-privatisation positions and more vociferously defended existing rights under threat from the bailout agreements, such as public ownership of electricity and telecommunications and progressive land taxation. The experience of AKEL reinforces wider findings that RLPs shift to more radical positions on exiting office.[28] AKEL also engaged in promoting more populist and quasi-patriotic or nationalist appeals. However, the key feature of AKEL's programmes through the period is a continuity and the crisis has not provoked major changes in terms of the party's ideology or world view.

Rather, the crisis simply re-confirmed existing pre-conceptions as AKEL interpreted what was going on through its existing discourse and ideological perspectives. According to AKEL, the economic crisis is a crisis in capitalism that resulted in a political/institutional crisis, and it is being managed by neoliberal responses that are determined by the balance of forces in the wider context of imperialism and the neocolonial hegemony of powerful Western countries. The European Union and the Eurozone are seen to primarily serve the economic interests of international capital and the military.

In late 2012 AKEL's leaders hinted at a shift to anti-Eurozone positions. However, this was aimed at exploiting the growth in Euroscepticism in the context of AKEL's return to opposition. Although AKEL commissioned international experts including economist Costas Lapavitsas (later a Syriza MP) to produce a report concerning the economic prospects for Cyprus if it existed outside the Eurozone and the Memorandum. It was released after the parliament voted through the last Memorandum legislation. After the party left office these proposals were quickly shelved.

AKEL is a party that has long downplayed the development of theories about social change and has given little to no role for intellectuals in the sense of celebrated party thinkers who influence the party line. It does not have a theoretical journal and no intellectuals are included in the leadership. AKEL's policies and slogans are generally determined by practical and electoral concerns, rather than being theoretically informed. This has always been the case and the crisis did not push the party to seek to develop a theoretical analysis of capitalism nor to seek a deep discussion of ideological issues.

Nor did AKEL seek to discuss the crisis in a more participatory or deliberative environment.

The party did however, develop its educational and research activities as the crisis unfolded. Within a year it established a second institute called 'Promitheas' (its other one being the Cyprus Labour Institute of the Pancyprian Federation of Labour [INEK-PEO]). Promitheas is run by an executive board of party supporters, hitherto inactive supporters and academics. Promitheas did not focus its activities on current affairs, but opted instead to work on historical and international themes. It has made only limited interventions in public debates on the crisis. INEK-PEO on the other hand, continued to work as before on economic and labour market issues. These issues became more important in the context of the crisis, but the leaders of AKEL largely ignored the criticisms of austerity measures that came from INEK-PEO.

AKEL produces both daily and weekly newspapers and also operates a radio station (ASTRA). However, its newspapers do little to reach out beyond core party supporters and have been constrained by the need to closely adhere to the party line.[29] The party's newspapers operate in the context of an absence of public political debate between party members. The newspapers gave blind support to government policy in 2008–2013 and were unable to develop a theoretical response to the economic crisis. Attempts to do this have been largely done by academics and activists who work outside the party and to the left of it. In particular, intellectuals (artists, journalists, teachers, academics) and liberal activists from the anti-capitalist Left with a sympathetic stance towards AKEL have used online social media (such as Facebook) and blogs to interact with AKEL supporters. As yet, no mechanism has been established to incorporate these 'outside' suggestions into AKEL's policymaking processes. Any ideological or discursive influence upon the party remains selective, essentially informal and very indirect.

The most systematic left-wing intellectual response to the crisis in Cyprus has come from the alternative weekly electronic newsletter *Defteri Anagnosi*, which appeared in early 2012 and provides a detailed commentary of public affairs and international politics. This newsletter was originally established by far left activists and has promoted independent but AKEL-friendly positions with a higher level of debate on socio-economic issues than can be found in AKEL's newspapers. *Defteri Anagnosi* refrained from articulating a full-fledged Marxist analysis of the causes of the economic crisis or overly theoretical language but offered a broadly leftist analysis and called for social control of the banking system, and criticised the 'colonial Troika' and local 'predatory capital'. *Defteri Anagnosi* became relatively popular among AKEL supporters, offered backing to the otherwise isolated AKEL government and challenged the criticisms made of it elsewhere in the media.

The publication has criticised the bourgeois economic and political power-holders of the 'deep state' in Cyprus but also defended the policies of the Christofias government. The influence of *Defteri Anagnosi* upon AKEL is apparent in the way that AKEL's leaders have drawn on its arguments in public debates.

Developments within the Greek Left have placed pressures on AKEL. The leaders of AKEL have refused to take sides between the Greek Communist Party (KKE), its 'brother', with which it shares a common world view, and Syriza, whose actual policies are more in tune with AKEL's. AKEL also meets Syriza most regularly at European-level meetings and shares with Syriza an experience of governing in the context of a crisis-ridden south European country. In effect, AKEL's party base and in particular, middle-level cadres remain divided in regards to the 'Greek question' with a significant section being pro-KKE. The youth organisation of AKEL has a long tradition of close relations with the KKE, in part, because the majority of students that support AKEL have been educated in Greece and have participated in KKE-led protests. This group promotes appeals that resemble the KKE's anti-imperialist approach and tends to look suspiciously upon any kind of negotiation or 'constructive engagement' with Western capitalist powers. Not surprisingly then, those voicing support for the KKE's policy during the crisis are also those who appear to adopt an anti-imperialistic, hard line approach in relation to the prospects for a solution to the Cyprus problem.

Consequently, AKEL's leaders have been careful to limit internal discussion on developments in Greece that might give room for divisions to emerge between those supporting Syriza and those seeking a more revolutionary approach similar to that of the KKE. Since Syriza shifted towards continued implementation of Memorandum-led austerity, AKEL has limited itself to vague statements of support for the struggles of the Greek people and has rarely spoken about developments within Greece. It has not crossed the line of identifying the policies of the Anastasiades government with those of the Tsipras government.

It is also apparent that the imperialist strand of thought in AKEL's programmes is largely used in an opportunistic way, rather than being a factor that determines AKEL's policies. It certainly did not prevent the Christofias government from making energy and military deals with Israel and it did not obstruct its signing of the EU Constitution nor the EU Fiscal Stability Agreement. The use of anti-imperialist rhetoric with regards to the Cyprus problem is also selective, one-dimensional and not based on a theoretical analysis of the 'national question'. More importantly, it is an easy position to take, as it often overlaps with the hegemonic nationalism of the centre parties.[30] This approach portrays foreign elites as a threat to the true interests of an equally homogeneous 'Cypriot people'. Thus the crisis has rendered AKEL's anti-imperialism more prone to patriotic and nationalist discourse. This was expressed in slogans adopted at the end of 2012 and the beginning of 2013, which described a conflict between Germany and the Cypriot people and called on the Cypriots to defend their sovereignty against the Troika. Such an approach may win votes but may also become a focal point for internal divisions.

The Extra-Parliamentary Left in Cyprus

The extra-parliamentary Left in Cyprus has been persistently weak during the crisis and unable to challenge AKEL's hegemony over the broader space of left-wing egalitarianism, anti-imperialism and even left-wing ecology. The most significant initiative has been the formation of the Committee for a Radical Left Rally (ERAS) in 2011, a coalition of various groups and individuals that began to enlist members and held a few protests. The group ran a press office and sought to develop analyses of the crisis and alternative policy solutions. It was, however, unable to consolidate itself and disintegrated in 2013. Disagreements about its relationship with AKEL were central to its collapse and in particular, its role became unclear after AKEL moved into opposition. The main area of activity for the extra-parliamentary Left has therefore been found in its attempt to contribute to public debate on the crisis rather than in promoting protest. These developments have meant that the extra-parliamentary Left in Cyprus remains essentially inexistent in organisational terms with a weak capacity for mobilisation. Demonstrations and solidarity marches usually attract only between 20 and 100 activists. The electoral coalition Action (*Drasy-Eylem*) that formed in 2014 in order to contest the European elections is illustrative of these weaknesses. It was the first bi-communal ticket contesting elections, but polled less than 1 per cent and was unable to attract the support of even the Far Left.

CONCLUSION

AKEL has never been an overtly 'radical' RLP, but has nevertheless long stood to the left of social democracy and has at the same time been central to the Cypriot political system. It was able to dominate the Left and allowed little room for the emergence of alternative radical left political forces, or for the emergence of a strong social democratic party. Cypriot Trotskyists and new leftists have always been marginalised as AKEL dismissed forms of Marxism that diverged from orthodox Soviet teachings and never recognised the significance of 'contamination' (to use a term that was popular in Italy) from social movements.

AKEL headed the government when the international economic crisis unfolded in Cyprus. It was damaged by this development and it gradually realised that its choices were very limited. Subsequently, AKEL attempted to implement 'mild austerity measures' and then agreed to a 'fair' memorandum with the Troika. Although the crisis had potentially similar economic and political ramifications to other southern European countries, the fact that the main radical left actor was directing the crisis response rather than trying to mobilise against it was critical. Instead of fundamentally rethinking its policies or linkages, AKEL focused all its energies on supporting the government and defending it from concerted attack from the opposition parties. So the potential for internal organisational or programmatic change was stymied.

Therefore, the crisis did not force AKEL's leaders to substantially rethink its understanding of capitalism, its positions on European integration nor its organisational practices. We find a high degree of continuity in its policies, rhetoric and internal party organisation. The party was generally unable to adapt to the changing circumstances by developing new 'left-wing answers' to the problems brought by the crisis. It was able, however, to maintain its dominance of the Left in Cyprus, subsuming other alternative and radical Left initiatives and thwarting the development of new forces to its left. Those who abandoned AKEL or criticised it have remained relatively disorganised and failed to challenge its extensive societal reach. Therefore, AKEL did not really experience competition from the Left that might have propelled change, and where it did, it was relatively insignificant. These factors help to explain the puzzlingly limited adaptation within AKEL during the years of the crisis.

NOTES

1. Giorgos Seferis 'Argonautica', 1948. Alternative translation at http://www.poetryfoundation.org/poem/181958.

2. For a detailed account of AKEL's policies in office and its lack of success see Giorgos Charalambous and Gregoris Ioannou, 'Party systems, party-society linkages and contentious acts: Cyprus in a comparative south European perspective' (forthcoming).

3. Ibid.

4. Giorgos Charalambous, *Political Culture and Behaviour in the Republic of Cyprus during the Crisis* (Nicosia: Peace Research Institute Oslo – Cyprus Centre, 2014).

5. Andreas Panayiotou, 'Lenin in the coffeeshop,' *Postcolonial Studies* 9, no. 3 (2006): 267.

6. Makarios Drousiotis, *The First Partition* (Athens: Alfadi, 2005); Peter Loizos, *The Greek Gift: Politics in a Cypriot Village* (Bibliopolis: Mannheim and Mohnesse 2004).

7. Makarios was the first president of independent Cyprus (1960–1974 and 1974–1977) and took Cyprus into the NAM on its founding in 1961.

8. Richard Dunphy and Tim Bale. 'Red Flag Still Flying? Explaining AKEL – Cyprus's Communist Anomaly,' *Party Politics* 13, no. 3 (2007): 287.

9. Drousiotis, *The First Partition*; Loizos, *The Greek Gift.*

10 Antonis A. Ellinas and Yiannos Katsourides, 'Organisational Continuity and Electoral Endurance: The Communist Party of Cyprus,' *West European Politics* 36, no. 4 (2013): 859–82.

11. Giorgos Charalambous and Christophoros Christophorou, 'The Cypriot Communists Between Protest and the Establishment: A Second Look at AKEL's Linkages with Society,' in *Party-Society Relations in the Republic of Cyprus: Political and Societal Strategies*, ed. Giorgos Charalambous and Christophoros Christophorou (Abingdon: Routledge, 2015), 19–46.

12. Charalambous and Christophorou, 'The Cypriot Communists Between Protest and the Establishment'; Giorgos Charalambous and Christophoros Christophorou, 'A Society within Society: Linkage in the Case of the Cypriot Communist Party,' *South European Society and Politics* 18, no. 1 (2013): 101–19.

13. Gregoris Ioannou, 'Employment in Crisis: Cyprus 2010–2013,' *The Cyprus Review* 26, no. 1 (2014): 107–26.

14. Andreas Panayiotou, 'Οι Τράπεζες, τα ΜΜΕ και οι Προσπάθειες Συγκάλυψης, Μετατόπισης και Λογοκρισίας των Σκανδάλων,' [The Banks, the Mass Media and the Attempts at Covering, Silencing and Censoring the Scandals], accessed 5 February 2014, http://koinonioloyika.blogspot.com/2013/01/blog-post_23.html.

15. Ibid.

16. The explosion caused the deaths of fourteen people and destroyed the island's largest electrical power station. This event allowed the opposition parties to launch vicious attacks on the Christofias government for its 'ineptitude' and contributed to an erosion of trust in the government. See Giorgos Charalambous and Gregoris Ioannou, 'No Bridge Over Troubled Waters: The Cypriot Left Heading the Government 2008–2013,' *Capital and Class* 39, no. 2 (2015): 265–86; D. Kanol and Giorgos Charalambous, 'Fluctuations in Public Trust in Government in Cyprus: Why Context Matters,' Unpublished manuscript 2015.

17. *Phileleftheros* 9 November 2011, Front page. 'Σε βαθιά νερά επιτήρησης' [In deep probation waters]; *Phileleftheros* 11 November 2011, 10. 'Τελεσίγραφο κυρώσεων από ΕΕ' [Ultimatum for sanctions by the EU].

18. Pegasiou Adonis, 'The Cypriot Economic Collapse: More Than a Conventional South European Failure,' *Mediterranean Politics* 18, no. 3 (2013): 333–51; Panayiotou 'Οι Τράπεζες'.

19. This was a consequence of the understanding that austerity could no longer be delayed and that fiscal restraint and wage cuts were seen as inevitable. It was in this context that Kazamias, the AKEL finance minister, introduced the 'third package' of economic measures. See *Phileleftheros* 21 November 2011, 10. 'Την αναγκαιότητα των μέτρων θα εξηγήσει σε όλους ο Καζαμίας' [The need for measures will be explained to everybody by Kazamias].

20. Ioannou, 'Employment in Crisis: Cyprus 2010–2013', 107–26; Charalambous, *Political Culture and Behaviour in the Republic of Cyprus During the Crisis.*

21. In the middle of the international economic crisis, Cypriot banks were investing billions in Greek sovereign bonds, buying from the secondary market (mainly German banks), at a time when most other banks were selling. The investments of Cypriot banks in Greek sovereign bonds were completely derailed following the voluntary private sector involvement in the Greek debt haircut in February 2012 as part of the Eurogroup agreement. See Pegasiou 'The Cypriot Economic Collapse: More Than a Conventional South European Failure', 344.

22. Panayiotou, 'Οι Τράπεζες'.

23. Charalambous and Christophoros, 'The Cypriot Communists Between Protest and the Establishment'.

24. Pancyprian Federation of Labour (PEO) (2012) Ανακοίνωση Γενικού Συμβουλίου 1/12/2012 [Announcement by General Council].

25. Dimitris Trimithiotis, 'Communication and Interactions Between Parties and Youth Organisations in Cyprus', in *Party-Society Relations in the Republic of Cyprus: Political and Societal Strategies,* ed. Giorgos Charalambous and Christophoros Christophorou (Abingdon: Routledge, 2015). Charalambous and Christophorou, 'The Cypriot Communists Between Protest and the Establishment'; Gregoris Ioannou, 'The Connection between Trade Unions and Political Parties in Cyprus,' in Ibid.

26. Charalambous and Christophorou, 'The Cypriot Communists Between Protest and the Establishment', 30–1.

27. Myrto Tsakatika and Marco Lisi, '"Zippin' up my Boots, Goin" Back to my Roots': Radical Left Parties in Southern Europe,' *South European Society and Politics* 18, no. 1 (2013): 19.

28. Olsen, Jonathan, Michael Koß and Dan Hough, eds. *Left Parties in National Governments* (Basingstoke: Palgrave, 2010).

29. ASTRA does have broader reach beyond the narrow core circles of party supporters, but this is a consequence of its general entertainment function and the social and cultural content of its programmes (rather than its content being strictly focused on political news and analysis). It is also open to comments from the public.

30. Vassilis Protopapas, 'Empty Vessels? The Center Parties' Linkages with Society,' in *Party-Society Relations in the Republic of Cyprus: Political and Societal Strategies*, ed. Giorgos Charalambous and Christophoros Christophorou (Abingdon: Routledge, 2015), 69–90.

Chapter 15

Greek Radical Left Responses to the Crisis

Three Types of Political Mobilisation, One Winner

Costas Eleftheriou

The economic crisis had a visibly dramatic impact on Greek politics, creating such political instability that the mainstream parties collapsed in two elections in 2012. The traditional two-partyism based on competition between the social democratic Panhellenic Socialist Movement (PASOK) and conservative New Democracy (ND) ended.[1] The implosion of PASOK created new political opportunities for the three main RLPs – the Coalition of the Radical Left (Syriza), the Communist Party of Greece (KKE) and Democratic Left (Dimar). Moreover, the economic crisis caused a rapid deterioration in living standards and enhanced Eurosceptic and anti-German sentiment as several austerity packages and three bailout agreements were implemented (in 2010, 2011 and 2015).[2] The Greek radical Left, and in particular Syriza, responded to this changing environment by trying to present a governing alternative to the electorate based on an anti-austerity platform and through forming links with protests.[3] Syriza came to the fore of debates surrounding the economic crisis and became the main party of the opposition after the 2012 double elections (May and June) and it entered government following the January 2015 election.

In this chapter, the responses of the Greek radical Left to the economic crisis are analysed in order to examine the changing nature of party competition in Greece. It is argued that the three RLPs' strategic responses were strongly shaped by their pre-crisis ideological, programmatic and organisational characteristics. This meant that while all three parties seemed to initially adapt to the changing crisis environment, only one of them – Syriza – was ultimately able to take advantage of the favourable conditions and to translate them into significant levels of electoral success. The chapter shows how under Alexis Tsipras' leadership, Syriza successfully combined intense engagement in grassroots activism, anti-austerity appeals and office-seeking to transcend the traditional Greek radical left electorate by attracting large numbers of disenchanted PASOK voters. In contrast, the KKE missed the chance to expand because it was unwilling to compromise its ideological purity, thus losing ground to its more moderate left-wing rival. Meanwhile, Dimar transformed from a radical left to social democratic position, and became gradually isolated from emerging social protests.

THE GREEK RADICAL LEFT: A BACKGROUND

Since 1974 the 'Third Hellenic Republic' has witnessed a high degree of competition between RLPs corresponding to different ideological currents.[4] The historic absence of a social democratic contender until 1974 meant that left politics became monopolised by the communist tradition. However, following a split in the KKE in 1968, Greek RLPs became divided over their positions towards the Soviet Union. This dualism became a defining feature of the Greek radical Left until 2009 as an 'orthodox' party, represented by the original KKE, positioned itself on a pro-Soviet basis and the 'reformist' current, represented by the Eurocommunist KKE-Interior, held a critical stance towards the Soviet Union.[5] Until 1986 both parties favoured convergence with PASOK; nevertheless in 1988 the KKE and the Greek Left (EAR) – the refounded KKE-Interior – cooperated to create the Coalition of Left and Progress (*Synaspismós*), an electoral coalition formed on an anti-PASOK basis.[6] Synaspismós competed in three consecutive elections (June 1989, November 1989, 1990) and it remained the only way in which the two main RLPs cooperated.[7]

After the collapse of the Soviet Union, the KKE suffered another split in 1991.[8] This took place as an 'orthodox' majority opted for the withdrawal of the party from the Synaspismós coalition, while a 'modernising' minority insisted on the continuation of the coalition and its subsequent transformation into a single party. The departure of the 'modernisers' meant that the KKE took an increasingly 'orthodox' or 're-bolshevised' orientation while the foundation of Synaspismós as a single party in 1993 incorporated a number of those leaving or expelled from the KKE. These developments meant that the dualist nature of the Greek radical Left resurfaced as the 'orthodox' current was represented by the KKE and the 'reformist' current by the internally fragmented Synaspismós. While the first was characterised by strict internal homogeneity, the latter consisted of a number of tendencies but also two discrete factions ('reform communist' and 'democratic socialist').

The two parties also adopted different organisational paths that were decisive in shaping their responses to the economic crisis.[9] The KKE's *vanguardist strategy* was forged in the 1990s. It is one of the last West European communist parties to promote a traditional Marxist-Leninist party model.[10] The party's 15th Congress (22–26 May 1996) presented the party as the main heir and guarantor of the Soviet political tradition. The KKE uses democratic centralism as the basic principle of managing its intra-party organisation.[11] Consequently, it does not tolerate factionalism and prioritises internal cohesion. Moreover, the KKE creates ancillary organisations in trade unions, business associations, student unions, farmers and women's associations that function under its tight control. In 1999, a 'quasi trade union structure' called PAME (All Workers' Militant Front), was founded to coordinate these organisations.[12] This organisational development enabled the party to appeal to less privileged strata of Greek society.[13] The party also retains its influence in middle-class groups, which have been a defining feature of the social base of Greek communism since 1974.[14]

The KKE has promoted an explicitly anti-capitalist and Eurosceptic discourse. Its anti-capitalism was expressed through anti-imperialist rhetoric that described Greece as an economy in a dependency position in relation to other advanced capitalist economies.[15] This conceptualisation remained until the party's 17th Congress in 2005, when the notion of 'dependence' began to gradually disappear from party documents.[16]

Opposition to European integration has been one of the KKE's main priorities.[17] Notwithstanding a few exceptions, it has consistently argued that the European Union promotes 'capitalist integration' that intensifies capital's rule over the working class, erodes industrial relations in member states and destroys Greece's productive capacity (by imposing a tertiary sector based economy on Greece). To the KKE, European integration is a negative development for working-class movements. The European Union is an 'alliance of wolves', and its primary purpose is to exploit and suppress European peoples. It is however, destined to dissolve itself in the event of a widespread capitalist crisis, which the party argues is inevitable.

In this sense, the KKE argues that the only viable political counterweight for Greece's accession to the European Union is to promote a socialist path of development, the so-called 'Popular Power' (*Laiki Exousia*).[18] For the KKE, Greece's participation in the European Union, and later in the Eurozone, makes any attempt for a left alternative strategy impossible, while a possible exit of the country from the European Union will be doomed if not accompanied by a 'genuine' socialist orientation. The KKE argues that as European integration has advanced, the room for independent policymaking has shrunk as the institutions of the Greek state (from central to local government) have become powerless. In this context, the KKE has, since 2003, recused itself from claiming control of municipalities and rejected any collaboration with other political parties. Thus, its Euro-rejectionism has become combined with a rejection of taking government responsibility. This was to affect KKE strategy during the economic crisis when it was faced with the challenge of participating in a 'left' government.

Conversely, Synaspismós was a pluralist and fragmented party. In organisational terms it was 'centralised with relatively autonomous local branches': essentially meaning that it had a strong bureaucracy but loose control over its grassroots.[19] Indeed, it emphasised intra-party democracy (intra-party referenda, tolerance of factions and tendencies, deliberative structures) and informal arrangements for retaining the party's cohesion (e.g. unanimous resolutions of party bodies through deliberation between factions). One of its most defining features was the permanent functioning of factions, something that gave an image of being a 'confederation'. Synaspismós' two main political currents were 'reform communists' (called 'leftists'), who kept a 'soft-Eurosceptic' stance and 'democratic socialists' (called the 'renewers'), who championed a critical Europeanism.[20]

Synaspismós' links with civil society underwent significant changes. Until 2000, it enjoyed influence in certain trade unions – mainly public-sector employees, school teachers and bank employees. It focused on electoral campaigns and on promoting its public image in the mass media, especially in the newly formed private television stations. After 2000, however, the party re-examined its linkage strategies and aligned itself with the Global Justice Movement, by organising the so-called 'Greek Social Forum' as part of the European Social Forum. This shift towards social movements was promoted by Synaspismós' youth wing, and significantly strengthened this group to become a significant intra-party actor. Compared with the KKE, Synaspismós' appeals were mainly directed towards educated middle-class groups.

The reform communist faction assumed control of Synaspismós after its 3rd Congress (29 June to 2 July 2000) by supporting its long-standing president Nicos Konstantopoulos. This shift had two consequences: first Synaspismós changed its critical pro-EU positions and assumed a soft form of Euroscepticism by voting against the ratification of the Nice Treaty in the Parliament. Second, it refocused Synaspismós' orientation towards political coalitions. Subsequently, Synaspismós initiated a search for 'common political ground' with other small RLPs and left-leaning groups. Such dialogue ultimately led to the formation of the electoral coalition Syriza at the 2004 parliamentary elections.[21]

After Synaspismós' 4th Congress (9–12 December 2004) and under the leadership of Alekos Alavanos, the Syriza coalition helped Synaspismós to direct its appeals to young people.[22] Alavanos selected 33-year-old ex-youth wing leader Alexis Tsipras as the party's candidate for the Athens municipality in the 2006 local elections. Tsipras' candidacy was the starting point for his rise to the leadership and this provided him with the opportunity to gain a reputation beyond the narrow confines of youth wing politics. Syriza also initiated its involvement in societal mobilisation and it sought to become the 'spokesperson' of movements in the public sphere. This 'back to society' strategy was rewarded with a positive result for Syriza at the 2007 general elections with 5.04 per cent of the vote.[23]

Nevertheless, this radical shift was not well-received by the democratic socialist minority in Synaspismós. The *Ananeotiki Pteryga* (Renewers' Wing) faction led by Fotis Kouvelis was suspicious of the Syriza project, which it saw as a 'leftist' political formation undermining the party's pro-European identity. In this context, and after Tsipras' election as Synaspismós leader in 2008, Pteryga started to develop party-like structures (e.g. parallel informal groups in main party bodies) and opposed almost every resolution taken by the party's Central Committee and Executive Secretariat. In this sense, Synaspismós' minority faction favoured a different political project that included a coalition strategy with PASOK and Ecologists-Greens and moderate positions on the evolution of the European project. Unyielding tensions between the two factions defined Synaspismós' intra-party politics for the next few years, leading the party to split in 2010.

The gap between the two factions became increasingly apparent when Ananeotiki Pteryga's four MPs refused to vote against the ratification of the Lisbon Treaty in the Greek Parliament, contrary to the party's official position.[24] The party was also divided over responses to the December 2008 riots. The Syriza and Synaspismós leaders, Alavanos and Tsipras respectively, chose to provide the 'student uprising' with critical support, in stark contrast to condemnation of the violent demonstrations from across the political spectrum.[25] This position appeared to undermine Syriza's rising standing in public opinion polls and allowed Pteryga, to attack the majority faction for its 'ambiguous' position on 'political violence'. In February 2009, Tsipras presented a new party programme, which was 'killed' by Pteryga, and co-existence between the factions was preserved only on electoral grounds – because a split might result in both parties losing parliamentary representation.

Syriza achieved feeble results in European and national elections in 2009, and this exacerbated divisions within Synaspismós. The Synaspismós leadership was considering enhancing Syriza into a consolidated political coalition rather than merely an electoral one. For Pteryga this was out of the question, since it feared that Synaspismós would be dissolved into Syriza. What was at stake was firstly party identity – a radical left, pro-movement, soft Eurosceptic identity versus a left legalistic and dogmatically pro-European identity. Secondly, the development of Syriza threatened to undermine Pteryga's ability to shape party strategy, gain positions in the party bureaucracy and to access the party's resources and state subsidies. As a result, at Synaspismós'

6th Congress (3–6 June 2010), Pteryga left the party and soon created Dimar. Subsequently, Syriza was left with a young and popular leader and a more explicitly radical left orientation.

THE SOCIOPOLITICAL IMPACT OF THE CRISIS (2010–2015)

The austerity packages that were implemented in the context of Greece's loan agreements were a catalyst for widespread economic and sociopolitical change.[26] As the established political parties collapsed, new parties formed on both the left and the right of the ideological spectrum, partly as a consequence of emergent social movements. The shifts in party competition were related to a general recomposition of Greek social structure, which was caused by austerity policies that provoked a deep recession. From 2008 to 2012 Greek GDP decreased by over 20 per cent and net national disposable income fell by 22 per cent. Unemployment rose from 7.2 per cent to 23.6 per cent (by 2016 it exceeded 27 per cent, with youth unemployment at 64 per cent).[27] Almost 229,000 small enterprises closed down in 2008–2014. The economic crisis impoverished large segments of the Greek population, principally wage earners in both public and private sectors and self-employed and small businesspeople. These social groups were the backbone of PASOK's support base and since the latter introduced austerity policies, it suffered a major loss of support, which significantly strengthened the non-PASOK Left.[28]

The 'Memoranda' (bailouts agreed with the Troika) had significant impact on the functioning of party democracy in Greece as 'Memorandum' policies replaced decisions made by parliament. For example, the unilateral revision of Memoranda terms by Government and the Troika occurred without prior discussion or ratification by parliament. Critics argued that the Government and the Troika had ceased to be accountable to representative institutions. At the level of intra-party democracy, PASOK's shift from pro-distribution to pro-austerity policies in 2010 and ND's shift from an anti-Memorandum to pro-Memorandum position in late 2011 were also taken without approval from the parties' collective bodies or membership. In both cases, marginalisation of the parties' middle-level elites and members was considered as *sine qua non* to the implementation of the austerity measures.

The political crisis also had implications for the relationship between party elites and civil society. There was an 'explosion' of formal collective action mainly through the traditional trade unions.[29] The General Confederation of Greek Commerce (GSEE) organised nearly 27 general strikes, while even the business associations of the SMEs participated with shop closures and demonstrations.[30] Moreover, the failure of negotiations over the minimum wage paved the way for more contentious demonstrations and strategies.

In most cases civil society groups battled against the government's proposals while mainstream elites condemned popular protests as being 'populist' and 'irresponsible'.[31]

Such responses did little to stop the emergence of several regional movements that promoted civil disobedience, the emergence of new trade unions and the Greek 'Indignants' movement, which appeared in mid-2011.[32] The Indignants organised mass gatherings, marches, occupations and other radical actions placing further strains on the political system while at the same time championing direct democracy and citizen participation in the elections in order to take advantage of the changing political opportunity structure. Furthermore, 'reformed' and new unions frequently used types of civil disobedience such as sit-ins, occupations and even mass hunger strikes as they distanced themselves from traditional trade union tactics. Finally, 'Can't Pay, Don't Pay' committees formed to defend those unable to pay their bills and 'solidarity' citizen groups created committees for offering food, meals and clothing to the homeless, unemployed and immigrants.[33] These forms of collective action and mass opposition towards austerity policies provided significant opportunities for RLPs to expand their appeal.[34]

RADICAL LEFT RESPONSES TO THE CRISIS

Organisational Responses and Linkage Strategies

Before 2009, both the KKE and Synaspismós organised links with civil society through their ancillary organisations to campaign on economic, educational or environmental issues. These parties, however, always prioritised enhancing their electoral support over other goals. The crisis, however, altered such strategies. In particular, when Synaspismós split in 2010, a deep strategic dilemma was apparent as debates emerged regarding whether it was possible to work inside a coalition government with PASOK to mitigate the negative consequences of austerity policies, or whether a staunch oppositional position against the Memorandum was preferable.

The splinter group from Synaspismós, which became Dimar, pursued an office-seeking strategy and sought to explore cooperating with PASOK in order to become a reliable left governmental party. Therefore, it did not need to develop a mass organisation (its membership never exceeded 4,000–5,000). While Dimar retained links with professional unions (doctors, lawyers and university professors) and NGOs, it was reluctant to participate in mass demonstrations or contentious movement activity. While it declared its support for the Indignants, it pointed out that democratisation and changes in the political system had no connection with the vague rhetoric of extra-parliamentary protests that threatened to weaken democracy.[35] Dimar's party organisation became the equivalent of a 'modern cadre party'.[36]

In contrast, Syriza initially became more policy-seeking, as it preserved links with social movements and converged with the protesters that opposed the Memorandum. Yet after its success in the May 2012 elections, its leaders pushed it in a more office-seeking direction as it contemplated the prospect of a 'government of the Left'. This caused a major strategic division as it had to decide whether abolishing the Memorandum was a prerequisite for the viability of the government of the Left, or whether such a government was an end in itself that would eventually initiate the demise of the Memorandum. Major intra-party clashes took place around this tension, involving the new majority faction of 'Left Unity' supporting Alexis Tsipras and the minority 'Left Platform' led by Panagiotis Lafazanis. The pro- or anti- 'Government of the Left' cleavage superseded the previous internal fractional politics within Syriza.

The post-2012 attempt to re-establish Syriza as an office-seeking party had two organisational phases: (a) the enlargement of the party's membership and (b) the redefinition of its linkage strategies. As for the first, the new unified Syriza claimed to have almost 33,000 members before its Founding Congress (July 2013).[37] This was a significant increase on the old Synaspismós, which along with its Syriza counterparts (after the departure of Dimar), could count nearly 15,000 members.[38] This rise is impressive given that Syriza has a relatively undeveloped party organisation. Nevertheless, its members/voters ratio still remains lower than 2 per cent. This means that the party's rapid electoral expansion was not followed by an equivalent expansion in party membership or a change in its political personnel. In fact, while Syriza attracted swathes of disillusioned PASOK voters, the actual impact of this shift on the party organisation was minimal. For example, at the 2013 Congress, Syriza's new Central Committee was comprised predominantly of ex-Synaspismós cadres and only of two ex-PASOK cadres (of 201 members). The same also applied for the parliamentary group after the June 2012 elections (4 of 71 MPs). This phenomenon can be partly explained by the suspicion that traditional Syriza members held towards the ex-PASOK newcomers, who were considered as unreliable and excessively moderate: accordingly, the older members tried to insulate the party's leading bodies from the newcomers.

The second phase involved the launching of a new linkage strategy vis-à-vis civil society. The crisis created a favourable environment for the formulation of an active model of political mobilisation. This saw Syriza participating in strikes through formal trade union structures. At the regional level there were mass demonstrations – for example in Iraklio at Crete, the fifth largest city in Greece – which were not under the control and guidance of the 'party in central office'. This is revealing of the real nature of Syriza's mobilisation strategy, which was based on the autonomous activity of local activists. While Syriza's leaders rarely initiated actions, they supported and defended them in the public sphere, a stance of great importance given that they were presented by the government and the media as dangerous, un-democratic, anti-system movements. Moreover, the party endorsed emergent civil disobedience movements.[39] This approach was to play an important part in shaping Syriza's electoral success.

Most of Syriza's movement activity occurred through 'solidarity networks', which it created in municipalities.[40] These activities involved the provision of food and medicine and free lessons to students. Syriza's tactics created spaces of solidarity and built links to PASOK's social base. Finally, Syriza partici-pated informally but actively in the 'Indignants' movement.[41] Syriza activists co-organised some of the assemblies in Syntagma Square and a number of cities. It attempted to connect the 'square movements' with the other strikes and demonstrations. A good example is the general strike in Athens on 25–26 June 2012, where both the strikers and the Indignant protesters participated. That Syriza managed to capitalise on the 'squares movement' is indicated by June 2012 being the moment that its electoral support expanded further.

The post-2012 office-seeking strategy entailed increased emphasis on the activities of the parliamentary group, further autonomy of the party leader vis-à-vis the party organisation and submission of the movement activity to the goal of the government of the Left. It was implied that the demands of the movements could be fulfilled by a left government. As a result, the party prioritised electoral mobilisation and many activists from social movements became MPs for Syriza or joined its administrative personnel. However, this did not imply a decisive distancing from the movements; almost 25 per cent of Syriza's MP's wages were spent on supporting solidarity networks and 20 per cent of Syriza MPs before 2015 considered their intra-parliamentary activity as an extension of their movement activity.[42] Hence Syriza emphasised par-ticipatory linkage as a way of preparing its members and sympathisers for election campaigning and governmental responsibilities. Simultaneously, in terms of environmental linkages, the party's ties to civil society organisations and social movements were subjugated to office-seeking. This involved top-down practices, with ancillary organisations being increasingly coordinated to promote 'permanent electoral alertness'.

In contrast, the KKE's vanguardist approach relied on a single organisa-tion, the trade union front PAME. This centralised organisation coordinates party-affiliated trade unions and their members. The party views PAME as one of the most important means of attracting support. PAME functioned to prevent convergence between KKE trade unionists and those of other parties. PAME has also promoted the creation of work-place cells instead of local branches. This strategy has led to a loss of the KKE's electoral capacity, but at the same time it strengthened its working-class identity.

The KKE recognised the importance of the protests from 2010 to 2015; however, its leaders protected its homogeneity through exerting control over its participation in collective actions. For example, the KKE criticised the Indignants for not allowing parties to participate in its procedures and denied its members the chance to participate in the movement on an individual basis. Alternatively, the KKE initiated several enterprise-level strikes, with the most prominent being the 272-day strike (October 2011 to July 2012) in the steel factory 'Greek Halyvourghia' in Aspropyrgos.[43] The Halyvourghia strike was a turning point for the KKE's strategy since it mobilised its resources via PAME to support the strikers. The KKE tried to highlight Halyvourghia as a nationwide example of a 'correct' militant mobilisation ('The whole Greece to become a Halyvourghia'). The eventual failure of the strike was downplayed by the party leadership because it highlighted the limitations of the KKE's linkage strategy.

Strategic Responses and Government Potential

PASOK was the 'paradigmatic' party of the Third Hellenic Republic, and therefore its 2012 electoral collapse (when it lost 75 per cent of its voters) was a major event in Greek politics.[44] Most of PASOK's former voters switched to Syriza and Dimar.[45] Both parties managed to articulate their appeals in order to correspond with the two faces of PASOK – the traditional Centre-Left of the 1980s headed by Andreas Papandreou and the modernising 'Third way'-style PASOK of the 1990s expressed by Costas Simitis.[46] In 2012, Syriza came closest to the positions of Andreas Papandreou's PASOK, while Dimar clung to more pro-modernising PASOK positions. Such attempts to win over PASOK supporters presented a major change, given that Greek RLPs had historically either tried to converge with PASOK to gain influence or to differentiate themselves from PASOK in order to ensure their survival.

Opposition to Memorandum policies was crucial for the de-alignment of Greek party system.[47] It produced new parties and mainstream parties now made unusual coalitions. For example, until October 2011 the conservative ND held a staunch anti-Memorandum position, in opposition to PASOK's austerity policies – from a pro-taxpayers' and a pro-small owners' perspective. After that October, it supported a coalition government led by ex-Governor of the Bank of Greece Loukas Papademos with PASOK and the radical right party LAOS, in order to facilitate a new bailout agreement – the so-called 'Second Memorandum' (November 2011). LAOS, which had been on the rise after the 2009 elections, voted in 2010 in favour of the Memorandum along with PASOK's MPs and supported the Papademos government. After it became evident that LAOS was losing supporters to the extreme right Golden Dawn party, it switched to an anti-Memorandum position until its demise at the 2012 elections. The Independent Greeks party came from a group of ND MPs that rejected their party's pro-Memorandum U-turn and managed to secure a significant share of votes at the 2012 elections by defending ND's previous anti-Memorandum position. Finally, Golden Dawn, a hitherto marginalised neo-Nazi group, became a significant party after 2012 through an anti-system, xenophobic discourse coupled with criticism of the Memorandum.[48]

Syriza ruled out any collaboration with PASOK, since the latter was perceived as the political 'proprietor' of the First Memorandum – and the Memoranda policies generally. Two groups of disenchanted PASOK supporters could be identified within Syriza: the 'New Militant' and the 'Unified Social Front' (EKM). Syriza used both groups to present candidates that could appeal to PASOK voters. Moreover, several PASOK cadres and MPs included themselves in the ballots without any association with these two groups. Tsipras also appealed to traditional PASOK voters by defending Andreas Papandreou's policies in the 1980s including those on the National Health System, democratisation and expansionary fiscal policies; he contrasted these with (then PASOK leader) George Papandreou's austerity measures to appeal to PASOK supporters.

As for the Right, Syriza held a position of strategic tolerance towards ND, as long as the latter was moving on an anti-Memorandum trajectory. Alexis Tsipras was praised for his 'patriotic' stance by right-wing pundits. Syriza's anti-Troika appeals were also extremely popular with right-leaning social groups. After October 2011, when ND leader Antonis Samaras switched to a pro-Memorandum position, Syriza re-initiated the familiar 'anti-two-partyism' appeals and tried to attract those parts of the ND electorate that still opposed the Memorandum policies. With this in mind, it is perhaps less surprising that before the May 2012 elections, Tsipras did not rule out cooperation with the nationalist Independent Greeks party – a split from ND – in a potential government.

Dimar was more eager to form a coalition with PASOK; after all, this was one of the main reasons for its departure from Synaspismós. Dimar sought collaboration with PASOK at the 2010 local elections in running candidates for the municipalities of Athens and Salonika. After the 2012 elections and until mid-2013 it participated in a coalition government with ND and PASOK under the justification of preserving Greece's membership of the Eurozone. In contrast, the KKE intensified its hostility towards PASOK and the other RLPs alike. This insular approach helps to explain why the KKE was the only RLP that failed to benefit from PASOK's collapse (see Tables 15.1 and 15.2).

PASOK's collapse also increased the governing potential of Greek RLPs. How did they respond to this challenge? The KKE rejected Syriza's proposals for government cooperation both before and after the 2012 elections. For the KKE, the idea of a left government was futile and such strategies would be against the interests of the Greek working class. After 2012, the KKE

Table 15.1 National Election Results of Greek RLPs 1993–2015 (percentage share of the vote and number of seats)

	1993	1996	2000	2004	2007	2009
KKE	4.54 (9)	5.61 (11)	5.52 (11)	5.90 (12)	8.15 (22)	7.54 (21)
SYN	2.94 (0)	5.12 (10)	3.20 (6)	n/a	n/a	n/a
Syriza	n/a	n/a	n/a	3.26 (6)*	5.04 (14)*	4.60 (13)*
Dimar	n/a	n/a	n/a	n/a	n/a	n/a

	May 2012	June 2012	January 2015	September 2015
KKE	8.48 (26)	4.51 (12)	5.47 (15)	5.55 (15)
SYN	n/a	n/a	n/a	n/a
Syriza	16.78 (52) **(a)**	26.89 (71) **(b)**	36.34 (149) **(b)**	35.46 (145) **(b)**
Dimar	6.11 (19)	6.26 (17)	0.49 (0) **(c)**	6.29 (1) **(d)**

Key: * as electoral coalition; (a) as Syriza-EKM; (b) as a single party; (c) as Greens-Democratic Left; (d) in coalition with PASOK. Dimar secured one seat of 17 in total.
Source: Ministry of Internal Affairs, Electoral Results, ekloges.ypes.gr.

Table 15.2 European Parliament Elections Results of Greek RLPs (1994–2014) (percentage share of the vote and number of seats)

	1994	1999	2004	2009	2014
KKE	6.29 (2)	8.67 (3)	9.48 (3)	8.35 (2)	6.07 (2)
SYN	6.25 (2)	5.16 (2)	4.16 (1)	n/a	n/a
Syriza	n/a	n/a	n/a	4.70 (1)	26.60 (6)
Demar	n/a	n/a	n/a	n/a	1.20 (0)

Source: Ministry of Internal Affairs, Electoral Results, ekloges.ypes.gr.

highlighted Syriza as its main adversary and claimed that it functioned as 'born-again' social democracy. For the KKE, the only path to 'socialism' was 'popular power' as a transitional state of affairs that would include the 'socialisation of the means of production, 'central planning' and eventually 'disengagement' from the European Union. In that sense, the idea that there would be a left government inside the European Union and without a genuine will for a 'clash' with monopoly capital or the 'imperialist-capitalist supranational alliances' was considered as insincere. The KKE refused to see the collapse of PASOK as an opportunity to govern and remained reluctant to hold positions in public office. Following the 2010 local elections it controlled only one municipality and after the 2014 local elections only three municipalities.

Post-2010, Dimar saw governmental participation as the main task of a 'responsible Left'. In the 2012–2013 coalition government it held two important ministerial posts (internal affairs and administrative reform, and justice) and contributed policy experts to the government's official discussions with the Troika. However, during its year-long spell in government two problems were evident: (a) the party's political personnel were unprepared for managing government responsibilities, in terms of producing bills and justifying

policies; and (b) communication gaps between Dimar and its coalition partners – especially ND – created a degree of confusion. Dimar was unable to
handle Troika demands (for instance, in relation to the IMF's call for the
dismissal of civil servants) and clashed with ND on issues of human and
civil rights (e.g. over anti-racism legislation) and the closure of Greek Public
Television. Dimar's exit from the government coalition in July 2013 was the
beginning of the end for its significance in party competition as its electoral
support evaporated in just one year.

Tsipras first presented the idea of a government of the Left before the
May 2012 elections. At first this was conceptualised in terms of 'left unity',
but after the 2012 elections the aim increasingly became a single-party
Syriza government. Syriza presented the government of the Left on an anti-
Memorandum basis and Tsipras drew parallels with both the National Libera-
tion Front (EAM) – the communist-led resistance organisation during Axis
occupation – and United Democratic Left (EDA) – the left party in post-war
Greek politics. This was an attempt to present the goal of achieving power as
a historic challenge for the Greek Left.

Consistent with its new office-seeking aim, Syriza's leadership remodelled
the party's organisation in 2012–2015. Rapid expansion of its electoral base
in 2012 critically challenged its organisational capacities. Therefore, party
cadres were switched from chiefly oppositional duties to preparing for government. The parliamentary group's role vis-à-vis the party organisation was
also upgraded as the former became the main locus of decision-making. Due
to its increased size, the parliamentary group now employed most of Syriza's
personnel. Moreover, a programme committee led by leading figure and later
Deputy Prime Minister Yannis Dragassakis was initiated to formulate Syriza's
governing programme. The role of the party leader in developing Syriza's
international links was strengthened as Tsipras made a number of visits across
Europe. Tsipras' image was also enhanced through his nomination as the European Left's candidate to be the president of the European Commission in 2014.

By the end of 2014 Syriza rejected the remnants of Dimar as being possible
coalition partners and sought to govern alone. Nevertheless, after the 2015
elections, Syriza accepted the Independent Greeks as a coalition partner. The
latter were ready to suppress ideological differences with Syriza in order to
enter office and vital common ground existed between the parties in their
anti-Memorandum appeals.

Programmatic Responses: Opposing Austerity and the EU's Management of the Crisis

This section analyses Greek RLPs' interpretations of the crisis and whether
they understood the crisis as being primarily endogenous (stemming from

problems in Greek society) or as primarily exogenous (imposed by the European Union's management of Greece's economic problems). Until the 2012 elections Syriza (and Synaspismós) interpreted the crisis in Greece as being both a by-product of a general crisis at the European level and as a result of the long-standing mismanagement by the parties that dominated domestic politics during the pre-crisis years. Therefore, on the one hand Syriza criticised the European Union's management of the crisis and blamed the Memorandum for causing an acute social crisis. On the other hand, it criticised PASOK and ND for exploiting opportunities to impose 'Shock Therapy' reforms. For Syriza, these two developments confirmed the need to struggle against the domination of neoliberalism at both the European and national levels.

At the same time, Syriza's majority faction took a critical pro-Euro position challenging the view that a Grexit would produce positive results for the Greek people. In the wake of the imposition of the first Memorandum, Synaspismós' 2010 Congress passed a resolution to promote an 'Alternative Programme for the Progressive Exit from the Crisis' that involved: the 'disengagement' from the Memorandum through direct loans by the ECB, renegotiation of the debt and partial debt relief; the 'socialisation' of the banking system; the 'productive reconstruction of Greek economy' with emphasis on preserving social protection and forwarding 'an alternative model of development under a public investments programme'.[49] Syriza/Synaspismós also proposed the issuing of 'Eurobonds' for indebted countries and advocated the formation of an anti-austerity alliance between Greece and southern European countries facing similar problems.

Conversely, Syriza's minority faction favoured a 'Plan B' that involved tackling the crisis through the gradual return to national currency. While they did not propose the total reorientation of Syriza's programme towards the Plan B, they insisted that the party should accept the possibility of the drachma if an intra-Eurozone solution was impossible.[50] In fact, the only notable figure to campaign fully for Plan B was former Synaspismós leader Alekos Alavanos, who after leaving the party in 2010 formed the Plan B movement to contest the 2014 European Parliamentary elections (it attained just 0.2 per cent).

Expansion at the May 2012 elections forced Syriza to elaborate more specific programmatic positions for the subsequent June 2012 elections. Nevertheless, its electoral programme was directed towards the Greek public with only minor references to EU management of the crisis. This can be explained by its pursuit of an electoral strategy that emphasised domestic aspects of the crisis in order attract PASOK and ND supporters. Nevertheless, at the presentation of the party's economic programme, Yannis Dragassakis pinpointed that 'it is not our choice to exit the Euro, but neither can we consent to the continuation of policies that offer no guarantee for the survival of our society and our country'.[51] He also declared that

> the crisis in Greece does not constitute a 'national peculiarity', but is part of a broader European crisis, with both endogenous and external causes. It is only within a framework of a common European solution that the particular and existing problems of Greece can be dealt with.[52]

Tsipras also made explicit references to 'a direct abolition of the Memorandum' as soon as Syriza assumed office, its substitution by a 'National Recovery Plan' and its 'renegotiation' with fairer terms.[53] Here, the 'renegotiation' presupposed the 'abolition' of the Memorandum.

After 2012, Syriza's leaders gradually moved to more 'realist' programmatic positions focused on governmental responsibility. Nevertheless, the discourse of official documents of Syriza's Congress and Central Committee were always more radical than the day-by-day discourse articulated by Tsipras and leading party cadres. For example, Syriza's Founding Congress (July 2013) underscored the radical left character of the party through declaring that 'we will cancel the Memoranda and the [respective] implementing laws' and also that 'we will renegotiate the loan contracts and cancel their onerous terms'.[54] Moreover, Tsipras described the 2014 European Parliament elections as 'a referendum for the Memoranda, Troika and inhumane austerity' as the party re-emphasised the EU-management dimension of the crisis.[55]

Syriza's 'realism' became more prominent during the January 2015 elections. The narrative of 'renegotiation' became its main appeal, while the goal of abolishing the Memoranda as a prerequisite for such a renegotiation was downplayed. Syriza's main programmatic document was the so-called 'Thessaloniki Programme' (September 2014), which analysed four areas: 'confronting the humanitarian crisis', 'restarting the economy and promoting tax justice', 'regaining employment' and 'transforming the political system to deepen democracy'.[56] This set out a roadmap for the first six months of a Syriza government for managing the Greek crisis without abolishing the Memoranda. The cost of the programme reached 12 billion Euros, which would be financed from tackling tax evasion and re-distributing funds from the National Strategic Reference Framework and the Hellenic Financial Stability Fund. The 'abolition of the Memorandum' would now come after the renegotiation in the form of a new 'just agreement'.

Conversely, the KKE's programmatic positions changed very little after May 2010. For the KKE, unlike Syriza, the emergence of the crisis was neither a contingent development caused by a 'corrupt' political elite that

mismanaged the public debt nor a 'collusion' of foreign and domestic economic interests that subjugated Greek people to the austerity demands of
a specific group of countries. On the contrary, the Greek crisis was part of
'a generalised crisis of over-production, over-accumulation of capital'.[57]
Therefore, the crisis was a crisis of the capitalist system that occurred at the
global level because of the dramatic burdens on minor economies within
supranational 'imperialist' entities like the European Union. In that sense, the
Greek economy 'being part of the capitalist barbarity of the European Union,
interwoven with the IMF, involved in the imperialist rivalries among the EU,
the US, China and Russia, is involved in the race for a share in the markets
[and] ... will always be considered less productive and competitive'.[58] Consequently, the position of Greece in the European division of labour made any
economic strategy inside the European Union futile.

In this context, a left government would still fail to challenge the main
cause of the recession, which is the EU framework and the capitalist system
in general. For the KKE 'the epoch of the bourgeois-democratic revolutions
has ended' and the time is right for the socialist transformation of Greek
society and the realisation of 'popular power'.[59] The latter was conceptualised
by the party's 19th Congress (April 2013), as a 'social coalition' (between
the working-class, self-employed, poor farmers, women, the young) that 'has
movement characteristics in a line of rupture and overthrow'.[60]

Therefore, to the KKE the 'Memorandum' was a by-product of a general
crisis and its abolition was considered an inadequate response. This argument
was used to justify the KKE's rejection of cooperation with Syriza. However,
after the 2012 elections, the KKE prioritised the abolition of the Memoranda,
in an attempt to halt the exodus of voters to Syriza. The KKE held a rather
ambiguous position on the prospect of a Grexit as it rejected exiting the
Eurozone without prior advances in the socialist goals of 'popular power',
central planning and 'productive reconstruction'. Without these, an exit from
the Eurozone was seen as catastrophic for the Greek working class. While the
KKE claimed to have accurately predicted the crisis, this convoluted position
contributed to its failure to benefit from this 'ideological advantage'.

Finally, Dimar maintained a moderate position on these issues. It saw
Greece's Eurozone and EU membership as its main goals and thereby justified programmatic compromises in office. Dimar stressed that although the
crisis in Greece was connected to international developments, it was *primarily* a Greek phenomenon rooted into the shortcomings of its party system
and social problems. A 'responsible left' party, Dimar declared, should not
give in to temptations of 'populism' or extreme 'leftism' but should promote
'modernisation' through 'europeanisation' to address the crisis. Thus, Dimar
considered austerity to be a 'necessary evil' for Greece to remain inside the
European Union.

CONCLUSION

The Greek crisis opened up major opportunities for the Greek radical Left, yet only Syriza, a formerly minor party, was able to benefit. Syriza's formation as an 'open' coalition and inclusive approach to ex-PASOK supporters was instrumental in its success in the 2012 elections. This development was not, however, based on clientelism, which was a major feature of PASOK's strategy. Instead, Syriza's active involvement with anti-austerity protest movements enabled it to present itself as the principal left-wing advocate of the anti-Memorandum movement. This meant that many KKE voters also switched to Syriza in 2012.

At the same time, internal debates inside Syriza became polarised. On the one hand, Syriza's programme took a 'realist' direction as the majority sought a socially just solution within the Eurozone framework, and increasingly governmental office. However, the anti-Euro stance of the minority faction within Syriza meant that it also appealed to Eurosceptic parts of the electorate. Eventually, the rise of Tsipras as a 'national leader' enabled Syriza to broaden its appeal and, at least initially, to transcend problems arising from internal divisions. The party gradually distanced itself from social movement activity as it redirected its resources towards achieving electoral success, and cultivated the image of a credible party of government from 2012 to 2015. The January 2015 elections saw Syriza transition from an oppositional role to being a party of government that presents policies of a social democratic orientation.

Dimar enjoyed rising support in early 2012, and sought a role as a governing party. In 2012 it appealed to former PASOK voters with a 'modernising' orientation. However, its participation in the Samaras government after June 2012 undermined its soft anti-Memorandum profile, while Syriza's impressive advance forced it to make an ideological transition to mainstream social democratic positions. Its exit from government after one year undermined its image as a 'responsible' governing left party. From 2013 to 2015 the party initiated several coalitional strategies in order to ensure its survival – with the Greens, PASOK and even with Syriza – but it proved unable to maintain a significant position in the party system.

Finally, the KKE failed to exploit the opportunities presented by the economic crisis. For the first time in two decades the radical Left had the opportunity to develop its coalition potential. It was, however, Syriza, the KKE's main antagonist, which while being internally fragmented, was better positioned to exploit the disenchantment triggered by austerity policies. The KKE's domineering approach towards mobilisation meant that it failed to shape protests after the imposition of the Memorandum, and it ultimately became further marginalised in what was a changing political environment.

NOTES

1. Christos Lyrintzis, 'Greek Politics in the Era of Economic Crisis: Reassessing Causes and Effects', *GreeSE Paper* 45 (2011): 1–25, accessed 22 October 2015, http://eprints.lse.ac.uk/33826/1/GreeSE_No45.pdf.

2. Susannah Verney, 'Waking the "Sleeping Giant" or Expressing Domestic Dissent? Mainstreaming Euroscepticism in Crisis-stricken Greece,' *International Political Science Review* 36 (2015): 279–95. Zinovia Lialiouti and Giorgos Bithimitris, '"The Nazis Strike Again": The Concept of German Occupation, Party Strategies and Mass Perceptions Under the Prism of the Greek Economic Crisis,' in *Nation States Between Memories of World War II and Contemporary European Politics*, ed. Christian Karner and Bram Mertens (London, NJ: Transaction Publishers, 2013), 155–72.

3. Stathis Gourgouris, 'Left Governmentality in Reality,' *AnalyzeGreece!*, 20 January 2015, http://www.analyzegreece.gr/topics/elections-250102015/item/65-stathis-gourgouris-left-governmentality-in-reality.

4. Stathis Kalyvas and Niko Marantzidis, 'Greek Communism 1968–2001,' *Eastern European Politics and Societies* 26 (2002): 665–90; Myrto Tsakatika and Costas Eleftheriou, 'The Radical Left's Turn towards Civil Society in Greece: One Strategy, Two Paths,' *South European Society and Politics* 18 (2013): 81–99.

5. Richard Clogg, *Parties and Elections in Greece: The Search for Legitimacy* (Durham: Duke University Press, 1987), 171–81.

6. Costas Eleftheriou, 'The "Uneasy Symbiosis": Factionalism and Radical Politics in Synaspismós' (paper presented at the 4th Hellenic Observatory PhD Symposium, London, 19–21 June 2009).

7. Susannah Verney, '"Compromesso Storico": Reunion and Renewal on the Greek Left,' *Journal of Communist Studies* 5 (1989): 200–6.

8. George Doukas, 'The Thirteenth Congress of the KKE: Defeat of the Renovators,' *Journal of Communist Studies* 7 (1991): 393–8.

9. Tsakatika and Eleftheriou, 'The Radical Left's Turn'.

10. Luke March, *Radical Left Parties in Europe* (Oxford and New York: Routledge, 2011).

11. KKE, *Καταστατικό του Κομμουνιστικού Κόμματος Ελλάδας* (Athens: Central Committee of KKE, 1996).

12. Tsakatika and Eleftheriou, 'The Radical Left's Turn'.

13. Costas Eleftheriou, 'Ρωγμές στον μονόλιθο; Το ΚΚΕ στις εκλογές του 2012', in *2012: Ο διπλός εκλογικός σεισμός*, eds. Yannis Voulgaris and Ilias Nicolacopoulos (Athens: Themelio, 2014), 151–84.

14. Ibid.

15. KKE, *Πρόγραμμα του Κομμουνιστικού Κόμματος Ελλάδας* (Athens: Central Committee of KKE, 1996).

16. Eleftheriou, 'Ρωγμές στον μονόλιθο'.

17. Giorgos Charalambous, *European Integration and the Communist Dilemma: Communist Party Responses to Europe in Greece, Cyprus and Italy* (Farnham: Ashgate, 2013), 59–93.

18. KKE, *Το Πρόγραμμα του ΚΚΕ* (Athens: Central Committee of KKE, 2013).

19. Eleftheriou, 'The "Uneasy Symbiosis"'.

20. Myrto Tsakatika, 'Από ένα "κριτικό ναι" σε ένα "φιλοευρωπαϊκό όχι." Τί έχει αλλάξει στον ευρωπαϊκό προσανατολισμό του Συνασπισμού;' *International and European Politics* 14 (2009): 143–61.

21. Tsakatika and Eleftheriou 'The Radical Left's Turn'.

22. Giorgos Katsambekis, 'Populism in post-democratic times. Greek politics and the limits of consensus' (paper presented at the 61st Political Studies Association Annual Conference, London, 19–21 April 2011).

23. Michalis Spourdalakis, '2007 Greek Elections: Signs of Major Political Realignment. Challenges and Hopes for the Left', *Studies in Political Economy* 82 (2008): 171–86.

24. Tsakatika, 'Από ένα "κριτικό ναι" σε ένα "φιλοευρωπαϊκό όχι."'.

25. Kevin Ovenden, *Syriza: Inside the Labyrinth* (London: Pluto Press, 2015), 52.

26. Valia Aranitou, Efthimios Papavlassopoulos and Michalis Spourdalakis, 'The Greek Political System: From Multi-level Governance to the "Stability Program"' (paper presented at the 22nd World Congress of the International Political Science Association, Madrid, 8–12 July 2012).

27. Christos Laskos and Euclid Tsakalotos, *Crucible of Resistance: Greece, the Eurozone & the World Economic Crisis* (London: Pluto Press, 2013), 91–112.

28. Costas Eleftheriou and Chrisanthos Tassis, *ΠΑΣΟΚ: Η άνοδος και η πτώση (;) ενός ηγεμονικού κόμματος* (Athens: Savvalas, 2013).

29. Lefteris Kretsos, 'Greece's Neoliberal Experiment and Working Class Resistance,' *WorkingUSA* 15 (2012): 517–27.

30. Thanassis Tsakiris and Valia Aranitou, '"Under the Weight of the Social": Reactions of the Social Representation System and Anti-systemic Challenges During the era of the Memorandum' (paper presented at the 22nd World Congress of the International Political Science Association, Madrid, 8–12 July 2012).

31. Jenny Lialiouti and Giorgos Bithymitris, 'Implications of the Greek Crisis: Nationalism, Enemy Stereotypes and the European Union', in *The European Union beyond the Crisis: Evolving Governance, Contested Policies, Disenchanted Publics*, ed. Boyka Stefanova (Lanham, Boulder, New York and London: Lexington Books, 2014), 257.

32. Lefteris Kretsos, 'Union Responses to the Rise of Precarious Youth Employment in Greece,' *Industrial Relations Journal* 42 (2011): 453–72; John Karamichas, 'Square Politics: Key Characteristics of the Indignant Mobilizations in Greece' (paper presented at the 62nd PSA Annual International Conference, Belfast, 3–5 April, 2012).

33. Tsakiris and Aranitou, 'Under the Weight of the Social'.

34. Wolfgang Rüdig and Georgios Karyotis, 'Who Protests in Greece? Mass Opposition to Austerity,' *British Journal of Political Science* 44 (2014): 487–513.

35. Demar, 'Ανακοίνωση της Δημοκρατικής Αριστεράς για την πολιτική κατάσταση, την κινητοποίηση των πολιτών και την οικονομία', 6 June 2011.

36. Ruud Koole, 'The Vulnerability of the Modern Cadre Party in the Netherlands', in *How Parties Organize: Change and Adaptation in Party Organizations in Western Democracies*, ed. Richard S. Katz and Peter Mair (London: Sage, 1994), 278–303.

37. Costas Eleftheriou, 'Η ελληνική ριζοσπαστική αριστερά και η κρίση (2010-2015): Όψεις μιας μεγάλης ανατροπής', *Synchrona Themata* 71 (2015): 130–1.
38. Eleftheriou, 'The Uneasy Symbiosis'.
39. Tsakiris and Aranitou, 'Under the Weight of the Social'.
40. Michalis Spourdalakis, 'The Miraculous Rise of the "Phenomenon SYRIZA"', *International Critical Thought* 4 (2014): 364.
41. Tsakatika and Eleftheriou, 'The Radical Left's Turn'.
42. Danae Koltsida, 'Η Κοινοβουλευτική Ομάδα του ΣΥΡΙΖΑ μετά τις διπλές εκλογές του 2012: ρήξη (και) στις σχέσεις εκπροσώπησης;' (ΜΑ thesis, University of Athens, 2013).
43. Giorgos Bithymitris, 'Union Militancy during Economic Hardship: The Strike at the Greek Steel Company "Hellenic Halyvourgia,"' *Employee Relations* 38 (2016), 373–89.
44. Eleftheriou and Tassis, *ΠΑΣΟΚ*.
45. Yannis Mavris, 'Greece's Austerity Election', *New Left Review* 76 (2012): 100.
46. Eleftheriou and Tassis, *ΠΑΣΟΚ*.
47. Yannis Mavris, 'The Greek Party System in the era of the Memorandum: Parties and Party System in Transition', *AnalyzeGreece!*, 5 January 2015, accessed 16 February http://www.analyzegreece.gr/topics/elections-250102015/item/28-the-greek-party-system-in-the-era-of-the-memorandum-parties-party-system-in-transition.
48. Antonis A. Ellinas, 'The Rise of Golden Dawn: The New Face of the Far Right in Greece,' *South European Society and Politics* 18 (2013): 556–9.
49. Synaspismós, 'Πολιτική Απόφαση 6ου (έκτακτου) Συνεδρίου του Συνασπισμού της Αριστεράς των Κινημάτων και της Οικολογίας', 2010, accessed 16 February http://www.syn.gr/6osynedrio/polapofasi.pdf.
50. See Laskos and Tsakalotos, *Crucible of Resistance*, 130–45.
51. Yannis Dragassakis, 'The Economic Program of SYRIZA-EKM', *Socialist Project E-Bulletin* 653 (2012), accessed 16 February, http://www.socialistproject.ca/bullet/653.php.
52. Ibid.
53. Alexis Tsipras, 'Ομιλία Αλέξη Τσίπρα, Προέδρου της ΚΟ του ΣΥΡΙΖΑ/ΕΚΜ κατά την παρουσίαση του προγράμματος του συνδυασμού', 1 June 2012, accessed 16 February 2016, http://www.syn.gr/gr/keimeno.php?id=27218.
54. Syriza, 'The political resolution of the 1st congress of SYRIZA', July 2013, accessed 16 February 2016, http://www.syriza.gr/article/id/53894/The-political-resolution-of-the-1st-congress-of-SYRIZA.html#.ViYRGX7hDIV.
55. Syriza, 'Η υπομονή μας τέλειωσε! 25 Μαΐου 2014: ΨΗΦΙΖΟΥΜΕ ΚΑΙ ΦΕΥΓΟΥΝ!', 2014, accessed 16 February 2016, https://left.gr/news/i-ypomoni-mas-teleiose-25-maioy-2014-psifizoyme-kai-feygoyn.
56. Syriza, 'The Thessaloniki Programme', September 2014, accessed 16 February 2016, http://www.syriza.gr/article/SYRIZA---THE-THESSALONIKI-PROGRAMME.html.

57. Eleni Mpellou, 'The International Economic Crisis and the Position of Greece. The theses of KKE,' *International Communist Review* 1 (2009), accessed 16 February 2016, http://www.iccr.gr/site/en/issue1/the-international-economic-crisis-and-theposition-of-greece-the-theses-of-kke.html.

58. Aleka Papariga, 'Speech of the General Secretary of the CC, Al. Papariga, at the nationwide demonstration of the party on 15 May' 15 May 2010, accessed 16 February 2016, http://interold.kke.gr/News/2010news/2010-06-22-omilia-aleka-15may/view.html.

59. Giorgos, Marinos, 'The character of the contemporary era as the basic element which defines the strategy of the Communist Parties and the experience of the KKE,' 23 March 2012, accessed 16 February 2016, http://interold.kke.gr/News/news2012/2012-03-28-brazil.

60. KKE, 'Political Resolution of the 19th Congress of the KKE', April 2013, accessed 16 February 2016, http://inter.kke.gr/en/articles/Political-Resolution-of-the-19th-Congress-of-the-KKE/.

Chapter 16

Riders on the Storm

United Left and Podemos during the 2008 Great Recession

Luis Ramiro[1]

RLPs have traditionally been relatively successful in Spain. It is also one of the few countries in which they have experienced significant growth during the Great Recession. The Communist Party of Spain (*Partido Comunista de España*, PCE) first, and, since 1986, United Left (*Izquierda Unida*, IU) – an organisation the PCE created and within which it has always been the most relevant actor – have been represented in parliament since the first democratic elections of 1977. However, their electoral trajectory has been characterised by electoral fluctuations and fragility. The PCE/IU's vote share in national legislative elections has oscillated between 3.7 and 10.5 per cent. However, the Great Recession opened a remarkable period of transformation for the Spanish radical Left. This change encompasses three main elements. First, initial growth was followed by a considerable crisis for the more 'established' RLP, IU. Second, the radical Left fragmented and a new RLP, Podemos (We Can) achieved dramatic and rapid growth. Finally, the aftershocks of the economic crisis positioned radical left support at a historic high with a strong showing for Podemos and a weak showing for IU in the 2015 elections.

These three developments make the Spanish radical Left's trajectory during and after the post-2008 crisis complex, as it involves opposing trends for the two main constituent parties. Podemos' growth was based on attracting voters and activists from – among others – IU. Indeed, the very existence of IU was threatened by its electoral losses and organisational weakening during the later years of crisis. In the next pages, the evolution of Podemos and IU will be examined through an analysis of the political, organisational and electoral consequences of the Great Recession. I argue that IU's travails are rooted in its classical ideological radical left traditions, which mean that it has struggled to reinvent its traditional modes of organising. In contrast, Podemos articulates a more novel left-populist message, and possesses an organisation that combines centralisation and presidentialisation with high levels of inclusiveness in decision-making. This new amalgam explains its record levels of support. Before describing these contrasting trajectories, the chapter analyses the state of the radical Left before the crisis began.

THE SPANISH RADICAL LEFT BEFORE THE GREAT RECESSION: CRISIS AND CHANGE

Compared with the Spanish Socialist Workers' Party (*Partido Socialista Obrero Español*, PSOE), the PCE was a very small organisation during the 1920s and 1930s, the two first decades after its foundation.[2] The party increased its influence on Spanish politics during the Civil War (1936–1939) and during the clandestine struggle against the Francoist dictatorship (1939–1975). During the 1970s and the democratic transition, the PCE moderated very significantly in line with the Eurocommunist project.[3] Under the leadership of Santiago Carrillo, the PCE attempted to extend its dominant role during the clandestine struggle to the new democratic circumstances, aiming to overtake the PSOE as the leading left-wing actor. However, as with Eurocommunist strategies elsewhere, there was little ultimate gain for the communist party, albeit that its restraint helped accomplish a relatively peaceful transition to democracy. The two first democratic elections in 1977 and 1979 foreshadowed the future imbalance within the Spanish Left, with the PSOE becoming the major party despite its relative organisational weakness during the dictatorship.

During the first half of the 1980s, the PCE suffered a very intense organisational and electoral crisis, the main outcome of which was the foundation of IU, a new umbrella organisation (originally an electoral coalition) in which the communists were the major internal actor.[4] This strategy involved two dimensions. The organisational dimension consisted in IU being a new type of organisation, intended to be more open, inclusive, decentralised and governed by grassroots democratic principles. The political dimension meant the adoption of a left-wing programme combining traditional socialist principles with 'new politics' policies (environmentalism, feminism and pacifism).

However, IU has encountered considerable instability.[5] In electoral terms, the party grew between 1986 and 1996. Then followed a period of decline that lasted through the three following elections (2000, 2004 and 2008). Thus, until the consequences of the 2008 crisis were clearly felt, the trajectory of IU followed an almost perfect inverted U (see Table 16.1). It took until 1996, under the leadership of Julio Anguita, for IU finally to reach support levels similar to those gained by the PCE in 1979; but IU's subsequent decline took it back to levels (3.8 per cent) slightly less than the 1982 nadir that had prompted the creation of IU in the first place. The 2000 elections, still with Anguita as the leader, were disastrous. A new leader, Gaspar Llamazares, oversaw further deterioration in 2004 and 2008. Only in the first elections (2011) following the onset of the Great Recession was there a partial electoral recovery for IU. In sum, the Spanish radical Left represented by IU has been unable to achieve electoral stability since the 1970s.

Nor has the situation been very stable from an organisational point of view. IU began as an electoral coalition but has evolved via unification of its internal components into a model in which (despite the persistence of some constituent parts) the common organisation (IU) finally works as a conventional party. The most important founding party, the PCE, still exists as a political party, even though its influence, resources and internal cohesion have greatly diminished.[6] Nevertheless, the PCE remains IU's most important and most structured internal actor, and its leaders and activists play key roles in defining IU policies and strategies. The organisational model that IU has developed resembled that of a party with well-structured factions, with the small parties within IU (mainly the PCE and the smaller *Izquierda Abierta* [Open Left]) operating as the functional equivalents of factions.

Nevertheless, IU's changing organisational model (from coalition to 'party') is not the only feature making it unstable.[7] More significant is that its evolution has been characterised by organisational conflicts that have ended in major splits. The largest and most traumatic one took place in 1997 when the moderate faction (that had founded the internal New Left Democratic Party) left after several of its members were sanctioned by the IU leadership.[8]

The split weakened IU in regions including Galicia, Comunidad Valenciana, Cantabria and Castilla-La Mancha, and it has not been an isolated event. IU also suffered significant fissures giving birth to new regional-level left-wing organisations in the Basque Country (in 2009 and 2011), Comunidad Valenciana (in 2008), Balearic Islands (2010) and Madrid (2015). The period of Anguita's leadership experienced conflictual relations with IU's former sister union *Comisiones Obreras* (Workers' Commissions, CC OO), the largest Spanish trade union; and with its former sister organisation in Catalonia, Initiative for Catalonia Greens (*Iniciativa per Catalunya Verds*, ICV). Additionally, IU's relationship with the Spanish Greens, who have run in electoral coalition with IU several times, has always been unstable.

Finally, the organisational strategy has frequently fallen short of its original goals of founding a 'new type of political organisation' or a 'social and political movement' different from traditional parties. Indeed, the party has hardly been ground-breaking regarding internal procedures. IU has traditionally been a very decentralised organisation but the efforts to foster membership involvement in designing party policies have in practice been unsuccessful, and the reforms regarding the role of individual members in candidate and leader selection have been neither very innovative nor inclusive.[9] In terms of participatory linkage, IU has not significantly altered the internal distribution of power in favour of its members.

However, in terms of programmatic and political strategy, the creation and evolution of IU entailed a thorough renewal of Spanish radical left policies and platforms. Since 1989, IU has fully embraced the turn towards the new politics and new left policies common to some other RLPs.[10] In terms of the relevance of environmental policy, minority rights, individual freedoms and, in general, post-materialist priorities, IU has combined traditional democratic socialist and left-wing principles with those of the new Left.[11]

This programmatic turn was combined with loyalty to traditional radical left principles and symbols. The PCE's decision not to disband but to continue as a political party within IU had significant effects on IU. These were most visible in its general ideological approach and foreign policies, as signalled by, for example, continuing solidarity with Castro's Cuba or with the Chávez/Maduro governments in Venezuela. From this point of view, IU mixed a considerable degree of policy renewal with socialist and Marxist ideological traditionalism. Discussions about IU's ideological direction have oscillated between avoiding explicit ideological definition (apart from an assertive left-wing orientation) and an increasingly firm socialist emphasis in more recent years. During the relatively recent electoral and organisational crisis of 2000–2008, the then-leader, Llamazares, made several attempts to adopt a sharper red-green (or eco-socialist) direction and to abandon more traditional socialist ideology. Such proposals were made amidst internal divisions and acute electoral decline, and were defeated by the majority of communist activists. Thus, IU was experiencing severe problems at the point (2008) when Spain entered the worst economic crisis it has experienced during the democratic period.

THE 2008 GREAT RECESSION: NEW OPPORTUNITIES FOR THE RADICAL LEFT

During most of the 1990s and 2000s Spain experienced remarkable economic growth and it became one of the EU's five largest economies. However, during this period the economy also suffered major imbalances, principally a trade deficit, low competitiveness, sky-rocketing house prices and, consequently, high private indebtedness. One of the most important consequences was a housing bubble of colossal proportions. The third quarter of 2008 saw the international financial crisis put an abrupt end to economic growth as Spain entered recession in 2009 and GDP fell again in 2010.[12] While this ended in 2011, the economy shrank once again in 2012 and the situation worsened dramatically as Spain experienced a collapse in the residential property market and the housing industry, and unemployment grew. Moreover, a major crisis occurred in the savings banks and in 2012 Spain felt forced to negotiate a bailout of its financial sector and to inject capital into its weakened banks. The fall in tax revenues, increased expenditure on unemployment benefits, the bailout of the financial sector, and the rise in the debt servicing costs, all resulted in disastrous consequences on public finances. The ratio of debt-to-GDP rose to almost 100 per cent by the end of 2014.

One of the most important sociopolitical consequences of the Great Recession for Spain was the rise of unemployment. Among EU countries, Spain has traditionally suffered from comparatively high unemployment rates. The economic crisis had a major impact on Spain's labour market, which consisted of a large contingent of low skilled workers and workers in temporary jobs. Finally, the level of youth unemployment rose dramatically (in 2014, 53 per cent of those younger than 25 were unemployed, according to Eurostat). Such a social and economic situation had significant political effects.

The political consequences of the Great Recession unfolded in three stages. The first started in 2008, when the first symptoms of economic downturn appeared but were not yet felt by the public. This stage ended in 2011 with the first general elections held under the Great Recession. The second stage began after the 2011 general election, with the conservative People's Party (PP) forming a new government, and ended with the 2014 European Parliament (EP) elections, which were the second elections in Spain during the Great Recession. Finally, a third (and ongoing) stage started after the EP election results shook Spanish party politics in a significant and unanticipated way with the emergence of Podemos. The following section analyses the electoral dynamics in these three periods and the consequences of the crisis for the radical Left.

Although signs of crisis were already apparent by the March 2008 general elections, the incumbent PSOE had been praised for Spain's positive economic performance over the previous years. Accordingly, the PSOE won the 2008 elections in a social and political climate that did not anticipate the coming economic problems. When the economic downturn became apparent, the PSOE government temporarily used expansionary measures before abandoning this strategy for austerity policies and budget cuts in 2010. The austerity policies even included a constitutional reform before the 2011 general elections to cap the budget deficit.

Dissatisfaction with the state of the economy and government policies soon led to social mobilisation. The PSOE government reacted by changing their candidate for the upcoming 2011 general elections. However, as predicted by retrospective economic voting models, it lost the elections and the main opposition party, the right-wing PP, gained an overall majority.[13] Nevertheless, the

Table 16.1   General Election Results: PCE/IU and Podemos

Election Year	Share of Votes	Number of MPs	Share of MPs
1977	9.3	19	5.4
1979	10.8	23	6.6
1982	4.0	4	1.1
1986	4.6	7	2.0
1989	9.1	17	4.9
1993	9.6	18	5.1
1996	10.5	21	6.0
2000	5.5	8	2.3
2004	5	5	1.4
2008	3.8	2	0.6
2011	6.9	11	3.1
2015	3.7 (IU)	2 (IU)	0.6 (IU)
	20.7 (Podemos)	69 (Podemos)	19.7 (Podemos)

Note: the figures include the votes and MPs that ICV won in Catalonia except for 2000 when the agreement between ICV and IU was broken and both parties ran separately. In 2015 IU ran as United Left-Popular Unity and one of the MPs was not an IU member; three other IU members were elected MPs within broad left-wing coalitions (which included Podemos, ICV, other organizations and independent activists) in Galicia and Catalonia, and they were part of the Podemos parliamentary group. Podemos' results include also those of the coalitions within which it ran in Catalonia, Galicia and Comunidad Valenciana, although many of their MPs did not belong to Podemos and four of them (from the Valencian nationalist party *Compromís*) decided not to be part of Podemos' parliamentary group after the elections.
Source: www.parties-and-elections.eu.

2011 elections also resulted in electoral gains for some smaller parties such as IU, which was headed by a new party leader (Cayo Lara) and it abruptly reversed its almost decade-long period of electoral decline (Table 16.1).

The second period started when the PP, right after taking office in 2011, implemented austerity policies just as the outgoing PSOE government had done. As a result, public support for the PP and Prime Minister Mariano Rajoy plummeted. Yet, *both* the government and the mainstream opposition were subject to high levels of public dissatisfaction. While the PSOE was tarnished by its recent government experience and policy U-turns, the PP's promises of a quick fix to the economic problems were unfulfilled. This environment of broken promises and expectations by the two large mainstream parties created a crisis of trust in political parties and politicians to the point that they were perceived, alongside economic troubles, as one of the most important problems facing the country. The discovery of corruption scandals affecting the highest levels of the PP added to the sense of a political crisis, and contributed to rising levels of political mobilisation and protest (Figure 16.1).

Consequently, between 2011 and 2014 public opinion polls showed weakening electoral support for the PP and PSOE and the strengthening of some minor parties, in particular IU – in a context strongly reminiscent of that analysed by Kriesi.[14] This was the context for the second elections within the recessionary electoral cycle, the May 2014 EP elections. The very nature

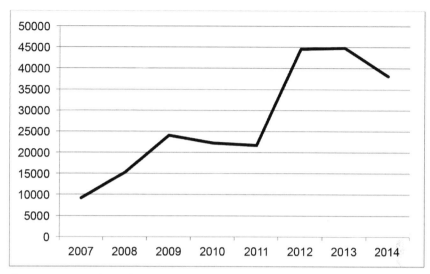

Figure 16.1 Number of Demonstrations, 2007–2014. *Source*: Spanish Ministry of Internal Affairs.

of EP elections as 'second-order' ones favoured votes for opposition, minor, radical and protest parties and IU was expected to expand. However, just five months before the elections, a political development initially deemed only relevant among radical left milieux took place: in January 2014 a new RLP, Podemos, formed.[15]

Podemos was designed and developed by a relatively small group of experienced activists around its young leader, Pablo Iglesias. Some of them had been advisers and consultants to the IU leadership or had worked for IU in electoral campaigns (including Pablo Iglesias); others had links to a small RLP of Trotskyist origins, Anti-Capitalist Left (which had been part of IU), and others still were linked to progressive social movements. The party originally grew through the personal and political networks of its founders (many of them academics) and it took advantage of the wave of mobilisation that began in May 2011 with sit-in protests in dozens of Spanish cities (the '15M' or *Indignados* movement). Indeed, many Podemos local branches were populated by activists from these protests. Podemos' founders anticipated that the economic, social and political crises, and the discredited two-party (PP and PSOE) dominance, opened a window of opportunity for the emergence of a new political force.

Podemos' original goal was extremely ambitious; the party aimed not at being just another opposition party, but to win government in the next general elections. As anticipated, the deep economic crisis, high unemployment levels, dissatisfaction with the two mainstream parties, and the comparatively high level of social mobilisation acted as ideal 'socio-economic facilitators' for the creation of Podemos.[16] Additionally, Podemos' founders were fully-aware that the forthcoming EP elections, as second-order elections with a highly proportional electoral system, were ideal for maximising electoral support for a new party. As such, the EP elections were a very promising 'institutional facilitator' for the Podemos operation.[17]

Finally, the founders of Podemos perceived important deficiencies in IU that, in their interpretation, made the traditional radical Left unsuited to taking political and electoral advantage of the crisis. The formation of Podemos supports arguments that the behaviour of competing parties can act as a 'political facilitator' in the creation of new parties.[18] IU's behaviour in the months prior to the launching of Podemos directly contributed to the desire by the Podemos founders to act as 'political entrepreneurs' by creating a new party. The founders thought that IU's leaders had demonstrated a lack of innovation and a conservatism that left them unable to understand the 'systemic' crisis that Spain was experiencing. According to this interpretation, IU's leaders had shown an inability and unwillingness to build an open and broad coalition of social and political actors that would allow it to benefit from opportunities presented by the EP elections. It was the failure to build such a new umbrella organisation, in which non-party activists such as themselves might feel comfortable, that convinced future Podemos leaders that IU was an inappropriate political tool.[19] Whether or not this is an accurate assessment of IU's politics, it contributed to the decision to form a new political party.

Certainly, not only did IU not promote such a new umbrella organisation during 2013 but it also failed to react in any noticeable way to the new challenger party between January (when Podemos was launched) and May 2014 (when the EP elections took place). Moreover, IU first refused to accept the conditions outlined by Iglesias in January 2014 to reach an electoral agreement that could have perhaps averted competition between Podemos and IU (a common electoral list elaborated through open primaries). Secondly, IU selected their candidates in a conventional way without trying to counterbalance the presence of the new challenger. In both cases it could be argued that IU underestimated the electoral threat posed by Podemos.

Ultimately, the results of the 2014 EP elections confirmed some of the expectations of the second-order thesis.[20] The results for the two largest mainstream parties were the worst on record and minor opposition parties of various types obtained resounding electoral successes. IU gained 10 per cent of the vote and progressed from its poor results in the previous EP elections of 2009, sustaining its increase in support in the 2011 general elections. However, the most important result was the 8 per cent of the votes and five MEPs gained by Podemos. The result was not only a success given the recent formation of the party, but also a surprise because the party's rise had been unexpected as the polls had forecast a vote share of between one and 3 per cent. In contrast, the outcome for IU – positive as it was – fell short of predictions.

Consequently, the 2014 EP elections were an electoral earthquake that dramatically changed the dynamics of Spanish politics and signalled the beginning of the third political period of the Great Recession. Soon after the elections, polls showed a sharp rise in support for Podemos. Polls conducted between the summer of 2014 and January 2015 placed the new party level-pegging with PSOE and PP, and even sometimes in the lead. Thus, the 2014 EP elections meant not only a change in party preferences but also heralded an increase in electoral volatility and a complete party system transformation. The polls suggested that IU was among the losers from these changes and that it was losing between 40 and 50 per cent of its 2011 general election electorate as these voters now declared their intention to support Podemos.

These forecasts were confirmed by the results of the 2015 local and regional elections. Positive results in the local elections hardly compensated for IU's disastrous regional results. The party fell out of regional parliaments in some of its former strongholds (e.g. Madrid and Comunidad Valenciana). While Podemos had decided not to run in local elections to protect its brand from the dangers of accelerated party formation and uncontrolled growth of local branches, the general outcome was positive for it. Integrated in broad alliances (sometimes including IU and often led by non-partisan candidates), the party became part of the local government of some of the most important Spanish cities. The regional elections were also a relative success for Podemos. Despite being unable to overtake the PSOE, it gained representation in almost all regional parliaments and, supporting the PSOE, it played a decisive role in the ousting of the PP from many regional governments.

The rapid rise of Podemos and the decline in support for IU also had internal consequences for the latter; the party felt forced to design a new strategy and many IU activists (and even leaders) lost confidence in the party. On the opposite side, Podemos was relatively successful even if the regional elections results started to signal that its strategy of entering national government might be more difficult than anticipated. Indeed, polls at the beginning of 2015 showed that the party had lost momentum (Figure 16.2).

The December 2015 general elections confirmed this pattern. For several months during 2015 Podemos and IU had informally discussed an electoral alliance. With Podemos enjoying excellent prospects, it had less of an incentive than IU to establish an alliance. Podemos' leader Pablo Iglesias repeatedly rejected an agreement with what he considered a too ideologically traditional IU. The latter's prime-ministerial candidate, Alberto Garzón, who de facto headed the organisation in an attempt to reverse its electoral decline, insisted that political change was unthinkable without an agreement between the parties. In fact, Garzón's IU believed so intensely in the need for an agreement that when Podemos finally rejected the possibility in October 2015, IU needed to redesign its entire strategy just three months before the general elections. In this extremely difficult situation, IU also had to improvise

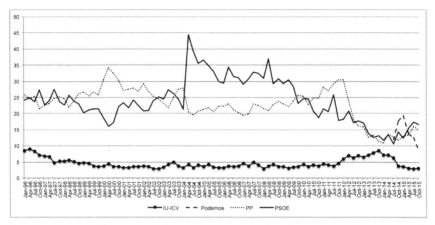

Figure 16.2 Intention to Vote for PP, PSOE, IU and Podemos, January 1996 to July 2015. *Source*: Center for Sociological Research (Centro de Investigaciones Sociológicas).

candidate selection via open primaries that included independent candidates, and formed a new electoral umbrella, 'Popular Unity' (*Unidad Popular*).

Podemos preferred to form coalitions with other left-wing parties in Catalonia, Comunidad Valenciana and Galicia, where such parties were particularly strong.[21] The small green party *Equo* accepted being part of Podemos lists, and in Galicia and Catalonia IU's regional federations were part of Podemos' left-wing coalitions, introducing a significant lack of internal coherence to IU's overall electoral strategy. The electoral results, although anticipated, were a disaster for IU as IU-Popular Unity only gained 2 MPs (both in the district of Madrid) and 3.7 of the national vote. Conversely, the elections proved an outstanding success for Podemos and its broad regional coalitions. Despite falling short of its initially unrealistic goal of overtaking the PSOE in its first general elections and winning office, Podemos gained 21 per cent of the vote, just one point below the PSOE. While this result placed Podemos in a position never enjoyed by the Spanish radical Left before, IU had to confront an electoral and organisational situation that again threatened its very existence.

POST-CRISIS PROGRAMMATIC AND ORGANISATIONAL TRANSFORMATION

Political Impacts

The Great Recession altered not only the electoral make-up of the Spanish radical Left but also its internal organisation. The start of the crisis found IU renewing its leadership amidst a significant change to its dominant faction.

As already indicated, the 2000–2008 period was extraordinarily challenging for IU for several reasons. First, the new leader, Llamazares, could not stop the party's electoral decline when confronted with a PSOE that had been revitalised through its role in opposition in 1996–2004. Second, from 2004 to 2008, IU had faced a relatively popular and reformist PSOE minority government, and regularly provided parliamentary support to it. Llamazares faced the difficult balance of opposing the PSOE while trying to influence the minority government. The 2008 general elections results proved disastrous; by winning a single MP (Llamazares himself) IU seemed close to collapse. Llamazares resigned and a party congress elected a successor amidst major internal fragmentation.

The new IU leadership signalled a break with the previous one in terms of personnel and strategy. At the 2008 party congress a list of activists close to Llamazares lost to a list headed by Cayo Lara. While it was previously common for PCE members to support different factions within IU, and the 2008 IU congress was no exception, the PCE leadership strongly supported Lara's winning list. In fact, the PCE had been the main opposition to Llamazares for most of the time he had been leading IU. While Llamazares had suggested the need for IU to engage in a process of ideological renewal, the PCE had opposed this project and defended the need to stress IU's ultimate class and socialist nature.[22] The PCE and allies within IU had strongly criticised the 'conditional support' that IU under Llamazares' leadership had lent to the 2004–2008 PSOE government. In this regard, the new IU leadership in 2008 was controlled by a new dominant faction (or coalition of factions) in which the PCE leadership had a prominent role. In strategic terms, the new IU leadership defended IU adopting a purely oppositional role vis-a-vis the PSOE government.

In this sense, the Great Recession did not immediately induce a change in the IU, but its leadership was already in a state of flux. After 2008, the new IU leadership took a more adversarial tone towards the PSOE and this was cemented by the policies implemented by the PSOE as the crisis unfolded and austerity policies were introduced from 2010. The recession and austerity measures only intensified the ongoing changes in IU's strategy, which were a product of its electoral crisis and the change in the party's dominant coalition.

How did the radical Left interpret the Great Recession? For IU, the economic crisis in Spain and wider crisis in the Eurozone were seen as a confirmation of previous analyses. The Great Recession triggered little discernible rethinking of party policy. On the one hand, IU argued that the economic crisis was a crisis of the capitalist system caused by its neoliberal drift.[23] On the other hand, regarding its European dimension, the crisis was understood as a corroboration of IU's opposition to the Maastricht Treaty. IU thought that the European Union had long been dominated by neoliberal ideas. However, it viewed this treaty as having intensified the neoliberal project through the

Euro, EU economic and budgetary policies, and the roles assigned to the different EU institutions. To IU the 2008 crisis both showed this project to be fully flawed and confirmed the legitimacy of its fight against neoliberalism and its soft Euroscepticism.[24]

Furthermore, IU argued that the development of the crisis and the austerity policies promoted by the European Union and other international institutions would create a 'market dictatorship'. IU criticised not only the neoliberal and austerity policies, but also the way in which they were 'imposed' by undemocratic institutions upon national governments and the people of Europe.[25] In this regard, IU interpreted the crisis as a loss of popular and national sovereignty, democratic rights and freedoms. According to IU, Europe and particularly the South European countries experiencing bailouts and austerity programmes were experiencing a 'silent coup d'Etat' by anti-democratic institutions (the Troika: the IMF, the ECB, the EC).

Such views entailed no substantive modification of IU's soft Eurosceptic policy, merely changes to the content of its policies. What IU called for was essentially what it had traditionally defended: a 're-foundation' of the European Union. IU did not reject the EU project, it did not propose leaving the Euro, and the party still supported the need for 'more EU'. The party nuanced its EU policy discourse to emphasise the need to preserve national sovereignty alongside increased integration.[26] Further amendments were a strengthened assertion of the socialist character of IU's 'project'. Previously, IU's diverse internal components avoided any explicit ideological self-definition, although IU has always considered itself as located within a broad conception of democratic socialism. Nevertheless, the emphasis on its socialist nature has been more frequent since 2008 and in particular since 2012. The same might be argued about its anti-capitalist appeals.

This interpretation of the international and EU nature of the crisis, and rejection of the policies implemented in response to them, resonates with IU's view of the crisis within Spain. In IU's analysis, Spain is experiencing a 'regime crisis'. Spanish capitalism is thought to be experiencing an 'organic crisis' that affects the type of economic development imposed since the 1980s and a crisis of the political and party system generated since the democratic transition of the 1970s. All the core political institutions, rules and procedures that emerged from the democratic transition, such as the monarchy, the constitution and the mainstream parties, were demonstrated to be unsuitable by the 2008 crisis.

The tone of IU's interpretation of the Spanish crisis was pessimistic. The austerity policies promoted by both the PSOE and PP, the constitutional reform promoted by the two large mainstream parties in 2011, and the policy constraints imposed by the Troika, led to a breakdown of Spanish democracy, and a permanent subversion of social, economic and political rights.[27] The PP and PSOE were considered to be the defenders of a broken social, economic and political system.[28] In this way, after 2008 IU strengthened its long-standing argument that there were no differences between the conservative PP and social democratic PSOE.

However, while IU's national cadres made critical statements of the PSOE, its Andalusian regional federation approved forming a regional government coalition with the PSOE in 2012 (a decision approved by IU's Andalusian members in a referendum).[29] Similarly, after the 2015 local elections, IU agreed a large number of local coalition governments with the PSOE. Therefore, despite the rhetoric, and traditional tensions and competition with the PSOE, IU's practice remained more nuanced.

Did Podemos develop a significantly different interpretation of the crisis? One of the most interesting features of the fragmented radical Left in Spain is that Podemos has not introduced many new proposals that differ from those already sought by IU. The parties share broadly similar interpretations of the crisis and policies to solve it.[30] Both parties see the international economic crisis to have resulted from the hegemony of neoliberal economic policies. The parties' policies also belong to the same radical left and democratic socialist traditions and their policies towards the European Union are quite similar. Although Podemos decided not to enter the Party of the European Left (PEL), identifying it with the same ideological traditionalism that they criticised in IU, it belongs – as IU does – to the GUE/NGL parliamentary group in the EP. Podemos' leader was the GUE/NGL candidate for the presidency of the EP, and it has warm relations with PEL parties such as Syriza and Bloco de Esquerda. Like IU, Podemos does not defend an exit from the European Union nor from the Eurozone, while criticising the direction of EU policies. Thus, overall there is no clear differentiation between the two on programmatic grounds. Indicatively, it was only after an electoral agreement between IU and Podemos was finally rejected by the latter that IU expressed its most explicit criticism towards Podemos' populist strategy.

Some clear commonalities can also be identified between the parties regarding the nature of the crisis within Spain. Both interpret it as a 'regime crisis' that affects all the political institutions and actors on which the current democratic period has been founded. Podemos has emphasised how the 1970s transition to democracy sowed the seeds of contemporary problems. IU takes a similar approach and even criticises the PCE's role during the transition. Both parties also agree on the need for a new constitution.[31]

What differentiates Podemos from IU in terms of its programmatic positions is that while the policies of Podemos are categorically to the left of the PSOE (and similar to the ones defended by the radical Left), it has deliberately avoided declaring itself as left-wing. The spokespeople of Podemos have repeatedly argued that they consider the left-right divide an obsolete political dimension.[32] From their point of view, what the current Spanish crisis reflects is a clear opposition between the interests of 'the people' and those of 'the caste', the elite or the oligarchy.

In this way Podemos' discourse strongly corresponds to some of the key pillars of populism.[33] This conflict between a benign people and a corrupt elite is almost the only relevant divide, thus leading the party to avoid reference to other social actors or political categories linked to traditional socialist or left-wing discourse. The divide certainly connected with citizens' mistrust towards parties and politicians in the context of the crisis and recurrent corruption scandals. Some of Podemos' founders, who have an academic professional background, have made frequent use of Ernesto Laclau's arguments, and explicitly recognised that the party uses populist appeals.[34] Additionally, while sharing IU's recent emphasis on regaining popular sovereignty, Podemos' discourse has used some (civic) nationalist tones that are not common in IU.[35]

The second specificity of the new party is found in its strategy, which has prioritised vote-maximisation. Podemos has focused on valence issues and whenever possible avoided issues requiring a clear stance that could alienate moderate or non-ideological voters. This firm catch-all strategy, which avoids any link with socialism or traditional ideologies and evades the left-right divide, made Podemos an exceptional RLP. However, this initial strategy became increasingly unsuitable in Podemos' later stages of development. Podemos started to participate in the daily business of the EP and after the May 2015 regional elections it supported PSOE regional governments. It has also participated in local governments in important cities within broad progressive coalitions (as in Madrid, Barcelona, or Zaragoza), and ran the September 2015 Catalan regional elections in coalition with the IU's Catalan regional federation and the Initiative for Catalonia Greens. In these processes, Podemos could not avoid demonstrating a more conventional left-wing orientation. Unsurprisingly, the public (including Podemos supporters) consistently places Podemos as an RLP in the polls, and the party has been unable to accomplish its initial goals of breaking ideological barriers and attracting moderate voters, despite being very successful in appealing to former PSOE voters.[36] Consequently, some strategic alteration to its image during its first months of existence has been apparent, and the party moved in a clearer left-wing direction after the December 2015 general elections.

Organisational Impacts

The Great Recession initiated significant organisational changes in the Spanish radical Left. The development of Podemos entails a major departure from traditional models of party organisation. Podemos aimed to avoid conventional party structures and to build a new type of horizontal, participatory and inclusive organisation. While this ambitious goal has been attempted on many occasions, the experience of Podemos stands out. Party membership grew exponentially in the months after its May 2014 EP election success, reaching figures of around 250,000 members and hundreds of local branches were formed. These membership figures are comparable to those of the PSOE and PP and much higher than the modest 50,000 members customarily declared by IU. The members of Podemos have plenty of online participation opportunities, and important party decision-making processes (candidate and leader selection, electoral platform elaboration) are decided through online 'one member, one vote' procedures.

However, the practical implementation of these procedures falls short of original expectations and Podemos' own self-image.[37] The goal of building a grassroots democratic party has clashed with the presence of a strong and very presidentialised central leadership.[38] Many party activists critical of Podemos' leaders have warned of declining activity in its local branches. The party's internal electoral rules unquestionably favour central and majority faction control. Moreover, levels of participation in Podemos' internal electoral processes declined dramatically in its two first years of existence.[39] As might be expected, Podemos' leaders benefit internally from their key role in the party's foundation (most party founders held party leadership positions), their undeniable success and their presence in the media; but on top of that they have promoted a set of internal rules that guarantees them a considerable degree of central control and produces a power distribution unfavourable to individual members.

Podemos' organisational innovations have arguably been disseminated to other Spanish parties and in particular IU. The leadership of IU was aware of the membership participation deficit in their party and it never fully embraced using 'one member, one vote' primaries for candidate or leader selection.[40] However, things started to change soon after the decline of IU's electoral support in summer 2014, when many IU leaders and regional organisations implemented primaries to select IU's candidates, and the IU-Popular Unity candidates for the December 2015 general elections were selected through open primaries. In the field of candidate selection, at least, IU introduced a more inclusive set of practices during this period.

The consequences of the Great Recession for the relationship between Spanish RLPs and social movements are less clear. The post-2011 wave of mobilisation reintroduced debates around party-movement linkages, the building of sociopolitical movements, the respective role of parties and movements in the task of political transformation, and the problem of cultural hegemony. These are long-standing classic topics of discussion within RLPs, however, neither IU nor Podemos have proposed particularly original contributions to this century-long debate.

This wave of mobilisation had several components: new loosely structured movements such as the 15M, new single-issue groups (e.g. movements campaigning against house repossessions and in defence of public provision of education and healthcare), and trade unions. IU embraced a self-critical evaluation of its approach to the newest of these social movements. Defining the 15M *Indignados* movement as the most relevant since the 1970s, IU criticised itself for having been unable to answer the demands of the movement.[41] Regarding other movements, IU showed its traditional support to unions, often asking them to escalate the conflict, and sometimes criticising moderate union strategies. Overall, IU's approach to social movements consisted in willingness to contribute to the creation of a social and political bloc, able to create 'hegemony' in Gramscian terms. It would participate in the social movements, express their demands, represent them, while seeking to avoid controlling them. How this should be practically implemented, beyond IU members' participation in those movements, remains unclear.

Podemos shares the aim of avoiding to be seen to control, direct or even represent, social movements. It has enjoyed a somewhat less problematic relationship with the newest ones – whereas its relationship with the unions has been less salient. Links between Podemos and the newest social movements are obviously of an informal nature and are fostered by those Podemos activists who formerly participated in the 15M and other new anti-austerity protests. Some Podemos activists came directly from these mobilisations to the task of party formation without previous political experience. The network of former 15M activists was beneficial to the territorial expansion of Podemos, although the impulse towards party creation was more a top-down design by some (mostly Madrid-based) activists than any bottom-up initiative by social movement networks. Therefore, contrary to a common view among commentators abroad, Podemos was not created as the political branch of the movements nor is it the result of the social movements' political maturation. In any case, as with IU, the main connection between Podemos and the social movements is in terms of significant overlap of their policy goals.

CONCLUSION

The Great Recession has shaken the Spanish party system at every level; it modified voters' party preferences, and gave birth to new parties. In particular, the experience of what was one the deepest economic crises in Spanish contemporary history has transformed the Spanish radical Left. There has, however, been continuity in terms of the radical Left's ongoing instability. During the first years of the Great Recession and until the end of 2013, IU grew to a point close to its historical maximum support. Then, after the May

2014 EP elections, the party experienced a drastic decline as a substantial part of its former voters were attracted by the new RLP Podemos. While IU declined to minimum levels of support, Podemos was able to grow to the point of rivalling the larger mainstream parties, PSOE and PP.

The arrival of Podemos represented a significant upheaval for the Spanish radical Left. While the policies of Podemos and IU are hard to differentiate, the new challenger's strategy, organisation and ideological stances are in stark contrast not only to those of IU but also to the West European radical Left in general. Podemos is, possibly, the closest example of the ideal-typical radical left 'social populist' party that has existed to date.[42] Besides this, Podemos has gone further than any other party in the West European radical left family in its attempt to avoid the traditional left-right divide through a catch-all and vote-maximising strategy (including the highly successful Syriza). Compared with Syriza, Podemos shows some distinct features. Despite some similar political stances, Podemos is a completely new and different actor in organisational terms, and its assertive populism stands out when compared to the much weaker radical left-populist themes used by parties such as the Dutch SP or the German Die Linke.[43]

Spain offers a case in which there has been competition between a new radical left-populist party and a traditional RLP during the Great Recession. Podemos' aversion to forming a nationwide agreement with a too ideologically-anchored IU and its sudden success contributed to reinforcing IU's electoral decline and organisational weakening, and triggering a soul-searching exercise within IU's leadership. All this suggests a future of far-reaching changes within the Spanish radical Left, as it confronts (for the first time) internal competition for voters, activists and resources. Overall, the Great Recession has both benefited and transformed the Spanish radical Left, to the extent that it will never be the same.

NOTES

1. This work has been supported by the Spanish Ministry of Economy and Competitiveness [grant number CSO2012-38665].

2. Rafael Cruz, *El Partido Comunista de España en la Segunda República* (Madrid: Alianza, 1987).

3. Juan Antonio Andrade, *El PCE y el PSOE en (la) transición* (Madrid: Siglo XXI, 2015).

4. Luis Ramiro, *Cambio y adaptación en la izquierda. La evolución del Partido Comunista de España y de Izquierda Unida* (Madrid: Centro de Investigaciones Sociológicas, 2004).

5. Ramiro, *Cambio y adaptación en la izquierda*.

6. Ibid.

7. Luis Ramiro, 'Entre coalicion y partido: la evolución del modelo organizativo de Izquierda Unida,' *Revista Española de Ciencia Política* 1 (2000): 237.

8. Juán Luis Paniagua and Luis Ramiro, *Voz, Conflicto y Salida. Un Estudio sobre Faccionalismo: Nueva Izquierda, 1992-2001* (Madrid: Editorial Complutense, 2003).

9. Luis Ramiro and Tania Verge, 'Impulse and Decadence of Linkage Processes: Evidence from the Spanish Radical Left,' *South European Society and Politics* 18 (2013): 41.

10. Luke March, *Radical Left Parties in Contemporary Europe* (Abingdon: Routledge, 2011).

11. Raúl Gómez, Laura Morales and Luis Ramiro, 'Varieties of Radicalism: Examining the Diversity of Radical Left Parties and Voters in Western Europe,' *West European Politics* 39 (2016): 351.

12. Eloísa Ortega and Juan Peñalosa, *The Spanish economic crisis: key factors and growth challenges in the Euro area* (Madrid: Banco de España, 2012).

13. Mariano Torcal, 'The Incumbent Electoral Defeat in the 2011 Spanish National Elections: The Effect of the Economic Crisis in an Ideological Polarized Party System', *Journal of Elections, Public Opinion and Parties* 24 (2014): 203–21.

14. Hanspeter Kriesi, 'The Political Consequences of the Economic Crisis in Europe: Electoral Punishment and Popular Protest,' in *Mass Politics in Tough Times*, ed. Nancy Bermeo and Larry M. Bartels (Oxford: Oxford University Press, 2014), 297.

15. Jacobo Rivero, *Podemos. Objetivo: Asaltar los cielos* (Barcelona: Planeta, 2015); Igncio Torreblanca, *Asaltar los cielos. Podemos o la política después de la crisis* (Madrid: Debate, 2015).

16. Charles Hauss and David Rayside, 'The Development of New Parties in Western Democracies Since 1945,' in *Political Parties: Development and Decay*, ed. Louis Maisel and Joseph Cooper (Beverly Hills: Sage, 1978), 31. Airo Hino, *New Challenger Parties in Western Europe* (London: Routledge, 2012).

17. Hauss and Rayside, 'The development of new parties'; Hino, *New Challenger Parties*.

18. Simon Hug, 'The Emergence of New Political Parties from a Game Theoretic Perspective,' *European Journal of Political Research* 29 (1996): 169. Simon Hug, *Altering Party Systems: Strategic Behavior and The Emergence of New Political Parties in Western Democracies* (Ann Arbor: University of Michigan Press, 2001).

19. 'Conversaciones Ctxt and Juan Carlos Monedero', *Ctxt*, September, 2015, accessed 20 December 2015, http://ctxt.es/es/20150916/Politica/2249/#.VfnJIjN-Bkj4.facebook.

20. Karlheinz Reif and Hermann Schmitt, 'Nine Second Order National Elections: A Conceptual Framework for the Analysis of European Election Results,' *European Journal of Political Research* 8 (1980): 3.

21. The Initiative for Catalonia Greens (ICV), and the group around the independent mayor of Barcelona; the left-wing Valencian nationalists of *Compromís*; and the left-wing Galician nationalists of Left Galician Alternative.

22. Luis Ramiro, 'Electoral Competition, Organizational Constraints and Party Change: The Communist Party of Spain (PCE) and United Left (IU), 1986–2000,' *Journal of Communist Studies and Transition Politics* 20 (2004): 1.

23. IU, *X Asamblea Federal* (Madrid, 2012).

24. Margarita Gómez-Reino, Iván Llamazares and Luis Ramiro, 'Euroscepticism and Political Parties in Spain', in *Opposing Europe? The Comparative Party Politics of Euroscepticism*, Volume 1, ed. Paul Taggart and Aleks Szczerbiak (Oxford: Oxford University Press, 2008).

25. IU, *X Asamblea*.

26. Ibid.

27. Ibid.

28. Ibid.

29. Interestingly, IU remained in the Andalusian government until it was expelled from it by the PSOE regional prime minister. Despite growing dissatisfaction with the coalition government among IU rank-and-file and leaders, IU remained loyal to the coalition government agreement and it was the PSOE prime minister who broke it up, expelling IU regional ministers and calling snap elections for January 2015.

30. Pablo Iglesias, 'Understanding *Podemos,*' *New Left Review* 93 (2015): 7.

31. For Podemos see Sol Gallego-Díaz and Jacobo Rivero, 'La campaña de infamias y acoso va a ir a más,' *Ctxt*, January 2015, accessed 20 December 2015, http://ctxt.es/es/20150115/politica/92/La-campaña-de-infamias-y-acoso-va-a-ir-a-más-España-Rebelión-en-la-periferia-sur.htm.

32. Gallego-Díaz and Rivero, 'La campaña'.

33. Cas Mudde, *Populist Radical Right Parties in Europe* (Cambridge: Cambridge University Press, 2007). Luis Ramiro and Raúl Gómez, 'Radical Left Populism during the Great Recession: Podemos and its Competition with the Established Radical Left', *Political Studies* (June 22, 2016). doi: 10.1177/0032321716647400.

34. Íñigo Errejón, 'Spains's *Podemos*: An inside view of a radical left sensation', *Links* (2014), accessed 20 December 2015, http://links.org.au/node/3969.

35. Podemos defends a version of Spanish civic nationalism, very often stressing that the nation is the people (*la patria es el pueblo*), and avoiding traditional Spanish nationalism that usually rejects the ethno-national diversity of Spain.

36. Ramiro and Gómez, 'Radical Left Populism during the Great Recession'; José Fernández-Albertos, *Los votantes de Podemos* (Madrid: Catarata, 2015).

37. Thomas Poguntke, *Alternative Politics: The German Green Party* (Edinburgh: Edinburgh University Press, 1994).

38. Beatriz Gimeno and Carmen San José, 'Aún estamos a tiempo', eldiario.es, 9 July 2015, accessed 20 December 2015, http://www.eldiario.es/zonacritica/tiempo_6_407419278.html.

39. Álvaro Carvajal, 'La participación toca fondo en las polemicas primarias de *Podemos,*' *El Mundo*, 23 July 2015, accessed 20 December 2015, http://www.elmundo.es/espana/2015/07/23/55affbf1e2704e98178b458d.html.

40. Ramiro and Verge, 'Impulse and Decadence of Linkage Processes'.

41. IU, *X Asamblea*. Vera Gutiérrez, 'Qué le ha pasado a Izquierda Unida,' *El País*, 12 June 2015, accessed 20 December 2015, http://politica.elpais.com/politica/2015/06/12/actualidad/1434135099_152388.html.

42. March, *Radical Left Parties*.

43. Teun Pauwels, *Populism in Western Europe* (Abingdon: Routledge, 2014).

PART III

TOWARDS AN INTERNATIONAL RESPONSE?

Chapter 17

To EU or Not To EU?

The Transnational Radical Left and the Crisis

Michael Holmes and Simon Lightfoot[1]

European integration poses an unusual challenge for transnational parties of the radical Left. The current neoliberal nature of the European Union has hindered the development of international cooperation among RLPs. In the broadest sense, a transnational party is one that operates in more than one country, but in a specifically European context, it refers to federations established by national parties in order to facilitate their collaboration in the European Union. Two distinct types can be identified: groups working together in the European Parliament (EP), and wider federations – sometimes referred to as Euro-parties – which seek to coordinate in the broader setting beyond the EP.[2] For some, this indicates a gradual Europeanisation of parties – there is an assumption that organisational cooperation is a prelude to closer policy cooperation and, inevitably, greater acceptance of the European Union as a political arena in which to compete.[3]

However, the picture has never been quite so straightforward for the 'mosaic' radical Left, and the situation has become even more occluded with the Eurozone crisis.[4] This chapter will evaluate whether RLPs have moved beyond just minimum engagement, and will identify the main pressures for – and against – deepening collaboration. While the crisis might seem to have offered an opportunity for closer cooperation and more coherent radical left programmes at the European level, instead the agreements remain largely at the rhetorical level.

This chapter will begin with a brief overview of the development and evolution of the two main European transnational groups of the radical Left, the Group of the European United Left/Nordic Green Left (GUE/NGL) and the Party of the European Left (PEL). It illustrates how the two groups are interlinked. The chapter then examines how they have responded to the Eurozone crisis. It outlines the programmatic approaches they have sought to adopt, both in terms of criticisms of policies being implemented and the advocacy of alternatives. It then evaluates the strategic responses that have emerged, paying particular attention to how the transnational groups of the radical Left have sought to build a united position among their own member parties and to the extent to which they have engaged with actors outside their own groups.

A number of key issues emerge from our analysis. First of all, it illustrates an ongoing problem of the transnational radical Left: the lack of unity both within and between the groups. Secondly, it highlights the problem of reconciling the contradictory impulses of a generally Eurosceptic outlook with the realities of working at EU level. Finally, it raises the thorny old problem of purity of opposition versus the messy compromises of being in (or even just seeking) actual political power. We argue that there was a divided response among the radical Left that illustrates the tension within the movement around European integration. Those parties who reject the European Union outright adopted different positions on austerity to those parties who support European cooperation but not in the current form of the European Union.[5] In many cases, the divisions *between* RLPs are as big as the divisions between the radical Left and other political families.[6] In general, our analysis concludes that rather than provide an opportunity for RLPs to present a coherent and united response, the Eurozone crisis has actually exacerbated tensions and difficulties for them at the EU level, contributing to the radical Left not fulfilling its potential for growth, despite a good result in the 2014 EP elections and in some national contexts since the crisis.

THE GUE/NGL AND PEL

Transnational parties in the European Union have developed along two lines. There are usually separate organisations representing the parliamentary and extra-parliamentary components, with greater or lesser degrees of cooperation between them depending on the party family involved. The parliamentary group is made up of Members of the European Parliament (MEPs) and deals with the day-to-day business of the Parliament.[7] It is regulated by EP rules.[8] Euro-parties are made up of associated member parties, which might not have any MEPs (or even national MPs) and which might not even be from member states of the European Union. Euro-parties have evolved more slowly than EP groups, but most European party families now belong to some such grouping.[9] Generally, EP groups have tended to be accorded the primary position because of their parliamentary role – they have real political work to do and real political roles to fill. However, Euro-parties have the potential to be more significant in terms of trying to manufacture a broader consensus, particularly in terms of developing common positions and manifestos for European elections.

The radical Left features one of the more pronounced disparities between an EP group and its Euro-party, and it is worth setting out their rather convoluted histories. On the parliamentary side, the Communist and Allies Group in the EP was founded in 1973. However, the split between the French and Italian communist parties (PCF and PCI) meant that there were 'glaring and increasing policy divergences between the Group components',[10] to the extent that the Communist and Allies Group 'never operated as a Group, met infrequently, and [was] fragmented into national delegations'.[11] These divisions also found their way into the EP chamber, with the Group 'seldom agreeing on a common line in committee or plenary meetings'.[12] This was largely due to the increasingly pro-European tone emanating from the Italian PCI set against the persistent anti-EU stance of the French PCF.

The Group limped on until the 1989 EP elections, when it split into two: a more reformist GUE and a more hard-line Left Unity. The GUE group disappeared in 1993, when its large contingent of Italian communists left to join the Party of European Socialists. Following the 1994 election, however, the remnants of GUE and Left Unity were able to put aside their differences to form a single Confederation of the European United Left.[13] In 1995, this group was joined by various Nordic green-left parties, including the Swedish Left Party and the Finnish Left Alliance, to form the present-day GUE/NGL conglomeration (see Table 17.1).

The GUE/NGL has struggled to operate as a unitary group, with the result that the Group has found it hard to formulate a coherent political line or strategy.[14] This trend was exacerbated after the 2004 enlargement with the absorption of new parties in the group from Central and Eastern Europe (CEE).[15] There are always issues connected with integrating new parties after enlargement and the CEE enlargement threw up some specific challenges for the radical Left. The new members included some very unreformed parties, such as the Czech KSČM[16]; the lack of appetite for radical left politics among the CEE electorates led to a sharp fall in the size of the Group in 2004 (see Table 17.2).

If the struggle of the EP group has been long and difficult, the journey to the creation of a transnational Euro-party has been even harder.[17] Parties could see the need for some degree of cooperation in the EP due to the nature of the EP rules, but Euro-parties of all political views have struggled to institutionalise in this fashion for a number of reasons. Most crucial has been the issue of sovereignty, with parties anxious to preserve national prerogatives. In the case of RLPs there has also been major discussion around European integration, with parties divided as to the extent to which a Euro-party in some way legitimises the integration process. This is perhaps most evident within the German Die Linke/PDS, where there was considerable internal debate over the European Constitutional Treaty (ECT).[18]

Table 17.1   Member-parties of GUE/NGL after the 2014 EP Election

Cyprus	Progressive Party of Working People (AKEL)	2
Czech Rep.	Communist Party of Bohemia and Moravia (KSČM)	3
Denmark	People's Movement Against the EU	1
Finland	Left Alliance (*Vasemmistoliitto*)	1
France	Left Front (*Front de Gauche*)	3
	Union for Overseas (*L'Union pour les Outremer*)	1
Germany	Left (*Die Linke*)	7
	Independent	1
Greece	Coalition of the Radical Left (*Syriza*)	6
Ireland	Sinn Féin (SF)	3
	Independent	1
Italy	Tsipras List (*Lista Tsipras*)	2
	Independent	1
Netherlands	Socialist Party (SP)	2
	Party for the Animals (PvdD)	1
Portugal	Portuguese Communist Party (PCP)	3
	Left Bloc (*Bloco de Esquerda*)	1
Spain	Podemos	5
	United Left (IU)	4
	Basque Country Unite (*EH Bildu*)	1
	Left Alternative – Galicia	1
Sweden	Left Party (*Vänsterpartiet*)	1
UK	Sinn Féin (SF)	1
Total		**52**

Source: European Parliament, 'MEPs – Confederal Group of the European United Left', Brussels: European Parliament, no date http://www.europarl.europa.eu/meps/en/search.html?politicalGroup=4277 (accessed 25 July 2015).

Table 17.2   Seats of the Radical Left in the European Parliament, 1979–2014

Election	EP Total	Group	Seats[a]	Percentage[b]
1979	410	COM	44	10.7
1984	434	COM	41	9.5
1989	518	GUE	28	8.1[c]
1994	567	GUE	28	4.9
1999	626	GUE/NGL	42	6.7
2004	732	GUE/NGL	41	5.6
2009	736	GUE/NGL	35	4.8
2014	**751**	**GUE/NGL**	**52**	**6.9**

Abbreviations: COM – Communists and Allies; GUE – European United Left; LU – Left Unity; NGL – Nordic Green Left.

Notes: [a]Total seats held at outset of Parliament; [b]Radical Left seats as % of total seats in EP; [c]Combined figure for GUE and Left Unity.

Source: European Parliament, *Les élections européennes et nationales en chiffres/European and national elections figured out.* Directorate-General for Communication – Public Opinion Monitoring Unit, 2014. Online at http://www.europarl.europa.eu/pdf/elections_results/review.pdf (accessed 28 July 2015).

These obstacles to the establishment of Euro-parties were again partially overcome as a result of external organisational pressures. The introduction of a Party Regulation, which formalised rules for Euro-party funding,[19] coupled with internal pressure from some key parties such as the German PDS, saw many RLPs put aside years of ideological disagreement and hostility to European integration to form a Euro-party in 2004. As the Euro-party itself saw it, 'It was high time to build up a more concrete collaboration, to convey a common profile of the European Left.'[20] The PEL was founded in 2004 with 18 member parties drawn from 16 countries (including some non-EU states such as Moldova and Switzerland) and a further nine observer parties. Further parties have subsequently joined the PEL (see Table 17.3).

The PEL recognises its own diversity, stating broadly that membership 'is open to any left party and political organisation in Europe that agrees with

Table 17.3   Member-parties of the Party of the European Left, 2015

Austria	Communist Party of Austria (KPÖ)
Belarus	Belarusian Party of the Left 'Free World'
Belgium	Communist Party-Wallonie/Bruxelles
Bulgaria	Bulgarian Left
Czech Rep	Communist Party of Bohemia and Moravia (KSČM)
	Party of Democratic Socialism (PDS)
Denmark	Red-Green Alliance (*Enhedslisten*)
Estonia	Estonian Left Party
Finland	Finnish Communist Party
	Left Alliance
France	Left Party
	United Left
	French Communist Party
Germany	The Left
	German Communist Party
Greece	Syriza
Hungary	Workers' Party of Hungary 2006
Italy	Communist Party of Italy
	Communist Refoundation Party
Luxembourg	The Left
Moldova	Party of Communists of the Republic of Moldova
Portugal	Left Bloc
Romania	Socialist Alliance Party
Slovakia	Communist Party of Slovakia
Spain	United Left Alternative
	United Left (IU)
	Spanish Communist Party (PCE)
Switzerland	Swiss Labour Party
Turkey	Freedom and Solidarity Party

Source: 'EL-parties', http://www.european-left.org/about-el/member-parties (accessed 26 July 2015).

the aims and principles of the ... Manifesto and accepts the ... statutes'.[21] It specifies that 'member Parties ... are socialist, communist, red-green and other democratic left parties of the member states and associated states of the EU that work together and establish various forms of co-operation at all levels of political activity in Europe, based on the agreements, basic principles and political aims laid down in the ... Manifesto'. This diversity, however, contributes to considerable tensions within the PEL, particularly concerning party sovereignty. This is reflected in Article 1 of the PEL statutes, which sets out that it is a 'flexible, decentralised association of independent and sovereign European left-wing parties and political organizations which works on the basis of consensus'.[22] Statements like this indicate that the PEL is the least institutionalised Euro-party.

Links between the EP Group and the Euro-party have been slow to develop, and there is less coherence between the two organisations in terms of membership than there is with other EP groups.[23] Indeed, the GUE/NGL report of 2004 stated that the Group does not have a unanimous position on the organisation of European political parties.[24] A number of the parties that sit in the GUE/NGL Group are either not members of the PEL or only have observer status (compare tables 17.1 and 17.3). As Gomez et al. argue, the choice of which grouping to join links to a parties' self-definition and as a result the membership of the radical left grouping appears more fluid than other ideological groupings; for example, the Finnish VAS, the Italian Rifondazione and Syriza have joined the PEL but a major party (KKE) has never been part of the PEL and even left the GUE/NGL in 2014.[25] Following the 2014 EP elections we see that divisions between RLPs have become more pronounced. The 2014 EP elections produced 'remarkable vote and seat gains' for the radical Left but the divide between those parties affiliated to the PEL (24 MEPs) and GUE/NGL (25 MEPs) grew.[26]

This creates a complex situation where there are a number of lines of division at the transnational level. Most evident is an ideological one, expressed particularly in terms of attitudes towards communism – with many parties basing their identity on a clear and unequivocal rejection of any links with old-style communism. There are also, however, one or two parties who persist with a more dogmatic position: as Hanley notes, the past has left a 'deep mark on the left parties' psyche'.[27] Second, there is a practical feature – the differences in significance between different parties. Some are large parties with a strong presence both in their national parliaments and in the EP, while others are no more than micro-parties. This creates inevitable tensions about leadership, with parties from the GUE/NGL tending to be more assertive by virtue of the platform and status of their EP seats. These ideological and practical issues both tend to feed into an over-arching debate about approaches to European integration, which will be examined further in the next section.

THE TRANSNATIONAL RADICAL LEFT
AND EUROPEAN INTEGRATION

The very act of forming EP groups and Euro-parties implies a certain degree of commonality of outlook and purpose, something not shared equally by all parties. This has made it particularly difficult for the transnational parties to adopt clear and coherent positions on integration and on the European Union. Of course, European integration is a very broad term meaning different things to different people. It is probably worth considering it as three aspects. First of all, European integration can be taken to refer to the principle of closer cooperation between European states. Second, it can refer to the specific policies being followed. Third, it can mean the current organisational structure of the European Union.

Given the internationalist rhetoric that suffuses left-wing politics, it is hardly surprising that RLPs tend to be supportive of the principle of European cooperation. This is evident at the transnational level. Initially, the communist group in the EP was primarily an organisational convenience, and there was little or no attempt to build common stances.[28] During the 1980s, this had begun to change and by the time GUE was established in 1989, its founding declaration stated that it was 'firmly committed to European integration' while their rivals in the Left Unity group 'avoided the anti-European integration language so frequently used by the constituent parties'.[29] When these two merged together, the broad acceptance of integration remained evident. As already noted, European integration poses particular challenges for RLPs. The support of the transnational radical Left for European integration is clearly conditional. Both the GUE/NGL and the PEL have no difficulty in identifying the areas where they see flaws in the European Union. First among these is the EU's economic approach, particularly its perceived neoliberalism. This is closely associated with criticism of the weakness of the EU's social policies and its environmental commitments. In addition, the European Union's foreign and security policy is criticised, with the European Union seen as being far too closely linked to NATO and the United States. As Hough and Handl argue, in the case of the EP group, the 'GUE/NGL will continue to oppose militarization, neoliberalism and the alleged dangers of economic globalization'.[30]

This takes us into the key debate about the relationship between the radical Left and European integration. Dunphy and March argue that the relationship is categorised by a distinction between those parties that fear that EU membership restricts their sovereignty versus those who see the advantages of European-level cooperation (Europeanism and Sovereignism).[31] If we combine this analysis with a focus on radical left Euroscepticism we can see that for some nationalism and sovereignism interconnect.[32] This produces the classic divide between supporters of a reformed 'social Europe' and those parties who advocate the breakup of the European Union, considered as a necessary step to free their countries from neoliberal external constraints and to adopt progressive national macroeconomic policies. The latter position is supported by several orthodox communist parties (KKE, PCP, AKEL), radical left parties (the Swedish V) and other parties (e.g. Danish People's Movement Against the EU).

However, we see more merit in the position adopted by Keith, offering more nuance regarding the EU question and in particular transnational cooperation. He characterises the Eurosceptic Left using four categories: Rejectionist; Conditional; Compromising; and Expansionist/Integrationist.[33] The first two categories range from rejection of the European Union to conditional Euroscepticism where parties accept some form of confederal Europe but are concerned about compromising the sovereignty of the nation-state. Compromising Eurosceptic parties tend to support EU cooperation at the European level as is. In contrast, Integrationist parties accept the notion of EU cooperation but reject the current structures in favour of supranational policies and structures that further a federal socialist Europe. We argue that this last category appears to best explain the standard response from the transnational radical Left, while explaining the apparent contradiction between support for the principle of European cooperation (the first aspect) and criticism of many facets of EU policies (the third aspect).

The Expansionist/Integrationist response is to call for a different kind of Europe. Again, this is a prominent feature of both the GUE/NGL and PEL. A core GUE/NGL assertion is that 'another Europe is possible'.[34] This is echoed by the PEL, which argues for 'a deep-rooted social and democratic transformation of Europe'[35] and has set out a programmatic platform calling for 'a Europe refounded on a democratic, solidarity-based, social, ecological and peaceful basis'.[36] Overall, this suggests that the transnational radical Left is quite comfortable with the *idea* of integration. Indeed, even two of their regular criticisms noted above – that the European Union's social and environmental policies are too weak – can be interpreted as indicating desire for a stronger European policy, not as a rejection of the idea of integration.

To this point, the transnational radical Left's story appears quite consistent. They approve of the idea of European cooperation, but have significant reservations about the policies associated with the current direction of the European Union project. But while this could potentially form the basis of a very coherent position for the GUE/NGL, the PEL and their constituent parties, instead the reality is that the transnational groups remain weak. This is due to the third aspect of integration, the organisational framework of the European Union.

Once again, there is agreement in the GUE/NGL and in the PEL that the European Union suffers from a serious democratic deficit. However, the question of how to deal with that dearth – and beyond that, the question of how to try to construct the 'Other Europe' that the radical Left regularly talks about – is where the real problems emerge. For some constituent parties, there is a commitment to change the European Union, although they tend to be rather imprecise about how this could actually be achieved. But others argue that the organisational arrangements of the European Union render it virtually impossible to reform.[37] We even see this division connected to the Euro-party configurations. Therefore, we see the Danish EL and Syriza in PEL, while more rejectionist parties such as the Swedish V and PCP refuse the join the PEL while remaining in the GUE/NGL group. Divisions within the radical Left also saw the KKE leave the GUE/NGL group, citing the allegedly increasingly centralised organisation of the GUE/NGL, its accommodation with austerity and ideological disagreements as reasons for leaving.[38] These organisational/membership changes in both GUE/NGL and the PEL since the much-improved 2014 election results have somewhat slowed the trajectory that the PEL, in particular, was on. Having the 50 or so radical left MEPs split three ways weakens the opportunity for the radical Left to influence the agenda within the EP.

This lack of unity when it comes to the crucial aspect of how to deal with the European Union is written into the core principles of both the GUE/NGL and the PEL. The EP group defines itself explicitly as a 'confederal group', and declares that 'confederalism for us means respecting and preserving the diversity of identities and opinions of our members'.[39] For a number of its constituent parties, it is precisely that looseness, that lack of an enforced common position that makes the group bearable. Similarly, the PEL recognises that it is 'not a force free of contradictions, having differing views on many issues'.[40]

In overall terms, we can see that the membership changes above mean that there is increasingly common cause in relation to European integration *within* both the GUE/NGL and PEL, suggesting a gradual movement towards working together in a European framework, and even an increasing acceptance of the European Union by the radical Left as a whole. Having said that, significant divisions between parties over whether or not to accept the European Union do persist. These features are neatly captured if we look briefly at the transnational radical Left during the debates around the ECT and the Treaty of Lisbon.[41] Throughout the debates, the GUE/NGL showed consistent lines of argument, calling for 'another Europe', criticising the 'constitutionalisation of the liberal model' and warning of a deepening democratic deficit, although when it came to trying to advance an overall common position, 'the members of the group appeared to be quite divided over the ECT'.[42] Indeed, the sole GUE/NGL full member of the EP delegation to the European Convention, Sylvia-Yvonne Kaufmann, was to end up leaving her party and the group.[43] The PEL was in a different position, as it was only just being established at the same time as the ECT was being shaped. The PEL position was to be critical, while acknowledging that a political agreement on the issue of a European constitution would be valuable.[44] So while the GUE/NGL remained more reticent, there were signs that the PEL was inching the radical Left towards a more pro-EU stance. If that is the case, how has it been affected by the financial crisis?

THE FINANCIAL CRISIS

The unfolding financial crisis posed a number of significant issues for the radical Left. There are three distinct aspects worth considering. First of all, there is the international dimension of the crisis. Far from being just a European event, it has affected many other countries. Second, there is the manner in which the crisis has impacted on the European Union's economic and social policies. And third, there is the way it has impacted on the European Union's political structures.

The international nature of the crisis is very clear, with most analyses identifying the collapse of the US sub-prime lending market as a key trigger. This is something that should have played into the hands of the radical Left. It corroborated their arguments that the European Union was part of a global capitalist structure and that the European Union's image of being a 'nicer' form of capitalism was flawed. However, despite some vague calls for wider alliances with similar parties around the world, the actual policy statements of both the GUE/NGL and PEL are firmly European in their approach. As a PEL document notes, 'We are faced with a crisis of the capitalist system that affects every region of the world, without exception. Nevertheless, the crisis in the EU is specific in nature.'[45] This reflects the intensity of the challenges being faced within the EU setting.

The crisis has had very specific consequences for the European Union for two reasons. First of all, the constitutional structure of the European Union means that policies are much more rigid, with only a very limited capacity for changing the direction of governance. Policies are embedded in treaties, which have to be negotiated by all member states, so once they have been agreed, it becomes very difficult to alter them. Second, those policies already lean strongly towards market-driven prescriptions.[46] Third, the European Union has been particularly affected because of the single currency. The existence of the Euro imposes significant constraints on the policies of Eurozone member states. The result has been the requirement for bailout programmes in five countries, with the consequence being the enforcement of stringent austerity programmes.[47] Many other EU countries have also been required to implement austerity measures in order to avoid the need for bailouts.[48]

The transnational radical Left has responded primarily with a defensive approach. They have sought to oppose the policies, and the PEL's manifesto for the 2014 European elections is littered with this kind of language: 'stop austerity plans', 'no to privatisation', 'regain power over finance', 'refuse the Transatlantic Trade and Investment Partnership', 'resist armaments policy' etc.[49] To some extent this reflects a real sense of being under attack: 'Demolishing the achievements of the labour movement is the united global project of the neoliberal, right wing forces.'[50] It also reflects the positions adopted by key member parties[51]; furthermore, many Europeans undoubtedly see their economic and social expectations being eroded, so the radical Left has had a ready-made agenda to promote. This agenda also corresponds to the beliefs and attitudes of many of the member parties' core voters.[52]

RLPs have concentrated on an appeal to preserving conditions (at least in the short run) rather than trying to present an alternative. This is evident in their stance on social welfare in the PEL's 2014 European manifesto. In a section titled 'For a social Europe, for a Europe of rights', the manifesto states, 'Our goal is to guarantee the fundamental human rights of all Europeans, men and women, by universal access to these rights, through public services and social security systems, managed by the public.'[53] It goes on to list 12 specific rights, which would not seem out of place in even the mildest centre-left social democratic manifesto.[54]

There is, of course, more than that. Both radical left transnational groups have presented their economic solutions to the crisis. However, it is noteworthy that these provide extensive analysis of the crisis but are less vociferous when it comes to proposing actual alternative policies. The PEL presented one 17-page document on the crisis, which was dominated by critique but which devoted less than a page to summarising a few brief policy prescriptions – a European Convention to renegotiate national debts, a framework for establishing a European public bank, democratic control of the European Central Bank (ECB) and tax reform.[55] Something very similar is evident from the GUE/NGL.[56]

Opposition to the proposed Transatlantic Trade and Investment Partnership (TTIP) is another common factor across the GUE/NGL and PEL. But TTIP is also another example of the extent to which both groups tend to emphasise opposition rather than the promotion of alternatives. The oppositional strategies – to TTIP and to the wider context of EU policies on the crisis – can be explained partly because there is plenty to oppose for the radical Left, and because opponents of the European Union's current economic and social direction inevitably have to respond to the drives coming from Brussels. Partly it represents good political sense, since social democratic parties have grown reluctant to defend the traditional welfare state, leaving a considerable constituency who are more interested in protecting what they have rather than promoting a completely new model. But it also reveals the underlying reality that while it is relatively easy for the constituent parties to agree on what they do not like, it is far trickier to get them to agree on what they do like.

This relates strongly to the final aspect of the financial crisis, its impact on the European Union's political structures. The radical Left has consistently criticised the European Union for its perceived democratic deficit. This has been reinforced by the crisis in two ways. First of all, it has exacerbated the weakness of democratic control of key EU policies. A particular touchstone of this is the way that the ECB runs the Euro without any real democratic input. As the PEL's president Pierre Laurent put it, 'The European Central Bank and the euro are at the exclusive service of the financial markets' rather than the people.'[57]

A second aspect of the growing democratic dilemma is the undermining of national political systems. The cases are well known – the imposition of technocratic administrations in Greece and Italy, the strict limitations on policy choice that are demanded of governments in bailout countries, and the rejection of the outcomes of national referendums and elections. The response of the radical Left to this mantra of 'There Is No Alternative' was to insist on 'Another Europe', and to consistently express strong solidarity with all anti-austerity movements throughout the European Union.[58]

However, this is an area that once again begins to expose the tensions behind the façade of agreement among RLPs in the transnational groups. For some, the solidarity stems from a sense of internationalism. But for others, it is as much to do with a desire to respect national sovereignty from the depredations of the European Union. As vice-chair of the Communist Party of Finland Elli Tuomi noted, 'There's a special challenge in strengthening the fight against austerity politics in Northern parts of Europe; to build a common struggle, based on solidarity, from Southern Europe to North, from West to East.'[59] This is particularly evident in the GUE/NGL, where there is superficial agreement. Parties including the Danish Red-Green Alliance, the Swedish Left and the Finnish Left Alliance, however, show an underlying concern that harmonisation of standards at a European level will inevitably mean a lowering of the high social standards in their countries. In addition, they can face a degree of competition on the issue of protecting social welfare from the Far Right.

So, to quote a certain radical left leader from an older generation, what is to be done? In particular, what approach should be adopted towards European integration to best respond to the crisis? Is the European Union the problem or the answer? The transnational radical Left is very clear in arguing that the current European Union is failing, while advocating another Europe. It even hints that this might require a very significant rupture with the present-day European Union: 'We propose a break in order to found a new European project, one which is based on the interests of the peoples and respect for their sovereignty, in order to restore a sense of meaning to European integration.'[60] Within the GUE/NGL there have been clear attempts to link the discussions about austerity to the issue of long-term unemployment and to broaden the focus away from Greece. Interestingly there has been at least one attempt to share ideas around a 'left' response to austerity with Social Democrats and Greens, something that has heightened the divisions with the rejectionist parties.[61]

There is also the issue of the strategic/intellectual responses to the crisis. Here we see the intellectual responses reflecting the positions outlined above. The Expansionist/Integrationist parties created *Plan B in Europe*, launched in late 2015 by former Die Linke leader Oskar Lafontaine from Germany, Italian deputy and economist Stefano Fassina, leader of France's Left Party Jean-Luc Mélenchon and from Greece former deputy and parliamentary speaker Zoe Kostantopoulou and ex-finance minister Yanis Varoufakis. The Plan calls for a summit to develop a new common plan for the Left in Europe.[62] A sign of division lies with the fact that the proposal for a *Plan B* Summit has not received support from other elements of the European Left despite the agenda being almost blank to encourage debate. Instead of supporting *Plan B*, the GUE/NGL group reiterated their three-pronged platform for reform at a European level. This more conditional position involved: democratising the European Union and its financial institutions; raising wages and social services while taxing the rich; and beginning large programmes of public investment to stimulate growth and jobs.[63] The strategic response from parties that reject the European Union was set out in the INITIATIVE framework, which was 'against the EU, its parties and policies'.[64]

Thus on the radical Left we have at least three strategic responses to the European Union and the crisis, making assertions that 'we need action not just rhetoric' unintentionally ironic.[65] Calls for another Europe remain persistently vague, as there is no agreement as to concrete plans or ideas about what a reformed European Union would look like, and this is perhaps precisely because there is no consensus or agreement about how to reform it. Instead, the transnational radical Left continues to work best by agreeing to disagree about the core issue – is the European Union worth trying to reform and save, or should it be abandoned? This lack of a unified strategy is creating problems in specific national contexts. For example, in France, existing tensions have been exacerbated with the Left Party supporting *Plan B*, while the PCF has backed Tsipras and the mainstream GUE/NGL strategy.

Furthermore, such tensions have if anything been exacerbated by the financial crisis. For the parties that are opposed to the EU project, the crisis is irrefutable evidence that the European Union is pursuing a fundamentally flawed programme. For the PEL, 'there will be no maintaining of the status quo or going backwards. If the current choices are upheld, the EU will increasingly be reduced to an authoritarian management board and producer of social regression, threatening any idea of solidarity and European justice.'[66] But for others, the depth of the crisis is evidence that economic, social and political systems have become so deeply and irretrievably interconnected that they can only be addressed through significant European integration. As Finnish Communist Party chairman Juha-Pekka Väisänen noted, 'Withdrawal from the euro would not automatically lead to more progressive policies. The main problems are the role of financial markets and the power of big capital.'[67]

A related issue is the political contradiction of the crisis. When RLPs are elected to government, it is a consequence of hostility towards 'mainstream' parties (usually of the Centre-Left) and electoral pledges to withstand austerity. The harsh reality of office often highlights the limited room for policy manoeuvre that modern governments have, in part of course due to EU and Eurozone rules. Therefore we saw Syriza forced to accept EU/IMF rules and other RLPs in power forced to compromise/tone down their rhetoric as a result.[68] Keith highlights that the very parties that did well in countries hit hardest by austerity were the ones forced to implement the policies of austerity.[69] We also saw a change in rhetoric from the more populist RLPs such as Podemos, who have been forced to dampen their critique of the European Union and austerity to ensure they could not be accused of backtracking on commitments. We have seen signs of how these tensions played out within the transnational groupings already, making maintaining unity over the coming parliamentary term even harder.[70]

CONCLUSION – TO EU OR NOT TO EU?

The conventional view of Europeanisation seemed to fit the transnational radical Left until recently. There was clear evidence of an organisational coming-together among these parties, with the evolution of the GUE/NGL group and the founding of the PEL. There were also emerging indications of increasing policy congruence. This can be seen across the three levels discussed in this chapter. First of all, the two key transnational radical left organisations are strongly supportive of the normative ideal of European integration, although this masks very strong alternative views among some constituent parties. Secondly, they have very clear criticisms of the economic and social policies being pursued by the European Union. For the transnational groups, there is little difficulty in securing support for common statements on policy in this way. But it is the third aspect that creates the difficulties. The constituent parties simply do not agree about how to interpret the political system of the European Union, and that immediately blocks the transnational groups from any kind of effective intervention. There also appears to be very little intellectual leadership in radical left opposition to the European Union. As it stands in 2015 criticising is easy, constructing an alternative is proving harder.

The Eurozone crisis has changed the situation partially. The normative commitment to the idea of integration remains broadly intact and we find a broad consensus on economic and social policy. But as we have argued, while the parties agree about what they do not like, they struggle to agree about what should be done. So instead of continued growth in policy congruence, there has been evidence of a stalling in party coordination. It is not so much a growth of divisions over policy, more of a case that the parties have been unable to seize the moment of the economic crisis by presenting a strong, coherent and united alternative. This is strongly connected to the third aspect. The crisis has polarised opinion about the European Union within the transnational radical Left. For some parties, such as the rejectionist KKE and the PCP, it has confirmed anti-EU convictions. But for others, such as the initiators of the *Plan B in Europe*, it has reinforced a belief that the only way to respond to global capitalist pressures is through some form of European-level Union.

The transnational radical Left has always had to accommodate different outlooks on integration, from sceptic to supportive. But the crisis has pushed both viewpoints further away from each other. They share an extensive critique of the EU project, but find it hard to agree to any common programme for changing it. The rhetoric of 'Another Europe' is not matched by any roadmap for getting there. The Plan B debates show that while the critique of the European Union from a radical left perspective is easy, putting details into the Plan is much harder. This is a major challenge for the Expansionist/ Integrationist parties and the PEL, which seems to be the main vehicle for this view of the European Union.

There are some grounds for suggesting that RLPs could develop strong common positions. But neither the GUE/NGL nor the PEL have sought to push for much actual collaboration. Instead, the emphasis has been on voluntary consensus rather than any degree of enforced compliance. This is good as a means of preserving the two transnational bodies as operational vehicles, but it weakens the overall voice of the radical Left on the European stage. The parties agree on the principle of integration and many specific policies, but on the fundamental question of whether the European Union itself can be reformed, that agreement breaks apart. Instead, the groups have relied on the old formula of agreeing to disagree. Thus the radical Left has not been able to capitalise on its recent successes and as a result left the field open to political forces with different ideological positions to prosper.

NOTES

1. We would like to thank Donal Walsh for his excellent research assistance. This chapter builds upon a paper presented at the Workshop on 'Another Europe is possible? The radical left and the European union,' Political Studies Association annual conference Edinburgh 2010.

2. Simon Lightfoot, *Europeanising Social Democracy? The Rise of the Party of European Socialists* (London and New York: Routledge, 2005).

3. See Tapio Raunio, 'Political Parties in the European Union,' in *Handbook of European Union Politics*, ed. Knud Erik Jørgensen, Mark A. Pollack and Ben Rosamond (London: SAGE, 2007), 247–62; Stefano Bartolini, 'The Strange Case of Europarties,' in *The Domestic Party Politics of Europeanisation: Actors, Patterns and Systems*, ed. Erol Külahci (Colchester: ECPR Press, 2012).

4. See Luke March, 'Beyond Syriza and Podemos, other radical left parties are threatening to break into the mainstream of European politics,' EUROPP, accessed 7 March 2016, http://blogs.lse.ac.uk/europpblog/2015/03/24/beyond-syriza-and-podemos-other-radical-left-parties-are-threatening-to-break-into-the-mainstream-of-european-politics/.

5. Dan Keith, 'Opposing Europe, Opposing Austerity: Radical Left Parties and the Eurosceptic Debate', in *The Routledge Handbook of Euroscepticism*, ed. Nick Startin and Simon Usherwood (Abingdon: Routledge, 2016, forthcoming); Michael Holmes, 'Contesting Integration: The Radical Left and Euroscepticism', in *Euroscepticism as a Transnational and Pan-European Phenomenon: The Emergence of a New Sphere of Opposition*, ed. Nick Startin, John FitzGibbon and Ben Leruth (London: Routledge, forthcoming); Giorgos Charalambous, 'All the Shades of Red: Examining the Radical left's Euroscepticisms,' *Contemporary Politics* 17, no. 3 (2011): 299–320.

6. See Keith, 'Opposing Europe'.

7. See Steven van Hecke, 'Do Transnational Party Federations Matter? (… why should we care?),' *Journal of Contemporary European Research* 6, no. 3 (2010): 395–411; and Stephen Day, 'Between "Containment" and "Transnationalization,"' *Acta politica* 49 (2014): 5–29.

8. Each grouping must contain a minimum number of parties from a minimum number of EU member states or MEPs are seen as unattached. Unattached MEPs tend to have extremely limited power and resources, something that beset the early communist grouping. See Richard Dunphy, *Contesting Capitalism? Left Parties and European Integration* (Manchester: Manchester University Press, 2004), 54.

9. Dimitri Almeida, *The Impact of European Integration on Political Parties: Beyond the Permissive Consensus* (London: Routledge, 2012).

10. Dunphy, *Contesting Capitalism?*, 65.

11. David Bell, 'Western Communist Parties and the European Union', in *Political Parties and the European Union*, ed. John Gaffney (Manchester: Manchester University Press, 1996), 138.

12. Andrea Volkens, 'Policy Changes of Parties in European Parliament Party Groups', in *Democratic Politics and Party Competition: Essays in Honour of Ian Budge*, ed. Judith Bara and Albert Weale (London and New York: Routledge, 2006).

13. Not without problems – the largest national delegation at the time, the Spanish United Left, had an intense debate as to whether to join GUE or the Greens.

14. Dunphy, *Contesting Capitalism?*, 172.

15. Dan Hough, 'Learning From the West: Policy Transfer and Programmatic Change in the Communist Successor Parties of Eastern and Central Europe,' *Journal of Communist Studies and Transition Politics* 21, no. 1 (2005): 1–15.

16. Dan Hough and Vladimir Handl, 'The Post-communist Left and the European Union: The Czech Communist Party of Bohemia and Moravia (KSČM) and the German Party of Democratic Socialism (PDS),' *Communist and Post-Communist Studies* 37, no. 3 (2004): 319–39.

17. Richard Dunphy and Luke March, 'Seven Year Itch?: The European Left Party: Struggling to Transform the EU,' *Perspectives on European Politics and Societies* 14, no. 4 (2013): 520.

18. Knut Roder, 'The German Left from Laeken to Lisbon,' in *The Left and the European Constitution: From Laeken to Lisbon,* ed. Michael Holmes and Knut Roder (Manchester: Manchester University Press, 2012), 103–5.

19. Regulation 2004/2003 of the European Parliament, accessed 26 July 2015, http://eur-lex.europa.eu/legal-content/EN/TXT/?uri=URISERV:l33315.

20. 'About the EL', accessed 23 March 2015, http://www.european-left.org/about-el.

21. 'Statute of the Party of the European Left', accessed 30 July 2015, http://www.european-left.org/propos-de-la-ge/documents.

22. 'About the EL.'

23. Luke March, *Radical Left Parties in Europe* (London: Routledge, 2011); Dimitri Almeida, *The Impact of European Integration on Political Parties: Beyond the Permissive Consensus* (London: Routledge, 2014); Dunphy and March, 'Seven Year Itch?'.

24. GUE/NGL, Activity report, 1999–2004, Brussels: GUE/NGL, 2004.

25. Raul Gómez, Laura Morales and Luis Ramiro, 'Varieties of Radicalism. Examining the Diversity of Radical Left Parties and Voters in Western Europe,' *West European Politics* (In press for print version, electronic version available http://www.tandfonline.com/doi/abs/10.1080/01402382.2015.1064245#.VcS1UiRG9E5).

26. Oliver Treib, 'The Voter Says no, but Nobody Listens: Causes and Consequences of the Eurosceptic vote in the 2014 European Elections,' *Journal of European Public Policy* 21, no. 10 (2014): 1541–54; Paulo Chioccetti, 'The Radical Left at the 2014 European Parliament Election', in *The Left in Europe after the EU Elections: New Challenges*, ed. Cornelia Hildebrant (Berlin: Rosa Luxemburg-Stiftung, 2014), 7–14; Thilo Janssen, *The Parties of the Left in Europe* (Berlin: Rosa Luxemburg Foundation, 2013).

27. David Hanley, *Beyond the Nation State: Parties in the Era of European Integration* (London: Palgrave MacMillan, 2008), 152.

28. Bell, 'Western Communist Parties'.

29. Dunphy, *Contesting Capitalism?*, 70.

30. Ibid., 333.

31. Dunphy and March, 'Seven Year Itch?'.

32. Daphne Halikiopoulou, Kyriaki Nanou and Sofia Vasilopoulou, 'The Paradox of Nationalism: The Common Denominator of Radical Right and Radical Left Euroscepticism,' *European Journal of Political Research* 51 (2012): 504–39.

33. See Keith, 'Opposing Europe'.

34. GUE/NGL, Review of activities, 2009–2011, accessed 30 July 2015, http://www.guengl.eu/uploads/publications-documents/Mid-term_EN.pdf.

35. PEL, 'Peace, development and employment with rights,' final declaration, 2nd PEL Congress, Prague, November 2007.

36. PEL, 'Escaping from austerity, rebuilding Europe,' draft programme, 4th PEL Congress, Madrid, December 2013.

37. See Giorgos Charalambous, *European Integration and the Communist Dilemma: Communist Party Responses to Europe in Greece, Cyprus and Italy* (Farnham: Ashgate, 2013).

38. See http://inter.kke.gr/en/articles/Statement-of-the-Central-Committee-of-the-KKE-on-the-stance-of-the-KKE-in-the-EU-parliament/, accessed 7 March 2016.

39. GUE/NGL, http://www.guengl.eu/group/about/, accessed 7 March 2016.

40. 'Statute of the Party of the European Left.'

41. Michael Holmes and Knut Roder (eds), *The Left and the European Constitution: From Laeken to Lisbon* (Manchester: Manchester University Press, 2012).

42. Olga Laletina, 'The European United Left-Nordic Green Left,' in *The European Constitution and its Ratification Crisis: Constitutional Debates in the EU Member States*, ed. Nina Eschke and Thomas Malick (Bonn: Zentrumfür Europäische Integrationsforschung, Rhenische Friedrich-Wilhelms-Universität, 2006); Simon Lightfoot, 'Left Parties at the EU Level: Influencing the Convention,' in *The Left and the European Constitution: From Laeken to Lisbon*, ed. Michael Holmes and Knut Roder (Manchester: Manchester University Press, 2012), 27.

43. Formally titled the Convention on the Future of Europe, this was an extraordinary institution intended to act as a kind of constitutional assembly, with the aim of simplifying and synthesising the European Union's multiple treaties into an integrated constitutional document. See Jo Shaw et al., *Convention on the Future of Europe: Working towards an EU Constitution* (London: Federal Trust, 2003). On Germany, see Knut Roder, 'The German Left from Laeken to Lisbon,' 95–117 in Holmes and Roder (eds), *The Left and the European Constitution*.

44. Lightfoot, 'Left parties at the EU level,' 29.

45. PEL, 'Unite for a left alternative in Europe,' draft document, 4th PEL Congress, Madrid, December 2013.

46. Bernard Moss, *Monetary Union in Crisis: The European Union as a Neoliberal Construction* (Basingstoke: Palgrave, 2004).

47. Greece (first bailout €110bn May 2010; second bailout €130bn July 2011; at time of writing a third bailout is being negotiated), Ireland (€85bn, November 2010), Portugal (€78bn, May 2011), Spain (€100bn, June 2012) and Cyprus (€10bn, March 2013).

48. Notably Italy, although a number of CEE states have also undergone similar measures.

49. PEL, *Manifesto for the 2014 European Elections*.

50. Juha-Pekka Väisänen, 'We are Family,' speech to IVth Congress of the Party of the European Left, Madrid 15 December 2013, accessed 2 April 2015, http://www. skp.fi/2013-12-12/we-are-family-jp-vaisanen-speech-in-european-left-congress-in-madrid-13-15-12-2013.

51. Giorgos Charalambous and Iasonas Lamprianou, 'Societal Responses to the Post-2008 Economic Crisis among South European and Irish Radical Left Parties: Continuity or Change and Why?,' *Government and Opposition* (2014), available on CJO2014. doi:10.1017/gov.2014.35.

52. Luis Ramiro, 'Support for Radical Left Parties in Western Europe: Social Background, Ideology and Political Orientations,' *European Political Science Review* (In press for print version, electronic version available http://dx.doi.org/10.1017/ S1755773914000368); Mark Visser, 'Support for Radical Left Ideologies in Europe,' *European Journal of Political Research* 53, no. 3: 541–58; Luke March and Charlotte Rommerskirchen, 'Out of Left Field? Explaining the Variable Electoral Success of European Radical Left Parties,' *Party Politics* 21, no. 1 (2015): 40–55.

53. PEL, *Manifesto for the 2014 European Elections.*

54. For example, 'Right to decent work, increase the wages,' 'Right to health care and health protection', 'Universal right to public education,' 'LGBT rights' etc.

55. 'Unite for a left alternative in Europe,' draft document, 4th PEL Congress, Madrid, December 2013.

56. GUE/NGL, *Review of Activities 2012-2014* (Brussels: GUE/NGL).

57. *Manifesto for the 2014 European Elections.*

58. See, for instance, GUE/NGL, *Review of Activities*, 9–10.

59. 'European Left against austerity politics', speech to IVth Congress of the Party of the European Left, Madrid 15 December 2013, accessed 2 April 2015, http://www. skp.fi/2013-14-12/-european-left-against-austerity-politics-emmi-tuomi-cpfinland-vice-chairperson-speech-in-iv-congress-of-the-party-of-the-european-left-parties.

60. Final political document PEL Congress 2013 *Unite for a Left Alternative in Europe,* www.european-left.org/sites/default/files/final_political_doc.

61. See http://www.guengl.eu/news/article/greece-austerity-and-growth, accessed 7 March 2016.

62. Jean-Luc Mélenchon, 'Pour un Plan B en Europe,' blog posting, 11 September 2015, accessed 6 December 2015, http://melenchon.fr/2015/09/11/pour-un-plan-b-en-europe/.

63. See https://www.greenleft.org.au/node/60305, accessed 7 March 2016.

64. See http://www.initiative-cwpe.org/en/sections/the-initiative-in-the-european-parliament/, accessed 7 March 2016.

65. GUE/NGL, *Review of Activities.*

66. 'Unite for a left alternative in Europe,' draft document.

67. Väisänen, 'We are Family.'

68. See Yannis Stavrakakis and Girogos Katsambekis, 'Left-wing Populism in the European Periphery: The Case of SYRIZA,' *Journal of Political Ideologies* 19, no. 2 (2014): 119–42; Keith, forthcoming.

69. See Keith, 'Opposing Europe'.

70. Gómez et al., 'Varieties of Radicalism.'

Chapter 18

Conclusion

The European Radical Left: Past, Present, No Future?

Daniel Keith and Luke March

After nearly a decade of the international financial crisis and its repercussions, what is the state of the European radical Left? To what degree has the Great Recession fundamentally altered the party family's long-term trajectories? This concluding chapter synthesises our main research foci on the reasons for the divergent growth of the party family and the precise impact of the crisis. We will first look briefly at the state of the radical Left on the eve of the crisis in 2008, then summarise the specific impacts of the crisis on the parties we have examined, in particular their intellectual, electoral and organisational processes. We will draw some general conclusions about the impact of the crisis on the radical Left before making longer-term prognoses.

In the introduction, we outlined three groups of hypotheses for how the crisis should affect the Left – the *radical surge, no change* and *success shock* theses. Each finds some confirmation in this chapter. This is ostensibly paradoxical, because they are *prima facie* conflicting arguments. However, the fact that they all have some validity in some cases is an indication of how fractured and nationally specific European RLPs' crisis responses have been. Overall, we find the radical surge and success shock theses the most convincing, and this itself is no paradox. The Great Recession has produced demonstrably improved external conditions for RLPs; however, the majority have been unable to exploit these to the full, and the gap between expectations and achievements has in turn created significant difficulties. The crisis has certainly engendered change on the radical Left, but this is usually limited, circumscribed and by no means 'radical'.

ON THE EVE: STABILISATION VS. DECLINE; MUTATION VS. FRAGMENTATION

When analysing the state of the communist movement in 1994, Martin Bull characterised its recent past as 'ambiguity' (over the balance between Soviet and nation-state imperatives), 'decline' and 'fragmentation' (the demise of parties' support bases because of socio-economic and sociocultural changes).[1] He expressed serious doubts over the communists' future as a party family. A decade later, March and Mudde expressed qualified optimism that the party family was undergoing processes of 'decline *and* mutation'.[2] The former was most notable in the continuing attrition of the traditional communist parties. However, it was being partially compensated by newly cohesive policies and ideological approaches (principally 'social populism') and societal links (e.g. with the global justice movement).

Other works also argued that in the decade prior to the crisis the radical Left was slowly recovering from the traumatic external shock of the Soviet collapse, with increased orientation towards national government participation, enhanced emphasis on participatory and environmental linkages and incremental efforts to agree and organise internationally, most noticeably via the European Left Party (PEL), founded in 2004.

The chapters in this volume do not fundamentally challenge this picture of partial pre-crisis consolidation. There was a slight recovery in aggregate RLP electoral performance across Europe in the 1990s and early 2000s, along with a decrease in national-level fragmentation, although electoral performance generally did not rebound to 1980s levels (Luke March, this volume). Formerly antagonistic groups were uniting to form new parties, such as the Left Bloc in Portugal, Die Linke and the Front de Gauche (Freire and Lisi; Amieke Bouma; Escalona and Vieira, this volume). International efforts were driving greater policy congruence and even Europeanisation in support of 'Another Europe' (Holmes and Lightfoot, this volume). Contrary to earlier expectations, communist parties in Cyprus, Portugal and Greece exhibited a stubborn longevity, while other parties such as the Dutch SP were able to successfully employ flexible strategies even prior to the crisis (Dan Keith, this volume). Even the revolutionary extreme Left was getting in on the act, with, for example, the Irish Socialist Party holding a Dáil seat from 1997 to 2007. The new orientation towards government was shown in the increasing pragmatism and ideological moderation of formerly protest parties such as the Dutch SP and German Die Linke, while the Cypriot AKEL became the first RLP to lead a national coalition in the Eurozone in February 2008.

At the same time, our chapter contributions demonstrate the ongoing weaknesses of the European radical Left. Demand-side conditions across Europe have generally been propitious for the survival and flourishing of RLPs. For example, in the Czech Republic, 'socio-economic conditions, Euroscepticism, conservative national values and the past success of the communist party played crucial roles in stabilising the place of the KSČM on the political scene' (Handl and Goffin, this volume). There are of course exceptions – in Ireland, the Catholic/Nationalist political culture has proved hostile to class politics (Richard Dunphy, chapter 10), whereas in Latvia, the Soviet legacy combined with the dominant Latvian ethnic nationalist culture has marginalised left-wing politics as pro-Russian (Cheskin and March, chapter 12). Overall though, across Europe the potential ideological support for RLPs is larger (11 per cent) than its electoral success (7.2 per cent) (March, chapter 2).

That support rarely matches potential means that supply-side explanations are vital in explaining variation in RLP success. As noted throughout, RLPs have gained traction by both critiquing social democrats and appropriating their former policies, an approach that forces social democrats to engage with them or risk vote loss. Prior to the crisis, this strategy rarely managed to significantly weaken the social democrats (except perhaps in the Netherlands). With the exception of Cyprus, social democrats remained hegemonic on the Left. Moreover, in several cases, notably the Czech Republic, Western Germany and Latvia, RLPs were unable to overcome fully their historical social stigma. In Latvia, the Left's isolation was reinforced by strict citizenship policies and an informal *cordon sanitaire* by the ethnic Latvian parties.

Perhaps more problematic still was the internal supply side (i.e. intra-party politics). Offsetting tendencies towards party consolidation was the persistence of internal conflict. For instance, divisions between the PCE and other constituent parts of the Spanish United Left over issues such as relations with the Socialists contributed to the United Left's secular decline (Luis Ramiro, this volume). Die Linke remained ideologically and regionally divided during its formation process, with a party programme only emerging in 2011, four years after foundation. Moreover, in both Portugal and Greece, divisions in the radical Left were made very apparent by the persistence of two significant parties representing 'old left' (conservative communist) and 'new left' (democratic socialist) profiles. The latter were in turn internally fractious.

A related issue was that of identity. Whereas for Bull, 'ambiguity' largely dissipated when the collapse of the Soviet Union allegedly ended tensions between national and international imperatives, our chapters show many instances of identity issues, with the balance between national and international still salient. In many cases this was the persistence of long-standing ideological motifs. For most of the communist parties analysed here, the collapse of the Soviet Union involved more continuity than change. Indeed, the Greek KKE 're-bolshevised' during the 1990s (Costas Eleftheriou, chapter 15). Other parties such as the Czech KSČM and Cypriot AKEL have continued to nourish their long-term traditions, albeit with increasing pragmatism and the downplaying of contentious ideological debate. In the former party, ideological stasis results from the dominance of pragmatists who defer to the conservative/traditionalist majority as well as the party's debilitated intellectual life (Handl and Goffin); the latter has always been risk-averse, centralised and never an overtly 'radical' RLP (Charalambous and Ioannou, this volume). Other parties have struggled with trying to form a radical identity clearly distinct from social democrats, not least the SP and its 'social democracy plus' strategy. Indeed, the dominant tendency has been movement from unabashed anti-capitalism to a Keynesian position arguing that neoliberalism is more cause than symptom of capitalist crisis (David Bailey, this volume).

Similar tendencies were evident in party linkages. Confirming Tsakatika and Lisi's arguments, all parties gave at least lip service to the concept of environmental linkage, even when (as with the KSČM) they had little practical ability to interact effectively with civil society.[3] Other communist parties (especially AKEL) continued to attempt to liaise with traditional class-based affiliated social movements. Non-communist parties tried to form links with the global justice movement. However, prior to the crisis, these links were often characterised by mutually antipathetic views over the meaning of representation (David Bailey, this volume). In particular, many of the newer social movements saw RLPs as integral to the representative politics they wished to transcend.

The international realm also showed a similar combination of fusion and fission. RLPs partially managed to overcome the utter fragmentation of the movement, and by the early 2000s had formed relatively coherent fora for rudimentary co-operation at EU level, principally the GUE/NGL in the European parliament and the 'Euro-party', the PEL. But prior to the crisis, neither had built up much integrative momentum. As Holmes and Lightfoot show, they were poorly interlinked, were missing several prominent European RLPs, and above, all, had failed to move from confederal co-operation towards something more genuinely transnational.

To sum up the status quo ante, by September 2008, the radical left party family was hardly a cohesive enough actor ideally positioned to exploit the crisis in a collectively strategic way. Writing about the position of the radical Left in the late 1980s, the Italian communist Lucio Magri argued that 'the social forces antagonistic to the system today appear largely divided, or boxed in, between subalternity and revolt, integration and utopianism; a unifying perspective still lies far beyond their practice and culture'.[4] Two decades later, this reproach was still substantially true, consolidating processes notwithstanding. What was also evident was that the ambiguity continuum between international and national tendencies had been shifted decisively to the latter, potentially making the issue still *worse*. RLPs had become increasingly nationally specific; a major actor in Cyprus, a minor actor in many countries, irrelevant in many more. The movement towards polycentrism and 'national Communism' in train since the 1970s had clearly proceeded apace.[5] New momentum at EU level implied that national siloism could be overcome, but was hardly yet a sufficient launching-pad to provide an internationalist solution to the international crisis.

THE PRESENT: THE IMPACT OF THE GREAT RECESSION

In the introduction, we identified three principal areas where we wanted to trace the effect of the Great Recession on RLPs: *intellectual/programmatic responses*; *organisational responses* and *electoral responses*. We now take each of these in turn.

Intellectual/Programmatic Responses

In general, our country cases accord with Costas Eleftheriou's observation (chapter 15) that 'RLPs' strategic responses were strongly shaped by their pre-crisis ideological, programmatic and organisational characteristics'. For many parties, the crisis simply confirmed existing ideological preconceptions, despite the absence of obvious dividends from existing stances. This tendency was particularly evident for conservative communists like the Greek KKE, Latvian Socialist Party, Portuguese PCP and the conservative/traditionalist elements of the KSČM. Such parties/tendencies interpreted the crisis as a manifestation of the cyclical crisis tendencies within capitalism and generally tended towards passivity rather than enhanced mobilisation, as if waiting for capitalism's contradictions to do their work for them. Despite their Leninist heritage and revolutionary self-image, the absence of more active interventions is fully explicable given these parties' ageing activist profiles and largely introverted strategies as guardians of the pro-Soviet subculture (e.g. the LSP has been more attentive to Soviet memory politics than the crisis; the KSČM's intellectual elite is 'exhausted', according to Handl and Goffin). Such parties have not risked fundamentally new approaches that might compromise their organisational and electoral stability, even when (as in the KKE's case), the result was to be outflanked by Syriza, a formerly junior party whose ability to adopt more flexible strategies was much more developed.

One feature of these parties' ideological traditionalism is 'particularist revolutionary anti-globalism' (Handl and Goffin, chapter 11); what we might alternatively see as indebtedness to Stalin's 'socialism in one country'. They argue that their position within the 'imperialist' division of labour makes transnational strategies within the European Union futile and therefore concentrate on building 'popular power' within the nation-state. This limits their inclination to international solidarity except with other (mostly tiny) communist forces. Hence their lack of enthusiasm for groups such as the PEL and lack of full engagement with the Greek crisis. Where they have even taken a strong position (not evident in the LSP's case), they have supported the KKE's ambiguously pro-Grexit positions rather than Syriza. Even the relatively moderate reform communist AKEL has been lukewarm in support for Syriza because of historical ties to its 'brother' the KKE. In the KSČM's case, the legacy of national communism reinforces its support for fiscal rectitude and low state indebtedness, further undermining solidarity with Greece.

In several cases (albeit not the KKE's) ideological traditionalism is reinforced by a lack of strong external incentives to change position (e.g. the Czech Republic's relatively mild crisis and the ethnicisation of the crisis in Latvia diminish the scope for international solidarity). The Ukraine crisis in 2014 further transformed international aspects of the European Union's crisis from economics and markets to questions of geopolitics and minorities. The Portuguese PCP did undergo a major shift at the end of 2015 in lending support to the socialist minority government and thereby ending its long-term strategic isolation. As Freire and Lisi argue, this is less an example of the PCP's ideological change than the left-wards tilt of socialist voters and pressure from the Left Bloc in particular.

Even other less doctrinaire parties show a mixture of ideological and strategic motives for making limited or vague intellectual responses to the crisis. For example, although they are very different parties, both the Icelandic Left-Greens and Cypriot AKEL are relatively pragmatic actors who have governed during the crisis. The governing experience involved adopting improvised, emergency policies, which were far from an ideal-typical radical left programme (including in both cases, implementing austerity). Therefore, after being ejected from government, neither was in a strong position suddenly to adopt a substantive radical critique. In AKEL's case, opposition has indeed been associated with some radicalisation (including increased Euroscepticism), but most efforts have been directed towards defending the record of the Christofias government. In the Left-Green's case, as Silja Bára Ómarsdóttir and Andrés Ingi Jónsson show, governmental participation was accompanied by significant dissent and defections. Yet since the dissenters have largely chosen an 'exit' route, this has left a smaller and more consolidated party, which even though a 'sharp turn to the left' has reaffirmed party identity, now has little incentive to fundamentally rethink previous positions.

Some moderate change is noted in several of our cases, principally Germany, France, Portugal (the BE) and Ireland. During the crisis, Germany's Die Linke has had to find a difficult balance between its traditional accent on consolidating the European Left and its national domestic context, which (like the Czech Republic) has externalised the crisis and is unsympathetic towards debtor nations. For Die Linke, the theoretical development of a crisis response (through Transformation Theory) has helped organisational consolidation by giving 'a common reference point against neoliberalism' (Amieke Bouma, this volume) and contributing to the formation of the new party programme. However, this has supplemented existing ideas and organisational strategies rather than fundamentally changing Die Linke's direction. The party remains, as before, internationalist, Europeanist and pro-Euro. Nor has the reformulation brought any obvious electoral dividends.

The crisis has played a similar function for the French Front de Gauche, acting as the ideological cement for this new radical left alliance (Escalona and Vieira, this volume). Nevertheless, the alliance's formation preceded the crisis, which has at best brought out different accents in party responses, rather than adding anything substantively new (perhaps excepting eco-socialism, which however has not yet been accepted as doctrine by the French radical Left). Since the crisis, the French radical Left has certainly become more Eurosceptic, but this is partially attributable to longer-term processes (e.g. the movement against the European Constitutional Treaty and bridge-building between the French Communist Party and the broader 'left of the left'). In Portugal, the main ideological trend has also been a hardening of Eurosceptic positions, which has allowed the Left Bloc and Portuguese Communist Party to find more common policy positions. It has still not changed their underlying philosophy however: the Left Bloc remains in favour of Eurozone membership and progressive change within the European Union (and even moderated somewhat in 2015), while the PCP is 'nationalist' and wants to exit the Eurozone.

For the Irish radical Left, the main ideological effect is the emergence of trends who look towards Podemos and enhanced organic grassroots interaction with the social movements. As Richard Dunphy shows (chapter 10), this tendency has been accelerated both by the profusion of left Independents and dissatisfaction with the feuding sectarianism of the Marxist Left and the faux-radical 'social republicanism' of Sinn Féin.

It's a similar story at EU level: the crisis has modified, but not fundamentally changed the emergent Europeanisation of the radical Left's principal EU-level bodies, the GUE/NGL and PEL (Holmes and Lightfoot, this volume). In this case, the change is, symptomatically, mostly negative. While the normative commitment to the idea of European integration (the 'Expansion-ist/Integrationist' consensus) remains intact and there is a solid consensus over economic and social policy, the crisis has 'polarised opinion about the EU within the transnational radical left' so that beyond day-to-day policy co-operation and rhetorical unity about 'Another Europe', a 'strong, coherent and united alternative' cannot be discerned. Indeed, the crisis has latterly seen the emergence of possibly contradictory initiatives, such as *Plan B in Europe* and now Yanis Varoufakis' Diem25 movement (officially launched in February 2016), which exist alongside the main bodies of the transnational radical Left, and may grow to compete with them.[6]

The two countries where there has undoubtedly been the most substantive programmatic change are Greece and Spain. However, whereas these are usually considered as two very similar examples of 'new' left-wing populist parties, our chapters do highlight significant differences between them. Podemos is most clearly a new party that has articulated an archetypally populist appeal. It tries to transcend left-right divisions in the political system, presenting itself as the political articulation of the 15M movements and mobilising around the moral people vs. corrupt political caste dichotomy adapted from Chávez's Venezuela. Nevertheless, it has been forced to develop a clearer radical left profile over time, as well as to emphasise more 'responsible' policy positions.

Syriza in contrast is a new constellation of previously existing organisations, principally Synaspismós. The crisis directly affected Synaspismós' internal composition, since in 2010 the proto-social democratic 'Renewers' defected to form the Dimar party; this allowed Syriza greater organisational consolidation around a radical left identity. Apart from populism, its most evident ideological innovation is its self-presentation as the 'government of the Left' and its increasing emphasis on office-seeking, which allowed it to draw on the heritage and support of the former centre-left PASOK party. As a product of potentially incompatible traditions, Syriza's positions have been shot through with contradictions, as evident in its strategic divisions over whether abolishing the Memorandum was a prerequisite for the viability of the government of the Left, or vice versa.

The alleged proliferation of populism deserves analysis, since it has been seen as one of the key results of the crisis. Apart from the obvious cases of Syriza and Podemos, it is clear that other parties have dabbled with populism, albeit to a less sustained or successful degree. One reason why Sinn Féin has surpassed the Marxist Left in Ireland is that it has been able to combine 'nationalist populism' with eclectic left-leaning policy positions, even though this position is partially compromised by its record in government in Northern Ireland (Dunphy, this volume). Conversely, the Marxist Left remains wedded to traditional Trotskyist ideological sectarianism, wherein 'streaks' of populism have failed to supplant 'class-against-class' politics. Many of the left Independents more effectively exploit locally based anti-Dublin populism. Other parties such as the Danish Red-Green Alliance have debated moving to more left-populist positions, albeit so far without resolution. At the same time, there is no universal populist moment. This volume confirms how some erstwhile populist parties (principally the Dutch SP) have largely jettisoned their populism in a search for governing responsibility. Others (e.g. the

KSČM and Die Linke) have elements of populism as part of their protest appeal (noticeably the KSČM's slogan of 'with the people, for the people', used for over a decade). However, neither party has a clear ideological direction, with numerous internal tendencies contesting their position.

Organisational Responses

Given parties' innate conservatism, significant organisational change is unlikely to occur for its own sake, but rather would most likely be accompanied by larger ideological or strategic change. Given the aforementioned general absence of fundamental ideological/strategic changes, we should hardly expect fundamental organisational post-crisis responses either. So it proves.

There are many parties, again most noticeably the conservative communists, where the watchword is organisational stability. The crisis has seen the continuation of previous tendencies, whereby parties such as the PCP and KKE try to preserve traditional hegemonic ties with class-based organisations. They have engaged with the crisis to the degree that they have tried to lead and harness traditional working-class revolt, in some cases successfully (for instance the PCP remains much more rooted in the trade unions than the Left Bloc). However, they retain a tendency to isolationism (most noted in the KKE and its PAME organisation, which tries to teach protesters 'correct' militant mobilisation).

The LSP and KSČM have been less effective still, mirroring their ideological passivity with organisational passivity. The LSP lamented its weak ties to trade unions, but the crisis saw little advancement and even the defection of the United Latvia youth organisation from the party. Only the KSČM's moderniser minority 'appear[s] to actually seek an intensive exchange of ideas with social movements' (Handl and Goffin, this volume). Most innovative thinking occurs outside the party, since many leftists consider the KSČM an obstacle to a modern radical Left.

Another significant 'no change' party is the Spanish United Left. As Luis Ramiro shows, owing to ideological traditionalism and internal instability (including debilitating splits), the IU has failed to achieve its original goals of becoming a new type of 'social and political movement' different from traditional parties. Its efforts to include individual members in candidate and leader selection have been 'neither very innovative nor inclusive' and it has become too decentralised without becoming correspondingly democratic. The perception that the party was rigid, conservative and incapable of creating a broad anti-austerity umbrella was the principal reason Podemos' founders gave for setting up their own party. It was only after Podemos' success that IU's leaders improvised derivative experiments with open candidate selection – too little, too late.

Most of the other parties observed have changed their organisational strategies only slightly. For instance, the Dutch SP has made minor adjustments to its long-established linkage strategies (office-seeking combined with internal centralisation and extra-parliamentary mobilisation). The SP preserves a high degree of centralisation and leadership dominance that allows strategic flexibility; this has minimised organised intra-party opposition or party splits during the crisis. Poor electoral results contributed to the resignation of party leader Agnes Kant, but Emile Roemer survived an identical (but more disappointing) result in 2012. The most obvious changes in linkage involve the party trying to wean the trade unions from the Labour party, as well as participating in anti-austerity protests and forging links with Occupy. However, in general the party has seen the newer movements as relatively weak and deserving little special attention.

France and Germany represent similar processes of new left unity projects that preceded the crisis and have continued through it in a process of incremental change and consolidation. Both the Front de Gauche and Die Linke have used the crisis to expand their links with anti-austerity groups (including Blockupy in the case of the latter). Yet neither group has developed fully effective forms of participatory or environmental linkage, largely because of internal divisions. The FdG is clearly less consolidated, still containing constituent parties with different traditions and ambitions (e.g. the pro-socialist position of the PCF versus the more movement-oriented Trotskyist traditions). Die Linke is a genuine party, but still contains a twin leadership and internal pluralism such that a unified response to the crisis has been absent. It is significant that it took serious intra-party discussion before effective links could be formed with Blockupy.

Moderate change and internal fission is most evident among the Irish Marxist Left. To the degree that the Socialist Party and Socialist Workers' Party now co-operate in broader anti-austerity alliances, which are focused less on ideology than concrete campaigns (e.g. against water charges), these parties have learnt from some of the more successful RLPs in recent times. However, the cumbersome name of their current project (Anti-Austerity Alliance-People Before Profit) indicates that this is far from an integrated initiative. As Richard Dunphy shows, it is the left Independents who may have the best chance of developing close links with social movements, local initiatives and new ways of 'doing' politics via a 'mass movement' party. However, at present, such a party remains only a theoretical possibility.

The Portuguese Left Bloc was formerly one such 'successful' RLP, with an apparently ideal-typical organisation combining centralisation and democratisation. Its three constituent founding parties formed as internal factions with an apparently stable controlled factionalism within the party. But, as Freire and Lisi show, this combination came under increasing stress during the crisis as initially poor electoral results and the retirement of long-standing party figurehead Francisco Louçã prompted an increase in internal dissent over the party's strategic direction and alleged internal centralisation. A protracted internal crisis contributed to further electoral decline and party splits before being resolved in November 2014 with a rethinking of the model of party leadership to create a more consensual party leadership body, the permanent commission of six members. This has so far been successful, with the new spokesperson Catarina Martins being an 'electoral asset', and a clearer more moderate and office-seeking strategy contributing to renewed electoral success. However, the party model still contains weaknesses, with relatively volatile connections to social movements, in decline in any case.

Forced organisational change is also evident in the case of the Cypriot AKEL and Icelandic Left-Greens, in these cases caused by their fraught participation in government. AKEL has managed the most organisational continuity, given its extensive democratically-centralised organisation and hegemony over the Left and social movements. Its main strategy in government was to deradicalise protest and to co-opt its affiliated organisations into the role of 'managing discontent – staging symbolic protest and ensuring that reactions were controlled' (Charalambous and Ioannou, chapter 14). Its approach to social movements was top-down and similar to that taken by the conservative communist parties. Newer social movement structures were created under party control or as online communities and independent intellectuals were allowed to develop more autonomous (but necessarily atomised) critiques. The strategy was successful in terms of minimising organised opposition to the party strategy, less so in terms of responding to the crisis more proactively or avoiding electoral defeat.

Like AKEL, the Left-Greens found themselves unprepared for government, but in this case, their smaller and less consolidated party organisation was given a severe buffeting under the pressure of contentious policy discussions such as the Icesave dispute and EU membership. Former strengths (the autonomous role for MPs and a lean party organisation) became severe weaknesses when the parliamentary group suddenly doubled in size and its party activists became embroiled in support for the MPs and parliamentary group: the party struggled to maintain engagement in grassroots activism and campaigns. Its parliamentary group and party organisation suffered numerous defections and splits. Yet the aforementioned dissident 'exit' has preserved the party's organisation and parliamentary group largely unscathed.

Dramatic organisational change is notable in only two of our case studies, Syriza and Podemos. It is notable that our contributors show little consensus over how to treat these parties. For David Bailey they are 'new anti-austerity RLPs' with unique ties to social movements and their struggles for authentic representation; for Óscar García Agustín and Martin Bak Jørgensen, Podemos is similarly an example (along with the Slovenian IDS) of a party with a unique ability to engage with social movements' struggle for democracy and new ways of doing politics via transversal strategies that include 'subjectivities excluded from the representative system'.

Other authors are less sanguine. The Irish Independents cited by Dunphy compare Podemos' alleged emergence from the mass movements with Syriza's top-down co-optation of them. Eleftheriou argues that Syriza's perceived inclusivity relative to the KKE's insistence on ideological purity was instrumental in it gaining new supporters, but agrees that Syriza played more of a role in legitimating social mobilisation than initiating it (e.g. via local 'solidarity networks'), and that this was accompanied by significant organisational centralisation, distancing from social movements and office-seeking 'realism' even prior to taking office.

Something similar, however, could be said of Podemos. It is an entirely new organisation (albeit formed from IU's cadres), and has undoubtedly been the most radically organisationally innovative of any party examined here. Luis Ramiro argues that 'Podemos entails a major departure from traditional models of party organisation', horizontal, participatory and inclusive, involving plenty of online participation opportunities, including in important party decision-making. Nevertheless, he also argues that Podemos' original leadership cadres have taken advantage of social movement mobilisation, with the emergence of a very presidentialised central leadership, alongside declining internal participation. In his view, Podemos 'was not created as the political branch of the movements nor is it the result of the social movements' political maturation'.

In sum, with the principal exceptions of Podemos and (only partially) Syriza, radical organisational change has been conspicuous by its absence. Most parties have continued established patterns with at best minor tinkering, and when modifications have occurred they have most been a reactive response (e.g. to electoral decline, leadership change or the pressures of government) than a proactive exploitation of opportunities. Organisational conservatism has won out.

Electoral Responses

Electoral responses to the crisis are much more divergent. Chapter 1 noted that there has been a marginal 'crisis bounce' for the radical Left across Europe, but that national-level trajectories differ markedly. Our chapters confirm this national variability. There are several parties who actually lost votes and/or seats in the most crisis-hit elections, principally the KSČM (2010), the SP (2010 and 2012) and the LSP (2010–2014). Others have had an initial boost that they have struggled to maintain (e.g. Die Linke and the

Icelandic Red-Greens in 2009, the Spanish IU in 2011). Others still (e.g. the PCP) have been relatively stable. In some countries, the radical Left was and remains marginal (e.g. the United Kingdom, and for that matter Austria and most of Eastern Europe). There are few countries where the radical left has made sustained growth (e.g. Denmark, Ireland). In only a handful has it made a genuine breakthrough (Slovenia, Spain and Greece).

What accounts for such divergence? In line with what our contributors have argued throughout, and particularly Luke March (chapter 2), we can posit an ideal-typical model of how the crisis should affect political parties (Figure 18.1).

This figure illustrates the most significant elements that we would expect to lead to RLP success, but is by no means exhaustive. These are grouped into *demand-side factors* (long-term socio-economic and electoral variables), *external supply-side factors* (party-system and institutional factors) and *internal supply-side factors* (factors internal to RLPs themselves). As already noted, the expectation is that even pre-crisis, the demand-side is conducive to RLP success in most countries. However, it will be particularly so where has been a tradition of strong class cleavages, a radical left 'legacy' (e.g. a strongly performing RLP in the communist era) and poor socio-economic performance perhaps allied to Eurosceptic and/or protest sentiment. The demand side is a necessary but not a sufficient 'breeding ground'; 'clever exploitation' of external conditions is required, meaning that the supply side is the main facilitator and/or catalyst for RLP success.

In terms of the specific effect of the Great Recession, in chapter 1 we referred to Kriesi and Pappas' characterisation of an economic crisis (measurable by decreasing GDP growth, increasing unemployment and government debt) and a political crisis (evidenced by rising electoral volatility, decreasing satisfaction with national democracy and trust in national parliaments). They acknowledged that this classification was broad-brush and minimalistic, and might have to be supplemented with other nationally specific factors. From our volume's chapters, we would add that the perception that the economic crisis has led to increased hardship, poverty and inequality should be important for RLP support; similarly, the perception that political elites are imposing austerity measures that are exacerbating this impact is also crucial (although the population may actively or passively support austerity measures).

Turning to the supply side, we have indicated that facilitating institutional factors are important.[7] When electoral systems are not very proportional, or there are high parliamentary thresholds, these generally weaken small parties' prospects, and RLPs are no exception. Particularly in Eastern Europe, RLPs have faced legal restrictions (Latvia being our principal example; with many former party members unable to run for public office and the LSP unable to employ the communist name).

Daniel Keith and Luke March

	Demand-side factors			External supply-side factors		Internal supply-side factors		Result
	Long-term electoral/cultural sympathies	Economic crisis	Political crisis	Institutional facilitators	Political facilitators	RLP ideology/strategy	RLP organisation	
Example factors	Strong class cleavages: strong ideological support for left parties; history of electorally strong left parties; high Eurosceptic sentiment	Decreasing GDP growth, increasing unemployment, government debt; rise in inequality and poverty	Rising electoral volatility, decreasing satisfaction with national democracy and trust in national parliament; austerity measures; corruption scandals or specific governmental crises	Low electoral thresholds, proportional electoral system, absence of legal restrictions on parties/candidates	Lack of effective crisis engagement from mainstream parties (esp. social democrats); social movement mobilisation	Flexible/pragmatic responses, open to new ideas and approaches (e.g. populism, new alliances, governmental participation)	Unified but flexible organisation lacking serious internal dissent/splits; responsive and popular leadership; strong links with social movements	RLP success

Figure 18.1   Ideal-Typical Model for Post-Crisis RLP Success. *Source:* Authors' calculations.

'Political facilitators' mainly refer to the behaviour of competitors (above all social democratic parties). Social democrats' inability to provide a cohesive critique of the crisis, to protect their supporters from it, and in many cases their intimate involvement in the very processes that caused the crisis will likely be a major incentive to RLPs to protest the 'neoliberalisation' of social democracy. We can expect this to boost populist arguments that the 'establishment parties' are identikit. Where the political elite as a whole is seen as unresponsive, incompetent and/or corrupt, we might expect the prospects for sustained extra-parliamentary social movement mobilisation to increase commensurably.

Such circumstances still need skilled party strategies to exploit them and 'seize the day'. Examples of such strategies include the general openness to new social and electoral alliances, and ideological flexibility, including pragmatism focusing on specific popular social campaigns. Populism is relevant here, since it helps downplay traditional RLP ideological verities in favour of a more emotive identitarian appeal that mobilises the dispossessed against incumbent elites. We have noted how various RLPs were indeed attempting to adopt elements of such strategies before the crisis, albeit with variable success.

The final element is party organisation, where a difficult balance must be struck. Parties need to be unified enough to avoid perennial 'Pythonisation', but flexible enough to accommodate new approaches, respond to incentives and change tack if necessary (i.e. conversely to avoid the inflexible unity of traditional democratic centralist parties). Party leadership needs to be internally strong, but also able reach beyond the party faithful and communicate effectively with the electorate, even if it need not be 'charismatic' as such.

We can now use these criteria to help illustrate our case studies (Table 18.1). Chapter 1 noted that the average vote change for RLPs since September 2008 was 2.7 per cent. We can therefore categorise parties as 'very successful' (above-average growth), 'moderately successful' (growth, but below average) and 'unsuccessful' (zero or negative growth) in the context of the international economic crisis.

Table 18.1 highlights several important issues. First, very few of our cases actually show very successful post-crisis results. Two of these are Podemos and Syriza, whose vote gains (approximately 20 per cent each) dwarf the remainder. The third is Sinn Féin, which, given its eclectic and inconsistent position, is a dubious gain for the radical Left. Second, the majority of parties (nine) are only 'moderately successful' with vote gains between zero and 2.6 per cent, reinforcing the fact that for the most part, RLPs' gains are incremental. Three parties are thoroughly unsuccessful. Third, the fact that the crisis (and demand-side factors generally) play only a contextual role is shown by the divergent fortunes of competing RLPs *within* the most crisis-ridden

Table 18.1 Explaining Our Case Studies' Post-Crisis Trajectories

	Demand-side Factors			External Supply-side Factors		Internal Supply-side Factors			
	Long-term Electoral or Cultural Sympathies	Economic Crisis	Political Crisis	Institutional Facilitators	Political Facilitators	RLP Ideology/ Strategy	RLP Organisation	Vote Change	No of Strong/ Positive Factors
Very Successful RLPs									
Spain (Podemos)	Mixed: once strong but declining RLP	Strong	Strong	Positive	Positive: social movement mobilisation and social democrat (sd) involvement in austerity	Positive: populist office-seeking strategy	Positive: New, flexible organisation with innovative strategies	+20.7	6
Greece (Syriza)	Positive: strong RLP history	Strong	Strong	Positive	Positive: social movement mobilisation and discrediting of political class	Positive: populist office-seeking strategy	Positive: increasingly centralised and dissenters choose 'exit'	+19.0	7
Ireland (Sinn Féin)	Negative: Catholicism, nationalism and weak class cleavages	Strong	Strong	Negative: STV system facilitates party splits and independents	Positive: social movement mobilisation and sd involvement in austerity	Positive: flexible office-seeking strategy	Positive; internally centralised	+5.0	5
Moderately Successful RLPs									
France (Left Front)	Mixed: once strong but declining RLP	Weak	Weak	Negative: presidentialism; electoral system disadvantages smaller parties	Mixed: moderate austerity	Mixed: some crisis response but internal divisions	Mixed: unificatory project but persistent internal divisions between constituent parties	+2.6	0
Portugal (BE)	Positive: strong RLP history	Strong	Strong	Positive	Largely positive: social movement mobilisation (but declining) and sd involvement in austerity	Mixed: divisions then office-seeking strategy	Mixed; internal divisions but addressed in 2014	+2.0	5
Iceland (VG)	Positive: strong RLP history	Strong	Strong	Positive	Mixed: RLP brought to government by crisis but unable to stay in power	Positive: office-seeking strategy	Mixed: multiple internal divisions but dissenters choose 'exit'	+2.0	5
Ireland (AAA – PBP)	Negative: Catholicism, nationalism and weak class cleavages	Strong	Strong	Negative: STV system facilitates party splits and independents	Positive: social movement mobilisation and sd involvement in austerity	Negative: movement towards coalition but sectarian	Negative: frequent schisms	+2.0	3
Germany (Die Linke)	Mixed: strongholds in East vs anti-communism in West	Weak	Weak	Mixed: 5 per cent electoral threshold	Mixed: sd involvement in grand coalition but minimal austerity	Mixed: some crisis response but internal divisions	Mixed: unificatory project but persistent internal tensions	+1.6	0

	Demand-side Factors			External Supply-side Factors		Internal Supply-side Factors			
	Long-term Electoral or Cultural Sympathies	*Economic Crisis*	*Political Crisis*	*Institutional Facilitators*	*Political Facilitators*	*RLP Ideology/ Strategy*	*RLP Organisation*	*Vote Change*	*No of Strong/ Positive Factors*
Spain (United Left)	Mixed: once strong but declining RLP	Strong	Strong	Positive	Positive: social movement mobilisation and social democrat involvement in austerity	Negative: lack of proactive response to crisis paves way for Podemos	Negative: persistence of internal ideological/ strategic disputes	+1.5	4
Cyprus AKEL	Positive: hegemonic RLP	Strong	Strong	Positive	Negative: RLP brought to government by crisis and unable to stay in power	Negative: concentration on defending governing record	Mixed: lack of internal rethinking but preserves hegemony over left	+1.6	4
Portugal (PCP)	Positive: strong RLP history	Strong	Strong	Positive	Positive: social movement mobilisation and sd involvement in austerity	Mixed: some crisis response and movement to governmental participation, but largely policy-seeking	Mixed: stable but not dynamic	+0.4	5
Czech Republic (KSČM)	Mixed: communist subculture vs. anti-communism	Strong	Strong	Mixed: 5 per cent electoral threshold	Mixed: corruption scandals but low social mobilisation	Negative: no obvious crisis response and internal divisions	Negative: moribund internal party life	+0.3	2
Unsuccessful RLPs									
Latvia (LSP)	Negative: socialism associated with pro-Sovietism	Strong	Weak	Negative: 5 per cent electoral threshold; anti-communist legislation	Positive: social movement mobilisation and right-wing austerity	Negative: no obvious crisis response	Mixed: stable but evidence of disaffection	N/a: lost seats	2
Greece (KKE)	Positive: strong RLP history	Strong	Strong	Positive	Positive: social movement mobilisation and discrediting of political class	Negative: focus on sectarian isolation	Negative: stable but isolationist	–1.9	5
Netherlands (SP)	Positive: RLP embedded in community and strong populist/ Eurosceptic traditions	Weak	Weak	Positive	Mixed: Sd in government but minimal austerity	Mixed: continuation of moderation and office-seeking but lack of distinction from sd	Positive: centralised, stable and flexible	–6.8	3

Source: Authors' calculations from data in this volume.

countries: the KKE, IU and Irish Trotskyists have been left far in the wake of Syriza, Podemos and Sinn Féin. The common element is the ideological/ strategic inflexibility of the former relative to the latter.

Fourth and relatedly, when parties are unsuccessful, supply-side factors are at least as relevant as demand-side factors, and usually more so. For example, in Latvia, the country with the world's worst crisis-related fall in GDP, the radical Left has made no ground. Whereas some of the reasons are demand-side issues (e.g. the subordination of class to ethnic cleavages), it is supply-side factors (the ability to politicise these cleavages, the LSP's inability to develop an independent, post-Leninist profile, and the *cordon sanitaire* placed around the 'Russian' parties), that are just as salient. Similarly, the relative absence of crisis phenomena in the Netherlands would not lead us to expect great growth for the SP, but its dramatic vote loss (Table 18.1) needs explanation. The table is admittedly partially misleading, because the SP gained its best ever vote in 2006, thereby exaggerating its decline (its post-crisis results are still over 3 per cent above its pre-2006 levels). Nevertheless, as Dan Keith's chapter shows, 2012 was an excellent opportunity for the party to capitalise on protest sentiment, an opportunity missed owing to the SP's 'social democracy plus' strategy, which made it vulnerable to losing votes to Labour once the latter ran an effective campaign.

Table 18.1 is also perhaps deceptive when it comes to the Cypriot AKEL, which is classed as a 'moderately successful' party. Yet, as Charalambous and Ioannou show, the full brunt of the crisis hit Cyprus only in 2011, and therefore AKEL's 2011 parliamentary election result does not fully indicate its post-crisis performance. Moreover, since Cyprus is a presidential system, AKEL's failure to keep hold of executive power after the 2013 presidential election gives reason to classify it as having been unsuccessful.

Another apparent distortion is the characterisation of the Czech case as comprising both strong economic and political crises when categorised under the Kriesi and Pappas framework. This *prima facie* conflicts with some of our authors' observations. For instance, Handl and Goffin note that the financial crisis was relatively short-lived, directly affected just one election (2010), while the Czech Republic maintained relatively low poverty and unemployment levels throughout. Nevertheless, they do concede that economic growth remained sporadic after 2008 and that crisis had ongoing (and growing) political consequences, such as the crumbling 'fragile stability' of the party system and the emergence of new parties trading on disappointment with the established parties. This accords with Vlastimil Havlik's view that, even though the crisis did not reach the intensity of some other countries, it nevertheless did have a significant and negative impact.[8] However, in other respects, the Kriesi and Pappas framework seems robust. For example, our authors concur that France and Germany were among the countries least hit by the financial crises, albeit for different reasons. Once again, this reinforces the persuasiveness of supply-side explanations. It is not the economic shock per se that has catalytic affect, but how it is perceived and politicised.

Die Linke and the Front de Gauche also deserve further comment, since they have made modest vote gains despite not having any strongly facilitative demand or supply-side factors. This is consistent with their growth as part of a regroupment process on the left involving high-profile social democrat dissidents that precedes the crisis and has marginally capitalised on it. Their electoral trajectory supports this diagnosis, with the strongest results in the parliamentary elections in 2009, and relative stagnation thereafter.

In sum, the electoral picture shows that dramatic advances are rare, and when they occur are the product of complex interrelated factors. Syriza and Podemos are clearly very distinct, not just in terms of having a huge vote increase, but also in terms of possessing nearly a 'full house' of beneficial facilitating factors. That Syriza possesses all of them shows how unique it is, with remarkably propitious combination of external and internal factors. Externally, Greece has suffered from a violent socio-economic cataclysm resulting in political polarisation, unparalleled in Europe (except Ukraine, for obviously very different reasons). Relatedly, the complete collapse of the mainstream left PASOK allowed Syriza to appropriate much of PASOK's electoral space, activists and organisation. Syriza's 'magic formula' for electoral success includes populist overtones that can unite different ideological tendencies by articulating popular anger against the 'oligarchy' and a pragmatic but principled approach to power (clear anti-austerity principles, but 'realist' demands and flexible coalition strategies with ostensible ideological opponents such as the Independent Greeks).

Podemos has certain similarities with and even advantages over Syriza: it has a still more developed populist ideology, a more media-savvy leader in Pablo Iglesias, and the above-mentioned presidentialist but inclusive party structure. All of this grants it still greater authenticity as a 'new' force battling the corrupt establishment 'caste'. That said, it has faced a less propitious external environment than Syriza, with the Spanish Socialists and the party system so far more resilient than in Greece. Moreover, as Luis Ramiro argues, had the United Left not underestimated Podemos, its rise could have been avoided from the start. Therefore, Syriza and Podemos show ideal-typical 'growth blueprints' for other RLPs, but are unlikely to foster quite such abundant growth in less fertile soil.

PARTY RESPONSE TO CRISIS IN THE AGGREGATE: NATIONAL CRISES, NATIONAL OUTCOMES?

In the introduction, we set out three competing groups of hypotheses derived from common understandings of the crisis. It is consistent with what we have said above that RLPs represent very diverse phenomena in each country, above all in terms of electoral and societal impact, and their crisis responses are filtered through a complex range of nationally specific factors. Therefore we should not expect any hypothesis to find universal validity. However, we can still identify common trends. Our first argument, the *radical insurgency thesis* finds general corroboration in the improvement in RLPs' average electoral ratings post-crisis, however modest. Moreover, RLPs have had at best below-average growth in countries not relatively strongly hit by the crises (e.g. Netherlands, France, Germany and Denmark).

Hypothesis 1a, that a deep economic crisis enables increasing support for the radical Left would appear to have general, but not always nationally-specific, validity. Hypothesis 1b, that a deep economic crisis combined with political crisis increases RLP support is more persuasive, particularly since it explains the main exceptions to H1a: in neither Latvia or the United Kingdom has a deep economic crisis been accompanied by a political crisis. Moreover, the countries most strongly hit by combined economic and political crises, especially the latter where the political establishment has been shaken to the core, have experienced the closest thing to a radical left 'insurgency', as spearheaded by Syriza and Podemos. We might also latterly add Portugal to this category: both Portuguese RLPs have individually experienced modest growth, but in 2015 and they were able to put aside historic differences and support a socialist government for the first time.

Our third sub-hypothesis H1c, that those parties that have most developed their populist appeal benefit in conditions of combined economic and political crises also finds general support. Populism has been a key part of both Podemos and Syriza's appeal, and is also evident in streaks across the Irish left spectrum. Clearly, populism is an ideology ideally placed to flourish in conditions of perceived people-elite polarisation. There appears to be a vicious circle in action; such conditions encourage populism, which in turn exacerbates the people-elite dichotomy. Populism clearly needs intent and effect: most other RLPs have populist elements but have not had incentives to develop this into core parts of their ideological appeal, which in turn potentially reduces their mobilisation potential.

This confirms that the crisis has been a major opportunity for the Left. What it does not confirm is the argument that victory in some countries can create a 'democratising chain reaction' across the continent.[9] This appears a version of Lenin's flawed theory of imperialism, and takes no account of intervening national or supply-side variables.

Our second argument, the *'no change' thesis*, finds some corroboration but on the whole is somewhat exaggerated. This thesis argues that there is no ideological trend in executive power rotation. There is admittedly no substantial movement for or against the radical Left here. Some RLPs have participated in executive power for the first time during the crisis (in Greece, Iceland, Denmark and now Portugal). This is a significant development for the radical Left itself but is the continuation of an existing trend of increasing governing aspirations (indeed AKEL was in office before the crisis). Moreover, the general rule that incumbents are judged retrospectively on their achievements is not one the radical Left has been able to shuck: both AKEL and the Left-Greens claimed policy achievements but were unable to avoid association with the crisis over which they had presided.

The main problem with this thesis is what it misses: focus on executive rotation ignores wider changes in the electorate such as rising electoral volatility and the emergence of protest parties of right and left, which may fundamentally alter the political climate without even challenging for office. Moreover, the argument that there has been no ideological movement in executive patterns depends on ones' viewpoint. From the radical left perspective, the normal course of executive rotation between centre-left, centre-right, liberal and occasionally right-wing populist parties indicates strengthening of the elite neoliberal consensus during the crisis. This argument is also overstated, but the inability of parties such as AKEL, Syriza and the Left-Greens to challenge the consensus indicates it is not baseless.

We developed two related hypotheses for this argument: that RLPs will not benefit from the crisis unless they become viable governing alternatives to incumbent parties (H2a), and that the main benefits will only occur in the very rare cases where RLPs become the dominant governing partner (H2b). The former finds some support: Syriza, Podemos, Sinn Féin and latterly BE have certainly been boosted when they have made their governing aspirations clear. Conversely, the Dutch SP's 2012 opinion poll lead foundered over concerns about its governing capabilities. Nevertheless, parties can still make significant gains when governing is a remote possibility (as with Syriza's initial breakthrough in 2012). The second hypothesis is much less plausible: gains for most parties (such as the Left-Greens or BE) have rarely been accompanied by realistic aspirations of becoming *dominant* governing partners, although governing aspirations have certainly often helped them increase support relative to other RLPs in their country.

Our third and final argument was the *'success shock' thesis*: that the crisis is more challenge than opportunity. This argument finds much corroboration within our volume: with a few notable exceptions, the crisis is at best an opportunity missed. Ideological and organisational conservatism has been the rule. Significant responses have generally occurred due to ongoing intra-party processes, and are not necessarily instigated by obvious external shocks like electoral defeats.

We can certainly identify the two 'success shocks' at the heart of this thesis. The 'electoral success shock' (when RLPs struggle to deal with unprecedented electoral success) is evident in the behaviour of AKEL and the Left-Greens in government and Syriza both before and after gaining power: unpreparedness for office, a lack of robust or appropriate party organisations, and sometimes simply lack of professional experience and/or competence have been evident. Conversely the 'dashed expectations shock', the failure to benefit from perceived golden opportunities has also been evident in the conduct of parties such as the BE, SP, FdG and Die Linke: it is not so much individual election results that cause disappointment, but the longer-term perception of underperforming. To some degree the BE and SP have resolved this with recently improved electoral/polling results, but the stalling of momentum has been evident in the latter cases.

Our related hypotheses were that ideological reasons make RLPs ill-prepared to benefit from the crisis (H3a) and that the conservative communists and the revolutionary extreme Left are least able to benefit from the crisis (H3b). Both these hypotheses find significant substantiation from our chapters. Of course, there are other reasons for RLPs to be ill-prepared, mentioned above, but ideological reasons are paramount. Whereas it is certainly true that many RLPs have tried to become more 'normal' office-seeking actors, turning from 'pariahs to players', this hardly means that they are fully de-ideologised.[10] The primary evidence of continued ideologisation is the number of parties using the crises to corroborate existing paradigms; second, while many parties are governed by office-seeking Realos, there is evident internal contestation over policy, with significant tendencies such as Syriza's former Left Platform seeking more maximalist policies. Third, with the exception of AKEL, which largely co-opted dissent, it is still arguable that RLPs struggle more than most party families in office, because of the gap between their ideological aspirations and the constraints of office. Finally, ideological proclivities are evident in parties' approaches to Europe. Holmes and Lightfoot note how most of the transnational radical Left agrees on the normative ideal of European integration, and on most concrete policies, but has no shared understanding of the European Union as an entity. The ability to agree over specifics but not the general is the clearest indication of a 'radical' viewpoint that sees structural and system-level factors as vital to its world view.

The argument that the conservative communists and the revolutionary extreme Left are least of all able to benefit from the crisis finds corroboration everywhere. The former parties have stagnated electorally and organisationally during the crisis. With the exception of the Irish Marxist Left (and also, it must be noted, the Labour Party of Belgium), the latter have not made parliamentary breakthroughs during the crisis and remain, as before, marginal.

In sum, that the crisis is both opportunity *and* threat is no paradox: traditionally the radical Left has faced a 'radical dilemma' of the trade-off between policy purity and efficacy and a temptation to 'radicalism through failure' where a lack of success paradoxically reinforces radical identity and the unreformability of the 'system'.[11] Given this ideological heritage, it is less surprising that a single-minded pursuit of electoral gain remains neither uncontested nor straightforward.

THE FUTURE: STILL WAITING FOR THAT DAY?

Κρίσις (*krisis*) in Ancient Greek meant so much more than 'crisis': it included 'judgement', 'choice' and a 'turning point' in a disease. To that extent, even as the most pernicious effects of the Crisis dissipate, Europe's radical Left is still in *krisis* as it remains at the juncture between marginality and the mainstream. To extend the medical metaphor, whereas Bull saw the communist movement as 'dead' in 1994, today's radical Left is in recovery, but hardly back to full health.[12] Relative to 1994, today's radical Left has regained the rudiments of a European movement, but remains more a collection of national stories than a convincing international narrative. This, as we have shown throughout, is both strength and weakness: strength, because RLPs can respond more flexibly and innovatively to national conditions than they ever could under Soviet tutelage; weakness, because neoliberal capitalism, and its cyclical crises, are an international phenomenon that appear immune to merely national remedies. What then are the prospects for today's radical Left? Do their crisis experiences show that this turning point can be the road to greater strength? There are three broad scenarios that we can envisage: first a renewed surge; second a return to decline; and third, the most likely trajectory in our view, incremental gains and 'muddling through'.

The Renewed Surge

Syriza and Podemos have shown many the way to go: and these 'movement party' models are already being emulated in unlikely places.[13] Even without direct emulation, there are diverse new left-wing initiatives being formed on the fringes of European party systems, such as the Polish *Razem* and the Workers' Front in Croatia, some of which may have good prospects. Jeremy Corbyn's leadership of the UK Labour Party can be seen as part of the same phenomenon: the radical Left is moving from the margins.[14] The numerous initiatives to re-found Europe can be seen as a sign of diversity and innovation.

Although at the time of writing, a modicum of financial stability has returned to Europe, the Greek crisis is by no means resolved, and in many places elsewhere the crisis and accompanying austerity have left a legacy of lower growth and higher unemployment that will take years to ameliorate (in the best scenarios). We have argued that the growth potential for the radical

Left was significant before the crisis; it will certainly remain more than sufficient to maintain reinvigorated RLPs for the foreseeable future.

While Syriza's capitulation to the TINA imperative of the August 2015 Third Memorandum shocked and dispirited many on the radical Left, its governing experience is still in evolution and may yet have a more measured ultimate outcome. At the least, it has failed to have the predicted deflating effect on RLP fortunes elsewhere, as the later 2015 elections in Spain and Portugal showed. Syriza still has many defenders who argue that it was not a 'strategic defeat' but a retreat and 'the only way to avoid the disastrous social, economic and political consequences'.[15] As David Bailey argues in his chapter, that the radical Left is losing its illusions about the European Union may even give scope for anti-capitalist, anti-representational viewpoints to grow.

Crisis Redux

A more negative view would argue that if no universal surge has occurred earlier, it will not now: the moment has passed. What if 2015 marked the high water mark before RLPs return to their previous irrelevance? Syriza's poll-rating is already in free fall and its government may end ignominiously. The radical Left is no nearer showing that it can make a difference in office. Declining results for the standard-bearers are likely to prove self-perpetuating: if the Left has the feeling of 'if not now – then when' and the perception of the crisis as a 'missed opportunity shock' becomes more widespread, this may have lasting ramifications for the Left's fragile credibility.[16] This view would make much of the exceptionality of Syriza and Podemos, particularly their reliance on propitious external circumstances, not least the 'Pasokification' of the social democrats. Although social democrats are certainly under threat elsewhere, the degree of implosion noted in Greece has not been replicated even in Spain, and absent such an all-encompassing crisis, will not be. The new pan-European initiatives are a sign of division, not strength, and have already been subject to telling criticism.[17]

In addition, an anti-capitalist, anti-representational critique might appear intellectually viable, but who are the agents of such a critique? Most successful RLPs are so strongly wedded to a 'reformist' anti-neoliberal, pro-representation critique that rapid strategic transformation is hard to envisage. But the more 'revolutionary' options are meagre. Such a critique would need to rely on three competing and relatively small constituencies: left-wing intellectuals, conservative communist parties and the revolutionary extreme Left.[18] Regarding the latter, Bailey himself notes that the Popular Unity group emerging from Syriza suffered an electoral fiasco. But in the absence of an electoral route, what prospects do such forces have?

A more damning critique still would argue that the tide of mainstream opinion in the European Union has moved decisively to the right. Not only did RLPs fail to fulfil the hopes of 2015, but the economic crisis is being increasingly subsumed to the refugee and immigration crisis in everyday political discourse. One might see evidence for this in Germany, where the emergent refugee crisis 'took the wind out of Die Linke's sails' (Amieke Bouma, this volume). McGowan and Keith's chapter also shows that because the radical left takes fundamentally internationalist and solidaristic approaches to immigration and asylum, it has not matched the Right's ability to frame immigration as a focal point for people's insecurity. In such circumstances, the populist Right will benefit, whereas it is 'the beginning of the end for Europe's radical left'.[19]

Incremental 'Muddling Through'

It is consistent with our view of the Janus-faced nature of crisis that we would expect both of the above pressures to play out to some degree. It is customary for leftists and analysts of the Left (particularly those of a Marxian bent) to think in terms of linear progress, 'leaps forward', 'wars of position' etc., and indeed we have used such terms in our work. Yet the recent history of the radical Left rarely shows such a clear picture of victory and defeats. Consider the Όχι vote, considered a 'catharsis' one week, but undermined by Syriza's own retreat the next. Generally, today's radical Left is too diverse, too nationally idiosyncratic and too reactive to progress in such a modular fashion. The very same reasons mean that it has been both unable to come up with a coherent response to the crisis, and that its constituent parts are unlikely to respond in a unified coherent way.

On balance, though we would tend towards a sober view of the immediate future, without accepting the most doom-laden scenarios. The threat of a crisis of capitalism has passed, capitalism has been stabilised, with at best limited gains for the radical Left. To this degree the 'window of opportunity' is closing and may not reopen for a considerable time. On the other hand, with the principal possible exception of the ailing and ageing conservative communists, the radical Left is now stable enough in most party systems to survive periods of more adverse conditions and recover. It is clear that any road to recovery will involve addressing more proactively twin challenges. First, how to become more flexible than hitherto within national party systems (potentially adopting *elements* of the innovative ideological and organisational approaches most evident in Podemos, without necessarily the full package).

Second, RLPs would need to develop more coherent and unified responses transnationally (with the weaknesses of the GUE/NGL and PEL most needing attention). Many on the transnational European Left agree, arguing that even the negative events of 2015 helped the radical Left's strategic thinking by starkly illustrating 'what its possibilities and limits are within the European Union's neoliberal architecture'. The consequence is that 'for the left … there can be no return to organisation on a purely national basis'.[20] This is easy to say, of course, but it may need to be repeated much in future.

NOTES

1. Martin J. Bull, 'The West European Communist Movement: Past, Present, Future,' in *West European Communist Parties After the Revolutions of 1989,* ed. Martin J. Bull and Paul Heywood (Basingstoke: Macmillan, 1994), 203–22. This chapter consciously references this earlier work in its structure and headings.

2. Luke March and Cas Mudde, 'What's Left of the Radical Left? The European Radical Left after 1989: Decline *and* Mutation', *Comparative European Politics* 3 (2005): 23–49.

3. Myrto Tsakatika and Marco Lisi, '"Zippin' up My Boots, Goin' Back to My Roots": Radical Left Parties in Southern Europe', *South European Society and Politics* 18, no. 1 (2013): 1–19.

4. Lucio Magri, *The Tailor of Ulm: A Possible History of Communism* (London: Verso Books, 2011), 418.

5. R. Neal Tannahill, *Communist Parties of Western Europe: A Comparative Study* (Westport: Greenwood Press, 1978), 242.

6. http://diem25.org/.

7. Cf. Charles Hauss and David Rayside, 'The Development of New Parties in Western Democracies since 1945', in *Political Parties: Development and Decay*, ed. Louis Maisel and David Cooper (London: Sage, 1978), 31–57.

8. Vlastimil Havlík, 'The Economic Crisis in the Shadow of Political Crisis: The Rise of Party Populism in the Czech Republic,' in *European Populism in the Shadow of the Great Recession*, ed. Hanspeter Kriesi and Takis S. Pappas (Colchester: ECPR Press, 2015), 202.

9. Cesar Rendueles and Jorge Sola, 'Podemos and the Paradigm Shift,' *Jacobin*, 13 April 2015, https://www.jacobinmag.com/2015/04/podemos-spain-pablo-iglesias-european-left/.

10. Jonathan Olsen et al., 'From Pariahs to Player? Left Parties in National Governments,' in *Left Parties in National Governments*, ed. Jonathan Olsen, Michael Koß and Dan Hough (Basingstoke: Palgrave, 2010), 1–15.

11. As discussed in Luke March, *Radical Left Parties in Europe* (Abingdon: Routledge, 2011), 13–14.

12. Bull, 'The West European Communist Movement: Past, Present, Future,' 213.

13. For instance, the Scottish RISE, http://www.rise.scot/#intro.

14. Albeit that this is hardly the victory for the radical Left it is often claimed, since the Labour Party has not adopted radical left policies (e.g. the dissolution of NATO), and there has been no obvious electoral dividend.

15. Michalis Spourdalakis, 'Rekindling Hope: Syriza's Challenges and Prospects,' in *The Enigma of Europe*, ed. Walter Baier, Eric Canepa and Eva Himmelstoss, Transform! Yearbook 2016 (London: Merlin Press, 2016), 222.

16. Luke Cooper and Simon Hardy, *Beyond Capitalism? The Future of Radical Politics* (Winchester: Zero Books, 2012), 2.

17. See George Souvlis and Samuele Mazzolini, 'An Open Letter to Yanis Varoufakis,' *LeftEast* (29 March 2016), http://www.criticatac.ro/lefteast/an-open-letter-to-yanis-varoufakis/; and the response: Yanis Varoufakis, 'What's DiEM25, Really? Reply to Open Letter by Souvlis & Mazzolini,' *LeftEast* (2 April 2016), http://www.criticatac.ro/lefteast/varoufakis-reply-to-souvlis-mazzolini/.

18. See for instance the debate 'Syriza in power: whither Greece?' between Stathis Kouvelakis and Alex Callinicos, https://www.youtube.com/watch?v=1paxMRddO0M.

19. Cas Mudde, 'Podemos, and the Beginning of the End for Europe's Radical Left,' *The Guardian*, 21 December 2015, http://www.theguardian.com/commentisfree/2015/dec/21/podemos-europe-radical-left-party-syriza-pablo-iglesias-spanish-elections.

20. Walter Baier, Eric Canepa and Eva Himmelstoss, 'The Enigma of Europe,' in *The Enigma of Europe*, ed. Walter Baier, Eric Canepa and Eva Himmelstoss, Transform! Yearbook 2016 (London: Merlin Press, 2016), 7–9.

Bibliography

Adamovsky, Ezequiel. 'Autonomous Politics and its Problems: Thinking the Passage from Social to Political.' Choike.org, 2006, accessed 30 November 2015, http://www.choike.org/documentos/adamovsky_autonomous.pdf.

Agustín, Óscar García. 'Podemos som postkrise-parti: Mellem populisme og radikalisme'. *Arbejderhistorie* 1 (2015): 34–57.

Akkerman, Tjitske. 'Immigration Policy and Electoral Competition in Western Europe. A Fine-Grained Analysis of Party Positions Over the Past Two Decades.' *Party Politics* 21 (2015): 54–67.

Allemagna, Lilian and Stéphane Alliès. *Mélenchon le plébéien.* Paris: Editions Robert Laffont, 2012.

Allen, Kieran. 'The Defeat of Syriza and its Implications for the Irish Left', 23 accessed August 2015, www.peoplebeforeprofit.ie/2015/07/the-defate-of-syriza-and-its-implications-for-the-irish-left.

Almeida, Dimitri. *The Impact of European Integration on Political Parties: Beyond the Permissive Consensus.* Abingdon: Routledge, 2014.

Alþingi. '"Störf þingsins." 132. fundur'. *Alþingi.* 15 April 2009, accessed 30 June 2015, http://www.althingi.is/skodalid.php?lthing=136&lidur=lid200904 15T103240.

Alonso, Sonia and Sara Claro da Fonseca. 'Immigration, Left and Right.' *Party Politics* 18, no. 5 (2012): 865–84.

Anastasakis, Othon. 'The Far Right in Greece and the Theory of the Two Extremes.' *Open Democracy,* 31 May 2013, https://www.opendemocracy.net/othon-anastasakis/far-right-in-greece-and-theory-of-two-extremes-0.

Anderson, Perry. 'Renewals'. *New Left Review* 1 (2000): 1–20.

Andolfatto, Dominique and Fabienne Greffet. 'La "semi-cartellisation" du parti communiste français.' In *Les systèmes de partis dans les démocraties occidentales. Le modèle du parti-cartel en question,* edited by Yohann Aucante and Alexandre Dézé, 321–46. Paris: Presses de Sciences Po, 2008.

Andolfatto, Dominique. *PCF: de la mutation à la liquidation*. Paris: Editions du Rocher, 2006.

Andrade, Juan Antonio. *El PCE y el PSOE en (la) transición*. Madrid: Siglo XXI, 2015.

Aranitou, Valia, Efthimios Papavlassopoulos and Michalis Spourdalakis. 'The Greek Political System: from Multi-level Governance to the "Stability Program"'. Paper presented at the 22nd World Congress of the International Political Science Association, Madrid, 8–12 July 2012.

ARD, Panorama, 17 December 2015, accessed 18 February 2016, http://www.ardmediathek.de/tv/Panorama/Panorama-die-ganze-Sendung/Das-Erste/Video?documentId=32347834&bcastId=310918.

Arter, David. '"Communists We Are No Longer, Social Democrats We Can Never Be": The Evolution of the Leftist Parties in Finland and Sweden'. *Journal of Communist Studies and Transition Politics* 18, no. 3 (2002): 1–28.

Arzheimer, Kai. 'Working Class Parties 2.0? Competition Between Centre Left and Extreme Right Parties.' In *Class Politics and the Radical Right*, edited by Jens Rydgren. London: Routledge: 2013.

Åslund, Anders and Valdis Dombrovskis. *How Latvia Came Through the Financial Crisis*. Washington, DC: Peterson Institute of International Economics, 2011.

Åslund, Anders. *The Last Shall Be the First: The East European Financial Crisis*. Washington, DC: Peterson Institute for International Economics, 2010.

Auers, Daunis. 'An Electoral Tactic? Citizens' Initiatives in Post-Soviet Latvia.' In *Citizens' Initiatives in Europe: Procedures and Consequences of Agenda-Setting by Citizens*, edited by Maija Setälä and Theo Schiller, 53–65. Basingstoke: Palgrave, 2012.

Auers, Daunis. 'The October 4th 2014 Parliamentary Election in Latvia.' *EPERN*, 28 October 2014, https://epern.wordpress.com/2014/10/28/the-october-4th-2014-parliamentary-election-in-latvia/.

Autain, Clémentine. 'Prendre la mesure du tournant historique.' *Regards*, 17 July 2015, accessed 23 July 2015, http://www.regards.fr/je-vois-rouge-par-clementine/article/prendre-la-mesure-du-tournant.

Azam, Nicolas. 'Européanisation et dynamique de changement partisan – Le Parti communiste français et l'Union européenne (1989-1999).' *Politique européenne* 43, no. 1 (2014): 46–67.

Baier, Walter, Eric Canepa and Eva Himmelstoss. 'The Enigma of Europe'. In *The Enigma of Europe*, edited by Walter Baier, Eric Canepa and Eva Himmelstoss, 7–9. Transform! Yearbook 2016. London: Merlin Press, 2016.

Bailey, David J. 'Palliating Terminal Social Democratic Decline at the EU-level?' In *European Social Democracy During the Global Economic Crisis: Renovation or Resignation?* edited by David J. Bailey, Jean-Michel De Waele, Fabien Escalona and Mathieu Vieira, 233–51. Manchester: Manchester University Press, 2014.

Bailey, David J. 'Resistance is Futile? The Impact of Disruptive Protest in the "Silver Age of Permanent Austerity".' *Socio-Economic Review* 13, no. 1 (2015): 5–32.

Bailey, David J. 'The Transition to "New" Social Democracy: The Role of Capitalism, Representation, and (hampered) Contestation.' *British Journal of Politics and International Relations* 11, no. 4 (2009): 593–612.

Bailey, David J. and Stephen R. Bates. 'Struggle (or its absence) during the Crisis: What Power is Left?' *Journal of Political Power* 5, no. 2 (2012): 195–216.

Bailey, David J. *The Political Economy of European Social Democracy: A Critical Realist Approach*. London: Routledge, 2009.

Bailey, David J., Jean-Michel De Waele, Fabien Escalona and Mathieu Vieira. 'Introduction'. In *European Social Democracy during the Global Economic Crisis: Renovation or Resignation?* edited by David J. Bailey, Jean-Michel de Waele, Fabien Escalona and Mathieu Vieira, 1–15. Manchester: Manchester University Press, 2014.

Bailey, David. 'The European Left after Recession and Representation: Social Democracy or Bust?.' *E-International Relations*, 14 June 2015, http://www.e-ir.info/2015/06/14/the-european-left-after-recession-and-representation-social-democracy-or-bust/.

Bale, Tim. 'Cinderella and Her Ugly Sisters: The Mainstream and Extreme Right in Europe's Bipolarising Party Systems.' *West European Politics* 26, no. 3 (2003): 67–90.

Bale, Tim. 'Turning Round the Telescope: Centre-right Parties and Immigration and Integration Policy in Europe.' *Journal of European Public Policy* 15, no. 3 (2008): 315–30.

Bale, Tim, Christoffer Green-Pedersen, Andre Krouwel, Kurt Richard Luther and Nick Sitter. 'If You Can't Beat Them, Join Them? Explaining Social Democratic Responses to the Challenge from the Populist Radical Right in Western Europe.' *Political Studies* 58, no. 3 (2010): 410–26.

Bale, Tim and Richard Dunphy. 'In from the Cold? Left Parties and Government Involvement since 1989.' *Comparative European Politics* 9, no. 3 (2011): 269–91.

Barry, Ellen. 'Latvia Is Shaken by Riots Over Its Weak Economy.' *The New York Times*, 14 January 2009, http://www.nytimes.com/2009/01/15/world/europe/15latvia.html?_r=0.

Bartels, Larry M. 'Ideology and Retrospection in Electoral Responses to the Great Recession'. In *Mass Politics in Tough Times*, edited by Larry Bartels and Nancy Bermeo, 185–223. Oxford University Press, 2014.

Bartolini, Stefano. 'The Strange Case of Europarties.' in *The Domestic Party Politics of Europeanisation: Actors, Patterns and Systems*, edited by Erol Külahci. Colchester: ECPR Press, 2012.

Baumgarten, Britta. 'Geração À Rasca and Beyond: Mobilisations in Portugal after 12 March 2011.' *Current Sociology* 61 (2013): 457–73.

BE. *Começar de novo*. Lisbon: BE 1999.

BE. *Compromisso Eleitoral – Bloco de Esquerda 2011: Mudar de Futuro, Pelo Emprego e Pela Justiça Fiscal*. Lisbon: BE, 2011.

BE. *Declaração da Comissão Política do Bloco de Esquerda*. Lisbon: BE, 2013.

BE. *Recuperar o que é Nosso. Manifesto Eleitoral Legislativas 2015*. Lisbon: BE, 2015.

BE. *Resolução Aprovada na VIII do Bloco de Esquerda 2011: A Esquerda Contra a Dívida*. Lisbon: BE, 2013.

Bell, David. 'Western Communist Parties and the European Union.' In *Political Parties and the European Union*, edited by John Gaffney, 220–34. London and New York: Routledge, 1996.

Bell, David and Byron Criddle. 'The Decline of the French Communist Party.' *British Journal of Political Science* 19, no. 4 (1989): 515–36.

Bergh, Johannes and Tor Bjrgarklund. 'The Revival of Group Voting: Explaining the Voting Preferences of Immigrants in Norway.' *Political Studies* 59 (2011): 308–27.

Bergmann, Eiríkur. 'The Icesave Dispute: Case Study into Crisis of Diplomacy during the Credit Crunch.' *ECPR General Council.* 2014.

Bermeo, Nancy and Jonas Pontusson. 'Coping with Crisis: An Introduction.' In *Coping with Crisis: Government Reactions to the Great Recession*, edited by Nancy Bermeo and Jonas Pontusson, 1–31. New York: Russel Sage Foundation, 2012.

Bernaciak, Magdalena, Rebecca Gumbrell-McCormick and Richard Hyman. *Trade Unions in Europe Innovative Responses to Hard Times*. Berlin: Friedrich Ebert Stiftung, April 2014.

Bernburg, Jón Gunnar, Berglind Hólm Ragnarsdóttir and Sigrún Ólafsdóttir. 'Hverjir tóku þátt í búsáhaldabyltingunni?' In *Þjóðarspegillinn* 2010, edited by Helga Ólafs and Hulda Proppé. Reykjavík: Félagsvísindastofnun Háskóla Íslands, 2010.

Betz, Hans-Georg. *Radical Right-Wing Populism in Western Europe*. New York: St. Martin's Press, 1994.

Bisky, Lothar. 'European Parliament Elections: Ambivalent Results for the Left.' *Transform! European Network for Alternative Thinking and Political Dialogue*, 2009. http://transform-network.net/journal/issue-052009/news/detail/Journal/european-parliament-elections-ambivalent-results-for-the-left.html.

Bithymitris, George. 'Union Militancy during Economic Hardship: The Strike at the Greek Steel Company "Hellenic Halyvourgia."' *Employee Relations* 38 (2016).

Bird, Karen, Thomas Saalfeld and Andreas Wust. *The Political Representation of Immigrants and Minorities: Voters, Parties and Parliaments in Liberal Democracies*. London: Routledge, 2010.

Bloom, Stephen. 'The 2010 Latvian Parliamentary Elections.' *Electoral Studies* 30, no. 2 (2011): 379–83.

Blyth, Mark. *Austerity : The History of a Dangerous Idea*. Oxford and New York: Oxford University Press, 2013.

Bosco, Anna. 'Four Actors in Search of a Role: The Southern European Communist Parties.' In *Parties, Politics, and Democracy in the New Southern Europe*, edited by P. Nikiforos Diamandouros and Richard Gunther, 329–87. Baltimore: The Johns Hopkins University Press, 2001.

Bosco, Anna. *Comunisti. Trasformazioni di partito in Italia, Spagna e Portogallo.* Bologna: Il Mulino, 2000.

Boucek, Françoise. 'Rethinking Factionalism: Typologies, Intra-party Dynamics and Three Faces of Factionalism.' *Party Politics* 15, no. 4 (2009): 455–85.

Bouma, Amieke. 'Left without Its Party: Interest Organizations of Former GDR Elites and the Transformation of the PDS/Linke'. In *Radical Left Movements in Europe*, edited by Magnus Wennerhag, Christian Fröhlich and Grzegorz Piotrowski. Farnham: Ashgate, forthcoming, 2016.

Bozóki, Andras and John T. Ishiyama, eds. *The Communist Successor Parties of Central and Eastern Europe*. Armonk: M. E. Sharpe, 2002.

Braemer Michael, 'Vælgerne: EL er de mindst stuerne.' *Ugebrevet A4*, October 2014, accessed 30 November 2015, http://www.ugebreveta4.dk/vaelgerne-el-er-de-mindst-stuerene_19867.aspx.

Brangsch, Lutz. 'Haben wir etwas gelernt? Was Syrizas scheitern für Linke in der Europäischen Union bedeutet.' *Rosalux* 3 (2015): 19–20.

Bratsis, Peter. 'The End of TINA.' *Jacobin*, 13 January 2015, https://www.jacobin-mag.com/2015/01/syriza-greece-election-tina/.

Brie, André, Michael Brie and Michael Chrapa. 'Für eine moderne sozialistische Partei in Deutschland. Grundprobleme der Erneuerung der PDS.' *RLS-Standpunkte* 7 (2002), https://www.rosalux.de/publication/15621/fuer-eine-moderne-sozialist-ische-partei-in-deutschland-grundprobleme-der-erneuerung-der-pds.html.

Brie, Michael and Cornelia Hildebrandt. 'Solidarische Mitte-Unten Bündnisse und Anforderungen an Linke Politik.' *Luxemburg. Gesellschaftsanalyse und Linke Praxis* 2 (2015), http://www.zeitschrift-luxemburg.de/solidarische-mitte-unten-buendnisse/.

Bull, Martin J. 'The West European Communist Movement: Past, Present, Future'. In *West European Communist Parties After the Revolutions of 1989*, edited by Martin J. Bull and Paul Heywood, 203–22. Basingstoke: Macmillan, 1994.

Callinicos, Alex. 'Thunder on the Left.' *International Socialism*, 26 June 2014, http://isj.org.uk/thunder-on-the-left/.

Candeias, Mario, Lukas Obendorfer and Anne Stecker. 'Neugründung Europas? Strategische Orientierungen.' *Europalinks. Beilage der Tageszeitung neues deutschland in Zusammenartbeit mit der Zeitschrift Luxemburg* (February 2014): 3–5, accessed 17 March 2016, https://www.neues-deutschland.de/artikel/923336.eine-vision-einstieg-in-ein-anderes-europa.html.

Candeias, Mario. 'From a Fragmented Left to Mosaic'. *Zeitschrift Luxemburg*, April 2010, http://www.zeitschrift-luxemburg.de/from-a-fragmented-left-to-mosaic/.

Candeias, Mario. 'Nichts mehr wie zuvor. Den Widerstand für ein anders Europa von Unten zusammenbringen.' *Rosalux* 3 (2015): 15–16.

Canovan, Margaret. 'Trust the People! Populism and the Two Faces of Democracy.' *Political Studies* 47, no. 1 (1999): 2–16.

Carlens, Sebastian. 'Wohin geht Die Linke?' *Junge Welt* (18 June 2015): 3.

Carles, Alexis. 'Mélenchon, de la Gauche au Peuple 2/2.' *Ballast*, 11 March 2015, accessed 12 June 2015, http://www.revue-ballast.fr/melenchon-de-la-gauche-au-peuple-22/.

Carvajal, Álvaro. 'La participación toca fondo en las polemicas primarias de Podemos.' *El Mundo*, 23 July 2015, accessed 20 December 2015, http://www.elmundo.es/espana/2015/07/23/55affbf1e2704e98178b458d.html.

Caselli, Francesco and Wilbur J. Coleman. 'On the Theory of Ethnic Conflict'. *Journal of the European Economic Association* 11 (2013): 161–92.

Cautrès, Bruno. 'Le vote Mélenchon. Le poids de l'héritage communiste et les limites d'une dynamique.' In *Le vote normal*, edited by P. Perrineau, 111–32. Paris: Presses de Sciences Po, 2013.

Charalambous, Giorgos and Christophoros Christophorou. 'The Cypriot Communists Between Protest and the Establishment: A Second Look at AKEL's Linkages with Society.' In *Party-Society Relations in the Republic of Cyprus: Political and Societal Strategies*, edited by Giorgos Charalambous and Christophoros Christophorou, 19–46. Abingdon: Routledge, 2015.

Charalambous, Giorgos and Iasonas Lamprianou, 'Societal Responses to the Post-2008 Economic Crisis among South European and Irish Radical Left Parties: Continuity or Change and Why?' *Government and Opposition*, 2014.

Charalambous, Giorgos and Christophoros Christophorou. 'A Society within Society: Linkage in the Case of the Cypriot Communist Party.' *South European Society and Politics* 18, no. 1 (2013): 101–19.

Charalambous, Giorgos and Gregoris Ioannou. 'No Bridge Over Troubled Waters: The Cypriot Left Heading the Government 2008–2013.' *Capital and Class* 39, no. 2 (2015): 265–86.

Charalambous, Giorgos and Gregoris Ioannou. 'Party Systems, Party-society Linkages and Contentious Acts: Cyprus in a Comparative South European Perspective' (forthcoming).

Charalambous, Giorgos. 'Taking Party Ideology Development Seriously.' *Rivista Italiana di Scienza Politica* XLIV, no. 2 (2014): 193–216.

Charalambous, Giorgos. *European Integration and the Communist Dilemma: Communist Party Responses to Europe in Greece, Cyprus and Italy.* Farnham: Ashgate, 2013.

Charalambous, Giorgos. *Political Culture and Behaviour in the Republic of Cyprus During the Crisis.* Nicosia: Peace Research Institute Oslo – Cyprus Centre, 2014.

Charalambous, Giorgos. 'All the Shades of Red: Examining the Radical Left's Euroscepticism.' *Contemporary Politics* 17, no. 3 (2011): 299–320.

Cheskin, Ammon. 'History, Conflicting Collective Memories, and National Identities: How Latvia's Russian-Speakers are Learning to Remember.' *Nationalities Papers* 40, no. 4 (2012): 561–84.

Cheskin, Ammon. *Russian Speakers in Post-Soviet Latvia: Discursive Identity Strategies.* Edinburgh: Edinburgh University Press, 2016.

Chioccetti, Paulo. 'The Radical Left at the 2014 European Parliament Election.' In *The Left in Europe after the EU Elections: New Challenges*, edited by Cornelia Hildebrandt Rosa Luxemburg Stiftung, 7–14, Berlin, 2014.

Chiocchetti, Paolo. 'The Radical Left at the 2014 EP Election'. *Transform!*, 27 June 2014, http://www.transform-network.net/en/blog/blog-2014/news/detail/Blog/-c5f323c33b.html.

Chrapa, Michael. 'Interne Konfliktpotentiale und Modernisierungschancen der PDS. Situation, Anforderungen, Optionen.' *UTOPIE Kreativ* 113 (2000): 276–83.

Christensen, Paul T. 'Socialism after Communism?: The Socioeconomic and Cultural Foundations of Left Politics in Post-Soviet Russia'. *Communist and Post-Communist Studies* 31, no. 4 (1998): 345–57.

Chubb, Basil. *The Government and Politics of Ireland.* Oxford: Oxford University Press, 1970.

Císař, Ondřej. 'The Left in the Beginning of the 21st Century.' In *Trajectories of the Left*, edited by Lubomír Kopeček, 11–28. Brno: CDK, 2005.

Clark, Alistair, Karin Bottom and Colin Copus. 'More Similar than they'd Like to Admit? Ideology, Policy and Populism in the Trajectories of the British National Party and Respect.' *British Politics* 3, no. 4 (2008): 511–34.

Clausen, Per. 'Ehl. opfordrer til at stRGAtte flygtninge under jorden.' Published 14 September 2009, accessed 20 September 2015, https://enhedslisten.dk/artikel/ehl-opfordrer-til-sttte-flygtninge-under-jorden-11483.

Clogg, Richard. *Parties and Elections in Greece: The Search for Legitimacy.* Durham: Duke University Press, 1987, 171–81.

Coakley, John and Michael Gallagher. *Politics in the Republic of Ireland.* London: Routledge, 2010, fifth edition.

Coffé, Hilde and Rebecca Plassa. 'Party policy position of Die Linke: A continuation of the PDS?' *German Politics* 16, no. 6 (2010): 721–35.

Colau, Ada 'First we take Barcelona ...', *Open Democracy* 20 May 2015, https://www.opendemocracy.net/can-europe-make-it/ada-colau/first-we-take-barcelona

Colau, Ada. 'Making the democratic revolution happen,' *Diario Público*, 5 December 2014, http://adacolau.cat/en/post/making-democratic-revolution-happen.

Cole, Alistair M. 'Factionalism, the French Socialist Party and the Fifth Republic: An Explanation of Intra-party Divisions.' *European Journal of Political Research* 17 (2009): 77–94.

Conti, Nicolò, and Vincenzo Memoli. 'The Multi-Faceted Nature of Party-Based Euroscepticism'. *Acta Politica* 47, no. 2 (April 2012): 91–112.

Cooper, Luke and Simon Hardy. *Beyond Capitalism? The Future of Radical Politics.* Winchester: Zero Books, 2012.

Copenhagen Post. 'Justice Ministry grants seven year old second chance at residency.' Published online 9 January 2012, accessed 20 September 2015, http://cphpost.dk/news14/immigration-denmark/justice-ministry-grants-seven-year-old-second-chance-at-residency.html.

Corbière, Alexis. 'Au PG, notre "plan B" envisage la sortie de l'euro.' *Marianne*, 27 July 2015, accessed 27 July 2015, http://www.marianne.net/alexis-corbiere-au-pg-notre-plan-b-envisage-sortie-euro-100235722.html.

Crespy, Amandine. 'La cristallisation des résistances de gauche à l'intégration européenne: les logiques de mobilisation dans la campagne référendaire française de 2005'. *Revue internationale de politique comparée* 15, no. 4 (2008): 589–603.

Crouch, Colin. *The Strange Non-Death of Neoliberalism.* Cambridge, UK: Polity Press, 2011.

Cruz, Rafael. *El Partido Comunista de España en la Segunda República.* Madrid: Alianza, 1987.

Cuperus, Rene. 'Electoral Bloodbath for Dutch Labour.' *Policy Network* 26 March 2014 Policy Network, accessed 10 August 2015, http://www.policy-network.net/pno_detail.aspx?ID=4604&title=Electoral-bloodbath-for-Dutch-Labour-.

Daiber, Birgit, Cornelia Hildebrandt and Anna Striethorst (eds.). *Von Revolution bis Koalition. Linke Partein in Europa.* Berlin: Karl Dietz Verlag, 2010.

Daiber, Birgit. 'Über den Gebrauchswert der Linksparteien.' In *Von Revolution bis Koalition. Linke Parteien in Europa*, edited by Birgit Daiber, Cornelia Hildebrandt and Anna Striethorst, 39–48. Berlin: Karl Dietz Verlag, 2010.

Dahlström, Carl and Anders Sundell. 'A Losing Gamble. How Mainstream Parties Facilitate Anti-immigrant Party Success.' *Electoral Studies* 31 (2012): 353–63.

Dahlström, Carl and Peter Esaiasson. 'The Immigration Issue and Anti-Immigrant Party Success in Sweden 1970-2006: A Deviant Case Analysis.' *Party Politics* 19 (2011): 343–64.

Damro, Chad. 'Market Power Europe'. *Journal of European Public Policy* 19, no. 5 (2012): 682–99.

Daniel, Philip, Ruud De Mooij, Thornton Matheson and Geerten Michielse. 'Iceland: Advancing Tax Reform and the Taxation of Natural Resources.' *IMF.* Country Report No 11/138. 2011.

Day, Stephen. 'Between "Containment" and "Transnationalization."' *Acta Politica* 49 (2014): 5–29.

de Giorgi, Elisabetta, Catherine Moury and João Pedro Ruivo. 'Governing Portugal in Hard Times: Incumbents, Opposition and International Lenders.' *Journal of Legislative Studies* 21 (2015): 54–74.

de Jong, Alex. 'From Sect to Mass Party', *Jacobin*, 10 July 2014, accessed 1 September 2015, https://www.jacobinmag.com/2014/10/from-sect-to-mass-party/.

de Jong, Alex. 'Netherlands Elections: A Hangover Instead of an Earthquake.' *International Journal of Socialist Renewal* 12 September 2012.

de Jong, Alex. 'The Long March of the Dutch Socialist Party.' In *Institute for Research and Education Working Paper 35*. Amsterdam: Institute for Research and Education, 2014.

de Jong, Dennis. 'De Euro Heeft Een Plan B Nodig', SP, 23 November 2010, accessed 1 September 2015, https://www.sp.nl/nieuws/2010/11/jong-euro-heeft-plan-b-nodig.

de Jong, Dennis. Europese Bankenwetgeving Gatenkas, 16 April 2013, https://www.sp.nl/nieuws/2013/04/jong-europese-bankenwetgeving-gatenkaas, accessed 1 September 2015.

de Jong, Dennis. *The Euro has a Plan B,* SP, accessed 20 September 2014, http://www.sp.nl/nieuwsberichten/8151/101123-de_jong_de_euro_heeft_plan_b_nodig.html.

Deegan-Krause, Kevin and Tim Haughton. 'A Fragile Stability. The Institutional Roots of Low Party System Volatility in the Czech Republic, 1990-2009.' *Czech Journal of Political Science* 7, no. 3 (2010): 227–41.

della Porta, Donatella. 'Del 15M a Podemos: resistencia en tiempos de recesión.' *Encrucijadas. Revista Crítica de Ciencias Sociales* 9 (2015): 1–11.

Demar. 'Ανακοίνωση της Δημοκρατικής Αριστεράς για την πολιτική κατάσταση, την κινητοποίηση των πολιτών και την οικονομία', 6 June 2011.

Demirovic, Alex. 'Regieren reicht nicht. Der Fall Griechenland zeigt: Europa muss radikal demokratisiert werden.' *Rosalux* 3 (2015), 13–4.

Die Linke, 'Mitgliederzahlen 2014', accessed 28 August 2015, http://www.die-linke.de/partei/fakten/mitgliederzahlen/.

Die Linke, 'Programme of the Die Linke Party', Resolution of the Party Congress, Erfurt, 21–23 October 2011, en.die-linke.de/fileadmin/download/english_pages/programme_of_the_die_linke_party_2011/programme_of_the_die_linke_party_2011.pdf.

Die Linke, 'Programmentwurf', accessed 28 August 2015, http://www.die-linke.de/programm/programmdebatte/leitantrag-an-den-erfurter-parteitag/programmentwurf/.

Die Linke. 'Für ein Ende der neoliberalen Traurigkeit – Europa anders machen. Resolution des Bielefelder Parteitages.' Resolution adopted at the Die Linke party congress 6–7 June 2015, *Disput* (June 2015): 55–6.

Die Linke. 'GUE/NGL – die Fraktion der LINKEN im Europäischen Parlament', accessed 1 December 2015, http://www.dielinke-europa.eu/article/8985..html.

Die Linke. 'Programmatische Eckpunkte – Programmatisches Gründungsdokument der Partei DIE LINKE. Beschluss der Parteitage von WASG und Linkspartei. PDS am 24. und 25. März 2007 in Dortmund', accessed 18 February 2016, http://www.die-linke.de/fileadmin/download/dokumente/alt/programmatische_eckpunkte.pdf.

Die Linke. *100% Sozial. Wahlprogramm zur Bundestagswahl 2013*, accessed 17 March 2016, http://www.die-linke.de/die-linke/wahlen/archiv/archiv-fruehere-wahlprogramme/wahlprogramm-2013/wahlprogramm-2013/.

Documentatiecentrum Nederlandse Politieke Partijen. 'SP ledentallen' 1992–2015. 25 February 2015, accessed 1 September 2015, http://dnpp.ub.rug.nl/dnpp/pp/sp/leden.

Dolejš, Jiří. 'CO s řeckými dluhy?.' *Blog Aktuálně.cz*, 20 June 2011, accessed 10 July 2015, http://blog.aktualne.cz/blogy/jiri-dolejs.php?itemid=13516.

Dolejš, Jiří. 'Ekonomická krize a krize ekonomů.' *Blog Aktuálně.cz*, 6 April 2010, accessed 10 July 2015, http://blog.aktualne.cz/blogy/jiri-dolejs.php?itemid=9435.

Dolejš, Jiří. 'Je tu krize – zbavme se stereotypů.' Blog Aktuálně.cz, 9 February 2009, accessed 10 July 2015, http://blog.aktualne.cz/blogy/jiri-dolejs.php?itemid=5844#more.

Dolejš, Jiří. 'Sýček Klaus o fiskální unii.' *Blog Aktuálně.cz*, 14 December 2010, accessed 10 July 2015, http://blog.aktualne.cz/blogy/jiri-dolejs.php?itemid=11588.

Dolejš, Jiří. 'Vláda nemá lék na hospodářský propad.' *Parlamentní listy*, 16 March 2013 accessed 10 July 2015, http://www.parlamentnilisty.cz/arena/politici-volicum/Dolejs-KSCM-Vlada-nema-lek-na-hospodarsky-propad-265648.

Dolejš, Jiří. 'Základní směry v diskusi o socialismu v 21. Století.' *KSČM, 2012*, accessed 23 August 2015, https://www.kscm.cz/nazory-a-polemika/61135/zakladni-smery-v-diskusi-o-socialismu-v-21-stoleti?previev=archiv.

Doran, James. 'Democratic Wealth and Building up the Institutions of the Left.' *openDemocracy*, 15 October 2013, http://www.opendemocracy.net/ourkingdom/james-doran/democratic-wealth-and-building-up-institutions-of-left.

Doukas, George. 'The Thirteenth Congress of the KKE: Defeat of the Renovators.' *Journal of Communist Studies* 7 (1991): 393–8.

Dragassakis, Yannis. 'The Economic Program of SYRIZA-EKM', *Socialist Project E-Bulletin* 653 (2012), accessed 16 February 2016, http://www.socialistproject.ca/bullet/653.php.

Drda, Adam and Petr Dudek. 'Kdo ve stínu čeká na moc. Čeští komunisté po listopadu 1989.' Praha: Paseka, 2006.

Drousiotis, Makarios. *The First Partition*. Athens: Alfadi, 2005.

Dunphy, Richard and Luke March. 'Seven Year Itch?: The European Left Party: Struggling to Transform the EU.' *Perspectives on European Politics and Societies* 14, no. 4 (2013): 520–37.

390 Bibliography

Dunphy, Richard and Stephen Hopkins. 'The Organizational and Political Evolution of the Workers' Party of Ireland.' The Journal of Communist Studies 8, no. 3 (1992): 91–118.
Dunphy, Richard and Tim Bale. 'Red Flag Still Flying? Explaining AKEL – Cyprus's Communist Anomaly.' Party Politics 13, no. 3 (2007): 287–304.
Dunphy, Richard and Tim Bale. 'The Radical Left in Coalition Government: Towards a Comparative Measurement of Success and Failure'. Party Politics 17, no. 4 (2011): 488–504.
Dunphy, Richard. 'In Search of an Identity: Finland's Left Alliance and the Experience of Coalition Government.' Contemporary Politics 13, no. 1 (2007): 37–55.
Dunphy, Richard. 'The Workers' Party and Europe: Trajectory of an Idea.' Irish Political Studies 7 (1992): 21–39.
Dunphy, Richard. Contesting Capitalism?: Left Parties and European Integration. Manchester: Manchester University Press, 2004.
Edinaya Latviya. '"Edinaya Latviya": Rubiks Nas Obmanul.' United Latvia Webpage, 10 June 2010, http://www.vienotalatvija.lv/index.php?option=com_content&view=article&id=113%3A-l-r-&catid=3%3Anewsflash&Itemid=11&lang=ru.
Egilsson, Gunnar Smári. 'Vantar fleiri mál til að vera á móti'. Fréttablaðið 20 January 2003: 14.
Einarsdóttir, Lára Hanna. 'Ári síðar – þingið og byltingin'. eyjan.is. 23 January 2010, accessed 30 June 2015, http://blog.pressan.is/larahanna/2010/01/23/ari-sidar-thingid-og-byltingin/.
EL. 'Udlændingepolitik og statsborgerskab.' Published online 29 October 2013, accessed 20 September 2015, http://enhedslisten.dk/artikel/udlpercentC3percentA6ndingepolitik-og-statsborgerskab-71981.
EL. 'SpRGArgsmål og svar om flygtninge i Europa.' Published Online 2015, accessed 20 September 2015, http://enhedslisten.dk/spoergsmaal-og-svar-om-flygtninge-i-europa.
El-Ojeili, Chamsy. Beyond Post-Socialism: Dialogues with the Far-Left. Basingstoke: Palgrave Macmillan, 2015.
Eleftheriou, Costas and Chrisanthos Tassis. ΠΑΣΟΚ: Η άνοδος και η πτώση (;) ενός ηγεμονικού κόμματος. Athens: Savvalas, 2013.
Eleftheriou, Costas, 'The "uneasy symbiosis": Factionalism and Radical Politics in Synaspismós'. Paper presented at the 4th Hellenic Observatory PhD Symposium, London, 19–21 June 2009.
Eleftheriou, Costas. 'Η ελληνική ριζοσπαστική αριστερά και η κρίση (2010-2015): Όψεις μιας μεγάλης ανατροπής', Synchrona Themata 130–1 (2015).
Eleftheriou, Costas. 'Ρωγμές στον μονόλιθο; Το ΚΚΕ στις εκλογές του 2012.' In 2012: Ο διπλός εκλογικός σεισμός, edited by Yannis Voulgaris and Ilias Nicolacopoulos, 51–184. Athens: Themelio, 2014.
Ellinas, Antonis A. 'The Rise of Golden Dawn: The New Face of the Far Right in Greece'. South European Society and Politics 18 (2013): 556–9.
Ellinas, Antonis A. and Yiannos Katsourides. 'Organisational Continuity and Electoral Endurance: The Communist Party of Cyprus.' West European Politics 36, no. 4 (2013): 859–82.

Enhedslisten, *Partiprogram* 1996, accessed 30 November 2015, http://www.arbejder-museet.dk/index.php?option=com_docman&task=cat_view&gid=21&Itemid=238.

Erlingsdóttir, Auður Lilja. 'The Left in Iceland'. In *From Revolution to Coalition – Radical Left Parties in Europe*, edited by Birgit Daiber, Cornelia Hildebrandt and Anna Striethorst, 41–9. Berlin: Rosa-Luxemburg-Foundation, 2012.

Errejón, Iñigo and Chantal Mouffe. *Construir pueblo. Hegemonía y radicalización de la democracia*. Barcelona: Icaria, 2015.

Errejón, Íñigo, 'Spains's *Podemos*: An inside view of a radical left sensation.' *Links* (2014), accessed 20 December 2015, http://links.org.au/node/3969.

Escalona, Fabien and Mathieu Vieira. 'France'. In *The Palgrave Handbook of Social Democracy in the European Union*, edited by Jean-Michel De Waele, Fabien Escalona and Mathieu Vieira, 127–62. Basingstoke and New York: Palgrave Macmillan, 2013.

Escalona, Fabien and Mathieu Vieira. 'Le sens et le rôle de la résistance à l'UE pour le Parti de gauche'. *Politique européenne* 43, no. 1 (2014): 68–92.

Escalona, Fabien and Mathieu Vieira. 'The Radical Left in Europe. Thoughts About the Emergence of a Family'. *Fondation Jean-Jaurès* (2013): 1–17.

EuroMemo Gruppe. 'EuroMemorandum 2015, Die Zukunft der Europäischen Union. Stagnation und Polarisierung oder eine grundlegende Neuausrichtung?' Supplement to the *Zeitschrift Sozialismus* 3 (2015).

Eurostat. 'Unemployment Statistics', Eurostat accessed 1 September 2015, http://ec.europa.eu/eurostat/statistics-explained/index.php/Unemployment_statistics.

Eyjan.is. 'VG með kröfu um riftun Magma-samningsins – Samfylkingin áminnt', 24 July 2010, accessed 5 November 2015, http://eyjan.pressan.is/frettir/2010/07/24/vg-med-krofu-um-riftun-magma-samningsins-samfylkingin-ihugi-sina-stodu/.

Fagerholm, Andreas. 'What Is Left for the Radical Left? A Comparative Examination of the Policies of Radical Left Parties in Western Europe before and after 1989'. *Journal of Contemporary European Studies* (2016): doi:10.1080/14782804.2016. 1148592.

Fernández-Albertos, José. *Los votantes de Podemos*. Madrid: Catarata, 2015.

Filardo, Andrew, Jason George, Mico Loretan, Ma Guonan, Anella Munro, Ilhyock Shim, Philip Woodridge, James Yetman and Haibin Zhu. 'The International Financial Crisis: Timeline, Impact and Policy Responses in Asia and the Pacific'. BIS Papers. Bank for International Settlements, July 2010, http://www.bis.org/publ/bppdf/bispap52c.pdf.

Filip, Vojtěch. 'Nabízíme spolupráci všem, kteří vyznávají levicové myšlenky', accessed 10 July 2015, http://www.kscm.cz/article.asp?thema=3892&item=48984.

Finn, Daniel. 'Order Reigns in the Hague: The Dutch Elections and the Socialist Party'. *New Left Review* 77 (2012): 71–80.

Fitzgerald, Laura. 'Organised Left Force or Disparate Independents?.' *The Socialist* 93 (July–August 2015).

Flesher Fominaya, Cristina. 'Autonomous Movement and the Institutional Left: Two Approaches in Tension in Madrid's Anti-globalization Network.' *South European Society & Politics* 12, no. 3 (2007): 335–58.

Flesher Fominaya, Cristina. 'Debunking Spontaneity: Spain's 15M/*Indignados* as Autonomous Movement.' *Social Movement Studies: Journal of Social, Cultural and Political Protest* 14, no. 2 (2014): 142–63.

Flesher Fominaya, Cristina. 'Redefining the Crisis/Redefining Democracy: Mobilising for the Right to Housing in Spain's PAH Movement.' *South European Society and Politics* (forthcoming).

Fondation Copernic. 'Appel des 200 contre le Traité constitutionnel européen', accessed 11 February 2016, http://www.fondation-copernic.org/index.php/2004/10/14/appel-des-200-contre-le-traite-constitutionnel-europeen-octobre-2004/.

Foucault, Martial and Florent Gougou. 'Regard rétrospectif sur les élections municipales de mars 2014. Un vote sanction dans la logique des élections intermédiaires.' *Revue Politique et Parlementaire* 1075 (2015): 109–27.

Framkvæmdanefnd um einkavæðingu 2003. *'Einkavæðing 1999-2003'*. Reykjavík: 2003.

Frampton, Martyn. *The Long March: The Political Strategy of Sinn Féin, 1981-2007*. Basingstoke: Palgrave Macmillan, 2009.

Framsóknarflokkurinn. 'Ályktun um stjórnlagaþing frá flokksþingi.' 19 January 2009, accessed 5 November 2015, http://wayback.vefsafn.is/wayback/20090403105814/http:/www.framsokn.is/Flokkurinn/Fyrir_fjolmidla/Frettir/?b=1,3719,news_view.html.

Franks, Ben. 'The Direct Action Ethic: From 59 Upwards.' *Anarchist Studies* 11, no. 1 (2003): 16–41.

Freire, André, Marco Lisi and Inês Lima. 'Crise económica, política de austeridade e o potencial de coligação da "esquerda radical" portuguesa.' In *Crise Económica, Políticas de Austeridade e Representação Política*, edited by André Freire, Marco Lisi and José Manuel Leite Viegas, 385–410. Lisbon: Assembleia da República, 2015.

Freire, André, Emmanouil Tsatsanis and Inês Lima. 'Portugal in Times of Crisis: Value Change and Policy Representation.' In *Values, Economic Crisis and Democracy*, edited by Malina Voicu, Ingvill C. Mochmann and Hermann Dülmer. Abingdon: Routledge 2016 forthcoming.

Freire, André. 'The Condition of Portuguese Democracy during the Troika's Intervention, 2011-2015.' *Portuguese Journal of Social Science* 15 (2016 forthcoming).

Friðriksson, Ingimundur. 'Aðdragandi bankahrunsins í október 2008.' *Seðlabanki Íslands*. 2009.

FSCS. "£4.5bn paid out to nearly 230,000 UK customers – FSCS reveals Icesave's impact five years after its collapse." *FSCS*. 8 October 2013, accessed 30 June 2015, http://www.fscs.org.uk/uploaded_files/07_icesave_five_year_anniversary_08_10_13_final_pdf.pdf.

Fukuyama, Francis. 'Where Is the Uprising from the Left?' *Spiegel Online*, 2 January 2012, http://www.spiegel.de/international/world/0,1518,812208,00.html.

Gallego-Díaz, Sol and Jacobo Rivero, 'La campaña de infamias y acoso va a ir a más.' *Ctxt*, January 2015, accessed 20 December 2015, http://ctxt.es/es/20150115/politica/92/La-campaña-de-infamias-y-acoso-va-a-ir-a-más-España-Rebelión-en-la-periferia-sur.htm.

Gamble, Andrew. *The Spectre at the Feast: Capitalist Crisis and the Politics of Recession*. Basingstoke: Palgrave Macmillan, 2009.

Gayle, Damien, 'Anti-austerity Protests: Tens of Thousands Rally Across UK,' *The Guardian*, 20 June 2015, accessed 30 November 2015, http://www.theguardian.com/world/2015/jun/20/tens-thousands-rally-uk-protest-against-austerity.

Généreux, Jacques. 'La priorité, c'est de sauver l'Europe, pas l'euro.' *Rue 89*, 16 November 2013, accessed 10 June 2015, http://rue89.nouvelobs.com/2013/11/16/jacques-genereux-priorite-cest-sauver-leurope-leuro-247475.

Généreux, Jacques. *Nous on peut!* Paris: Seuil, 2011.

Gerodimos, Roman. 'The Ideology of Far Left Populism in Greece: Blame, Victimhood and Revenge in the Discourse of Greek Anarchists.' *Political Studies* 63, no. 3 (2015): 608–25.

Gills, Barry K. 'The Return of Crisis in the Era of Globalization: One Crisis, or Many?' *Globalizations* 7, no. 1–2 (2010): 3–8.

Gimeno, Beatriz and Carmen San José, 'Aún estamos a tiempo.' eldiario.es, 9 July 2015, accessed 20 December 2015, http://www.eldiario.es/zonacritica/tiempo_6_407419278.html.

Gíslason, Björn Valur. 'Besta ríkisstjórn lýðveldissögunnar.' 30 September 2013, accessed 12 February 2016, http://www.bvg.is/blogg/2013/09/30/besta-rikisstjorn-lydveldissogunnar.

Gohlke, Nicole and Janine Wissler. 'Escaping the Euro Dream.' *Jacobin Magazin*, 31 July 2015, https://www.jacobinmag.com/2015/07/germany-greece-austerity-grexit/.

Gómez-Reino, Margarita, Iván Llamazares and Luis Ramiro. 'Euroscepticism and Political Parties in Spain.' In *Opposing Europe? The Comparative Party Politics of Euroscepticism*, volume 1, edited by Paul Taggart and Aleks Szczerbiak. Oxford: Oxford University Press, 2008.

Gómez, Raúl, Laura Morales and Luis Ramiro. 'Varieties of Radicalism: Examining the Diversity of Radical Left Parties and Voters in Western Europe.' *West European Politics* 39, no. 2 (2016): 351–79.

Gourgouris, Stathis, 'Left Governmentality in Reality,' *AnalyzeGreece!*, 20 January 2015, http://www.analyzegreece.gr/topics/elections-250102015/item/65-stathis-gourgouris-left-governmentality-in-reality.

Graeber, David. 'The New Anarchists.' *New Left Review* 13 (2002): 61–73.

Grétarsdóttir, Guðfríður Lilja. 'Ríkisábyrgð á lántöku Tryggingarsjóðs innstæðueigenda og fjárfesta.' 21 August 2009, accessed 12 February 2016, http://www.althingi.is/altext/raeda/137/rad20090821T203143.html.

Greve, Bent. 'Denmark: Still a Nordic Welfare State After the Changes of Recent Years?' *Challenges to European Welfare Systems*, 159–76. Springer International Publishing, 2016.

Grospič, Stanislav 'Soupeření dolaru s euroem a co je za tím.' *KSČM*, 4 March 2010, accessed 10 July 2015, https://www.kscm.cz/nazory-a-polemika/46809/grospic-soupereni-dolaru-s-eurem-a-co-je-za-tim?previev=archiv.

Grzymała-Busse, Anna. *Redeeming the Communist Past. The Regeneration of Communist Parties in East Central Europe*. Cambridge: Cambridge University Press 2002.

Guðjónsson, Elías Jón. 'Mikilvæg skilaboð utanríkisráðherra.' *24 stundir*. 15 April 2008, accessed 30 June 2015, http://www.mbl.is/greinasafn/grein/1207015/.

GUE/NGL. 'About the group.' 2013, accessed 30 July 2015, http://www.guengl.eu/group/about.

GUE/NGL. *Activity report, 1999-2004*. Brussels: GUE/NGL, 2004.

GUE/NGL. *Review of activities 2012-2014*. Brussels: GUE/NGL.

GUE/NGL *Who we are, what we work for*, accessed 30 July 2015, http://www. guengl.eu/uploads/publications-documents/EN_web.pdf.

GUE/NGL, *Review of activities, 2009-2011*, 2011, accessed 30 July 2015, http:// www.guengl.eu/uploads/publications-documents/Mid-term_EN.pdf.

Gunnarsdóttir, Halla. 'Stjórnlagaþing gæti tekið til starfa í haust', *Morgunblaðið*, 30 January 2009: 14.

Gutiérrez, Vera 'Qué le ha pasado a Izquierda Unida.' *El País*, 12 June 2015, accessed 20 December 2015, http://politica.elpais.com/politica/2015/06/12/actuali-dad/1434135099_152388.html.

Hábová, Vlasta. 'Idea Levicového fóra.' *Britské listy*, 13 May 2013, accessed 20 July 2015, http://blisty.cz/art/68452.html.

Halikiopoulou, Daphne, Kyriaki Nanou and Sofia Vasilopoulou. 'The Paradox of Nationalism: The Common Denominator of Radical Right and Radical Left Euros-cepticism.' *European Journal of Political Research* 51 (2012): 504–539.

Halikiopoulou, Daphne. 'Far-Left Euroscepticism in the 2014 European Parliament Elections: A Cross-Europe Comparison'. In *Is Europe Afraid of Europe? An Assessment of the Result of the 2014 European Elections*, edited by Kostas Infatis, 244–56. Athens: The Wilfried Martens Centre for European Studies, 2014.

Haló Noviny. 'Úvodní vystoupení předsedy ÚV KSČM Vojtěcha Filipa na VIII. Sjezdu.' 21 May 2012, accessed 5 August 2015, http://www.halonoviny.cz/articles/view/324759.

Hancox, Dan. 'Why Ernesto Laclau Is the Intellectual Figurehead for Syriza and Podemos'. *The Guardian*, 9 February 2015, http://www.theguardian.com/commentisfree/2015/feb/09/ernesto-laclau-intellectual-figurehead-syriza-podemos.

Handl, Vladimír. 'Choosing between China and Europe? Virtual Inspiration and Policy Transfer in the Programmatic Development of the Czech Communist Party.' *Journal of Communist Studies and Transition Politics* 21, no. 1 (2005): 123–41.

Hanley, David. *Beyond the Nation State*. London: Palgrave Macmillan, 2008.

Harðarson, Ólafur Þ. and Gunnar Helgi Kristinsson. 'Iceland.' *European Journal of Political Research* 49 (2010): 1009–16.

Harðarson, Ólafur Þ. and Gunnar Helgi Kristinsson. 'Iceland.' *European Journal of Political Research* 52 (2014): 101–4.

Harðarson, Ólafur Þ. 'Republic of Iceland.' In *World Encyclopedia of Political Systems and Parties*, edited by Neil Schlager and Jayne Weisblatt, 569–580. New York: Facts on File, 2006.

Harvey, David. *A Brief History of Neoliberalism*. Oxford: Oxford University Press, 2005.

Hauss, Charles and David Rayside. 'The Development of New Parties in Western Democracies since 1945.' In *Political Parties: Development and Decay*, edited by Louis Maisel and Joseph Cooper, 31–57. Beverly Hills: Sage, 1978.

Havlik, Vlastimil. 'The Economic Crisis in the Shadow of Political Crisis: The Rise of Party Populism in the Czech Republic'. In *European Populism in the Shadow of the Great Recession*, edited by Hanspeter Kriesi and Takis S. Pappas, 199–216. Colchester: ECPR Press, 2015.

Heller, Josef. 'Bída analýzy aneb Co překroutili analytici ČSSD,' *Alternativy* 14 (2003).

Hildebrandt, Cornelia. 'DIE LINKE in Deutschland.' In *Von Revolution bis Koalition. Linke Parteien in Europa*, edited by Birgit Daiber, Cornelia Hildebrandt and Anna Striethorst, 154–72. Berlin: Karl Dietz Verlag, 2010.

Hino, Airo. *New Challenger Parties in Western Europe*. Abingdon: Routledge, 2012.

Hoffmann, Hannah. 'Man muss immer wieder von vorn anfangen können.' *Clara* 22 (14 December 2011).

Holloway, John. *Change the World Without Taking Power: The Meaning of Revolution Today: New Edition*. London: Pluto, 2005.

Holmes, Michael and Knut Roder, eds. *The Left and the European Constitution: From Laeken to Lisbon*. Manchester: Manchester University Press, 2012.

Holmes, Michael. 'Contesting Integration: The Radical Left and Euroscepticism.' In *Euroscepticism as a Transnational and pan-European Phenomenon: The Emergence of a New Sphere of Opposition*, edited by Nick Startin, John FitzGibbon and Ben Leruth. London: Routledge, forthcoming.

Holubec, Stanislav. 'Die radikale Linke in Tschechien.' In *Die Linke in Europa. Analyse der linken Parteien und Parteiallianzen*, edited by Birgit Daiber and Cornelia Hildebrandt, 116–25. Berlin: Dietzverlag, 2009.

Hooghe, Liesbet, Ryan Brigevich Bakker, Catherine de Vries, Erica Edwards, Gary Marks, Jan Rovny, Marco Steenbergen and Milada Vachudova. 'Reliability and Validity of the 2002 and 2006 Chapel Hill Expert Surveys on Party Positioning.' *European Journal of Political Research* 49 (2010): 687–703.

Hough, Dan and Vladimír Handl. 'The Post-communist Left and the European Union: The Czech Communist Party of Bohemia and Moravia (KSČM) and the German Party of Democratic Socialism (PDS).' *Communist and Post-Communist Studies* 37, no. 3 (2004): 319-39.

Hough, Dan and Michael Koß. 'Populism Personified or Reinvigorated Reformers?' The German Left Party in 2009 and Beyond.' *German Politics and Society* 91, no. 27 (2009): 76–91.

Hough, Dan. 'Learning From the West: Policy Transfer and Programmatic Change in the Communist Successor parties of Eastern and Central Europe.' *Journal of Communist Studies and Transition Politics* 21, no. 1 (2005): 1–15.

Hough, Dan. 'From Pariah to Prospective Partner? The German Left Party's Winding Path Towards Government.' In *Left Parties in National Governments*, edited by Jonathan Olsen, Michael Koß and Dan Hough, 138–54. Basingstoke: Palgrave, 2010.

Hozák, Dalibor. 'Usnesení VIII. sjezdu KSČM a realita.' *Dialog 289*, October 2012, accessed 5 August 2015, http://www.komsomol.cz/clanky/2594_dialog_sjezd.html.

http://www.landskjor.is/media/frettir/Urslit2009_mai2009.pdf (accessed 30 June 2015).

Hug, Simon. 'The Emergence of New Political Parties from a Game Theoretic Perspective.' *European Journal of Political Research* 29 (1996): 169–90.

Hug, Simon. *Altering Party Systems: Strategic Behavior and The Emergence of New Political Parties in Western Democracies*. Ann Arbor: University of Michigan Press, 2001.

Huke, Nikolai, Mònica Clua-Losada and David J. Bailey. 'Disrupting the European Crisis: A Critical Political Economy of Contestation, Subversion and Escape.' *New Political Economy* 20, no. 5 (2015): 725–51.

Iglesias, Pablo. 'Spain on Edge.' *New Left Review* 93 (2015): 23–42.

Iglesias, Pablo. 'Understanding Podemos.' *New Left Review* 93 (2015): 7–22.

Ijabs, Ivars. 'After the Referendum: Militant Democracy and Nation-Building in Latvia.' *East European Politics & Societies* (2015), doi:10.1177/0888325415593630.

Ikstens, Janis. 'Does Europe Matter? The EU and Latvia's Political Parties'. In *The European Union and Party Politics in Central and Eastern Europe*, edited by Paul Lewis and Zdenka Mansfeldova, 86–106. Basingstoke: Palgrave, 2006.

Ikstens, Janis. 'Latvia.' In *The Palgrave Handbook of Social Democracy in the European Union*, edited by Jean-Michel De Waele, Fabien Escalona and Mathieu Vieira, 470–87. Basingstoke: Palgrave Macmillan, 2013.

Infratest Dimap. 'ARDDeutschlandTREND September 2015. Eine Studie im Auftrag der Tagesthemen', accessed 17 March 2016, https://www.tagesschau.de/inland/deutschlandtrend-399.pdf.

Initiative for Democratic Socialism, *Manifesto of the Initiative for Democratic Socialism* (2013), accessed 30 November 2015, http://www.demokraticni-socializem.si/programski-dokumenti/manifesto-of-the-initiative-for-democratic-socialism/.

Institut für Gesellschaftsanalyse. 'Die gesellschaftliche Linke in den gegenwärtigen Krisen.' *Kontrovers* 2 (2009), https://www.rosalux.de/fileadmin/rls_uploads/pdfs/kontrovers/kontrovers_02-09.pdf.

International Workingmen's Association, 1864, 'General Rules', October 1864, http://www.marxists.org/archive/marx/iwma/documents/1864/rules.htm

Ioannou, Gregoris. 'Employment in crisis: Cyprus 2010–2013.' *The Cyprus Review* 26, no. 1 (2014): 107–26.

Ioannou, Gregoris. The Connection between Trade Unions and Political Parties in Cyprus.' In *Party-society Relations in the Republic of Cyprus*, edited by Giorgos Charalambous and Christophoros Christophorou. Abingdon: Routledge 2015.

Ishiyama, John T. and Andras Bozóki. 'Adaptation and Change: Characterizing the Survival Strategies of the Communist Successor Parties'. *Journal of Communist Studies and Transition Politics* 17 (2001): 32–51.

IU. *X Asamblea Federal*. Madrid, 2012.

IWW, 1905. 'Preamble to the IWW Constitution', http://www.iww.org/culture/official/preamble.shtml.

Jankowski, Michael, Sebastian Schneider and Markus Tepe. 'Ideological Alternative? Analyzing Alternative für Deutschland candidates' ideal points via black box scaling.' *Party Politics*. Published online before print, 12 January 2016. 1–13. doi: 10.1177/1354068815625230.

Janssen, Roel. 'How Anti-Euro Sentiment is Fuelling the Rise of the Dutch Socialists.' *The Guardian*, 15 May 2012, accessed 10 September 2014, http://www.theguardian.com/commentisfree/2012/may/15/anti-euro-sentiment-rise-dutch-socialist-party.

Janssen, Thilo. *The Parties of the Left in Europe. A Comparison of Their Position on European Policy Leading into the 2014 European Elections*. Berlin: Rosa-Luxemburg-Stiftung, 2013.

Jeffries, Stuart. 'Why Marxism Is on the Rise Again'. *The Guardian*, 4 July 2012, http://www.theguardian.com/world/2012/jul/04/the-return-of-marxism.

Jerez, Ariel and Carolina Bescansa, 'Coyuntura fluida y nuevo sujeto constituyente.' *El Diario*, 2 February 2013, accessed 30 November 2015, http://www.eldiario.es/zonacritica/Coyuntura-fluida-nuevo-sujeto-constituyente_6_99100110.html.

Jessop, Bob. 'The Symptomatology of Crises, Reading Crises and Learning from Them: Some Critical Realist Reflections.' *Journal of Critical Realism* 14, no. 3 (2015): 238–71.

Jessop, Bob. *State Theory: Putting Capitalist States in their Place*. Cambridge: Polity, 1990.

Jóhannsson, Guðni Th. 'Búsaháldabylting? Hvaða búsáhaldabylting?' *gudnith.is*. 2010, accessed 30 June 2015, http://gudnith.is/efni/b%C3%BAs%C3%A1haldabylting_hva%C3%B0a_b%C3%BAs%C3%A1haldabylting_2010.

Johansen, Inger. 'The Danish People's Party – A Success Story' Situation on the Left.' In *Europe After the EU Elections*, edited by Cornelia Hildebrant, 95–100. Rosa Luxemburg-Stiftung, Berlin, 2014.

Johansen, Inger. 'The Left and Radical Left in Denmark.' In *From Revolution to Coalition, Radical Left Parties in Europe*, edited by Birgit Daiber, Cornelia Hildebrandt and Anna Striethorst, 10–26. Berlin: Rosa Luxemburg-Stiftung, 2012.

Jónasson, Ögmundur. 'Gróði og samfélag.' *ogmundur.is*. 1 November 2006, accessed 30 June 2015, http://ogmundur.is/samfelagsmal/nr/2896/.

Jónasson, Ögmundur. 'Staða efnahagsmála.' 21 March 2006, accessed 5 November 2015, http://www.althingi.is/altext/raeda/132/rad20060321T140101.html.

Jónsson, Birkir Jón. 'Stefna ríkisstjórnarinnar, skýrsla forsætisráðherra. 'Þingræða.' *Alþingi*. 4 February 2009, accessed 30 June 2015, http://www.althingi.is/altext/raeda/136/rad20090204T203725.html.

Joordinarybloggs, 'After the Election: What Next for Left Unity.' *Facing Reality*, 24 May 2015, accessed 30 November 2015, https://bloggingjbloggs1917.wordpress.com/2015/05/24/after-the-election-what-next-for-left-unity/.

Jørgensen, Martin Bak and Óscar García Agustín. 'The Postmodern Prince: The Political Articulation of Social Dissent.' In *Politics of Dissent*, edited by Martin Bak Jørgensen and Óscar García Agustín, 31–52. Frankfurt am Main: Peter Lang, 2015.

Jubulis, Mark. *Nationalism and Democratic Transition: The Politics of Citizenship and Language in Post-Soviet Latvia*. Oxford: University Press of America, 2001.

Kalyvas, Stathis and Niko Marantzidis. 'Greek Communism 1968–2001.' *Eastern European Politics and Societies* 26 (2002): 665–90.

Kanol, D. and Giorgos Charalambous. 'Fluctuations in Public Trust in Government in Cyprus: Why Context Matters.' Unpublished manuscript 2015.

Karamichas, John. 'Square Politics: Key characteristics of the indignant mobilizations in Greece'. Paper presented at the 62nd PSA Annual International Conference, Belfast, 3–5 April 2012.

Karitzis, Andreas. 'The "SYRIZA Experience": Lessons and Adaptations'. *openDemocracy*, 17 March 2016, https://www.opendemocracy.net/can-europe-make-it/andreas-karitzis/syriza-experience-lessons-and-adaptations-0.

Katsambekis, Giorgos. 'Populism in post-democratic times. Greek politics and the limits of consensus'. Paper presented at the 61st Political Studies Association Annual Conference, London, 19–21 April 2011.

Katsambekis, Giorgos. 'Left Wing Populism and the Dutch SP: An Interview with Professor Gerrit Voerman.' *Populismus Interventions* 2 (2015), accessed 1 September 2015, Available at: http://www.populismus.gr/wp-content/uploads/2015/05/interventions2-voerman.pdf.

Katsembekis, Giorgos. 'The Rise of the Greek Radical Left to Power: Notes on Syriza's Discourse and Strategy.' *Linea Sur* 9 (2015): 152–61.

Katz, Richard S. and Peter Mair, eds. *How Parties Organize: Change and Adaptation in Party Organizations in Western Democracies*. Sage Publications Ltd, 1994.

Keith. Dan. 'Opposing Europe, Opposing Austerity: Radical Left Parties and the Eurosceptic Debate'. In *The Routledge Handbook of Euroscepticism*, edited by Nick Startin and Simon Usherwood. Abingdon: Routledge, 2016, forthcoming.

Keith, Dan. 'Party Organisation and Party Adaptation: Western European Communists and Successor Parties'. DPhil Thesis, University of Sussex, 2011.

Keith, Dan. 'Radical Left Parties and left movements in Northern Europe and Scandinavia.' In *Radical Left Movements in Europe*, edited by Magnus Wennerhag, Christian Fröhlich and Grzegorz Piotrowski. Farnham: Ashgate, forthcoming, 2016.

Keith, Dan. 'Ready to Get their Hands Dirty: The Dutch Socialist Party and Groen-Links.' In *Left Parties in National Governments*, edited by Jonathan Olsen, Michael Koß and Dan Hough, 155–72. Basingstoke: Palgrave, 2010.

Kelly, Fiach. 'Sinn Féin has taken a hit on its exposed Left flank.' *The Irish Times* (13 October 2014).

Kelly, Fiach. 'The Anti-Austerity Alliance and the People Before Profit Alliance.' *The Irish Times*, 3 February 2016, accessed 3 February 2016, http://www.irishtimes.com/election-2016/the-anti-austerity-alliance-and-people-before-profit-1.2520628.

Kipping, Katja and Bernd Riexinger. 'Asylrecht ist Menschenrecht.' 13 January 2016, accessed 16 March 2016, http://www.die-linke.de/nc/mediathek/videos-pressekonferenzen/archiv/2016/januar/.

Kipping, Katja and Bernd Riexinger. 'Die Kommende Demokratie: Sozialismus 2.0. Zu den Aufgaben und Möglichkeiten einer Partei der Zukunft im Europa von Morgen.' 24 April 2015, accessed 17 March 2016, http://www.katja-kipping.de/de/article/887.die-kommende-demokratie-sozialismus-2-0.html.

Kipping, Katja. 'Eine starke LINKE ist die Garantie dafür, dass sozialen Worten soziale Taten folgen.' Speech at the 2013 Die Linke party congress, 15 June 2013, http://www.die-linke.de/index.php?id=12344.

Kirn, Gal. 'The emergence of the new left party in Slovenia: Initiative for Democratic Socialism,' *Chronosmag* March 2014, accessed 21 March 2015, http://chronosmag.eu/index.php/g-kirn-the-emergence-of-the-new-left-party-in-slovenia-initiative-for-democratic-socialism.html.

Kirn, Gal. 'Slovenia's Social Uprising in the European Crisis: Maribor as Periphery from 1988 to 2012.' *Stasis* 2, no. 1 (2014): 106–29.

Kitschelt, Herbert, Zdenka Mansfeldova, Radoslaw Markowski and Gabor Toka. *Post-Communist Party Systems: Competition, Representation, and Inter-Party Cooperation.* Cambridge: Cambridge University Press, 1999.

Kitschelt, Herbert. 'Left-Libertarian Parties: Explaining Innovation in Competitive Party Systems.' *World Politics* 40 (1988): 194–234.

Kitschelt, Herbert. 'Social Movements, Political Parties, and Democratic Theory.' *The Annals of the American Academy of Political and Social Science.* 528 (1993): 13–29.

KKE. *Programme of the KKE* (2013), http://inter.kke.gr/en/articles/Programme-of-the-KKE/.

KKE. 'Political Resolution of the 19th Congress of the KKE', April 2013, accessed 16 February 2016, http://inter.kke.gr/en/articles/Political-Resolution-of-the-19th-Congress-of-the-KKE/.

KKE. Καταστατικό του Κομμουνιστικού Κόμματος Ελλάδας. Athens: Central Committee of KKE, 1996.

KKE. Πρόγραμμα του Κομμουνιστικού Κόμματος Ελλάδας. Athens: Central Committee of KKE, 1996.

KKE. Το Πρόγραμμα του KKE. Athens: Central Committee of KKE, 2013.

Klein, Dieter. 'Eine zweite Grosse Transformation und die Linke.' *Kontrovers* 1 (2010), https://www.rosalux.de/fileadmin/rls_uploads/pdfs/kontrovers/kontrovers_01-2010_web.pdf.

Klein, Dieter. *Das Morgen tanzt im Heute. Transformation im Kapitalismus und über ihn hinaus.* Hamburg: VSA Verlag, 2013.

Klein, Dieter. *The Second Great Transformation and the Left.* Brussels: RLS, 2010.

Kliman, Andrew. *The Failure of Capitalist Production: Underlying Causes of the Great Recession.* London: Pluto Press, 2012.

Klonza, Věra. 'Kolapsy a regenerace společensko-ekonomických systémů. Naše současná situace a možnosti jejího aktivního ovlivnění.' *25 let budování kapitalismu v České republice.* Sborník vystoupení na XXXVI Pražské teoreticko-politické konferenci, Praha 8. 11. 2014, 75–95. Praha: KSČM Praha Východ, 2014.

Kolsto, P. and B. Tsilevich. 'Patterns of Nation Building and Political Integration in a Bifurcated Postcommunist State: Ethnic Aspects of Parliamentary Elections in Latvia'. *East European Politics & Societies* 11, no. 2 (1 March 1997): 366–91. doi: 10.1177/0888325497011002008.

Koltsida, Danae. 'Η Κοινοβουλευτική Ομάδα του ΣΥΡΙΖΑ μετά τις διπλές εκλογές του 2012: ρήξη (και) στις σχέσεις εκπροσώπησης;' (MA thesis, University of Athens, 2013).

Koole, Ruud. 'The Vulnerability of the Modern Cadre Party in the Netherlands.' In *How Parties Organize: Change and Adaptation in Party Organizations in Western Democracies,* edited by Richard S. Katz and Peter Mair, 278–303. London: Sage, 1994.

Korsch, Felix and Volkmar Wölk. *National-Konservativ und Marktradikal. Eine politische Einordnung der 'Alternative für Deutschland'. Analysen* series. Berlin: Rosa-Luxemburg-Stiftung, 2014.

Korsika, Anej and Luka Mesec. 'Slovenia: From Spontaneous Protests to Renewal of the Social Left.' *Kurswechsel* 1 (2014): 80–8.

Korsika, Anej. 'The formation of a European Movement is Key.' *LeftEast* 14 March 2014, accessed 30 November 2015, http://www.criticatac.ro/lefteast/interview-anej-korsika-ids-1/.

Košťál, Zdeněk. 'Dvě poznámky.' *25 let budování kapitalismu v České republice.* Sborník vystoupení na XXXVI Pražské teoreticko-politické konferenci, Praha 8. 11. 2014. Praha: KSČM Praha Východ, 2014, 74–8.

Kouvelakis, Stathis. 'Syriza's Magic Equation.' *Jacobin*, 9 February 2015, https://www.jacobinmag.com/2015/02/tsipras-parliament-speech-austerity/.

Koyama, Yoji. 'Economic Crisis In The Baltic States: Focusing On Latvia.' *Economic Annals* 55, no. 186 (2010): 89–114.

Kretsos, Lefteris. 'Greece's Neoliberal Experiment and Working Class Resistance,' *WorkingUSA* 15 (2012): 517–27.

Kretsos, Lefteris. 'Union Responses to the Rise of Precarious Youth Employment in Greece'. *Industrial Relations Journal* 42 (2011): 453–72.

Kriegel, Annie. *The French Communists: Profile of a People.* Chicago: University of Chicago Press, 1972.

Kriesi, Hanspeter and Takis S. Pappas. 'Populism during Crisis: An Introduction'. In *European Populism in the Shadow of the Great Recession*, edited by Hanspeter Kriesi and Takis S. Pappas, 1–19. Studies in European Political Science. Colchester: ECPR Press, 2015.

Kriesi, Hanspeter. 'The Political Consequences of the Economic Crisis in Europe: Electoral Punishment and Popular Protest.' In *Mass Politics in Tough Times,* edited by Nancy Bermeo and Larry M. Bartels, 297–333. Oxford: Oxford University Press, 2014.

KSČM. 'Address delivered by Comrade Vojtech Filip, chairman of the Central Committee of the Communist Party of Bohemia and Moravia (CPBM) at the 13th World Meeting of Communist and Workers' Parties in Athens.' 2011, accessed 8 July 2015. https://www.kscm.cz/international/60503/address-delivered-by-comrade-vojtech-filip-chairman-of-the-central-committee-of-the-communist-party-of-bohemia-and-moravia-cpbm-at-the-13th-world-meeting-of-communist-and-workers-parties-in-athens.

KSČM. 'Main Tasks & Aims of the Party's Work after KSCM's VIII Congress.' 2012, accessed 10 July 2015, https://www.kscm.cz/our-politics/documents/65189/main-tasks-aims-of-the-partys-work-after-kscms-viii-congress.

KSČM. 'Otevřený volební program KSČM pro volby do PS PCR 2010', accessed 2 July 2015, www.kscm.cz/viewDocument.asp?document=5481.

KSČM. 'Programme of Renewal.' 2008, accessed 10 July 2015, https://www.kscm.cz/our-party/our-programms/39786/.

KSČM. 'Řešení řecké krize přijetím jednostranných opatření povede k diskreditaci levicové politiky. 17.07.215', accessed 5 August 2015, https://www.kscm.cz/politika-kscm/stanoviska-kscm/99605/reseni-recke-krize-prijetim-jednostrannych-opatreni-povede-k-diskreditaci-levicove-politiky.

KSČM. 'Socialismus pro 21. Století.' 2008, accessed 10 July 2015, https://www.kscm.cz/nase-strana/sjezdy-kscm/vii-sjezd-kscm/35668/socialismus-pro-21-stoleti.

KSČM. 'Socialismus pro 21. Století.' 2012, accessed 10 July 2015, https://www.kscm.cz/volby-a-akce/viii-sjezd-kscm-v-liberci/dokumenty/64118/socialismus-v-21-stoleti.

KSČM. 'Speech by cme. Vojtech Filip, Chairman of Communist Party of Bohemia & Moravia's Central Committee, to be delivered on 15th International Meeting of Communist and Workers' Parties, Lisbon 2013.' 2013, accessed 10 July 2015, https://www.kscm.cz/international/82172/speech-by-cme-vojtech-filip-chairman-of-communist-party-of-bohemia-moravias-central-committee-to-be-delivered-on-15th-international-meeting-of-communist-and-workers-parties-lisbon-2013.

KSČM. 'Statements, Elections in the European Union – hope for change.' 2012, accessed 9 July 2015, https://www.kscm.cz/our-politics/statements/64022/elections-in-the-european-union-hope-for-change.

KSČM. 'The CPBM at the Turn of the Millennium.' 2008, accessed 10 July 2015, https://www.kscm.cz/our-party/our-programms/39787/.

KSČM. 'The Declaration Communist Party of Bohemia & Moravia's International Conference, Prague, May 23–24, 2015', accessed 8 July 2015, https://www.kscm.cz/our-politics/international-conferences/international-conference-22-24-05-2015/98740/the-declaration-communist-party-of-bohemia-moravias-international-conference-prague-may-23-24-2015.

KSČM. 'The Lisbon Treaty.' 2008, accessed 10 July 2015, https://www.kscm.cz/rewrite_url.asp?rew_thema=political-opinions&rew_item=39980&rew_other=.

KSČM. 'The Natural Child of Capitalism.' 2008, accessed 10 July 2015, https://www.kscm.cz/rewrite_url.asp?rew_thema=political-opinions&rew_item=40724&rew_other=.

KSČM. 'Volby do EP 2009', accessed 10 July 2015, www.kscm.cz/volby-a-akce/volby-do-ep-2009.

KSČM. 'Vystoupení předsedy ÚV KSČM Vojtěcha Filipa na 14. zasedání ÚV KSČM 28. 3. 2015', accessed 5 May 2015, https://www.kscm.cz/stanoviska-tiskove-konference-projevy/projevy/96712/vystoupeni-predsedy-uv-kscm-vojtecha-filipa-na-14-zasedani-uv-kscm-28-3-2015.

KSČM. Zpráva ÚV KSČM o činnosti strany v období od VII. do VIII. sjezdu KSČM. 2012.

Kunštát, Daniel. 'Strana, která neumírá. 'K příčinám stability volební podpory KSČM.' *Naše společnost* 12, no. 2 (2014): 15–23.

Kunštát, Daniel. 'Za rudou oponou. Komunisté a jejich voliči po roce 1989.' *Sociologické nakladatelství* (2013): 288–90.

Laclau, Ernesto. *On Populist Reason*. London: Verso, 2007.

Lakoff, George, Howard Dean and Don Hazen. *Don't Think of an Elephant!: Know Your Values and Frame the Debate--The Essential Guide for Progressives*. White River Junction: Chelsea Green, 2004.

Laletina, Olga. 'The European United Left-Nordic Green Left'. In *The European Constitution and its Ratification Crisis: Constitutional Debates in the EU Member States,* edited by Nino Eschke and Thomas Malick, Bonn: ZentrumfürEuropäischeIntegrationsforschung, Rhenische Friedrich-Wilhelms-Universität, 2006.

Landskjör. 'Úrslit kosninga til Alþingis 25. Apríl 2009.' *landskjor.is*. Landsvirkjun, 'Fljótsdalur Power Station', accessed 5 November 2015, http://www.landsvirkjun. com/Company/PowerStations/FljotsdalurPowerStation/.

Laskos, Christos and Euclid Tsakalotos. *Crucible of Resistance: Greece, the Eurozone & the World Economic Crisis*. London: Pluto Press, 2013.

Laurent, Pierre. 'Une sortie de la zone euro n'empêche pas la pression des marchés.' *Marianne*, 25 July 2015, accessed 27 July 2015, http://www.marianne.net/ pierre-laurent-sortie-zone-euro-n-empeche-pas-pression-marches-100235637. html.

Larson, Thomas. 'Heading Towards a Change of Government in Denmark.' *EU Observer*. Published online 14 September 2011, accessed 20 September 2015, https://euobserver.com/political/113620.

Lavelle, Ashley. 'Postface: Death by a Thousand Cuts'. In *European Social Democracy during the Global Economic Crisis : Renovation or Resignation?*, edited by David J. Bailey, Jean-Michel De Waele, Fabien Escalona and Mathieu Vieira, 270–83. Manchester: Manchester University Press, 2014.

Lavelle, Ashley. *The Death of Social Democracy: Political Consequences in the 21st Century*. Aldershot: Ashgate, 2008.

Lees, Charles, Dan Hough and Dan Keith. 'Towards an Analytical Framework for Party Mergers: Operationalising the Cases of the German Left Party and the Dutch Green Left.' *West European Politics* 33, no. 6 (2010): 1299–317.

Left Party. *Partiprogram på lättläst svenska*: Stockholm, 2015, accessed 20 September 2015, Available at: http://www.vansterpartiet.se/assets/Partiprogram-met-lattlast-svenska.pdf.

Left Party. 'Handledning Flyktingmottagande.' Stockholm: Left Party, 2015, accessed 20 September 2015, http://www.vansterpartiet.se/assets/Handledning-flyktingmottagande1.pdf.

Left Party. 'Parliamentary Motion 2013/14:A301.' Published online 3 October 2013, accessed 20 September 2015, http://www.riksdagen.se/sv/Dokument-Lagar/ Forslag/Motioner/Inkludering-och-antidiskrimine_H102A301/?text=true.

Left Party. *Strategy for the Future of the Left Adopted by the Left Party's 39th Congress 5-8 January 2012*. Stockholm: Left Party, 2012.

Left Party. 'Party Programme.' January 2012, accessed 20 September 2015, http:// www.vansterpartiet.se/material/partiprogram.

Left Party. 'Förbättrat flyktingmottagande'. Stockholm: Left Party, 2008, http://www. vansterpartiet.se/assets/frbttrat_flyktingmottagande.pdf.

Left Unity, 'Final motions and amendments.' 21–22 November 2015, accessed 30 November 2015, http://leftunity.org/motions-passed-at-left-unity-conference/.

Left Unity. 'Policy passed at Left Unity National Conference Manchester', 29 March 2014, accessed 21 March 2016, http://leftunity.org/policy-passed-at-left-unity-conference-29-march-2014/.

Lialiouti, Jenny and Giorgos Bithymitris. 'Implications of the Greek Crisis: Nationalism, Enemy Stereotypes and the European Union.' In *The European Union beyond the Crisis: Evolving Governance, Contested Policies, Disenchanted Publics*, edited by Boyka Stefanova, 249–68. Lanham: Lexington Books, 2014.

Lialiouti, Zinovia and Giorgos Bithimitris. '"The Nazis Strike again": The Concept of German Occupation, Party Strategies and Mass Perceptions under the Prism of the Greek Economic Crisis.' In *Nation States between Memories of World War II and Contemporary European Politics*, edited by Christian Karner and Bram Mertens, 155–72. London, NJ: Transaction Publishers, 2013.

Lightfoot, Simon. 'Left Parties at the EU Level: Influencing the Convention.' In *The Left and the European Constitution: From Laeken to Lisbon*, edited by Michael Holmes and Knut Roder, 18–34. Manchester: Manchester University Press, 2012.

Lisi, Marco. 'New Politics in Portugal: The Rise and Success of the Left Bloc.' *Pôle Sud* 30 (2009): 127–44.

Lisi, Marco. 'Rediscovering Civil Society? Renewal and Continuity in the Portuguese Radical Left.' *South European Society and Politics* 18 (2013): 21–39.

LKS. 'PROGRAMMA Ob"edineniya Politicheskikh Organizatsii "Za Prava Cheloveka v Edinoi Latvii" Na Vyborakh 9-Go Seima'. *LKS Web Page*, 2006, http://zapchel.lv/index.php?lang=ru&mode=party&submode=program&page_id=3989.

LKS. 'Programma ZaPChEL Na Vyborakh 10-Go Seima.' *LKS Web Page*, 2010, http://zapchel.lv/index.php?lang=ru&mode=party&submode=program&page_id=10629.

LKS. 'Programma ZaPChEL Na Vyborakh Rizhskoi Dumy 2009 G.' *LKS Web Page*, 2009, http://zapchel.lv/index.php?lang=ru&mode=party&submode=program&page_id=10628.

Lobo, Marina Costa and Pedro C. Magalhães. 'Room for Manoeuvre: Euroscepticism in the Portuguese Parties and Electorate.' *South European Society and Politics* 16 (2011): 81–104.

Lobo, Marina Costa. 'A União Europeia e Os Partidos Políticos Portugueses: Da Consolidação à Qualidade Democrática.' In *Portugal Em Mudança (1986–2006)*, edited by Marina Costa Lobo and Pedro Lains, 77–96. Estoril: Princípia, 2007.

Loizos, Peter. *The Greek Gift: Politics in a Cypriot Village*. Bibliopolis: Mannheim and Mohnesse 2004.

LSDSP. 'Latvijas Sociāldemokrātiskās Strādnieku Partijas (LSDSP) īsā Programma [The Concise Programme of the Social Democratic Party of Latvia (LSDSP}', accessed 25 January 2016, http://www.lsdsp.lv/faili/upload/programma.pdf.

LSP. 'Otchetnyi Doklad Pravleniya i Politicheskogo soveta SPL XI s"ezdu Sotsialisticheskoi Partii Latvii Na XIX S"ezde.' *Sotsialist Latvii* 2, no. 51 (2008): 8–9, http://latsocpartija.lv/ru/activities/paper/.

LSP. 'Otchetnyi Doklad Pravleniya Sotsialisticheskoi Partii Latvii Na XIX S"ezde.' *LSP*, 12 January 2016, http://latsocpartija.lv/ru/news/234/.

Lublin, David. 'The 2012 Latvia Language Referendum.' *Electoral Studies* 32, no. 2 (2013): 385.

Lucardie, Paul and Gerrit Voerman. 'The Netherlands.' *EJPR Political Data Yearbook* 49, no. 7 (2010): 1095–101.

Lucardie, Paul and Gerrit Voerman. 'The Netherlands.' *EJPR Political Data Yearbook* 50, no. 7 (2011): 1070–6.

Lucardie, Paul and Gerrit Voerman. 'The Netherlands.' *EJPR Political Data Yearbook* 51, no. 1 (2012): 215–20.

Lucardie, Paul. 'The Netherlands.' *EJPR Political Data Yearbook* 48, no. 7 (2009): 1130–2.

Luxemburg, Rosa. *Reform or Revolution*. London: Militant Publications, 1900 [1986], https://www.marxists.org/archive/luxemburg/1900/reform-revolution/.

Lyrintzis, Christos, 'Greek Politics in the Era of Economic Crisis: Reassessing Causes and Effects'. *GreeSE Paper* 45 (2011): 1–25, accessed 22 October 2015, http://eprints.lse.ac.uk/33826/1/GreeSE_No45.pdf.

Magri, Lucio. *The Tailor of Ulm: A Possible History of Communism*. London: Verso, 2011.

Maiguashca, Bice, Jonathan Dean and Dan Keith. 'Pulling Together in a Crisis? Anarchism, Feminism and the Limits of Left-wing Convergence in Austerity Britain.' *Capital & Class* (2016): 0309816815627388.

Mailand, Mikkel. 'Austerity Measures and Municipalities: The Case of Denmark.' *Transfer: European Review of Labour and Research* 20, no. 3 (2014): 417–30.

Mair, Peter, Wolfgang C. Müller and Fritz Plasser. 'Introduction: Electoral Challenges and Party Responses'. In *Political Parties and Electoral Change : Party Responses to Electoral Markets*, edited by Peter Mair, Wolfgang C. Müller and Fritz Plasser, 1–19. London: Sage, 2004.

Mair, Peter. 'The Electoral Universe of Small Parties.' In *Small Parties in Western Europe*, edited by Ferdinand Müller-Rommel and Geoffrey Pridham, 41–70. London: Sage, 1991.

Mair, Peter. *Party System Change: Approaches and Interpretations*. Oxford: Oxford University Press, 1997.

Makarov, Victor. 'Latvian Political Culture: Democratic or Authoritarian Bias? An Interpretation Attempt Based on a Survey Study,' Baltic Forum, 2002, http://www.balticforum.org/files_uploads/files/vm_survey2002-1.pdf.

Manetta, Francesco, 'Podemos co-founder criticizes mainstream drift in his own party.' *El País*, 30 April 2015, http://elpais.com/elpais/2015/04/30/inenglish/1430403454_148415.html?rel=mas.

March, Luke and André Freire. *A Esquerda Radical em Portugal e na Europa: Marxismo, Mainstream ou Marginalidade?* Porto: Quid Novi, 2012.

March, Luke and Cas Mudde. 'What's Left of the Radical left? The European Radical Left after 1989: Decline *and* Mutation.' *Comparative European Politics* 3, no. 1 (2005): 23–49.

March, Luke and Charlotte Rommerskirchen, 'Out of Left Field? Explaining the Variable Electoral Success of European Radical Left Parties.' *Party Politics* 21, no. 1 (2015): 40–55.

March, Luke. 'Beyond Syriza and Podemos, other radical left parties are threatening to break into the mainstream of European politics.' EUROPP, accessed 7 March 2016, http://blogs.lse.ac.uk/europpblog/2015/03/24/beyond-syriza-and-podemos-other-radical-left-parties-are-threatening-to-break-into-the-mainstream-of-european-politics/.

March, Luke. 'Radical Left Parties and Movements: Allies, Associates or Antagonists.' In *Radical Left Movements in Europe*, edited by Magnus Wennerhag, Christian Fröhlich and Grzegorz Piotrowski. Farnham: Ashgate, forthcoming, 2016.

March, Luke. 'From Vanguard of the Proletariat to Vox Populi: Left-Populism as a "Shadow" of Contemporary Socialism.' *SAIS Review* 27, no. 1 (2007): 63–77.

March, Luke. 'Problems and Perspectives of Contemporary European Radical Left Parties: Chasing a Lost World or Still a World to Win?.' *International Critical Thought* 2, no. 3 (September 2012): 314–39.

March, Luke. 'Squashed Tomatoes – Will the SP Miss the Target?.' Extremis Project 10 September 2012, accessed 1 September 2015, http://extremisproject. org/2012/09/squashed-tomatoes-will-the-socialist-party-miss-the-target/.

March, Luke. 'The Russian Duma "opposition": No Drama out of Crisis?' *East European Politics* 28, no. 3 (2012): 241–55.

March, Luke. 'What We Know and Do Not Know about the Radical Left (and What Do We Want to Know?)'. Paper presented at ECPR General Conference, Bordeaux, 2013.

March, Luke. *Contemporary Far Left Parties in Europe From Marxism to the Mainstream?* Berlin and Bonn: Friedrich Ebert Stiftung, 2008.

March, Luke. *Radical Left Parties in Europe.* Abingdon: Routledge, 2011.

Marinos, Giorgos. 'The character of the contemporary era as the basic element which defines the strategy of the Communist Parties and the experience of the KKE'. 23 March 2012, accessed 16 February 2016, http://interold.kke.gr/News/news2012/2012-03-28-brazil.

Marioulas, Julian. 'The Greek Left.' In *From Revolution to Coalition, Radical Left Parties in Europe*, edited by Birgit Daiber, Cornelia Hildebrandt and Anna Striethorst, 292–309. Berlin: Rosa Luxemburg-Stiftung 2012.

Market and public opinion research centre. 'Piederības Sajūta Latvijai: Mazākumtautību Latvijas Iedzīvotāju Aptauja [Feeling of Belonging to Latvia: A Survey of Latvia's Inhabitants]'. June 2014, http://www.mk.gov.lv/sites/default/files/editor/atskaite_piederiba_08_2014.pdf.

Marković, Goran. 'Challenges of the Czech Radical Left.' *Journal of Contemporary Central and Eastern Europe* 21, no. 1(2013): 67–85.

Mason, Paul. 'Trying to Understand Syriza.' 14 May 2012, accessed 20 September 2015, Available at: http://www.bbc.co.uk/news/world-europe-18056677.

Mauzé, Gregory. 'The Left and Migrants: How to Think about Struggles in Common by Migrants, Non-migrants and Minorities?.' Published online 21 June 2013, accessed 1 March 2016, http://www.transform-network.net/cs/blog/blog-2013/news/detail/Blog/the-left-and-migrants-how-to-think-about-struggles-in-common-by-migrants-non-migrants-and-minoriti.html.

Mavris, Yannis. 'The Greek party system in the era of the Memorandum: Parties and party system in transition', *AnalyzeGreece!*, 5 January 2015, accessed 16 February, http://www.analyzegreece.gr/topics/elections-250102015/item/28-the-greek-party-system-in-the-era-of-the-memorandum-parties-party-system-in-transition.

Mayer, Margit and John Ely, eds. *The German Greens: Paradox between Movement and Party.* Philadelphia: Temple University Press, 1998.

Mayer, Nonna. *Ces Français Qui Votent FN.* Flammarion, 1999.

Mbl.is. 'Greinir á um kosningar.' 28 January 2009, accessed 30 June 2015, http://www.mbl.is/frettir/innlent/2009/01/28/greinir_a_um_kosningar/.

Mbl.is. 'Ingibjörg vill kosningar í vor.' 21 December 2009, accessed 30 June 2015, http://www.mbl.is/frettir/innlent/2009/01/22/ingibjorg_vill_kosningar_i_vor/.

Mbl.is. 'Kerfið fjarri því hrunið.' 22 November 2008, accessed 30 June 2008, http://www.mbl.is/greinasafn/grein/1256305/.

Mbl.is. 'Ögmundur ítrekar andstöðu við stjórnlagaráð.' 26 February 2011, accessed 30 June 2015, http://www.mbl.is/frettir/innlent/2011/02/26/itrekar_andstodu_vid_stjornlagarad/.

McGee, Harry. 'Sinn Féin prepares for government where compromises await.' *The Irish Times* (23 June 2014).

McInnes, Neil. *The Communist Parties of Western Europe.* London; New York: Published for the Royal Institute of International Affairs by Oxford University Press, 1975.

McKearney, Tommy. *The Provisional IRA: from Insurrection to Parliament.* Dublin: Pluto Press Ireland, 2011.

Meißner, Herbert. 'Geht es um die Transformation des Kapitalismus oder der Partei Die Linke? Über Täuschungsmanöver der gehobenen Art.' *RotFuchs* 17, no. 209 (2015): 15.

Mélenchon, Jean-Luc. 'Pour un Plan B en Europe.' blog posting, 11 September 2015, accessed 6 December 2015, http://melenchon.fr/2015/09/11/pour-un-plan-b-en-europe/.

Metro. 'Roemer (SP): PvdA onbetrouwbaar en ongeloofwaardig.' *Metro*, 31 January 2015, accessed 1 September 2015, http://www.metronieuws.nl/binnenland/2015/01/roemer-sp-pvda-onbetrouwbaar-en-ongeloofwaardig.

Metro. 'Roemer: Kabinet wist van naheffing', accessed 1 September 2015, http://www.metronieuws.nl/nieuws/2014/10/roemer-sp-kabinet-wist-van-naheffing 26 October 2014.

Meulenbelt, Anja. 'Afscheid van de SP- de lange versie', 5 August 2014, accessed 1 September 2015, http://www.anjameulenbelt.nl/weblog/2014/08/05/afscheid-van-de-sp-de-lange-versie/.

Meves, Helge. 'Das Selbstverständnis der PDS, der Neoliberalismus und die Mitte-Unten-Optionen.' *UTOPIE kreativ* 152 (2003): 525–35.

Moore, Suzanne. 'Forget the Greens – if the UK wants a truly leftwing party, it might have to grow its own.' *The Guardian*, 28 January 2015, accessed 30 November 2015, http://www.theguardian.com/commentisfree/2015/jan/28/forget-greens-grow-your-own-leftwing-party-election.

Moschonas, Gerassimos. 'The EU and the Identity of Social Democracy'. *Renewal* 17 (2009): 11–20.

Moss, Bernard. *Monetary Union in Crisis: The European Union as a Neo-liberal Construction.* Basingstoke: Palgrave, 2004.

Moulds, Josephine. 'Estonia and Latvia: Europe's Champions of Austerity?' *The Guardian*, 8 June 2012, sec. World news, http://www.theguardian.com/world/2012/jun/08/estonia-latvia-eurozone-champions-austerity.

Mpellou, Eleni. 'The International Economic Crisis and the Position of Greece. The Theses of KKE'. *International Communist Review* 1 (2009), accessed 16 February 2016, http://www.iccr.gr/site/en/issue1/the-international-economic-crisis-and-theposition- of-greece-the-theses-of-kke.html.

Mudde, Cas. 'After One Year in Government, Syriza and Greece Are More Isolated Than Ever'. *The World Post*, 25 January 2016, http://www.huffingtonpost.com/theworldpost/.

Mudde, Cas. 'Podemos, and the Beginning of the End for Europe's Radical Left'. *The Guardian*, 21 December 2015, sec. Opinion, http://www.theguardian.com/commentisfree/2015/dec/21/podemos-europe-radical-left-party-syriza-pablo-iglesias-spanish-elections.

Mudde, Cas. 'The Far Right in the 2014 European Elections: Of Earthquakes, Cartels and Designer Fascists'. *The Washington Post*, 30 May 2014, https://www.washingtonpost.com/news/monkey-cage/wp/2014/05/30/the-far-right-in-the-2014-european-elections-of-earthquakes-cartels-and-designer-fascists/.

Mudde, Cas. 'The Populist Radical Right: A Pathological Normalcy.' *West European Politics* 33, no. 6 (2010): 1167–86. doi:10.1080/01402382.2010.508901.

Mudde, Cas. 'The Populist Zeitgeist.' *Government and Opposition* 39, no. 4 (2004): 541–56.

Mudde, Cas. 'The War of Words Defining the Extreme Right Party Family'. *West European Politics* 19, no. 2 (1996): 225–48.Mudde, Cas. (2012) 'The Dutch Elections and the Eurosceptic Paradox.' *Open Democracy* 2012, accessed 1 September 2015, http://www.opendemocracy.net/cas-mudde/dutch-elections-and-eurosceptic-paradox.

Mudde, Cas. *Populist Radical Right Parties in Europe*. Cambridge: Cambridge University Press, 2007.

Mudde, Cas. *The Relationship Between Immigration and Nativism in Europe and North America*. Washington: Migration Policy Institute, 2012.

Murphy, John A. 'Why we should be wary of Sinn Féin in government.' *The Irish Times* (8 July 2014).

Murphy, Paul. 'Why Syriza Capitulated and the Alternative Road of "Rupture."' *The Socialist* 93 (July to August 2015).

Nakai, Ryo. 'The Influence of Party Competition on Minority Politics: A Comparison of Latvia and Estonia.' *Journal on Ethnopolitics and Minority Issues in Europe* 13, no. 1 (2014): 57–85.

NRC. 'Harry van Bommel: SP-top overweegt nieuwe partijnaam'. 2 June 2012, accessed 1 September 2015, http://www.nrc.nl/nieuws/2012/06/02/harry-van-bommel-sp-top-overweegt-nieuwe-partijnaam/.

NRC. 'Marijnissen: coalitie tussen PvdA en VVD kost ze geloofwaardigheid'. 23 September 2012, accessed 1 September 2015, http://www.nrc.nl/nieuws/2012/09/23/marijnissen-pvda-en-vvd-zijn-ongeloofwaardig-als-ze-coalitie-vormen/.

NRC. 'SP wil in cabinet en is bereid tot compromissen'. 1 June 2012, accessed 1 September 2015, http://www.nrc.nl/nieuws/2012/06/01/sp-wil-in-kabinet-en-is-bereid-tot-compromissen/.

NRC. 'SP-standpunt over EU-boete levert geen zetels op'. 19 August 2012, accessed 1 September 2015, http://www.nrc.nl/verkiezingen/2012/08/19/sp-standpunt-over-eu-boete-levert-geen-zetels-op/.

NRC. 'Buitenlandse media waarschuwen voor anti-Europa-partij van Roemer'. 31 August 2012, accessed 1 September 2015, http://www.nrc.nl/stevendejong/2012/08/30/buitenlandse-media-waarschuwen-voor-anti-europa-partij-van-roemer/.

NRC. 'Buitenlandse media waarschuwen vooranti-Europa-partij van Roemer'. 30 August 2012, accessed 1 September 2015, http://www.nrc.nl/stevendejong/2012/08/30/ buitenlandse-media-waarschuwen-voor-anti-europa-partij-van-roemer/.

NRC. 'Insiderspanel: kan de PvdA zich nog profileren ten opzichte van de SP?' 22 August 2012, accessed 1 September 2015,_http://www.nrc.nl/verkiezingen/2012/08/22/ insiderspanel-kan-de-pvda-zich-nog-profileren-ten-opzichte-van-de-sp/.

NRC. 'Marijnissen voorziet 45 zetels voor SP'. 28 August 2012, accessed 1 September 2015, http://www.nrc.nl/verkiezingen/2012/08/28/marijnissen-voorziet-45-zetels-voor-sp/.

NRC. 'Peiling De Hond: verlies SP vooral door terugkerende PvdA-stemmers'. 2 September 2012, accessed 1 September 2015, http://www.nrc.nl/verkiezingen/2012/09/02/ peiling-de-hond-verlies-sp-vooral-door-terugkerende-pvda-stemmers/.

NRC. 'PvdA-voorzitter: Nederland kan zich geen kabinet met SP permitteren'. 3 August 2012, accessed 1 September 2015, http://www.nrc.nl/nieuws/2012/08/03/ pvda-voorzitter-nederland-kan-zich-geen-kabinet-met-sp-permitteren/.

NRC. 'Roemer onder vuur om 'rabiate standpunten' over begrotingstekort', 16 August 2012, accessed 1 September 2015, http://www.nrc.nl/verkiezingen/2012/08/16/ roemer-onder-vuur-om-eu-dreigement/.

NRC. 'Wientjes noemt SP-programma rampzalig', 25 August 2012, accessed 1 September 2015, http://www.nrc.nl/verkiezingen/2012/08/25/wientjes-noemt-sp-programma-rampzalig/.

NU. 'Gesthuizen wil "linkse en activistische" SP in de regering.' NU 30 August 2015, accessed 5 September 2015, http://www.nu.nl/politiek/4115846/gesthuizen-wil-linkse-en-activistische-sp-in-regering.html.

NU. 'SP Had No Plan B in Campaign.' *NU*, 13 September 2012, accessed 1 September 2015, http://www.nu.nl/.

Nunns, A. 'More than a Demonstration, Less than a Revolt.' *Red Pepper* 183 (2012): 17–19.

Ó Broin, Eoin. *Sinn Féin and the Politics of Left Republicanism.* London: Pluto Press, 2009.

Occupy London. 'Economics Statement' 2011, 6 December 2011, http://occupylondon.org.uk/about/statements/statement-on-economy/.

Odmalm, Pontus and Tim Bale. 'Immigration into the Mainstream: Conflicting Ideological Streams, Strategic Reasoning and Party Competition.' *Acta Politica* (2014), accessed 20 September. doi: 10.1057/ap.2014.28.

OECD. 'Migration and Foreign Born Population.' 2015, accessed 1 March 2016, https://data.oecd.org/migration/foreign-born-population.htm.

OFCE. 'Austerity and purchasing power in France.' 5 January 2015, accessed 19 August 2015, http://www.ofce.sciences-po.fr/blog/austerity-purchasing-power-france/.

Office of Citizen and Migration Affairs. 'Latvijas Iedzivotaju Sadalijums Pec Nacionala Sastava Un Valstiskas Piederibas (The Division of Latvia's Inhabitants by Nationality and Citizenship).' 1 January 2015, http://www.pmlp.gov.lv/lv/assets/ documents/statistika/01.01.2015/ISVN_Latvija_pec_TTB_VPD.pdf.

Olsen, Jonathan, Dan Hough and Michael Koß. 'From Pariahs to Players? Left Parties in National Governments'. In *Left Parties in National Governments*, edited by Jonathan Olsen, Michael Koß and Dan Hough, 1–15. Basingstoke: Palgrave, 2010.

Olsen, Jonathan, Michael Koß and Dan Hough, eds. *Left Parties in National Governments*. Basingstoke: Palgrave, 2010.

Opálka, Miroslav. 'Podklad k vystoupení na semináři SPaS 26. dubna 2012. Téma – sociální politika' 2012, accessed 5 August 2015, https://www.kscm.cz/viewDocument.asp?document=5769.

Ortega, Eloísa and Juan Peñalosa. *The Spanish Economic Crisis: Key Factors and Growth Challenges in the Euro Area*. Madrid: Banco de España, 2012.

Otjes, Simon and Tom Louwerse. 'Populists in Parliament: Comparing Left-Wing and Right-Wing Populism in the Netherlands.' *Political Studies* 63, no. 1 (2015): 60–79.

Otjes, Simon and Gerrit Voerman. 'The Netherlands.' *EJPR Political Data Yearbook* 2014 53, no. 1 (2014): 229–34.

Otjes, Simon and Gerrit Voerman. 'The Netherlands', *EJPR Political Data Yearbook* 52, no. 1 (2013): 162–9.

Ovenden, Kevin. *Syriza: Inside the Labyrinth*. London: Pluto Press, 2015.

Ozoliņš, Aivars. 'Nebalsotāji Atbalstīs Rubiku (Non-Voters Support Rubiks).' *Diena*, 6 October 2006, http://www.diena.lv/arhivs/nebalsotaji-atbalstis-rubiku-12925970.

Pabriks, Artis and Aiga Štokenberga. 'Political Parties and the Party System in Latvia.' In *Post-Communist EU Member States: Parties and Party Systems*, edited by Susanne Jungerstam-Mulders, 51–68. Aldershot: Ashgate, 2006.

Pabriks, Artis and Aldis Purs. *Latvia: The Challenges of Change*. Abingdon: Routledge, 2002.

Panayiotou, Andreas. 'Lenin in the Coffeeshop.' *Postcolonial Studies* 9, no. 3 (2006): 267–80.

Panayiotou, Andreas. 'Οι Τράπεζες, τα ΜΜΕ και οι Προσπάθειες Συγκάλυψης, Μετατόπισης και Λογοκρισίας των Σκανδάλων' [The Banks, the Mass Media and the Attempts at Covering, Silencing and Censoring the Scandals], accessed 5 February 2014, http://koinonioloyika.blogspot.com/2013/01/blog-post_23.html.

Paniagua, Juán Luis and Luis Ramiro. *Voz, Conflicto y Salida. Un Estudio sobre Faccionalismo: Nueva Izquierda, 1992-2001*. Madrid: Editorial Complutense, 2003.

Panitch, Leo and Sam Gindin. 'The Current Crisis: A Socialist Perspective'. In *The Great Credit Crash*, edited by Martijn Konings, 370–95. London: Verso, 2010.

Papariga, Aleka. 'Speech of the General Secretary of the CC, Al. Papariga, at the nationwide demonstration of the party on 15 May'. 15 May 2010, accessed 16 February 2016, http://interold.kke.gr/News/2010news/2010-06-22-omilia-aleka-15may/view.html.

Pappas, Takis S. 'Populist Hegemony in Greece'. *openDemocracy*, 25 September 2015, https://www.opendemocracy.net/can-europe-make-it/takis-s-pappas/populist-hegemony-in-greece.

Patterson, Henry. *The Politics of Illusion: A Political History of the IRA*. London: Serif, 1997.

Patton, David F. 'Germany's Left Party.PDS and the "Vacuum Thesis": From Regional Milieu Party to Left Alternative?' *Journal of Communist Studies and Transition Politics* 22, no. 2 (2006): 206–27.

Pauwels, Teun. *Populism in Western Europe: Comparing Belgium, Germany and the Netherlands*. Abingdon: Routledge, 2014.

PCP. *Compromisso por Uma Política Patriótica e de Esquerda – Legislativas de 2011*. Lisbon: PCP, 2011.

PCP. *Declaração Programática do PCP para as Eleições para o Parlamento Europeu 2014*. Lisbon: PCP, 2014.

PCP. *Políticas Patrióticas e de Esquerda. Soluções para um Portugal com Futuro*. Lisbon: PCP, 2014.

PCP. *Política Patriótica e de Esquerda. Soluções para um Portugal com Futuro*. Lisbon: PCP, 2015.

PCP. *Programa e Estatutos aprovados no XIX Congresso. Uma Democracia Avançada, os Valores de Abril no Futuro de Portugal*. Lisbon: PCP, 2012.

Pegasiou Adonis. 'The Cypriot Economic Collapse: More Than a Conventional South European Failure.' *Mediterranean Politics* 18, no. 3 (2013): 333–51.

PEL. 'Peace, development and employment with rights.' final declaration, 2nd PEL Congress, Prague, November 2007.

PEL. 'Escaping from austerity, rebuilding Europe.' draft programme, 4th PEL Congress, Madrid, December 2013a.

PEL. *'Unite for a left alternative in Europe'*, draft document, 4th PEL Congress, Madrid, December 2013b.

PEL. *Manifesto for the 2014 European elections*, 2014.

PEL. (nd) 'Statue of the Party of the European Left', accessed 30 July 2015, http://www.european-left.org/propos-de-la-ge/documents.

People Before Profit Alliance. *Vote Brid Smith. Send a Working Class Fighter to the European Parliament*. Dublin: European Election Manifesto, 2014.

Pettai, Vello and Marcus Kreuzer. 'Party Politics in the Baltic States: Social Bases and Institutional Context.' *East European Politics & Societies* 13, no. 1 (1998): 148–89.

Pina, Christine. 'L'extrême-gauche, la vraie gauche?' In *Les partis politiques français*, edited by Pierre Bréchon, 181–203. Paris: La documentation française, 2011.

Podemos. 'Turning outrage into political change,' English translation of the 2014 Podemos manifesto: *Mover ficha*, https://hiredknaves.wordpress.com/2014/01/20/podemos-translated-manifesto/.

Poguntke, Thomas. *Alternative Politics: The German Green Party*. Edinburgh: Edinburgh University Press, 1994.

Polášek, Martin, and Novotný, Vilém, Perottino, Michael and col. 'Mezi masovou a kartelovou stranou. Možnosti teorie při výkladu vývoje ČSSD a KSČM v letech 2000-2010.' (Praha: Slon, 2012).

Porcaro, Mimmo. 'Occupy Lenin.' In *Socialist Register: The Question of Strategy*, edited by Leo Panitch, Greg Albo and Vivek Chibber, 84–97. London: Merlin Press, 2013.

Prager Frühling Magazine. 'This is a movement. Massendissidenz in Merkelland? Überlegungen zur Flüchtlingspolitikkrise.' *Rosalux* 3 (2015): 6–7.

Prentoulis, Marina and Lasse Thomassen. 'The Winds Are Changing: A New Left Populism for Europe'. *openDemocracy*, 27 January 2015, http://www.opendemocracy.net/can-europe-make-it/marina-prentoulis-lasse-thomassen/winds-are-changing-new-left-populism-for-europe.

Protopapas, Vassilis. 'Empty Vessels? The Center Parties' Linkages with Society.' In *Party-Society Relations in the Republic of Cyprus: Political and Societal Strategies*, edited by Giorgos Charalambous and Christophoros Christophorou, 69–90. Abingdon: Routledge, 2015.

Pudal, Bernard. *Un monde défait: les communistes français de 1956 à nos jours.* Bellecombe-en-Bauges: Editions du Croquant, 2009.

Ramirez, Gloria M. *The Fire and the Word: A History of the Zapatista Movement.* San Francisco: City Light Books, 2008.

Ramiro, Luis and Raúl Gómez. 'Radical Left Populism during the Great Recession: Podemos and its Competition with the Established Radical Left', *Political Studies* (June 22, 2016). doi: 10.1177/0032321716647400.

Ramiro, Luis. 'Support for Radical Left Parties in Western Europe: Social Background, Ideology and Political Orientations.' *European Political Science Review* 8, no. 1 (Febraury 2016): 1–23.

Ramiro, Luis and Tania Verge. 'Impulse and Decadence of Linkage Processes: Evidence from the Spanish Radical Left.' *South European Society and Politics* 18 (2013): 41–60.

Ramiro, Luis. 'Electoral Competition, Organizational Constraints and Party Change: The Communist Party of Spain (PCE) and United Left (IU), 1986–2000.' *Journal of Communist Studies and Transition Politics* 20 (2004): 1–29.

Ramiro, Luis. 'Entre coalicion y partido: la evolución del modelo organizativo de Izquierda Unida.' *Revista Española de Ciencia Política* 1 (2000): 237–68.

Ramiro, Luis. *Cambio y adaptación en la izquierda. La evolución del Partido Comunista de España y de Izquierda Unida.* Madrid: Centro de Investigaciones Sociológicas, 2004.

Ransdorf, Miloslav. 'Ekonomická mapa pro sjezd modrých mimoňů', accessed 20 July 2015, http://www.ransdorfmiloslav.com/clanky/ekonomicke/ekonomicka-mapa-pro-sjezd-modrych-mimonu.

Ransdorf, Miloslav. 'Sedíš-li na mrtvém koni, sesedni!'. *25 let budování kapitalismu* 124–6.

Raunio, Tapio. 'Political Parties in the European Union.' In *Handbook of European Union Politics*, edited by Knud Erik Jørgensen, Mark A. Pollack and Ben Rosamond, 247–62. London: SAGE, 2007.

Rehmann, Jan. *Connective Party or Return to a 'War of Maneuver'?* Berlin: Rosa Luxemburg Stiftung, 2013.

Reif, Karlheinz and Hermann Schmitt. 'Nine Second Order National Elections: A Conceptual Framework for the Analysis of European Election Results.' *European Journal of Political Research* 8 (1980): 3–44.

Reißig, Rolf. *Gesellschafts-Transformation im 21. Jahrhundert. Ein neues Konzept sozialen Wandels.* Wiesbaden: VS Verlag für Sozialwissenschaften, 2009.

Reitan, R. 'Coordinated Power in Contemporary Leftist Activism'. In *Power and Transnational Activism*, edited by T. Olsen, 51–72. Abingdon: Routledge, 2011.

Rendueles, Cesar and Jorge Sola. 'Podemos and the Paradigm Shift'. *Jacobin*, 13 April 2015, https://www.jacobinmag.com/2015/04/podemos-spain-pablo-iglesias-european-left/.

Riexinger, Bernd. 'Eine Vision: Einstieg in ein anderes Europa.' *Europalinks. Beilage der Tageszeitung Neues Deutschland in Zusammenartbeit mit der Zeitschrift Luxemburg* (February 2014): 23–4, accessed 17 March 2016, https://www.neues-deutschland.de/artikel/923336.eine-vision-einstieg-in-ein-anderes-europa.html.

Riexinger, Bernd, Pierre Laurent, Maite Mola and Theodoros Paraskevopoulos. 'Hoffnung für einen demokratischen Aufbruch in Europa.' 17 February 2015, http://www.die-linke.de/nc/die-linke/nachrichten/detail/artikel/hoffnung-fuer-einen-demokratischen-aufbruch-in-europa/.

Right2Water. *Policy Principles for a Progressive Irish Government*. Dublin: Right2Water 2015.

Rivero, Jacobo. *Podemos. Objetivo: Asaltar los cielos*. Barcelona: Planeta, 2015.

Roder, Knut. 'The German Left from Laeken to Lisbon.' In *The Left and the European Constitution: From Laeken to Lisbon*, edited by Michael Holmes and Knut Roder, 95–117. Manchester: Manchester University Press, 2012.

Rodrik, Dani. *The Globalization Paradox*. Oxford: Oxford University Press, 2012.

Rooduijn, Matthijs and Tjitske Akkerman. 'Flank Attacks. Populism and Left-Right Radicalism in Western Europe'. *Party Politics*, 2015. doi:10.1177/1354068815596514.

Roos, Jerome and Leonidas Oikonomakis. 'We are Everywhere! The Autonomous Roots of the Real Democracy Movement'. Paper delivered at 7th annual ECPR general conference, Sciences Po Bordeaux, 4–7 September 2013, https://www.academia.edu/4342422/The_Autonomous_Roots_of_the_Real_Democracy_Movement.

Rosa-Luxemburg-Stiftung. 'Flüchtlinge wilkommen – Refugees welcome? Mythen und Fakten zur Migrations- und Flüchtlingspolitik.' *Luxemburg Argumente* 8, no. 2 (2015): 45–50.

Rose, Richard. 'New Baltic Barometer III: A Survey Study.' *Studies in Public Policy* 284 (1997).

Rose, Richard. 'New Baltic Barometer VI: A Post-Enlargement Survey'. *Studies in Public Policy* 401 (2005).

Rosenkvist, Marianne et al., 'Enhedslistens forspildte muligheder – Hvad kan vi lære af Folketingsvalget 2015?' *Modkraft*, 14 July 2015, accessed 30 November 2015, http://modkraft.dk/blog/marianne-rosenkvist/enhedslistens-forspildte-muligheder-hvad-kan-vi-l-re-af-folketingsvalget.

Rubiks, A. and F. Stroganov, eds. *SPL: Istoriya v Dokumentakh*. Riga: Latvijas Sociālistiskā partija, 2006.

Rüdig, Wolfgang and Georgios Karyotis. 'Who Protests in Greece? Mass Opposition to Austerity.' *British Journal of Political Science* 44 (2014): 487–513.

S.M. 'The Bernie Manifesto: How Much of a Socialist Is Sanders?' *The Economist*, 1 February 2016, http://www.economist.com/blogs/democracyinamerica/2016/02/bernie-manifesto.

Samman, Amin. 'Making Financial History: The Crisis of 2008 and the Return of the Past.' *Millennium* 42, no. 2 (2014): 309–30.

Savov, Penčo. 'Teoreticko-analytické pracoviště KSČM a komunisté. Materiál k VII. Sjezdu KSČM je pro marxisty-leninovce nepřijatelný', *Dialog* (18) 234, 3.

Schraad-Tischlera, Daniel and Christian Kroll. 'Social Justice in the EU – Cross-country Comparative.' *Social Inclusion Monitor Europe (SIM).* Güttersloh: Bertelsmann Stiftung, 2014.

Serrano, Manuel Nunes Ramires, 2015. 'Why is there no Syriza in Portugal?', accessed 30 December 2015, https://www.opendemocracy.net/democraciaabierta/manuel-nunes-ramires-serrano/why-is-there-no-syriza-in-portugal.

Seymour, Richard. 'Left Unity: A Report from the Founding Conference.' *New Left Project* 1 December 2013, accessed 30 November 2015, http://www.newleftproject.org/index.php/site/article_comments/left_unity_a_report_from_the_founding_conference.

SF. 'Plads Til Alle Der Vil', accessed 20 September 2015, http://sf.dk/det-vil-vi/et-mangfoldigt-danmark/udlaendinge-og-integration. Copenhagen: SF, 2014.

SF. *Socialdemokraternes og SF's Forslag Til en Integrationsreform for Danmark.* Copenhagen: SF, 2011.

Shambaugh, Jay C. 'The Euro's Three Crises'. Brookings Papers on Economic Activity, Spring 2012, http://www.brookings.edu/about/projects/bpea/latest-conference/shambaugh.

Shaw, Jo, Paul Magnette, Lars Hoffman and Anna Vergès Bausili, *Convention on the Future of Europe: Working Towards an EU Constitution.* London: Federal Trust, 2003.

Sigbjörnsson, Björn Þór. 'Óskhyggja og fögur orð duga skammt.' *Fréttablaðið.* 26 July 2008.

Sigfússon, Steingrímur J. 'Byggjum framtíð á fjölbreytni.' 19 October 2001, accessed 5 November 2015, http://eldri.vg.is/wp-content/uploads/2013/02/Setningarr%C3%A6%C3%B0a-Steingr%C3%ADms.pdf.Sigfússon, Steingrímur J. 'Fjármálafyrirtæki.' 14 October 2003, accessed 5 November 2015, http://www.althingi.is/altext/130/10/r14143923.sgml.

Sigfússon, Steingrímur J. 'Setningarræða.' 21 October 2005, accessed 5 November 2015, http://eldri.vg.is/wp-content/uploads/2013/02/Setningarr%C3%A6%C3%B0a-Steingr%C3%ADms-J.-Sigf%C3%BAssonar1.pdf.

Sigfússon, Steingrímur J. 'Umræður utan dagskrár (skuldastaða þjóðarbúsins).' 10 March 2003, accessed 5 November 2015, http://www.althingi.is/altext/130/03/r10160721.sgml.

Sigfússon, Steingrímur J. et al. 'Tillaga til þingsályktunar um aðgerðir til að tryggja efnahagslegan stöðugleika', accessed 13 September 2015, http://www.althingi.is/altext/131/s/1014.html.

Sigurbjörnsson, Stefán Rafn. 'Tóku skarpa vinstri beygju á Selfossi.' *Visir.is* 26 October 2015, accessed 5 November 2015, http://www.visir.is/toku-skarpa-vinstri-beygju-a-selfossi/article/2015151029193.

Sile, Vija and Ilze Dzalbe. 'The Financial Crisis and the Discourses of Latvia's Political Parties.' *European Integration Studies* 5 (2012): 102–8.

Simiti, Marilena. 'Rage and Protest: The case of the Greek Indignant movement', GreeSE Paper No. 82 Hellenic Observatory Papers on Greece and Southeast Europe, February 2014, http://www.lse.ac.uk/europeanInstitute/research/hellenicObservatory/CMS%20pdf/Publications/GreeSE/GreeSE-No82.pdf.

Sinn Féin. *Introducing Martina Anderson, MEP.* Derry, 2015.

Sinn Féin. *Putting Ireland First.* Dublin: European election manifesto, 2014.

Sjálfstæðisflokkurinn, 'Endurreisn atvinnulífsins: Uppgjör, umfjöllun, álit, hugmyndir og tillögur vegna stóðu og framtíðar íslensks atvinnulífs.' 2009, accessed 5 November 2015, http://www.framtidarnefnd.is/sm/u/d/Endurreisn_atvinnul%C3%ADfsins.pdf.

Skipper, Pernille. 'Tale: KRGAbenhavn er for alle.' 26 May 2013, accessed 20 September 2015, https://enhedslisten.dk/artikel/tale-kbenhavn-er-alle-71430.

Skuland, Brita. 'The Impact of Historical Conflicts and Cleavages on the Formation of New Political Oppositions in Latvia.' University of Oslo, 2005.

Slačálek, Ondřej. 'Opatrně s tou pravdou', *A2Alarm*, 2015, accessed 10 July 2015, http://a2larm.cz/2014/02/opatrne-s-tou-pravdou/.

Smith, Graham. 'The Ethnic Democracy Thesis and the Citizenship Question in Estonia and Latvia.' *Nationalities Papers* 24, no. 2 (1996): 199–216.

Socialist Party. *We Can't Afford to Live: Shift the Burden to the Super-Rich.* Dublin: European Election Manifesto, 2014.

Soeiro, José. 'Da Geração À Rasca Ao Que Se Lixe a Troika. Portugal No Novo Ciclo Internacional De Protesto.' *Sociologia* XXVIII (2014): 55–79.

Souvlis, George and Samuele Mazzolini. 'An Open Letter to Yanis Varoufakis', *LeftEast*, 29 March 2016, http://www.criticatac.ro/lefteast/an-open-letter-to-yanis-varoufakis/.

SP. *Handvest 2000.* Rotterdam: SP, 1991.

SP. *A Better Europe Starts.* Amersfoort: SP, 2006.

SP. *A Better Netherlands for the Same Money: Election Programme 2006-2010.* Amersfoort: SP, 2006.

SP. *Lessons from the Credit Crisis.* SP: Amersfoort: 2008.

SP. *Crisis Plan SP: A New Course for Netherlands* Amersfoort: SP, 2009.

SP. *Better Netherlands for Less money: Election Programme 2011-2015.* Amersfoort: SP, 2010.

SP. 'De Jong wil referendum over Europese Economische Regering.' 14 November 2011, accessed 1 September 2015, https://www.sp.nl/nieuws/2011/11/jong-wil-referendum-over-europese-economische-regering.

SP. 'Bonusverbod Voor alle Banken en Verzekeraars.' SP, 31 January 2012, accessed 1 September 2015, http://www.sp.nl/nieuwsberichten/11251/120131-pvda_en_sp_bonusverbod_voor_alle_banken_en_verzekeraars.html.

SP. 'Nieuw Vertrouwen: Verkiezingsprogramma 2013-2017.' Amersfoort: SP, 2012. https://www.sp.nl/verkiezingen/2012/programma/gedeelde-toekomst.

SP. *European Election Manifesto: 'No to this EU'.* Amersfoort: SP, 2014.

SP. 'Kandidaat-Vooritters: Maak Kennis Met Sharon Gestuizen en Ron Meyer.' 14 August 2015, accessed 1 September 2015, https://www.sp.nl/nieuws/2015/08/kandidaat-voorzitters-maak-kennis-met-sharon-gesthuizen-en-ron-meyer.

SP. 'Kom naar de red de zorg demonstratie.' 21 August 2015, accessed 1 September 2015, https://www.sp.nl/nieuws/2015/08/kom-naar-red-zorg-demonstratie.

Special Investigation Commission. 'Ágrip um meginniðurstöður skýrslunnar.' *Skýrsla Rannsóknarnefndar Alþingis* 1, 2010.

Special Investigation Commission. 'Appendix II.' *Skýrsla Rannsóknarnefndar Alþingis* 8, 2010.

Special Investigation Commission. 'Einkavæðing og eignarhald bankanna.' *Skýrsla Rannsóknarnefndar Alþingis* 1, 2010.

Special Investigation Commission. 'Stefna stjórnvalda um stærð og starfsemi íslenskra fjármálafyrirtækja.' *Skýrsla Rannsóknarnefndar Alþingis* 1, 2010.

Special Investigation Commission. 'Orsakir falls íslensku bankanna – ábyrgð, mistök og vanræksla'. *Skýrsla Rannsóknarnefndar Alþingis* 7, 2010.

Spehr, Christoph. 'Wem gehört die Partei? Moderne Linkspartei, Offene Organisation, Offener Sozialismus.' In *Parteien und Bewegungen. Die Linke im Aufbruch*, edited by Michael Brie and Cornelia Hildebrandt, 44–57. Berlin: Karl Dietz Verlag, 2006.

Spiegel Online. 'Merkel's Unintended Creation: Could Tsipras' Win Upset Balance of Power in Europe?' *Spiegel Online*, 30 January 2015, http://www.spiegel.de/international/europe/greek-election-makes-euro-zone-exit-real-possibility-a-1015907.html.

Spiegel Online. 'Schuldenstreit mit Griechenland: Grünen-Wähler begrüßen Merkels Krisenkurs.' 14 July 2015, accessed 1 December 2015, http://www.spiegel.de/politik/deutschland/griechenland-gruenen-waehler-lieben-angela-merkels-kurs-a-1043649.html.

Spiegel Online. 'Übergriffe in Silvesternacht: Union plant nach Kölner Gewaltexzessen schärfere Gesetze.' 8 January 2016, accessed 18 February 2016, http://www.spiegel.de/politik/deutschland/koeln-cdu-plant-schaerfere-gesetze-und-schnelle-abschiebung-a-1071069.html.

Spourdalakis, Michalis. '2007 Greek Elections: Signs of Major Political Realignment. Challenges and hopes for the Left.' *Studies in Political Economy* 82 (2008): 171–86.

Spourdalakis, Michalis. 'Rekindling Hope: Syriza's Challenges and Prospects'. In *The Enigma of Europe*, edited by Walter Baier, Eric Canepa and Eva Himmelstoss, 221–28. Transform! Yearbook 2016. London: Merlin Press, 2016.

Spourdalakis, Michalis. 'The Miraculous Rise of the "Phenomenon SYRIZA".' *International Critical Thought* 4, no. 3 (2014): 354–66.

Statistics Iceland. 'General Elections to the Althingi 27 April 2013.' *Statistical Series, Elections*. 2015.

Stavrakakis, Yianiis and Giorgos Katsambekis, 'Left-wing Populism in the European Periphery: The Case of SYRIZA.' *Journal of Political Ideologies* 19, no. 2 (2014): 119–42.

Steiner, Barbara. 'The Swedish Left Party.' In *From Revolution to Coalition, RLPs in Europe*, edited by Birgit Daiber, Cornelia Hildebrandt and Anna Striethorst, 65–77. Berlin: Rosa Luxemburg Stiftung 2012.

Steger, Manfred B. and Erin K. Wilson. 'Anti-Globalization or Alter-Globalization? Mapping the Political Ideology of the Global Justice Movement.' *International Studies Quarterly* 56, no. 3 (2012): 439–54.

Stjórnarráð Íslands. 'Ríkisstjórnatal frá stofnun lýðveldis', accessed 30 June 2015, http://www.stjornarrad.is/Rikisstjornartal/.

Stjórnarráð Íslands. 'Samstarfsyfirlýsing ríkisstjórnar Samfylkingarinnar og Vinstri-hreyfingarinnar – græns framboðs', accessed 30 June 2015, http://www.stjornarrad.is/media/Skjol/rikisstjorn_8mai09.pdf. 2009.

Stjórnarráð Íslands. 'Verkefni ríkisstjórnar', accessed 30 June 2015, http://www.stjornarrad.is/media/rikisstjorn/verkefni-rikisstjornar.pdf. 2011.

Streeck, Wolfgang. 'The strikes sweeping Germany are here to stay', *The Guardian* 22 May 2015, http://www.theguardian.com/commentisfree/2015/may/22/strikes-sweeping-germany-here-to-stay.

Striethorst, Anna. *Members and Electorates of Left Parties in Europe.* Berlin: Rosa Luxemburg-Stiftung, 2011.

Striethorst, Anna. 'Aktuelle Themen und Debatten der europäischen Linksparteien.' In *Von Revolution bis Koalition. Linke Parteien in Europa*, edited by Birgit Daiber, Cornelia Hildebrandt and Anna Striethorst, 49–66. Berlin: Karl Dietz Verlag, 2010.

Striethorst, Anna. 'Mitglieder und Elektorate von Linksparteien in Europa.' In *Von Revolution bis Koalition. Linke Parteien in Europa*, edited by Birgit Daiber, Cornelia Hildebrandt and Anna Striethorst, 89–113. Berlin: Karl Dietz Verlag, 2010.

Šūpule, Inese. 'The Construction of National and Ethnic Identity in Online Discussions on Referenda Initiatives in Latvia.' *Baltic Journal of European Studies* 2, no. 1 (2011): 119–37.

Süssner, Henning. 'Sweden: The Long March to a Coalition.' In *The Left in Government in Latin America and Europe*, edited by Birgit Daiber. Brussels: Rosa Luxemburg-Stiftung, 2010.

Synaspismós. 'Πολιτική Απόφαση 6ου (έκτακτου) Συνεδρίου του Συνασπισμού της Αριστεράς των Κινημάτων και της Οικολογίας'. 2010, accessed 16 February 2016, http://www.syn.gr/6osynedrio/polapofasi.pdf.

Syriza. 'The political resolution of the 1st congress of SYRIZA'. July 2013, accessed 16 February 2016, http://www.syriza.gr/article/id/53894/The-political-resolution-of-the-1st-congress-of-SYRIZA.html#.ViYRGX7hDIV.

Syriza. 'The Thessaloniki Programme'. September 2014, accessed 16 February 2016, http://www.syriza.gr/article/SYRIZA---THE-THESSALONIKI-PROGRAMME.html.

Syriza. 'Τι είναι και τι θέλει ο Συνασπισμός Ριζοσπαστικής Αριστεράς' (Founding Statement). Published online July 2013, accessed 20 September 2015, http://www.syriza.gr/page/idrytikh-diakhryksh.html#.VfQCQbxViko.

Syriza. 'Η υπομονή μας τέλειωσε! 25 Μαῖου 2014: ΨΗΦΙΖΟΥΜΕ ΚΑΙ ΦΕΥΓΟΥΝ!'. 2014, accessed 16 February 2016, https://left.gr/news/i-ypomoni-mas-teleiose-25-maioy-2014-psifizoyme-kai-feygoyn.

Syriza. ΟΙ ΠΡΟΣΦΥΓΙΚΕΣ ΚΑΙ ΜΕΤΑΝΑΣΤΕΥΤΙΚΕΣ ΡΟΕΣ ΕΙΝΑΙ ΕΝΑ ΟΙΚΟΥΜΕΝΙΚΟ ΖΗΤΗΜΑ, http://www.syriza.gr/theseis/pros_diavoulefsi_metanasteytiko.pdf. Syriza, Athens, 2014.

Syriza. *The Election Programme of Syriza for the Election 6 May 2012.* Athens: Syriza, 2012.

Tagesschau.de. 'Bundestagsabstimmung zu Griechenland.' 19 August 2015, accessed 26 January 2015, https://www.tagesschau.de/inland/griechenland-abweichler-101.html.

Tannahill, R. Neal. *Communist Parties of Western Europe: A Comparative Study.* Westport: Greenwood Press, 1978.

Taylor-Gooby, Peter. 'Root and Branch Restructuring to Achieve Major Cuts: The Social Policy Programme of the 2010 UK Coalition Government.' *Social Policy & Administration* 46, no. 1 (2012): 61–82.

Tejerina, Benjamin, Ignacia Perugorría, Tova Benski and Lauren Langman. 'From Indignation to Occupation: A New Wave of Global Mobilization.' *Current Sociology* 61, no. 4 (2013): 377–92.

Telegraaf. 'Roemer: Samsom is ongeloofwaardig.' 17 March 2015, accessed 1 September, 2015, http://www.telegraaf.nl/verkiezingen/ps2015/23813194/___Samsom_is_ongeloofwaardig___.html.

Thorvaldur, Gylfason. 'Democracy on Ice: A Post-Mortem of the Icelandic Constitution.' *open Democracy*, 19 June 2013, http://www.opendemocracy.net/can-europe-make-it/thorvaldur-gylfason/democracy-on-ice-post-mortem-of-icelandic-constitution.

Tilly, Charles. *From Mobilization to Revolution.* Reading, MA: Addison-Wesley, 1978.

Torcal, Mariano. 'The Incumbent Electoral Defeat in the 2011 Spanish National Elections: The Effect of the Economic Crisis in an Ideological Polarized Party System.' *Journal of Elections, Public Opinion and Parties* 24 (2014): 203–21.

Tormey, Simon. *The End of Representative Politics.* Cambridge: Polity, 2015.

Torreblanca, Ignacio. *Asaltar los cielos. Podemos o la política después de la crisis.* Madrid: Debate, 2015.

Trading Economics. 'International Migration Data', accessed 1 March 2016, http://www.tradingeconomics.com/greece/international-migrant-stock-percent-of-population-wb-data.html.

Treib, Oliver. 'The Voter Says no, but Nobody Listens: Causes and Consequences of the Eurosceptic vote in the 2014 European Elections.' *Journal of European Public Policy* 21, no. 10 (2014): 1541–54.

Trimithiotis, Dimitris. 'Communication and Interactions Between Parties and Youth Organisations in Cyprus.' In *Party-Society Relations in the Republic of Cyprus: Political and Societal Strategies*, edited by Giorgos Charalambous and Christophoros Christophorou, 166–82. Abingdon: Routledge, 2015.

Troost, Axel. 'Die Flüchtlingsfrage als europäische und gesamtdeutsche Aufgabe.' 4 September 2015, accessed 1 December 2015, http://www.die-linke.de/nc/die-linke/nachrichten/detail/artikel/die-fluechtlingsfrage-als-europaeische-und-gesamt-deutsche-aufgabe/.

Tsakatika, Myrto and Costas Eleftheriou. 'The Radical Left's Turn towards Civil Society in Greece: One Strategy, Two Paths.' *South European Society and Politics* 18 (2013): 81–99.

Tsakatika, Myrto and Marco Lisi. '"Zippin' up my Boots, Goin' back to my Roots": Radical Left Parties in Southern Europe.' *South European Society and Politics* 18, no. 1 (2013): 1–19.

Tsakatika, Myrto. 'Από ένα 'κριτικό ναι' σε ένα 'φιλοευρωπαϊκό όχι'. Τί έχει αλλάξει στον ευρωπαϊκό προσανατολισμό του Συνασπισμού.' *International and European Politics* 14 (2009): 143–61.

Tsakiris, Thanassis and Valia Aranitou. '"Under the weight of the social": reactions of the social representation system and anti-systemic challenges during the era of the Memorandum'. Paper presented at the 22nd World Congress of the International Political Science Association, Madrid, 8–12 July 2012.

Tsatsanis, Emmanouil. 'Hellenism under Siege: The National-Populist Logic of Antiglobalization Rhetoric in Greece'. *Journal of Political Ideologies* 16, no. 1 (2011): 11–31.

Tsipras, Alexis. 'Ομιλία Αλέξη Τσίπρα, Προέδρου της ΚΟ του ΣΥΡΙΖΑ/ΕΚΜ κατά την παρουσίαση του προγράμματος του συνδυασμού'. 1 June 2012, accessed 16 February 2016, http://www.syn.gr/gr/keimeno.php?id=27218.

Tuomi, Emmi. 'European Left against austerity politics.' speech to IVth Congress of the Party of the European Left, Madrid 15 December 2013, accessed 2 April 2015, http://www.skp.fi/2013-14-12/-european-left-against-austerity-politics-emmi-tuomi-cpfinland-vice-chairperson-speech-in-iv-congress-of-the-party-of-the-european-left-parties.

Unkovski-Korica, Vladimir. 'Where Next, after Syriza? A View from the Left in South-Eastern Europe'. *Counterfire*, 8 February 2016, http://www.counterfire.org/articles/analysis/18164-where-next-after-syriza-a-view-from-the-left-in-south-eastern-europe.

Vail, Mark I. and Benjamin T Bowyer. 'Poverty and Partisanship: Social and Economic Sources of Support for the Far Left in Contemporary Germany'. *Comparative European Politics* 10, no. 4 (2011): 505–24.

Väisänen, J. P. 'We are family', speech to 4th Congress of the Party of the European Left, Madrid 15 December 2013, accessed 2 April 2015, http://www.skp.fi/2013-12-12/we-are-family-jp-vaisanen-speech-in-european-left-congress-in-madrid-13-15-12-2013.

van Apeldoorn, Bastiaan. 'The Struggle over European Order: Transnational Class Agency in the Making of "Embedded Neo-Liberalism"'. In *Social Forces in the Making of the New Europe : The Restructuring of European Social Relations in the Global Political Economy*, edited by Andreas Bieler and Adam David Morton. Basingstoke: Palgrave, 2001.

van der Steen, P. 'De doorbraak van de "gewone mensen"-partij: De SP en de Tweede-Kamerverkiezingen.' In *Kroniek 1994*, edited by Joop Hippe, Paul Lucardie and Gerrit Voerman. Groningen: DNPP, 1994.

van Hecke, Steven. 'Do Transnational Party Federations Matter? (… why should we care?).' *Journal of Contemporary European Research* 6, no. 3 (2011): 395–411.

van Kessel, Stijn. 'Dutch Populism During the Crisis.' In *European Populism in the Shadow of the Great Recession,* edited by Hanspeter Kriesi and Takis Pappas, 107–22. Colchester: ECPR, 2015.

van Kessel, Stijn and Andre Krouwel. 'Fishing in the Same Pond? Comparing the Electorates of the Socialist Party and the Freedom Party in the Netherlands.' Paper for the Dutch-Flemish annual political science conference Politicologenetmaal, 1 June 2012.

van Kessel, Stijn and Saskia Hollander. 'Europe and the Dutch Parliamentary Election September 2012.' *European Parties, Elections and Referendums Briefing Paper* 71. Sussex: Sussex European Institute, 2012.

van Spanje, Joost. 'Contagious Parties: Anti-Immigration Parties and Their Impact on Other Parties' Immigration Stances in Contemporary Western Europe.' *Party Politics* 16, no. 5 (2010): 563–86.

Varoufakis, Yanis. 'What's DiEM25, Really? Reply to Open Letter by Souvlis & Mazzolini'. *LeftEast*, 2 April 2016, http://www.criticatac.ro/lefteast/varoufakis-reply-to-souvlis-mazzolini/.

Vasilopoulou, Sofia. 'Far-Right Euroscepticism in the 2014 European Parliament Elections'. In *Is Europe afraid of Europe?* edited by Kostas Ifantis. Athens: Wilfried Martens Centre, 2014.

Vasilopoulou, Sofia and Daphne Halikiopoulou. *The Golden Dawn's 'Nationalist Solution': Explaining the Rise of the Far Right in Greece*. Basingstoke: Palgrave Macmillan, 2015.

Verge, Tania and Dan Hough. 'A Sheep in Wolf's Clothing or a Gift from Heaven? Left-left Coalitions in Comparative Perspective.' *Regional and Federal Studies* 19 (2009): 37–55.

Verney, Susannah. '"Compromesso Storico": Reunion and Renewal on the Greek Left.' *Journal of Communist Studies* 5 (1989): 200–6.

Verney, Susannah. 'Waking the "Sleeping Giant" or Expressing Domestic Dissent? Mainstreaming Euroscepticism in Crisis-stricken Greece.' *International Political Science Review* 36 (2015): 279–95.

Verrier, Benoît. 'Chronique d'une rupture. De Socialisme et République au Mouvement des Citoyens'. *Politix* 12, no. 45 (1999): 87–113.

Viðskiptablaðið. 'Lausn að handan.' 30 July 2008, accessed 5 November 2015, http://www.vb.is/skodun/lausn-a-handan/15242/.

Viðskiptablaðið. 'Ögmundur segir af sér ráðherradómi.' *Viðskiptablaðið*. 30 September 2009, accessed 30 June 2015, http://www.vb.is/frettir/4369/.

Vilhjálmsson, Ingi Freyr. 'Halldór og Guðni skrifuðu undir.' *dv.is*. 9 October 2013, accessed 30 June 2015, http://www.dv.is/frettir/2013/10/10/halldor-og-gudni-skrifudu-undir-4ZOMBY/.

Vinstrihreyfingin – grænt framboð. 'Ályktun um stóriðju og virkjanir.' ályktanir landsfundar VG 2001, 12–13, accessed 5 November 2015, http://eldri.vg.is/wp-content/uploads/2013/02/%C3%81lyktanir-landsfundar-2001.pdf.

Vinstrihreyfingin – grænt framboð. 'Friðsöm alþjóðahyggja', accessed 5 November 2015, http://vg.is/stefnan/fridsom-althjodahyggja/.

Vinstrihreyfingin – grænt framboð. 'Landsfundarályktanir 2015', accessed 5 November 2015, http://vg.is/landsfundaralyktanir-2015/.

Vinstrihreyfingin – grænt framboð. 'Ríkisstjórnarsamstarf með Samfylkingu', accessed on November 5, 2015, http://vg.is/um-vg/flokksradsfundir/mai-2009/.

Vinstrihreyfingin – grænt framboð. 'Samþykkt á landsfundi 2009', accessed 5 November 2015, http://vg.is/wp-content/uploads/2015/02/Landsfundaralykanir_2009.pdf.

Vinstrihreyfingin – grænt framboð. 'Stefnan', accessed 5 November 2015, http://vg.is/stefnan/.

Vísir. 'Markaðurinn í mínus og krónan fellur áfram.' *Vísir*. 18 March 2008, accessed 30 June 2015, http://www.visir.is/markadurinn-i-minus-og-kronan-fellur-afram/article/200880318021.

Vísir.is. 'Rúm 60% segja já við Icesave.' 25 February 2011, accessed 30 June 2015, http://www.visir.is/rum-60-prosent-segja-ja-vid-icesave/article/2011702259957.

Visser, Mark, Marcel Lubbers, Gerbert Kraaykamp and Eva Jaspers. 'Support for Radical Left Ideologies in Europe.' *European Journal of Political Research* 53, no. 3 (2014): 541–58.

Voerman, Gerrit and Paul Lucardie. *Sociaal-democraie nu definitief verdeeld: Met volwassen SP is het adonnement van de PvdA opde linkse stem verlopen.* Groningen: DNPP, 2007.

Voerman, Gerrit. 'Een politieke kameleon'. *Vlaams marxistisch tijdschrift* 38 (2004): 48.

Voerman, Gerrit. 'The Disappearance of Communism in the Netherlands.' In *Communist and Post-Communist Parties in Europe*, edited by Uwe Backes and Patrick Moreau. Gottingen: Vandenoek and Ruprecht, 2008.

Volkens, Andrea. 'Policy Changes of Parties in European Parliament Party Groups'. In *Democratic Politics and Party Competition: Essays in Honour of Ian Budge*, edited by Judith Bara and Albert Weale, 56–81. London and New York: Routledge, 2006.

Volkens, Andrea. 'Policy changes of European Social Democrats, 1945-98.' In *Social Democratic Party Policies in Contemporary Europe*, edited by Giuliano Bonoli and Martin Powell, 21–42. London: Routledge, 2004.

Weisbrot, Mark and Rebecca Ray. 'Latvia's Internal Devaluation: A Success Story?' Centre for Economic and Policy Research, 2011, http://www.cepr.net/documents/publications/latvia-2011-12.pdf.

Weisenthal, Joe. 'I Just Saw The Most Feared Man In All Of Europe'. *Business Insider*, 14 June 2012, http://www.businessinsider.com/alexis-tsipras-rally-2012-6.

Wirries, Clemens. 'A Party for the "Ordinary People": The Socialist Party of the Netherlands.' In *From Revolution to Coalition – Radical Left Parties in Europe*, edited by Birgit Daiber, Cornelia Hildebrant and Anna Striethorst, 144–62. Berlin: Rosa Luxemburg Stiftung, 2012.

Wood, Lesley J. *Direct Action, Deliberation, and Diffusion: Collective Action After the WTO Protests in Seattle.* Cambridge: Cambridge University Press, 2012.

Workers' Party. 'Contribution by the Workers' Party of Ireland to the 17th International Meeting of Communist and Workers' Parties', accessed 2 November 2015, http://workersparty.ie/wpi-contribution-to-international-meeting/.

World Bank. GDP Growth Rate, World Bank, accessed 1 September 2015, http://data.worldbank.org/indicator/NY.GDP.MKTP.KD.ZG/countries/NL?display=graph.

Wright, Anthony. 'Social Democracy and Democratic Socialism'. In *Contemporary Political Ideologies*, edited by Roger Eatwell and Anthony Wright, 78–99. London: Pinter, 1993.

Wroth, Will. 'Rise and rise of the Dutch Socialist Party: New Perspectives for Socialism or Naïve, Hip, Left Parliamentarism?' *International Journal of Socialist Renewal* 1 September 2012.

Zariski, Raphael. 'Party Factions and Comparative Politics: Some Preliminary Observations.' *Midwest Journal of Political Science* 4, no. 1 (1960): 372–90.

ZDF Politbarometer. 'Merkel stürtzt ab'. 15 January 2016, accessed 18 February 2016, http://www.zdf.de/ZDFmediathek/beitrag/video/2646638/Politbarometer-Merkel-stuerzt-ab#/beitrag/video/2646638/Politbarometer-Merkel-stuerzt-ab.

Zimmer, Gabi. 'Three proposals for a real rescue package for Greece and its people. Statement by GUE/NGL President Gabi Zimmer on the Greek bailout deal.' 15 August 2015, http://www.guengl.eu/news/article/three-proposals-for-a-real-rescue-package-for-greece-and-its-people.

Index

Notes: The following abbreviations have been used: n = note; page references for figures and tables are italicised.

Greens:
  competition with RLPs, 34;
  electoral performance, 4
GroenLinks (GreenLeft) (Netherlands),
  157–59
Grzymała-Busse, Anna, 236
GUE/NGL. *See* Confederal Group of
  the European United Left/Nordic
  Green Left
Gysi, Gregor, 134

Harmony Centre (SC) (Latvia), 233,
  234, 236, 242;
  office seeking, 238;
  programmatic response to the
    International Economic
    Crisis, 243;
  Russian identity, 239–40, 243;
  Ukraine crisis, 243–44
Hartz IV, 134, 138, 143
Havlik, Vlastimil, 370
Hildebrandt, Cornelia, 11
Hollande, Francois, 124
Holloway, John, 57
Hough, Dan, 339
Hudson, Kate, 76
Hue, Robert, 116–17, 127
Hungary, 337;
  RLP electoral performance, 33, 35

Iceland:
  constitutional revision, 182;
  and the International Economic
    Crisis, 13, 176–79, 181–82, 183;
  participatory budgeting, 46;
  party system, 174–75, 177;
  proposed EU membership, 18,
    173, 182;
  RLP electoral performance, 175;
  RLP membership, 185
Icesave, 173, 180–91, 363
Iglesias, Pablo, 7, 64, 80, 198,
  317–19, 371
Independent Greeks (ANEL), 100,
  298–99, 301, 371

Indignants (*Indignados*), 4, 44, *55*, 60,
  295, 297, 317, 326
INITIATIVE of Communist and
  Workers' Parties, *10–11*
Initiative for Democratic Socialism
  (Slovenia) (IDS), 72, 74;
  electoral alliances, 81;
  electoral performance, 80–81;
  extra-Parliamentary links, 74–75, 78,
    83, 364;
  formation, 78;
  organisation, 75, 364;
  populism, 74–75, 78;
  profile, 78
intellectuals, 119, 130n5, 211, 213,
  217–18, 224, 225, 281–83, 347,
  356–57
international communist movement, 6,
  10–11
International Economic Crisis
  (Great Recession 2008–), 3, 13;
  definition, 12, 46, 52, 61;
  impact of, 71;
  political impact, 4, 12, 16–17, 38,
    46–47, 52, 61, 89
International Meetings of Communist
  and Workers' Parties (IMCWP),
  11, 219, 235
International Monetary Fund (IMF), 7,
  46, 127, 173, 175, 178–80, 183,
  186, 192, 301, 304, 322, 346
International Socialist Tendency, *11*
Intersectional politics, 72, 77–79, *84*
Intra-party power balance, 16, 36, 147,
  263, 291–96, 355, 362, 373
Iraq War, 147
Ireland:
  independent radical left politicians,
    181, 194, 200, 205–7, 359–60;
  and the International Economic
    Crisis, *13*, 191–93, 204;
  EU membership, 196;
  Marxism, 196, 198–99, 360, 374;
  party system, 191, 193;
  populism, 198, 206, 360;

internal divisions, 120;
organisation, 120;
profile, 120, 126;
programmatic response to the
International Economic Crisis,
126–27;
membership, 122
Left Party (Sweden):
electoral performance, *91*, 102,
104–5;
Euroscepticism, 340–41, 344;
European level links, 335, 341;
extra-parliamentary links, 102;
immigration policies, 93–96;
and the radical right, 90, 100–1
Left Platform (Greece), 66, 296, 374
left-populism, 4, 9, 12, 15, 17, 32, 34,
37–38, 46, 60, 72, 74, 76, 78, 80,
82, 85, 106, 282, 323–24, 327,
354, 360, 371–72;
eastern Europe, 74;
populist socialists and social
populists, 9, 12, 354;
southern Europe, 2, 46, 60, 80,
323–24, 327, 371;
vote maximisation, 327, 371, 374;
office seeking, 43
Left Unity (European Parliamentary
group), 335, 338
Left Unity (UK) *10*, 72, 74;
electoral performance, 76, 80, 83, 85;
links to social movements, 76,
79, 85;
profile, 76, 79
Lenin, 372
Leninism, 8, 44;
eastern Europe, 212, 214, 212, 231,
247;
Soviet Union, 10, 31, 247;
western Europe, 31, 36, 156, 198–99
Liberal Democrats (UK), 76
Lisbon Treaty, 41, 215, 293, 341
LKP. *See* Communist Party of Latvia
Llamazares, Gaspar, 313–14, 321
Loach, Ken, 76

Louçã, Francisco 263, 362
LSP. *See* Latvian Socialist Party (LSP)

Maastricht Treaty, 321
Maoism, 8–9, *10*;
Netherlands, 155–56;
Portugal, 255
Marchais, Georges, 37, 116–17, 119
Marijnissen, Jan, 37, 156, 162, 164–66
Martins, Catarina, 264, 266, 363
Marx, Karl, 6, 219
Marxism-Leninism, 8, 10, 36, 44, 156,
198, 214, 221, 231, 247
Mélenchon, Jean-Luc, 115, 117–20,
128, 148, 345
the Memorandum, 7, 27, 41, 45, 128,
140, 147, 256, 260, 267, 277–79,
282–84, 286, 294–96, 302–4, 375
Merkel, Angela, 59, 138–42
Meyer, Ron, 162
Miliband, Ed, 82
modernisation crisis, 31
Moldova:
electoral performance, 29, 39;
RLP in government, 41
Momentum (UK), 83
Monedero, Juan Carlos, 74
Mudde, Cas, 5, 32, 89, 107, 165, 354

NATO:
bombing of Yugoslavia, 147;
opposition to, 7, 157, 175, 215, 237,
242, 339
neoliberalism:
and the International Economic
Crisis, 5;
opposition to, 7, 14, 38, 41, 45, 54,
56–57, 65, 322, 339, 355;
social democracy and, 4, 34,
53, 118
Netherlands:
and the International Economic
Crisis, *13*, 157–58;
Party system, 156, 157–59;
protests, 161;

List of Contributors

Óscar García Agustín is an Associate Professor at the Department of Culture and Global Studies at Aalborg University, Denmark. His main research areas include discourse theory, critical studies, and political and social change. With Christian Ydesen he has co-edited the book *Post-Crisis Perspectives: The Common and its Powers* (2013) and with Martin Bak Jørgensen he has coedited the books *Politics of Dissent* (2015) and *Solidarity without Borders. Gramscian Perspectives on Migration and Civil Society* (2016). He is author of *Discurso y autonomía zapatista* (2013) and *Sociology of Discourse: From Institutions to Social Change* (2015).

Amieke Bouma is Lecturer in European Studies at the University of Amsterdam and PhD researcher in History at VU University Amsterdam. Her research interests include post-socialist historiography and radical left politics in Europe. She is currently finishing her dissertation on interest organizations of former GDR functionary elites in unified Germany; preliminary results of this research have been published as 'Strategies of Complaint: Interest Organizations of GDR Staatssicherheit Co-workers after German Reunification', in *Laboratorium: Russian Review of Social Research* 6, no. 3 (2014): 27–54. Her previous research on the interrelations between national ideology and historiography in Turkmenistan resulted in the article 'Turkmenistan: Epics in Place of Historiography', in *Jahrbücher für Geschichte Osteuropas* 59, no. 4 (2011): 559–85.

David Bailey is Senior Lecturer in Politics at the University of Birmingham. His research and teaching focuses on left parties, protest, the critical political economy of European integration, and the relationship between each of these three things. He has recently published in *New Political Economy*,

Socio-Economic Review, and *British Politics*, and is currently working on a co-authored book with Mònica Clua-Losada and Nikolai Huke, titled *Beyond Defeat: Disrupting (the Critical Political Economy of) Neoliberal Europe*, in which the authors highlight how neoliberal Europe has been (and is being) contested. He is also the review essays editor for *Comparative European Politics* and the reviews editor for *Capital & Class*.

Giorgos Charalambous is Senior Research Consultant at the Cyprus Centre of the Peace Research Institute Oslo. He also lectures at the University of Cyprus. Currently he is President of the Cyprus Association of Political Science. His work concentrates on political parties, left radicalism, political behaviour and southern Europe. His publications have appeared or are forthcoming in such journals as *Mobilization, European Political Science Review, Government and Opposition, Italian Political Science Review* and *Communist and Post-Communist Studies*, among others. He is the author of *European Integration and the Communist Dilemma* (2013) and co-editor of *Party-Society Relations in the Republic of Cyprus* (2015).

Ammon Cheskin is Lecturer in Nationalism and Identity at Central and East European Studies, the University of Glasgow. He holds a PhD and MRes in Russian, Central and East European Studies from the University of Glasgow, an MA in Interpreting and Translation (Russian) and a BA in Russian and Politics from the University of Bath. His research focuses on complex issues of minority and national identity with reference to foreign policy and nation and state building. Most of his current projects examine Russia's compatriot policies and discourses and the reception of these policies in Ukraine and the Baltic states. He is the author of *Russian Speakers in Post-Soviet Latvia: Discursive Identity Strategies* (2016), published by University of Edinburgh Press. His articles have appeared in *Europe-Asia Studies, Nationalities Papers, East European Politics, Ethnopolitics* and the *Journal of Baltic Studies*.

Richard Dunphy is a Senior Lecturer in Politics at the University of Dundee. His principal research interests are in Irish politics, the European Left, and sexual politics. His books include *The Making of Fianna Fáil Power in Ireland, 1923–1948* (1995), *Sexual Politics* (2000), *The European Mosaic*, 3rd edition (2006 – co-edited with Gowland and Lythe), *Europe, Globalisation and Sustainable Development* (2004 – co-edited with Barry and Baxter), and *Contesting Capitalism? Left Parties and European Integration* (2004). In addition he has published various articles and book chapters on Irish and European politics, sexual politics, and left parties. He is currently completing a book with Luke March (Edinburgh) for Manchester University Press on the

European Left Party. He has engaged in collaborative research projects on left parties in coalition governments (with Tim Bale, University of Sussex), on the European Left and European integration (with Luke March, University of Edinburgh). He is Associate Editor of the journal *European Politics and Societies*.

Costas Eleftheriou is a PhD candidate in political science at the National and Kapodistrian University of Athens. His research interests include perspectives in Greek party politics focused on left parties. He is the co-author of *PASOK: The Rise and Fall of a Hegemonic Party* (2013, in Greek) and his research has been published in academic journals such as *South European Society and Politics* and *Greek Political Science Review*.

Fabien Escalona is completing his PhD at Sciences Po Grenoble and teaches at Sciences Po Lyon in France. He is also an associated researcher at Cevipol, ULB (Université Libre de Bruxelles) in Belgium. His research interests focus on the transformations of European social democracy, but also on the emergence of a radical left family and the contemporary developments in French politics. He is co-editor of *The Palgrave Handbook of Social Democracy in the European Union* (2013) and *European Social Democracy during the Global Economic Crisis* (2014). He wrote a chapter on the French PS in *The Three Worlds of Social Democracy* edited by Ingo Schmidt (2016) and produced several policy analyses published by think-tanks (Robert Schuman Foundation, Jean Jaurès Foundation) and press media (Slate, Mediapart).

André Freire is an Associate Professor with Agrégation/Habilitation, Head of the Doctoral Programme in Political Science at ISCTE-IUL (Lisbon University Institute), and Senior Researcher at CIES-IUL. He is a participant in several international research networks (CSES, CCS, PARTIREP, PARE-NEL, EES, among others; for more details see here: http://er.cies.iscte-iul. pt/). Freire has published (in different languages) several books, book chapters, and papers in academic journals about left–right (mass and elite) ideology, electoral behaviour, political attitudes, political institutions, political elites and political representation. His most recent four articles appeared in *Communist and Post-Communist Studies*, *Comparative European Politics*, *Journal of Political Ideologies*, and *South European Society and Politics*.

Andreas Goffin is a PhD student at the Institute of International Area Studies, Charles University Prague. In his research he focuses on system transformation, communist successor parties and European integration in Germany and Central Europe. His PhD thesis deals with the influence of the European integration process and European crises on the parties Die Linke and KSČM.

Vladimír Handl is a Lecturer and Researcher at the Institute of International Studies (Department for German and Austrian Studies) at the Faculty of Social Studies of the Charles University, Prague. He also works at the Institute of International Relations, Prague (part time) and was a research fellow at the Institute of German Studies (University of Birmingham) in 1996–2000/2002–2003 and a visiting fellow at a number of German research institutions. He is a graduate of the Moscow State Institute of International Relations. His main research interests include German foreign policy, Czech–German relations and transition of the communist parties in Central Europe. He published on the Czech communist party in the Journal *Communist and Post-Communist Studies* and *Journal of Communist Studies and Transition Politics*, most recently in the German Journal *Osteuropa* (nos. 5–6, 2013).

Michael Holmes is a Senior Lecturer in Politics and International Relations at Liverpool Hope University. His main area of research has been on the impact of European integration on political parties, and especially parties of the Left. In this area, his publications include *The Development of the Irish Labour Party's European Policy: from Opposition to Support* (2006) and *The Left and the European Constitution: from Laeken to Lisbon* (edited with Knut Roder; 2012). He is also currently working on a study of The Left and the Euro-zone Crisis. He has also published research on Ireland's relationship with the European Union, including *Ireland and the EU: Nice, Enlargement and the Future of Europe* (editor, 2005).

Gregoris Ioannou is a sociologist who works as an Adjunct Lecturer at Frederick University and the University of Cyprus teaching a variety of courses in the fields of social science, culture and communication. He has been engaged in research in the fields of oral and social history, employment and trade unionism, migration and social movements, digital public sphere and media framing. Aspects of his work have been published in international peer-reviewed journals such as *Mobilization: An International Quarterly*, *Mediterranean Politics*, *Bulgarian Ethnology*, *Working USA: The Journal of Labor and Society*, *Capital and Class*, *The Cyprus Review* and as chapters in several edited volumes. His current research interests include the impact of the economic crisis on South European labour markets, the portrayal of the crisis in the media and contentious politics and political upheavals in South European societies.

Andrés Ingi Jónsson is an active member of the Left-Green Movement in Iceland. With a background in journalism, he was one of the experts working with the Constitutional Council, formed after the financial crisis to rewrite Iceland's constitution. He served as the political advisor to two ministers during the 2009–2013 left-wing government. He has an MA in War, Violence and Security from the University of Sussex.

Martin Bak Jørgensen is an Associate Professor at Department for Culture and Global Studies, Aalborg University, Denmark where he is Research Director of Centre of the Studies of Migration and Diversity (CoMID). He works within the fields of sociology, political sociology and political science. He has published books such as *Politics of Dissent* (2015; co-authored with Óscar García Agustín), *Solidarity Without Borders: Gramscian Perspectives on Migration and Civil Society Alliances* (2016; co-authored with Óscar García Agustín) and *Politics of Precarity: Migrant Conditions, Struggles and Experiences* (2016; co-edited with Carl-Ulrik Schierup). He has published articles in journals such as *Internal Migration Review*, *Critical Sociology*, *Journal of International Migration and Integration* and *British Journal of International Politics*.

Daniel Keith is a Lecturer in Politics at the University of York. He wrote his PhD at the University of Sussex on the programmatic adaptation of west European communist parties. He has recently published articles on the Left, including 'Non-mainstream left parties and women's representation in Western Europe' with Tania Verge in *Party Politics* and 'Pulling together in a crisis? Anarchism, feminism and the limits of left-wing convergence in austerity Britain' with Bice Maiguashca and Jonathan Dean in *Capital & Class*. Daniel's research on communist parties includes the article 'On the (non) distinctiveness of Marxism-Leninism: The Portuguese and Greek communist parties compared' published in *Communist and Post-Communist Studies* (with Giorgos Charalambous). Daniel's other research interests include internal party organisation, political leadership and Euroscepticism.

Simon Lightfoot is a Senior Lecturer in European Politics at the University of Leeds. His research interests include transnational European political parties, especially the Party of European Socialists. His publications include *Europeanizing Social Democracy?: The Rise of the Party of European Socialists* (2005).

Marco Lisi is an Assistant Professor in the Department of Political Studies, Nova University of Lisbon and researcher at IPRI. His research interests focus on political parties, electoral behaviour, democratic theory, political representation and election campaigns. He has published several articles in national and international journals. His latest books are *Party Change, Recent Democracies and Portugal: Comparative Perspectives* (Lexington, 2015) and *Political Representation in Times of Bailout: Evidence from Greece and Portugal* (co-edited, 2016).

Luke March is a Professor of Post-Soviet and Comparative Politics at Politics and International Relations, University of Edinburgh, and Deputy Director of the Princess Dashkova Russian Centre, University of Edinburgh. His main research interests include the politics of the European (radical) Left, Russian domestic and foreign politics, nationalism, populism, radicalism and extremism in Europe and the former Soviet Union. He has published in a range of journals including *Party Politics, Comparative European Politics, Europe-Asia Studies* and *East European Politics*. His books include *The Communist Party in Post-Soviet Russia* (2002), *Russia and Islam: State, Society and Radicalism* (edited with Roland Dannreuther, 2010) and *Radical Left Parties in Europe* (2011).

Francis McGowan is a Senior Lecturer in the Department of Politics at the University of Sussex. He has published extensively on EU politics and policy-making, particularly in the area of energy and environmental policy. Recent publications include 'Regulating Innovation: European Responses to Shale Gas Development', *Environmental Politics* (2014).

Silja Bára Ómarsdóttir is an Adjunct Lecturer at the Faculty of Political Science at the University of Iceland. Her research, which is mainly on Icelandic foreign and security policy, is grounded in feminist approaches and narrative analysis. Her latest book *Rof: Frásagnir kvenna af fóstureyðingum* (2015) is on women's experiences of abortion in Iceland and was shortlisted for two literature prizes in Iceland. She has published on peace and violence, for example, in *State Violence and the Right to Peace* (2009), *International Handbook of War, Torture, and Terrorism* (2012), and *International Handbook on Peace and Reconciliation* (2013).

Luis Ramiro (PhD, European University Institute, Florence) is an Associate Professor at the School of History, Politics and International Relations, University of Leicester. His research centres on parties and political behaviour. His most recent publications have focused on the vote for radical left parties (*West European Politics, European Political Science Review*), on the support for radical left populism (*Political Studies*), on the electoral effect of party primaries (*Party Politics*) and on parties and social movements' activists (*Party Politics*).

Mathieu Vieira is a PhD candidate at Sciences Po Grenoble, France, and Université Libre de Bruxelles, Belgium. His research interests include the transformations of social democracy and the radical left in Europe and the metropolitisation of politics in France. He is co-editor of *Une droitisation de la classe ouvrière en Europe?* (2012), *The Palgrave Handbook of Social Democracy in the European Union* (2013) and *European Social Democracy During the Global Economic Crisis. Renovation or Resignation?* (2014).